# Learning to Teach

## FIFTH EDITION

## Richard I. Arends
*Central Connecticut State University*

McGraw Hill

Boston   Burr Ridge, Il   Dubuque, IA   Madison, WI   New York   San Francisco   St. Louis
Bankok   Bogata   Caracas   Lisbon   London   Madrid
Mexico City   Milan   New Delhi   Seoul   Singapore   Syndey   Taiei   Toronto

# McGraw-Hill Higher Education ⚛

*A Division of The* **McGraw-Hill** *Companies*

LEARNING TO TEACH, FIFTH EDITION

Published by McGraw-Hill, an imprint of The McGraw-Hill Companies, Inc., 1221 Avenue of the Americas, New York, NY 10020. Copyright © 2000, 1998, 1994, 1991, 1988 by The McGraw-Hill Companies, Inc. All rights reserved. No part of this publication may be reproduced or distributed in any form or by any means, or stored in a database or retrieval system, without the prior written consent of The McGraw-Hill Companies, Inc., including, but not limited to, in any network or other electronic storage or transmission, or broadcast for distance learning.

Some ancillaries, including electronic and print components, may not be available to customers outside the United States.

♲  This book is printed on recycled, acid-free paper containing 10% postconsumer waste.

3 4 5 6 7 8 9 0 QPD/QPD 0 9 8 7 6 5 4 3 2 1

ISBN 0–07–232164–4

Vice president and editor-in-chief: *Thalia Dorwick*
Editorial director: *Jane E. Vaicunas*
Sponsoring editor: *Beth Kaufman*
Developmental editor: *Cara Harvey*
Marketing manager: *Daniel M. Loch*
Project manager: *Christine Schultz*
Media technology project manager: *James Fehr*
Senior production supervisor: *Sandra Hahn*
Coordinator of freelance design: *Rick D. Noel*
Cover/interior designer: *Ellen Pettengell*
Cover image: *©Ad Stock Images—Image no. 0897GEO6200332*
Photo research coordinator: *John C. Leland*
Photo research: *Connie Gardner Picture Research*
Supplement coordinator: *Stacy A. Patch*
Compositor: *Carlisle Communications, Ltd.*
Typeface: *9.5/12 Palatino*
Printer: *Quebecor Printing Book Group/Dubuque, IA*

The credits section for this book begins on page 481 and is considered an extension of the copyright page.

### Library of Congress Cataloging-in-Publication Data

Arends, Richard.
    Learning to teach / Richard I. Arends. — 5th ed.
        p.   cm.
    Includes bibliographical references and index.
    ISBN 0–07–232164–4
    1. Teaching. 2. Effective teaching. I. Title.

LB1025.3 .A74   2001                    00–039438
371.102—dc21                            CIP

www.mhhe.com

# About the Author

Richard I. Arends is Professor of Educational Leadership at Connecticut State University, where he also served as dean of the School of Education for nine years. Before coming to Connecticut, Professor Arends was on the faculty and chair of the department of curriculum and instruction at the University of Maryland, College Park. He received his Ph.D. in education from the University of Oregon, where he was on the faculty from 1975 to 1984. A former elementary, junior high, and high school teacher, his special interests are teacher education, organizational development, and school improvement.

Professor Arends has authored or contributed to over a dozen books on education, including the *Second Handbook of Organization Development in Schools, Systems Change Strategies in Education, Classroom Instruction and Management,* and *Exploring Teaching.* He has worked widely with schools and universities throughout North America, in Jamaica, and in the Pacific Rim, including Australia, Samoa, Palau, and Saipan.

The recipient of numerous awards, he was selected in 1989 as the outstanding teacher educator in Maryland and in 1990 received the Judith Ruskin Award for outstanding research in education from the Association for Supervision and Curriculum Development. From 1995 to 1997, Professor Arends held the William Allen (Boeing) Chair in the School of Education at Seattle University.

# Contents in Brief

**Part 3**

## The Organizational Aspects of Teaching      407

### Resource Handbook

# Contents

**Part 2**

*The Interactive Aspects of Teaching*   229

Chapter 7

**Presentation   232**

Overview of Presentation Teaching   234

# Features Index

## Research Summary

## Spotlight on Technology

## Tailoring Teaching for Inclusive Classrooms

# Preface

Learning to be a teacher is a long and complex journey full of excitement and challenge. It begins with the many experiences we have with our parents and siblings; it continues as we observe teacher after teacher through sixteen to twenty years of schooling. It culminates, formally, with professional training but continues through a lifetime of teaching experiences.

## Purpose and Audience

This is the fifth edition of *Learning to Teach.* It is intended for students taking courses in teacher education, commonly labeled General Methods of Teaching. A variety of other course titles—Analysis of Teaching, Study of Teaching, Principles and Practices of Teaching, or Strategies of Teaching—are sometimes used. Whatever its title, the course's content normally focuses on general models, strategies, and skills that apply to teaching in all subject areas and at all grade levels. Such courses are routinely offered in secondary education and in elementary education programs.

Although these courses vary somewhat among institutions, most of them seem to share the following general goals. Most instructors want their students to:

1. Begin developing a repertoire of basic teaching models, strategies, and skills.
2. Understand the dynamics of teaching, both inside and outside the classroom.
3. Begin developing an awareness and appreciation of the knowledge base that supports current practices in teaching.
4. Begin developing skills with which to observe, record, and reflect on teaching.

To help achieve these general course goals, I have tried to produce a text with the following characteristics.

## Content of the Fifth Edition

In the fifth edition of *Learning to Teach,* I have tried to provide a comprehensive and balanced view of teaching. To accomplish this, I organized the book into an initial chapter and three parts. The first chapter, "The Scientific Basis for the Art of Teaching," introduces the book, explores the meaning of effective teaching, and considers the processes and stages beginning teachers go through on the way to becoming accomplished teachers. This initial chapter also lays out the major themes of the book as well as the contemporary social context that has an impact on teachers and their work.

Parts One, Two, and Three, which constitute the heart of the book, are organized around concepts of what teachers do. These sections assume that all teachers are asked to perform three important functions. They are asked to lead a group of students, the *leadership aspects of teaching;* they are asked to provide students with direct, face-to-face instruction, the *interactive aspects of teaching;* and they are expected to work with colleagues and others to perform the *organizational aspects of teaching.* Readers will soon find that these different aspects of a teacher's job are not always discrete; the teacher does not always perform one independently of the others. These different aspects, however, are convenient organizers for helping teacher candidates make sense out of the bewildering array of events associated with teaching today in a complex society.

## Theory-Practice Connections

*Learning to Teach* strives to provide readers with the theory and rationale that underlie and support the specific principles and practices being described. Readers are also shown why a recommended principle or procedure works the way it does, not just how to execute it effectively. Because models, principles, and procedures of teaching were not invented yesterday, sometimes a short history lesson is also provided. A good example of this can be found in the discussion of cooperative learning and problem-based instruction. Even though significant developments have helped refine these approaches to teaching during the past decade, readers will find that the basic models, including the theory and rationale, are lodged firmly in the mainstream of democratic thought and reach as far back as Horace Mann and John Dewey.

## Knowledge Base Focus

Because *Learning to Teach* strives to develop the point of view that there is a knowledge base that can and should guide teaching practice, each chapter has a section entitled "Theoretical and Empirical Support." This section provides a broad sampling of the research that underlies and supports the recommended teaching practices found in the latter part of each chapter. In addition, each chapter contains a boxed "Research Summary" of an important research study pertaining to the chapter topic. The studies have been selected to illustrate not only some aspect of the knowledge base that supports the topics under discussion but also particular modes of inquiry practiced by educational researchers. Some of the studies are more traditional empirical studies, whereas others represent contemporary qualitative approaches. Many of studies are considered classics, and together they cover fifty years of educational research. Although highly compressed, these summaries are truthful to the investigators' methods and conclusions and, collectively, they reflect the variety and richness of methods used by educational researchers over time and around the world. This is an important feature of *Learning to Teach.* Much progress has been made in clarifying and organizing the knowledge base on teaching. It is important for teachers in the twenty-first century to have a command of the specialized knowledge that has accumulated over the past half century and more. This will set them apart from the average person and provide them, as professionals, with some guarantees that they are using best practice.

Finally, the Resource Handbook found at the end of the text contains two research-oriented units. The first of these offers a succinct guide to reading and understanding the research literature available through professional journals. Anyone planning to be a serious student of teaching must learn to consume this literature, and this handbook unit provides a good beginning. The second unit of the handbook provides a succinct guide to action research, a practice that will become increasingly common as the professionalization of teaching continues its long evolution.

## Major Features of This Revision

As with previous editions, revisions were based on my own experience in teaching the text as well as on systematically gathered feedback from users across the country and from colleagues at my own university. Although the general goals, themes, and features of the previous editions have remained constant, many revisions have been in response to user feedback, as well as to developments in the expanding knowledge base on teaching and significant societal changes now occurring. The most significant changes in this edition are described below.

**Expanded Coverage and Thorough Update of All References.** Much has been learned about teaching and learning since the first edition of *Learning to Teach.* I have strived particularly hard in both the fourth and fifth editions to include new concepts and research in the field and to update all references. This has resulted in over one hundred new references, as well as new discussions on several topics including alternative assessment; use of portfolio in student assessment; the way research is conceived and conducted; cognitive/constructivist views of teaching and learning; self-regulated learning; scaffolding; memory and how the brain works; motivation; and portfolio development for teachers.

**New Emphasis on Technology.** As more computers are found in classrooms and as more instructional materials become available on CD-ROMs and software programs, teachers must remain abreast of these developments. It is particularly important for new teachers to be able to step into their first classroom equipped with the knowledge and skills to use computer and telecommunication technologies. It is beyond the scope of *Learning to Teach* to provide a comprehensive introduction to educational technology. However, this edition includes a feature in each chapter titled "Spotlight on Technology." This feature highlights software and other computer technologies pertaining to the particular chapter topic. It also describes how teachers have used these technologies and directs readers to resources and websites for more information.

**New Emphasis on Inclusion.** Over the past twenty-five years, schools have been encouraged by Congress and the courts to include more students with a wide range of disabilities in the regular classroom. Under a practice known as inclusion, teachers often struggle with how to adapt their instruction to help students with special needs. Users of *Learning to Teach* were unanimous in their feedback that more was needed on inclusion beyond the chapter in previous editions on multicultural education. As a result, the chapter on multicultural education has been expanded to include much more on inclusion and special education. More important, however, a new feature has been added to each chapter titled "Tailoring Teaching for Inclusive Classrooms." This feature describes how teachers can tailor and adapt their teaching strategies and instructional practices to the wide range of abilities and students with special needs found in most classrooms today. I am very excited about this feature and hope you agree.

**New Cases for "Reflection and Portfolio."** Although many aspects of teaching can be guided by the knowledge base, many other aspects have more than one point of view and require teacher problem solving and reflection. Beginning and ending cases have been written for this edition of *Learning to Teach* that allow teacher candidates to reflect on important issues related to the chapter topic and to compare their ideas and opinions to those of experienced teachers. These cases can be used as springboards for class discussion and have been designed so a reflective essay on a case can become an exhibit in the candidate's professional portfolio.

**More Concise Chapters and Content Coverage.** Over the years of revising *Learning to Teach*, the number of chapters increased, and each chapter became longer and longer. This happens because those who use the book recommend more topics for addition than for elimination. It also happens because it is very painful to remove words from a book after so much energy has gone in to writing them. However, I made every effort to delete chapters and to make those that survived more concise. Except in Chapter Four, where I added new materials on inclusion and special education, each chapter has been trimmed to make *Learning to Teach* more readable as well as less time-consuming. Many users, although they had praise for the content of the chapters on learning strategies and school improvement, reported that they simply did not have time in their courses to cover these topics. As a result of this feedback, I have eliminated the chapter on learning strategies that appeared in the fourth edition and provide a shortened version of it as part of the Resource Handbook. This shortens the book while keeping it responsive to the needs of some users who want this information. I have also eliminated the chapter on school improvement, again believing this to be an important topic for beginning teachers but recognizing the time limits of teacher education programs.

## Resource Handbook

The easily referenced handbook at the end of the book brings together previously scattered reference material dealing with (1) reading and understanding research, (2) conducting action research, and (3) learning strategies. While such information is not central to most courses of this type, its inclusion here makes the book more responsive to the needs of more advanced courses and students and to instructors who cover these topics.

## Chapter Pedagogy and Learning Aids

To increase the accessibility and readability of *Learning to Teach*, previous pedagogical features have been maintained and some new ones added. Chapter outlines appear at the beginning of each chapter and lengthy point-by-point summaries conclude each chapter. Lists of key terms appear at the end of each chapter and are tied to a glossary at the end of the book. The book also has a very detailed topic and author index.

In addition, several new pedagogical features have been added to increase student learning and to enhance the text's usefulness. New marginal notes highlight main ideas and define important concepts. At the end of each major section, the "Check for Understanding" feature allows readers to quiz themselves before going on. This edition has also been enhanced with an engaging new design, an expanded photo program, and increased use of charts and graphs to illustrate important points.

## Teaching and Learning Resources

This edition of *Learning to Teach* is accompanied by an expanded number of supplemental resources and learning aids for instructors and students.

## For the Instructor*

*Learning to Teach* is accompanied by a revised **instructor's manual** and **bank of test questions** as well as a **computerized test bank** (available for both Macintosh and IBM-compatible computers).

We are very excited to announce the availability of an **original video** developed especially for and linked to this new edition. The video depicts the different models of instruction to help them come alive for students.

Create your own course website using PageOut! Simply plug the course information into a template and click one of sixteen designs. The process takes no time at all and leaves instructors with a professionally designed website. Powerful features include an interactive course syllabus that lets you post content and links, an online gradebook, lecture notes, bookmarks, and even a discussion board where students can discuss course-related topics. For an example, please visit www.mhhe.com/pageout.

## For the Student

This edition also provides extensive supplements for the student. Some aspects of teaching cannot be learned by merely studying theory-based or research-based knowledge. To truly understand what effective teaching is all about, teacher candidates must actively observe others teach, engage in dialogues about teaching, and reflect on both their own and others' teaching experiences. To help promote such active learning experiences, I have included over one hundred pages of structured observations, interviews, and reflection and portfolio guides in the attached *Manual for Observation, Reflection, and Portfolio.* These resources constitute a helpful field guide that assists teacher candidates in gathering and interpreting data, examining their own related experiences, and developing a professional portfolio. Watch for the *Manual for Observation, Reflection, and Portfolio* icon at the end of each chapter.

An important resource for the student is the **Making the Grade CD-ROM** located in the inside back cover of the text. Packaged free with each new copy of the text, this interactive study tool allows students to test their mastery of text material with chapter-by-chapter quizzes. All quizzes are graded instantly. The CD includes a learning styles assessment to help students understand how they learn and, based on that assessment, how they can use their study time most effectively. The CD also offers two different guides to the Web. The Internet Primer explains the essentials of online research, including how to get online and find information once you are there. The Guide to Electronic Research guides students through using web-based information databases and explains how to evaluate the quality of online information.

## For the Instructor and the Student

Finally, for both the instructor and student, the *Learning to Teach* **Online Learning Center Website** is available at **www.mhhe.com/ltt.** This site includes numerous resources for both the instructor and student including study questions, online activities, and web links. The website icon at the end of each chapter reminds students to visit the site for additional resources and activities to extend their learning.

## Student Feedback

As with previous editions, I encourage students to provide feedback about any and all aspects of the text. Please e-mail me at arends@CCSU.edu.

## Acknowledgments

Because the field of teaching and learning is becoming so comprehensive and so complex, I have relied on colleagues to assist in writing about topics outside my own area of expertise. Outstanding contributions were made in previous editions by chapter authors Dr. Richard Jantz, Dr. Virginia Richardson, and Dr. Nancy Winitzky.

I also want to acknowledge and extend my thanks to the many students in my principles of teaching classes at the University of Maryland, particularly those in the Master's Certification Program, for their willingness to ask questions and provide reactions to every aspect of the book. Similarly my co-teachers and colleagues over the years—Drs. Hilda Borko, Sheri Castle, Shelley Clemson, Lenore Cohen, Pat Christensen, Neil Davidson, Margaret Ferrara, Paulette Lemma, Ronald Moss, Susan Seider, Carole Shmurak, Nancy Hoffman, Karen Riem, Jim Henkelman, Frank Lyman, Joe McCaleb, Roger Zieger, and Linda Mauro—have not only been a source of support but have provided important input for early versions of the manuscript as well as for this revision. My administrative assistant, Lisa Manousos, provided helpful assistance throughout the revision process and also was a constant source of support, as were our graduate assistants Kristen Oberg and Elizabeth Hayes. Elizabeth made significant contributions to the fifth edition by working on the margin notes, tracking down permissions, and helping identify websites. She, along with Nancy Hoffman, wrote the study questions found in the CD-ROM.

Many reviewers and users also contributed very useful reactions and critiques that have resulted in a much improved text. Reviewers of previous editions include Mary Crisp, *Western Kentucky University;* Carmen Dumas, *Nova University;* Susan Geis and Jean Shaw, *University of Mississippi;* John Hoffman, *Northeast Missouri State University;* Harriet Johnson, *Augsburg College;* Larry Kortering, *University of Delaware;* W. C. Martin, *University of West Florida;* Rita Moretti, *Niagara University;* Karna Nelson and Sam Perez, *Western Washington University;* Steve Penn, *Vincennes University;* George Rawlins, *Austin Peay State University;* and Kinnard White, *University of North Carolina.*

I would like to extend a special thanks to the reviewers who provided feedback during the revision of this new edition.

Bonnie Buckland, Lincoln Memorial University
Elizabeth S. Foster-Harrison
Thomas John Graca, University of Texas at Arlington
Janice Grow, Truman State University
Nancy J. Hadley, Angela State University
Duane Inman, University of Memphis
Mary Jondrow, University of Arizona
Howard L. Jones, University of Houston
Kathi Kearney, Iowa State University
Mark S. Kostin, Georgia Southern University
Robert Locatelli, University of Nevada, Las Vegas
Marc Mahlios, University of Kansas
Sandra F. Mark, Kean University
Rita N. Moretti, Niagara University
John Nidds, Dowling College
Claudia M. Pagliaro, University of Pittsburgh
John P. Strouse, Ball State University

My current editors, Beth Kaufman and Cara Harvey, have been super to work with and a constant source of encouragement, support, and great ideas. Finally, thanks to the team that brought the book through production: Jane Vaicunas, Dan Loch, Christine Schultz, James Fehr, Sandy Hahn, Rick Noel, John Leland, and Stacy Patch.

I extend thanks to my original editor, Lane Akers, who had faith in the book from the beginning and who has provided so much valuable assistance, advice, and support over the years of our relationship.

**Richard I. Arends**

## *Qualifications

As a full-service publisher of quality education products, McGraw-Hill does much more than just sell textbooks to your students. We create and publish an extensive array of print, video, and digital supplements to support instruction on your campus. Orders of new (versus used) textbooks help us to defray the cost of developing such supplements, which is substantial. Please consult your local McGraw-Hill sales representative to learn about the availability of the supplements to accompany *Learning to Teach*.

# Learning to Teach

# Chapter 🍎 One

# The Scientific Basis for the Art of Teaching

## Reflecting on **Learning to Teach**

If you are like many students, you begin this book and this course with a sense of excitement and challenge, perhaps also some concerns. You have decided you want to be a teacher, but you also know some of the challenges teachers face today, and you know you have a lot to learn if you are going to meet these challenges. Before you read this chapter, take a few minutes to think about teachers, teaching, and education today.

🍎 *Think about the best teachers you have had. Do you still know their names? Why were they good teachers? How did they influence your life?*

🍎 *Think about teachers you didn't think were very good. Why didn't you consider them good teachers? Regardless of how good they were, did they have any influence on your life?*

🍎 *Which aspects of teaching do you look forward to the most? Which aspects give you the greatest concern? What do you see as the major challenges facing teachers today?*

🍎 *Think about education in general. Do you believe most schools are doing a good job? Or do you believe schools are in lots of trouble and need serious reform? Do you see yourself as a person who can help schools become better?*

Teaching offers a bright and rewarding career for those who can meet the intellectual and social challenges of the job. Despite the spate of reports over the past decade critical of schools and teachers, most citizens continue to support our schools and express their faith in education. The task of teaching the young is simply too important and complex to be handled entirely by parents or through the informal structures of earlier eras. Modern society needs schools staffed with expert teachers to provide instruction and to care for children while parents work.

**Best practices are those teaching methods, processes, and procedures that have been shown to be effective in helping students learn.**

In our society, teachers are given professional status. As experts and professionals, they are expected to use **best practice** to help students learn essential skills and attitudes. It is no longer sufficient for teachers to be warm and loving toward children, nor is it sufficient for them to employ teaching practices based solely on intuition, personal preference, or conventional wisdom. Contemporary teachers are held accountable for using teaching practices that have been shown to be effective, just as members of other professions, such as medicine, law, and architecture, are held to acceptable standards of practice. This book is about how to learn and to use best practice—practice that has a **scientific basis.** It is aimed at helping beginning teachers master the knowledge base and the skills required of a professional.

**Teaching has a scientific basis—its practices are based on research and scientific evidence.**

This book also explores another side of teaching: the **art of teaching.** Like most human endeavors, teaching has aspects that cannot be codified or guided by scientific knowledge alone but instead depend on a complex set of individual judgments based on personal experiences. Nathaniel Gage (1984) of Stanford University, one of the United States' foremost educational researchers, some years ago described the art of teaching as:

> an instrumental or practical art, not a fine art aimed at creating beauty for its own sake. As an instrumental art, teaching is something that departs from recipes, formulas, or algorithms. It requires improvisation, spontaneity, the handling of hosts of considerations of form, style, pace, rhythm, and appropriateness in ways so complex that even computers must, in principle, fall behind, just as they cannot achieve what a mother does with her five-year-old or what a lover says at any given moment to his or her beloved. (p. 6)

**Teaching is also an art based on teachers' experiences and the wisdom of practice.**

Notice some of the words chosen by Gage to describe the art of teaching—*spontaneity, pace, rhythm.* These words describe aspects of teaching that research cannot measure very well but that are nonetheless important characteristics of best practice and are contained in the wisdom of experienced and expert teachers. This book strives to show the complexity of teaching—the dilemmas faced by teachers and the artistic choices that effective teachers make as they perform their daily work. It also presents an integrated view of teaching as a science and as an art, and emphasizes that what we know about teaching does not translate into easy prescriptions or simple recipes.

This chapter begins with a brief historical sketch of teaching, because the basic patterns of teaching today are intertwined in the web of history and culture, which impact the processes of learning to teach. This introduction is followed by the perspective about effective teaching that has guided the design and writing of *Learning to Teach.* The final section of the chapter describes a portion of what is known about the processes of learning to teach. It tells how beginners can start the process of becoming effective teachers by learning to access the knowledge base on teaching, accumulating the wisdom of practice, and reflecting on their experiences.

# 🍎 *Historical Perspective on Teaching*

Conceptions of teaching reflect the values and social philosophy of the larger society, and as these change, so too does society's view of its teachers. To understand the role of the teacher in today's society requires a brief historical review of some of the important changes that have taken place in teaching and schooling over the past three centuries.

*Effective teaching requires an integrated view of the science and art of teaching; there are no simple recipes.*

## Role Expectations in Earlier Times

The role of teacher, as we understand it today, did not exist in the colonial period of our national history. Initially, literate individuals, often young men studying for the ministry, were hired on a part-time basis to tutor or teach the children of the more wealthy families in a community. Even when schools started to emerge in the eighteenth century, the teachers selected by local communities did not have any special training, and they were mainly middle-class men who chose to teach while they prepared for a more lucrative line of work.

Common, or public, schools came into existence in the United States between 1825 and 1850. During this era and for most of the nineteenth century, the purposes of schools were few and a teacher's role rather simple, compared to today. Basic literacy and numeracy skills were the primary goals of nineteenth-century education, with the curriculum dominated by what later came to be called the three Rs: reading, writing, and arithmetic. Most young people were not required (or expected) to attend school, and those who did so remained for relatively brief periods of time. Other institutions in society—family, church, and work organizations—held the major responsibility for child rearing and helping youth make the transition from family to work.

*Standards for teachers in the nineteenth century emphasized the conduct of their personal lives over their professional abilities.*

*Vast changes in the nineteenth century determined many elements of the educational system we have today.*

**Figure 1.1**  *Sample Nineteenth-Century Teacher Contract*

I promise to take a vital interest in all phases of Sunday-school work, donating of my time, service and money without stint for the benefit and uplift of the community.

I promise to abstain from dancing, immodest dressing, and any other conduct unbecoming a teacher and a lady.

I promise not to go out with any young man except as it may be necessary to stimulate Sunday-school work.

I promise not to fall in love, to become engaged or secretly married.

I promise to remain in the dormitory or on the school grounds when not actively engaged in school or church work elsewhere.

I promise not to encourage or tolerate the least familiarity on the part of any of my boy pupils.

I promise to sleep eight hours a night, eat carefully...

Source: Brenton (1970), p. 74.

Teachers were recruited mostly from their local communities. Professional training of teachers was not deemed important, nor was teaching necessarily considered a career. Teachers by this time were likely to be young women who had obtained a measure of literacy themselves and were willing to "keep" school until something else came along. Standards governing teaching practice were almost nonexistent, although rules and regulations governing teachers' personal lives and moral conduct could, in some communities, be quite strict. Take, for example, the set of promises, illustrated in Figure 1.1, that women teachers were required to sign in one community in North Carolina. This list may be more stringent than many others in use at the time, but it gives a clear indication of nineteenth-century concern for teachers' moral character and conduct and apparent lack of concern for teachers' pedagogical abilities.

## Twentieth-Century Role Expectations

By the late nineteenth and early twentieth centuries, the purposes of education were expanding rapidly, and teachers' roles took on added dimensions. Comprehensive high schools as we know them today were created, most states passed compulsory attendance laws that required all students to be in school until age 16, and the goals of education moved beyond the narrow purposes of basic literacy. Vast economic changes during these years outmoded the apprentice system that had existed in the workplace, and much of the responsibility for helping youth to make the transition from family to work fell to the schools. Also, the arrival of immigrants from other countries, plus new migration patterns from rural areas into the cities, created large, diverse student populations with more extensive needs than simple literacy instruction. Look, for example, at the seven goals for high school education issued by a committee appointed by the National Education Association in 1918, and notice how much these goals exceed the focus on the three Rs of earlier eras:

1. Health
2. Command of fundamental processes
3. Worthy home membership
4. Vocational preparation
5. Citizenship
6. Worthy use of leisure time
7. Ethical character*

Such broad and diverse goals made twentieth-century schools much more comprehensive institutions as well as places for addressing some of the societal reforms that have characterized this century. Schools increasingly became instruments of opportunity, first for immigrants from Europe and later for African Americans, Hispanics, and other minority groups who had been denied equal access to education. Expanding their functions beyond academic learning, schools provided such services as health care, transportation, extended day care, and breakfasts and lunches. Schools also took on various counseling and mental health functions—duties that earlier belonged to the family or the church—to help ensure the psychological and emotional well-being of youth.

Obviously, expanded purposes for schooling had an impact on the role expectations for teachers. Most states and localities began setting standards for teachers that later became requirements for certification. Special schools were created to train teachers in the subject matters they were expected to teach and to ensure that they knew something about **pedagogy**. By the early twentieth century, teachers were expected to have two years of college preparation; by the middle of the century, most held bachelor's degrees. Teaching gradually came to be viewed as a career, and professional organizations for teachers, such as the National Educational Association and the American Federation of Teachers, took on growing importance both for defining the profession and for influencing educational policy. Teaching practices of the time, however, were rarely supported by research, and teachers, although expected to teach well, were judged by vague global criteria, such as "knows subject matter," "acts in a professional manner," "has good rapport," "dresses appropriately." However, progress was made during this period, particularly in curriculum development for all the major subject areas, such as reading, mathematics, social studies, and science. Also, major work was accomplished in helping to understand human development and potential.

**The study of the art and science of teaching is called pedagogy.**

## Teaching Challenges for the Twenty-First Century

No crystal ball can let us look fully into the twenty-first century, which we have just begun. Certain trends, however, are likely to continue, and some aspects of education and teaching will remain the same, while others may change rather dramatically. On one hand, the tremendous changes occurring in the way information is stored and accessed with computers and over the Internet will certainly change many aspects of education. Today and in the future, the World Wide Web has the potential of connecting students to a vast array of resources not previously available. Many believe that the Internet will become, if it hasn't already, the primary medium for information and will substantially redefine other forms of print and visual publications. This in turn will cause educators to redefine many lessons and assignments they give to students.

*These goals were named the Seven Cardinal Principles. Some historians believe that they were symbolic statements of hope that reveal what schools in the new industrial society aspired to do rather than descriptions of reality.

On the other hand, it is likely, at least in the immediate future, that society will continue to require young people to go to school. Education will remain committed to a variety of goals and some new ones may be added, but **academic learning** will remain the most important. It is not likely that the physical space called *school* will change drastically in the foreseeable future. Organizing and accounting for instruction will change, but if history is a guide, this change will come slowly. Schools will likely continue to be based in communities, and teachers will continue to provide instruction to groups of children in rectangular rooms.

Contemporary reform efforts show the potential of bringing new and radical perspectives about what academic learning means and how it can best be achieved. New perspectives also are emerging as to what constitutes *community* and its relationship to the common school. The nature of the student population and the expectations for teachers are additional factors that likely will change drastically in the decades ahead.

### Teaching in a Multicultural Society.

The United States is a multicultural society. Today, this situation is no longer a question of values or policy. It is a fact, a condition of our culture. The challenge for teachers in the twentieth-first century is to transform schools and approaches to teaching that were created at a time when most of the students had a Western European heritage and spoke English to meet the needs of a much more diverse student population. Harold Hodgkinson (1983) wrote that "every society is constructed on a foundation of **demographic assumptions.** When these assumptions shift, as they do from time to time, the result is a major shock throughout the society" (p. 281). Schools in the United States have been experiencing such a demographic shock over the past thirty years, and it will continue to affect schools and teachers well into the twenty-first century. The most important demographic shift involves the increasing number of students who have ethnic or racial heritages that are non-European, for whom English is a second language, and who live in poverty. Nationwide, the proportion of these young people has increased from less than one-fifth in 1970 to about one-third today. It is predicted that students from minority groups will reach 40 percent by the year 2010. (See *Conditions of Education*, 1996, and *Youth Indicators*, 1996.) In some states, such as California, New Mexico, Texas, and Florida, students from non-European or non-English-speaking backgrounds already comprise over 50 percent of the public school population. Although this demographic shift is most pronounced in large urban areas, it is not confined to inner cities alone. Today, many schools in suburban communities, and even rural areas such as Idaho, are characterized by racial and ethnic diversity.

Linguistic diversity constitutes one of the most rapidly growing shifts, as an increasing number of non-English-speaking children enter the public schools. The number of limited-English students has doubled nationwide over the past two decades (Office of Bilingual Education, 1998), with 3.2 million now enrolled in public schools. At the beginning of the twenty-first century, about 16 percent, of children had a first language other than English. The majority of these children speak Spanish as their first language, but many other languages are represented, including Arabic, Vietnamese, Russian, and Tagolog. Look, for example, at the many different languages spoken in homes in the United States shown in Figure 1.2.

A trend throughout the history of schools has been to extend educational opportunities to more and more students. Compulsory attendance laws early in the century opened the doors to poor white children; the now-famous Supreme Court decision, *Brown* v. *Board of Education of Topeka* (1954), extended educational opportunities to African American children. The Education for All Handicapped Children Act of 1975

---

*Today, society holds teachers accountable for using best practice and for the academic learning of their students.*

*We live in a multicultural society; it is a condition of our culture.*

*Today, about 16 percent of children in school have a first language other than English.*

**Figure 1.2** *Languages Spoken in U.S. Homes*

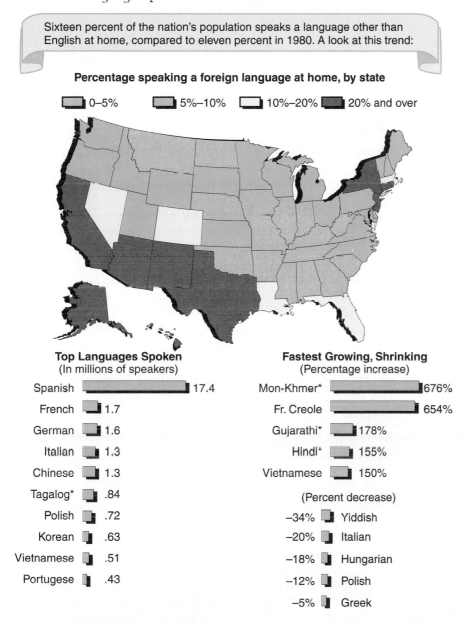

Sixteen percent of the nation's population speaks a language other than English at home, compared to eleven percent in 1980. A look at this trend:

**Percentage speaking a foreign language at home, by state**

0–5%    5%–10%    10%–20%    20% and over

**Top Languages Spoken**
(In millions of speakers)

Spanish 17.4
French 1.7
German 1.6
Italian 1.3
Chinese 1.3
Tagalog* .84
Polish .72
Korean .63
Vietnamese .51
Portugese .43

**Fastest Growing, Shrinking**
(Percentage increase)

Mon-Khmer* 676%
Fr. Creole 654%
Gujarathi* 178%
Hindi* 155%
Vietnamese 150%

(Percent decrease)

−34% Yiddish
−20% Italian
−18% Hungarian
−12% Polish
−5% Greek

*Tagalog is a language of the Philippines; Mon-Khmer is a language of Cambodia; Hindi and Gujarathi are languages of India.

Source: After *Spokesman Review* (1993), p. 2A; Office of Bilingual Education, 1998.

brought an end to policies that prevented children with disabilities from getting an education and changed the enrollment patterns in schools. Figure 1.3 shows the changes in the number of children served by special education between 1977 and 1999. Notice that for all disabilities, the population being served increased from 8 percent in the 1970s to almost 13 percent by the mid-1990s.

**Figure 1.3** *Number of Children with Disabilities Served by Special Education as a Percentage of Total Public (K–12) School Enrollment*

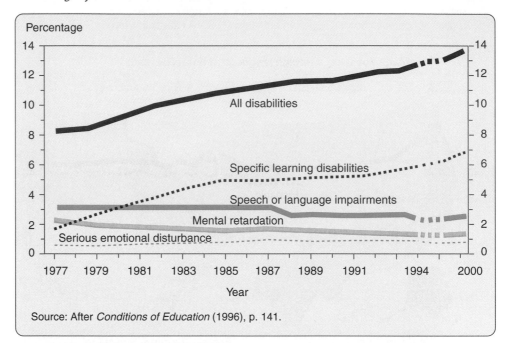

Source: After *Conditions of Education* (1996), p. 141.

*Schools today must accommodate a wide variety of learning and cultural differences.*

Another demographic factor that affects schools and teachers is that many children who attend public schools today live in poverty. In fact, some observers argue that poverty has replaced race as the most urgent issue facing the nation and that poverty is at the core of most school failure. Figure 1.4 shows the percentage of children under 18 years old who live below the poverty level. Note that the percentage of children living in poverty decreased rather substantially between 1960 and 1970 but increased steadily in the 1980s and 1990s.

**Figure 1.4** *Percentage of Children under 18 Years Old Who Live in Families with Incomes below the Poverty Level*

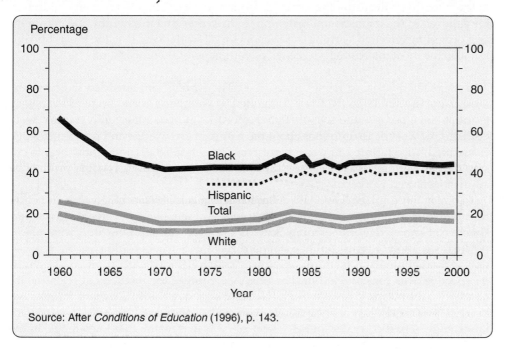

Source: After *Conditions of Education* (1996), p. 143.

These trends have significance for teaching and for those preparing to teach in at least three important ways.

First, for both social and economic reasons, many people in the larger society will remain committed to providing educational opportunities to all children. Society will also demand that minority and handicapped students do well in school. Some of these students will come from homes of poverty; others will come from homes in which parents do not speak English; some will be emotionally or physically different from their classmates. These students will experience school differently than those whose parents were educated in our schools and who have prepared their children for them. Working with youth from diverse cultural backgrounds and with various special needs will necessitate that teachers have a repertoire of effective strategies and methods far beyond those required previously. Teachers will also have to be able to adapt curriculum to make it more suitable for those who may find school devastatingly difficult or irrelevant to their lives.

Second, it is likely that schools will continue to be scrutinized for racial and ethnic balance in their student and teacher populations. This means that during the next several decades, teachers can expect to experience complex social and organizational arrangements in which school enrollment boundaries will be changed often, efforts will be made to diversify student populations through open enrollment and magnet school programs, and teachers themselves may be moved from school to school more often than in the past.

Finally, and perhaps most important, the voices of minority and immigrant communities and those who don't speak English will no longer be ignored. Parents of these children will no longer tolerate schools with inadequate materials and untrained

**Today's schools require teachers who have a repertoire of effective teaching strategies so the needs of all children can be met.**

teachers. They will not allow their children to be automatically grouped by ability and placed in noncollege-bound tracks. They will demand a curriculum and approaches to teaching that will ensure the same academic and social success for their children as for children in the mainstream. Listening to the voices of a multicultural community and providing effective learning experiences for all students will be the most difficult, but also the most interesting, challenge of your generation of teachers.

**Teaching for the Construction of Meaning.** The schools you attended were, for the most part, very similar to the schools attended by your parents and perhaps even your grandparents, because the schools that evolved in the late nineteenth century were built around a set of assumptions about the nature of knowledge and how knowledge is acquired. Also factored in was a corresponding set of beliefs about how best to ensure that all young citizens acquire this knowledge and, in turn, become productive adult citizens and workers.

> The traditional view of knowledge holds that there are "truths" and an objective reality that humans have access to and can learn through discovery.

Our contemporary educational system has its roots in the late nineteenth and early twentieth centuries and is based on a factory model of schooling and an **objectivist perspective** of knowledge and learning. Schools, like the factories of the time, were places where instruction or tasks could be standardized and teachers could pass on information to their students in the form of known "truths." Knowledge, from an objectivist perspective, was constant and unchanging. Accordingly, the methods of scientific inquiry were the means to discovering a fixed and objective reality. Teachers, from an objectivist perspective, were individuals who had acquired a "chunk" of important knowledge in particular disciplines. Their role was to transmit that knowledge, in the form of facts, concepts, and principles, to students. Since knowledge was known and fixed (relatively speaking), formal schooling governed by this perspective aimed to organize what was known into a set curriculum for all students to learn. In turn, school success was demonstrated through student mastery of the curriculum, as measured by standardized achievement tests. This perspective has led to the testing movement observed over the past two decades: students in almost every state are required to demonstrate that they have mastered specified knowledge. Increasingly, those who do not pass their state's mastery tests are held back from promotion to the next grade and required to attend summer school.

> A constructivist perspective holds that learning is a social and cultural activity, that knowledge is somewhat personal, and that learners construct meaning through experience and interaction with others.

An alternative to the objectivist perspective, and one that has gained respectability in some educational circles over the past two decades, is known as **constructivism.** Rather than viewing knowledge as fully known, fixed, and transmittable, the **constructivist perspective** holds that knowledge is somewhat personal, and meaning is constructed by the learner through experience. Learning is a social and cultural activity in which learners construct meaning that is influenced by the interaction of prior knowledge and new learning events. Tobin (1992) wrote that from a constructivist perspective, "learning should focus . . . not only on the manner in which an individual attempts to make sense of phenomena, but also on the role of the social in the mediation of learning" (p. 3). The school's curriculum, from this perspective, is no longer considered a document of important information but instead a set of learning events and activities through which students and teachers, jointly negotiate meaning.

**Teaching for Active Learning.** The system of schooling we created in the nineteenth century rested on a perspective that learning was a passive activity. Rectangular rooms, fixed seating, and blackboards and lecterns at the front of classrooms were designed for the effective transmission of knowledge from teachers as their students sat quietly taking notes.

Learning from a constructivist perspective is not viewed as passively receiving information from the teacher but instead as actively engaging in relevant experiences and having opportunities for dialogue so meaning can evolve and be constructed. Learning takes place not in passive classrooms but in communities characterized by high levels of participation and engagement. We will repeatedly come back to the idea that learning is the process of making sense out of experience in *Learning to Teach,* and you will come to see that teaching for active learning will require drastic changes in teacher behavior as contrasted to the teachers you have observed for most of your life.

**Learning Ability Is More Than Language and Math.** Traditional theories and practices have held that individuals have specific mental abilities. At the turn of the last century, psychologists such as Alfred Binet in France and Lewis Terman at Stanford University developed tests aimed at measuring human intelligence and abilities. These tests were used widely in Europe to determine who could benefit from advanced schooling. In the United States, they were soon employed to help place students in instructional groups based on their abilities as well as to help determine who was fit to serve in the army. Even though IQ tests have fallen into disfavor over the past half century, tests of basic skills and those that measure more general knowledge, such as the Scholastic Aptitude Test (SAT), have replaced them and are used widely to make decisions about where students should be placed in school and where they can go to college. A century of work has left us with three unresolved questions: Is intelligence one or many things? Is intelligence inherited? And, can intelligence be accurately measured?

Many practicing educators today believe that IQ tests and tests of general knowledge have little to do with an individual's ability or capacity for learning but instead reflect one's social and cultural background. Children from families and communities that reflect the cultural mainstream, for instance, often do better on these tests than the children of parents who live in poverty or who just immigrated to the United States and whose primary language is not English.

Finally, some contemporary psychologists, such as Howard Gardner (1984, 1999), challenge the idea that there is general intelligence, as suggested by Spearman (1927). Instead, this research has shown that intelligence and ability are much more than the single dimension of language usage and logical thinking as measured by most intelligence and aptitude tests. According to Gardner, there are at least eight separate intelligences, including: linguistic, logical-mathematical, spatial, musical, bodily-kinesthetic, interpersonal, intrapersonal, and naturalist. Individuals differ in their strengths in the various intelligences. Unfortunately, today's schools too often emphasize only success as determined by language and mathematical abilities and ignore the other six intelligences. We will come back to this issue in later chapters of *Learning to Teach.*

**Teaching and Choice.** Once we move away from notions of fixed curriculum and fixed ways of knowing, we can also start questioning the efficacy of the standardized school. For example, do all students need to be exposed to the same ideas in particular subjects, at the same time and in the same manner? Should all students be required to go to the same type of school with the same curriculum and for the same lengths of time? An increasing number of policy makers and educators are saying no to these types of questions, and alternatives are being sought to the standard public school.

Alternatives to the standard school are found in many suburban areas of the country today. Normally these alternatives consist of magnet or special-focus schools, where curriculum is designed around the performing arts or science and technology. This type of alternative is financed by public funds, but students and their parents can choose the alternative over other more traditional schools in the community.

A trend more pronounced in schools situated in the larger cities in the United States, where student populations are most diverse and where resources to support public education are scarcest, are privatization and charter schools. For instance, several large city school systems from Florida to California have contracted with private firms to run some of their schools, with the intent of making a profit. In the spring of 1992, the president of Yale University resigned from Yale to manage Whittle Industries' Edison Project. Today, Edison runs seventy-nine for-profit schools all over the country, serving thirty-eight thousand students (*Education Week,* 1999).

Another trend over the past decade related to school choice has been the home schooling movement. Many reasons have prompted parents to take on the responsibility of educating their own children. Some belong to fundamental religious groups that fear that the secular nature of public schools will dilute their children's faith. Others want to keep their children separated from youth culture and the drugs and violence perceived to characterize the public schools in their communities. Still others want to express their right to have their children experience a "monocultural" rather than a multicultural community. Regardless of the reasons, as of 2000, many families were educating their children at home, and this trend presents the same kinds of challenges to public education as do other forms of school choice.

The latest trend in school choice has been the charter school movement. Charter schools are publicly funded schools conceived and started by parents, citizens, or teachers; in some ways, they operate like private schools in that they are independent of the local public school districts and exempt from many of the local and state regulations imposed on public schools. After individuals or groups obtain a charter from a school district or the state government, they are then given public monies to operate the school and are held accountable by the chartering agency for meeting prespecified standards. As of 2000, over twenty-five states had enacted charter-school laws, and over seventeen hundred charter schools had been started.

School choice and privatization have their critics as well as their advocates. Advocates maintain that private, profit-driven schools will introduce an element of competition into the educational system and that schools, once freed from the bureaucratic structures and political processes that have come to characterize many large city schools, will provide superior education for students for the same or lower cost through innovative programming and more effective use of human resources. Many people are willing to allow these experiments to proceed because of beliefs that the public schools simply are not functioning as they should.

On the other hand, many educators and concerned citizens worry that private schools will not accept the more difficult-to-teach students, thus making the public schools more and more the home for the most helpless and hopeless young people in our society. Some research evidence seems to bear this out. Others are concerned about the values and moral system reflected, either formally or informally, in for-profit schools. Still others are afraid that the best teachers in the country will be drawn to for-profit schools, leaving the less capable to teach those students who need good teachers the most.

**Teaching and Accountability.** Until very recently, teachers had minimal preparation and few expectations as to performance. However, standards during the twentieth century began to emphasize liberal arts preparation and some exposure to pedagogy. During the early part of the twentieth-first century, this trend will accelerate rather dramatically. Beginning teachers will increasingly be required to demonstrate their knowledge of pedagogy and subject matter prior to certification, and they will be held **accountable**

*Giving parents a choice in the schools their children attend challenges the traditional concept of the standardized school.*

*Today's teachers are held accountable for their teaching practices and for what their students learn.*

*The best teachers show
concern for their students
and feel responsible for
their learning.*

for using best practice throughout their careers. For instance, as of 1999, all but one state
required some type of testing before issuing an initial certificate to teach. Most states are
using the Praxis tests developed by the Educational Testing Service (ETS), but alternative and more performance-based tests are being considered in a number of states.

Current trends in teacher testing are likely to continue and to lead to extended training
programs for teachers. Many of you using this book may be in extended programs now.
Most extended programs are characterized by the teacher candidate obtaining a bachelor's degree with a subject matter major, followed by a master's degree in pedagogy.

Before getting a license to teach, you may be required to demonstrate through examination your knowledge and skill in teaching. Competency in academic subject matter
will no longer be sufficient, particularly for teaching in classrooms that are culturally diverse and contain students with various special needs. Neither will liking children, in
and of itself, be enough for tomorrow's teachers. Twenty-first-century teachers will be
required to have a command of various knowledge bases (academic, pedagogical, social, and cultural) and to be reflective, problem-solving professionals. The following description of teachers appeared in *A Nation Prepared: Teachers for the Twenty-First Century*,
sponsored by the Carnegie Forum on Education and the Economy (1986):

> Teachers should have a good grasp of the ways in which all kinds of physical and social
> systems work; a feeling for what data are and the uses to which they can be put; an ability to
> help students see patterns of meaning where others see only confusion; an ability to foster
> genuine creativity in students; and the ability to work with other people in work groups that
> decide for themselves how to get the job done. They must be able to learn all the time, as the
> knowledge required to do their work twists and turns with new challenges and the progress
> of science and technology. Teachers will not come to the school knowing all they have to
> know, but knowing how to figure out what they need to know, where to get it, and how to
> help others make meaning out of it.
>
> Teachers must think for themselves if they are to help others think for themselves, be able
> to act independently and collaborate with others, and render critical judgment. They must
> be people whose knowledge is wide ranging and whose understanding runs deep. (p. 25)

Arthur Wise (1995), the president of the National Council for the Accreditation of
Teacher Education (NCATE), made a similar statement about the knowledge and skills
teachers will need to demonstrate in the future.

*spotlight on Technology*

## Is School Out?

In 1992, L. Perelman wrote a particularly provocative book around the idea that schools as we know them are obsolete.

In *School's Out: Hyperlearning, the New Technology and the End of Education* (1992), Perelman uses the term *hyperlearning* to denote the speed and connectedness of learning as he develops the thesis that new technology in the form of computers, information networks, and multimedia will give everyone access to learning, something not possible when the schools we now have were created. Instead of learning occurring within the "classroom box," learning in the future will permeate every form of social activity. Instead of learning being confined to children, it will be the province of everyone at every age.

Perelman argues that it makes no sense to reform schools and that reform efforts such as school choice or higher standards only serve as a diversion from the main things that need to happen, which include:

- Complete privatization of education
- Replacement of school buildings with learning channels on television and the information superhighway
- Abolition of all credentialing systems (including those for teachers), which he believes choke progress
- Creation of national technological schools that would exist without campuses or faculty

Although Perelman's book was written almost a decade ago, many of his speculations seem to have come true. With home schooling, distant learning, and Web-based instruction, perhaps schools as formal organizations are becoming less dominant, and a great deal of learning is occurring informally through families, peer groups, work organizations, and computer networks. This, of course, raises a number of provocative questions for educators and individuals preparing for a career in teaching. What would the end of schools as we know them mean to learners? Could they obtain through informal means the type of education required in a technologically advanced society? What would it mean to teachers? Would teaching careers even exist? If we did away with credentials, how would quality control be provided for consumers of medical, legal, or educational services?

Teachers should be able to use strategies for developing critical thinking and problem solving. They should be able to use formal and information evaluation strategies to ensure continuous student learning. They should be versed in educational technology, including use of the computer and other technologies for instruction and student evaluation. Prospective teachers should be skilled in classroom management and be able to collaborate effectively with parents and others in the community. They should know and use research-based principles of effective practice proven to be effective. In other words, teachers should be able to explain why they decide to use a certain strategy or teach a particular idea in a certain way. In short, prospective teachers should demonstrate competence, needed knowledge, and acceptable proficiency. (p. 5)

In 1986, the Carnegie Task Force on Teaching as a Profession recommended establishing a career ladder for teachers and the creation of a National Board for Professional Teaching Standards (NBPTS). NBPTS was formed the following year and is currently governed by a 63-member board of directors, mostly K–12 teachers but also including administrators, curriculum specialists, state and local officials, union and business leaders, and college and university professors. The national board has designed procedures to assess the competence of experienced teachers, and it issues a national teaching certificate to those who meet its rigorous standards. National certification is voluntary, and the national certificate is not intended to replace the continuing or advanced certificate offered by the states. Currently, no specific extrinsic rewards, such as a higher salary, accompany national certification. However, some teacher groups argue that a reward system will be required if national certification is to become widespread.

When fully realized, the national board will offer certificates in more than thirty fields, categorized by subject matter and developmental level of students. Certification will be available to teachers either as generalists or specialists in subject areas or special education.

**Teaching and Technology.** It is likely, as our society completes its transition into the informational age, that schools will change just as they did when we moved from an agrarian to an industrial society during the nineteenth century. Although we certainly don't know exactly how schools will look by the mid-twenty-first century, futurists have argued that formal schooling, as currently conceived and practiced, will be as out-of-date in the enterprise of learning as the horse and buggy are in the modern transportation system.

Throughout *Learning to Teach,* you will find box summaries on particular aspects of technology. These boxes are included to help you see how almost everything teachers do today is influenced by technology and how many aspects of teaching can be enhanced by technology. The Spotlight on Technology box in this chapter explores an interesting thesis developed a few years ago by L. Perelman, namely that schools as we know them are no longer needed.

**✓ Check for Understanding**

- How have teacher roles evolved over the years, and what forces have contributed to these changes? What revisions to traditional schooling do you foresee?

- What demographic shifts have led to changes in the student population, and how have these trends impacted schools and teachers?

- What are six major teaching challenges of the twenty-first century?

# 🍎 A Perspective on Effective Teaching

Central to the process of learning to teach are views about how children learn, the primary goals of teaching, and definitions of an effective teacher. The goals of teaching in a complex society are diverse, and trying to define an effective teacher has long occupied the thoughts of many. For example, in the media we have traditional images of effective teachers, such as the kindly Miss Dove and the bumbling but caring Mr. Chips. More recently, the effectiveness of the rigid and authoritarian Joe Clark has been described, as has that of James Escalante of *Stand and Deliver* fame, who gets his students to accomplish extraordinary feats.

Within the educational community there has been a remarkable diversity in the definition of effective teaching. Some have argued that an effective teacher is one who can establish rapport with students and a nurturing, caring environment for personal development. Others have defined an effective teacher as a person who has a love for learning, a superior command of a particular academic subject and transmits his or her subject effectively to students. Still others argue that an effective teacher is one who can activate student energy to work toward a more just and humane social order.

The content of a teacher education curriculum is itself a statement about what effective teachers need to know. Clinical experiences and tests for certification, such as Praxis I or Praxis II, make similar statements, as do the assessment systems used in schools to evaluate and counsel beginning teachers.

The purposes of teaching and conceptions of the effective teacher are also central to writing a book about learning to teach and influence its plan, its organization and unifying themes, and the choice of topics to include. The following section describes the point of view of *Learning to Teach* on these matters.

## The Ultimate Goal of Teaching

Citizens in a diverse and complex society such as ours expect their schools to accomplish many different goals. For example, here are a few that appear regularly in the popular press: teach basic academic skills, build student self-esteem, prepare students for college, promote global understanding, prepare students for work, transmit cultural heritage. The multiple purposes of education can become overwhelming unless teachers can focus their teaching goals. *Learning to Teach* takes the position that the ultimate purpose of teaching is *to assist students to become independent and self-regulated learners.* This purpose does not negate other purposes of education, but instead it serves as an overarching goal under which all other goals and teacher activities can be placed. This primary purpose stems from two underlying assumptions. One is the contemporary view that knowledge is not entirely fixed and transmittable but is something that all individuals, students and adults alike, actively construct through personal and social experiences. The second is the perspective that the most important thing that students should learn is *how to learn.*

## A View of the Effective Teacher

The concept of effective teaching that has guided the planning and writing of *Learning to Teach* does not include any of the stereotypes embodied in Mr. Chips, Joe Clark, or Miss Brooks; neither does it include an argument about whether academic competence is more important than nurturance or vice versa. Effective teaching requires at its baseline individuals who are academically able, who have command of the subjects they are required to teach, and who care about the well-being of children and youth. It also requires individuals who can produce results, mainly those of student academic achievement and social learning. These characteristics are prerequisites for teaching, but they are insufficient without four higher-level attributes:

1. Effective teachers have *personal qualities* that allow them to develop **authentic** human relationships with their students, parents, and colleagues and to create democratic, **socially just classrooms** for children and adolescents.
2. Effective teachers have positive dispositions toward knowledge. They have command of at least three broad **knowledge bases** that deal with subject matter, human development and learning, and pedagogy. They use this knowledge to guide the science and art of their teaching practice.
3. Effective teachers command a **repertoire** of teaching practices known to stimulate student motivation, to enhance student achievement of basic skills, to develop higher-level thinking, and to produce self-regulated learners.
4. Effective teachers are personally disposed toward **reflection** and problem solving. They consider learning to teach a *lifelong process,* and they can diagnose situations and adapt and use their professional knowledge appropriately to enhance student learning and to improve schools.

These attributes of effective teachers are illustrated in Figure 1.5.

In *Learning to Teach,* these attributes of an effective teacher are crucial themes and have been woven into each of the chapters in the book. The word *theme* is used here as it is used to describe a theme song in a Broadway musical—a song that recurs often throughout the production and becomes associated with the main ideas and characters in the play. Readers will find the themes summarized here referred to again and again throughout the book.

*The ultimate purpose of teaching is to help students become independent and self-regulated learners.*

*The knowledge bases that inform teaching consist of information accumulated over time from research and from the wisdom of experienced teachers.*

*A teacher's repertoire consists of the number of teaching approaches and strategies he or she is able to use to help students learn.*

*Effective teaching requires careful and reflective thought about what a teacher is doing and the effects of his or her action on students' social and academic learning.*

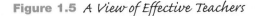

**Figure 1.5** *A View of Effective Teachers*

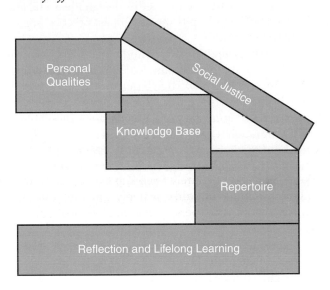

## Personal Qualities for Developing Authentic Relationships

For many years, people believed that a teacher's personal qualities were the most important attributes for effective teaching. In general, teachers who were warm and loving were thought to be more effective than those who were perceived to be cold and aloof. Like most beliefs, this one had a measure of truth to it. It also left an incomplete picture, because effective teaching requires much more than being warm and loving toward children.

Our perspective encompasses a view that it is important for teachers to have caring dispositions toward children and youth and to believe in the abilities of all children to learn. As will be described in later chapters, all too often teachers do not hold high expectations for all children. Instead, they sometimes have perceptions that some students, mainly those from minority groups, are not capable of learning, and as a result, they restrict these students' opportunities to learn. It is critical that tomorrow's teachers break the cycle of failure built into our educational system by creating classroom learning communities that are democratic and socially just.

Our perspective also encompasses the view that teachers must possess sufficient interpersonal and group skills to establish authentic relationships with their students and their colleagues. It is from these relationships that student motivation to engage in learning is maximized. Similarly, it is from authentic relationships with colleagues that schoolwide goals are developed and accomplished.

> Establishing authentic relationships with students is a prerequisite to everything else in teaching.

## Knowledge Base to Guide the Art of Practice

Effective teachers have control over a knowledge base that guides what they do as teachers, both in and out of the classroom. In fact, professionals by definition have control over information (the knowledge base) that allows them to deal with certain matters more insightfully and more effectively than the average person. At the same time, no professionals, including doctors, engineers, and lawyers, have a complete knowledge base from which to find answers to every question or problem. Not every problem can be solved by the use of best practice—patients die, design ideas fail, and legal cases are lost. The same is true in teaching. Despite the use of best practice, some students do not learn and others drop out of school.

It is important for those learning to teach to understand what is meant by the *knowledge bases* for teaching and to understand the strengths and limitations of the scientific research that informs the current knowledge bases for teachers. It is also important to point out that, though the knowledge bases for teaching are still young and not yet complete, in contrast to the fragmentary and inconsistent knowledge bases of two or three decades ago, the situation today is vastly improved.

Three questions about the knowledge base for teaching are important to consider: (1) What does it mean to have a knowledge base about teaching, and what domains of knowledge are most relevant? (2) How do teachers access and use knowledge? (3) What are the limits of current knowledge on teaching and learning?

**Nature and Domains of Knowledge.** Scientific knowledge is essentially knowledge about relationships between variables. In the social sciences or applied sciences (such as education), this means that knowledge exists about how one variable is related to another and, in some instances, how one set of variables under certain conditions affects others. In education, the variables that have been most studied, and those most relevant to learning to teach, are those associated with student learning and with how student learning is affected by teacher behavior. Lee Schulman (1987) has attempted to organize the important domains of knowledge for teachers into seven categories:

> There are several domains of knowledge that inform teaching, some of which stem from research and others from the experiences of practicing teachers.

1. *Content knowledge,* or knowledge of the particular subjects to be taught such as mathematics, English, history.
2. *Pedagogical content knowledge,* that is, the special amalgam of content and pedagogy that is uniquely the province of teachers; their own special form of professional understanding.
3. *Knowledge of learners* and their characteristics.
4. *General pedagogical knowledge,* with special reference to those broad principles and strategies of classroom management and organization that appear to transcend subject matter.
5. *Knowledge of educational contexts,* ranging from the workings of the group or classroom, to the governance and financing of school districts, to the character of communities and cultures.
6. *Curriculum knowledge,* with particular grasp of the materials and programs that serve as "tools of the trade" for teachers.
7. *Knowledge of educational ends, purposes, and values* and their philosophical and historical grounds. (pp. 2–3)

*Learning to Teach* explores primarily the knowledge bases associated with categories 3, 4, and 5. In particular, it synthesizes and describes the enormous body of knowledge that has been created in the past thirty years and informs our understanding of how students learn; the factors that motivate learning; how leadership can be provided to manage complex instructional settings; and, specifically, the links that have been found between teacher expectations and behaviors and student achievement. At one time, what we knew about these topics and relationships was very limited. Currently, we can be confident of considerable knowledge in several areas, some of which have been validated experimentally and replicated under varying conditions.

**Teacher Use of Knowledge.** Educational philosopher Gary Fenstermacher (1986) has proposed that the major value of educational research for teachers is that it can lead to the improvement of their **practical arguments.** His argument for this position goes something like the following.

The knowledge and beliefs that teachers, as well as other professional practitioners, hold are important not only for their own sake but also because they prompt and guide action. Actions taken by practitioners are guided by a number of premises—beliefs held to be just and true and linked together in some logical format. Sometimes these premises and the underlying logic have been made explicit by the practitioner; many times, however, they are not consciously aware of their practical arguments. Fenstermacher (1986) provides the following example of a teacher's practical argument used to support the methods she used to teach reading.

A practical argument is the reasoning, based on knowledge and beliefs, that is used by teachers as they make pedagogical decisions.

1. It is extremely important for children to know how to read.
2. Children who do not know how to read are best begun with primers.
3. All nonreaders will proceed through the primers at the same rate (the importance of learning to read justifies this standardization).
4. The skills of reading are most likely to be mastered by choral reading of the primers, combined with random calling of individual students.
5. This is a group of nonreaders for whom I am the designated teacher.

Action: (I am distributing primers and preparing the class to respond in unison to me.) (p. 46)

In this example, premise 1 is a statement of value, on which most people concur. Premise 5 is a statement of fact, presumed to be accurate. Premises 2, 3, and 4, however, are beliefs held by the teacher about how children learn and about pedagogy. These beliefs influence the actions of using primers and choral reading. In this particular instance, these beliefs are simply not supported by the research on reading instruction.

Fenstermacher pointed out that the results of research, and knowledge of "best" practice, if known, could lead this teacher to doubt her beliefs and subsequently rethink the premises undergirding her pedagogical behavior and instructional practices. Knowing about and using research becomes a process of understanding, doubting, and challenging the beliefs we hold about how children learn and about the best practices to employ to enhance this learning. It is in contrast to taking actions based on tradition, conventional wisdom, or folklore.

Research on teaching, then, can dispel old wives' tales about teaching, just as other research can dispel myths about aspects of the physical and social world outside education. For this reason, it is important for teachers to have a firm grasp of the knowledge base on teaching, including its application in various settings. Everyone, however, should be cautious and remember that teaching is a tremendously complex process that continually departs from fixed recipes and formulas. We should also remember the limits of educational research and current knowledge about teaching.

**The Limits of Research.** There are several reasons research can inform classroom practice in some instances and not in others.

***No Fast Formulas or Recipes.*** Even though principles and guidelines for best practice exist for today's teachers, beginning teachers should not jump to the conclusion that principles based on research will work all the time, for all students, or in all settings. That simply is not true. Instead, teaching and learning are very situational. What works

**There are no easy prescriptions or simple recipes for teaching effectively.**

with one group of students in one setting will not necessarily work with another group someplace else. Similarly, strategies and approaches used by expert, experienced teachers cannot necessarily be emulated by a novice teacher. Teachers must take explanations and principles and apply them within the capacity of their own abilities and skills and within the contextual confines of particular groups of students, classrooms, and communities.

*Explanations Are Not Automatically Recommendations.* Practicing teachers often ask researchers to make recommendations based on their research. Some examples of the types of questions they ask include: Should we use ability groupings in third-grade classrooms? What are the best concepts to teach in tenth-grade social studies? How can I motivate John, who comes to school tired every morning? The reply to such questions has to be that research alone cannot provide answers to such specific practical problems. For example, take the question about what to teach in tenth-grade social studies. Even though a researcher might provide empirical information about what other school districts teach in the tenth grade or about the abilities of most 15-year-olds to understand historical concepts, this would not tell a teacher what concepts to teach, given a particular group of students, the goals of a particular social studies curriculum or teacher, and the community values—all crucial factors to consider.

**Societal views and community values influence what and how teachers teach.**

*Explanations Are Not Inventions.* A final limitation of research is that it focuses on existing practice. The descriptions and explanations about what teachers currently do are valuable but should not preclude the invention or use of new practices. The two examples that follow may help to highlight the importance of this point.

Many of the research-based practices for classroom management stem from studies in which researchers compared the classroom management procedures used by researcher-defined effective teachers with those used by less effective teachers. From this research, patterns of effective classroom management practices have emerged. However, these results do not mean that better practices are not to be invented. It simply means that compared to the range of current practices, we can say that some classroom management procedures are better than others under certain conditions.

Along the same line, much of the research on effective teaching has been done in classrooms that represent the more traditional patterns of teaching—a single teacher working with whole groups of students for the purpose of achieving traditional learning objectives—student acquisition of basic information and skills. Although this research, like the classroom management research, can inform us about best practices within the confines of the traditional paradigm, it does not tell us very much about worthwhile innovations and new paradigms that may exist in the future.

## Repertoire of Effective Practice

Effective teachers have a repertoire of best practices. *Repertoire* is a word used mainly by people in music and the theater to refer to the number of pieces (such as readings, operas, musical numbers) a person is prepared to perform. Obviously, more experienced and expert performers have larger, more diverse repertoires than novices do. This is also true for teachers.

This book emphasizes that effective teachers have diverse repertoires and are not restricted to a few pet practices. This is in contrast to some arguments from earlier eras intended to prove the superiority of one approach to another—for example, inductive versus deductive teaching, the lecture versus discussion method on the use of phonics

**Figure 1.6** *Three Aspects of Teaching*

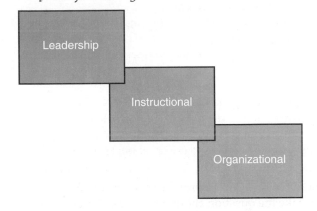

to teach reading versus a whole-language approach. This debate is futile and misdirected. No single approach is consistently superior to any other in all situations. Instead, many teaching approaches are appropriate, and the selection of a particular model depends on a teacher's goals, the characteristics of a specific group of learners, and community values and expectations.

The teaching practices described in this book comprise a minimum number of models, strategies, and procedures that should be in a beginning teacher's repertoire. Some are large and complex models of teaching; others are rather simple procedures and techniques. The practices described are obviously not all that exist; effective teachers add to their repertoires throughout their careers.

The concept of repertoire carries with it the idea that a course of action is linked to various aspects of the job. To use the music analogy again, an accomplished musician may have one repertoire for performances of classical music, one for appearances in nightclubs or pop concerts, and perhaps another for family get-togethers. Just as this text was designed around a particular perspective of teaching, so too was it constructed around a conception of what teachers do and the repertoire required in three domains of their work.

Teachers, regardless of their grade levels, their subject areas, or the types of schools in which they teach, are asked to perform three important functions. They provide leadership to a group of students, they provide direct, face-to-face instruction to students, and they work with colleagues, parents, and others to improve classrooms and schools as learning organizations. These three aspects of teachers' work are illustrated in Figure 1.6. Obviously, these aspects are not always discrete, nor does the teacher always perform one aspect of the job independently of the others. These labels, however, are convenient organizers for helping beginning teachers make sense out of the bewildering array of events associated with teaching in a complex school setting.

**Leadership.** In many ways, a contemporary teacher's roles are similar to those of leaders who work in other types of organizations. Leaders are expected to plan, to motivate others, to coordinate work so individuals can work interdependently, and to help formulate and assess important organizational goals.

The leadership view of teaching has sometimes been criticized. Critics argue that it grew out of the industrial age concept of the efficient manager and that this image makes people think about schools the same way they think about factories and thus overemphasize the technical and skill side of teaching. The "teacher as leader"

*Teachers provide leadership to their students through planning, motivation, and the facilitation of learning.*

metaphor can also lead to excessive attention to control, orderliness, and efficiency at the expense of creativity and spontaneity.

Regardless of past misuse of the "teacher as leader" metaphor, there are indeed many parallels between the work they perform. *Learning to Teach* presents these leadership skills in a manner that does not violate the artistic side of teaching, that is, teacher creativity and spontaneity.

**The most important aspect of teachers' work is providing face-to-face instruction to students in classrooms.**

*Instructional.* When most people think about what teachers do, they think of the day-by-day instruction of students. The overall framework for thinking about this aspect of teaching comes mainly from three sources: (1) the "models of teaching" concept developed by Bruce Joyce and Marsha Weil (1972, 1996); (2) the teaching strategies and procedures that have resulted from the research on teaching over the past forty years (Gage, 1963; Travers, 1973; Wittrock, 1986; Richardson, 2000); and (3) the wisdom of practice contained in the repertoire of experienced teachers.

Over the years, many different teaching approaches have been created. Some were developed by educational researchers investigating how children learn and how teaching behavior affects student learning. Others were developed by classroom teachers experimenting with their own teaching in order to solve specific classroom problems. Still others were invented by psychologists, industrial trainers, and even philosophers such as Socrates.

**The term *teaching model* is used to describe an overall approach to or plan for instruction. The attributes of teaching models are a coherent theoretical framework, an orientation toward what students should learn, and specific teaching procedures and structures.**

Joyce and Weil (1996) labeled each of these approaches a **teaching model.** A model, as defined here, is more than a specific method or strategy. It is an overall plan, or pattern, for helping students to learn specific kinds of knowledge, attitudes, or skills. A teaching model, as you will learn later, has a theoretical basis or philosophy behind it and encompasses specific teaching steps designed to accomplish desired educational outcomes.

Each model differs in its basic rationale or philosophical base and in the goals the model has been created to achieve. Each model, however, shares many specific procedures and strategies, such as the need to motivate students, define expectations, or talk about things.

Teachers need many approaches to meet their goals with a diverse population of students. A single approach or method is no longer adequate. With sufficient choices, teachers can select the model that best achieves a particular objective, the model that best suits a particular class of students, or the models that can be used in tandem to promote student motivation, involvement, and achievement.

In *Models of Teaching* (1996), Joyce and Weil identify and describe over twenty major models or approaches to teaching. But how many of these should there be in a beginning teacher's repertoire? Obviously, it is unrealistic to ask a beginner to master all the models—that is a lifelong process. To require command of only a single model is equally unrealistic. It seems fair and practical to ask beginning teachers to acquire a modest repertoire during the initial stages of their career. Therefore, we have selected six models that, if learned well, can meet the needs of most teachers. These are: presentation, direct instruction, concept teaching, cooperative learning, project-based instruction, and classroom discussion. In Table 1.1, you will find that the first three teaching models—presentation, direct instruction, and concept teaching—are based on more traditional perspectives about student learning and rest on teacher-centered principles of instruction. Cooperative learning, problem-based instruction and discussion, on the other hand, stem from a constructivist perspective of learning and learner-centered approaches to teaching.

**Table 1.1** *Classification of Six Models of Teaching*

| Traditional/Teacher-Centered | Constructivist/Student-Centered |
|---|---|
| Lecture/presentation | Cooperative learning |
| Direct instruction | Problem-based instruction |
| Concept teaching | Classroom discussion |

**Organizational.** The common view of teaching focuses mostly on classroom interactions between teachers and students, and as such it is insufficient for understanding the reality of teaching in contemporary schools. Teachers not only plan and deliver instruction to their students; they also serve as organizational members and leaders in a complex work environment.

Not only are schools places where children learn; they are also places where adults carry out a variety of educational roles—principal, teacher, resource specialist, aide, and so forth. Schools are both similar to and different from other workplaces. Similarities include the ways coordination systems are designed to get the work of the school accomplished. Beginning teachers will find that adults who work in schools are pretty much like adults who work in any other organization. They strive to satisfy their own personal needs and motives in addition to achieving the mission of the school. At the same time, those of you who have worked in other organizations (perhaps during the summer or in a previous career) will find some unique aspects of the school workplace. These include norms that give teachers a great deal of autonomy in their work but isolate them from their colleagues; clients (students) who do not voluntarily participate in the organization; and because the school is highly visible

**In addition to working with students, teachers today are expected to work with other adults in the school setting for the purpose of schoolwide planning and coordination.**

*Working with other teachers is an important aspect of a teacher's job.*

politically, diverse and unclear goals that reflect the multiple values and beliefs of contemporary multicultural society.

Schools are also places, like other organizations, that need to be changed as things change in the larger society around them. Many people preparing to teach have strong idealistic drives to make education and schools better. This idealism, however, is not always supported with sound strategies for putting good ideas into practice, even though the knowledge base on educational change and school improvement has increased substantially over the past two decades. A knowledge base now exists to explain why many earlier education reform efforts failed, and this knowledge can be applied to school improvement ideas you may want to implement.

Building a repertoire of organizational skills is important for two main reasons. First, your ability to perform organizational roles and to provide leadership within the school as well as the classroom will greatly influence your career. It is through performing organizational roles well that beginning teachers become known to other teachers, to their principals, and to parents. It is also how they become influential professionally with their colleagues and beyond the confines of their schools. Conversely, a beginning teacher's inability to perform organizational functions effectively is the most likely reason for dismissal. Many teachers who are terminated in their early years are dismissed not for instructional incompetence but for their inability to relate to others or to attend to their own personal growth and psychological well-being within a complex organizational setting.

A second reason for learning organizational skills is because researchers and educators are starting to understand that student learning is related not only to what a particular teacher does but also to what teachers within a school do in concert. To work toward schoolwide effectiveness requires such organizational skills as developing good relationships with colleagues and parents, engaging in cooperative planning, and agreeing on common goals and common means for achieving those goals. The effective teacher is one who has a repertoire for entering into schoolwide and communitywide dialogue about important educational issues.

*Student learning not only depends on what teachers do in their classrooms; it is also strongly influenced by what teachers and parents in particular schools do in concert.*

## Reflection and Problem Solving

Many of the problems faced by teachers are situational and characterized by their uniqueness. Unique and situational cases call for "an art of practice," something that cannot be learned very well from reading books. Instead, effective teachers learn to approach unique situations with a problem-solving orientation and learn the art of teaching through reflection on their own practice.

In addition, many of the problems facing teachers become problems of values and priorities that scientific knowledge can help explain but cannot help decide. An observation from Schön (1983) underscores the value-laden world of practicing teachers.

> Practitioners are frequently embroiled in conflicts of values, goals, purposes and interests. Teachers are faced with pressure for increased efficiency in the context of contracting budgets, demands that they rigorously "teach the basics," exhortation to encourage creativity, build citizenship, and help students to examine their values. (p. 17)

If knowledge cannot provide a complete guide for effective practice, how do practitioners become skilled and competent in what they do? Again Schön (1983) provides valuable insights. He argues that there is an irreducible element in the art of professional practice and that gifted practitioners, whether they are engineers, scientists, managers, or teachers, display their artistry in their day-to-day practice. And, though

✓ **Check for Understanding**

- What are the major characteristics of effective teachers?

- What specific personal qualities are typically exhibited by effective teachers?

- What areas of teaching and learning have been scientifically studied, producing a knowledge base for educators to use?

we don't always know how to teach the art of practice, we do know that for some individuals it is learnable.

*Learning to Teach* strives to present its textual information in such a way as to alert you to the areas of teaching where our knowledge is fragmented and incomplete and to possible teaching situations in which you will be required to exhibit individual problem solving and reflection. Many of the learning aids found in the student manual that accompanies this text will assist you in becoming problem solving in your orientation and reflective about your teaching practice. Reflection and problem solving are complex dispositions and skills and are not easily learned. However, as you read previously, the art of professional practice is learnable, and it is experience, coupled with careful analysis and reflection, that produces this learning.

## 🍎 Learning to Teach

Some teachers, like fine wines, keep getting better with age. Others do not improve their skills even after years of practice and remain at about the same skill level as the day they first walked into a classroom. Why is it that some teachers approach the act of teaching critically and reflectively; are innovative, open, and altruistic; are willing to take risks with themselves and their students; and are capable of critical judgment about their own work? Conversely, why do others exhibit exactly the opposite traits?

Becoming truly accomplished in almost any human endeavor takes a long time. Many professional athletes, for example, display raw talent at a very early age, but they do not reach their athletic prime until their late twenties and early thirties and then only after many years of dedicated learning and practice. Many great novelists write their best pieces in their later years only after producing several inferior and amateurish works. The biographies of talented musicians and artists often describe years of pain and dedication before the subjects reached artistic maturity. Becoming a truly accomplished teacher is no different. It takes purposeful actions fueled by the desire for excellence; it takes an attitude that learning to teach is a lifelong developmental process in which one gradually discovers one's own best style through reflection and critical inquiry.

This section describes some of the things we know about the process of learning to teach and emphasizes that learning to teach is a lifelong and developmental process, not one limited to the period of time between the first methods class and the date a teaching license is acquired. Few effective teachers are born that way. Rather, they become increasingly effective through attention to their own learning and development of their own particular attributes and skills.

### Models of Teacher Development

As you will read later, contemporary views about how children learn also apply to how teachers learn. As applied to teaching, it means that individuals develop cognitively and affectively through stages. As we learn to teach, we process experiences through our existing cognitive structures. Obviously, individuals entering teaching have a rather complex cognitive structure about teaching because they have spent so many hours observing teachers during their years in school. As we gain new experiences, growth occurs and we progress to a more complex stage. Growth, however, is not automatic and occurs only when appropriate experiences provide a stimulus to a person's

✓ **Check for Understanding**

- Why should a teacher's repertoire of strategies be as diverse and flexible as possible?

- What are the three major aspects of a teacher's job?

- In what ways are the leadership challenges faced by teachers similar to those of individuals in other lines of work?

- Why must teachers maintain an open mind and be reflective about their practice?

**Becoming a truly accomplished teacher takes a long time, fueled by an attitude that learning to teach is a lifelong process.**

cognitive and emotional growth. When environmental conditions are not optimal, that is, are either too simple or too complex, then learning is retarded. In other words, as people learning to teach become more complex themselves, their environments must also become correspondingly more complex if they are to continue developing at an optimal rate. Although it is not possible to readily change many of the environments you will experience as you learn to teach, you can, nonetheless, try to seek out environments and experiences that will match your level of concern and development as a teacher.

What this means is that becoming a teacher, like becoming anything else, is a process in which development progresses rather systematically through stages with a chance of growth remaining static unless appropriate experiences occur. The following are specific developmental theories about how people learn to teach.

**Stages of Development and Concern.** The late Frances Fuller studied student teachers, beginning teachers, and more experienced teachers at the University of Texas in the late 1960s and early 1970s. During the 1980s, Sharon Feiman-Nemser (1983), then a researcher at Michigan State University, also identified several stages **novice teachers** go through in the process of becoming **expert teachers.** Her stages are similar to those of Fuller, and the two are combined in the following list.

> **Novice teachers go through rather predictable stages in the process of becoming accomplished.**

1. *Survival stage.* When people first begin thinking about teaching and when they have their first classroom encounters with children from in front of rather than behind the desk, they are most concerned about their own personal survival. They wonder and worry about their interpersonal adequacy and whether or not their students and their supervisors are going to like them. Also, they are very concerned about classroom control and worry about things getting out of hand. In fact, many beginning teachers in this initial stage have dreams about students getting out of control.

2. *Teaching situation stage.* At some point, however—and this varies for different individuals—beginning teachers start feeling more adequate and pass beyond the survival stage. Various aspects of controlling and interacting with students become somewhat routinized. At this stage, teachers begin shifting their attention and energy to the teaching situation itself. They start dealing with the time pressures of teaching and with some of the stark realities of the classroom, such as too many students, inappropriate instructional materials, and perhaps their own meager repertoire of teaching strategies.

3. *Pupil concern and mastery stage.* Eventually, individuals mature as teachers and find ways of coping or dealing with survival and situational concerns. During this stage, teachers master the fundamentals of teaching and classroom management. These become effective and routine. It is only then that teachers reach for higher-level issues and start asking questions about the social and emotional needs of students, being fair, and the match between the teaching strategies and materials and pupil needs and learning.

The Fuller and Feiman-Nemser models are useful for thinking about the process of learning to teach. Their principles help to put present concerns in perspective and to prepare beginners to move on to the next and higher level of concern. For example, a beginning teacher who is overly worried about personal concerns might seek out experiences and training that build confidence and independence. If class control takes too much mental and emotional energy, a beginning teacher can find ways to modify that situation. An aid that can help you to measure your concerns at this point in your career is included in the Student Manual that accompanies *Learning to Teach.*

**Implications of Developmental Models for Learning to Teach.** As beginning teachers go through the process of learning to teach, the developmental models conceptualized by Sprinthall and Thies-Sprinthall, Fuller, and Feiman-Nemser have numerous implications. First, these models suggest that learning to teach is a developmental process in which each individual moves through stages that are simple and concrete at first and later more complex and abstract. Developmental models thus provide a framework for viewing your own growth.

Second, you can use the models to diagnose your own level of concern and development. This knowledge can help teachers to accept the anxiety and concerns of the beginning years and, most important, to plan learning experiences that will facilitate growth to more mature and complex levels of functioning.

## Early Influences on Teaching

It appears that some aspects of learning to teach are influenced by the experiences that people have with important adult figures, particularly teachers, as they grow up and go through school. In the early 1970s, Dan Lortie, a sociologist at the University of Chicago, spent several years studying why people become teachers, what kind of a profession teaching is, and what experiences affect learning to teach. As part of his study, he interviewed a rather large sample of teachers and asked them what experiences most influenced their teaching. Many experienced teachers told Lortie that early authority figures, such as parents and teachers, greatly influenced their concepts of teaching and their subsequent decision to enter the field. Lortie's study and his results are summarized in Research Summary 1.1.

This is the first example of the research summaries you will find in each chapter of *Learning to Teach.* These summaries are included to help you get a feel for some of the research that has been carried out in education and to help you develop an appreciation for the knowledge base on teaching. The boxed research summaries, such as the Lortie study, were chosen either because they are considered classics in particular fields or because they illustrate the variety and richness of method found in educational research.

The format used to present Lortie's research is one that will be followed throughout the book when research reports are summarized. The problem the researcher addressed is presented first, followed by brief descriptions about who was studied and the types of procedures used. When needed, pointers are provided to help you read the research. Each research summary concludes with a description of important findings and statements about the implications of the research for practice.

This format is used because it is important that you become knowledgeable about the research base on teaching and learning, and it is equally important that you learn how to read, critique, and use research. At the end of this book is a special section called "Reading and Using Research." This section provides further insight into the nature of research on teaching and a practice exercise for reading research; you may want to read it before going on.

A great deal is known about the process of learning to teach that goes beyond the scope of this chapter. However, by way of summary, those learning to teach should enter the process valuing the experiences they have had and recognize that they already

✔ **Check for Understanding**

- What are the three stages that teachers typically go through during the process of becoming an effective teacher?

- What forces seem to influence many teachers when they initially make the decision to enter the profession? What are the advantages and disadvantages of this situation?

# How Do Early Experiences Influence Our View of Teaching?

What do we know about the influences on our decision to become teachers, and how do all those experiences we have as students influence our view of teaching? These were among several questions asked by Daniel Lortie in what has become a classic study about teachers and teaching.

**Problem and Approach:** Lortie was interested in a variety of issues about teaching as an occupation, particularly the organization of the teacher's work, the sentiments teachers have about their work, and the "ethos" of the teacher's occupation as contrasted to other occupations.

**Sample and Setting:** Lortie collected information from a number of sources. The focus here is on the data he collected through extensive interviews with ninety-four teachers from five towns in the Boston metropolitan area and from a national survey conducted by the National Education Association in the late 1960s.

**Procedures:** By Lortie's own account, his methods included "historical review, national and local surveys, findings from observational studies by other researchers, and content analysis of intensive interviews" (p. ix). His sample from the five towns around Boston included selecting school systems that were broadly representative of American education; he then randomly selected teachers from within the five systems. He interviewed the teachers about the attractions of teaching and various other features of their careers, using techniques he developed in earlier studies on the legal profession.

**Pointers for Reading Research:** The researchers who carried out many of the studies used in this book reported their results in numeric form and summarized them in data tables. Lortie's data are presented not in tabular format but, instead, as direct quotes from the people he interviewed. Information quoted directly from interviews is quite easy to read and to understand. However, readers of this type of research information always need to ask themselves questions about the data, such as: Did the researcher conduct the interviews in such a way that respondents provided honest and accurate information? From many possibilities, did the researcher se-

lect quotes that were representative of what the total sample reported, or did he or she select quotes to represent a particular point of view or bias? Are the conclusions reached by researchers using interview data consistent with the information the data contain?

**Results:** Lortie's study is large and complex and has many insights into teaching and teachers. Here are some of his findings about why people go into teaching and the influence of early experiences on their teaching.

**Interview Data:** One teacher interviewed shows the influence of early adult figures on her decision to teach:

My mother was a teacher, her sisters were teachers—it's a family occupation. I always wanted to go into teaching. I can't remember when I didn't want to. . . . I remember as a little girl sometimes seeing teachers have a hard time. I thought, well, I will be careful because some day I'll be on the other side of the desk. (p. 61)

Lortie also found that teaching is one of the few professions in which the practitioner has been in the client (student) role for an extended period (several hours each day for sixteen years) before switching to the professional role. It comes as no surprise that teachers told Lortie that their own teaching was greatly influenced by the teaching they had received as students. The following excerpts from Lortie's interviews illustrate this influence.

The teacher I had in sixth grade was good, interesting. There are a few things I used this year that I remember having done in her room. (p. 63)

There was one particular teacher in my eighth and ninth grades. She was very hard, very strict, and used to say, "I know some of you don't like me since I'm so strict; but when you get out of school and think back, a lot of you will probably think of me as being the best teacher." She really was. She probably taught me how important classroom discipline was. (p. 64)

My second-grade teacher was kind. She knew it was a terrific change for me to come all the way from Iowa and she'd take the time to talk to me, to take away some of the fright. I never forgot that and when new youngsters come into my room I always try to team them up with someone. I have a special word for them. (p. 64)

I had a college professor. . . . This is the man who had more to do with my techniques than any other person. (p. 64)

I had her in United States history and she whetted my appetite for history. . . . I may be one of her products. I think I am. (p. 64)

**Discussion and Implications:** It is obvious that prior experiences with their own teachers have affected and will continue to influence the ways teachers think and act about teaching. In some ways this is positive, since it provides beginners with many models over the years. However, relying too completely on these early experiences may make

teachers rather conservative in trying new approaches. Many of the standard practices used by former teachers may not represent best practices, given current knowledge about teaching and learning. Also, if beginning teachers rely too heavily on their prior experiences, that may prevent them from being sufficiently reflective and analytical toward their work.

Lortie, D. (1975). *School-teacher: A sociological study.* Chicago: University of Chicago Press.

know a lot about teaching. At the same time, they should also accept that they have much to learn. Effective teachers must learn to execute complex and particularly effective procedures and methods. They must also challenge their existing perceptions and learn how to think like experienced teachers. This is not always easy, because expert and novice teachers think differently. Mastering the behaviors and thought processes of teaching are among the most important challenges of learning to teach and when accomplished can bring the most cherished rewards.

## 🍎 *Summary*

### Scientific Basis for the Art of Teaching

Teaching has a scientific basis that can guide its practice; it also has an artistic side.

### Historical Perspective on Teaching

- The role of the teacher is a complex one that has been shaped by historical and contemporary forces. Expectations for teachers have changed. In the eighteenth and nineteenth centuries, the primary concern was the teacher's moral character, whereas today we are more concerned about the teacher's pedagogical abilities.
- Today, almost one-third of our students come from non-Western European backgrounds, many speak English as their second language, and a large proportion of them are poor. These three factors in combination are reshaping the teacher's role. Teachers are expected to work in complex multicultural educational settings and to provide good educational experiences for all children.
- Teachers today are expected to help students construct their own knowledge and to be actively involved in their own learning.

- Increasingly, teachers are expected to have advanced preparation and to demonstrate their knowledge of both subject matter and pedagogy.

### A Perspective on Effective Teaching

- Effective teachers possess personal qualities for developing authentic relationships with their students, understand the knowledge base on teaching and learning, can execute a repertoire of best practices, have attitudes and skills necessary for reflection and problem solving, and consider learning to teach a lifelong process.
- The scientific basis of teaching is learned mainly through studying research and the wisdom of practice accumulated by the profession. From scientific knowledge certain teaching principles and propositions have been derived that can inform best teaching practices.
- Principles based on research, however, cannot be translated directly into fixed recipes and formulas that will work all the time. This is true because teaching is situational, and the characteristics of particular students, classrooms, schools, and communities affect what works and what doesn't.

- Repertoire refers to the number of strategies and processes teachers are prepared to use. Effective teachers develop a repertoire of methods and skills to successfully carry out various aspects of their work.
- A teacher's work can be conceptualized around three main functions: leadership, instructional, and organizational.
- The leadership aspects of teaching refer to the leadership roles teachers are expected to play in their classrooms, such as providing motivation, planning, and allocating scarce resources.
- The instructional aspects of teaching refer to methods and processes teachers employ as they provide day-by-day instruction to students.
- The organizational aspects of teaching refer to teachers' work in the school community, including work with colleagues, parents, and school leadership personnel.
- Effective practice includes abilities to approach classroom situations in reflective and problem-solving ways.

## Learning to Teach

- Learning to teach is developmental and a lifelong process. Teachers go through predictable stages. At first they are concerned about survival, later about their teaching situation, and finally about the social and academic needs of their pupils.
- Parents and teachers often influence a person's decision to enter teaching and affect a teacher's vision of teaching. Memories of favorite teachers, however, may not be the best models for developing one's own teaching style, because these teachers may not have been as effective as they seemed.
- Learning to teach is a complex process, and information that is useful to experienced teachers may not have the same value for beginners.

## 🍎 Key Terms

| | | |
|---|---|---|
| best practice | constructivist perspective | leadership aspects of teaching |
| scientific basis of teaching | accountability | instructional aspects of teaching |
| art of teaching | authentic relationship | organizational aspects of teaching |
| pedagogy | socially just classroom | teaching model |
| academic learning | knowledge base | novice teachers |
| demographic assumptions | repertoire | expert teachers |
| objectivist perspective | reflection | |
| constructivism | practical arguments | |

## 🍎 Books for the Professional

Barzun, J. (1991). *Begin Here: The Forgotten Conditions of Teaching and Learning.* Chicago: University of Chicago Press. This little book features various essays and articles written by Jacques Barzun during his long career that describe his vision about what it means to teach and to learn and what is required of teachers and schools if they are to be effective.

Fosnot, C. T. (1989). *Enquiring Teachers, Enquiring Learners.* New York: Teachers College Press. This book does a wonderful job of taking concepts such as constructivist perspectives, teacher empowerment, and reflection and showing how they relate to classroom learning and how they can be put into practice to help beginners learn to teach.

Gage, N. L. (1978). *The Scientific Basis of the Art of Teaching.* New York: Teachers College Press. This book discusses the value of educational research and how it has produced useful knowledge that supports practice.

Gardner, H. (1993). *Multiple Intelligences: The Theory in Practice.* New York: Basic Books. This is the book in which Gardner describes his theory of multiple intelligences and discusses how this perspective can impact schools of the future.

Joyce, B., Weil, M., and Showers, B. (1996). *Models of Teaching* (5th ed.). Englewood Cliffs, N.J.: Prentice Hall. This book is a must. It provides more information on the models of teaching described here, plus many others.

Oakes, J., and Lipton, M. *Teaching to Change the World.* Boston: McGraw-Hill, 1999. An excellent little book about teaching from a constructivist, social-cultural perspective. Provides a nice critique of problems facing today's schools and offers concrete suggestions for reform for teachers.

Richardson, V. (ed.). (2000). *Handbook of Research on Teaching* (4th ed.). New York: Macmillan. This book is the most authoritative review of the mountain of research on teaching. Beginning teachers will find many of the chapters tough going; however, it is an invaluable reference work.

Russell, T., and Munby, H. (eds.). (1992). *Teachers and Teaching: From Classroom to Reflection.* New York: Falmer Press. A very timely book of readings on reflective teaching with particular attention to Schön's concept of "reflection-into-action." Contributors represent the United Kingdom, the United States, Australia, and Canada.

Schön, D. A. (1983). *The Reflective Practitioner.* San Francisco: Jossey-Bass. This book explores the complexity of learning to become a professional and emphasizes the importance of developing skills for "reflection in action."

Warren, D. (ed.). (1989). *American Teachers: Histories of a Profession at Work.* New York: Macmillan. This collection of essays provides excellent insight into the history of teaching in the United States, including efforts to reform the profession over two centuries. Essays provide a perspective about how current reforms efforts in education are linked to the past.

## 🍎 *The Professional Portfolio*

Many beginning and experienced teachers today are preparing what are known as "professional portfolios." A portfolio is a collection of ideas, artifacts, and products that provide an authentic means for teachers to represent their views on teaching, their work, and their students' work.

Portfolios are not just something you do one time. Instead, they are useful for keeping a record of professional growth over a lifetime of learning to teach. They are particularly useful for displaying your work when interviewing for a teaching position. Many teacher education programs require teacher candidates to build a portfolio early in their program so it can evolve and mature as the candidate grows and changes. Some states also require portfolios as part of the evaluation process for beginning teachers.

At the end of each chapter of *Learning to Teach,* you will find a feature called Reflection and Portfolio. This feature has been designed to help you reflect on the important ideas covered in the chapter and to develop a product that can be placed in your portfolio.

Items most teachers put in their portfolios include reflective essays showing how they think about teaching and learning, artifacts such as sample units of work or lesson plans, and samples of their students' work, particularly work that shows how the teacher has impacted student learning. Some teachers also include photos and videos showing classroom teaching and student interaction.

There is no particular format to follow in a portfolio. However, the portfolio, like all work, should be neat, organized, and creative. Most important, the portfolio should represent you. More information and portfolio activities can be found in the Student Manual that accompanies *Learning to Teach.* Below is a suggestion for your first portfolio entry.

## Reflection & Portfolio

You have just completed your student teaching, and the professor you had last year for your methods class has asked you to provide your perspective on effective teaching to her class. You are pleased that the professor has asked you to do this. At the same time, you know that coming up with a definitive answer about what constitutes effective teaching is no easy task. So, you start asking yourself: What is the perspective that guided my action while I was student teaching? How were my teaching practices tied to my views about student learning? How were my teaching practices influenced by research? How did my own experiences or those of my cooperating teachers influence them? Reflect on answers to these questions as you prepare your presentation and compare them to the views expressed by the teachers below. You may also want to turn this reflective essay into an exhibit on effective teaching for your portfolio.

### Theresa Carter

If I were asked to provide students in a methods class my perspective on effective teaching, I would emphasize two important things: knowledge and passion for my subject, and ability to relate to students. Mainly, I hold a constructivist perspective about how students learn. This means that it is not enough merely to present information to students, have them take notes, and then give it back to me on a test. I want students to build and develop their own knowledge and meaning. This requires that I know my subject well enough so I understand the nuances of the field and so I can create lessons that connect new subject matter to what my students already know. Also, I need to be able to explain things in response to student questions and in ways they understand.

"I think effective teachers must also show students that they really care about them as individuals. It is the kind of caring where teachers hold high expectations for the student's work, where they take the time to provide each student with in-depth and constructive feedback, and where they pay attention to what students are doing in aspects of their lives that extend beyond the classroom."

### Dean Kleinert

I think effective teachers are those who hold their students to very high standards. Perhaps I am old-fashioned, but I believe that students should learn the things adults deem important. There is a body of knowledge and a set of skills to be mastered if students are to be successful in life. The best way to promote student learning is to be clear about what is expected of students and be modestly authoritarian in regard to demands for learning and classroom behavior. This is what gives teachers respect; this is what produces good learning year after year.

# Part 1 🍎 *The Leadership Aspects of Teaching*

**T**his part of *Learning to Teach* is about the leadership aspects of teaching. Teachers, like leaders in other settings, are expected to provide leadership to students and to coordinate a variety of activities as they and students work interdependently to accomplish the academic and social goals of schooling. Teacher leadership is critical, because if students are not motivated to participate in and persist with academic learning tasks, or if they are not managed effectively, all the rest of teaching can be lost. Yet these complex functions must be performed in classrooms characterized by fast-moving events and a large degree of unpredictability, and unlike many of the instructional aspects of teaching that can be planned ahead of time, many teacher leadership roles require on-the-spot judgments.

This part focuses on five important leadership functions: planning, motivating students and building productive learning communities, creating inclusive and multi-cultural classrooms, managing classroom groups, and assessing and evaluating student progress. Even though each function is described and discussed in a separate chapter, in the real day-to-day life of teaching, the distinctions are not nearly so tidy. When teachers plan, as described in Chapter 2, they are also setting conditions for allocating time, motivation, and building productive learning communities, the subjects of Chapters 3 and 4. The way students behave and how they are managed on any particular day, the focus of Chapter 5, cycles back to influence future plans and resource allocation decisions, as does evaluation and grading, the focus of Chapter 6.

There is a substantial knowledge base on each aspect of teacher leadership that can provide a guide for effective practice. There is also considerable wisdom that has been accumulated by teachers over the years to help beginning teachers get started with learning to plan, to allocate resources, and to deal with students in group settings.

You will discover as you read and reflect on the leadership aspects of teaching that providing leadership in classrooms is no easy matter and cannot be reduced to simple recipes. Instead, leadership is tightly connected to specific classrooms and schools, and what works in general may not work in any specific case. Learning to read specific situations and to act on them effectively in real classrooms through reflection and problem solving is one of the most important challenges facing beginning teachers. When mastered, this is a most rewarding ability.

# Chapter Two

# Teacher Planning

## Reflecting on **Planning**

Think about personal experiences you have had in your life that required considerable planning. Examples might be planning what college to attend, for a wedding, or for an extended trip. They might also include experiences for which you did not plan. Divide these experiences into two categories: experiences that were well planned and experiences that were not well planned. Now consider the following questions:

🍎 *What did the well-planned experiences have in common?*

🍎 *What did the poorly planned experiences have in common?*

🍎 *What were the consequences, if any, of good planning? Of poor planning?*

Now think about your own planning skills. Are you the type of person who likes to plan? Do you make to-do lists? Do you think through each step of an activity before you begin? Or are you the type of person who feels more at home with allowing experiences to go unplanned and letting things evolve?

🍎 *How do you think your own attitudes toward planning might influence your teaching and the planning required of teachers?*

Even though planning and making decisions about instruction are demanding processes that call for rather sophisticated understanding and skills, teachers do not have to feel overwhelmed. Most of you have planned trips that required complicated travel arrangements. You have planned college schedules, made to-do lists, and survived externally imposed deadlines for term papers and final examinations. Graduation celebrations and weddings are other events most people have experienced that require planning skills of a high caliber. Planning for teaching may be a bit more complex, but the skills you already have can serve as a foundation on which to build.

This chapter describes some of what is known about the processes of teacher planning and decision making. The rationale and knowledge base on planning, particularly the impact of planning on student learning and on the overall flow of classroom life, are described, as are the processes experienced teachers use to plan and make decisions. Also included is a rather detailed explanation of specific planning procedures and a number of aids and techniques used for planning in education and other fields. The discussion that follows strives to capture the complexity of teacher planning and decision making and to show how these functions are performed by teachers under conditions of uncertainty. Although the chapter's emphasis is on the planning tasks carried out by teachers in solitude prior to instruction, attention is also given to the varied in-flight decisions teachers make in the midst of teaching lessons to students.

## 🍎 *Perspective on Planning*

**Careful planning is required for many aspects of modern life.**

People today express great confidence in their ability to control events through sophisticated planning. The importance given to planning is illustrated by the many special occupational roles that have been created for just this purpose. For example, a professional cadre of land-use planners, marketing specialists, systems analysts, and strategic planners, to name a few, work full-time putting together detailed, long-range plans to influence and direct the economy and ensure appropriate military efforts. Family planning, financial planning, and career planning are topics taught to students in high schools and universities and to adults in many settings.

**Good planning involves allocating the use of time, choosing appropriate methods of instruction, creating student interest, and building a productive learning environment.**

Planning is also vital to teaching. One measure of the importance of planning is illustrated when you consider the amount of time teachers spend on this activity. Clark and Yinger (1979), for example, reported that teachers estimate they spend between 10 percent and 20 percent of their working time each week on planning activities. The importance of planning is illustrated in another way when you consider the wide variety of educational activities affected by the plans and decisions made by teachers, as described by Clark and Lampert (1986):

> Teacher planning is a major determinant of what is taught in schools. The curriculum as published is transformed and adapted in the planning process by additions, deletions, interpretations, and by teacher decisions about pace, sequence, and emphasis. And in elementary classrooms, where a teacher is responsible for all subject matter areas, planning decisions about what to teach, how long to devote to each topic, and how much practice to provide take on additional significance and complexity. Other functions of teacher planning include allocating instructional time for individuals and groups of students, composing student groupings, organizing daily, weekly, and term schedules, compensating for interruptions from outside the classroom and communicating with substitute teachers. (p. 28)

*Careful planning is required for many aspects of modern life.*

Indeed, the process of learning to teach is described by some as that through which teacher candidates learn to decide what curriculum content is important for students to learn and how it can be enacted in classroom settings through the execution of learning activities and events (Doyle, 1990).

This chapter will emphasize the importance of planning and highlight that there is much more to planning than good lesson plans. Most important, it will attempt to convey the message that planning is complex and that effective teachers believe "plans are made to be bent."

## Planning—The Traditional View

The planning process in all fields, including education, has been described and studied by many researchers and theorists. The dominant perspective that guides most of the thinking and action on this topic has been referred to as the **rational-linear model.** This perspective puts the focus on goals and objectives as the first step in a sequential process. Modes of action and specific activities are then selected from available alternatives to accomplish prespecified ends. The model assumes a close connection between those who set goals and objectives and those charged with carrying them out. Figure 2.1 illustrates the basic linear planning model.

This model owes its theoretical base to planners and thinkers in many fields. In education, the basic concepts are usually associated with early curriculum planners and theorists, such as Ralph Tyler (1950), and with later instructional designers, such as Mager (1962, 1984), Gagné and Briggs (1988), and Eby (1992). For both groups, good educational planning is characterized by carefully specified instructional objectives (normally stated in behavioral terms), teaching actions and strategies designed to promote prescribed objectives, and careful measurements of outcomes, particularly student achievement.

**The rational-linear approach to planning focuses on setting goals first and then selecting particular strategies to accomplish these goals. Nonlinear planning turns this around. Planners start by taking action and attach goals at some later time.**

**Figure 2.1** *Rational-Linear Planning Model*

Goals → Actions → Outcomes

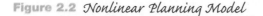

Figure 2.2 *Nonlinear Planning Model*

## Planning—An Alternative Perspective

✓ **Check for Understanding**

• Contrast the traditional, rational-linear view of planning with nonlinear perspectives.

• Can teachers effectively use both models to plan activities?

• In what ways do planning and decision-making activities impact other aspects of teaching?

During the last twenty-five years, many observers have questioned whether the rational-linear model accurately describes planning in the real world (Weick, 1979, and Fullan, 1995, for example). Its view that organizations and classrooms are goal-driven has been challenged, as has its view that actions can be carried out with great precision in a world characterized by complexity, change, and uncertainty.

Note that the rational-linear model found in Figure 2.1 is turned upside down in the **nonlinear model** in which what planners really do is start with actions that in turn produce outcomes (some anticipated, some not) and finally summarize and explain their actions by assigning goals to them. Proponents of this model of planning illustrated in Figure 2.2 argue that plans do not necessarily serve as guides for actions but instead become symbols, advertisements, and justifications for what people have already done. As will be shown later, this model may describe the way many experienced teachers actually approach some aspects of planning. Although they set goals and strive to get a sense of direction for themselves and their students, teachers' planning proceeds in a cyclical, not a straight linear fashion, with a great deal of trial and error built into the process. Indeed, experienced teachers pay attention to features of both the linear and nonlinear aspects of planning and accommodate both.

## 🍎 *Theoretical and Empirical Support*

The research on teacher planning and decision making is substantial and has grown significantly in the past three decades. It has shown that planning has consequences for what students learn, that beginning teachers and experienced teachers plan differently, and that experienced teachers do not always plan as expected. This research also illustrates the complexity of teacher planning and how certain kinds of planning can produce unanticipated and surprising results.

### Consequences of Planning

Both theory and common sense suggest that planning for any kind of activity improves results. Research also favors instructional planning over undirected events and activities, but as you will see, some types of planning may lead to unexpected results.

Planning processes initiated by teachers can give both students and teachers a sense of direction and can help students become aware of the goals implicit in the learning tasks they are asked to perform. Two important studies done at about the same time highlight the effects of planning on teacher behavior and its consequence for students.

Duchastel and Brown (1974) were interested in the effects of instructional objectives on student learning. At the time of their study, previous research results were contradictory, and some had failed to support the contention that clear objectives lead to higher student achievement. The researchers randomly assigned college students taking a course in communications at Florida State University into two groups. Subjects were asked to study several units on the topic of mushrooms. Twenty-four objectives had been written for each unit, and a specific test item had been written to correspond to each objective. Students in group 1 were given twelve of the twenty-four objectives to use as a study guide. Students in group 2 were not given any of the objectives, but they were told to learn as much as they could from the mushroom materials.

When the subjects were tested later, the researchers found that both groups scored the same on the total test. What is interesting and important, however, is the fact that the students who were given twelve of the twenty-four objectives to focus their learning outscored other students on test items associated with these twelve objectives. Of equal interest is that students without any objectives as study aids outscored their counterparts on the items associated with the other twelve objectives.

Duchastel and Brown concluded that learning objectives have a focusing effect on students, which leads to the recommendation that teachers make students aware of the objectives they have for their lessons. On the other hand, the researchers caution teachers to be careful because the study also illustrated how focusing too much on objectives may limit other important student learning.

John Zahorik (1970), working about the same time as Duchastel and Brown, was interested in the effects of planning on *teacher behavior*, particularly planning behaviors associated with identifying objectives, diagnosing student learning, and choosing instruction strategies. He wanted to find out if teachers who planned lessons were less sensitive to pupils in the classroom than teachers who did not plan.

Zahorik studied twelve fourth-grade teachers from four suburban schools near Milwaukee, Wisconsin. The twelve teachers in the study were randomly divided into two groups designated "teachers who planned" and "teachers who did not plan." Teachers in the planning group were given a lesson plan with objectives and a detailed outline on the topic of credit cards. They were asked to use it with their classes. Teachers in the nonplanning group were asked to reserve an hour of classroom time to carry out some unknown task—the task later to be announced as teaching about credit cards. All lessons were tape-recorded, and teacher behaviors were coded using a system designed to categorize the teachers' sensitivity to students.

Zahorik found *significant* differences between the teachers who had planned and those who had not planned. Teachers who planned were less sensitive to student ideas and appeared to pursue their own goals regardless of what students were thinking or saying. Conversely, teachers who had not planned displayed a higher number of verbal behaviors that encouraged and developed student ideas. Zahorik concluded that goal-based planning may inhibit teachers from being as sensitive to students as they could be.

The question that immediately arises from this study is, if goal-based planning makes teachers less sensitive to students, should teachers eliminate planning? Zahorik concluded that the answer is obviously no. Elimination of planning might "also bring about completely random and unproductive learning. If a lesson is to be effective, it would seem that some direction in the form of goals and experiences, no matter how general or vague, is needed" (p. 150).

Both the Duchastel and Brown and the Zahorik studies are interesting, because together they show the importance of goal-based planning; but they also warn that this

**Planning and the use of objectives have a focusing effect on students and their learning.**

**Planning can also have the unintended consequence of causing teachers to be insensitive to student needs and ideas.**

**Figure 2.3** *Consequences of Clear Instructional Goals and Objectives*

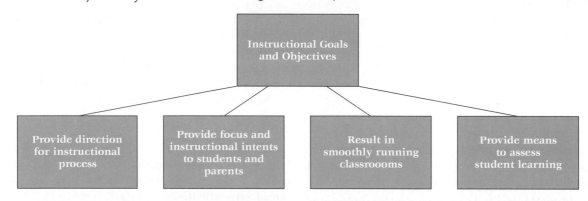

type of planning can lead to unanticipated consequences that are not always desirable. To resolve this dilemma, Zahorik recommends that teachers establish goals that focus on their own behavior. He states, "Along with the typical plan, which can be described as a plan for pupil learning, develop a teaching plan that identifies types and patterns of teacher behaviors to be used during the lesson" (p. 150).

*Careful planning by teachers can lead to smoothly running classrooms.*

Another consequence of teacher planning is that it produces a smoothly running classroom with fewer discipline problems and fewer interruptions. Chapter 5 is devoted to classroom management, so the research on this topic will not be highlighted here. It is important to note, however, that educational research for the past three decades has consistently found that planning is the key to eliminating most management problems. Teachers who plan well find they do not have to be police officers, because their classrooms and lessons are characterized by a smooth flow of ideas, activities, and interactions. Such planning encompasses the rules and goals teachers establish for their classrooms and emphasizes how responsible and businesslike classroom behavior is an integral part of learning. Figure 2.3 summarizes the consequences of having clear instructional goals and objectives.

## Planning and the Beginning Teacher

Researchers and educators also have puzzled over why it seems so difficult for beginning teachers to learn some of the important planning skills. One insight gleaned over the past few years is that it is difficult to learn from experienced teachers, not only because they think differently about planning, but also because they approach planning and interactive decision making differently. Three interesting studies highlight these differences.

Housner and Griffey (1985) were interested in comparing differences in planning and decision making of experienced and inexperienced teachers. They studied sixteen physical education teachers. Eight of the subjects had more than five years' experience; the other eight were preservice teacher candidates. The teachers were given sixty minutes to plan a lesson on how to teach soccer and basketball dribbling to 8-year-olds. The teachers then taught their lessons and were videotaped. Later the teachers viewed their lessons and told the researchers what they were thinking and the decisions they made while teaching. The results of their study are highlighted in this chapter's Research Summary.

Gael Leinhardt (1989) conducted a similar study and compared planning and lesson execution skills of experienced and inexperienced math teachers. Leinhardt found that

*Research Summary 2.1*

# Experience Makes a Difference in Planning

*Housner, L. D., and Griffey, D. G.* (1985). Teacher cognition. Differences in planning and interactive decision making between experienced and inexperienced teachers. *Research Quarterly for Exercise and Sport, 56,* 45–53.

**Problem:** Housner and Griffey were interested in the differences in planning and decision making of experienced and inexperienced teachers.

**Sample and Setting:** The researchers studied sixteen physical education teachers. Eight of the subjects had more than five years of teaching experience; the other eight were preservice teachers training to be physical education teachers.

**Procedures:** The teachers were given sixty minutes to plan a lesson on how to teach soccer and basketball dribbling skills to 8-year-old children. They were to teach two lessons, one for each of the skills. Subjects were told they could ask for more information if they needed it and to think aloud while planning so their thought processes could be recorded. Teachers then taught their lessons to students in groups of four. Lessons were videotaped, and teachers viewed their lessons with the researchers and told them what they were thinking and the decisions they made while teaching.

**Points for Reading Research:** Often researchers are interested mainly in presenting descriptive information about their study. In the data tables from the Housner and Griffey study you will find this situation. The researchers counted teacher behaviors in various categories and described these for the reader using straight percentage figures.

**Results:** In Table 2.1 are data about the kinds of decisions experienced and inexperienced teachers made during the planning period. The researchers divided these into two broad sets—activity decisions and instructional decisions; each set has several subsets.

Table 2.2 shows the types of cues that experienced and inexperienced teachers attended to as they taught the lesson and made in-flight decisions.

**Discussion and Implications:** Table 2.1 shows that experienced and inexperienced teachers differed in the percentage of their thinking that went into four categories: adaptations, management, verbal instructions, and assess/feedback. Experienced teachers planned ahead for more adaptations that might be needed in a lesson as it got underway and were more concerned than inexperienced teachers with establishing rules for activities and means for giving students feedback. Inexperienced teachers devoted a larger percentage of their planning to verbal instructions.

**Table 2.1** *Comparison of Types of Activity and Instructional Strategy Decisions Made by Experienced and Inexperienced Teachers*

| Activity Decisions | Exp. | Inexp. | Instructional Strategy Decisions | Exp. | Inexp. |
|---|---|---|---|---|---|
| Structure | 42.6% | 54.5% | Management | 13.4% | 4.8% |
| Procedures | 24.6 | 28.0 | Assess/feedback | 22.8 | 15.9 |
| Formations | 4.9 | 1.5 | Demonstrate | 7.9 | 7.9 |
| Time | 9.0 | 6.8 | Transitions | 5.5 | 6.4 |
| Adaptations | 18.9 | 9.1 | Focus attention | 18.9 | 19.1 |
| | | | Equipment use | 7.9 | 7.9 |
| | | | Verbal instruction | 19.7 | 34.9 |
| | | | Time | 3.9 | 3.2 |

Source: Adapted from L. D. Housner and D. G. Griffey (1985), p. 48.

Table 2.2 shows that experienced and inexperienced teachers varied in the types of cues they attended to while teaching the lesson. The experienced teachers were most attentive to student performance, whereas inexperienced teachers attended most often to student interest and were more interested in keeping the class on task. This study suggests that beginning teachers would do well to consider the following:

- When planning, submerge a natural tendency to think about verbal instructions and think more about ways to structure rules and routines, give feedback to students, and plan for contingencies.
- When teaching, pay attention to student performance as a basis for making in-flight decisions rather than the stated interests of students or their requests for changes in the lesson.

**Table 2.2** *Types of Cues Heeded by Experienced and Inexperienced Teachers During Interactive Teaching*

| Cues | Experienced | Inexperienced |
|---|---|---|
| Student performance | 30.1% | 19.0% |
| Student involvement | 27.4 | 22.6 |
| Student interest | 11.8 | 27.3 |
| Student requests | 3.2 | 7.7 |
| Student mood/feelings | 3.2 | 6.5 |
| Teacher's mood/feelings | 5.3 | 1.7 |
| Other | 19.0 | 15.2 |

Source: Adapted from L. D. Housner and D. G. Griffey (1985), p. 49

experienced teachers had more complete "mental notepads" and agendas compared to inexperienced teachers. They also built in and used many more checkpoints to see if students were understanding the lesson than did the inexperienced teachers. The experienced teachers, according to Leinhardt,

> weave a series of lessons together to form an instructional topic in a way that consistently builds upon and advances materials introduced in prior lessons. Experts also construct lessons that display a highly efficient within-lesson structure, one that is characterized by fluid movement from one type of activity to another. . . . Novice teachers' lessons, on the other hand, are characterized by fragmented lesson structures with long transitions between lesson segments. . . . Their lessons do not fit well together within or across topic boundaries. (p. 73)

Finally, in a study that is now considered a classic, Peterson and her colleagues (1978) found that experienced teachers do not always use what might be considered "best planning practices." Researchers gave twelve experienced elementary teachers objectives and materials and asked them to plan three lessons on a town in France. Their study produced important and interesting results. Experienced teachers in the study did not follow the common recommendation to start with objectives and learner outcomes. Instead, they planned content and instructional activities first, then came

*Planning skills can sometimes be difficult for beginning teachers to learn because the process itself cannot be directly observed.*

back to the objectives. This raises an interesting question about whether or not these planning patterns represent best planning practices.

The fact that experienced teachers attend to different planning tasks and cues from those attended to by inexperienced teachers presents some challenging problems for a beginning teacher. Unlike other acts of teaching, most teacher planning occurs in private places, such as the teacher's home or office. Also, by their very nature, planning and decision making are mental, nonobservable activities. Only the resulting actions are observable by others. Even when written plans are produced, they represent only a small portion of the actual planning that has gone on in the teacher's head. The private nature of planning thus makes it difficult for beginning teachers to learn from experienced teachers. Beginning teachers may ask to look at lesson plans, or they may talk to experienced teachers about planning and decision-making processes. However, many experienced teachers cannot describe in words the novice can understand the thinking that went into specific plans and decisions. This is particularly true of moment-to-moment planning decisions that characterize the rapid flow of classroom life, such as those described in the studies by Housner and Griffey and by Leinhardt. Teacher planning and decision making may be one of the teaching skills that research can be of most assistance in helping beginning teachers learn about the hidden mental processes of the experienced expert.

## 🍎 Planning Domains

Teacher planning is a complex process. Planning interacts with all other aspects of teaching and is influenced by many factors. Understanding the planning process and mastering the specifics of planning are important skills for beginning teachers.

### Planning and the Instructional Cycle

Teacher planning is a multifaceted and ongoing process that covers almost everything teachers do. It is also part of an overall instructional cycle. It is not just the lesson plans that the teachers create for the next day but also the in-flight adjustments they make

**✓ Check for Understanding**

- What are the benefits and consequences of good planning?

- How did Zahorik's study demonstrate that planning possibly impedes a teacher's level of sensitivity and flexibility? Does his research suggest that planning should be eliminated? Why or why not?

- In what ways do planning approaches of new teachers differ from those used by experienced teachers? How do you explain this, and what can the novice teacher do to improve planning?

**Figure 2.4** *Planning and the Instructional Cycle*

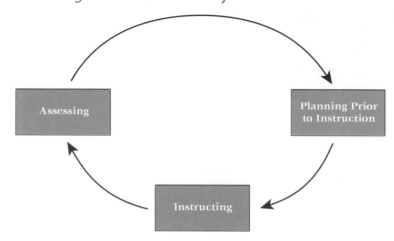

as they teach as well as the planning done after instruction as a result of assessment. Figure 2.4 illustrates the overall flow of planning as it is connected to the instructional cycle.

Notice in Figure 2.4 how some aspects of planning precede instruction and in turn precede assessment of student learning. The whole planning process, however, is cyclical. Assessment information influences the teacher's next set of plans, the instruction that follows, and so on. Further, the mental processes of planning vary from one phase of the cycle to the next. For example, choosing content can only be done after careful analysis and inquiry into students' prior knowledge, the teacher's understanding of the subject matter, and the nature of the subject itself. Most postinstructional decisions, such as the type of test to give or how to assign grades, can also be made as a result of consideration. Planning and decision making during instruction itself, on the other hand, most often must be done spontaneously, on the spur of the moment. Examples of decisions made at each phase of the cycle are listed in Table 2.3.

## The Time Spans of Planning

Teachers plan for different time spans, ranging from the next minute or hour to the next week, month, or year. If schoolwide planning or one's own career planning is involved,

**Table 2.3** *Three Phases of Teacher Planning and Decision Making*

| Before Instruction | During Instruction | After Instruction |
|---|---|---|
| Choosing content | Presenting | Checking for understanding |
| Choosing approach | Questioning | Providing feedback |
| Allocating time and space | Assisting | Praising and criticizing |
| Determining structures | Providing for practice | Testing |
| Determining motivation | Making transitions | Grading |
| | Managing and disciplining | Reporting |

**Figure 2.5** *Five Planning Time Spans*

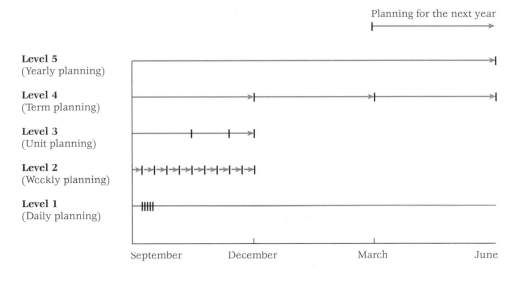

time spans may even cover several years. Obviously, planning what to do tomorrow is much different from planning for a whole year. However, both are important. Also, plans carried out on a particular day are influenced by what has happened before and will in turn influence plans for the days and weeks ahead.

Robert Yinger (1980) conducted an interesting and important study a few years ago that provides teachers with a model for thinking about the time dimensions of teacher planning. Yinger made a detailed study of one first- and second-grade elementary school teacher in Michigan. Using participant-observation methods, he spent forty full days over a five-month period observing and recording the teacher's activities. From this work, Yinger was able to identify the five time spans that characterized teacher planning: daily planning, weekly planning, unit planning, term planning, and yearly planning. Figure 2.5 illustrates these five time spans of planning and plots their occurrence across the school year.

Yinger also found that for each time span of planning, the teacher attended to the following four items: goals of planning, sources of information, form of the plan, and criteria for judging the effectiveness of planning. Table 2.4 summarizes these four aspects of planning for each of the five levels.

## 🍎 *The Specifics of Planning*

By now it must be obvious that planning is important and that teachers must consider a broad range of planning tasks. In this section, the primary tasks associated with teacher planning are described in some detail, starting with choosing what to teach and the use of instructional objectives and followed by the use of long-range and short-range plans and the tools available to teachers to accomplish planning tasks.

**Teachers plan for different time spans ranging from a few minutes to a full year.**

✔ **Check for Understanding**

• What are the three primary phases of the overall instructional cycle? What types of plans and decisions do teachers make at each phase?

• For what time spans must teachers establish plans? What factors did Yinger identify as common to each time span?

• Why is it important to develop unique plans for different time spans? How do these plans interrelate with each other, requiring modification as lessons evolve?

**Table 2.4** *Planning at Each Level of the Model*

| | Goals of Planning | Sources of Information | Form of the Plan | Criteria for Judging the Effectiveness of Planning |
|---|---|---|---|---|
| **Yearly planning** | 1. Establishing general content (fairly general and framed by district curriculum objectives). 2. Establishing basic curriculum sequence. 3. Ordering and reserving materials | 1. Students (general information about numbers and returning students). 2. Resources available. 3. Curriculum guidelines (district objectives). 4. Experience with specific curricula and materials. | General outlines listing basic content and possible ideas in each subject matter area (spiral notebook used for each subject). | 1. Comprehensiveness of plans. 2. Fit with own goals and district objectives. |
| **Term planning** | 1. Detailing of content to be covered in next three months. 2. Establishing weekly schedule for term that conforms to teacher's goals and emphases for the term. | 1. Direct contact with students. 2. Time constraints set by school schedule. 3. Resources available. | 1. Elaboration of outlines constructed for yearly planning. 2. A weekly schedule outline specifying activities and times. | 1. Outlines: comprehensiveness, completeness, and specificity of elaborations. 2. Schedule: comprehensiveness and fit with goals for term, balance. 3. Fit with goals for term. |
| **Unit planning** | 1. Developing sequence of well-organized learning experiences. 2. Presenting comprehensive, integrated, and meaningful content at an appropriate level | 1. Students' abilities, interests, etc. 2. Materials, length of lessons, set-up time, demand, format. 3. District objectives. 4. Facilities available for activities. | 1. Lists of outlines of activities and content. 2. Lists of sequenced activities. 3. Notes in plan book. | 1. Organization, sequence, balance, and flow of outlines. 2. Fit with yearly and term goals. 3. Fit with anticipated student interest and involvement. |
| **Weekly planning** | 1. Laying out the week's activities within the framework of the weekly schedule. 2. Adjusting schedule for interruptions and special needs. 3. Maintaining continuity and regularity of activities. | 1. Students' performance in preceding days and weeks. 2. Scheduled school interruptions (for example, assemblies, holidays). 3. Materials, aides, and other resources. | 1. Names and times of activities in plan book. 2. Day divided into four instructional blocks punctuated by A.M. recess, lunch, and P.M. recess. | 1. Completeness of plans. 2. Degree to which weekly schedule has been followed. 3. Flexibility of plans to allow for special time constraints or interruptions. 4. Fit with goals. |
| **Daily planning** | 1. Setting up and arranging classroom for next day. 2. Specifying activity components not yet decided on. 3. Fitting daily schedule to last-minute intrusions. 4. Preparing students for day's activities. | 1. Instructions in materials to be used. 2. Set-up time required for activities. 3. Assessment of class "disposition" at start of day. 4. Continued interest, involvement, and enthusiasm. | 1. Schedule for day written on the chalkboard and discussed with students. 2. Preparation and arrangement of materials and facilities in the room. | 1. Completion of last-minute preparations and decisions about content, materials, etc. 2. Involvement, enthusiasm, and interest communicated by students. |

Source: Yinger (1980), pp. 114–115

# Using Planning Tools

The computer can be a powerful tool for planning and keeping records. It can assist the teacher in organizing learning activities, keeping attendance records, and creating lesson plans and learning materials. Below are tools that are available to assist teacher planning.

- *Lesson planning software:* Software designed to organize lesson plans and tie particular plans to learning objectives.
- *Worksheet and puzzle tools:* Software designed to create worksheets and puzzles and link these to learning objectives.
- *Concept mapping tools:* Software for organizing ideas into conceptual maps or webs and showing relationships among various ideas.

- *Certificate production software:* Software for creating certificates that can be given students to reward achievement and special effort.
- *Poster and bulletin board production tools:* Software that enables teachers to create and print posters and other devices to post on bulletin boards and classroom walls.
- *Time and meeting management tools:* Software and handheld computers that allow teachers to plan, keep track of, and organize meetings, schedules, things to do, telephone numbers, and so on.

More general tools such as database software and spreadsheets included in software suites such as Clarisworks and Microsoft Office can also be helpful to teachers for keeping records and for a variety of other planning and organizing activities.

## Choosing Curriculum Content

The curriculum in most elementary and secondary schools is currently organized around the academic disciplines—history, biology, mathematics, and so forth—used by scholars to organize information about the social and physical worlds. And even though some curriculum reformers have repeatedly argued that this is an inappropriate way to organize content for young people, the current structures are likely to remain for some time. Consequently, an important planning task for teachers will continue to be choosing the most appropriate content from the various subject matter areas for a particular group of students. This is no small feat, because there is already much more to teach on any topic than time allows, and new knowledge is being produced every day.

Beginning teachers are often bewildered about where content comes from and the role teachers play in selecting it. In today's schools, deciding what to teach is no longer done by teachers independently. Instead, what-to-teach decisions are influenced by many factors, some of which are described below and portrayed in Figure 2.6

**Deciding what to teach is among the most difficult aspects of teacher planning because there is so much that could be learned and so little time.**

**Learned Society Standards.** Curriculum has traditionally been drawn from the various academic disciplines deemed central to an individual's education. Core disciplines have included English, history, geography, foreign languages, mathematics, and the sciences. Content from these subjects is sequenced over students' twelve years of schooling, and specific accomplishments in each subject are required for high school graduation. Each subject has a learned society or professional association that makes recommendations about what should be taught. Sometimes these recommendations are made in the form of **performance standards** for what students should learn.

**Performance standards define what students should know and be able to do and at what level they are expected to perform in various subjects.**

**State Curriculum Frameworks and Mastery Tests.** Over the past decade, state departments of education have exerted an increasing amount of influence over what is taught in schools. Today, most states have curriculum guides or frameworks, as they

**Figure 2.6** *Factors Influencing What Is Taught in Schools*

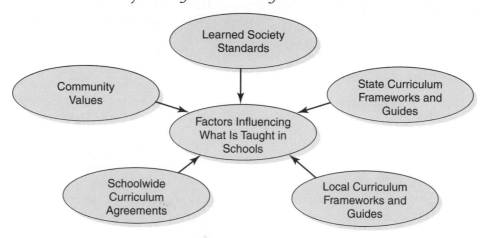

are often called, that define what students should know and be able to do as they proceed through the various levels of schooling. Curriculum frameworks in most states exist for each subject area and each grade level. Table 2.5 provides an illustration of performance standards found in one state's science framework.

Note how the overall goal for learning about the "evolution of scientific thought" is divided into specific performance standards for each level of instruction—early elementary, middle school, and high school. It is expected that teachers will provide learning experiences for students at the various levels that will ensure that students can meet the standards and ultimately the overall goal.

State frameworks have an important influence on what is taught in schools because mastery tests are usually built around the performance standards identified in the frameworks. These tests are administered to students every two or three years, normally in grades 4, 6, 8, and 10. Student scores are summarized by schools and/or school

**Table 2.5** *Illustration of Goals and Performance Standards in Science*

**Overall goal:** Students will learn the evolution of scientific thought, how science has influenced culture and society, and how groups from many countries have contributed to the history of science.

**K–12 Performance Standards**

| Educational experiences in **grades K–4** will ensure that students: | Educational experiences in **grades 5–8** will ensure that students: | Educational experiences in **grades 9–12** will ensure that students: |
| --- | --- | --- |
| Recognize (in grades K–2) that science is an adventure that people everywhere can take part in, as they have for many centuries | Recognize important contributions to the advancement of science, mathematics, and technology that have been made by men and women in different cultures at different times | Recognize that many Western as well as non-Western cultures (e.g., Egyptian, Chinese, Hindu, Arabic, Mayan) have developed scientific ideas and solved human problems through technology |

districts. Scores on mastery tests often are published in local newspapers so parents and citizens know how students in their school compare to students elsewhere in the state. It should be obvious that this situation heightens the influence of state curriculum frameworks.

**Community Values and Local Curriculum Frameworks.** Community values and societal viewpoints have an important influence on what is taught in schools, particularly in subjects that contain topics that are controversial. Larger societal views influence the content and standards that appear in the frameworks developed by professional associations, and local community values impact local curriculum frameworks. Movements in many communities to get schools "back to the basics" or to use a "phonetic approach" to teaching reading are two examples of how beliefs get translated into curriculum decisions at the local level. Actions in 1999 by the Kansas State Board of Education had the effect of reducing the amount of attention paid to evolution in that state's science curriculum, an issue that has been controversial for most of the past century.

> Deciding what to teach is value-laden and influenced greatly by societal and community viewpoints.

Many content decisions are made by experienced teachers and curriculum specialists in particular districts long before the student or first-year teacher steps into a classroom. Textbooks are selected and curriculum guides are often planned to parallel state frameworks. When this has occurred, they provide excellent tools for a beginning teacher to use. The experts who prepare these materials have taken considerable time to ask what should be taught and how various topics should be sequenced over time—both during the course of a year and over several years—as well as how local community values should be reflected in the school's curriculum. The job of beginning teachers becomes mainly that of making sure they understand the scope and sequence of this content and finding ways to interpret and teach it effectively to a particular group of students.

Some beginning teachers, however, may find themselves facing the time-consuming task of having to select content themselves. For instance, textbooks in some schools may no longer reflect current knowledge. In such a case, it is the beginning teachers' responsibility to plan ways to incorporate new knowledge into the curriculum, an action that generally requires taking something else out.

## Tools for Choosing Content

When beginning teachers face a situation in which they have to make content decisions without much assistance, they need to be aware of ideas and tools that can help them do this.

**Use Concepts of Economy and Power.** It has been observed that most teachers try to teach too much information and too much information that is irrelevant. Students are hampered in learning key ideas because of verbal clutter. Bruner (1962), among others, has argued that teachers should strive for **economy** in their teaching. Using economy means being very careful about the amount of information and the number of concepts presented in a single lesson or unit of work. The economy principle argues for taking a difficult concept and making it clear and simple for students, not taking an easy concept and making it difficult. It means helping students examine a few critical ideas in depth rather than bombarding them with unrelated facts that have little chance of making an impact on learning.

Bruner also described how the principle of **power** should be applied when selecting content. A powerful lesson or unit is one in which basic concepts from the subject area

**Figure 2.7** *Hypothetical Knowledge Structure*

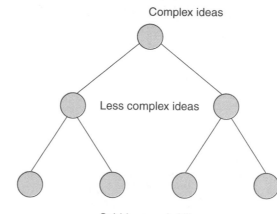

are presented in straightforward and logical ways. It is through logical organization that students come to see relationships between specific facts and among the important concepts of a topic.

**Attend to Knowledge Structures.** In every field there is much more to learn than it is possible to master in a single year or even a lifetime. Teachers must choose content based on the basic ideas and **structures of knowledge** for a particular field, taking into account, of course, their students' prior knowledge and abilities. In all fields of knowledge, advanced concepts and understandings are built in a more or less pyramid fashion on simpler ones, as illustrated in Figure 2.7. Notice how information is divided into more complex and abstract ideas and into simpler, less complex concepts and skills. Notice also that relationships exist among various subsets of ideas and understandings. We will discuss knowledge structures in more detail in later chapters.

Grant Wiggins and Jay McTighe (1998) have provided a simple but very useful framework for putting into operation the economy, power, and structure of knowledge principles, as illustrated in the nested rings in Figure 2.8. The background of the illustration represents the whole field of possible contents, which obviously can't be covered. The largest of the rings represents knowledge and skills that a teacher might determine that students should be familiar with, whereas the middle ring would be that knowledge that is determined to be very important. The students' education would be incomplete if they do not master these essentials. The third ring in the framework represent the "enduring" understandings, the big ideas that should remain with students after they have forgotten most of the details. Wiggins and McTighe offer four questions for teachers to ask as they select what to teach.

*Question 1:* To what extent does the idea, topic, or process represent a big idea having enduring value beyond the classroom?

*Question 2:* To what extent does the idea, topic, or process reside at the heart of the discipline?

*Question 3:* To what extent do students have misconceptions about the idea, topic, or process and find it difficult to grasp?

*Question 4:* To what extent does the idea, topic, or process offer potential for engaging students?

**Figure 2.8** *Establishing Curricular Priorities*

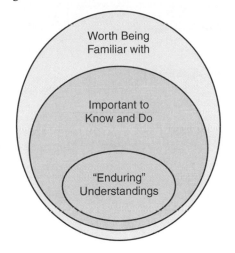

Source: Adapted from Wiggins and McTighe (1998).

**Content Matrix.** Another tool for helping teachers make wise content decisions is the **content matrix.** This device, illustrated in Table 2.6, is a planning tool that helps teachers integrate objectives and content for units of work.

This particular matrix is built around Bloom's "taxonomy of educational objectives." Bloom's taxonomy, which will be described in more detail later, conceptualizes objectives along a continuum from basic terms and facts up to higher-level thinking. Table 2.6 is an example of a content matrix developed by a health teacher for a unit on nutrition.

Making a behavioral content matrix like the one illustrated in Table 2.6 is a rather straightforward process. In this instance, the teacher has placed the categories of Bloom's cognitive domain along the top of the matrix. Running along the left side of the matrix is a list of the important topics the teacher wants to emphasize in this unit on nutrition. The numbers within the matrix represent the number of objectives the teacher considers desirable for each of the topics and in relation to the various levels of cognitive processes. Building a behavioral content matrix during the planning phase of a unit of work or a course of study takes time. However, it ensures well-balanced instruction. As with learning to use any other tools, practice and familiarity lead quickly to increased proficiency.

**Curriculum Mapping.** Even though teachers work together in the same school or school districts, they usually have only a sketchy knowledge about what each other teaches. Even teachers next door to one another lack information about what each is teaching. And although curriculum frameworks may list overall goals and standards, too often they remain mute on what teachers are doing day to day.

Heidi Hayes Jacobs (1997) has offered the idea of "curriculum maps" as a way for teachers in particular buildings or school districts to chart what they are doing and to help make sure neither gaps in important skills and understanding nor too much overlap and repetition occur.

**Curriculum mapping** begins with each teacher describing the processes and skills he or she emphasizes, the essential concept and topics he or she teaches, and the kind

---

*A content matrix is a planning tool that helps teachers connect course content to their objectives.*

**Table 2.6** *Sample Behavioral Content Matrix for a Unit on Nutrition.*

| | Student Behaviors | | | | | | | |
|---|---|---|---|---|---|---|---|---|
| | Knowledge | | | | | | | |
| Content/Topics | Terms | Facts | Comprehension Principles | Application Principles | Analysis | Synthesis | Evaluation | Total Objectives |
| Basic food components | 2 | | 1 | | | | | 3 |
| The balanced diet | | | 1 | 1 | | 1 | 1 | 4 |
| Four food group plan | 1 | | | | 1 | | | 2 |
| Dietary deficiencies | 1 | | 1 | | 1 | | | 3 |
| Special needs | | 1 | 1 | | | | | 2 |
| Making changes | | | | | 1 | 1 | 1 | 3 |
| Total objectives | 4 | 1 | 4 | 1 | 3 | 2 | 2 | 17 |

of learner outcomes expected. Then, depending on the situation, these descriptions are shared with other teachers across the school, and maps are constructed showing the school's curriculum, including gaps that may exist and topics that are unnecessarily taught more than once. Although beginning teachers will not be asked to be in charge of this process, understanding that it exists will help them enter into curriculum mapping and gain a clearer understanding of what is really going on in other teachers' classrooms and how what they are teaching fits in. Figure 2.9 illustrates two curriculum maps: One shows how literature and social studies are integrated in a fifth grade class; the other shows the life science program taught by a ninth grade interdisciplinary team.

**Check for Understanding**

- What are the major factors that influence teachers' decisions about what to teach?
- How can the principles of economy and power assist teachers in deciding what to teach?
- Contrast the Wiggins-McTighe questions with the principles of economy and power.
- What is the primary purpose of a curriculum map?

## Instructional Objectives

By definition, teaching is a process of attempting to promote growth in students. Student learning is the "bottom line" for teachers and for schools. The intended growth may be far-reaching, such as developing a whole new conceptual framework for thinking about science or acquiring a new appreciation for literature. It may be as precise and simple as learning how to tie a shoestring. **Instructional objectives** are statements that describe the teacher's intentions for students' growth and change. Instructional objectives are like road maps: They help teachers and their students know where they are going and when they have arrived at their destination. Like different kinds of road maps, some instructional objectives are simple. They are easy to make and to read. Others are more complex. For this reason, there are several different approaches to guide the writing of instructional objectives and a variety of formats to use. A major issue (sometimes controversial) has been differences among theorists and teachers about how specific or general instructional objectives should be.

**Instructional objectives describe a teacher's intent about what students should learn.**

**The Mager Format of Behavioral Objectives.** In 1962, Robert Mager wrote a book titled *Preparing Instructional Objectives* that set off a debate over the most desirable "form of a usefully stated objective" (p. i). The general message of Mager's work was the argument that for instructional objectives to be meaningful, they must clearly communicate

**Figure 2.9** *Two Examples of Curriculum Maps*

Fifth Grade Integrated Curriculum Map

| ORGANIZING CONCEPTS | NEW BEGINNINGS — | — | — | BALANCE — | — | EXPANSION — | — | — | INTERDEPENDENCE | — | ↑ |
|---|---|---|---|---|---|---|---|---|---|---|---|
| **MONTHS** | **AUGUST/ SEPTEMBER** | **OCTOBER** | **NOVEMBER** | **DECEMBER** | **JANUARY** | **FEBRUARY** | **MARCH** | **APRIL** | **MAY/JUNE** | | |
| Related Literature | The Talking Earth | Author Study | *Witch of Blackbird Pond* — | — ↑ | | *Caddie Woodlawn* | *Hatchet???* | Lit Set on Various Cultures — | ↑ Independent Reading | | |
| Seminar Selections | | | | | | | | | | | |
| Field Studies | Secuoyah-Energy Connections | | Williamsburg Jamestown | Nutcracker Ballet | | Channel 3 TV Station | | D.A.R.E. Picnic | | | |
| Forum/Current Events | Focus on people and countries making new beginnings | | | Focus on our struggle for independence | | Focus on immigration effects on our country | Focus on government regulation and its effects on citizens | Focus on USA events and how we live together as a nation | Focus on exploration in various fields (medicine, law, etc.) | | |
| Social Studies | 5 themes of Geography Explorers Native Americans | Colonization — | — ↑ | Declaration of Independence Bill of Rights and Constitution Branches of Government | Exploration Westward Expansion | Immigration to Ellis Island | | USA supply geography states and capitals | Interdependence of North Am. countries Interdependence of regions | | |

Ninth Grade Interdisciplinary Life Science Curriculum Map

| SUBJECT THEMES | QUARTER 1: TRUST | QUARTER 2: COMMUNICATION | QUARTER 3: TOLERANCE | QUARTER 4: RESPONSIBILITY |
|---|---|---|---|---|
| Health 9 | Drug Education (physiology & prevention) | Family Living (Role models, sex, birth control, AIDS prevention) | Drug Education (physiology & prevention) | Family Living (Role models, sex, birth control, AIDS prevention) |
| Biology 9 | Characteristics of Life (cells, biochemistry, metabolism) | Continuity of Life (reproduction & genetics) | Homeostasis (anatomy & physiology) | Patterns of Organization (evolution, ecology, & environment) |
| PA/Fitness | Cardiovascular Fitness (muscular strength & endurance) | Project Adventure (problem-solving skills) | Cardiovascular Fitness (muscular strength & endurance) | Project Adventure (problem-solving skills) |

Source: Adapted from Jacobs (1997).

# Individualizing Instruction through Planning

The process of planning affords teachers their greatest opportunity to individualize instruction and provide for diversity. Teachers can vary the time, materials, and learning activities required of students. In some instances, they can also vary what students are expected to learn.

### Keep Learning Objectives the Same for All Students

Sometimes things taught to students are so important that teachers do not have the luxury of tailoring their objectives to meet the needs of particular students. For example, all students are expected to know the answers to specific questions that appear on required mastery tests. These questions normally cover the basics in core curriculum areas: mathematics, reading and writing, the sciences, and history. Because students do not come to a teacher's class with the same backgrounds and abilities in these subjects, the teacher's plan must reflect ways to help them make progress according to their abilities. Normally, teachers do this by varying one of three aspects of instruction: time, materials, or learning activities.

*Vary Time.* Every experienced teacher knows that it takes some students longer than others to master particular content. To accommodate these differences, teachers devise plans with a common assignment but provide more time for students who need it to complete the assignment. To make this work, however, teachers must plan for the students who are likely to complete their work ahead of others. Generally, this means providing enrichment activities for students who complete the assignment quickly or making technology centers available to these students so they can pursue advanced topics of their choosing.

*Adapt Materials.* Another way teachers can tailor their instruction through planning is to vary the level of difficulty of the instructional materials. Some schools will have available textbooks that are written at different levels. In other schools, teachers will have to make their own adjustments. Materials can be adapted by rewriting, although this can be very time-consuming. Other ways to adapt materials include providing students with specially designed study guides or notes that make the materials easier to understand or making flashcards and other practice devices available.

*Use Different Learning Activities.* As will be explored in later chapters of *Learning to Teach,* students vary in the way they prefer to learn. Some students can glean a great amount of information from text, while others are more adept at listening to the teacher explain things. Some students like to deal with abstract ideas, while others are more successful when they are working with hands-on materials and projects. Still others learn as they talk about their ideas with each other. Effective teachers vary the teaching strategies they use, and they provide students with options for the learning activities they can use in pursuit of common learning goals.

### Vary the Learning Objectives

In some instances, teachers can vary the learning objectives they hold for students. For instance, students can be allowed to select topics within a unit of study that interests them or to accomplish projects that are consistent with their own abilities. The risk of this approach, as with instances when schools group students by ability, is that students in the slower groups or those who pursue less difficult or complex projects may fall farther and farther behind in the essential core content of the curriculum and never accomplish the objectives of their peers. These are decisions that each teacher will have to make for particular students and situations.

a teacher's instructional intent and should be very specific. Objectives written in the Mager format became known as **behavioral objectives** and required three parts:

- *Student behavior.* What the student will be doing or the kinds of behavior the teacher will accept as evidence that the objective has been achieved.
- *Testing situation.* The condition under which the behavior will be observed or expected to occur.
- *Performance criteria.* The standard or performance level defined as acceptable.

A simple mnemonic for remembering the three parts of a behavioral objective is to think of it as the STP approach: student behavior (S), testing situation (T), and performance criteria (P). Table 2.7 illustrates how Mager's three-part approach works and provides examples of each.

When teachers write behavioral objectives using the Mager format, the recommendation is to use precise words that are *not* open to many interpretations. Examples of precise words include *write, list, identify, compare.* Examples of less precise words are *know, understand, appreciate.* There are also recommendations about how to link the three parts of the instructional objective together using the following steps: Begin by noting the testing situation, follow this by stating the student behavior, and then write the performance criteria. Table 2.8 illustrates how behavioral objectives written in this format might look.

Mager's behavioral approach has been widely accepted among teachers and others in the educational community over the past three decades. Well-written behavioral objectives give students a very clear statement about what is expected of them, and they help teachers when it comes time to measure student progress, as you will see in Chapter 6. The behavioral approach, however, is not free from criticism.

Critics have argued that Mager's format leads to reductionism and, when used exclusively, it leads to neglect of many of the most important goals of education. Putting an emphasis on precision and observable student behaviors forces teachers to be specific in their objectives. To accomplish this specificity, they must break larger, more global educational goals into very small pieces. The number of objectives for almost any subject or topic could run well into the thousands, an unmanageable list for most

**Well-written behavioral objectives give students a clear statement of what is expected of them.**

**Table 2.7** *Sample Behavioral Objectives Using Mager's Format*

| Parts of the Objective | Examples |
|---|---|
| Student-behavior | Identify nouns |
| Testing situation | Given a list of nouns and verbs |
| Performance criteria | Mark at least 85 percent right |
| Student behavior | List five causes of the Civil War |
| Testing situation | Essay test without use of notes |
| Performance criteria | Four of five reasons |

**Table 2.8** *Three Parts of Behavioral Objectives Applied*

| Testing Situation | Student Behavior | Performance Criteria |
|---|---|---|
| Given a map . . . | The student will be able to: | At least 85 percent |
| Without notes . . . | Identify | Four of five reasons |
| With the text . . . | Solve | Correct to nearest percentages |
| | Compare | |
| | Contrast | |
| | Recite | |

teachers. The teacher also runs the risk of paying attention only to specific objectives, which are of minor importance in themselves, while neglecting the sum total, which is more important than all the parts.

Critics have also pointed out, and rightfully so, that many of the more complex cognitive processes are not readily observable. It is easy, for instance, to observe a student add two columns of numbers and determine if the answer is correct. It is not easy to observe the thought processes or the mathematical problem solving that goes into this act. Along the same line, it is rather easy to observe students recall the major characters in a Tolstoy novel. It is not so easy to observe and measure their appreciation of Russian literature or the novel as a form of creative expression. Critics worry that the emphasis on behavioral objectives may lead to the neglect of the more important aspects of education merely because the latter are not readily observed and measured.

**More General Approaches.** Several curriculum theorists, as well as measurement specialists, have developed alternative approaches to the behavior objective. Gronlund (1995), for example, illustrated how objectives can be written first in more general terms, with appropriate specifics added later for clarification. Gronlund, unlike the strict behaviorists, is more willing to use words such as *appreciate, understand, value,* or *enjoy* with his approach. He believes that although these words are open to a wide range of interpretations, they nonetheless communicate more clearly the educational intents of many teachers. Table 2.9 illustrates how an objective might look using the Gronlund format.

Notice that the initial objective is not very specific and perhaps not very meaningful or helpful in guiding lesson preparation or measuring student change. It does, however, communicate the overall intent the teacher wants to achieve. The subobjectives help clarify what should be taught and what students are expected to learn. They provide more precision yet are not as precise as the three-part behavior objective.

**Which Approach to Use?** The form and use of instructional objectives, as with many other aspects of teaching, are likely to remain subject to controversy and inquiry for a long time. The approach teachers use will be influenced somewhat by schoolwide policies, but in most instances, considerable latitude exists for individual preference and decisions. It is important to remember that the purposes behind instructional objectives are to communicate clearly to students a teacher's intents and to aid the teacher in assessing student growth. Common sense, as well as the research summarized earlier,

*Some critics believe that relying on specific student behaviors as the sole measure of learning does not provide evidence of larger learning goals that may not be observable.*

*Some educators advocate first writing global objectives and then writing specific objectives that are consistent with the larger (usually unobservable) ones.*

**Table 2.9** *More General Approach to Writing Objectives*

| Format | Example |
| --- | --- |
| Overall objective | Understands and appreciates the diversity of the people who make up American society. |
| Subobjective 1 | Can define diversity in the words of others and in his or her own words. |
| Subobjective 2 | Can give instances of how diverse persons or groups have enriched the cultural life of Americans. |
| Subobjective 3 | Can explore in writing how maintaining appreciation for diversity is a fragile and difficult goal to achieve. |

suggests adopting a middle ground between objectives stated at such a high level of abstraction that they are meaningless and a strict adherence to the behavioral approach. Gronlund's approach of writing a more global objective first and then clarifying it and getting as specific as the subject matter allows is probably the best advice at this time.

## Taxonomies for Helping Choose Instructional Objectives

Taxonomies are devices that help classify and show relationships among things. You already know about a variety of **taxonomies**; for instance, those that classify plants and animals in science. One very useful taxonomy, which serves as a tool for helping make decisions about instructional objectives, is Bloom's *Taxonomy of Educational Objectives* (1956).* Working with colleagues at the University of Chicago in the 1950s, Benjamin Bloom created a scheme that classifies educational objectives in a systematic fashion. Bloom's taxonomy, although almost a half-century old, is widely used as an aid in planning as well as in other aspects of teaching. For example, it can be used to assist in test construction and in choosing a questioning strategy, as later chapters describe. Bloom's taxonomy is divided into three large domains: the cognitive, the affective, and the psychomotor.

> **Taxonomies are classification systems that help arrange and show relationships among objects or ideas.**

**The Cognitive Domain.** Objectives in the **cognitive domain** are divided into six levels, according to Bloom's classification system. Each level specifies the type of cognitive, or thinking, process required of students, ranging from the simple to the more complex. The six levels in the cognitive domain and the associated cognitive processes expected of the learner are listed and described here.

> **The cognitive domain in Bloom's taxonomy classifies objectives in the thinking and reasoning processes.**

*Knowledge.* The student can recall, define, recognize, or identify specific information presented during instruction. The information may be in the form of a fact, a rule, a diagram, a sound, and so on.

*Comprehension.* The student can demonstrate understanding of information by translating it into a different form or by recognizing it in translated form. This can be through giving a definition in his or her own words, summarizing, giving an original example, recognizing an example, and so forth.

*Application.* The student can apply the information in performing concrete actions. These actions may involve figuring, writing, reading, handling equipment, and so forth.

*Analysis.* The student can recognize the organization and structure of a body of information, break this information down into its constituent parts, and specify the relationships between these parts.

*Synthesis.* The student can bring to bear information from various sources to create a product uniquely his or her own. The product can take a variety of forms—written, oral, pictorial, and so on.

*Evaluation.* The student can apply a standard in making a judgment on the worth of something—a concerto, an essay, an action, an architectural design, and so forth.

**The Affective Domain.** Schools spend most of their time on objectives related to cognitive matters. However, it is important to remember that other objectives for education exist that fall into the **affective domain** (for example, emotional responses to tasks). Bloom's taxonomy divides affective objectives into five categories. Each

> **The affective domain in Bloom's taxonomy classifies objectives for emotional responses.**

*Although not published at the time of this edition, Bloom's original work is being revised for publication within a year or two.

category specifies the degree of commitment or emotional intensity required of students. The five categories in the affective domain and the associated level of student response are listed here.

*Receiving.* The student is aware of or attending to something in the environment.
*Responding.* The student displays some new behavior as a result of experience and responds to the experience.
*Valuing.* The student displays definite involvement or commitment toward some experience.
*Organization.* The student has integrated a new value into his or her general set of values and can give it its proper place in a priority system.
*Characterization by value.* The student acts consistently according to the value and is firmly committed to the experience.

The Psychomotor Domain. We normally associate psychomotor activity most closely with physical education and athletics, but in fact, many other subjects require physical movement of one kind or another. Obviously, handwriting and word processing are tightly connected to all subjects. Work in laboratories for science students requires intricate use of complex equipment. Eye coordination is required for viewing all forms of visual art; hand coordination is required for producing this art. Moving from student to student, using audiovisual equipment, and communicating intentions with facial and hand gestures are examples of teacher skills in the psychomotor domain. Following are the six categories of objectives in the **psychomotor domain.** Notice that the categories range from simple reflex reactions to complex actions that communicate ideas and emotions to others.

The psychomotor domain in Bloom's taxonomy classifies objectives in the area of physical movement and coordination.

*Reflex movements.* Student's actions can occur involuntarily in response to some stimulus.
*Basic fundamental movements.* Student has innate movement patterns formed from a combination of reflex movements.
*Perceptual abilities.* Student can translate stimuli received through the senses into appropriate desired movements.
*Physical abilities.* Student has developed basic movements that are essential to the development of more highly skilled movements.
*Skilled movements.* Student has developed more complex movements requiring a certain degree of efficiency.
*Nondiscursive communications.* Student has the ability to communicate through body movement.

Bloom's taxonomies have not been free from criticism. The scheme, as you can see, classifies objectives from the most simple to the most complex. Some have misinterpreted this classification system, believing that it implies that simple (for example, knowledge objectives) are not as important as the more complex (for example, synthesis objectives). This was not Bloom's intent. Others have challenged the hierarchical ordering of the instructional objectives in Bloom's taxonomies. They argue, and rightfully so, that this ordering does not fit all fields of knowledge equally well. Finally, critics have pointed out that even experts in particular fields cannot distinguish objectives among the various levels. This has been particularly true for the higher levels in the cognitive domain, where the cognitive processes of analysis and synthesis commonly overlap.

Regardless of the criticism and identified weaknesses in the taxonomies, they remain popular with teachers and they have withstood the test of time. Perhaps like all taxonomies, the taxonomies of instructional objectives do not describe reality completely. Nonetheless, they provide a way of thinking about different kinds of instructional intents and thus become a valuable planning tool for teachers. They provide a good reminder that we want students to learn a variety of skills and to be able to think and act in a variety of straightforward as well as complex ways.

## Lesson Plans and Unit Plans

Instructional objectives are used in conjunction with **lesson plans,** and, as you saw from Yinger's research, teachers construct both short-term and long-term plans.

**Daily Planning.** A teacher's daily plan is the one that receives most attention. In some schools, it is required. In other schools, even the format for daily plans is prescribed. Normally, daily plans outline what content is to be taught, motivational techniques to be used, specific steps and activities for students, needed materials, and evaluation processes. The amount of detail can vary. During student teaching, cooperating teachers may require a beginning teacher to write very detailed daily plans, even though their own plans may be briefer.

> **Daily lesson plans normally outline the content to be taught, motivational techniques to be used, materials needed, specific steps and activities, and evaluation procedures.**

Most beginning teachers can understand the logic of requiring rather detailed daily plans at first. Think of the daily lesson plan as similar to the text of a speech to be delivered to a large audience. Speakers giving a speech for the first time need to follow a set of detailed notes or perhaps even a word-for-word text. As they gain experience, or as their speeches are gradually committed to memory from repeated presentations, they find less and less need for notes and can proceed more extemporaneously. Or think of using the plan as being similar to using a road map. Going to a location the first time requires careful and continuous attention to the map. After several trips, it can be discarded.

Daily plans can take many forms. The features of a particular lesson often determine the lesson plan format. For example, each of the teaching models described in Chapters 7 through 13 requires a somewhat different format, as you will see. A beginning teacher will find, however, that some schools have a preferred format that they require of all teachers. Usually, that format contains most, if not all, the features included in the sample lesson plan developed by faculty at Augsburg College and illustrated in Figure 2.10.

> **Lesson plans tend to vary according to the type of teaching model used.**

Observe that this lesson format includes a clear statement of objectives and a sequence of learning activities for the lesson, beginning with a way to get students started and ending with some type of closure and assignment. The lesson format also provides a means to evaluate student learning as well as the lesson itself.

**Weekly and Unit Planning.** Most schools and teachers organize instruction around weeks and units. A unit is essentially a chunk of content and associated skills that are perceived as fitting together in a logical way. Normally more than one lesson is required to accomplish a unit of instruction. The content for instructional units might come from chapters in books or from major sections of curriculum guides. Examples of units include such topics as sentences, the Civil War, fractions, thermodynamics, note taking, the heart, Japan, and the short stories of Hemingway.

> **Most teachers organize instruction around units that require multiple lessons spread over several days.**

Unit planning is, in many ways, more critical than daily planning. The unit plan links together a variety of goals, content, and activities the teacher has in mind. It determines the overall flow for a series of lessons over several days, weeks, or perhaps even months. Often it reflects the teacher's understanding of both the content and processes of instruction.

**Figure 2.10** *Sample Lesson Plan Format*

Lesson topic/subject_____ Grade level_____

**PREINSTRUCTIONAL PLANNING**

Objectives:                                                     Domains:
_____                  Cognitive
_____                  Affective
_____                  Motor/Skill

Materials/special arrangements/individual modifications:

**DURING INSTRUCTION**

Introduction/establishing set:

Sequence (syntax) of learning activities:

Closure:

Assignment:

**POSTINSTRUCTIONAL**

Evaluation of student learning:

   Formal:

   Informal:

Evaluation of the lesson (How did the lesson go? Revisions needed.)

SOURCE: Fleener

---

> **Unit plans should be put in writing, since they function as maps that connect several lessons and give teachers, students, and others an idea of where lessons are going.**

Most people can memorize plans for an hour or a day, but they cannot remember the logistics and sequencing of activity for several days or weeks. For this reason, teachers' unit plans are generally written in a fair amount of detail. When unit plans are put into writing, they also serve as a reminder later that some lessons require supporting materials, equipment, motivational devices, or evaluation tools that cannot usually be obtained on a moment's notice. If teachers are working together in teams, unit planning and assignment of responsibilities for various unit activities are most important. The content usually contained in a unit of instruction can be found in the sample unit plan illustrated in Figure 2.11.

Unit plans can also be shared with students because they provide the overall road map that explains where the teacher or a particular lesson is going. Through the communication of unit goals and activities, students can recognize what they are expected to learn. Knowledge of unit plans can help older students allocate their study time and monitor their own progress.

Over time, experienced teachers develop unit plans and supporting materials that can be reused. However, most beginning teachers will have to rely on textbooks and curriculum guides. There is nothing wrong with doing this, and the beginning teacher should not feel guilty about it. Most curriculum guides have been developed by experienced teachers, and even though their approach to subjects cannot be expected to fit the preferences of an individual teacher, they do provide a helpful overall design to fol-

**Figure 2.11** *Sample Unit Plan Format*

Title of unit_____

Unit rationale and introduction_____
_____

**OVERALL UNIT OBJECTIVES**

General Objective 1
Specific objective:_____
Specific objective:_____
General Objective 2
Specific objective:_____
Specific objective:_____

**UNIT CONTENT**

Major content and topics to cover

**SYNTAX FOR UNIT**

Major Activities and Overall Flow of Lessons
Day 1
Day 2
Materials and Other Resources Required

**MAJOR ASSIGNMENTS**

Long-range
Short-term
Bibliography and Other Student Aids

Assessment and evaluation _____
_____

low. Curriculum frameworks developed by most state departments of education can also provide valuable assistance with unit planning.

Two notes of caution are worth mentioning, however. First, some beginning teachers, particularly in middle schools and high schools, rely heavily on their college textbooks or the course and unit plans of their college instructors. These plans and materials are not ever appropriate for younger learners, who are not ready for the advanced content found in college courses. Second, there are teachers who, after several years of experience, still rely on textbooks for planning and sequencing their instruction. Teaching and learning are creative, evolutionary processes that should be keyed to a particular group of students at a particular point in time. Only when this is done can lessons rise above the humdrum and provide students with intellectual excitement.

**Yearly Plans.** Yearly plans are also critical but, because of the uncertainty and complexity in most schools, cannot be done with as much precision as daily or unit plans. The effectiveness of yearly plans generally revolves around how well they deal with the following three features:

*Overall Themes and Attitudes.* Most teachers have some global attitudes, goals, and themes they like to leave with their students. Perhaps a teacher in a mixed-race elementary classroom would like his or her students to end the term with a bit less bias or

**Most teachers have a few long-term global goals that can be achieved only by infusing them into many lessons and units during the year.**

misunderstanding and a bit more tolerance of people who are racially different. No specific lesson or unit can teach this attitude, but many carefully planned and coordinated experiences throughout the year can. Or perhaps a high school biology teacher would like students to understand and embrace a set of attitudes associated with scientific methods. A single lesson on the scientific method will not accomplish this goal. However, personal modeling and formal demonstrations showing respect for data, the relationships between theory and reality, or the process of making inferences from information can eventually influence students to think more scientifically. As a last example, a history teacher may want students to leave her class with an appreciation of the very long time frame associated with the development of democratic traditions. Again, a single lesson on the Magna Carta, the Constitution, or the Fourteenth Amendment will not develop this appreciation. However, building a succession of lessons that come back to a common theme on the "cornerstones of democracy" can achieve this end.

**Careful planning for the year helps teachers avoid the trap of covering too much content too superficially.**

*Coverage.*  There are few teachers who run out of things to do. Instead, the common lament is that time runs out with many important lessons still to be taught. Experienced teachers carry many of their yearlong plans in their heads. Beginning teachers, however, will have to take care to develop yearlong plans if they want to get past the Civil War by March. Planning to cover desired topics requires asking what is really important to teach, deciding on priorities, and attending carefully to the instructional hours actually available over a year's time. In most instances, teachers strive to teach too much, too lightly. Students may be better served if a reduced menu is planned. In short, most beginning teachers overestimate how much time is actually available for instruction and underestimate the amount of time it takes to teach something well. Careful planning can help minimize this error in judgment.

**Cycles of the school year can have strong effects on the plans teachers make.**

*Cycles of the School Year.*  Experienced teachers know that the school year is cyclical and that some topics are better taught at one time than another. School cycles and corresponding emotional or psychological states revolve around the opening and closing of school, the days of the week, vacation periods, the changes of season, holidays, and important school events. Some of these can be anticipated; some cannot. Nonetheless, it is important to plan for school cycles as much as possible. Experienced teachers know that new units or important topics are not introduced on Friday or the day before a holiday break. They know that the opening of school should emphasize processes and structures to facilitate student learning later in the year. They know that the end of the school year will be filled with interruptions and decreasing motivation as students anticipate summer vacation. They also know that it is unwise to plan for a unit examination the night after a big game or the hour following the Halloween party.

As beginning teachers, you will know something about these cycles and corresponding psychological states from your own student days. You can use this information, along with information provided by experienced teachers in a school, as you proceed with making long-range, yearly plans.

**Time-tabling Techniques to Assist Unit and Yearly Planning.**  There are several techniques to assist teachers in making clear and doable instructional plans that extend over several days or weeks or that include many specific, independent tasks to be completed before moving on. One such technique is **time-tabling.** A time table is a chronological map of a series of instructional activities or of some special project the teacher may want to carry out. It describes the overall direction of activities and any special products that may be produced within a time frame. The most straightforward time-

**Figure 2.12** *Gantt Chart, Museum Trip*

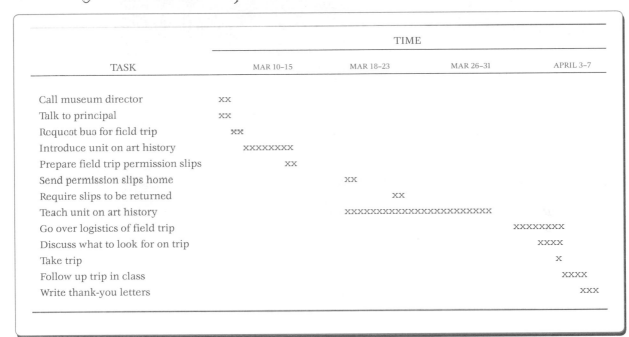

| TASK | TIME | | | |
| --- | --- | --- | --- | --- |
| | MAR 10–15 | MAR 18–23 | MAR 26–31 | APRIL 3–7 |
| Call museum director | xx | | | |
| Talk to principal | xx | | | |
| Request bus for field trip | xx | | | |
| Introduce unit on art history | xxxxxxxx | | | |
| Prepare field trip permission slips | xx | | | |
| Send permission slips home | | xx | | |
| Require slips to be returned | | | xx | |
| Teach unit on art history | | xxxxxxxxxxxxxxxxxxxxxxxxx | | |
| Go over logistics of field trip | | | | xxxxxxxx |
| Discuss what to look for on trip | | | | xxxx |
| Take trip | | | | x |
| Follow up trip in class | | | | xxxx |
| Write thank-you letters | | | | xxx |

tabling technique consists of constructing a special chart called a Gantt chart. A **Gantt chart** allows you to see the work pieces in relation to each other—when each starts and finishes. Gantt charts can be used similarly to previously described curriculum maps to show how particular content is to be covered over a period of time, such as a semester. They can also be used to plan logistics for instructional activities, such as the one illustrated in Figure 2.12 used by a teacher to plan a field trip to a local museum.

There are many formats for making time tables. Some teachers believe in evolving processes and prefer a more open and nonspecific approach. Others prefer just the opposite and write everything down in great detail. One's own personal philosophy and work style influence the exact approach and level of detail required. Regardless of the extent to which you choose to make time tables a part of your planning, it is at least important to consider their use, because they help planners recognize the limits of a very important and scarce resource—time.

The Spotlight on Technology box for this chapter described several tools that can assist teachers with planning and time-tabling.

**Other Planning Decisions.** Most of this discussion has been devoted to how teachers choose curriculum content, instructional objectives, and learning activities. There are, however, other decisions teachers make about their classroom that require advanced planning. For example, classroom teachers and students are expected to perform certain housekeeping activities such as taking attendance, keeping the classroom space safe and livable, making assignments, collecting papers, and distributing and storing materials. These tasks, like instructional tasks, require careful planning. Experienced teachers plan housekeeping tasks so thoroughly and efficiently that the naïve observer may not even notice they are occurring. A beginning teacher who has not planned

**Time tables are chronological maps showing how a series of instructional activities are carried out.**

*Often it is important for teachers to communicate their plans to parents.*

✔ **Check for Understanding**

Why are instructional objectives important to the teaching process, and what are their purposes?

• According to Mager, what three criteria need to be specifically defined and clarified so that students will completely understand what is expected of them and how they will be evaluated? What aspects of this approach have led to criticism?

• What are taxonomies? What are the three domains of learning categorized by Bloom's widely accepted *Taxonomy of Educational Objectives?* Are Bloom's classifications free from criticism?

• Although lesson plans vary between lessons and teachers, what common attributes are found in most good lesson plans?

• What are the differences between unit and daily plans, and how might such plans differ between teachers with different experience levels?

• How do time-tabling techniques assist with planning?

efficient ways to accomplish housekeeping routines will suffer from ongoing confusion and wasted instructional time. The following planning guidelines for routines derive from effective teachers' practice and from experience.

*Guideline 1.* Make sure detailed written plans exist for taking roll, giving assignments, collecting and distributing papers, and storing books and equipment.

*Guideline 2.* Distribute these written plans and procedures to students the first time a housekeeping activity occurs in a particular year or with a particular class.

*Guideline 3.* Provide students with time to practice routines and procedures, and give them feedback on how well they are doing.

*Guideline 4.* Post copies of the housekeeping plans on the bulletin board or on chart paper to serve as public reminders about how particular activities are to be carried out.

*Guideline 5.* Train student helpers immediately to provide leadership and assistance in carrying out routines. Students at all ages can and like to be in charge of taking roll, picking up books, getting and setting up the movie projector, and the like.

*Guideline 6.* Follow the plan that has been developed consistently, and make sure that plenty of time exists to carry out each activity, particularly early in the year.

*Guideline 7.* Be alert to ways housekeeping activities can become more efficient and seek feedback about how students think the housekeeping activities are going.

## 🍎 *Planning for Time and Space*

An additional overall aspect of teacher planning has to do with the use of time and space, resources over which teachers have considerable control. This includes how much time to spend on academic tasks in general, how much time to allocate to particular subjects, and where to place students, materials, and desks. Because there is much useful research on the relationship between teachers' use of classroom time and student achievement, we now look more carefully at this topic. Following that, we briefly consider the topic of classroom space. A more thorough discussion about the use of space can be found in Chapters 7 through 12, where particular teaching models are examined.

## Time

The management of classroom time is a complex and difficult task for teachers, although on the surface it appears to be a rather simple and straightforward matter. Fortunately, there is a well-developed knowledge base on the use of classroom time that can guide teacher planning in this area. Essentially, the research validates what experienced teachers have always known: The time available for instruction that appears to be so plentiful when the year begins soon becomes a scarce resource. Too often, inexperienced teachers find themselves racing through topics in as little time as possible in order to cover targeted content. Unfortunately, what appears to them an efficient use of time often produces little, if any, student learning. This suggests that the effective use of time is just as important as the amount of time spent on a topic. Current interest in the use of classroom time stems mainly from thought and research done in the 1960s and 1970s. A number of studies during that era produced three important findings (Stallings & Kaskowitz, 1974; Fisher et al., 1980; Rosenshine, 1980).

> **Research has validated that time available for instruction is far less than one might believe, even though it seems plentiful at the beginning of the year.**

1. Time allocated and used for specific tasks is strongly related to academic achievement. What the researchers found was that regardless of the specific methods used by teachers in particular programs, classrooms in which students spent the most time *engaged in academic work* were those in which students were making the highest achievement gains in reading and mathematics.

> **A direct relationship exists between time engaged in academic tasks and high achievement gains.**

2. Teachers varied considerably in the amount of time they allocated to particular studies. For instance, in one study researchers found some fifth-grade classrooms allocated sixty minutes each day to reading and language arts whereas others spent almost two and a half hours on these subjects.
3. Regardless of the amount of time a teacher allocated to a particular topic, the amount of time students were actually engaged in learning activities varied considerably. A large proportion of time was found to be devoted to nonacademic, noninstructional, and various housekeeping activities.

These time studies of the 1970s led Carol Weinstein and Andrew Mignano (1993) to differentiate instructional time into seven categories:

1. *Total time.* This is the total amount of time students spend in school. In most states, the mandated time consists of one hundred eighty days of school per year and from six to seven hours of school each day.
2. *Attended time.* This is the amount of time that students actually attend school. Sickness, broken heating systems, and snow days reduce the amount of attendance time from the total time required by law.
3. *Available time.* Some of the school day is spent on lunch, recess, pep rallies, and other extracurricular activities and, consequently, is not available for academic purposes.
4. *Planned academic time.* When teachers fill in plan books, they set aside a certain amount of time for different subjects and activities, called planned academic time.
5. *Actual academic time.* The amount of time the teacher actually spends on academic tasks or activities is called allocated time. This is also called **opportunity to learn** and is measured in terms of the amount of time teachers have their students spend on a given academic task.

> **Opportunity to learn is the time a teacher actually spends on academic tasks and activities.**

**Time on task is the amount of time students actually spend on a particular subject or learning activity.**

**Academic learning time is when students are engaged in academic subjects or activities at which they are successful.**

6. *Engaged time.* The amount of time students actually spend on a learning activity or task is called **engaged time** or **time on task.** This type of time is measured in terms of on-task and off-task behavior. If a teacher has allocated time to seatwork on math problems and the student is working on these problems, the student's behavior is on task. Conversely, if the student is doodling or talking about football with another student, the behavior is counted as off task.

7. *Academic learning time (ALT).* **Academic learning time** is the amount of time a student spends engaged in an academic task at which he or she is successful. It is the aspect of time most closely related to student learning.

The graph in Figure 2.13, developed by Carol Weinstein and Andrew Mignano (1993), shows how much time is available in each of the seven categories. Figure 2.13, based on the time studies described previously, shows how the almost eleven hundred hours of mandated time for schooling is reduced to slightly over three hundred hours when it comes to actual academic learning time, because there is slippage each step of the way. Thus, although there is great variation in the way school and classroom time is managed, the lesson from the research on how time is used clearly shows that far less academic learning time is available to teachers and students than initially meets the eye.

Time studies done by prominent educational researchers gained worldwide attention from both practitioners and researchers alike. If strong relationships existed between time on task and academic achievement, the obvious follow-up research would be to discover what some teachers do to produce classrooms with high on-task ratios and what can be done to help other teachers improve in this direction. Two domains of immediate concern were the ways teachers organized and managed their classrooms and the particular teaching methods they employed. More is said about these two topics in subsequent sections and chapters.

## Space

The arrangement of classroom space is critical and does not have simple solutions. Most important is the fact that the way space is used influences the way classroom participants relate to one another and what students learn. Consider, for example, how a

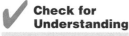
**Check for Understanding**

- What aspects of time and space planning do teachers have direct control of?

- What does research show about how teachers vary as to amount of time spent on similar subjects and work activities?

- What are the seven categories of instructional time as defined by Weinstein and Mignano? What factors detract from true instructional time, and how should teachers handle this?

- How might different types of lessons affect the way a teacher might arrange classroom space?

**Figure 2.13** *How Much Time Is There, Anyway?*

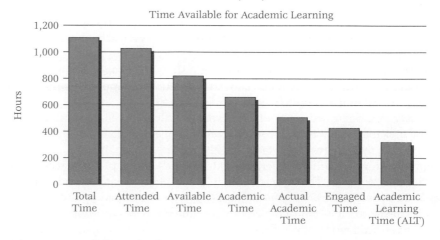

Source: After Weinstein and Mignano (1993).

teacher might conduct a discussion with students. The teacher and students could be arranged in a circle that permits equal communication among all parties or, as is more usual, the students could be arranged in straight rows with all information directed to and from a central figure (the teacher). In the latter arrangement, the discussion does not occur among students but between the students and the teacher. As this example shows, the way space is designed influences not only communication patterns but also power relationships among teachers and students. These relationships are important, because they may affect the degree to which students take ownership of the lesson and become independent learners.

Arrangements of students, desks, and chairs not only help determine classroom communication patterns and interpersonal relationships but also influence a variety of daily decisions teachers must make concerning the management and use of scarce resources. The choices involved are not clear-cut. Fortunately, a substantial body of research provides guidelines for teachers as they think about these decisions. Space arrangements to facilitate particular teaching models are described in some detail in subsequent chapters.

## 🍎 Summary

### Perspective on Planning

- Planning and making decisions about instruction are among the most important aspects of teaching, because they are major determinants of what is taught in schools and how it is taught.

- It is sometimes difficult to learn planning skills from experienced teachers, because most of their planning activities are hidden from public view.

- The traditional perspective of planning is based on rational-linear models characterized by setting goals and taking specific actions to accomplish desired outcomes. The knowledge base suggests that teacher planning and decision making do not always conform to rational-linear planning models. Newer perspectives on planning put more emphasis on planners' actions and reflections.

### Theoretical and Empirical Support

- Studies have shown that planning has consequences for both student learning and classroom behavior. It can enhance student motivation, help focus student learning, and decrease classroom management problems.

- Planning can have unanticipated negative effects as well; for example, it can limit self-initiated learning on the part of students and make teachers insensitive to student ideas.

- Experienced teachers and beginning teachers have different planning approaches and needs. Experienced teachers are more concerned with establishing structures ahead of time to guide classroom activities and plan ahead for the adaptations needed as lessons get under way. In general, beginning teachers need more detailed plans than experienced teachers do. They devote more of their planning to verbal instructions and respond more often to student interests.

### Planning Domains

- Teacher planning is multifaceted but relates to three phases of teaching: prior to instruction, in which decisions are made about what will be taught and for how long; the instructional phase, in which decisions are made about questions to ask, wait time, and specific orientations; and after instruction, where decisions are made about how to evaluate student progress and what type of feedback to provide.

- Planning cycles include not only daily plans but also plans for each week, month, and year. The details of these various plans differ, however. Plans carried out on a particular day are influenced by what has happened before and will in turn influence future plans.

### The Specifics of Planning

- One of the most complex planning tasks is choosing curriculum content. Standards and frameworks developed by professional societies and by state and local curriculum committees assist in making these decisions. A number of planning tools also can help teachers, including context matrices and curriculum mapping.

- The behavioral content matrix is a planning tool for helping teachers integrate their instructional objectives and course content.
- Curriculum mapping is a planning tool that allows groups of teachers to chart what they are teaching across grade levels and content fields. This type of planning identifies gaps and overlaps.
- Instructional objectives are statements that describe the student changes that should result from instruction. Behavioral objectives include statements about expected student behavior, the testing situation in which the behavior will be observed, and performance criteria. An objective written in a more general format communicates the teacher's overall intent but lacks the precision of a behavioral objective.
- Taxonomies are devices that help classify and show relationships between things. Bloom's taxonomy, which is the most widely used device in the field, classifies objectives in three important domains—the cognitive, the affective, and the psychomotor.
- Formats for lesson plans can vary, but in general, a good plan includes a clear statement of objectives, a sequence of learning activities, and a means of evaluating student learning.
- Unit plans cover chunks of instruction that can span several days or weeks. Like lesson plans, the format can vary, but a good unit plan includes overall objectives for the unit, major content to be covered, syntax or phases of the unit, major assignments, and assessment procedures.

- Time-tabling techniques, such as making a chronological map of a series of instructional activities, can assist with long-range planning tasks.
- Effective teachers know how to make good formal plans. They have also learned how to make adjustments when plans prove to be inappropriate or ineffective.

## Planning for Time and Space

- Time and space are scarce commodities in teaching, and their use should be planned with care and foresight.
- Research on time shows considerable variation from teacher to teacher on the amount of time allocated to different subject areas.
- The amount of time students spend on a task is related to how much they learn. Students in classrooms in which allocated time is high and a large proportion of students is engaged learn more than in classrooms where allocated time is low and students are found off task.
- Space—the arrangement of materials, desks, and students—is another important resource that is planned and managed by teachers. The way space is used affects the learning atmosphere of classrooms, influences classroom dialogue and communication, and has important cognitive and emotional effects on students.
- The use of time and space is influenced by the demands of the learning tasks. Effective teachers develop an attitude of flexibility and experimentation about these features of classroom life.

## 🍎 Key Terms

| | | |
|---|---|---|
| rational-linear model | instructional objective | time-tabling |
| nonlinear model | behavioral objectives | Gantt chart |
| performance standards | taxonomies | opportunity to learn |
| economy and power | cognitive domain | engaged time |
| structures of knowledge | affective domain | time on task |
| content matrix | psychomotor domain | academic learning time (ALT) |
| curriculum mapping | lesson plans | |

# 🍎 *Books for the Professional*

Eby, J. W. (1992). *Reflective Planning, Teaching and Evaluation in the Elementary School.* New York: Macmillan. This book provides an excellent description of planning processes and procedures and how these connect to teaching and evaluation.

Gardner, H. (1983). *Frames of Mind.* New York: Basic Books. This is the initial book to spell out the author's theory of multiple intelligences. An understanding of Gardner's ideas and theories is essential to effective teacher thinking and planning.

Gardner, H. (1991). *The Unschooled Mind: How Children Think and How Schools Should Teach.* New York: Basic Books. Gardner's attempt to provide specific advice to educators based on his theoretical work.

Gronlund, N. E. (1995). *How to Write and Use Instructional Objectives* (5th ed.). New York: Macmillan. This is a complete treatment of developing and using instructional objectives, written in nontechnical language.

Jacobs, H. H. (1997). *Mapping the Big Picture.* Alexandria, Va.: Association for Supervision and Curriculum Development. This little book explains the process of curriculum mapping, which teachers can use to integrate curriculum and assessment across subjects and grade levels.

Lerup, L. (1977). *Building the Unfinished: Architecture and Human Action.* Beverly Hills, Calif.: Sage Publications. Written by an architect, this book is not about teaching. It does, however, explore clearly and precisely the interaction between people and their environments and the impact of planning on this process. With examples from studies of fishing villages in Scandinavia and student housing at Berkeley, Lerup shows how planning processes, if they are to serve people, must be conceived as cyclical and interactive and remain open with a touch of the unfinished.

Mager, R. F. (1984). *Preparing Instructional Objectives* (2nd rev. ed.). Palo Alto, Calif.: D. S. Lake. This book, now a classic, makes a strong case for instructional objectives and tells why they should be stated clearly and precisely. It provides detailed instructions on how to become proficient in writing objectives.

Wiggins, G., and McTighe, J. (1998). *Understanding by Design.* Alexandria, Va.: Association for Supervision and Curriculum Development. The authors provide a detailed framework for teacher planning, beginning with two basic questions: What do we want students to know and be able to do, and what type of evidence will we accept that they have learned it?

# *Reflection & Portfolio*

Considerable debate has existed over the years about best practice in regard to teacher planning. On one side of the debate are those who hold behaviorist views about teaching and learning and who see planning as a rationale, linear process. This view would argue for detailed delineation of content and skills to be taught and careful use of behavioral objectives. On the other side of the debate are those who hold a more constructivist view of teaching and learning and who believe planning is not always linear and instead should take into account the complexity and serendipity of teaching and learning.

Write a reflective essay that gives your views on teacher planning in a way that would provide a principal who is considering hiring you with insight into the type of planner you will be. Compare your views with those of the two teachers below as you prepare to complete a final product for your professional portfolio.

### Jane DiGilio

I am the kind of teacher who spends a lot of time on planning. I start by writing out goals and objectives for my unit and all my daily lesson plans. I try to make these as behavioral as possible because I want them to define what I want

my students to learn. I then proceed with planning a variety of learning activities aimed at accomplishing my learning objectives. My lesson plans are very detailed, and seldom do I deviate from my plans. I am of the mind that "if you don't know where you are going, you are unlikely to get there."

### Penny Early

In my teacher education program, my professors emphasized the importance of tying all instructional activities to student learning outcomes. In an ideal world, I agree with this approach. However, in the real world, it just doesn't seem to work that way. As I plan, I normally start with big ideas I want students to understand. Sometimes I write these out; sometimes I don't. Also, over the years, I have developed many lessons that I know will interest the students and keep them engaged. I try to incorporate these highly motivational lessons into my teaching on a regular basis. Finally, I believe that students are mainly responsible for their own learning. My job is not to cram information and ideas into their brains. Instead, my job is to create learning experiences that will allow them to discover things on their own and to build knowledge out of experience. This calls for a different kind of planning that I find difficult to explain to others.

# Chapter Three

# Classrooms As Learning Communities

## *Reflecting on* **Classrooms as Learning Communities**

Before you read this chapter, think for a moment about some of the classrooms you experienced when you were in elementary or high school or, for that matter, classrooms you have been in as a college student. Some of these classrooms were definitely teacher-centered places where teaching practices were characterized by transmitting knowledge to students. Some were efficient, and students were well behaved. Others may have been out of control. Still others were places where students were friends with one another and where everyone worked hard to learn things that had meaning for them.

Below make two lists, one describing the attributes of classrooms that you thought led to positive learning communities and the other detailing attributes that were negative and prevented the development of a learning community.

Positive Attributes                        Negative Attributes

_____    _____

_____    _____

_____    _____

Now analyze your lists and reflect on what you think teachers did to make those classrooms the way they were; consider other factors that may have influenced the situation such as the type of student, physical conditions, and so on.

*Perspective of Classrooms As Learning Communities*

Fusion of the Individual and the Group

*Theoretical and Empirical Support*

Human Motivation

Features of Learning Communities

Research on Motivation and Learning Communities

*Strategies for Motivating Students and Building Productive Learning Communities*

Believe in Students' Capabilities

Avoid Extrinsic Motivation

Use Positive Feeling Tones

Build on Students' Interests

Accomplish Flow

Use Knowledge of Results

Attend to Student Needs

Attend to the Structures of Learning Goals

Facilitate Group Development

Making one's classroom a learning community is one of the most important things a teacher can do, even more important perhaps than the practices used in the more formal aspects of instruction. The classroom learning community influences student engagement and achievement, and it determines how a teacher's class will evolve from a collection of individuals into a cohesive group characterized by high expectations, caring relationships, and productive inquiry. Creating positive learning communities, however, is no simple task, nor are there easy recipes that will ensure success. Instead, it is a process of doing many things right and well and of having the courage to create classrooms that are different from many now found in schools. Let's begin this process by looking at two teachers who do this aspect of their work very well.

**Carolyn Barnes** has come to love her fifth-grade class. She is now in her third year of teaching at Woodville School. Her class is organized as a learning community, and she is pleased to be able to focus on the real learning needs of her students rather than being preoccupied with classroom management problems. She believes that her class is a democratic society in which she and the students are devoted to learning about themselves and the world around them. She sees herself as playing two roles—instructional leader and participant—in the community of scholarship they are building together. Barnes believes that what is learned must be socially constructed and that what is constructed affects what it is possible to learn. She finds herself reflecting frequently on the balance between initiating actions and responding to student initiatives within the class.

One of Barnes's students, Steve, is a good example of the payoff of her approach to teaching. Steve had a low opinion of himself and of schooling in general before he started in Carolyn's fifth-grade class. He didn't seem to care about anything. In fact, his favorite response to most everything was, "Who cares?" However, in Carolyn's learning community, students learn to trust their ability to think through problems in many areas of the curriculum. Steve first became excited when he discovered that he could solve simple algebraic problems. Later on, he found that he could apply his problem-solving skills in the social arena. The leadership Steve developed within his study team in dealing with mathematical problems helped him when he was faced with social problems within the team. Success in one area spread to other areas.

How did Carolyn Barnes get Steve to change so radically from a bored and indifferent nonparticipant to an enthusiastic learner? "It wasn't what I did so much," Carolyn says, "as what Steve's done for himself." Steve, however, thinks differently. He says, "Ms. Barnes's class is like a continuous debate. It's nothing like any class I've ever known." Steve is referring to the continuing discussions that characterize Barnes's class. No matter what the subject, students are involved in defining concerns, focusing on issues, gathering information, suggesting hypotheses, and defending their theories. Instead of focusing on facts and rote learning, students in Barnes's class strive to make sense of what they experience and to communicate that sense to others.

**Mark Hicks** now teaches social studies in the Walden Middle School in his midwestern home state. He found out about this job when he visited his parents during summer vacation several years after he started teaching. Walden is a professional development school associated with a nearby midwestern research university and located in an urban setting in a medium-size city. Hicks is a team leader in a . . . learning community that consists of 60 students. His team includes two interns from the university; an aide who is a specialist in reading; . . . a university professor who teaches language arts; and a graduate student who works as a researcher and documenter. The students are organized into study groups, and the whole group is organized into a cooperative learning community. The students leave their groups when it is time for them to take their mathematics, science, art, and physical education classes in different rooms and different groups. However, for half the day, the students are all together in one area of the school. Hicks is the instructional leader for social studies (including civics, history, geography, and economics), and the professor is the instructional leader for the language arts (literature, writing, speech, and drama). Mark also teaches one history class in the afternoon, for another learning-community group.

The whole group is also considered the home room for all 60 students. Insofar as possible, Hicks and his teaching colleagues organize their instruction themes around interdisciplinary issues. The students keep journals in which they write their thoughts and feelings about what they are studying and what is happening in the class. Their entries give Hicks insights into their fears and other emotions, as well as their cognitive development. Hicks is particularly interested in what the students understand and can use conceptually to build new ideas about the world they live in. The students are challenged to connect what they are studying in school with the outside world. For example, during a national election campaign one fall, the students organized into research groups and followed particular candidates, read their speeches, watched them on television, checked on their positions, and compared their voting records. The study groups prepared presentations for the whole group and made predictions about the election outcome.

After the elections, the students studied the results and compared them with their predictions. Where they missed the mark, the groups tried to find reasons for the difference between the outcomes and their predictions. This project combined many areas of knowledge and gave the students a feeling that what they were doing was relevant to the world around them. (after Putnam & Burke, 1992)

Classrooms like Carolyn's and Mark's do not happen by chance. Instead, they are the result of skillful planning and execution by their teachers. The intent of this chapter is to give you the understandings and skills to develop classrooms like Carolyn's and Mark's. The first section of the chapter provides an overview of motivation and the concept of learning communities. This overview is followed by a discussion of the theoretical and empirical support for these topics. The focus of the chapter then shifts to a discussion of specific actions teachers can take to motivate their students and to build productive learning communities. Several of the ideas introduced here will be revisited in Chapter 4, where the focus is on the nature of classrooms with students from diverse backgrounds, and in Chapter 5, on classroom management.

*Productive learning communities do not happen automatically. They require a lot of hard work on the part of teachers.*

You will discover as you study these three chapters that concepts that lead to productive learning communities are strongly connected to those that describe how teachers think about their students and about the diversity that characterizes today's classrooms. They also relate to how teachers go about creating approaches to classroom management that are caring and democratic.

# 🍎 *Perspective of Classrooms as Learning Communities*

The process of developing classrooms as learning communities necessitates teachers attending to many features of their students and their classrooms. Some of the ideas that inform this work date back many years. Other ideas are more recent. This section discusses three topics. First, a rather old perspective is presented, one that conceives of classrooms as places where individual and group needs are played out and where daily activity mirrors life outside of school. Second, a brief description is offered of human motivation and how teachers' choices of motivational strategies influence the development of learning communities. Finally, the concept of learning community itself and attributes that contribute to positive learning communities are described. An effort will be made throughout this section, and elsewhere in the chapter, to describe how most learning communities are today while pointing out how these can be changed for the future.

## Fusion of the Individual and the Group

The relationship between individuals and the group is complex in any setting and often fraught with dilemmas. In some ways, it mirrors the dilemma we have built into our larger system of government and economics in the United States. For instance, Americans value collective action, and we have built an elaborate system around democratic principles aimed at ensuring that the voices of citizens are heard and that actions are based on the will of the majority. We have many traditions such as singing the "Star-Spangled Banner" and saying the Pledge of Allegiance that define and promote our groupness. At the same time, we value liberty and have ensured through the Bill of Rights and subsequent laws that individuals can say what they want, believe what they want, bear arms, and pursue their lives without interference of others. This is the individual aspect of our lives.

The same dilemma exists in classrooms. We find a situation where, on the one hand, we want to establish communities that provide encouragement, safety, and support for individual learners. John Dewey (1916) observed a long time ago that children learn as they participate in social settings. More recently, scholars such as Jerome Bruner (1996) have argued that people create meaning out of relationships and membership in particular cultures. So groups and learning communities become an important aspect of learning. On the other hand, group life can limit an individual's initiative and promote norms opposed to creativity and academic learning. Let's look more closely at the relationships between these two features of classroom life.

Thinking about the individual-group connection stems from the work of early social psychologists, led by the famous Kurt Lewin (1939, 1956) and many of his colleagues who were interested in how a combination of individual needs and environmental conditions explain human behavior. Getzels and Thelan (1960) applied this work to education and developed a two-dimension model for considering the relationship between the needs of individual students and the conditions of classroom life. The first dimension of the model describes how, within a classroom, there are individuals with certain motives and needs. This perspective can be labeled the *individual dimension* of classroom life. From this perspective, particular classroom behavior results from the personality and attitudes of students and their actions to satisfy their individual needs and motives.

The second dimension of the model describes how classrooms exist within a social context and how certain roles and expectations develop within that setting to fulfill goals of the system. This dimension can be labeled the *group dimension* of the classroom. From this perspective, classroom behavior is determined by the shared expectations (norms) of the school and the classroom. Classroom life, thus, results from individually motivated students and teachers responding to each other in a social setting. It is out of this sustained development and interaction that learning communities evolve and produce desired social and academic learning.

> There are always built-in dilemmas in our society and in our classrooms between the needs of the group and the rights of individuals.

For teachers, the most important factor on the individual side of the model is motivation. This is true because, unlike a student's personality and other individual features that are rather stable and enduring, features of motivation are alterable, as will be described later in the chapter.

The concept of *learning community* is the most important factor on the social dimension of classroom life. A learning community, as contrasted to a collection of individuals, is a setting in which individuals within the community have mutual goals, have common relationships, and show concern for one another. It is a place in which people share tendencies and norms to feel and act in certain ways. These features are summarized in Table 3.1. Developing productive learning communities with these features is no easy task. However, for teachers who meet this challenge, no aspect of the job is more rewarding.

> The concept of *learning community* is most important when considering the social dimension of classroom life.

**Table 3.1** *Individual and Group Features of Productive Learning Communities*

| Individual | Group |
| --- | --- |
| • Students and teachers share common goals. | • Norms exist for expecting everyone to do their intellectual best. |
| • Students see themselves as feeling competent and self-determining. | • Norms exist for getting academic work done. |
| • Students see themselves as colleagues with high levels of attraction for one another. | • Norms exist for helping and being helped. |
| • Students and teachers reflect on past experiences and celebrate accomplishments. | • Norms support open communication and dialogue. |

✔ **Check for Understanding**

- What are the two major aspects of classroom life?
- What is the most important factor related to the individual aspect of classroom life? Why?
- What is the main feature of a classroom learning community?

# 🍎 *Theoretical and Empirical Support*

## Human Motivation

**Motivation** is usually defined as the processes within individuals that stimulate behavior or arouse us to take action. It is what makes us act the way we do. Think about this definition for a minute, and consider what arouses you to take action. What prompted you to get up this morning? Why did you choose to eat or ignore your breakfast? Why are you reading this book now rather than earlier or later? Is it because you find it interesting? Are you preparing for a classroom discussion on the topic? Or perhaps for a test? All these factors and more have the potential to arouse action. And, as you will discover later, often several factors combine to motivate individuals to act.

Psychologists make the distinction between two major types of motivation, intrinsic and extrinsic, as illustrated in Figure 3.1. When behavior is sparked internally by one's own interest or curiosity or just for the pure enjoyment of an experience, this is called **intrinsic motivation.** Lingering to watch the sun go behind the horizon on a beautiful evening is an example of intrinsic motivation. In contrast, **extrinsic motivation** kicks in when individuals are influenced to action from external or environmental factors, such as rewards, punishments, or social pressures. Intrinsic and extrinsic motivation are both important in classrooms. How teachers can use both to accomplish desirable behavior and learning is discussed more thoroughly later in the chapter.

Many theories have been proposed over the years that help explain human motivation. Some of these date back to the early part of the twentieth century, whereas others are of more recent origin. Here, our discussion of motivation is selective and follows the recent work of Graham and Weiner (1996), Spaulding, (1992), and Stipek (1996). In general, the discussion is limited to those aspects of motivation that help explain behavior within academic or achievement situations rather than behavior within a full range of situations. The discussion concentrates on four perspectives: reinforcement theory, needs theory, cognitive theory, and social learning theory.

**Intrinsic motivation causes people to act in a certain way because it brings personal satisfaction or enjoyment.**

**Extrinsic motivation is when individuals work for rewards that are external to the activity.**

**Figure 3.1** *Intrinsic and Extrinsic Motivation*

Reinforcement Theory. In the early twentieth century, **reinforcement theory** and behavioral theory dominated thinking about motivation. This approach to motivation emphasized the centrality of external events in directing behavior and in the importance of reinforcers. (Skinner, 1956). Reinforcers, whether positive or negative, are stimulus events that occur contingent with a behavior and increase the likelihood of particular behaviors. Reinforcers can be either positive or negative. **Positive reinforcers,** following desired behaviors, enhance the probability that the behavior will be repeated. **Negative reinforcers,** on the other hand, are stimulus events removed after particular behaviors. These stimuli also increase the likelihood of the behavior being repeated. In other words, people or animals repeat behavior to keep the negative reinforcer away—rats push a bar to avoid electric shock or kids do homework to avoid nagging by their parents or teachers. It is important to make distinctions between negative reinforcers and **punishments.** Punishments decrease the likelihood of a behaviors being repeated, or at least are intended to do so. For instance, if a rat removes the shock by pushing the bar, it will continue to push the bar, and that is negative reinforcement; if the rat gets a shock when it pushes the bar, it will stop pushing the bar, and that is punishment. If a student misbehaves and gets to leave class as a result, that is negative reinforcement; the student will continue to misbehave, assuming the class is more annoying than going to the principal's office. If a student misbehaves and gets detention after school, that is punishment, and it is supposed to stop the misbehavior.

Educators have embraced reinforcement theory* for a long time, and many of the practices found in contemporary classrooms stem from this perspective. The use of good grades, praise, and privileges are examples of incentives and rewards teachers have at their disposal to get students to develop desirable habits and to behave in certain ways. Negative reinforcers, such as bad grades, punishments, and loss of privileges, are used to discourage undesirable tendencies or actions. Behavior modification programs, the use of token economies, and assertive discipline (Alschuler, 1968; Cohen 1973; Cantor & Cantor 1976, 1995) are formal programs that have developed based on reinforcement theory and have been used widely in classrooms during the past thirty years. Although ideas stemming from behavioral theory still dominate many practices found in classrooms, they are increasingly in disrepute among reformers such as Kohn (1995, 1966), Noddings (1992), Oakes and Lipton (1999), who believe these practices contribute to many of the problems schools face today.

Needs Theory. Developed in the middle part of the twentieth century in part as a reaction to behaviorism and reinforcement theory, **needs theory** emphasizes that individuals are aroused to action by innate needs and intrinsic pressures, rather than by extrinsic rewards or punishments. There are several major variations within this overall theory, but three are of the most importance to classroom teachers.

Abraham Maslow, one of America's foremost mid-twentieth century psychologists, posited that human beings have a hierarchy of needs that they strive to satisfy. These needs were categorized by Maslow into seven levels. At the lower levels, needs exist to satisfy basic physiological requirements, such as food and shelter, to be safe, and to belong and be loved. The needs at the higher level of Maslow's hierarchy are more complex and refer to human growth needs, such as self-understanding, living up to one's potential, and self-actualization. Maslow's hierarchy of needs is illustrated in Figure 3.2.

According to Maslow, it is only when basic physical needs and the needs for love and self-esteem are met that individuals strive to meet higher-order needs. The classroom

A positive reinforcer is a stimulus such as a reward intended to get individuals to repeat desirable behavior.

A negative reinforcer is a stimulus that is removed, also intended to get individuals to repeat desired behaviors.

Punishments are stimuli intended to eliminate or reduce undesirable behaviors.

Needs disposition theory posits that people are motivated to take action to satisfy basic and higher-level needs.

*I want to thank Dr. Carole Shmurak for the examples and help she provided in describing reinforcement theory.

**Figure 3.2** *Maslow's Needs Hierarchy*

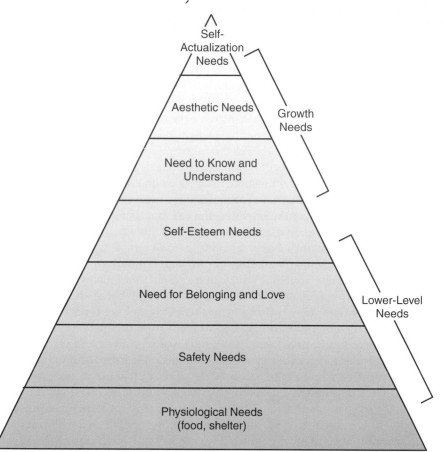

The desire to take action and to excel for the purpose of experiencing success and feeling competent is called achievement motivation.

Friendship and respect between classroom participants satisfy affiliation needs.

The desire to take action for the purposes of having control and a say in what's going on is called influence motivation.

implications of this situation are clear. Children who come to school without lower-level needs for food and security satisfied are unlikely to spend much energy in satisfying their higher-level needs for knowing and understanding. Students who lack a sense of belonging, either at home or at school, are less likely to seek knowledge of mathematics or history than they are to search for friends and colleagues.

David McClelland (1958), Atkinson and Feather (1966), and Alschuler and his colleagues (1970) took Maslow's more general needs theory and applied it to the specific needs relevant to teaching and classrooms. Sometimes called *needs disposition theory,* this theory of motivation suggests that individuals are motivated to take action and to invest energy in pursuit of three outcomes: achievement, affiliation, and influence.

The desire for achievement is evident when students try hard to learn a particular subject or when they strive to reach the objectives of particular tasks. Teachers manifest **achievement motives** as they strive to provide good instruction and act as competent professionals. **Affiliative motives** become important when students and teachers come to value the support and friendship of their peers. The motivation toward **influence** can be seen in those students who strive to have more control over their own learning and in those teachers who strive to have a larger say in the way schools are run. Students' feelings of self-esteem are related to feelings they have about their competence, affiliation, and influence. When these emotional states are frustrated by the activities in a classroom or a school, students become less involved in the school. When these states are frustrated for teachers, teachers are likely to feel incompetent, lonely, and power-less. Achievement motivation, or a student's "intent to learn," is the most important as-pect of this theory of motivation for classroom teaching.

A third cluster of ideas about the relationship between human needs and motivation is associated with the work of deCharms (1976), Deci and Ryan (1985), and Csikszent-mihalyi (1975, 1990). Although the ideas of these theorists differ in significant ways, they have in common the idea that people strive to satisfy needs for choice and self-determination in what they do and that actions taken as a result of internal pressures are more satisfying than those resulting from external influences.

DeCharms used the concepts of *origin* and *pawn* in his analysis. Pawns are persons who have no control over what happens to them. They are aroused to action not from in-trinsic values but from a sense of obligation or from external rewards. They always feel they are doing what others want them to do. Origins on the other hand, are in charge of their own behavior. They behave in particular ways because of themselves, not because of others. As origins, they resist external pressures such as orders and rules. DeCharms believed that tasks imposed externally, such as by a teacher, make people feel like pawns and dampen the internal motivation they may have to perform the task on their own. The implication of this point of view for classroom practices is considered in more detail later.

University of Chicago psychologist and educator Mihaly Csikszentmihalyi (1976, 1990) views the importance of self-determination in regard to motivation differently. For over two decades, Csikszentmihalyi has studied what he calls "states of optimal ex-perience," defined as times in people's lives when they experience total involvement and concentration as well as strong feelings of enjoyment. These types of experiences are called **flow experiences,** because the respondents Csikszentmihalyi studied often reported that what they were doing during the experience was so enjoyable "it felt like being carried away by a current, like being in a flow" (p. 127).

Perhaps you can think about a time in your life when you were doing something you became totally involved in. It could have been climbing a mountain, reading a novel, working on an old car, playing chess, engaging in a challenging run, or writing a poem. If you experienced flow, you were totally absorbed and concentrating on the activity alone, even to the point of losing track of time. In Csikszentmihalyi's (1990) words, "ac-tor and action become one," and participation is sustained because of intrinsic rather than extrinsic motivation (p. 127).

*During flow experiences, individuals experience pure enjoyment and total involvement.*

Obviously, the concept of flow has implications for education and for teaching. In fact, Csikszentmihalyi concluded that the main obstacles to student learning do not stem from the cognitive abilities of students but instead from the way we structure schools and from learning experiences that inhibit intrinsic motivation and corresponding flow experiences. Emphasis on external rules and evaluation and on rewards such as grades deters flow experiences for students. Similarly, standardized curricula and lessons that keep students in passive roles inhibit involvement and enjoyment.

**Cognitive Theory.** Cognitive theories provide a third perspective about human motivation. Like cognitive learning theorists, described elsewhere in this text, cognitive motivation theorists believe that individuals are aroused to action by their thinking. It is not external events or whether individuals are rewarded or punished that is important in explaining behavior, but instead it is the beliefs and attributions they hold about the event.

Attribution theories emphasize the way individuals come to perceive and interpret the causes of their successes and failures.

Bernard Weiner is a major cognitivist theorist, and his **attribution theory** is of particular importance to teachers. Attribution theory is based on the proposition that the ways individuals come to perceive and to interpret the causes of their successes or failures are the major determinants of their motivation, rather than innate needs or fixed earlier experiences. According to Weiner (1979, 1992, 1996), students attribute their successes or failures in terms of four causes: ability, effort, luck, and the difficulty of the learning task. Attributions can be classified as *internal* or *external*. Internal attribution occurs when individuals explain success or failure in terms of themselves; external attribution occurs when external causes are given. Attributing success to ability and effort are examples of internal attributions; luck and circumstances are external examples.

Attribution theory has several important implications for teachers. Students with high achievement motivation tend to associate their successes with their abilities and their failures with lack of effort. Conversely, students with low achievement motivation tend to attribute their successes to luck and their failures to lack of ability. There are ways in which teachers can change students' perceptions of themselves and the things around them. For instance, students can be taught to attribute their successes and failures to internal causes, such as effort, rather than to external causes, such as luck.

**Social Learning Theory.** A final perspective about motivation that has importance for teachers is Bandura's (1977) **social learning theory.** In some ways, social learning theory has similarities to both reinforcement and attribution theories. However, the important idea for teachers stems from Bandura's assertion that motivation is the product of two things: an individual's expectations about his or her chances of reaching a particular goal and the degree of value or satisfaction that will accrue if the individual achieves the goal. For instance, if a student who is working on a project for the local science fair believes that the project will win an award (high expectation) and if that reward is something he or she badly wants (high value), then motivation to work and persist until the project is done will be high. On the other hand, if either the expectation for success or the value of the reward is low, then perseverance will be low. The implications of this theory to teaching are clear. It is important to provide learning tasks that students value and have a high chance of completing successfully. The four perspectives about motivation are summarized in Table 3.2. Lessons for teachers and strategies that stem from these theories are described later.

## Features of Learning Communities

Now let's turn to the social dimension of classrooms and explore theories that explain the community aspect of classroom life. Let's do this by first looking into the classroom

## Using Technology as a Motivational Tool

Most teachers who use technology in their classrooms report the strong motivational aspects of computers and Internet resources. Many software programs today aim at being both entertaining and educational. Software with gamelike and competitive features is motivational to most students and can be used not only in schools but also purchased by parents for use at home. For instance, Math Magic software has an arcade-game format to help students learn basic math skills such as addition and subtraction. The aim of the game is to help Wizrow free an enchanted dragon from an evil dungeon. To free the dragon, students use a magic wand and must solve math problems correctly.

The fantasy setting and arcade format of the software seem to make students willing to spend considerable more time doing math this way than they would doing worksheets.

Motivation to achieve meaningful learning and higher-level goals is also important. Achieving higher-level goals requires students to do hard mental work and bear most of the responsibility for their own learning. This type of motivation is often highly personal. Working through tutorials or interacting with computer simulations and creative websites helps provide interesting challenges to students and helps them sustain the required mental activity to process and learn meaningful information and ideas.

Many teachers use educational software such as The Oregon Trail or Where in the World Is Carmen Sandiego, as well as free time on the Internet, as rewards for students who have worked hard or have completed their other work early.

**Table 3.2** *Four Perspectives of Motivation*

| Theory | Theorists | Main Idea |
|---|---|---|
| Reinforcement | Skinner | Individuals respond to environmental events and *extrinsic* reinforcement. |
| Needs | Maslow, Deci, McClelland, Csikszentmihalyi | Individuals strive to *satisfy needs* such as self-fulfillment, self-determination, achievement, affiliation, and influence. |
| Cognitive | Weiner | Individuals' actions influenced by their *beliefs and attributions,* particularly attributions about success and failure situations. |
| Social learning | Bandura | Individuals' actions influenced by the value particular *goals* hold for them and their *expectations* for success. |

of Marie Cuevas, a sixth-grade teacher at Martin Luther King Middle School. She meets daily with her students in an integrated science and language arts class. The students in her class have been heterogeneously grouped, meaning that all ability levels are represented. If we were to visit Ms. Cuevas' classroom on a typical day, we would likely see the following things going on.

Ms. Cuevas sits with a cluster of students in one corner of the room discussing a story they have just read on the life cycle of the Pacific Coast salmon, while several other students are working alone at their desks. They are writing their own stories about how salmon are threatened with extinction because hydroelectric activities have disturbed their breeding grounds. In another corner, a special education teacher is working with Brenda, a young girl who still reads at a second-grade level. Elsewhere, Ms. Cuevas' aide is administering a test to three children who were absent the previous Friday. At a far science table, a pair of students who are supposed to be practicing with a microscope are really discussing yesterday's football game. Overhearing their discussion, Ms. Cuevas stops to get them back on task. At the same moment, a squabble erupts between two students who are returning from the library. Ms. Cuevas asks the teacher's aide to resolve the conflict, then returns to the life-cycle discussion, in which irrelevant comments from Joey about last week's fishing trip with his father has caused it to drift.

As the class period draws to a close, the principal slips in to remind Ms. Cuevas that they have a short meeting scheduled during the lunch break and also to ask if she objects to having a small group of parents visit her next period. All this occurs as learning materials are being returned and readied for the next class, as today's homework assignments are collected, and as the squabble between the two students continues. (after Arends, 1996)

This scenario is not an atypical situation. Classrooms everywhere are extremely busy places, characterized by a variety of simultaneous activities: individual and group instruction, socializing, conflict management, evaluation activities, and in-flight adjustments for unanticipated events. In addition to being a specially designed learning community, classrooms are social settings where friendships form and conflicts occur. They are settings for parties, visits, and a myriad of other activities. Three basic ideas can help us understand the complexity of the classroom and will provide guidance on how to build a more productive learning community. These three dimensions are highlighted in Figure 3.3 and described in the following text.

**Classroom Properties.** One way to think about classrooms is to view them as **ecological systems** in which the inhabitants (teachers and students) interact within a specific environment (the classroom) for the purpose of completing valued activities and tasks. Using this perspective to study classrooms, Walter Doyle (1986) has pointed out that classrooms have six properties that make them complex and demanding systems.

*Multidimensionality.* This refers to the fact that classrooms are crowded places in which many people with different backgrounds, interests, and abilities compete for scarce resources. Unlike a dentist's or an optician's office where a narrow range of predictable events occur, a multitude of diverse events are planned and orchestrated in classrooms. Teachers explain things, give directions, manage conflict, collect milk money, make assignments, and keep records. Students listen, read, write, engage each other in discussion and conversation, form friendships, and experience conflict. Teach-

> **An ecological perspective views classrooms as places where inhabitants (teachers, students, and others) interact within a highly interdependent environment.**

**Figure 3.3** *Three Dimensions of Classrooms*

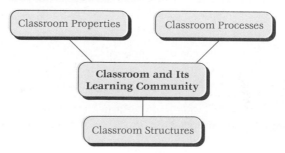

ers must learn to take these multidimensional activities into account and accommodate them in some manner.

*Simultaneity.* While helping an individual student during seatwork, a teacher must monitor the rest of the class, handle interruptions, and keep track of time. During a presentation, a teacher must explain ideas clearly while watching for signs of inattention, noncomprehension, and misbehavior. During a discussion, a teacher must listen to a student's answer, watch other students for signs of comprehension, and think about the next question to ask. Each of these situations illustrates a basic feature of classroom life—the simultaneous occurrence of difficult events that effective teachers must be able to recognize and manage.

*Immediacy.* A third important property of classroom life is the rapid pace of classroom events and their immediate impact on the lives of teachers and students. Teachers have hundreds of daily exchanges with their students. They are continuously praising, reprimanding, explaining, scolding, and challenging. Students also have hundreds of interactions with their teachers and with each other. Pencils are dropped, irrelevant comments are made, squabbles surface, and conflicts are resolved. Many of these events are unplanned, and their immediacy gives teachers little time to reflect before acting.

*Unpredictability.* Classroom events not only demand immediate attention, many take unexpected, unpredictable turns. Distractions and interruptions are frequent. Sudden illnesses, announcements over the intercom, and unscheduled visitors are common. Consequently, it is difficult to anticipate how a particular lesson or activity will go on a particular day with a particular group of students. What worked so well last year may be a complete flop this year. Even a lesson that produced enthusiasm and full participation first period may be greeted with stony silence during sixth period.

*Publicness.* In many work settings, people operate mostly in private or in view of only a few others. Doctors' diagnoses of patients' illnesses happen in the privacy of their offices; clerks and waitresses attend to their customers without much attention from others; technicians and accountants do their work unobstructed by an observing public. The classroom, however, is a very public place, and almost all events are witnessed by others. Teachers describe their existence as "living in a fishbowl." This feature of publicness or lack of privacy is just as acute for students. Student behavior is constantly being scrutinized by teachers, many of whom seem (from the students' perspective) to have eyes in the back of their heads. Students also watch each other with considerable interest. It is very difficult, therefore, for any aspect of one's classroom life, whether it is the score on the latest test or a whisper to a neighbor, to go unnoticed.

*History.* Classrooms and their participants gradually become a community that shares a common history. Classes meet five days a week for several months and thereby accumulate a common set of experiences, norms, and routines. Early meetings shape events for the remainder of the year. Each classroom develops its own social system with particular structures, organization, and norms. Though classrooms may look alike from a distance or on paper, each class is actually as unique as a fingerprint. Each class develops its own internal procedures, patterns of interaction, and limits. It is as if imaginary lines guide and control behavior within the group. In spite of day-to-day variation, there is a certain constancy in each class that emerges from its individual history.

**Distinctive features of classrooms—such as multidimensionality, simultaneity, immediacy, unpredictability, publicness, and history—that shape behavior of participants are called classroom properties.**

These properties directly affect the overall classroom environment and shape the behavior of participants. They have profound effects on teaching. As you will learn, some of these features can be altered by teachers, others cannot—at least not significantly. This aspect of teaching is revisited later in this chapter in the discussion of how teachers can provide leadership to students and help them manage group life.

Classroom Processes. Richard Schmuck and Patricia Schmuck (1997) developed a slightly different framework for viewing classrooms. They highlight the importance of interpersonal and group processes in the classrooms.

The Schmucks believe that positive learning communities are created by teachers when they teach students important interpersonal and group-process skills and when they help the classroom develop as a group. The Schmucks identify six group processes that, when working in relation to one another, produce a positive classroom community.

*Expectations.* In classrooms, people have expectations for each other and for themselves. The Schmucks are interested in how expectations become patterned over time and how they influence classroom climate and learning.

*Leadership.* This refers to how power and influence are exerted in classrooms and their impact on group interaction and cohesiveness. The Schmucks view leadership as an interpersonal process rather than as a characteristic of a person, and they encourage leadership to be shared in classroom groups.

*Attraction.* This refers to the degree to which people in a classroom have respect for one another and how friendship patterns within classrooms affect climate and learning. The Schmucks encourage teachers to help create classroom environments characterized by peer groups free from cliques, with no student left out of the friendship structure.

*Norms.* Norms are the shared expectations students and teachers have for classroom behavior. The Schmucks value classrooms with norms that support high student involvement in academic work but at the same time encourage positive interpersonal relationships and shared goals.

*Communication.* Most classroom interaction is characterized by verbal and nonverbal communication. The Schmucks argue for communication processes that are open and lively and have a high degree of participant involvement.

*Cohesiveness.* The final process refers to the feelings and commitments students and teachers have to the classroom group as a whole. The Schmucks advocate peer group cohesiveness but point out that it is important for this cohesiveness to be in support of academic work and member well-being.

Unlike the *properties* described by Doyle, classroom *processes* are highly influenced by the teacher's actions and can be altered to build productive classroom communities, as you will see later in this chapter.

Classroom Structures. The structures that shape classrooms and the demands particular lessons place on students offer an additional perspective on classrooms. Researchers, such as Gump (1967), Kounin (1970), and, more recently, Doyle (1992) and

---

**Interpersonal and group processes that help classroom participants deal with issues of expectations, leadership, attraction, norms, communication, and cohesiveness are important ingredients in developing productive learning communities.**

**Cohesiveness is determined by the feelings and commitments classroom participants have to the classroom group as a whole.**

**Figure 3.4** *Three Types of Classroom Structures and Relationship to Classroom Lessons and Activities*

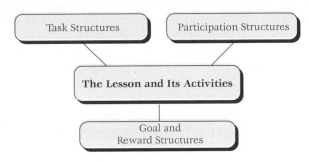

Doyle and Carter (1984), believe that behavior in classrooms is partially a response to the structures and demands of the classroom. This view of classrooms attends closely to the kinds of structures that exist within classrooms and to the activities and tasks students are asked to perform during particular lessons. Figure 3.4 shows how the lesson and its activities can vary in three important ways: structures of the learning task, structures for participation, and structures for establishing goals and providing rewards.

Unlike the classroom properties described earlier, which are mostly fixed, or classroom processes, which are highly alterable, the three structures highlighted in Figure 3.4 are sometimes fixed by tradition, but they can also be altered if a teacher chooses to do so. In fact, one might compare classroom structures to the designs of houses. The way space in a house is designed and partitioned can be thought of as the house's structure. This structure influences how people in the house normally interact with one another. For example, if all the rooms are small and closed off, it is difficult to have a party where lots of people can move around and interact easily. Conversely, if the house is wide open, it is difficult for individuals to find privacy. These structures influence certain types of behavior, but they do not guarantee or prevent specific behaviors. For example, you know of instances in which good parties have occurred in small spaces; you also know of instances in which ideal structural conditions have not produced positive interactions. Structures, however, can be changed. Using the house analogy again, walls can be removed to encourage wider interaction, or screens can be stationed to provide privacy. Classroom structures can also be changed. The following sections describe the three classroom structures in more detail.

> **Classroom structures are the ways classrooms are organized around learning tasks and participation and the ways goals and rewards are defined.**

*Classroom Task Structures.* The academic and social tasks and activities planned by teachers determine the kinds of work students carry out in classrooms. In this instance, *classroom tasks* refer to what is expected of students and the cognitive and social demands placed upon them to accomplish the task. **Classroom activities,** on the other hand, are the things students can be observed doing: participating in a discussion, working with other students in small groups, doing seatwork, listening to a lecture, and so forth. Classroom tasks and activities not only help shape the way teachers and students behave but also help determine what students learn.

**Task structures** differ according to the various activities required of particular teaching strategies or models used by teachers. As described in later chapters, lessons

**The work students are expected to do in classrooms and the cognitive and social demands placed on students as they perform particular lessons are called task structures.**

organized around lectures place far different demands on students than do lessons organized around small-group discussions. Similarly, the demands of students during discussion periods differ from those associated with seatwork.

Whereas some learning tasks and the demands they place on teachers and students stem from the nature of the learning activities themselves, others are embedded in the subjects being taught. Sometimes the academic disciplines (their concepts, organizing frameworks, and methods of revealing new knowledge) provide the basis for these differences. To understand this idea, think about the college classes you have taken in various disciplines and the demands placed on you as a learner in various situations. For instance, the task demands and your behavior when you were doing an experiment in the chemistry lab were different from the demands placed on you as you provided thoughtful analysis of a Shakespearean tragedy. Similarly, the task demands placed on you in anthropology to understand preliterate cultures were different from those required of you to understand the industrial revolution in European history.

Sometimes different task demands exist within particular academic subjects. A lesson aimed at teaching multiplication tables in arithmetic, for instance, makes a different set of demands on learners than does a lesson aimed at increasing skill in mathematical problem solving. Learning the names and locations of the major cities of the world requires different behaviors and actions for learners and teachers than a geography inquiry lesson exploring the importance of location in determining standard of living. A literature lesson on character development makes different demands than a spelling lesson.

The important thing to remember is that classroom task structures influence the thoughts and actions of classroom participants and help determine the degree of student cooperation and involvement. As later chapters emphasize, students need to be taught specific and appropriate learning strategies to help them satisfy the task demands being placed on them in classrooms.

**Goal structures determine the degree of interdependence sought among students. There are three different types of goal structures: cooperative, competitive, and individualistic.**

**Reward structures determine the ways in which rewards can be distributed within a classroom. There are three types: competitive, cooperative, and individualistic.**

*Goal Classroom and Reward Structures.* A second type of classroom structure is the way goals and rewards are structured. In Chapter 2, the concept of instructional goals was introduced. Instructional goals, you remember, were desired states a teacher had for students such as being able to spell a list of words or solve a mathematics problem. The concept of goal structure is different from that of instructional goals. **Goal structures** specify the type of interdependence required of students as they strive to complete learning tasks—the relationships among students and between an individual and the group. Johnson and Johnson (1994) and Slavin (1995) identified three different goal structures.

**Cooperative goal structures** exist when students perceive that they can achieve their goal if, and only if, the other students with whom they are working can also reach the goal.

**Competitive goal structures** exist when students perceive they can reach their goal only if other students do not reach the goal.

**Individualistic goal structures** exist when students perceive that their achievement of a goal is unrelated to achievement of the goal by other students.

The concept of goal structure is illustrated in Figure 3.5.

Classroom rewards can be categorized in the same manner as goals. **Reward structures** are competitive, cooperative, and individualistic. Grading on a curve is an example of a competitive reward structure, in that students' efforts are rewarded in

**Figure 3.5** *Three Different Goal Structures*

| Cooperative | Competitive | Individualistic |

comparison with other students. Winners in most field and track events are similarly competitive. In contrast, cooperative reward structures are in place when individual effort helps a whole group succeed. The reward system for a football team's effort (winning) is an example of a cooperative reward structure, even though the team as a whole is in competition with other teams.

Classroom goal and reward structures are at the core of life in classrooms and influence greatly both the behavior and learning of students. Regardless of a teacher's personal philosophy on the use of rewards, the current reality is that student motivation centers around the dispensation of grades. In fact, Doyle (1979) argued that the primary features of classroom life are the way students engage in academic work and how they "exchange [their] performance for grades." The way teachers organize goal and reward structures determines which types of goals are accomplished and how the exchange occurs.

*Classroom Participation Structures.* Additionally, teaching and learning are influenced by classroom **participation structures.** Participation structures, according to Cazden (1986), determine who can say what, when, and to whom. These structures include the way students take turns during group lessons and the way they ask questions and respond to teacher queries. These structures also vary from one type of lesson to another. During a lecture, for example, student participation is limited to listening to the teacher and perhaps individually taking notes. A discussion or recitation connected to a lecture, on the other hand, requires students to answer questions and to give their ideas. Listening to one another is another expectation for students during a discussion or a recitation, as is raising one's hand to take a turn. When the teacher plans seatwork for students, the prescribed participation is normally to work alone and to interact one-on-one with the teacher when help is required. Small-group and cooperative learning activities obviously require a different kind of participation on the part of students. Small-group activities require that students talk to each other, and cooperative learning activities require joint production of academic tasks. Chapters 10, 11, and 12 provide additional information about participation structures and describe steps teachers can take to increase the amount of student participation in their classrooms.

*Sociocultural Perspective.* A final perspective and the most contemporary one about classrooms as learning communities stems from sociocultural theorists and school reformers who have been heavily influenced by the work of Dewey, Piaget, and Vygotsky. This perspective views the traditional classroom as a place designed to promote certain types of formal learning and envisions classroom settings in the future that will be modeled after more informal settings in which individuals learn naturally. Often

**Participation structures help determine who can say what, when, and to whom during classroom discourse.**

these settings are described as those that enhance authentic learning, where students are involved in inquiry that helps them construct their own meaning, and where talk and action by teachers and students strive for social justice. Authentic learning is defined as students' accomplishments that have significance and meaning in the real world, not just in the classroom. Constructing one's own knowledge means being actively involved in inquiry that builds on what one already knows, rather than being treated to fixed knowledge defined and transmitted by the teachers.

Oakes and Lipton (1999) have summarized the sociocultural perspective. They argue that the pedagogy associated with this perspective cannot be translated into a "proven set of best practices" but instead evolves from "qualities of the learning relationships among teachers and students . . . and practices cannot be judged independently of the cultural knowledge students bring with them to school" (p. 196).

They do, however, posit a set of guidelines, not too much different than those described by the Schmucks, that teachers can use to construct learning communities that are authentic and socially just. These include:

- Teachers and students are confident that everyone learns well.
- Lessons are active, multidimensional, and social.
- Relationships are caring and interdependent.
- Talk and action are socially just.
- Authentic assessment enhances learning.

## Research on Motivation and Learning Communities

The research literature on classrooms and motivation is extensive and represents scholarship from many fields: psychology, social psychology, group dynamics, and social context of teaching. This section provides interesting studies to give beginning teachers insights into the way some of this research is carried out and to provide examples of some important findings. The studies cover a span of a half century and focus on the effects of classroom environments on motivation, how teacher behaviors influence motivation and group life, and how students themselves can influence each other and their teachers.

**Relationship Between Classroom Environments and Motivation.** One of the most difficult aspects of teaching is to get students to persist at learning tasks. Some students persist longer than others, and some tasks appear to be more interesting than other tasks to some students. Researchers have been interested for a long time in how classroom environments influence student motivation. The general finding is that environments characterized by mutual respect, high standards, and a caring attitude are more conducive to student persistence than other environments.

In an interesting and unique study conducted in the 1970s, Santrock studied the relationships between some of the dimensions of the classroom environment—happy and sad moods—and students' motivation to persist on learning tasks. Santrock randomly assigned first- and second-grade children into different treatment groups. On the way to a classroom, students were told a happy story and a sad story. The experimenter acted happy in relating a happy story and sad in relating the sad story. The various classrooms involved were decorated in one of two ways: with happy pictures, or with sad pictures. In the room, the children were asked to work at a task at which they were interrupted from time to time and asked to think either happy, or sad thoughts. Students could stop working on the task whenever they liked.

**Students persist longer in their studies and learning tasks if the learning environment is happy and positive.**

**Researchers have known for a very long time that students respond more favorably to teachers who are democratic than to teachers who are authoritarian.**

Students thinking happy thoughts who experienced a happy experimenter in a happy room persisted much longer at the learning task than did students thinking sad thoughts with a sad experimenter in a sad room. This type of result is important because it indicates that persistence at a task for a student is not simply a function of the child's self-control or interest but can be influenced by the environment and by aspects of the environment under the teacher's control—room decor and happy moods.

**Relationship between Leadership and Group Life.**  For many years, teachers have known that what they do influences the behavior of their students. Furthermore, many educators believe that a teacher's behavior should be "democratic" in character, thus reflecting the larger societal values about the way people should interact with one another. Take, for example, the following comments written by John Dewey over seventy-five years ago:

> We can and do supply ready-made "ideas" by the thousand; we do not usually take pains to see that the one learning engages in significant situations where his own activities generate, support, and clinch ideas—that is, perceived meanings or connections. This does not mean that the teacher is to stand off and look on; the alternative to furnishing ready-made subject matter and listening to the accuracy with which it is reproduced is not quiescence, but participation, sharing, in an activity. In such shared activity the teacher is a learner, and the learner is, without knowing it, a teacher—and upon the whole, the less consciousness there is, on either side, of either giving or receiving instruction, the better. (Dewey, 1916, p. 176)

But what effects do democratic behaviors and procedures have on students and group life? This question was first explored well over a half century ago in a set of classic studies conducted by Kurt Lewin, Ron Lippitt, and Richard White (Lewin, Lippitt & White, 1939; Lippitt & White, 1963). The researchers studied 11-year-old boys who volunteered to form clubs and to participate in a series of club projects. Clubs such as the Sherlock Holmes Club, Dick Tracy Club, and Secret Agents Club were formed, and club leaders (teachers) were taught to exhibit three different forms of leadership: authoritarian leadership, democratic leadership, and laissez-faire (passive) leadership. The boys were observed as they participated in club activities, including a time when the leader purposively left the boys on their own.

The researchers found that the boys reacted to authoritarian leadership by becoming rebellious and that they were much less involved than the boys under democratic leadership. What was most telling, however, was the boys' behavior when the leaders were out of the room. Boys under authoritarian and laissez-faire leadership stopped working as soon as the leader was absent. Boys in the democratic group, on the other hand, kept working, and certain boys even stepped in and provided leadership to the group.

Many educators have concluded from this and many similar studies over the past fifty years that teacher behavior has important influences on students' willingness to cooperate and stick to learning tasks. Teachers who are too strict and directive may get a lot of work from their students if they are physically present, but that involvement will drop off once close supervision is removed.

Certain motivational strategies used by teachers have also been the focus of considerable research, particularly over the past two decades. Of particular interest have been those strategies used by teachers that support student motivation to learn. An example of this research is highlighted in the Research Summary for this chapter.

**Effects of Students' Behavior on Each Other and on Their Teachers.**  Studies such as the one described in the Research Summary focus on the influence that teacher behavior has

# Can Particular Strategies Influence Students' Motivation to Learn?

*Marshall, H. H. L. (1987).* Motivational strategies of three fifth-grade teachers. *Elementary School Journal* 88, 135–150.

An enduring concern among teachers is how to motivate students. Keen observers of classrooms have long recognized subtle differences among classroom environments. Some are friendly; others are not. Some are learning oriented; in others, students avoid work. But how do environments get that way, and how do teachers' use of learning and motivational strategies influence the learning orientations of their classrooms? These were questions that Hermine Marshall explored in a very interesting and provocative study.

**Problem and Approach:** Marshall was interested in strategies used by teachers that motivate students to learn. Her study is important for two reasons. One, the questions she asked are central to teachers' work. And two, her findings provide concrete recommendations for teachers' actions. Her study is also interesting because it illustrates what can be learned when researchers choose to study a few teachers in depth rather than many superficially.

**Sample and Setting:** In earlier studies, Marshall developed the idea that classrooms can be classified as having one of three orientations toward learning.

- *Learning-oriented classrooms.* Classroom in which teachers emphasized to students the challenges and enjoyment of learning.
- *Work-oriented classrooms.* Classrooms in which teachers motivated students to complete their work for external reasons (e.g., rewards such as grades or threats such as detention).
- *Work-avoidance classrooms.* Classroom in which teachers seemed not to care and accepted minimal effort and incomplete work from their students.

Marshall selected three fifth-grade classrooms to participate in her study. Each one revealed one of the three motivational orientations. The three teachers in the study were expe-

rienced (a minimum of nine years' experience), and students in the three classrooms had similar backgrounds and abilities.

**Procedures:** To get acclimatized, trained observers visited the selected classrooms over a period of two to four weeks. They then observed each teacher for at least twelve hours during reading and math lessons and during selected whole-class instruction times. Observers kept a running record of classroom events, and they used an observation form that recorded teacher behavior in three categories: the way the teacher "framed" (began) lessons, the way the teacher refocused students' attention after the lesson was initiated, and the way the teacher encouraged students to take responsibility for their own learning. In addition, all three teachers were interviewed, and their students' achievement test scores in reading were analyzed.

**Results:** Table 3.3 displays Marshall's analysis of statements made by the three teachers to frame their lessons and statements made once the lesson had begun to maintain attention and engagement. Framing statements were divided into two categories: endogenous statements and exogenous statements. **Endogenous statements** emphasized the personal relevance of learning activities and communicated to students they were going to have fun and do well. **Exogenous statements,** on the other hand, included those that promised positive rewards, such as good grades, for getting work done, and sanctions, such as threats, if work was not completed. Refocusing statements were classified as being either positive or negative in their tone. The data displayed in Table 3.3 reveal some striking differences in the three classrooms and the ways teachers framed and refocused their lessons.

Teacher X framed her lessons with statements defined by the researchers as having mostly endogenous qualities. She emphasized the personal relevance of the lesson to students and told them they were going to have fun and that she expected everyone in class to do well. To maintain student engagement after initiating the lesson, Teacher X used positive motivational statements that challenged students to think (such as "I challenge you . . . "), or statements that alerted students to what was going to happen next, or statements that expressed enthusiasm or humor (such as "look bright-eyed and bushy-tailed, because this next part is going to present you with a real challenge").

Teacher Y, on the other hand, framed her lessons with exogenous statements. She made demands on students, promising rewards if they did well and punishment if they did not. Teacher Y was not observed using any strategies that alerted students and few that challenged them to think. Most of Teacher Y's refocusing statements merely redirected students to the task at hand. A large proportion of Teacher Y's refocusing statements, according to the researcher, had negative tones as contrasted to the positive tones associated with Teacher X's refocusing statements.

Teacher Z made few framing statements at all. She tended to begin lessons with matter-of-fact statements, such as "Open your books to page 382" or "All right, let's get started." Students were not encouraged to do well, nor were they threatened with punishment if their work was not completed. As you can see in Table 3.3, Teacher Z made few refocusing statements, and of those that were made, almost all were negative in tone.

Researchers reported that students in Teacher Z's classroom were often off task and wandered around the classroom while the teacher was trying to teach. In contrast, students in Teacher X's classroom appeared to be engaged almost all the time and on several occasions were observed asking the teacher for more work.

Marshall and her assistants also interviewed each teacher and compared gains made in reading between the beginning and the end of the school year. Interviews revealed that Teacher X believed all students have ability and can learn. Teacher Y, on the other hand, believed that she was the one responsible for student learning. Teacher Z didn't take responsibility for learning, nor did she think it was the students' responsibility.

In classroom X, students demonstrated almost a full year's growth in reading during the course of the year. In contrast, students in classroom Y gained almost a year and a half. Students in classroom Z made no gains in reading during the school year.

**Discussion and Implications:** Marshall's study points directly to the importance of teachers' expectations of their students and the relationships they built for getting them to engage in learning activities. Students in Teacher X's classroom were much more engaged and took on more responsibility for their own learning than did students in other two classrooms. This led Marshall to make the following observations about effective teachers in regard to the motivational strategies they employ.

1. Effective teachers view students as able and responsible and encourage students to take responsibility for their own learning.
2. Effective teachers begin and frame lessons with statements that challenge students. They convince their students that they are going to enjoy the lesson and that they will be successful in learning it.
3. As lessons proceed, effective teachers use encouragement, humor, and group-alerting statements to keep students interested and engaged.

At the same time, it is important to point out that it was the students in classroom Y who made the largest gains as measured by standardized achievement tests, the classroom in which the teacher made the most use of extrinsic and negative motivational strategies. This is an interesting finding and raises questions about motivation strategies, student engagement, and student learning outcomes.

**Table 3.3** *Comparison of Lesson-Framing and Lesson-Refocusing Statements*

|  | Teacher X | | Teacher Y | | Teacher Z | |
|---|---|---|---|---|---|---|
|  | **N** | **%** | **N** | **%** | **N** | **%** |
| Framing Statements: | | | | | | |
| Endogenous | 17 | 55 | 3 | 11 | 6 | 13 |
| Exogenous | 3 | 10 | 7 | 26 | 10 | 28 |
| Management Refocusing: | | | | | | |
| Positive | 43 | 53 | 9 | 9 | 6 | 5 |
| Negative | 2 | 5 | 56 | 58 | 34 | 28 |

Percentages of each type are of the total statements in the lesson and thus do not add up to 100 percent.

# Using Multidimensional Tasks to Build Community

One way teachers tailor their instruction for a diverse group of students is to make opportunities available for their students to work together on community activities and to pursue tasks that are motivational and challenging. Consider, for example, the learning situation in KimMan Thi Pham's eleventh grade history classroom described below.:

> The room is alive with activity. Desks are pushed to the edge of the classroom, accommodating various groups. Some students discuss how to share their recent experience of working with migrant farm workers in the fields. One student patiently charts a graph showing the economic breakdown of maintaining a large farm. Two students and I plan the presentation order. Other students complete a poster on the United Farm Workers, focusing on the leadership of Cesar Chavez and Philip Ver Cruz. Their photographs, news clippings, and markers are sprawled across the floor. Laughter erupts from the back of the room where four students debate the idea of dressing up as fruit while presenting information on the move-

ment of farm workers across the state following the peak harvest times of the fruit and vegetable season. Someone asks me if she can give her classmates a test after the presentation. "Certainly," I reply, "but consider—'What do you want them to know?'" The student thinks about the question while slowly returning to the group. Activity continues unabated until the final minutes. I remind students to document progress with a short journal entry highlighting individual concerns and feelings. Students write until the end of class. (Oakes & Lipton, 1999, pp. 209–210)

Elizabeth Cohen (1994) and Oakes and Lipton (1999) have called this type of learning situation "using multidimensional tasks." It emphasizes students working together on interesting tasks and problems where students can make contributions according to their own interests and abilities. According to Elizabeth Cohen, multidimensional tasks:

- Are intrinsically interesting, rewarding, and challenging.
- Include more than one answer or more than one way to solve the problem.
- Allow different students to make different contributions.
- Involve various mediums to engage the senses of sight, sound, and touch.
- Require a variety of skills and behaviors.
- Require reading and writing.

*The peer group has important influences on student behavior and their motivation to engage in learning activities.*

on students. Influence in the classroom group, however, does not always flow just from the teacher. Students also influence each other and can even influence their teachers. One particularly interesting line of inquiry over the years has been research that investigates how the student peer group, through both formal and informal interactions, affects attitudes and achievement. Peer group influences have been documented in studies of college dormitories and living houses (Newcomb, 1961, for example) and in many different public and private school settings. Much of the research shows that many students conform to peer group norms and that all too often these norms are in contradiction to those held by educators and teachers. James Coleman (1961) studied ten American high schools in the 1950s. He found many instances where the adolescent peer group supported norms for being popular and being athletic over the school's norms in support of academic achievement. This finding has been replicated in American high schools in every decade since Coleman's original work (see, for example, Ogee, 1994). Today, peer group pressure is used often to explain high dropout rates and low achievement of many inner-city youth.

## 🍎 Strategies for Motivating Students and Building Productive Learning Communities

Building productive learning communities and motivating students to engage in meaningful learning activity are major goals of teaching. Yet, many ingredients make up a student's motivation to learn. Success depends on using motivational strategies stemming from each of the perspectives described previously as well as on employing strategies that help a group of individuals develop into a productive learning community. Motivational and group development strategies, however, cannot be reduced to a few simple guidelines. No single dramatic event will produce motivation and a productive learning community. Instead, effective teachers employ strategies inter-dependently until motivation is a permanent aspect of their classrooms, where students' psychological needs are met, where they find learning activities that are interesting and meaningful, and where they will know they can be successful. Strategies to attain this type of classroom situation are described in the sections that follow.

### Believe in Students' Capabilities and Attend to Alterable Factors

There are many things that students take with them to school that teachers can do little about. For example, teachers have little influence over students' basic personalities, their home lives, or their early childhood experiences. Unfortunately, some teachers attend only to these aspects of their students, and such attention is mostly unproductive. It is true that social factors, such as students' backgrounds or their parents' expectations, influence how hard they work in school. Similarly, their psychological well-being, anxieties, and dependencies also affect effort. However, there is not much teachers can do to alter or influence these social and psychological factors. Instead, teachers are more effective in enhancing student motivation if they concentrate their efforts on factors that are within their abilities to control and influence.

The most important things that teachers can control are their own attitudes toward and beliefs about children, particular those they may have about students who come from different backgrounds than they do. Believing that every child can learn and that every child sees the world through his or her own cultural lenses can shift the burden of low engagement and low achievement from the child's background to where it often belongs—a nonunderstanding classroom and school.

### Avoid Overemphasizing Extrinsic Motivation

Most beginning teachers know much about how to use extrinsic motivation, because many common-sense ideas about human behavior rest on reinforcement principles,

✔ **Check for Understanding**

- Contrast reinforcement, needs, cognitive, and social learning theories of motivation. How does each inform a teacher's efforts to motivate students?

- What are the differences between extrinsic and extrinsic motivation?

- How are flow experiences defined?

- Contrast the classroom properties defined by Doyle with the classroom processes described by the Schmucks.

- How can classroom task and reward structures vary?

- Contrast the sociocultural perspective of learning communities with more traditional views.

- What features of a classroom environment help to produce students who persist longer on assigned tasks?

- Which leadership style has the most positive effect on student learning? On motivation? How does this approach compare to other leadership styles?

- How does student behavior influence the actions of the teacher and other students?

**Table 3.4** *Minimizing the Negative Effects of Extrinsic Motivation*

**Strategies for minimizing the negative effects of rewards on students' intrinsic motivation**

I. Use extrinsic rewards when there is no intrinsic motivation to undermine.
   A. Use extrinsic rewards when students feel too incompetent to experience intrinsic interest in the task at hand.
   B. Use extrinsic reward when the task is one for which no person is likely to find much intrinsic interest in completing.

II. Use extrinsic rewards in such a way that the likelihood of undermining students' perceptions of self-determination and control is minimal.
   A. Emphasize the informative, not the controlling, nature of extrinsic rewards.
      1. Tie grades given on specific assignments to detailed descriptive comments about the quality of the students' performance on the task.
      2. Use symbolic rewards, such as the teacher's initials, as record-keeping devices.
   B. Make the extrinsic reward the opportunity to make choices, to be self-determining.

Source: Spaulding (1992), p. 56.

**Teachers are more effective if they concentrate their efforts on things they can do something about.**

particularly on the principles of providing extrinsic rewards (positive reinforcers) to get desired behavior and using punishment to stop undesirable behavior. This theory of motivation is pervasive in our society. Parents get their children to behave in particular ways by giving them weekly allowances. They withhold these allowances or use "grounding" when their children behave inappropriately. People who work hard at their jobs are given merit raises; those who don't are fired. We give individuals medals for acts of bravery and put them in jail for acts of crime. Good grades, certificates of merit, praise, and athletic letters are extrinsic rewards used by teachers to get students to study and to behave in desirable ways. Poor grades, demerits, and detention are employed to punish undesirable behaviors.

**Although reinforcement theory is pervasive in our culture, effective teachers find ways to minimize its potentially harmful effects.**

On the surface, reinforcement theory makes good common sense, and certainly there may be instances in all aspects of life in which extrinsic supports are necessary. At the same time, extrinsic rewards do not always produce the intended results. For instance, providing extrinsic rewards for learning tasks that are already intrinsically interesting can actually decrease student motivation (see Chapter 6). Further, for any reward or punishment to serve as motivators they must be valued or feared. Many students in today's schools don't care about good grades. If that is so, then grades will not cause students to study. Similarly, if getting demerits or being assigned to detention are considered "badges of honor," as they are to some students, then they will not deter undesirable behavior. Effective teachers use extrinsic rewards cautiously and learn to rely on other means to motivate their students. Table 3.4 details particular strategies teachers can use to minimize the negative effects of extrinsic motivational strategies.

## Create Learning Situations with Positive Feeling Tones

Needs and attributional theories of motivation stress the important of building learning environments that are pleasant, safe, and secure and in which students have a degree of self-determination and assume responsibility for their own learning.

The overall learning orientation and tone of the classroom are critical. As observed in studies summarized in the previous section (Santrock, 1976; Marshall, 1989), teachers' attitudes and orientations toward particular learning situations have considerable influence on how students respond to learning situations. Some (e.g., Hunter, 1982) have used the term **feeling tone** to describe this aspect of the learning environment and have provided the following examples of simple things teachers can say to establish a positive, neutral, or negative feeling tone:

Positive:    "You write such interesting stories, I'm anxious to read this one."
Negative:   "That story must be finished before you're excused for lunch."
Neutral:     "If you aren't finished, don't worry; there'll be plenty of time later."

Students put forth more effort in environments with positive feeling tones and less in unpleasant learning environment. An important point for teachers to consider, if they choose to use unpleasant feeling tones to motivate students to complete a difficult learning task, is to return as soon as possible to a positive one: "I really put a lot of pressure on you, and you've responded magnificently," or "I know you were angry about the demands being made, but you should be proud of the improvement in your performance." Feeling tones in the classroom are not only the result of specific things teachers say at a particular moment; they are also the result of many other structures and processes created by teachers to produce productive learning communities, as later sections of this chapter describe.

> **Students put forth more effort in environments that have positive feeling tones, a condition where particular learning tasks are perceived as pleasant.**

## Build on Students' Interests and Intrinsic Values

Needs and attributional theories of motivation stress the importance of using intrinsic motivation and building on the students' own interests and curiosity. A teacher can do a number of things to relate learning materials and activities to students' interests. Here are some examples:

- *Relate lessons to students' lives.* Find things that students are interested in or curious about, such as popular music, and relate these interests to topics under study (Mozart, for instance).
- *Use students' names.* Using students' names helps personalize learning and captures students' attention. For example: "Suppose Maria, here, were presenting an argument for electing her friend, and Charles wished to challenge her position . . . , "or "John, here, has the pigmentation most commonly associated with Nordic races, whereas Roseanne's is more typical of Latinos."
- *Make materials vivid and novel.* A teacher can say things that make the ordinary vivid and novel for students. For example: "When you order your favorite McDonald's milkshake, it won't melt even if you heat it in the oven. That's the result of an emulsifier made from the algae we're studying," or "Suppose you believed in reincarnation. In your next life, what would you need to accomplish that you didn't accomplish satisfactorily in this life?"

> **Vivid and novel materials and examples can serve as powerful motivators for student learning.**

Using games, puzzles, and other activities that are inviting and carry their own intrinsic motivation is another way teachers make lessons interesting for students. Similarly, a variety of activities (field trips, simulations, music, guest speakers) and instructional methods (lecture, seatwork, discussion, small-group) keep students interested in school and their schoolwork.

It is important to highlight two cautions in using student interests for motivational purposes. Stressing the novel or vivid can sometimes distract students from learning a topic. Similarly, new interests are formed through learning about a new topic. Teachers who expose their students only to materials in which they are already interested prevent them from developing new interests.

## Structure Learning to Accomplish Flow

Schools and teachers can structure learning activities to emphasize their intrinsic value so students become totally involved and experience the type of flow described earlier. However, such total involvement, according to Csikszentmihalyi, is only possible with learning experiences that have certain characteristics.

**Highly motivational flow experiences require an appropriate level of challenge.**

First, flow experiences require that the challenge of a particular learning activity corresponds to the learner's level of skill. All the learner's skill is required, yet the activity cannot be so difficult that the participant becomes frustrated. Perhaps rock climbing can provide a good example of the need to match the degree of challenge and skill. If you are an advanced beginning rock climber, you will be bored if asked to climb the slightly sloping, fifteen-foot-high rock in your backyard. This would not require use of your skills or provide you with challenging practice. On the other hand, as an advanced beginner, you will become very frustrated and stressed if asked to climb El Capitan, one of the most challenging climbs in the United States. You will read later how experienced teachers plan lessons in which they balance the level of difficulty and the amount of challenge.

The definition of clear and unambiguous goals is another characteristic of learning experiences likely to produce flow. As you read in Chapter 2, lessons that make clear to students what is expected of them and what they are supposed to accomplish are more likely to produce extended engagement and involvement than are lessons with unclear goals and expectations. Finally, people who report having had flow experiences say they gained relevant and meaningful feedback about their activity as they were doing it, a feature of motivation discussed in the following section.

Establishing "flow" may not be as easy as it may seem, particularly in classrooms that are culturally and linguistically diverse. For instance, learning activities that may appear to be interesting and challenging to a white, middle-class teacher may have little meaning to students with different cultural heritages or who speak English as a second language. Failing to make meaningful connections with students can leave teachers frustrated with the lack of engagement on the part of students and students feeling that their voices are not being heard.

## Use Knowledge of Results and Don't Excuse Failure

**Feedback or knowledge of results is information given to students about their performance.**

**Feedback** (also called *knowledge of results*) on good performance provides intrinsic motivation. Feedback on poor performance gives learners needed information to improve. Both types of feedback are important motivational factors. To be effective, feedback must be more specific and immediate than a grade a teacher puts on a report card every six to nine weeks. In Chapter 8, Direct Instruction, specific guidelines for giving feedback are provided. This topic is also covered in Chapter 6 on testing and evaluation. It is enough to say here that feedback should be as immediate as possible (handing back corrected tests the day after an exam), as specific as possible (comments in addition to an overall grade on a paper), and nonjudgmental ("Your use of the word *that* is incorrect—you should have used *which* instead" rather than "What's wrong with you? We have gone over the difference between *that* and *which* a dozen times."). Additionally, feedback should focus on and encourage internal attributions—such as effort or lack of effort—rather than external attributions—such as luck or lack of ability. Feedback should help students see what they *did not* do rather than what they *cannot* do.

Sometimes teachers, particularly inexperienced teachers, do not want to embarrass students by drawing attention to incorrect performance. Also, it is sometimes easier to

*Feedback is important to eliminate incorrect performance—and to enhance student learning.*

accept students' excuses for failure than to confront them with the fact of their failure. These kinds of teacher actions are most often counterproductive. Teachers should not impose severe punishments for failures or use feedback that is belittling. At the same time, effective teachers know that it is important to hold high expectations for all students and that if things are being done incorrectly, this incorrect performance will continue and become permanent unless teachers bring it to the students' attention and provide instruction for doing it right.

## Attend to Student Needs, Including the Need for Self-Determination

You read in the discussion of needs theory that individuals invest energy in pursuit of achievement, affiliation, and influence as well as to satisfy needs for choice and self-determination. Most motivational research has focused on achievement motivation, and less is known about influence, affiliation, and the role of choice. All of these motives, however, play a role in determining the type of effort students will expend on learning tasks and how long they will persist. In general, students' influence and self-determination needs are satisfied when they feel they have some power or say over their classroom environment and their learning tasks. Cheryl Spaulding (1992) related an interesting story about how important choice and self-determination are to most people. Imagine the following scenario.

You are a person who loves to travel, and your favorite form of traveling is by car. Each summer you take off on a vacation, driving to and through some of the interesting places in this country. You prefer this sort of vacation because you enjoy discovering for yourself country inns and bed-and-breakfast homes run by unusual people in out-of-the-way places. This year an anonymous benefactor has awarded you with an all-expenses-paid, two-month driving tour through parts of the northeastern United States and Canada, a trip you have long wanted to take. To assist you, this benefactor has gone ahead and planned your itinerary, down to the minutest detail. Your travel route, including the specific roads on which you will travel, has been thoroughly mapped out so that you will never get off course. All your room and dinner reservations have already been made. Even your meals have been preordered for you. All you have to do to take advantage of this wonderful offer is agree to follow the planned itinerary down to the last detail. Would you accept this offer? Would this vacation be as enjoyable as your usual tours through the states? (p. 22)

Spaulding writes that the answers to these questions are likely to be no, because much of the pleasure derived from a driving tour comes from the freedom of being able to make choices on a moment-to-moment basis rather than having these decisions made by someone else.

Here are a few specific examples of how teachers can provide students choice and a sense of self-determination:

- Hold weekly planning sessions with students, assessing how well the previous week has gone and what they would like to see included in next week's lessons. Some experienced teachers use a technique called "pluses and wishes." On large newsprint charts, the teacher makes two columns and labels them as shown in Table 3.5. Together, students and teachers list their suggestions for all to consider. The teacher can use information from this list in his or her own planning and can come back to it to show students that particular lessons and activities were influenced by their input.
- Assign students to perform important tasks, such as distributing and collecting books and papers, taking care of the aquarium, taking roll, acting as tutors to other students, taking messages to the principal's office, and the like.
- Use cooperative learning and problem-based instructional strategies (see Chapters 10 and 11), because these approaches allow students considerable choice in the subject they study and the methods they use.

**Students look mainly to each other for satisfying their affiliation needs.**

Satisfying affiliative needs is also important. In most schools, it is the peer group that students look to for satisfying their affiliation needs. Unfortunately, norms for peer group affiliation often conflict with the strong achievement norms teachers would like to see. In some instances, very competitive cliques that exclude many students from both the academic and social life of the school are found. In other instances, peer group

**Table 3.5** *Pluses and Wishes Chart*

| Pluses | Wishes |
|---|---|
| The lecture on cells was clear. | We wish we had had more time on the experiment. |
| The group work was interesting. | We wish more students would cooperate. |
| We enjoyed the principal's visit. | We wish the test had been fairer. |

norms exist that apply negative sanctions to those students who try to do well in school work. Teachers can make needs for affiliation work in a positive way by following some of these procedures.

- Make sure that all the students in the class (even in high school) know one another's names and some personal information about each student.
- Initiate cooperative goal and reward structures, as described in Chapter 10.
- Take time to help the students in the classroom develop as a group, using procedures described in the following section.

## Attend to the Structure of Learning Goals and Difficulty of Instructional Tasks

Social learning theory reminds us of the importance of the ways learning goals and tasks are structured and carried out. Two aspects of learning goals and tasks should be considered here: goal structures and task difficulty.

You read earlier about three types of classroom goal structures: competitive, co-operative, and individualistic. Competitive goal structures lead to comparisons and win-lose relationships among students and make a student's ability, rather than ef-fort, the primary factor for success. Cooperative goal structures, on the other hand, lead to social interdependence, and shared activity makes student effort the primary factor for success. Chapter 10 goes into greater detail about how to set up coopera-tive goal structures.

Closely connected to the ways goals are structured is the level of difficulty of goals students choose for themselves. Students who set very high goals that are unachievable can be encouraged to rethink what might be more realistic goals. Similarly, students who always set low goals can be encouraged to raise their sights. The important thing for teachers to remember is that students are motivated to persevere longer in pursu-ing goals that are realistic and achievable.

An additional factor that can influence a student's motivation is associated with the actual degree of difficulty of the learning task and the amount of effort required to com-plete it. As described previously, tasks that are too easy require too little effort and pro-duce no feelings of success and, consequently, are unmotivational. At the same time, tasks that are too difficult for students, regardless of the effort they expend, will also be unmotivational. Effective teachers learn how to adjust the level of difficulty of learning tasks for particular students. Sometimes this means providing special challenges for the brightest in the class and providing more support and assistance for those who find a particular task too difficult. Effective teachers also help students see the connections between the amount of effort they put into a learning task and their successes and ac-complishments. This is done by discussing with students why particular efforts led to success and, conversely, why in other instances they led to failure.

> **Learning tasks that are too easy require too little effort and produce little feeling of success.**

## Facilitate Group Development and Cohesion

Developing a positive classroom environment will lead to enhanced motivation and heightened achievement. This requires attending to the social and emotional needs of students as well as their academic needs. Also, it requires helping students grow as a group. Sometimes people may not notice, but groups, like individuals, develop and pass through discernible stages in the process. Several social psychologists have stud-ied classrooms and found that classroom groups develop in similar patterns

(Schmuck & Schmuck, 1997; Putnam & Burke, 1992). The following stages of **group development** represent a synthesis of their ideas, with particular attention to the ideas identified by the Schmucks.

**Stage 1: Facilitating Group Inclusion and Psychological Membership.** Everyone wants to feel that they belong, that they are accepted by significant others. This is especially important in a classroom setting, because being a learner is a risky business. In order to have the courage to make the mistakes that are a natural part of learning, students need to feel they are in a safe environment. This feeling of safety comes only when students feel accepted and liked by those in their class. Therefore, early in classroom life, students will seek a niche for themselves in the classroom group. They will likely be on their good behavior and present a positive image. Teachers have considerable influence during this period because of their assigned authority. During this period, teachers should spend considerable time forging personal connections with students, helping them learn each others' names, and assisting them in building relationships with each other. When new students enter the group, special efforts must again be made to ensure their acceptance. What teachers do during the initial period of group development represents key first steps in creating a positive learning environment for students.

**Stage 2: Establishing Rules and Routines.** Think about when you become associated with a new group. Like most people, you are generally very concerned about what is expected of you and how you should behave toward others. Students always want to understand how a class will operate. What are the rules, procedures, policies, and expectations for behavior in the classroom? Sometimes this stage follows stage 1, but it can and often does happen concurrently. Effective teachers conduct lessons early in the year that weave academic expectations with interpersonal and behavioral expectations. They strive to establish an environment in which students can expect to work hard but also feel safe and supported. One day or one lesson is not sufficient to cement these norms; the process takes considerable time spread over several weeks. More about this aspect of classroom life is discussed in Chapter 5 under the topic of classroom management.

**Stage 3: Establishing Shared Influence and Collaboration.** It does not take very long, even with very young children, to facilitate psychological membership and establish rules and routines. However, inevitably, there will be problems. Members of the class soon enter into two types of power struggles. One struggle tests the authority of the teacher; the other establishes the peer group pecking order. These are signals that the classroom has entered stage 3, in which individuals begin struggling to establish their influence within the group. At this stage, it is important for teachers to show students that they have a voice in classroom decision making and that classroom life will be more satisfying if tensions among students can be resolved. Several techniques for dealing with tensions and conflict in the classroom are described in Chapters 5 and 6 and include classroom meetings, conflict resolution, active listening, and dealing with misbehavior. At this point, it is enough to know that such unpleasant experiences as challenges to the teacher's authority, fights between students, and off-task behavior are all normal occurrences on the road to establishing a positive classroom environment. A caution, however, is in order. If these tensions cannot be resolved and power relationships balanced, the group will not be able to move toward collaboration or into the next stage.

*Classroom groups go through stages in the process of developing into cohesive and effective groups.*

*Well developed groups are ready to work productively on academic goals.*

**Stage 4: Pursuing Individual and Academic Goals.** At this stage, the classroom group is functioning smoothly and productively. Students feel comfortable in the class and are confident that difficulties can be worked out. The frequency of conflicts and off-task behavior decreases, and when they do happen, they are dealt with quickly and effectively. At this time, the classroom enters a stage of development for working productively on academic goals. Students during this stage are very good at setting goals and accomplishing work. They "know the ropes," and little time is lost in miscommunication, conflict, or confusion. Teachers recognize this stage of their group's development and know that this is the time that the best teaching takes place. It is a time to communicate high expectations for students and to encourage them to aspire to high individual and group achievement. Good teachers are also aware that the group can also be pulled back into earlier stages during this period. If that happens, academic work will slow down as membership and power issues are again resolved.

**Stage 5: Accomplishing Self-Renewal, Transition, and Closure.** As the school year proceeds, teachers should help class members think about their continuous growth and about how to take on new and more challenging tasks. As the semester or year comes to an end, so too does the classroom group. Having worked side by side for several months, students develop close ties with each other, and teachers must address the heartache involved in the breaking of those ties. Similar moments of emotional strain can happen during the year as students move to new schools or as long vacations cause separations. The teacher's job in stage 5 is to watch for these emotional changes, be ready to assist the group in revisiting and reworking previous stages as needed, and to aid students in synthesizing and bringing to closure the bonds they have formed. Additionally, teachers must help prepare students for what is to come next—the next grade, teacher, or school. Table 3.6 summarizes the five stages of classroom development.

The Schmucks as well as others who study classroom groups are quick to point out, and rightfully so, that the stages of classroom development are not always sequential. Instead, they are often cyclical in nature, with many of the stages repeating themselves several times during the school year. When new students are placed in

✔ **Check for Understanding**

- Contrast the major strategies to accomplish motivation and a productive learning community.

- Why should teachers focus on controllable factors when attempting to heighten student motivation?

- When and how should extrinsic motivation be used? What cautions should be used?

- In what ways can teachers allow students to participate in classroom planning? How might this impact student motivation?

- What is meant by flow? Why are flow experiences often missing in formal education?

- How does a teacher's role as facilitator evolve through each stage of the classroom group's development?

- What effect does positive group development have on the classroom learning community?

**Table 3.6** *Schmucks' Stages of Classroom Development*

| Stage | Group and Member Needs and Behaviors |
| --- | --- |
| Stage 1: Inclusion and membership | Early in classroom life, students seek a niche for themselves in the peer group. Students want to present a good image and are on their good behavior. Teachers have great influence during this period because of their assigned authority. |
| Stage 2: Establishing rules and routines | Members are very concerned about what is expected of them. Students want to understand the way the class will operate and the rules that will govern their behavior. |
| Stage 3: Influence and collaboration | Members of the class enter into two types of power struggles. One tests the authority of the teacher; the other establishes the peer group pecking order. If tensions cannot be resolved and power relationships balanced, the group cannot move along productively to the next stage. |
| Stage 4: Individual and academic achievement | The classroom enters a stage of development for working productively on academic goals. Students during this stage can set and accomplish goals and work together on tasks. The classroom can also be pulled back into earlier stages during this stage. |
| Stage 5: Self-renewal/transition/closure | At this stage, members can think about their continuous growth and about taking on new and more challenging tasks. This is also a stage that can produce conflict, because change in tasks will perhaps upset earlier resolutions around membership. |

Source: After Schmuck and Schmuck (1997), pp. 178–187.

classrooms, membership issues again become important. Student growth in interpersonal skills keeps influence issues unstable and in constant flux. Larger societal issues cause change and a need to renegotiate norms associated with academic goals and performances.

The stages of classroom group development also have no *definite* time frames associated with them. The time it takes each group to work out issues associated with membership, influence, and task accomplishment depends on the skill of individual members within the class and the type of leadership the teacher provides. *General* time frames, however, can be inferred from the statements of experienced teachers. They report that membership issues consume students during the first month of school and that the most productive period for student learning and attention to academic tasks is between November and early May.

Teachers assist the development of the classroom group at each stage in the ways described and also by helping students understand that groups grow and learn in the same ways that individuals do. It is critical that teachers recognize that positive communication and discourse patterns are perhaps the single most important variable for building groups and productive learning environments. It is through classroom discourse that norms are established and classroom life defined. It is through discourse that the cognitive and social aspects of learning unite. Much more about this important topic is included in Chapter 12.

# 🍎 *Summary*

## Perspective of Classrooms as Learning Communities

- Motivating students and providing leadership for learning communities are critical leadership functions of teaching.
- A classroom community is a place in which individually motivated students and teachers respond to each other within a social setting.
- Classroom communities are social and ecological systems that include and influence the needs and motives of individuals, institutional roles, and the interaction between member needs and group norms.
- A productive learning community is characterized by an overall climate in which students feel positive about themselves and their peers, students' individual needs are satisfied so they persist in academic tasks and work cooperatively with the teacher, and students have the requisite interpersonal and group skills to meet the demands of classroom life.

## Theoretical and Empirical Support

- The concept of human motivation is defined as the processes within individuals that arouse them to action.
- Psychologists make distinctions between two types of motivation: intrinsic motivation, which is sparked internally, and extrinsic motivation, which results from external or environmental factors.
- Many theories of motivation exist. Four that are particularly relevant to education include reinforcement theory, needs theories, cognitive theories, and social learning theory.
- Reinforcement theory emphasizes the importance of individuals responding to environmental events and extrinsic reinforcements.
- There are several different needs theories. In general, these theories hold that individuals strive to satisfy internal needs such as self-fulfillment, achievement, affiliation, influence, and self-determination.
- Cognitive theories of motivation stress the importance of the way people think and the beliefs and attributions they have about life's situations.
- Social learning theory posits that individuals' actions are influenced by the value particular goals hold for them and their expectations for success with particular tasks.
- Three important features that help us understand classroom communities include classroom properties, classroom processes, and classroom structures.

- Classroom properties are distinctive features of classrooms that help shape behavior. Six important properties include multidimensionality, simultaneity, immediacy, unpredictability, publicness, and history.
- Classroom processes define interpersonal and group features of classrooms and include expectations, leadership, attraction, norms, communication, and cohesiveness.
- Classroom structures are the foundations that shape particular lessons and behaviors during those lessons. Three important structures include task, goal, and participation structures.
- Some classroom features can be altered by the teacher; others cannot. Some classroom properties, such as multidimensionality and immediacy, cannot be influenced readily by the teacher. Group processes and the classroom goal, task, reward, and participation structures are more directly under the teacher's control.
- Studies on classrooms and teaching show that student motivation and learning are influenced by the types of processes and structures teachers create in particular classrooms.
- Studies have also uncovered important relationships between teacher behaviors, student engagement, and learning. In general, students react more positively and persist in academic tasks in classrooms characterized by democratic as opposed to authoritarian processes and in classrooms characterized by positive feeling tones and learning orientations.
- Influence in classrooms does not flow just from the teacher. Studies show that students influence each other and the behavior of their teachers.

## Strategies for Motivating Students and Building Productive Learning Communities

- Effective teachers create productive learning communities by focusing on things that can be altered, such as increasing student motivation and encouraging group development.
- Factors associated with motivation that teachers can modify and control include the overall feeling tone of the classroom, task difficulty, students' interests, knowledge of results, classroom goal and reward structures, and students' needs for achievement, influence, affiliation, and self-determination.
- Although the use of extrinsic rewards makes good common sense, teachers should avoid overemphasizing this type of motivation.

- Teachers assist the development of their classrooms as a group by teaching students how groups grow and about the stages they go through and by helping students learn how to work in groups.

- Allocating time to building productive learning environments will reduce many of the frustrations experienced by beginning teachers and will extend teachers' abilities to win student cooperation and involvement in academic tasks.

## Key Terms

| | | |
|---|---|---|
| motivation | influence motives | individualistic goal structure |
| intrinsic motivation | flow experiences | reward structure |
| extrinsic motivation | attribution theory | participation structure |
| reinforcement theory | social learning theory | endogenous statements |
| positive reinforcers | ecological systems | exogenous statements |
| negative reinforcers | classroom activities | feeling tone |
| punishments | task structure | feedback |
| needs theory | goal structure | group development |
| achievement motives | cooperative goal structure | |
| affiliative motives | competitive goal structure | |

## Books for the Professional

Combs, A. W., Miser, A. B., and Whitaker, K. S. (1999). *On Becoming a School Leader.* Alexandria, Va.: Association for Supervision and Curriculum Development. This is an excellent little book about leadership from a person-centered point of view. Although written primarily for school leaders such as principals, it has good advice for teachers.

Csikszentmihalyi, M. (1990). *Flow: The Psychology of Optimal Experience.* New York: Harper and Row. This book describes Csikszentmihalyi's research and his theories about flow, or optimal, experiences. It is not written specifically for teachers; however, it is very readable and will be of interest to the beginning teacher who wants to explore theories of motivation in some depth.

Johnson, D. W., and Johnson, F. P. (1998). *Joining Together: Group Theory and Group Skills* (6th ed.). Englewood Cliffs, N.J.: Prentice Hall. This book is an excellent introduction to group theory with many practical exercises that can be used by teachers in the classroom.

Schmuck, R. A., and Schmuck, P. (1997). *Group Processes in the Classroom.* (7th ed.). Dubuque, Iowa: Brown & Benchmark.

This book provides a thorough review of group dynamics literature as it applies to the classroom as a learning group and includes many activities and ideas to help teachers build productive learning environments.

Shapiro, N. S., and Levine, J. L. (1999). *Creating Learning Communities.* San Francisco: Jossey-Bass. The focus of the discussion in this book is on college campuses. However, several chapters provide strong conceptualization and rationale for why learning communities are important.

Spaulding, C. L. (1992). *Motivation in the Classroom.* New York: McGraw-Hill. This book makes excellent connections between theory and practice in the field of motivation and is filled with practical ideas for teachers.

Stover, L. T., Neubert, G. A., and Lawlor, J. C. (1993). *Creating Interactive Environments in the Secondary School.* Washington, D.C.: National Education Association. This book provides good advice to secondary teachers on how they can build more satisfying and interactive learning communities in their classrooms.

## Reflection & Portfolio

The Lonely Student

It's mid-November, and Patti, a tenth grader, is sitting by herself again at lunch. Patti came to your school last year after her parents moved to the community from Florida. You have Patti in your homeroom and in your eighth grade English class. She is a pretty good student and moderately attractive, but she just hasn't been able to connect with other students or make any friends. You have noticed on several occasions that when friendships seem to be forming between someone and Patti, she goes overboard and gets too demanding, and soon the emerging friendship has disappeared. At other times, she seems overly shy. Of late, she seems to be distant in class, and her work is starting to fall off.

Think for a minute about this situation, then sketch out a reflective essay with the following questions in mind: Do you think teachers should have concerns for this kind of situation? What concerns for Patti would you have? Why do you think Patti is unable to make friends? What would you do to help Patti establish a good friendship?

Compare your ideas with those of the teachers below, and determine how you can make this type of reflection a document for your portfolio.

### Theresa Fried

There is no easy solution to this type of situation. However, I would be concerned about Patti. Even though she has been moderately successful in the academic aspect of school, it is obvious that she has not been able to negotiate any type of authentic relationship, something that is very important for most adolescents. All too often students who can't find a social niche for themselves move into groups at the fringe of school's social life and sometimes even turn to drugs and other kinds of antisocial behavior.

I think there are a number of steps teachers can take with a student like Patti. Using cooperative learning and making sure Patti is placed in a group with students who are socially skillful and who are open to new friendships is one positive thing to do. I would also try to build a positive relationship with Patti and get her to trust me. Then I could talk frankly to her about her situation and have a dialogue about what friendship means and how one goes about developing friend relationships.

### Jason Shotels

Although I feel sorry for this student and would worry that she might move into groups that don't care much about school, I don't think there is much I could do as a teacher. I am not trained to work with these kinds of problems. However, our school has an array of special programs and services to help students form friendships and get involved in extracurricular activities. One way I could help Patti would be to refer her to the counselor and have the counselor talk to her. Another way would be to recommend to Patti that she become involved in after-school activities and introduce her to the After-School Activities Coordinator. This would provide her with situations and settings in which she would meet other students. If I thought Patti's shyness was very serious, I might also treat it as a disability and consult with the special education faculty to see if Patti qualifies for special education assistance.

# Chapter 🍎 Four

# The Inclusive and Multicultural Classroom

## Reflecting on Teaching in Inclusive and Culturally Diverse Classrooms

As a teacher, it will be your responsibility to respond positively to cultural and linguistic diversity and to students with special needs. Before you read this chapter, answer the questions below about your understanding and sensitivities:

🍎 *Do I have an understanding of the cultures that may be represented in my classroom?*

🍎 *Am I aware of culture-based learning styles?*

🍎 *Are my expectations as high for students of color as for Anglo students?*

🍎 *Will I make conscious efforts to engage all students in learning activities?*

🍎 *Will I make conscious efforts to give equivalent attention and encouragement to all students?*

🍎 *Have I participated in programs that help people better understand diversity?*

🍎 *Am I open to identifying racial and cultural biases in myself, my students, and my curriculum materials?*

🍎 *Do I know how to use methodology that fosters integration (for example, cooperative learning)?*

🍎 *Will my instruction and methodology conflict with the cultural beliefs of any students in my classroom?*

🍎 *Do I know how to use a variety of tasks, measures, and materials in assessing student competencies to avoid inadvertent bias in assessment?*

SOURCE: Adapted from Sara LaBrec, *How to Respond to Your Culturally Diverse Student Population* (Alexandria, Va.: Association for Supervision and Curriculum Development, 1993).

Over the past half-century, the student population in America's public schools has changed dramatically. A short time ago, only a small portion of children and youth attended school. Immigrant and farm children were expected to work and help their families. Children who were physically disabled or who had severe learning problems either stayed home or were taught in special schools. Girls, until a very short time ago, were not expected to finish high school or go onto college.

Today, this has all changed. All children are expected to be in school, regardless of their race, gender, or physical or mental abilities. These children and youth bring with them a wide range of backgrounds, talents, and needs. Many also come from homes, impoverished and wealthy alike, where support and encouragement are in short supply. It is no longer acceptable to allow some students to be placed in special classrooms, to let others drop out, or to allow still others to pass from grade to grade without having mastered basic literacy and numeracy skills. Instead, schools belong to all children, and the learning potential of each child must be realized.

> **Today, all children are expected to be in school, and schools are expected to make sure all students reach their learning potential.**

Making classrooms inclusive and finding ways to help a widely diverse group of students find success is the *teaching challenge of the twenty-first century.* This chapter is designed to help you meet this important challenge. It begins by examining the nature of the challenge and tracing the history and rationale for inclusion and multicultural education. Current theoretical and empirical support for these topics are described, followed by recommendations on how teachers can create classrooms that are inclusive and that afford each student maximum opportunities to reach his or her potential.

## 🍎 *Perspectives on Inclusion and Multicultural Education*

> **Diversity refers to the variety among people that exists in schools and society. Equity refers to making conditions for everyone impartial, fair, just, and equal.**

Two major forces, **diversity** and **equity,** have provided the impetus for insisting on integrated classrooms where all children can learn. Diversity of contemporary societies and the increasing international interdependence spawned by rapid communication and transportation systems are realities. Also a reality is an increased societal concern about equity and fair treatment for groups that have traditionally experienced discrimination. Many of the same forces that gave rise to the American civil rights movement and movements throughout the world for greater equity and freedom have provided the impetus for a greater degree of social justice and equity in classrooms. This in turn has made it critical for beginning teachers to become culturally aware and instructionally effective with diverse groups of students.

### Examining the Challenge

The recognition of injuries suffered by a variety of groups in our society, the desire to right those wrongs, and the resurgence of pride in racial and ethnic heritage all converged on the classroom in the post–World War II era. This convergence, together with the growing awareness described in Chapter 1 that the United States is a truly multicultural society with a majority of public school students representing non-European cultures and speaking a multitude of languages, has changed forever the nature of teaching and learning in American schools.

*Today, schools are expected to include and help all students find success.*

The dream of success for all, however, has not been easy to realize, and many students still have restricted opportunities to learn. Textbook shortages still exist in many schools (Pyle, 1997), and schools attended by African American and Latino students still have limited access to some advanced courses required for college. Teachers in schools attended by minority students too often focus on basic skill instruction instead of developing inquiry and problem-solving skills. These schools are also more likely to have unqualified teachers, some of whom lack degrees or majors in the subjects they teach (Darling-Hammond, 1996). Perhaps most important, however, is the fact that minority students do less well in school than do students from European backgrounds. According to Jackson (1999), African American high school students score about one hundred points lower than whites on SATs. African American and Hispanic students also lag behind whites on the National Assessment of Educational Progress. While more African American and Hispanic students are completing high school than ever before, an important gap remains. For example, the African American high school completion rate increased from 59 to 87 percent between 1971 and 1997. White students, however, still have a higher (93 percent) rate of high school completion. This gap remains troubling to many (U.S. Department of Education, 1998).

**Even though the United States has experienced a sustained period of economic growth, prosperity has not been achieved by everyone.**

Even though the United States and other parts of the world experienced great economic prosperity in the 1990s, all individuals and groups did not advance equally. The overall poverty rate has been increasing, and the middle class is shrinking. Recent Bureau of the Census estimates of poverty indicate that 35.7 million Americans live below the poverty line—a twenty-eight year high—and that most of them are children. Reed and Sautter (1990) reported a decade ago that the United States had the highest rate of childhood poverty among industrial nations. Today, the rate remains high, with over 20 percent of children living in poverty. Homelessness is also a troubling problem. Families now account for one-third of the homeless; as many as half a million children in this country are homeless. Although beliefs about rugged individualism incline us to blame individuals for their distressing situations, studies indicate that economic achievement is best predicted by educational achievement, which in turn depends primarily on family socioeconomic status. This means that if you are poor, the educational and economic deck is stacked against you, making success much more difficult to attain.

The disabled are yet another disadvantaged group. Statistics on the physically and mentally disabled are not as complete as for other groups, but it is known that their unemployment and underemployment rates are very high. Unemployment rates as high as 36 percent have been cited, and the poverty rate for the disabled is estimated to be about 25 percent.

Some of you may be asking why schools should concern themselves with these larger social problems. It may be unfair, even unrealistic, to expect schools to remedy inequities that have existed in the larger society for a long time. At least three arguments can be advanced in response. The first is that these issues should be of major concern to every citizen, that it is incumbent on us as citizens to work toward the public good by trying to ameliorate these problems. Educators can do their part by making sure every young person gets equal opportunities to learn.

**In a multicultural and diverse world, teachers really have no choice except to create classrooms that are inclusive and multicultural.**

The second argument is that Americans have a strong belief in the power of education as the route to later success in life—economically, politically, and culturally. This belief is supported by research, which consistently shows that education is related to income. The argument has intuitive appeal as well, in that educated people are equipped with the tools to escape from poverty and to participate fully in our economic and political systems.

Third, we really have no choice. Each of us belongs to many different groups, as illustrated in Figure 4.1, and we live in a multicultural world. Our schools should reflect the groups represented there, and they should recognize the global aspect of modern life.

## Multicultural Education

**Multicultural education is an approach to teaching aimed at helping students recognize and value cultural diversity.**

For most educators, the term **multicultural education** has come to signify recognizing, understanding, and appreciating all cultural groups and the development of skills in working with diverse groups of students. Others (Billings, 1995; Oakes and Lipton, 1999), however, prefer a more activist view of the term, one that goes beyond the development of sensitivity, understanding, and interpersonal skills, and advocates some form of political action.

**Philosophical Roots.** The philosophy underlying multicultural education is cultural pluralism. Horace M. Kallen (1924), one of its major theorists, saw cultural pluralism as

**Figure 4.1** *Multigroup Membership*

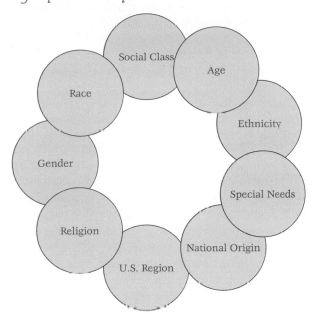

a step beyond two other competing ideologies—**Americanization** and the **melting pot.** Americanization was strongly promoted by prominent educators and politicians from the turn of the twentieth century well into the 1920s. Advocates believed that there existed an American race, culture, and value system that was based on the mores of northern Europe and that minority groups should forsake their own cultures and assimilate completely into this dominant American culture. Elwood P. Cubberley, a noted educator of the period, succinctly described the Americanization position:

> The southern and eastern Europeans are a very different type from the north Europeans who preceded them. Illiterate, docile, lacking in self-reliance and initiative and possessing none of the Anglo-Teutonic conceptions of law, order and government, their coming has served to dilute tremendously our national stock, and to corrupt our civic life. . . . Our task is to break up their groups or settlements, to assimilate and to amalgamate these people as part of our American race, and to implant in their children, so far as can be done, the Anglo-Saxon conceptions of righteousness, law and order and popular government, and to awaken in them reverence for our democratic institutions and for those things in our national life which we as a people hold to be of abiding worth. (Quoted in Krug, 1976, pp. 7–8)

The melting pot idea, although often confused with Americanization, was very different. Proponents of the melting pot believed that all ethnic groups had strengths and that in the "crucible" of America, these strengths would be merged into a new, superior culture. Rather than being contemptuous of cultural diversity, melting pot advocates welcomed diversity as a source of strength.

> They believed that the new emerging American culture must be built not on the destruction of the cultural values and mores of the various immigrant groups but on their fusion with the existing American civilization. . . . In the burning fires of the melting pot, all races were equal—all were reshaped and molded into a new entity. (Krug, 1976, p. 12)

**Americanization included the idea that one goal for education was to get minority groups to forsake their own cultures and assimilate into the dominant culture.**

**The melting pot ideology of education held that the strengths of minority cultures should be blended into a new, single, superior culture.**

**Cultural pluralism encourages minority cultures to maintain their distinctive identities within the larger culture and to value cultural diversity.**

**Cultural pluralism** rejects both the racism of Americanization and the concept of a single culture emerging from the melting pot. Cultural pluralism, while acknowledging the existence of a dominant American culture, also recognizes the strength and permanence of its diversity. This view normally purports that each cultural, racial, or ethnic group will accept some of the common elements of the dominant culture but should be constantly interacting with it and injecting into it new elements, to the benefit of all. The melting pot metaphor, with its implications of homogeneity, has been replaced with the salad metaphor, in which each ingredient is distinct and valued by itself, while at the same time contributing to the whole and bound together with a common dressing, that is, the dominant culture.

## Inclusive Classrooms

Another group of Americans to whom equal opportunities traditionally have *not* been extended are individuals who are disabled or have special needs that must be met if they are to successfully function in and out of school. Before the post–World War II era, not much attention was paid to this group of citizens, and those who did receive an education were more likely to do so in special schools. This has changed dramatically over the past twenty-five years as a result of legislation and court action. The landmark events have been the passage of Public Law 94-142, the Education for All Handicapped Children Act, in 1975 and the Americans with Disabilities Act of 1990. This legislation, along with numerous court decisions, was in response to inequalities and discrimination in services provided to children and adults with disabilities and special needs. In the case of education, some jurisdictions had barred disabled children from attending school because of their special needs; in others, the education such children received was often segregated and inferior to that received by other children. This legislation has changed all of this, as can be observed in Figure 4.2, which shows the dramatic increase in the number of children with disabilities being serviced by federally supported programs between 1977 and 1996.

**The practice of placing students with some types of disabilities in regular classrooms full or part time is called mainstreaming.**

The aim of the Education for All Handicapped Children Act was to ensure a free public education for all children in a setting that was most suitable for their needs. This legislation introduced the concept of **mainstreaming,** a strategy to move children out of special education and into regular classrooms (the mainstream) to the degree possible. At first, only children who were mildly disabled were placed in regular classrooms. The concept of **inclusion** followed on the heels of mainstreaming and promoted a wider goal, that of integrating all students, even those with severe disabilities, into regular classrooms.

**Inclusion is the practice of integrating students with disabilities fully into regular classrooms.**

Mainstreaming and inclusion are important, as you will read later, even if law did not mandate them. Other educational benefits accrue besides alleviating discrimination. For example, children with special needs have the opportunity to learn appropriate social and academic behavior from observing and modeling other children. Children without disabilities also benefit in that they are able to see firsthand the strengths and potential contributions, as well as the limitations, of their disabled peers. The school environment and society at large are thereby enriched.

**Least restrictive environment refers to the placement setting for students with disabilities that is most like the regular classroom.**

Public Law 94-142 and subsequent legislation rested on three premises: (1) students should be educated in the least restrictive environment; (2) each child with a special need should have an individual education plan; and (3) evaluation procedures should be nondiscriminatory.

Children are to be educated within the **least restrictive environment.** This means that to the extent possible, children with handicaps should be integrated into the reg-

**Figure 4.2** *Percentage of Children from Birth to Age 21 Who Were Served by Federally Supported Programs for Students with Disabilities, by Type of Disability: School Years Ending 1977–1996*

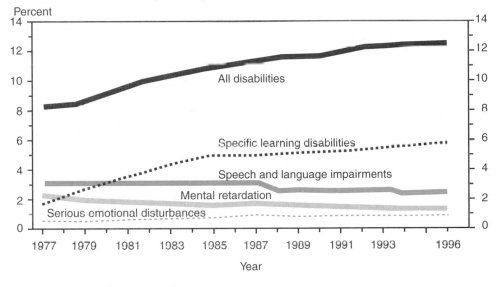

Number of children with disabilities who were served by federal programs as a percentage of total public K–12 enrollment

SOURCE: *Conditions of Education* (1998).

ular classroom. Those with very mild physical, emotional, and learning disabilities are to spend their entire school day in the regular classroom. Those with slightly more serious problems are to receive extra assistance from a special educator, either in or out of regular classrooms. As the disabilities grow more serious, the responsibility of the regular classroom teacher is further reduced, and the child is to receive a larger portion of his or her education in more specialized settings, culminating in a full-time residential school. In practice, the majority of disabled children who are mainstreamed attend regular classes for at least part of the day and have mild physical or learning disabilities.

Each disabled child is to have an **individualized educational plan (IEP).** IEPs are to be developed by a committee composed of the regular classroom teacher, the child's parents, the special education teacher, and any other staff who may be helpful, such as psychologists, speech therapists, or medical personnel. IEPs are required to contain information about the child's current level of academic performance, a statement of both long- and short-term educational goals, a plan for how these goals will be achieved, the amount of time the child will spend in the regular classroom, and an evaluation plan. The IEP, and the teacher's role in the process, will be described in more detail in a later section of this chapter.

School systems receive special federal funds for each labeled handicapped child, so the process of categorizing looms large in schools. Controversy reigns, however, about the desirability of labeling per se and the validity of current means for evaluating exceptionality. Advocates of labeling contend that it helps educators meet the special needs of the student and brings additional funding to bear where it is most needed. While they acknowledge the weaknesses of the current system of evaluation and

**A student's individualized education plan (IEP) specifies his or her level of functioning, long- and short-term educational goals, and how the student will be evaluated.**

placement, they argue that eliminating labeling amounts to throwing the baby out with the bath water.

Opponents counter that labeling creates more problems than it solves. For example, questions about equity arise because of the differential placement of boys, students of lower socioeconomic status, and minorities into special education programs and because the incidence of disabilities varies widely from state to state and district to district. Labels also cause perceived problems to be viewed as deficiencies inherent in the child, possibly causing deficiencies in the learning environment to be overlooked. Labels tend to become permanent; once placed in a special education program, students tend to stay there. Other students may ridicule labeled children, who may suffer diminished self-esteem as a consequence.

Finally, there exist few well-validated methods of instruction that are tied to the categories, and distinctions between the categories are blurry. No special interventions for the mildly mentally retarded, for instance, are distinct from those that might be used with any students experiencing academic difficulty (Reynolds, Wang, & Walberg, 1987; Wang, Reynolds, & Walberg, 1995).

## 🍎 Theoretical and Empirical Support

Values, philosophical perspectives, and politics influence the classroom practice of inclusion and multicultural education, and these are matters with which beginning teachers need to be concerned. At the same time, attention should be paid to a substantial knowledge base that describes what actually happens to children with special needs and from diverse cultures when they attend school and the best practices for working with these children. In this section, research on a variety of categories—race and ethnicity, language, gender, social class, and exceptionality—will be sampled to see what guidance it has to offer.

We should point out that the categories used to organize this section are social constructions. That is, while membership in any one category may be based on physical characteristics such as skin color or disability, these characteristics may signify different categories in different societies. For example, in the United States, a person with any African ancestry is usually considered black; in Puerto Rico, however, the same person may be classified as white if his or her social standing is high. A disability, too, may or may not constitute a handicap, depending on social factors. Ease in manipulating symbols, for example, is important in technological societies but less so in agrarian communities; a person lacking this skill is considered learning disabled in one society but not in the other. It is important to remember, as you read the sampled research, that these classifications are being used more for social purposes than because they have an independent basis in reality.

### Race, Ethnicity, and Culture

**Tracking.** The racial and ethnic inequalities that persist in society are mirrored in schools and classrooms. Over the years, accumulated evidence has shown that minority students receive a lower-quality education as a result of differing enrollment patterns, an unequal curriculum, tracking, and differential classroom interactions with teachers. Minorities are disproportionately placed in vocational and special education programs but are underenrolled in college preparatory and gifted programs. Even when the coursework is ostensibly the same, there are inequalities (Oakes, 1985).

**✔ Check for Understanding**

- What are the major changes that have occurred in American schools over the past half century? How do these translate into major challenges for teachers?

- What are the reasons teachers must create classrooms that are inclusive and multicultural?

- What does the term *multicultural education* mean, and how has it gained increased significance during the last century?

- Contrast the ideas found in the Americanization, melting pot, and cultural pluralism ideologies.

- What are the main features of inclusion as defined by legislation and judicial decisions over the past quarter of a century?

**Table 4.1** *Grouping-Related Differences in Learning Opportunities*

| Higher-Group Advantages | Lower-Group Disadvantages |
|---|---|
| Curriculum emphasizing concepts, inquiry, and problem solving | Curriculum emphasizing low-level facts and skills |
| Stress on students developing as autonomous thinkers | Stress on teaching students to follow rules and procedures |
| More time spent on instruction | More time spent on discipline or socializing |
| More active and interactive learning activities | More worksheets and seatwork |
| Computers used as learning tools | Computers used as tutors or electronic worksheets |
| More qualified and experienced teachers | More uncertified and inexperienced teachers |
| Extra enrichment activities and resources | Few enrichment opportunities |
| More engaging and friendly classroom atmosphere | More alienating and hostile classroom atmosphere |
| "Hard work" a likely classroom norm | "Not working" a likely classroom norm |

Source: Oakes and Lipton (1999), p. 303

Tracking represents a more formalized version of these curricular inequalities. Although tracking per se has fallen out of favor in many school districts, de facto tracking through advising in or out of college preparatory coursework is common. Many investigators have demonstrated the deleterious effects of tracking on classroom life and learning for minority students (Goodlad, 1984; Oakes, 1985; Oakes & Lipton, 1999; Rosenbaum, 1976). For example, the content and cognitive demands differ, with emphasis on memorization of basic facts and skills in lower-track classes and lower-ability groups, and emphasis on critical thinking, problem solving, and conceptual understanding in the upper tracks. Interestingly, heterogeneous and middle-track classes more closely resemble the higher track in learning goals and activities; in other words, minority students are more likely to receive a higher-quality education in mixed-ability classes and groups. Grouping-related differences are summarized in Table 4.1.

We return to the topic of teacher expectations and differential treatment later in this chapter.

**Cultural Deficit versus Cultural Difference.** Are the teachers and administrators who treat minority students differently than majority students bad, racist people? Not usually. They are responding in ways that are reasonable given mainstream beliefs about teaching, learning, and the uses of language and the ways the students behave. School staff and students often occupy different cultures with different ways of communicating and different beliefs and values. For example, Phillips (1972) studied the way Native American children learned at home and compared it to the way they were expected to learn in school. She observed that these children were silent in classroom lessons, sometimes even when asked a direct question by the teacher. Most Americans would assume that these children were extremely shy or that they had learning or linguistic disabilities—in the latter case, referring them to low-ability or special classes would

**Tracking (formal and de facto) limits educational opportunities for students placed in the lower tracks.**

make sense. However, Native American children are expected to learn by watching adults, not by interacting with them; they are to turn to older siblings, not adults, when they need assistance; and they are accustomed to a great deal more self-determination at home than is permissible in the school environment. In light of this information, their classroom behavior can be properly interpreted as an instance of cross-cultural miscommunication rather than a deficiency.

Another example of cultural discontinuity comes from a landmark study conducted several years ago. Heath (1983) documented the diverging communicative styles of working-class African Americans, middle-class African Americans and Euro-Americans in the Piedmont region of the Carolinas. One of the many cultural differences she found involved the use of questions. At home, working-class African American adults didn't ask children very many questions, and when they did, they were real questions, really seeking information that the adult didn't have. In school, however, teachers expected children to answer questions all the time, and the questions themselves were artificial in that the adults already knew the answer. From the students' perspective, these questions didn't make any sense at all, and there was difficulty bridging the cultural gap. These results have been replicated many times over the past decade.

**Cultural difference theory holds that the low achievement of minorities is explained by the discontinuity between home culture and school culture.**

*how does this apply to my students?*

Villegas (1991) elaborated on the **cultural difference theory** to account for the achievement difficulties minority students experience in schools. The vehicle for interaction in school is language, and if language is used by a subculture in ways different from the mainstream, then members of the subculture are at a disadvantage, as this and other studies document. As Villegas explained:

> Children whose language use at home corresponds to what is expected in the classroom have an advantage in the learning process. For these students, prior experience transfers to the classroom and facilitates their academic performance. In contrast, minority children frequently experience discontinuity in the use of language at home and at school. They are often misunderstood when applying prior knowledge to classroom tasks. (p. 7)

Villegas (1988 and 1991) has also criticized the work that blames school failure on home-school disjunctures and argues that this diverts attention from the existing inequalities that sustain the widespread failure of minority students. Villegas argues that the negative relationship between school and society is the problem and that solutions require finding more culturally sensitive political links between the school, its communities, and the larger society.

**The cultural deficit theory, now mainly discredited, accounts for the low achievement of minorities by postulating some defect in their culture or race.**

The cultural difference theory has come to replace the **cultural deficit theory** as the most viable explanation for the difference in achievement between minority and majority students. Various deficit theories have posited that minorities are genetically deficient in intelligence or have some other inherent defect that interferes with their ability to be successful in school. For example, Harvard psychologist Arthur Jensen in 1969 argued that children who came from poor families were intellectually inferior. A quarter of a century later, Herrnstein and Murray (1994) wrote *The Bell Curve: Intelligence and Class Structure in American Life*. This book, which argued that African Americans inherited lower IQs than whites, became a national best-seller.

These theories have been discredited, partly because of studies such as Heath's and Phillips's and because of analyses done by a variety of scholars over the past decade. For example, Gould (1996) in *The Mismeasure of Man* points out the statistical flaws in IQ testing. Jerome Bruner in *Acts of Meaning* (1990) and *Culture and Education* (1996) has shown how learning is social and cultural and how intelligence grows as people interact with each other in society. Finally, as you read in Chapter 1, Howard Gardner has provided an important perspective that individuals, regardless of race or culture, have many different intelligences, only one of which has been measured by the more traditional IQ tests.

## Language

*Dialects.* Clearly, language is a big factor in schooling. Not surprisingly, the United States enjoys a rich diversity of languages and dialects. Black English or Ebonics and Hawaiian Creole are a few of the major indigenous dialects. In the past, these and other dialects were considered inferior to English, and school people blamed the use of these "substandard" languages for childrens' poor academic performance (another manifestation of the cultural deficit theory). The school's remedy was to attempt to eliminate the use of the home dialect. This approach has not worked. Children do not improve academically when their language is suppressed and, in fact, may suffer negative emotional and cognitive consequences.

It is important to emphasize that people speaking a dialect are not speaking an error-ridden form of standard English. They are using a distinct language with its own complexity and its own rules. Use of the double negative, for example, an anathema in standard English, is correct in black English, as it is in many romance languages. Here is a further sampling of rules for black English (Jordan, 1988):

*The dialect used by some African Americans is called Ebonics.*

- Use a minimal number of words for every idea; this is the source for the aphoristic and poetic force of the language.
- Eliminate use of the verb *to be* whenever possible. This leads to the deployment of more descriptive and, therefore, more precise verbs.
- Never use the *-ed* suffix to indicate the past tense of a verb. (*Standard English:* She closed the door. *Black English:* She close the door. Or, she have close the door.)
- In black English, unless you keenly want to underscore the past tense nature of an action, stay in the present tense and rely on the overall context of your ideas for the conveyance of time and sequence. (pp. 368–369)

*like Angela Johnson books*

The whole issue of the use of dialects can become politically charged, as evidenced when the Oakland, California, School Board made Ebonics the language of instruction. The board later rescinded this policy, but only after considerable debate and cultural warfare. The important thing for teachers to remember is to be sensitive and not to make negative judgments about students' abilities based on the use of such dialects of English. Teachers should not assume that users of nonstandard English lack the intellectual capital to be academically successful. Below is how one teacher chose to deal with the language students bring to school.

> I vowed never to deliberately silence my students' voices. This vow is not easy to keep; it is something I struggle with daily. I am committed to creating a safe environment within my classroom, where my students feel comfortable expressing themselves regardless of the language that they bring with them, be it Ebonics, Spanglish, or other English dialects. But, to facilitate my students' acquisition of mainstream English, all of their assignments must be written in "standard" English. The majority of the time, I communicate with my students using standard English, but I feel that it is also necessary to model code switching in the classroom. I validate my students' primary language, but I do not feel the need to teach it. They come to class equipped with this language. (From Oakes and Lipton, 1999, p. 21)

*I can't do this, my IA can, enriches, esp. history lesson*

*Second Language Acquisition.* In addition to dialect diversity, the United States is home to a number of people for whom English is a second language. These students

**ESL is the acronym for "English as a second language."**

**LEP is the acronym for "limited English proficiency."**

are referred to as **ESL** (English as a second language) or **LEP** (limited English proficiency) students. There are over 200 Native American languages spoken in the United States, and a large minority of the U.S. population speaks Spanish. The influx of immigrants in recent years has brought many speakers of Vietnamese, Farsi, Korean, Russian, and dozens of other languages. For millions of American students, English is not the native tongue.

How do these children approach the problem of learning English? It is not an easy task. Communicative competence in any language consists of more than simply knowing its phonology (pronunciation), morphology (word formation), syntax (grammar), and lexicon (vocabulary). The speaker also must understand how to organize speech beyond the level of single sentences; how to make and interpret appropriate gestures and facial expressions; about the norms surrounding using the language in accordance with roles, social status, and in different situations; and finally, how to use the language to acquire academic knowledge (cognitive-academic language proficiency).

In first-language learning, these abilities are acquired over an extended period of time and in meaningful social interaction with others. Cummins (1981) estimated that non-English speakers require two years to attain basic communication skills but need five to seven years to develop cognitive-academic language proficiency (CALP). That is, children can get along on the playground and in social situations very readily, but they need much more time to become skillful in learning academic content in the medium of English.

It appears that the task of learning a second language is a creative one. Second-language learners do not passively soak up a new language; they must listen attentively, rely on social and other context cues to help them make guesses about how to use the language, test out their guesses, and revise accordingly.

**Language in the Classroom.** Schools are legally required to assist language-different children in learning English and school subjects. This came out of the 1974 Supreme Court ruling in *Lau* v. *Nichols,* arising from a class action suit by Chinese students in San Francisco against the school district. The Court reasoned that instruction presented in a language students could not understand amounted to denying them equal access to the educational system. The district's practice, common to many districts, had been simply to place LEP students in regular classrooms with native speakers. This **submersion approach,** allowing language minority students to sink or swim on their own, is no longer permissible.

**The submersion approach is the practice of simply placing LEP students in the classroom and expecting them to pick up English on their own.**

**Transitional bilingual programs place LEP students in classrooms where they are initially provided instruction in their native language along with English.**

**The goals of full bilingual programs are full oral proficiency and literacy in both languages.**

Schools have responded to the *Lau* v. *Nichols* mandate in a variety of ways. The most common is to provide ESL instruction in a pull-out program. ESL students are placed in regular classrooms for most of the day but attend separate classes in English instruction for part of the day. Another approach is to provide a **transitional bilingual program** for non-English-speaking students. In these programs, instruction is initially provided in the native language, with gradual increases in English until the student is proficient. ESL is a part of these programs, too. **Full bilingual programs,** in which the goal is full oral proficiency and literacy in both languages, are rare. Interestingly, research suggests that bilingualism brings with it several cognitive advantages, including heightened cognitive flexibility and a greater ability to analyze language (McCown & Roop, 1992).

Happily, researchers have also illuminated some methods that more effective teachers use to help language-minority students learn English and subject matter. Allen (1991) summarized this research:

They simplified their language, used gestures, and linked talk to a strong context. While the child's native language was used occasionally to explain concepts that were difficult to make clear in English, direct translation was not used, nor were the two languages mixed. These teachers were making their language comprehensible by keeping the learner's special needs in mind, involving the children in talk, and judiciously using the native language when necessary. (p. 290)

Guidelines for teachers can also be gleaned from the second-language learning literature. To learn to speak, read, and write in English requires a high input of English speech and print. Teachers who structure learning tasks and classroom interaction to maximize comprehensible English input help their students master the language. For example, effective teachers structure more teacher-student interaction and less peer interaction in a classroom in which most of the students are LEP, but in a classroom that is evenly divided between native speakers and LEP students, more peer interaction is appropriate.

Often the research on how children acquire English as a second language is forced to take a backseat to political pressures, as evidenced by the number of states that recently have passed legislation restricting bilingual education and the use of a student's native language in schools.

## Gender

Education has long been a field dominated by women. During the 1920s, for example, more than half of all elementary school principals were women. However, as schools and districts became larger and more urban, the percentage of women administrators declined; in the 1970s, only 13 percent were women. Current trends are again reversing this picture, and the proportion of women in administration is on the rise. Classroom teaching has been done primarily by women for well over a century.

Even though women predominate, gender bias has been a problem in the classroom. Complicating matters has been the controversy in recent years over whether gender differences exist in verbal and mathematical abilities and whether these differences are the result of differential socialization and education provided for boys as compared to that for girls. In a timely and persuasive meta-analysis (a technique for synthesizing and summarizing results from many individual studies, described further in Chapter 11), Linn and Hyde (1989) concluded that differences between boys and girls "were always small, that they have declined in the last 2 decades, that differences arise in some contexts and situations but not in others, and that educational programs can influence when differences arise" (p. 17). This is encouraging news for educators, because it fortifies our sense that we can and do make a difference in our students' lives.

The story about gender differences and bias, however, has a good side to it. Since 1971, girls have made definite strides in terms of graduating from high school and attending and graduating from college. For instance, in 1971, only about 78 percent of girls finished high school compared to almost 90 percent of boys. By 1996, this figure had essentially reversed. Also, in 1971, less than 40 percent of women had completed one year of college and less than 20 percent had graduated. In comparison, over 60 percent of men had completed one year and 30 percent had graduated. In 1996, almost 70 percent of women were going to college, compared to 50 percent of men. Also, a larger proportion of women than of men was graduating from college in 1996. (See *Conditions of Education,* 1998, and Koerner, 1999.)

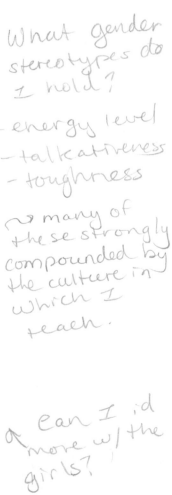
*[handwritten marginal notes: What gender stereotypes do I hold? — energy level — talkativeness — toughness — many of these strongly compounded by the culture in which I teach. Can I id more w/ the girls?]*

## Social Class

*Socioeconomic status (SES) is the term used to refer to variations among people based on income, family background, and relative prestige within the society.*

Two research studies show dramatically the differences that **socioeconomic status** (SES) can make on school learning. Cazden (1972) examined speech patterns, specifically sentence length, under differing contexts for a working-class (low-SES) child and a middle-class (middle-SES) child. She found that while they each gave their shortest utterances in the same context, an arithmetic game, their longest-sentence context varied: for the middle-class child, during a formal, story-retelling situation, and for the working-class child, during an informal, out-of-school conversation. In an earlier study, Heider, Cazden, and Brown (1968) found that while working-class and middle-class students' descriptions of animal pictures contained the same number of key attributes, working-class students required more prompts from the adult interviewer than middle-class students. If the interviewer hadn't persisted in requesting more information, student knowledge would have been underestimated.

These findings indicate that low-SES students have verbal abilities that may not be accessed by typical classroom tasks. As with any cultural group, people of each socioeconomic status behave in ways appropriate to their subculture. Middle-class teachers expect middle-class behavior, and when low-SES students behave differently, as these studies document, teachers' expectations about their abilities are negatively

*low SES behaviors → looks like less intelligent.*

*Schools can be organized to offset the negative impact of poverty.*

Research Summary 4.1

# What Influences Teachers' Expectations and to What Effect?

*Rist, R. C.* (1970). Student social class and teacher expectations: The self-fulfilling prophecy in ghetto education. *Harvard Educational Review*, 40, 411–451.

What is it that influences the way teachers think about their students? Does skin color make a difference? What about physical attractiveness or the clothes children wear? If expectations can be influenced, what impact does differential expectation have on students' achievement? Ray Rist set out to study some of these questions a number of years ago.

**Problem and Approach:** Previous studies showed that academic achievement was highly correlated with social class. However, researchers were not sure how schools and teachers helped reinforce this relationship. In the late 1960s, Ray Rist conducted an important study to find out what influence social class had on teachers' expectations and how teachers contributed to the achievement differential among social classes. This is an interesting study from a methodological perspective because Rist went right into the classroom to watch what was going on, and he studied the same group of children over a two-year period, something that doesn't happen all that often in educational research.

**Sample:** Rist studied a single class of children, located in an urban area. All the teachers, administrators, and students were African American.

**Procedures:** Data for this study were collected by means of 90-minute observation periods conducted twice weekly. Observations were conducted throughout the year while the children were in kindergarten and again when the same children were in the first half of their second-grade year. The classroom was also visited informally four times during first grade. Observers made a continuous handwritten account of classroom interaction and activity as it occurred. Additionally, a series of interviews was held with both the kindergarten and second-grade teachers.

**Results:** Rist documented that the kindergarten teacher used nonacademic data—namely, who was on welfare, a behavioral questionnaire completed by children's mothers, the teacher's own experience with and other teachers' reports about siblings, medical information, and the family structure—to make placement decisions. The teacher used this information, together with observations of the children's dress, physical appearance, and verbalizations during the first few days of school, to place children in low-, middle-, and high-ability groups on the eighth day of kindergarten. Children of like "ability" were seated together and received like instruction throughout the year. The teacher gave more positive attention to the children in the high group and spent more instructional time with them. She reprimanded the lows more often. The children in the low group were situated in the room such that when material was presented at the chalkboard, they could not see it. Children labeled as high ability frequently ridiculed those labeled as low ability.

When the students entered first grade, their new teacher also divided them into low-, middle-, and high-ability groups and seated them together. All the kindergarten highs became first-grade highs (group A), the former middle and low children became middle children (group B), and children who were repeating first grade constituted the new low group (group C). Only the group A children had completed the kindergarten curriculum and were able to start right away with the first-grade material. Groups B and C children spent the early part of their first grade year completing kindergarten lessons.

The second-grade teacher continued the low-middle-high grouping practice. Group A students became "Tigers," groups B and C students became "Cardinals," and repeating second-graders became "Clowns." By now, however, the teacher had test score data on which to base her decisions, as well as parental occupation and other social-class information. Of course, low children were at a disadvantage on these tests, because they had not been exposed to the same curriculum as the high children. The different groups were assigned different books for reading instruction and could not advance to the next book until the previous one was completed. Further, the teacher allowed no independent reading in which a child could finish a book on his or her own and move ahead. Thus, low children were locked into the low group, with no way of ever advancing into the higher group. Rist summed up his results with this statement: "The child's journey through the early grades of school at one reading level and in one social grouping appeared to be pre-ordained from the eighth day of kindergarten" (p. 435).

**Discussion and Implications:** Rist's findings shocked the educational community. He demonstrated that teachers' expectations and instructional decisions and actions were profoundly influenced by the social-class characteristics of children and that children who did not fit the middle-class mold suffered academically and emotionally. He concluded:

> It appears that the public school system not only mirrors the configurations of the larger society, but also significantly contributes to maintaining them. Thus, the system of public education in reality perpetuates what it is ideologically committed to eradicate—class

barriers which result in inequality in the social and economic life of the citizenry. (p. 449)

Rist's purpose was to expose the problem, not solve it, and thus he did not offer suggestions to teachers about how to avoid falling into the practices of those in his study. The last section of this chapter, however, will tackle this problem in some detail.

affected. Differing expectations result in differential student-teacher interactions, which result in poorer academic performance for low-SES students.

Another problem working-class students and minority children face is ability grouping and tracking. Low-SES students are disproportionately placed in low-ability groups and low-track classes. Instructional quality is poorer in these groups than in the higher groups. The criteria used to guide placement decisions are sometimes of dubious merit. Most often used are standardized aptitude test scores (the type administered in large groups, deemed least valid by test developers), and teachers' judgments. Unfortunately, teachers' judgments are influenced by race and class, and even when ability and teacher recommendation are equivalent, race and class are determining factors in placing children. The research highlighted in the Research Summary for this chapter, on pages 125–126, is a landmark study conducted by Ray Rist in 1970. He documented the impact of social class on grouping and instruction. In the thirty years since the publication of Rist's study, other researchers (Anyon, 1980; Goodlad, 1984; Hallinan & Sorensen, 1983; Oakes, 1985; Rosenbaum, 1976; Sorensen & Hallinan, 1986) corroborated his disturbing findings. However, recent experiments by Robert Slavin and his colleagues with Success for All Schools demonstrate that schools and classrooms can be organized with programs and processes that offset the impact of poverty and social class (Stevens & Slavin, 1995).

## Exceptionality

Mainstreaming and inclusion have been controversial, and debates continue over whether classes for students with disabilities should be self-contained, segregated, or diverse settings similar to the ones students will experience as adults. On the one hand, critics, including teachers and some parents, believe that schools have been too quick to place all kinds of students together, thus preventing different kinds of instruction and separate programs required to meet the special needs of particular children. Others (Shanker, 1995, for example) have argued that the practice of mainstreaming and inclusion is unrealistic and even harmful. The research is not totally clear on the issue, but there seems to be a few consistent findings, which are summarized below.

In 1995, several of America's foremost scholars on mainstreaming and inclusion reviewed and summarized the research on inclusion and special education practices (see Wang, Reynolds, & Walberg, 1995; Baker, Wang, & Walberg, 1995). Two important results stand out from their reviews.

**In general, research shows that students with disabilities who are educated in inclusive settings do slightly better compared to those who are placed in segregated settings.**

One, they cite numerous studies conducted in the 1980s and 1990s (Heller et al., 1982; Wang et al., 1992) that found the process of classifying special-needs students was ineffective and discriminatory. It seems that regardless of how well-intentioned the process, many students were misdiagnosed, and even when the diagnoses were accurate, the instruction provided to special students did not produce superior results.

They also report the results of three meta-analyses (Baker, 1994; Calberger & Kavale, 1980; and Wang & Baker, 1992). The meta-analyses included studies conducted over a fifteen-year period of time that used standardized achievement tests to measure academic outcomes and self, peer, teacher, and observer ratings to assess social relations with others. When inclusive versus noninclusive practices were compared, a small-to-moderate positive effect existed for academic and social learning of children with special needs in inclusive settings compared to learning in segregated settings. This means, according to Reynolds and Wang (1995), that "students educated in regular classes do better academically and socially than comparable students in noninclusive settings" (p. 34).

Finally, numerous questions have been asked by parents and teachers about the effects of inclusion on nondisabled students. Will inclusion reduce their academic progress? Will teachers give less attention to nondisabled students if disabled peers are in the same classrooms? Will nondisabled students pick up undesirable behaviors from students with disabilities?

Rarely in any of these studies were negative effects found for either students with special needs or their nondisabled peers in regular classrooms. For instance, in their review of the research on this topic, Staub and Peck (1995) reported that though the literature is not extensive, it is pretty consistent. Inclusion does not harm nondisabled students academically. Further, they reported studies, such as Peck and colleagues (1992) and Helmstetter (1993), in which nondisabled students who have been in inclusive classrooms report that they have *not* been left out of educational experiences or ignored by their teachers. Finally, case studies conducted by Staub herself (1996) showed that nondisabled children had *not* picked up any undesirable behaviors.

## 🍎 Creating Inclusive, Multicultural Classrooms

Most beginning teachers worry about what can be done in the classroom to work effectively with a diverse group of students and to assist students with special needs. Fortunately, a wealth of options is available for developing classrooms that are inclusive and multicultural. In fact, the array of options may be so large that it bewilders rather than assists the beginner in implementing an effective classroom program. In this section, strategies are organized and summarized to ease that process. Beginning teachers are encouraged to work first on their own knowledge and attitudes and to battle biases, stereotypes, and myths they may hold. Equally important, teachers need to make sure their curriculum is fair and culturally relevant and that they are using teaching strategies known to be effective with all kinds of students. Finally, it is important to improve classroom management and to alter the school organization so important learning goals can be achieved for all students.

Underlying all the recommendations made in this section is the importance of teachers valuing each and every student and challenging them to reach their highest potential. Claude Steele (1992) highlighted the themes of value and challenge. "If what is meaningful and important to a teacher is to become meaningful and important to a student, the student must feel valued by the teacher for his or her potential and as a person" (p. 78). If anything going on in the school—curriculum cast as remediation, or instruction cast as the pedagogy of poverty—diminishes students' sense of themselves as

## ✓ Check for Understanding

- Which categories have been predominantly studied, resulting in a substantial knowledge base from which teachers can draw when working with diverse students in inclusive classrooms?

- Contrast the cultural deficit theory with the cultural difference theory.

- What types of unequal treatment are sometimes experienced by minority students in the classroom?

- What types of language diversity issues do teachers have to overcome, and why is it critical that teachers be supportive of these differences?

- What specific problems are faced by students of low socioeconomic status?

- How is gender bias still a problem in classrooms? What progress has been made in this area?

- What are some benefits and special challenges faced by teachers as students with disabilities and special needs are included in regular classrooms? What does research tell about this practice?

valued people, students will be disinclined to identify with the goals of the school. Intellectual challenge goes hand in hand with valuing. "A valuing teacher-student relationship goes nowhere without challenge, and challenge will always be resisted outside a valuing relationship" (Steele, 1992, p. 78). Part of communicating that someone is valued is communicating high expectations.

## Developing Cultural Understandings and Self-Awareness

Developing wider cultural understandings and more self-awareness forms the first part of a strategy for working effectively in inclusive classrooms with a diverse group of students. Beginning teachers can work to improve their own knowledge and attitudes toward people different from them by taking the initiative to learn about the cultures represented in the communities where their students live and by striving to uncover and conquer their own biases.

Cultural Understanding. To familiarize yourself with local cultures, find and read books, magazines, and research articles, and take courses. To give you an idea of what can be gleaned from the literature on cross-cultural education, here are three excerpts from research that shed light on the effects of culture in the classroom. They provide those in the mainstream culture with a glimpse of what the mainstream culture looks like to a member of a minority culture.

A Navajo woman described her first school experience:

Well, my first deal is just getting to school. Just when you live all Navajo culture and you first start school and first see the brick buildings, you don't know what's inside them buildings. Especially when you've only been to trading post twice in your life before school. It's when you get there you see these long lines of kids with their mamas. All the kids throwing fits and cryin, hangin onto their mom. And your mom's standin there beside you sayin, "You can't be like them. You can't cry cause you're big girl now. You gotta go to school. Don't, don't shame me at the beginning. You gotta make me proud." . . .

So she took all of us to school, and she dropped me off there. . . . The ceilings were so high, and the rooms so big and empty. It was so cold. There was no warmth. Not as far as "brrr I'm cold," but in a sense of emotional cold. Kind of an emptiness, when you're hanging onto your mom's skirt and tryin so hard not to cry. And you know it just seems so lonely and so empty. Then when you get up to your turn, she thumbprints the paper and she leaves and you watch her go out the big, metal doors. The whole thing was a cold experience. The doors were metal and they even had this big window, wires running through it. And these women didn't smile or nothin. You watch your mama go down the sidewalk, actually it's the first time I seen a sidewalk, and you see her get in the truck, walk down the sidewalks. You see her get in the truck and the truck starts moving and all the home smell goes with it. You see it all leaving. (Quoted in McLaughlin, 1996, pp. 13–14)

An educational anthropologist described elementary classrooms in Mexico:

Characteristic of instruction in the *Primaria* was its oral, group interactive quality. . . . Students talk throughout the class period; teachers are always available to repeat, explain, and motivate; silent seat work is rare; and often a crescendo of sound . . . is indicative of instructional activity. The following observation of a first-grade classroom illustrates this pattern of verbal and physical activity:

As she instructs children to glue sheets of paper in their books and write several consonant-vowel pairs, the teacher sometimes shouts her directions to compete with the clamor of kids asking for glue, repeating instructions to each other, sharing small toys, sharpening pencils, asking to go to the bathroom, etc. This activity and "noise" is compounded by the large number in the classroom, 35, but things somehow seem to get done by some, if not all, students. Then teacher has the children recite the word pairs taped to the chalkboard. They shout these out loudly as a group as she points to each combination with an old broken broom handle. Sometimes she calls out the pairs in order; other times, out of order to check their attention. Then she calls individual children to the board, gives them the stick, they choose a pair of sounds, but then have to pronounce them loudly and quickly as she presses them for correct responses. (Macias, 1990, p. 304)

An example of cultural discontinuity in the classroom comes from a study of Hmong adults enrolled in an English language class (Hvitfeldt, 1986). These students refused to accept any democratic decision making, even of the most trivial kind. On one occasion, the teacher wanted to begin a review lesson by having the students draw numbers from a cup. When he held out the cup and said, "Who's first?" no one responded. After a long pause, one student said, "You teacher. You say." In Hmong culture, families and clans are extremely close and cooperative, viewing themselves as a single economic unit and looking exclusively to the male family head for all decisions. Given this background, it is not surprising that they resisted individual input into decisions.

Another avenue for familiarizing yourself with the cultures and backgrounds of your students is to reach out to people in the community to try to understand their points of view. Talk to your students and get to know them. The following story illustrates how participation in a community event helped one principal develop an important insight into the behavior of a large minority group in her school. Experiences like hers, coupled with observation and reflection, can help you bring your own biases to the surface and deal with them.

> Reaching out to parents and others in the school's community is an important avenue for understanding students and their cultural differences.

> I'm a principal at an urban elementary school with a high percentage of Pacific Islander kids. They often have a hard time in school—rowdy, easily distracted, quick-tempered—and I got some insight into why when their community invited me to a special ceremony at their church, a ceremony to recognize those kids who were doing well in school.
>
> I got there a few minutes early, and they showed me to the stage where guests of honor were to sit. I settled down expectantly for the event to begin. The starting time came and went, friendly people wandered in and out, and punctual me started getting nervous. Finally, things seemed to gel and they got under way, almost an hour late.
>
> They put on a very nice ceremony, showcasing each child individually on the stage, applauding each one, giving each a little remembrance. It was quite touching, and the kids were just beaming.
>
> The children all went back and sat down in the audience again, and the meeting continued on to several more items on the agenda. Well, the kids were fine for awhile, but as you might imagine, they got bored fast and started to fidget. Fidgeting and whispering turned into poking, prodding, and open chatting. I became a little anxious at the disruption, but none of the other adults appeared to even notice, so I ignored it, too. Pretty soon several of the children were up and out of their seats, strolling about the back and sides of the auditorium. All adult faces continued looking serenely up at the speaker on the stage. Then the kids started playing tag, running circles around the seating area and yelling gleefully. No adult response—I was amazed, and struggled to resist the urge to quiet the children. Then some of the kids got up onto the stage, running around the speaker, flicking the lights on and off, and opening and closing the curtain! Still nothing from the Islander parents! It was

not my place, and I shouldn't have done it, but I was so beyond my comfort zone that with eye contact and a pantomimed shush, I got the kids to settle down.

I suddenly realized then that when these children, say, come to school late, it doesn't mean that they or their parents don't care about learning or that they're a little bit lazy—that's just how all the adults in their world operate. When they squirm under desks and run around the classroom, they aren't trying to be disrespectful or defiant, they're just doing what they do everywhere else. Now I'm better equipped to help them develop the knowledge and skill they need to be successful in our school and our society, and I'm learning what it takes to get along in theirs. (Personal communication)

Beginning teachers will also find it helpful to develop understanding of intercultural interaction. Many training programs have been developed. Most aim to help people from any culture cope effectively with cross-cultural interaction in three broad areas of concern and potential misunderstanding: people's intense feelings, knowledge about cultural differences, and bases for cultural differences. Similar programs have been developed to sensitize people to the needs of those who are disabled.

**The anxious emotional response to the ambiguity and disconfirmed expectations that come from dealing with unfamiliar cultures is called culture shock.**

Whenever people meet and interact with others from a different culture, they experience predictable emotional reactions. When you find students in your class from a culture unfamiliar to you, you will likely feel anxiety, you may become upset because of disconfirmed expectations, and you will probably feel very discomfitted by the ambiguity of the situation. This **culture shock** is a normal reaction, however unpleasant, and will pass with time, as long as you make the effort to understand and accommodate the cultural gulf between you and your students, as the principal in the above story did. The danger is that people can react to their extreme discomfort by entrenching themselves in their prejudices, an unhelpful response.

There are a number of areas of cultural difference that seem to consistently cause trouble. Beginning teachers need to be alert to these. Cultures differ, for instance, in their attitudes toward work and the appropriate balance between being on task and socializing. Middle-class American culture tends to be very task-oriented, but many other cultures give more attention to social interaction. Cultures also vary in their sense of time. For many Americans, punctuality is an unquestioned virtue, and children in school are penalized for tardiness, turning work in late, and so on. But in many non-Western cultures, people are much more relaxed about time, do not regard punctuality as particularly sacred, and do not pay strict attention to deadlines. The amount of physical space deemed proper between people when conversing and norms about making eye contact are other key areas of difference.

Another area of possible misunderstanding is the relative weight put on the needs of the group versus the needs of the individual. American culture is very oriented to the individual, whereas in Japanese and some Native American cultures, more emphasis is placed on the group. Many Native American children, for example, do not want to be singled out for praise and attention, a situation that can be very disconcerting to their teachers. Finally, peoples' values differ, as Brislin and his colleagues (1986) described:

As part of their socialization, people learn to accept as proper a small set of ideas within such broad areas as religion, economics, aesthetics, political organization, and interpersonal relationships. Such learning becomes internalized and it affects attitudes, preferences, and views of what is desirable and undesirable. Understanding these internalized views . . . is critical in cross-cultural adjustment. (p. 41)

Teachers need to be aware of the bases of cultural differences, the underlying reasons behind the outward manifestations of cultural difference. One of these is that people of different cultures categorize and differentiate information differently; that is, they chunk information, combining and separating bits, in a variety of ways. A simple example comes from language comparisons. In English, there are the separate verbs *to like* and *to love*, while in French, one word, *aimer*, means both, and in Italian, no verb meaning "to like" exists. Speakers of these different languages categorize and differentiate experiences differently. It is easy to imagine the difficulties in communicating clearly when the parties interacting, even though they may both be speaking English, are relying on such divergent conceptions.

Another especially important area teachers need to watch for is learning style variations across cultures and among students with special needs. Teaching and learning clearly occur in all cultures, but preferred styles differ. In particular, in some cultures and domestic subcultures, teaching and learning are conducted *in context*, whereas in mainstream American schools, the predominant mode is *out of context*. What does "in-context learning" mean? It means that children acquire skills and knowledge at the point that they are needed and in real-life situations. For example, children may learn to use a paring knife in the context of helping their parents prepare meals, or they may learn how to multiply fractions in the context of doubling a recipe when company is coming. Out-of-context learning means that learning is unconnected to a real, immediate need. When parents play "what's this" games with infants or when math is broken down into discrete algorithms, each drilled separately before application to real math problems, then out-of-context learning is happening. Both kinds of teaching and learning are important, and both can clearly "work," but children accustomed to in-context learning are confused by out-of-context teaching.

Finally, cultures differ in their attributions, or judgments, about the causes of behavior. A polite smile construing friendliness in one culture may constitute a cold rebuff in another. Giving a friend academic assistance can mean helpfulness to one person, cheating to another. Erroneous attributions can obviously hinder the development of rapport between people of different cultures.

With so many areas of divergence, it is easy to see how students and teachers from different cultures could come into conflict with each other. Simply being aware of these potential sources of misunderstanding will reduce the risk that miscommunication will occur. When students and parents observe your efforts, they will feel that you do indeed value their experience.

**Self-Awareness.** Becoming aware of one's own biases, stereotypes, and expectations is just as important as developing cultural understandings. At the beginning of this chapter, you answered a series of questions about your cultural beliefs and sensitivities. Becoming aware of one's **expectations** for students who are different than oneself is probably the single most important action beginning teachers can take to create classrooms that are free of bias and instructionally effective.

**Self-Fulfilling Prophecy.** In 1968, Robert Rosenthal and Lenore Jacobson published *Pygmalion in the Classroom*. This book, instantly popular with professional and lay audiences, introduced the concept of the *self-fulfilling prophecy* and set off two decades of research and controversy about the effects of teacher expectations on student achievement and self-esteem. Rosenthal and Jacobson's research consisted of providing teachers in a particular elementary school information about several students in each of their classes. Teachers were told that a few students had been identified through a new test as "bloomers" and that they could expect these students to make large achievement

---

**Teachers need to be sensitive to the bases of cultural differences and how they can affect a student's classroom behavior.**

gains during the coming year. In fact, the students on whom teachers were given this information had been identified at random, and no special test information existed. As the year progressed, however, the identified bloomers, particularly those in the early grades, made significant gains in achievement. Rosenthal and Jacobson argued that these gains could be attributed to differential treatment received from the teachers as a result of their false expectations—thus the **self-fulfilling prophecy,** a situation in which inaccurate perceptions of students' abilities and subsequent acting on these perceptions make them come true over the years.

*Self-fulfilling prophecy refers to a situation in which teachers' expectations and predictions about student behavior or learning cause it to happen.*

Rosenthal and Jacobson's original study has been faulted because of its methodological weaknesses. (See Brophy & Good, 1974; Claiborn, 1969.) Their study, however, aroused the interest of the research community in the effects of teacher expectation on student achievement, and over the past two decades, researchers have found that though the effects of teacher expectations on students are not quite so straightforward as suggested in the Rosenthal-Jacobson study, they are, nonetheless, real.

Teacher expectations for individual students as well as for whole classes of students do indeed affect the kinds of interactions and relationships teachers have with students and, in some instances, what students learn. Teacher expectations create a cyclical pattern of behaviors on the part of both teachers and students. Drawing from the work of Good and Brophy (1987), this cyclical process is illustrated in Figure 4.3.

There are two important questions to ask about this process and teacher expectations. How are expectations created in the first place, and how do they get communicated to students?

In the classroom, as in all other aspects of life, people make impressions on us. The way students dress, the language they use, their physical features, as well as their interpersonal skills, influence the teacher. Information about a student's family or information gleaned from the school's records, even before the teacher meets a student, can also create impressions and expectations, as Rist's study demonstrated (Research Summary 4.1). As long as initial impressions are accurate, there is no problem. But when initial impressions are translated into inaccurate expectations about students and then used in differential treatment toward them, there is a problem.

**Figure 4.3** *Cyclical Process of Teacher Expectations*

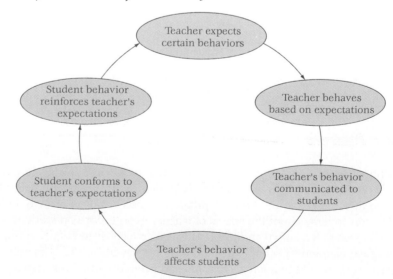

Once expectations (positive or negative) are formed, they are communicated to students in numerous ways. You can probably think of several instances when a particular teacher communicated expectations to you that influenced your attitude and work in that teacher's class. You may remember high expectations a teacher held for you. From the first day of class, she chose to single you out for important assignments; she wrote positive comments on your papers; and she called on you to answer difficult questions. It is likely that you worked hard for this teacher, perhaps even beyond your potential. Or you may remember an instance when a teacher had low expectations for you. Your work was seldom acknowledged publicly, and even though you raised your hand, you were seldom called on. If this behavior on the part of the teacher persisted, it is likely that you started to ignore your work in this class and concentrated your energies elsewhere.

Table 4.2 lists some of the ways that teachers communicate their expectations to students and how they behave differentially toward those for whom they hold high and low expectations. After you read the summary of teacher behaviors in Table 4.2, you will likely vow not to communicate low expectations to students in your classroom. This is a worthy goal but also one that requires more than just good intentions. It is good to know, however, that the goal can be achieved. **Differential treatment** does not occur in all teachers' classrooms. In fact, there is considerable difference among teachers in the degree to which they hold inaccurate expectations for students and act differentially toward students. Achieving a classroom free of inaccurate expectations and differential treatment can be difficult. Sometimes false expectations form because of the unconscious biases and stereotypes we have. It requires effort to change the way we think and behave even after we become aware of things we do unconsciously. At times, students for whom teachers have low expectations are those who are disruptive. Disruptive students often need more verbal and nonverbal interactions from the teacher

**Differential treatment refers to the difference in the educational experiences of the majority race, class, culture, or gender and those of minorities.**

**Table 4.2** *Teacher Differential Treatment of High- and Low-Expectation Students*

| Categories of Behavior | Teacher Behaviors |
| --- | --- |
| Praise and feedback | Rewarding inappropriate behaviors by lows. <br> Criticizing lows more often than highs for failure. <br> Praising lows less frequently than highs for success. <br> Briefer and less informative feedback to questions of lows. |
| Verbal interactions | Waiting less time for lows to answer. <br> Giving lows answers or calling on someone else. <br> Calling on lows less often to respond to questions. <br> Asking lows only easier, nonanalytical questions. |
| Interpersonal interactions | Generally paying less attention to lows. <br> Demanding less from lows. <br> Seating lows farther away from the teacher. <br> Less friendly interactions with lows. <br> Less nonverbal communication and responsiveness to lows. |
| Instructional strategies | Less use of effective but time-consuming methods with lows. <br> More seatwork and low-level academic tasks for lows. <br> Leaving lows out of some instructional activities. |

SOURCE: After Good and Brophy (1987), pp. 128–129.

that are negative or critical in tone. Similarly, the contributions of disruptive students can often be of low quality or careless. It is difficult, therefore, to call on low achievers or to use their ideas when their responses may disrupt the overall flow of a lesson, also an important goal for teaching. Later, a set of guidelines will be provided to help teachers overcome some of these difficulties.

**Sustaining Expectation Effect.** The discussion up to this point has focused on the self-fulfilling prophecy—a situation in which teachers hold inaccurate beliefs about particular students, act toward students based on these inaccurate beliefs, and over time, students match their behavior to the teacher's expectation. There is actually a second expectation effect that can occur. Labeled **sustaining expectation effect,** this condition exists when a teacher accurately reads a student's ability and behaves toward the student with this information but does not alter the expectation when a student improves or regresses over time. You can probably recall instances of this happening to you in classrooms as well as in other places. Perhaps you were an excellent English student. The essays you wrote for the teacher were always meticulously done. They were written with clarity, and you showed considerable creativity in the ways you created beautiful images with words. You always received an A for your effort. One week, however, you were recovering from the flu and were overwhelmed with other schoolwork. You had to write your essay in haste and with little thought or care. At this point, you simply didn't care about your grade; you just wanted to get it done. When the paper was returned marked with an A and a comment from the teacher, "Another superb piece of writing," you knew that your work had been judged not on its current value but on your previous history of producing good essays. The teacher sustained his or her high expectations for you even though your work was at a lower level.

> **Sustaining expectation effect occurs when teachers do not change their expectations about a student, even after the student's performance has changed.**

You can also probably think of instances when the sustaining expectation effect worked the other way. Perhaps you were notorious for not keeping up with your reading assignments in history. Every time the teacher called on you, you answered with silly and careless answers. This behavior made your classmates laugh. It also covered up your unpreparedness. You decided one day to stop this behavior. You started to read your assignments very carefully, and you came prepared to discuss your ideas in class. You raised your hand in response to the teacher's questions over and over, but someone else was always selected to recite. When you did get your chance, everyone started to laugh, including the teacher, before you could complete your point. This is another instance in which you had changed your behavior; you were working at a higher level, but past expectations were sustained by others (students and teachers), preventing them from accurately perceiving your improvement.

**Guidelines for Teachers.** In the classroom, as in all aspects of life, people make impressions on us, and we act on these impressions. In the classroom, the challenge obviously is to develop strategies to avoid negative expectations and to emphasize positive expectations. Several guidelines listed here can help teachers accomplish this goal.

1. Remember that a teacher's job is to teach all students, and assume an attitude that all students can learn. Communicate this positive belief in students to them.
2. Be very careful about how information from other teachers or information in the student's file is used.
3. During classroom discussions, strive to give all students equal access to public time. One way to do this is to prepare a stack of index cards with students' names. Shuffle the cards so the names come up at random; as you call on students, mix their cards back into the deck.

4. Systematically monitor the frequency and nature of verbal interactions with highs and lows, with members of different racial and ethnic groups, with boys and girls, with regular and exceptional students. Having another person observe and record these interactions provides the best objective record for analysis. Alternatively, you may want to videotape yourself and view the tape later to assess your actions.

5. Systematically monitor the frequency and nature of nonverbal interactions with highs and lows, with members of different racial and ethnic groups, with boys and girls, and with regular and exceptional students. Again, observers or videotape provide effective means for analyzing your interactions.

6. If ability grouping is used, find ways for it to remain flexible and open to change. Review group membership continuously. Argue with yourself that a student in a low or high group does not belong there.

7. Strive to be fair and consistent in the way student work is evaluated. On work that calls for subjective judgment (such as essays), periodically check for sustaining effect by taking the paper of a student who normally gets an A and argue with yourself that it really should be a C. Conversely, take a C paper and argue that it merits an A.

8. Strive to distribute rewards and privileges in a fair and consistent manner for high and lows, members of different racial and ethnic groups, boys and girls, regular and exceptional students.

9. Survey members of the class about how fairly they think the teacher treats them. A learning aid at the end of this chapter exists for this purpose.

10. Ask yourself whether your actions communicate value and challenge. Are you showing your students that you have confidence in their abilities by expecting excellence from them?

## Using a Fair and Relevant Curriculum

In addition to attending to their own understandings and attitudes, beginning teachers need to be prepared to make curricula decisions that will help their classrooms be more inclusive and multicultural. A prerequisite in any classroom is ensuring that the curriculum is relevant and free of bias. Normally, this requires teachers to move beyond the standard canons and become more inclusive in choice of content. For example, including literary works by prominent nonwhite authors in an American literature class is one action English teachers might take.

Next, teachers can evaluate for bias the textbooks and other materials they use. The forms of bias—linguistic, stereotyping, invisibility, imbalance, unreality, and fragmentation—are discussed in detail on page 137. Teachers can supplement learning activities with additional materials to redress bias. By the same token, when teachers make presentations, they need to supply examples and illustrations that are grounded in a variety of cultures. Finding such examples and illustrations will demand great initiative. One resource is practitioner journals; journals for teachers such as *Instructor, Arithmetic Teacher, Art Education, Social Studies*, and *Mathematics Teacher* are helpful. For example, one issue of *Arithmetic Teacher* (February 1991) describes a unit on teaching the geometry concept of tessalation through Native American art forms. The January 1995 issue of the journal *Education Leadership* was devoted to the topic of the inclusive school.

Alternatively, teachers can raise the issue of bias and discuss it directly with their students. Students themselves can analyze curriculum materials for bias and share their findings with peers. Class discussions can focus on the emotional impact of the various forms of bias, on the political conditions that give rise to bias, or on action that can be taken to correct it. Chapter 12 of this book provides guidelines for organizing effective discussions.

In addition to these minimal curricular reforms, there are three general approaches to incorporating multicultural aims and topics into the curriculum. One is the **single-group curriculum approach,** in which teachers set aside courses or units that present information on specific groups or cultures. Another method is the **topical approach.** It, too, consists of recognizing and teaching about nondominant cultures. However, it does so in a more limited way than does the single-group approach by devoting lessons to the heroes of various cultures; celebrating holidays of various cultures; and recognizing the art, music, literature, cuisine, and language of different cultures. For example, a third grade teacher might have a Mexican American theme party on Cinquo de Mayo with a piñata and tacos and might teach the children a few words in Spanish. Although these can be worthwhile educational activities, both approaches have problems. They emphasize differences between groups, not similarities, and so may have the undesired side effect of widening cultural gaps, rather than bringing cultures closer together. The topical approach can be quite superficial, and both approaches can be fragmented.

A third curricular strategy is called the **conceptual approach.** When teachers use this method, they incorporate a series of concepts associated with cultural pluralism into ongoing lessons. The conceptual approach identifies important concepts (for example, pluralism, interdependence, or communication) appropriate to the particular subject or grade level the teacher is teaching and then uses these concepts as the basis for lessons to promote multicultural understandings.

Here are a few examples of lessons using these concepts. The concept of pluralism could be infused into an intermediate school lesson on bar graphs, in which students plot the proportions of various ethnic and other groups in their community. The concept of interdependence could be infused into an elementary science unit on ecology. A secondary social studies lesson on voting rights could infuse the concept of exploitation.

Teachers using the conceptual approach first consider which of these concepts are complementary to material they are already teaching. Then, as opportunities arise, they incorporate the appropriate concepts into their lessons. In planning for such lessons, teachers couple the multicultural concept with the regular instructional objective and specify learning materials and activities that achieve both goals.

No matter which approach is used, teachers need to review their curricular decisions to ensure that they demonstrate to their students they are valued people and that they provide a complex curriculum, one that is challenging and culturally relevant to students. A culturally relevant curriculum is one that includes everyone and provides the voices of diverse people, particularly those who have been traditionally left out. For young black or Latino students, a curriculum lacking black or brown faces, traditions, literature, or music tells them that they don't count; it gives students from other groups the same message. Culturally relevant curricula, on the other hand, convey both value and challenge; are often thematic, integrating subject areas from diverse traditions; and often arise out of students' own questions so they can construct their own meaning.

Finally, much of a school's curriculum is communicated through textbooks and other materials. Researchers have identified curricular bias in many of the materials traditionally used in classrooms, and though progress has been made, teachers

**An approach to multicultural education in which special units or courses are devoted to a particular group or culture is called single-group curriculum.**

**A topical approach to multicultural education is one in which special lessons are devoted to studying heroes, holidays, art, or literature, of a particular culture.**

**A conceptual approach to multicultural education is one in which teachers incorporate a series of concepts associated with cultural pluralism into ongoing lessons.**

nonetheless need to be on the lookout and ensure that the materials they use are free of bias and stereotyping. Below are some forms of bias to watch for:

1. *Linguistic gender bias,* in which masculine terms and pronouns are used to refer to all people. This is easy to spot and easy to remedy. Simply replacing *he* with *they, mankind* with *people,* and so on corrects the problem.
2. *Stereotyping* is another problem. In some textbooks, white boys are depicted as brave, active, and successful, while boys of color and girls are shown in more passive and dependent situations.
3. *Invisibility* is another way cultural and gender bias finds its way into materials. Females and people of color are simply omitted or greatly underrepresented in both text and illustrations.
4. *Imbalance* is a related problem and refers to the situation in which only one aspect or interpretation of an issue or group of people is presented.
5. *Unreality* is another form of bias found in some textbooks and curriculum materials. In an attempt to avoid controversy, texts sometimes present an unrealistic picture of modern life, showing a nuclear family as typical, perhaps, instead of a single-parent or blended family.
6. *Fragmentation* occurs when information about women or minorities is not integrated into the body of a text but is presented in a separate chapter or box. This conveys the idea that their contributions are tangential to the mainstream and not important.

When teachers are working with materials that contain these biases, they need to supplement them with other books or illustrations that give balance to their instructional program. Teachers can also directly confront the curriculum biases with their students and use them as an opportunity to discuss their impact on all people.

## Using Authentic and Culturally Relevant Pedagogies

The strategies described in Part II of *Learning to Teach* form the basis for teaching in classrooms that are inclusive and multicultural. For example, direct instruction has been used widely and found effective for teaching basic skills to students with special needs. Cooperative learning has been shown to be effective in all kinds of urban classrooms with diverse student populations and in changing the attitudes of nondisabled students positively toward their peers who have disabilities. Therefore, attention here is on instructional strategies that are aimed particularly at the inclusive, multicultural classroom. The discussion draws heavily on the work of Gloria Ladson-Billings (1995), Cherry Banks and James Banks (1995), and Jeannie Oakes and Martin Lipton (1999). All of these educators have argued for a curriculum and a pedagogy that is culturally relevant and committed to equity.

There are a number of instructional strategies teachers can use to develop classrooms that are multicultural and inclusive. For instance, teachers can anchor instruction in students' prior knowledge and help them construct links between what they know and what they are to learn. By so doing, teachers will help students see commonalities and differences between cultures and will assist them in becoming multicultural. To do this effectively, though, teachers must actively seek out information about students' prior knowledge.

When teachers group students for instructional purposes, they can lean heavily on heterogeneous grouping and minimize ability grouping. The deleterious effects of

✔ **Check for Understanding**

- What steps can teachers take to develop cultural understanding and self-awareness?

- What are three broad areas of misunderstanding that commonly occur when people of different cultures come together?

- How do teachers subconsciously communicate their impressions of student ability levels and their expectations for students?

- Contrast self-fulfilling prophecy with the sustaining expectation effect.

- What are some guidelines that teachers can follow to ensure that they convey positive expectations to their students?

- What steps can teachers take to ensure they are using fair and relevant curricula in their classrooms? What are the types of bias to watch out for in curriculum materials?

**Cultural relevant pedagogy aims at making instruction culturally relevant by allowing students to construct knowledge on their own.**

tracking and the poor-quality instruction generally found in lower-ability groups and classes are well documented. (See Oakes, 1985; Oakes & Lipton, 1999.) Make sure that there are students of high, middle, and low ability in each learning group, and strive to achieve racial and ethnic balance.

Teachers can also design learning activities that mesh with a variety of learning styles. There are several style dimensions along which teachers can vary their instruction. One route is to incorporate visual, auditory, tactile, and kinesthetic modalities into lessons. Teachers can also apply cooperative as well as individualistic task and reward structures. Further, teachers can vary their lessons by making them more or less concrete or abstract and more or less formal or informal and by emphasizing in-context as well as out-of-context learning.

A related consideration in planning and presenting lessons is to capitalize on students' existing abilities. This is particularly crucial for exceptional or culturally different children, who may be ascribed low status by their mainstream peers. Teachers can use a technique called **assigning competence** with low-status students (Lotan & Benton, 1990). To assign competence, teachers first carefully observe their students while they work at a variety of tasks, focusing on the low-status children, and then identify the special abilities that these students have. They may be skilled in verbal reasoning, drawing, visual or spatial abilities, or other areas. Teachers then publicly and specifically draw the class's attention to the low-status student's special competence. Children who have been troubled by a lack of motivation and low achievement often bloom after teachers assign them competence. The story presented in Figure 4.4 illustrates the impact of assigning competence to one student.

An instructional element that should be an important part of your teaching is strategy instruction. One of the characteristics that distinguish good learners from poor is their ability to use a variety of strategies to read and write, to solve problems involving numbers, and to learn successfully. When teachers help at-risk students acquire the strategies they need to learn effectively, they give them the tools for school success. A large number of programs are available to support teachers in this goal. Many important strategies are described in the Resource Handbook. We will focus here on one of these: reciprocal teaching (Palincsar & Klenk, 1991).

**Reciprocal teaching is an approach to teaching reading in which peer teaching is used to help students master comprehension skills.**

**Reciprocal teaching** has been used with elementary and secondary students; with regular, special education, and at-risk students; and for teaching subject matter and reading comprehension. Research has documented the effectiveness of the approach.

Motivation is itself a major concern. You learned in Chapter 3 about needs theory and attribution theory and about the alterable factors impinging on students' willingness to engage and persist in learning tasks. Researchers have also studied specific strategies that promote motivation for at-risk students. The HOTS program (Pogrow, 1990, 1995) was developed for elementary students in remedial pull-out programs. Rather than providing additional drill on basic skills, as most pull-out programs do, students were challenged with difficult, ambiguous problems and were expected to discuss, question, and resolve problems for themselves with only modest help from the teacher. The program has been very effective in helping underachievers succeed in school, and part of the reason is that students find challenge and interaction much more motivating than "drill-and-kill." Abi-Nader (1991) described a successful program for Hispanic high school students that focused on priming them for college in part through future-oriented classroom talk. These students had been oriented to getting by day by day, and they were unaccustomed to planning and setting goals. Program classes are filled with references to the future, from specific lessons

**Figure 4.4** *A Story About Assigning Competence*

Alicia, a rather tall, bilingual Spanish-English-speaking second grader, was the type of youngster whom people barely noticed. She was not a discipline problem; she did not make demands on the teacher or the other students, nor did she actively participate in interactions. Alicia seldom raised her hand to answer questions, and she rarely voiced her opinions.

One day in April, while videotaping group interactions in Alicia's classroom, we focused on students who frequently exhibited low-status behavior. While working on the coordinates and measurement unit, Alicia had teamed up with another child in her group, Aneke. Their task was to draw life-sized representations of their bodies. The girls took turns, lying on large sheets of butcher paper and then outlining each other's bodies with a thick, felt-tip pen. After making the outlines, the children had to cut out the replicas and then color in their features and clothing.

Aneke had possibly the highest academic status in this second-grade classroom. She was petite, precocious, and popular. She knew the answer to almost every question the teacher asked. Her hand flew up at every opportunity. She was a delightful, outgoing child, who seemed to be skilled at everything she was asked to do.

Among the important skills needed by students in the second grade is the ability to use scissors and to cut accurately. However, as Alicia and Aneke set about to cut out their butcher paper bodies, it became apparent that Aneke, who was so accomplished academically, did not know how to use scissors properly, nor did she know how to follow the outline of the body to cut it out accurately. Aneke was distressed. She feared she would cut off her paper arms and legs. Patiently and expertly, Alicia guided Aneke through the procedure, coaching her exasperated partner on how to use the scissors and follow the outline.

When Alicia's teacher viewed the videotape of this incident with one of the authors, the teacher commented on the fact that this was the first time since school started that she had seen Alicia show real mastery on a skill relevant to a classroom task. During the next orientation, the teacher shared her observation with the class. She wanted all the children to realize that Alicia was particularly skilled at using scissors and that if ever they needed help cutting, they could turn to Alicia as a resource.

Coincidentally, the school was getting ready to present a musical called "Let George Do It." This colonial play required that each class be responsible for making a number of three-cornered hats. The second-grade teacher decided to put Alicia in charge of making these hats for her class. Alicia was to pick children to be on the committee, decide on what materials were needed, get the pattern from the teacher in charge of costumes, and see to it that the hats were made to specification. Since Alicia was perceived as the most accomplished "cutter" in her classroom, the committee looked to her for guidance.

Alicia took to the making of the three-cornered hats with tremendous enthusiasm. Again, it was the first time since September that her teacher had seen Alicia talking and working with other children in such an animated and empowered way. Alicia was now raising her hand more often during wrap-up, answering questions frequently and accurately. During this same period of time, the teacher also discovered that Alicia had good spatial reasoning and visual thinking skills. For example, when the task for her group was to draw a map of the classroom to scale, Alicia drew the map and then created an impressive three-dimensional model of the room. The teacher made sure that Alicia was assigned competence for this accomplishment also.

After the beginning of the next academic year, the opportunity arose to talk with Alicia's third-grade teacher. This teacher said that she would have never guessed that Alicia had been a low-status student for a large part of her second grade. Particularly during Finding Out/Descubrimiento, but also during many other parts of the day, Alicia interacted frequently and effectively with her classmates, raised her hand and answered questions correctly, and expressed her opinions readily. Children listening to Alicia were often observed going along with her suggestions. Alicia was greatly valued by her teachers and her classmates for her artistic and organizational skills. It appeared that Alicia was also performing better academically in almost every curricular area.

SOURCE: Lotan and Benton (1990), pp. 60–62.

that prepare them for future experiences (such as filling out sample financial aid forms), to describing situations they may encounter in college or in a professional career, to telling stories about graduates from the program and their successes in college and careers.

Teachers also have available to them many well-validated strategies to help all students accomplish learning goals. Cooperative learning has been mentioned several times; models such as STAD, Jigsaw, and group investigation, described in Chapter 10, have a remarkable research base backing their efficacy in increasing achievement, prosocial behavior, problem-solving abilities, and intergroup acceptance.

**Community problem solving,** a strategy similar to problem-based instruction described in Chapter 11, has also been found effective in multicultural classrooms. When using this strategy, teachers encourage students to identify concerns they have about their community or neighborhood and help them plan and carry out independent projects. In one case, students at a low-income-area elementary school decided to tackle the problem of a hazardous waste site in their neighborhood. In the process of confronting this problem, students had to plan, read up on environmental issues, and understand the danger of the various chemicals on their doorstep; write to their legislators and investigate the political process; organize and present their arguments for action effectively to a variety of audiences; and raise and manage money. In the context of a meaningful, important, and engaging activity, then, students developed skills in reading, writing, math, social studies, science, design and layout, and interpersonal communication.

## Using Authentic and Fair Assessment Strategies

One other factor should be considered in every lesson: assessment of student learning. Through both teacher-made and standardized tests, bias is often introduced into the classroom. To circumvent this bias, teachers need to do two things: (1) rely on a variety of methods for evaluating student learning—through written or oral tests, student reports and projects, observations, interviews, and discussions with parents and others who know the student—and (2) test at a variety of levels—recall, comprehension, application, analysis, synthesis, and evaluation. The goals of schooling are not high scores on culturally biased tests, after all, but rather are outcomes such as the ability to read independently for information and enjoyment, to solve problems involving numbers, to apply the lessons of history to current social problems, and so on. Whenever possible, assess students directly for achievement of these real goals, not just for the goal's proxy. Many teachers are beginning to use portfolios of student work to document student learning as an alternative to traditional tests. Analogous to artist's portfolios, students' portfolios are collections of student work samples that demonstrate progress in learning over time. Artwork, writing samples, research projects, journal entries, video clips of interaction in small groups, as well as tests and other materials can make up the contents of portfolios. These are also very useful in parent-teacher conferences.

*Relying on a number of different methods to assess what students know and can do helps eliminate cultural and class bias found in more traditional testing procedures.*

## Working with Students with Special Needs

The previous sections spoke mainly about how teachers can develop understandings and strategies for working with students from different racial, cultural, or ethnic groups. Beginning teachers also need understanding and skills for working with students with special needs. Although these are similar, important differences exist that are spelled out in the discussion that follows.

Most beginning teachers worry about what can be done in the classroom to assist special students. Several steps can be taken. First, as with all students, special-needs students will model teachers' intended and unintended behaviors and often live up to teachers' expectations, whether positive or negative. Positive, even-handed regard for all students is a prerequisite for effective teaching.

It is important for beginning teachers to know district policies pertaining to students with special needs and the teacher's role in the referral, screening, and IEP process. Familiarize yourself with district policies and procedures for referral and screening. Be alert for students with problems or special potential. Do you have any students whose academic work is well below or well above grade level? Do you have students whose behavior is well below or above the maturity level of their age mates? Do any of your students demonstrate especially low or high persistence at learning tasks? Are any of your students exceptionally creative? Typically, districts expect teachers to refer students exhibiting these characteristics—unusual academic performance, behavior, persistence, or creativity—to the appropriate colleagues for further evaluation.

Also, become aware of the specific categories of disabilities as prescribed by federal law. Students who have one of the disabilities described in Table 4.3 are eligible for special education services.

**Table 4.3** *Summary of Students with Disabilities*

| Federal Disability Category | Characteristic | Percentage of All Students Receiving Special Education Services |
|---|---|---|
| Learning disabilities (LD) | Dysfunctions in processing information; average intelligence; problems learning how to read, write, compute | 51% |
| Emotional disturbance (ED) | Difficulties in social and emotional areas; trouble with social relationships | 9% |
| Speech or language impairment | Speech is disordered and interferes with communication. | 21% |
| Mental retardation | Significant below-average mental functioning and cognitive abilities | 12% |
| Hearing impairment | Significant hearing loss; amount can vary | 1.3% |
| Visual impairment | Significant vision loss; amount can vary | 0.5% |
| Deaf-blindness | Significant vision and hearing disabilities | 0.1% |
| Orthopedic impairment | Serious physical disabilities; ability to move around impaired | 1.2% |
| Traumatic brain injury (TBI) | Intellectual and physical impairments resulting from brain injury | 0.1% |
| Autism | Developmental disability characterized by impairments in communication and social interactions | 0.5% |
| Multiple disabilities | Two or more interwoven disabilities | 1.8% |
| Other health impairments | Conditions resulting from chronic health problems or disease | 2.2% |

**Figure 4.5** *Steps in the IEP Process*

Step 1: Classroom teacher, special education teacher, and administrators identify through evaluation that the student is eligible. Parents must be involved and provide consent.

Step 2: Classroom and special education teachers, administrators, and parents develop an IEP and determine placement.

Step 3: Classroom and special education teachers and service providers implement and monitor the IEP.

Step 4: Classroom and special education teachers, parents, student, and others annually review IEP to see if goals have been achieved and to identify new goals and services.

Schools are required to have an individualized educational plan (IEP) for each student identified with a disability. In most school districts, IEPs are developed by a committee composed of the regular classroom teacher, the child's parents, the special education teacher, and any other staff who may be helpful, such as psychologists, speech therapists, or medical personnel. IEPs should contain information about the child's current level of academic performance, a statement of both long- and short-term educational goals, a plan for how these goals will be achieved, the amount of time the child will spend in the regular class, and an evaluation plan. The IEP is revised annually. Figure 4.5 shows the steps in the IEP process, and Figure 4.6 shows an example of a completed IEP.

Evaluation procedures used to assess special-needs students are tied to the IEP process and by law are to be nondiscriminatory. In screening children for special services, school officials are required to use a variety of tests and to consider the child's cultural background and language. The involvement of parents in the evaluation process is mandated, and no major educational decisions may be made without their written consent. Parents must be informed of intended school actions in their own language.

*Diagnosis and evaluation are important aspects of the IEP process.*

**Figure 4.6** *Sample Individualized Education Plan*

**Quentinburg Public Schools— Special Education Department**

**Individualized Education Program**

**Student Name:** Jillian Carol
**School:** Jefferson Elementary
**Primary lang.:** Home-English Student-English
**Program start date:** 8/28/97

**Date of Birth:** 4/2/87
**Grade:** 5
**Date of meeting:** 8/28/97
**Review date:** 8/28/98

**Services Required**

| | |
|---|---|
| *General Education* | Full-time participation with support from paraprofessional or special education teacher at least three hours weekly |
| *Resources* | Incidental as needed |
| *Self-Contained* | Speech/language therapy for language development |
| *Related Services* | 40 minutes/week |
| *Other* | |

***Justification for Placement (include justification for any time spent not in general education):*** Student's needs indicate that learning can appropriately take place in the general education classroom with appropriate supports provided. Support will include adapted materials as well as adult assistance up to three hours per week. Incidental time noted in the resource room is intended to preserve the option of one-to-one assistance on specific goals and objectives as needed, as determined by the teachers.

**Tests Used**

| | |
|---|---|
| *Intellectual* | WISC-III (Full Scale IQ = 64) |
| *Educational* | Woodcock Reading, Keymath |
| *Behavioral* | NA |
| *Speech/language* | |
| *Other* | |
| *Vision* | Within normal limits |
| *Hearing* | Within normal limits |

**Strengths (present level of functioning)**
Jillian enjoys talking with peers and adults.
Jillian is polite and well-mannered.
Jillian generally responds appropriately to directions.
Jillian likes to tell stories she creates.

**Weaknesses (present level of functioning)**
1. Below grade level in word identification (3.1) and reading comprehension (3.2)
2. Below grade level in vocabulary usage (2.1)
3. Below grade level in math computation and problem solving (1.6)

*(continued)*

**Figure 4.6** *(continued)*

**Annual Goal:** Jillian will improve her reading skills to approximately a 3.9 level.
**STO 1:** Jillian will read from a 3rd grade reader at 80 words per minute with fewer than 3 errors per minute.
**STO 2:** Jillian will answer with 80% accuracy comprehension questions about reading passages at a third-grade level.
**Evaluation:** Oral performance  **Person(s):** Special education teacher

**Annual Goal:** Jillian will use vocabulary at approximately a 3.0 level
**STO 1:** Jillian will tell a story using vocabulary from third grade reading materials.
**STO 2:** Jillian will use 3rd grade vocabulary when talking about her out-of-school activities.
**STO 3:** Jillian will learn at least 40 vocabulary words by using a word bank.
**Evaluation:** Oral performance, checklist  **Person(s):** Special education teacher
Classroom teacher

**Annual Goal:** Jillian will compute and problem solve at approximately a 2.5 level.
**STO 1:** Jillian will write answers to basic addition and subtraction facts with 100% accuracy.
**STO 2:** Jillian will accurately compute two-digit addition and subtraction problems without regrouping with 90% accuracy.
**STO 3:** Jillian will correctly solve word problems written at her reading level and at approximately a 2.5 difficulty level with 90% accuracy.
**Evaluation:** Written performance  **Person(s):** Special education teacher
Classroom teacher

**Team Signatures**

| | |
|---|---|
| *LEA Representative* | Eva Kim |
| *Parent* | Julia Carol |
| *Special Education Teacher* | Vera Delaney |
| *General Education Teacher* | |
| *Psychologist* | Nadine Showalter |
| *Counselor* | |
| *Speech/Language Therapist* | Ed Briggs |
| *Other* | |
| *Other* | |

SOURCE: Friend and Bursuck (1999), pp. 55–56.

Regarding specific lessons, teachers can develop learning materials and activities commensurate with the abilities of children with special needs, including the gifted, much as they adapt lessons to the individual differences of all students. In doing so, they should expect to work closely with resource teachers and other support personnel. Most schools have such support services readily available.

Cooperative learning strategies can also be used often, both to facilitate achievement and to help exceptional and regular students accept and appreciate each other. The following tips for teaching the mildly learning disabled or behaviorally disabled students most likely to be mainstreamed are adapted from recommendations offered by the National Information Center for Handicapped Children and Youth:

1. Use highly structured materials. Tell students exactly what is expected. Avoid distractions, such as colorful bulletin boards, in work areas.
2. Allow alternatives to the use of written language, such as tape recorders or oral tests.
3. Expect improvement on a long-term basis.
4. Reinforce appropriate behavior. Model and explain what constitutes appropriate behavior.
5. Provide immediate feedback and ample opportunities for drill and practice.

As you will see, these actions are not very different from many of the effective teaching behaviors described in Chapter 8. Careful task analysis and use of direct instruction are important tools for helping students with special needs. Not all agree, however, that these are the only effective teaching strategies for this population. Many (Curtis & Shaver, 1980; Haberman, 1992; Slavin, 1996) believe that instruction for students with special needs should stem from their interest and that strategies used by teachers should not emphasize basic information but promote ability to solve problems and think critically. They recommend strategies that resemble those recommended for gifted children—group investigation, community problem solving, and activities that emphasize active learning. Approaches such as cooperative learning and reciprocal teaching tell students that they all can learn, that they all can make a contribution to the learning process, and that all perspectives are valued. Community problem solving tells students that teachers care about their lives and their communities and provides opportunities for complex, meaningful, and motivating academic work.

Teachers also need to carefully think through the physical layout of their classrooms and make any changes that will facilitate easy movement for all students, particularly those who may require wheelchairs or special walking devices. They need to consider scheduling and time constraints and how these might affect special students. For example, the transition time between lessons may need to be extended for a student who is physically disabled and the downtime thus created for the students without disabilities properly managed. Likewise, highly able students will accomplish learning tasks very quickly, and thought must be given to how they can use their extra time meaningfully. Routines and procedures for such contingencies must be planned and taught to the whole class.

Teachers may also be called upon to assist students with special equipment, a topic that is highlighted in this chapter's Spotlight on Technology box. As always, they must accommodate individual differences and maintain communication with parents. And they must help exceptional and regular students work and play together. As with all students, students with special needs model teachers' intended and unintended behaviors, and they often live up to teachers' expectations, whether positive or negative. Positive, even-handed regard for exceptional students is a prerequisite for effective

**Tailoring Teaching for Inclusive Classrooms**

## Making Instructional Adaptations and Accommodations

Knowing how and when to adapt instructions to meet the needs of special students is one of the challenges facing beginning teachers. The following guidelines for when it is appropriate to make adaptations and when it is not draw on the work of Friend and Bursuck (1999).

- Make an adaptation only when you are sure that one is required. Adaptations take time and energy.
- Be certain that you have accurately diagnosed the student's problem or special need before making an adaptation. For instance, before adapting your classroom to meet the needs of a student with an attention problem, be sure the problem is not due to a hearing loss or some other physical impairment.

- Make sure you are dealing with a "can't," not a "won't," problem. Friend and Bursuck (1999) describe this situation as follows: "A can't problem is one in which the student, no matter how motivated, is unable to do what is expected. A won't problem implies that the student could do what is expected but is not motivated to do so. . . . A student unable to do what is expected might need an . . . (adapted) strategy; a student unwilling to do the work might need a management strategy. . . . For example, if a student failed a test because she didn't feel like working on the day of the test, a teacher's attempt to provide extra tutorial assistance would likely be a wasted effort" (p. 113).
- Keep the adaptation as simple as possible. In general, the closer an adapted condition or assignment is to what is going on in the regular classroom, the better it is for both teacher and student. It takes less time for the teacher, and the student is not unduly singled out.

It is very important for teachers to tailor their instruction to meet the needs of all students. However, instructional adaptations take time and should be used only when the teacher is quite sure that they are needed.

teaching, as are making curriculum relevant and using strategies known to work with students who have special needs.

Finally, learning how to use the right language when referring to students with special needs is important. This has become increasingly important as society's sensitivities to individuals with disabilities have grown. For example, most people today believe that it is not appropriate to refer to someone as "handicapped" because of the term's evolution. At one time, according to Friend and Busuck (1999), people with disabilities who had to resort to begging were referred to as "cap-in-handers." Later, they were called "hand-in-cappers," a term obviously similar to the contemporary term *handicapped*.

Some also prefer the term *challenged* instead of disabled when referring to students with special needs. For example, a person who cannot walk might be said to be physically challenged; a learning disabled student could be referred to as cognitively challenged. Some hold this preference because the term *challenge* communicates an obstacle that can be overcome, whereas *disabled* seems to convey a condition that is permanent. The term *disability*, however, remains acceptable, and you will find it used in most textbooks and other documents.

Although space does not allow an in-depth discussion of gifted and talented students, it is important to point out that they too have special needs that require a teacher's understanding and attention. Some of the same problems crop up for this population. Minority students are underrepresented in programs for the gifted, and methods for assessing giftedness are not well validated. Many of the strategies used with these students, such as group investigation and problem-based instruction (de-

*Spotlight on Technology*

## Assistive Technologies

*Computers provide valuable assistance to students with special needs*

Computers are an important part of today's inclusive classroom. Of particular importance is the variety of **assistive technologies** available to help students with special needs learn, regardless of their disability. Some of these devices are used to make available a wider range of educational opportunities than would otherwise be possible. For example, computer-assisted large print, Braille translations, and speech synthesizers can assist communication for students who have visual or speech impairments. Other technologies such as special switches can allow students who are physically disabled to turn on appliances and control other devices such as lamps or radios. Computerized "gait trainers" can help individuals with poor balance or control of their bodies learn how to walk.

Perhaps most important, however, is the assistive technologies that provide disabled students with access to computers and other modern communication technologies almost as readily as students without disabilities. Keyboards can be modified, for example, so one-handed or one-fingered typists can use them. Voice recognition programs allow physically disabled students to input text into a computer directly by speaking. Joy sticks have been developed that allow individuals to control the computer by pointing with their chin or their head. Needs for assistive devices are written into a student's IEP, and teachers are responsible for helping students learn how to use these devices in their classrooms.

---

scribed in Chapters 10 and 11) and higher-level thinking strategies (described in Chapter 9), would be appropriate for regular students as well. Unlike with special education programs, though, most school systems with gifted programs receive no additional monies from the federal government.

## Establishing Caring, Democratic Classroom Management

Classroom management frequently poses problems for new teachers, and these problems are exacerbated when teachers face a classroom full of students with diverse backgrounds and an array of special needs. Many of the ideas described in the next chapter speak directly to the management of inclusive, diverse classrooms. Management problems are kept to a minimum if teachers have well-planned rules and procedures that have been clearly communicated to and accepted by students. Classrooms are better learning communities when they are democratic and when all students have opportunities to air their views and grievances, such as in class meetings (described in Chapter 5). Students behave more appropriately when they know their teachers care for them, value them as individuals, and are committed to helping them achieve challenging goals. There are, however, some special issues for teachers to consider as they work in inclusive, diverse classrooms.

Researchers have found that classroom climate and teacher affect are vitally important to at-risk students. Schlosser (1992) studied thirty-one culturally diverse high school students who had been identified as potential dropouts by the district. For two years, she interviewed and observed both the students and their teachers in an attempt to identify those teaching practices most effective with this population. Students said that good teachers displayed the following behaviors:

> (a) noticing you and asking if you're in any trouble, (b) including topics of interest to students in classroom discussions, and telling you that you can come back after class if you want to talk more, and (c) listening to what you say without jumping at you. (p. 133)

Teachers who demonstrated that they cared about students by talking with them, finding out about their lives, and applying that information in the way they structured their classrooms were the most effective with at-risk students. These actions help create personalized learning environments, which are more successful because teachers:

> know more about student lives and backgrounds, are better able to draw on their students' experiences to bridge the gap between the known and unknown, and are more likely to understand what knowledge must be made explicit for students. (p. 138)

Problems will inevitably arise, however, and teachers may feel some conflict about how to approach difficulties with diverse students. For example, does enforcing school rules amount to denying respect for students' culture? Experienced teachers come to understand that respecting the culture of all students does not mean abandoning the rules of the school. Punctuality and other aspects of dominant culture may not be regarded as important elsewhere, but they are important in mainstream culture, and in order to be successful within that culture, all students must learn to abide by these norms when circumstances warrant it. Not enforcing such rules at school would be to perform a disservice to all students. However, the attitude and spirit with which rules are enforced need *not* be demeaning or punitive. Teachers can explain rules and consequences in a neutral way to students and parents and offer suggestions on how they might cope with such rules. Teachers can also make clear that rules at school apply only at school and that students are certainly free to express their own values within the context of their subcultures. By the same token, teachers and schools should be open to examining and changing their rules and policies, if these no longer serve the learning needs of their students and community.

Some students, because of particularly difficult life circumstances, such as acute poverty, homelessness, or fetal alcohol syndrome, may pose especially taxing classroom management and discipline problems for teachers. There are a number of actions teachers can take to ease these difficulties. One is to reframe the student's disruptive action. Adults tend to interpret the aggressive or challenging behaviors these children may display as malicious, when they may represent the only mechanism the student has for expressing overstimulation, frustration, or some other message as simple as "I need to go to the bathroom." The first step for teachers, then, is to figure out what the behavior means to the student. One tool to help develop hypotheses about the function of disruptive behavior is to maintain a behavioral log, tracking what kinds of behaviors happen under what circumstances. Others are close observation and referrals to specialists. Then teachers can help students develop nondisruptive alternatives to cope with their frustrations. This vignette by a clinical psychologist illustrates how children's coping behaviors may interfere with smooth classroom functioning:

[A] 4-year-old child was referred to me because he was "out of control in the classroom," had been cocaine-exposed prenatally, and was becoming increasingly aggressive toward the teacher.

When this little boy arrived for testing, my first impression was that he was nothing like what the teacher had described. He was friendly, polite, and . . . extremely cooperative. However, after about five minutes . . . the child announced he was done. I tried to persuade him otherwise by redirecting his attention to different items, pushing the table a little closer to him, and asking him to try a few more things. This attempt to make him continue when he wanted to quit was met with a behavioral outburst . . . screaming, kicking, and shoving. . . . I immediately pulled the table away, at which time the child ran out of the room.

I assumed the testing phase of the evaluation was over and started writing a few notes. . . . A few minutes later, however, the little boy returned . . . and said that he was ready to continue. After another 10 minutes or so . . . the child again said, "I'm done now," to which I replied, "That's fine." The child calmly got out of his chair, walked around the room for a minute, and then sat down to resume testing. This pattern was repeated. . . .

It was easy to see in a one-to-one testing situation that this child recognized the limits to his concentration and coped with increasing frustration by briefly removing himself. . . . It is equally easy to see, however, how this behavior created problems in the classroom. By wandering around, he would be disrupting the learning of other children. When the teacher tried to make him sit back down, she was increasing his frustration by removing from him the one method he had developed for coping. (Griffith, 1992, p. 34)

Griffith goes on to suggest that one solution to this impasse might be for the teacher to mark out a space on the floor with masking tape at the back of the room so the child would have a place to pace without disturbing others while they developed a larger repertoire of coping strategies.

Rootlessness, stress, and lack of a sense of control over their lives can also lead to special problems for homeless and extremely poor students. They may exhibit low tolerance for frustration and stimulation, short attention span, and distractability, typical reactions to high stress. These students, too, may benefit from instruction in alternate ways of coping with stress and frustration. Linehan (1992) offers several additional guidelines to make classroom life more hospitable for these students:

- Let the student "own" something in the classroom, perhaps a plant or a game—something that others must get their permission to handle.
- Give the student a classroom job to be responsible for, a stake in the life of the classroom.
- Don't confiscate their things or deny recess or physical activity as a punishment or to allow time for makeup work; they need a sense of personal control, and their outlets for activity may be limited.
- They may not have any quiet space to study in at their living quarters; if so, allow them to complete and store homework assignments at school.
- Transportation may be problematic; if so, don't penalize them for being late.
- Make sure students and parents are aware of the special services the school may offer, such as free lunch, free breakfast, bilingual activities, and other programs.
- Keep students' life circumstances confidential.

Most special-needs students will require extra teaching in communication skills, social skills, and making choices.

It is in the area of classroom organization, management, and discipline that teachers can most emphatically demonstrate an attitude of caring and valuing their students. Warmth, friendliness, asking questions about students' lives—these actions tell students you are concerned about what happens to them and help engender cooperation in times of conflict. Accommodating children with special needs and respecting cultural differences, within the boundaries of maintaining high expectations and promoting biculturalism, also foster feelings of mutual trust and respect.

## Considering Schoolwide Issues

Finally, it is important for teachers to be aware that all problems regarding inclusion and diversity cannot be solved in their own classrooms. Teachers can help effect reform at the school level that will make schooling more sensitive to students from diverse backgrounds and those with special needs. A number of programs and practices that require schoolwide implementation exist.

One of the most consistent findings from research is that tracking by ability does not promote achievement. Further, it has damaging consequences for minority students. A good place to start multicultural reforms, then, is to reduce or eliminate tracking. Many schools are beginning to experiment with reorganizing into teams of teachers and students, developing interdisciplinary curricula, relying heavily on cooperative learning in heterogeneous groups, and alternatives to standardized testing (Oakes, 1992; Oakes & Lipton, 1999).

There are also several school-level actions teachers can take to address the difficult life circumstances of students considered "at risk" due to poverty. Most schools offer free and reduced-price lunches for students, but only about 50 percent of these schools also offer free and reduced-price breakfasts. A smaller number of districts provide meals over the summer through the federal Summer Food Service Program. The connection between student learning and basic nutrition is not only self-evident but also well documented, so it behooves schools and districts that lack these basic programs to implement them.

School programs that target early intervention are also helpful. The effectiveness of one such program—Head Start—is well established. For every dollar invested in Head Start, many more are saved later on in reduced need for discipline and remediation, welfare, and criminal justice. Yet only about 20 percent of eligible children are served. The process of establishing a Head Start center is long and complex, but beginning teachers can lend their support to existing centers by promoting awareness among colleagues and parents and by lobbying for increased funding so that more low-income children can be served. Early identification and intervention with children who have been exposed prenatally to drugs and alcohol are also very important. To establish new programs or support existing ones, link with health and special education professionals in your school or district.

Recently, a move toward interagency collaboration has begun among educators concerned with at-risk students. As Guthrie and Guthrie (1991) argued: "A wide assortment of social service agencies has been organized to serve children and youth at risk; but the services often overlap, agencies are compartmentalized, and children are incorrectly referred" (p. 17). To improve services, they advocate that these agencies coordinate their work with schools to provide assistance that is comprehensive, preventive, and child-centered. Again, linking with health, special education, and social service professionals is the first step in streamlining interagency collaboration.

Another important avenue to improve the educational outcomes of low-income students is community involvement. When parents and other community members are involved in the life of the school through tutoring programs, mentoring programs, school improvement committees, parent education, site-based governance, or other activities, students benefit (Epstein, 1991; Nettles, 1991).

Three schoolwide intervention programs are especially noteworthy: Accelerated Schools (Levin, 1997), Success for All (Madden et al., 1992; Stevens & Slavin, 1995), and

✔ **Check for Understanding**

- How can a teacher improve performance by assigning confidence to students?

- What teacher behaviors and attitudes foster feelings of trust in children with special needs?

- What is an IEP, and what are the major steps in the IEP process?

- What are some examples of school programs that teachers can become involved in to promote inclusion and multicultural education?

- Why are caring classroom management processes important in inclusive and multicultural classrooms?

Yale psychiatrist James Comer's (1988) program initiated in New Haven, Connecticut, schools. These programs share characteristics such as parent involvement, decentralized decision making, and application of research-based instructional innovations. All three have proved highly effective in raising the achievement of at-risk students.

A word about being a new teacher and an agent for change at the same time is in order. All the programs and practices described in this chapter are worthwhile, important, and ought to be put into place in the public schools. Indeed, there is much public support for action to alleviate racial intolerance in the schools (71 percent of Americans favor such action, according to a recent Gallup poll). Unfortunately, because of a variety of factors (lack of funds, time, awareness), many schools have inadequate programs or lack them entirely. You are urged to make working for multicultural reform part of your professional agenda. You probably have concerns about your ability to successfully carry out these reforms. As a newcomer to a large, complex organization, you will not have a lot of clout, but you will have some. When you make proposals that are backed by solid research, administrators and colleagues will be more likely to listen. When you talk with parents and patrons and enlist their support, you will be more likely to effect change. It is also wise to prioritize your reform goals and focus your limited energy on only one or two projects at a time. Chapter 13 presents more detailed information on the processes of individual and organizational change and of improving schools.

## 🍏 *Summary*

### Perspectives on Inclusion and Multicultural Education

- Over the past half century, the student population in American schools has changed dramatically. Making classrooms inclusive and finding effective ways to teach a diverse group of students is the teaching challenge of the twentieth-first century.

- Today's classrooms are characterized by diversity. It is critical for teachers to develop classrooms that treat all students equally, regardless of their gender, racial or ethnic heritage, or learning difficulties.

- For educators, *multicultural education* involves learning to recognize, understand, and appreciate cultural groups—whether based on racial, ethnic, language, gender, or other differences—and developing skills in working with diverse groups of students.

- *Inclusion* is an effort to extend educational opportunities to students with special needs, a group that traditionally has been segregated and has received inferior educational opportunities.

- In creating inclusive, multicultural classrooms, effective teachers adopt an ecological perspective and view their classrooms as a system of interconnected elements—students, teachers, learning materials, instruction, and goals—all of which interact to produce or inhibit student learning.

### Theoretical and Empirical Support

- The knowledge base on multicultural education and inclusion can help teachers to understand particular cultures, what happens to children of different cultures and disabilities in school, and how to develop a strong teaching repertoire to use with a diverse student population.

- Studies over the years have shown that minority students receive a lower-quality education as a result of enrollment patterns, tracking and grouping patterns, and differential interactions with teachers.

- Language diversity must be respected, and bilingual skills must be encouraged and developed for students who do not speak the dominant language.

- Gender bias exists in schools and classrooms because of linguistic bias and stereotyping.

- Socioeconomic status has rather dramatic effects on school learning, mainly because of tracking and grouping and because of differential interactions with teachers.

- Traditionally, students with disabilities have received an inferior education. Current efforts to mainstream and include students with special needs are aimed at correcting this situation.

### Creating Inclusive, Multicultural Classrooms

- As with many other aspects of teaching, knowledge, self-understanding, and reflection about intercultural interactions are essential for teachers in developing inclusive, multicultural classrooms and schools.

- Teachers attend to their personal development by improving their own knowledge and attitudes toward people of different cultures and by becoming aware of their cultural biases.
- Teachers' expectations affect relationships with students, what they learn, and students' perceptions of their own abilities. Teachers can learn to be aware of and minimize their biases about students of different backgrounds.
- Teaching processes that can be employed to promote multicultural education include anchoring instruction to students' prior knowledge, meshing learning activities to students' learning styles, capitalizing on students' existing abilities, and using fair and relevant curriculum.
- Teachers' responsibilities for working with special-needs students include helping with the IEP process and adapting instruction and other aspects of teaching so all students can learn.
- Specific teaching models and strategies available to accomplish multicultural learning goals include direct instruction, cooperative learning, reciprocal teaching, and community problem solving.
- Teachers must evaluate and adapt their curriculum, instruction, and schools in keeping with the dual goals of valuing and challenging all their students.

## 🍎 Key Terms

| | | |
|---|---|---|
| diversity | cultural difference theory | self-fulfilling prophecy |
| equity | cultural deficit theory | differential treatment |
| multicultural education | ESL | sustaining expectation effect |
| Americanization | LEP | single-group curriculum approach |
| melting pot | submersion approach | topical approach |
| cultural pluralism | transitional bilingual program | conceptual approach |
| mainstreaming | full bilingual program | assigning competence |
| inclusion | socioeconomic status | reciprocal teaching |
| least restrictive environment | culture shock | community problem solving |
| individualized educational plan (IEP) | teacher expectations | assistive technologies |

## 🍎 Books for the Professional

Bank, J. A. (1994). *Multiethnic Education: Theory and Practice.* Boston: Allyn and Bacon. This is a very readable text on multicultural education written by one of the foremost authorities in the field.

Bennett, C. I. (1995). *Comprehensive Multicultural Education: Theory and Practice* (3rd ed.). Boston: Allyn and Bacon. This book has provided a comprehensive overview of multicultural education for over a decade.

Cushner, K., McClelland, A., and Safford, P. (1996). *Human Diversity in Education: An Integrative Approach* (2nd ed.). New York: McGraw-Hill. This book gives a thorough presentation of the issues surrounding multicultural education in the broadest sense and further develops sensitivity to problems inherent in intercultural interaction in schools through didactic presentation, case studies, and critical incidents.

Friend, M., and Bursuck, W. (1999). *Including Students with Special Needs.* (2nd ed.). Boston: Allyn and Bacon. A very readable textbook that provides classroom teachers with a thorough and practical guide for working with special-needs students.

Garcia, R. (1992). *Teaching in a Pluralistic Society: Concepts, Models, and Strategies.* New York: HarperCollins. This book provides teachers with down-to-earth advice on how to teach in multicultural classrooms.

Means, B., Chelemer, C., and Knapp, M. S. (1991). *Teaching Advanced Skills to At-Risk Students: Views from Research and Practice.* San Francisco: Jossey-Bass. This book gives an excellent, detailed explanation about how to teach high-level, complex goals to at-risk students. Strategies for language arts and mathematics at both elementary and secondary levels are described.

Oakes, J., and Lipton, M. (1999). *Teaching to Change the World.* New York: McGraw-Hill. An excellent book on how teachers can address issues of inclusion and diversity. The authors provide a careful analysis of the education received by most poor and minority students today, and they make a passionate plea for change while offering concrete things beginning teachers can do.

Tomlinson, C. A. (1999). *The Differentiated Classroom: Responding to the Needs of All Learners.* Alexandria, VA: Association for Supervision and Curriculum Development. A book specifically for teachers that provides and explains real-life examples of how they can tailor and differentiate instruction to meet the needs of today's diverse student population.

## *Reflection & Portfolio*

During your first year of teaching, you have been assigned to a high school interdisciplinary team. With one other teacher, you are responsible for teaching literature, writing, and history to a group of forty-seven ninth graders. You meet with your student in 80-minute blocks of time three times a week.

You like this assignment, but it presents you with some real challenges. Students in your classroom are about equally mixed among three racial and ethnic groups. In the larger community, these groups have traditionally *not* gotten along very well with each other. In addition, three of your students have been diagnosed as having behavior disorders; two have learning disabilities; and one is physically disabled.

The major problem is that the students just don't seem to get long with one another. Students from the three racial and ethnic groups hang out mostly with members of their own group. It's not that they are impolite to one another; they simply ignore anyone outside their own group. Some students make fun of the students with behavior disorders from time to time. Although things are not out of control from a classroom management perspective, the overall climate is not positive. It is not the type of learning environment you want for your classroom.

What would you do to make the learning environment more productive and to help students in your group get along better? Where would you start? Which of your actions would involve instruction? Group development? Are there outside resources that you might call upon? Write a reflective essay for your portfolio on this problem and then compare what you write to what the experienced teachers below have said.

### *Ron Mosely*

I definitely would tackle this problem through instruction. I would start immediately using cooperative learning groups for all aspects of instruction. I would make sure that each group had representatives from the three racial and ethnic groups and that each group had one of the special-needs students. I would make sure that all assignments were set up in such a way that students had to work together and each student's success was tied to the group's accomplishments. It is only through this type of real-life interaction and cooperation that the biases and animosities that students hold for each other can be changed.

I would also teach a number of lessons aimed at showing each of the racial and ethnic groups in a very positive light and how disabled persons have made important contributions to our society. Hopefully, this would break down some of the stereotypes that students often hold about individuals who are different from themselves.

### *Cassandra Garcia*

This is the type of situation that demands action on two fronts, one short-term, the other more long-term. For the short term, I would have some of the special education and counseling personnel provide human relations training for students in the class. I would want them to emphasize how to get along with one another, how to communicate in positive ways, and how to resolve conflict situations without resorting to anger or force. I would also like them to provide students with experiences through which they would get to know each other on a personal level. I think this would help students listen to each other a little better and display less indifference toward one another.

On a longer-term basis, I would work to establish an environment of trust between the students and myself and among the various groups of students. I would use "classroom meetings" to help students discuss their problems and differences. I know that it will take a long time to develop the type of learning environment I envision. I will have to remain patient and to expect many setbacks along the way.

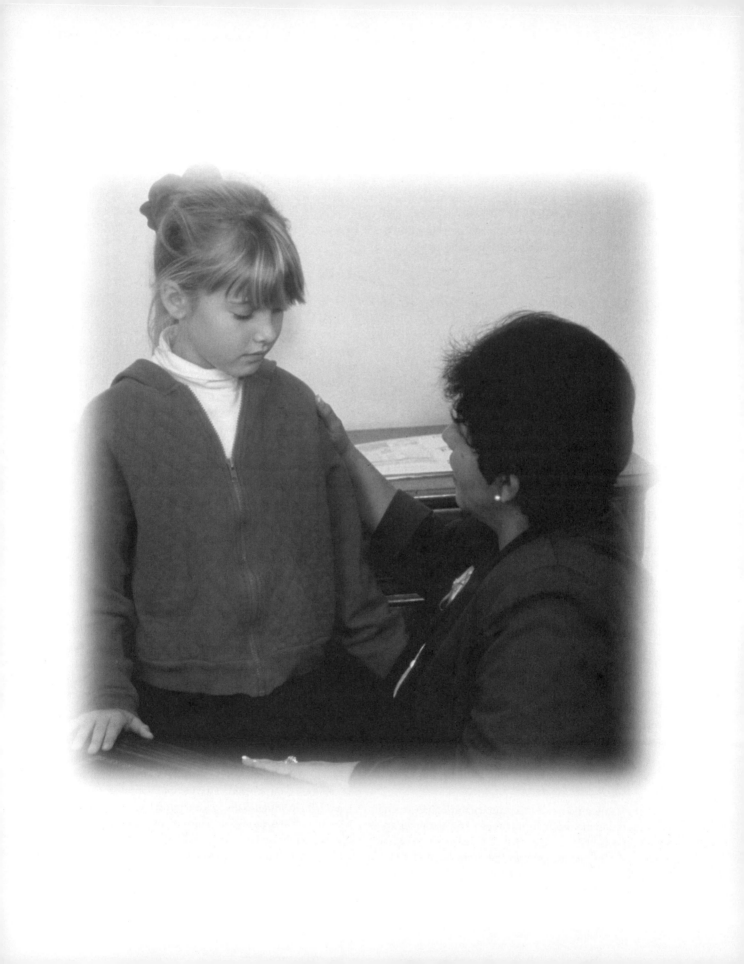

# Chapter Five

# Classroom Management

## Reflecting on **Classroom Management**

Beginning teachers report that the most difficult aspect of their first years of teaching is classroom management. They worry about it; they even have recurring nightmares about this issue. Before you read this chapter, reflect a bit about your own experiences with this topic as a student. What stands out in your mind about the ways your teachers managed their classrooms?

*Think about those who were strong disciplinarians and very strict. What did they do in regard to classroom management? How did you respond to this type of teacher and classroom? How did other students respond? What were the advantages of this type of management? Disadvantages?*

*Now think about teachers who were very lax. What did they do in regard to classroom management? How did you respond to this type of teacher and classroom? How did other students respond? What were the advantages of this type of management? Disadvantages?*

*Finally, write down the kind of classroom manager you want to be. Will you be strict? Lax? Friendly? What about your students? Do you want them to behave because you say they should? Or have you thought about helping your students develop self-discipline?*

**Effective classroom management exists within the context of democratic learning communities**

When teachers talk about the most difficult problems they experienced in their first years of teaching, they mention **classroom management** and discipline most often. Although a rich knowledge base on classroom management has been developed, beginning and student teachers continue to feel insecure about managing their first classrooms, and they spend many sleepless nights worrying about this issue.

Many of these anxieties are, in fact, similar to the anxieties experienced by people in any field when they are asked to assume positions of leadership and to exert influence for the first time. Nonetheless, gaining a repertoire of basic classroom management understandings and skills will do much to reduce the anxiety that naturally accompanies one's first classroom assignment. Describing the important concepts and skills associated with classroom management is the aim of this chapter. The first section of the chapter builds on the conceptual frameworks introduced in Chapter 3 and then presents a sampling of key research studies from the classroom management literature. In the final section of the chapter are specific and concrete procedures beginning teachers can use as they prepare for effective classroom management within the context of a democratic learning community.

## 🍎 *Perspective on Classroom Management*

**Effective teachers have a repertoire of management strategies to be used as situations dictate.**

**There is more than one perspective on effective classroom management.**

Although this chapter has a point of view, as you will discover, it also is eclectic in regard to the specific classroom management procedures. For example, you will find procedures that have grown out of the research that shows how effective management is connected to teachers' abilities to be "with it," to use effective instructional strategies, and to make lessons interesting for their students. At the same time, the shortcomings of this perspective are described, and approaches stemming from child-centered theorists are also presented for consideration. Multiple perspectives and approaches are provided because they exist in today's schools, and as beginning teachers, you will not always be free to choose the approach you think best. Some schools, for instance, will have a very definite behavioral approach to classroom management; all teachers will be expected to develop rules and procedures in their classrooms consistent with this approach. Other schools will foster more humanistic, child-centered approaches to classroom management. Finally, as is the case with most aspects of teaching, the most effective classroom managers are those with a repertoire of strategies and approaches that can be used with students as particular situations dictate.

Many of the ideas for understanding classroom management were presented in previous chapters and need only brief mention here. For example, the idea that the teacher's biggest job is to develop a democratic learning community where all students are valued, respect one another, and are motivated to work together remains central for thinking about classroom management. The same is true for the idea that good classroom management requires teachers who can create authentic relationships with their students and develop an "ethic of care." There are, however, two more ideas that can provide additional perspective on effective classroom management.

First, *classroom management is possibly the most important challenge facing beginning teachers.* A new teacher's reputation among colleagues, school authorities, and students will be strongly influenced by his or her ability to perform the managerial functions of teaching, particularly creating an orderly learning environment and dealing with student behavior. Sometimes, beginning teachers think this is unfair and argue that schools and principals put too much emphasis on order as contrasted to learning. Perhaps it is unfair. Nonetheless, a teacher's leadership ability is tested in the arena of man-

*Classroom management is one of the most important challenges beginning teachers face.*

agement and discipline, and when something goes wrong, it is known more quickly than other aspects of teaching. More important, without adequate management, little else can occur. Dunkin and Biddle (1974) pointed out this important fact over two decades ago when they wrote that "management of the classroom . . . forms a necessary condition for cognitive learning; and if the teacher cannot solve problems in this sphere, we can give the rest of teaching away" (p. 135).

Second, *classroom management and instruction are highly interrelated.* An important perspective stressed in the first part of this chapter is what Brophy and Putnam (1979), Evertson and Emmer (1998), and Putnam and Burke (1996) have called **preventive management.** This perspective has dominated views about classroom management for over two decades. Classroom management is not an end in itself; it is merely one part of a teacher's overall leadership role. In this regard, classroom management cannot be separated from the other aspects of teaching. For example, when teachers plan carefully for lessons, as described in Chapter 2, they are doing much to ensure good classroom management. When teachers plan ways to allocate time to various learning activities or consider how space should be used in the classroom, they are again making important decisions that will affect classroom management. Similarly, all the strategies for building productive learning communities described in Chapter 3, such as helping the classroom develop as a group, attending to student motivation, and facilitating honest and open discourse, are also important components of classroom management.

Further, each teaching model or strategy a teacher chooses to use places its own demands on the management system and influences the behaviors of both teachers and learners. The instructional tasks associated with giving a lecture, for example, call for behaviors on the part of students that are different from those needed for tasks associated with learning a new skill. Similarly, behavioral demands for students working together in groups are different from those required for working alone on a seatwork assignment. Instructional tasks are integrally related not only to the problem of instruction but also to the problems of order and management. Teachers who plan appropriate classroom activities and tasks, who make wise decisions about time and space allocation, and who have a sufficient repertoire of instructional strategies will be building a learning environment that secures student cooperation on learning tasks and minimizes discipline problems.

Finally, alternative perspectives to the preventive approach exist and stem mainly from the work of child-centered theorists such as John Dewey and the Swiss educator

**Preventive management is the perspective that many classroom problems can be solved through good planning, interesting and relevant lessons, and effective teaching.**

✔ **Check for Understanding**

- Why do most people consider classroom management the most important challenge for beginning teachers?

- How is classroom management linked to other aspects of instruction?

- What examples can you give to demonstrate that order in the classroom is considered so important by most educators?

"I'D LIKE TO OVERWHELM THEM WITH INSTRUCTIONAL EXCELLENCE, BUT I'M NOT ABOVE WINNING THROUGH INTIMIDATION."

SOURCE: Martha F. Campbell, Phi Delta Kappan

**The child-centered perspective to classroom management is critical of approaches aimed at controlling students.**

Johann Pestalozzi, as well as an array of twentieth-century humanistic reformers such as Abraham Maslow and Carl Rogers. This perspective is critical of processes aimed at controlling students and instead focuses on the basic goodness of children and youth. Educators holding this perspective argue for treating children in schools humanely and respectfully and for creating learning communities characterized by what Nel Noddings (1992, 1998) has called an "ethic of care." These settings assist student development not only academically but also socially and emotionally.

## 🍎 Theoretical and Empirical Support

Three traditions have guided the theory and research on classroom management: reinforcement theory, ecological and group processes perspective, and child-centered views. This section is organized around these three perspectives.

### Reinforcement Theory

You read in Chapter 3 how **reinforcement** and behavioral theory dominated thinking about motivation in the early part of the twentieth century. This perspective has also had a strong influence on classroom management. Remember that reinforcement theory emphasizes the centrality of external events in directing behavior and the importance of positive and negative reinforcers (Skinner, 1956). Teachers who apply behavioral principles to classroom management use rewards in the form of grades, praise, and privileges to reinforce desired behavior and punishments, such as bad grades, reprimands, and loss of privileges, to discourage undesirable tendencies or actions.

Many times this approach has focused on the individual student and has sought to understand the causes of a particular student's classroom behavior rather than causes that may stem from the features of the classroom group or the teaching situation.

This tradition has been led mainly by clinical and counseling psychologists, such as Dreikurs (1968), and Dreikurs and Grey (1968) and by behavioral psychologists and those who apply behavioral theory, such as Canter and Canter (1976, 1997). Their practice has focused on such psychological causes as insecurity, need for attention, anxiety, and lack of self-discipline as well as on sociological causes such as parent overprotection, bad peer relationships, or disadvantaged backgrounds. Recommendations to teachers stemming from this research normally emphasize ways to help individual students through counseling or behavior modification and show less concern for managing the classroom group. Behavior modification programs, the use of token economies, and assertive discipline (Alschuler, 1968; Cohen, 1973; Cantor & Cantor, 1976, 1997) are formal programs that have developed based on reinforcement theory and have been used widely in classrooms during the past thirty years. Although many of the behavioral-oriented programs have shortcomings, they nonetheless are found in many schools today, and beginning teachers should be knowledgeable about them. These will be described later in the chapter.

> Behavioral approaches often emphasize how to control the behavior of individual students as compared to considering the classroom group and overall learning situation.

## Classroom Ecology and Group Processes

In Chapter 3, several ideas were described that help explain classroom life from an ecological perspective, and the work of such researchers as Barker (1968), Doyle (1979, 1986), Gump (1967), and Kounin (1970) were cited. The ecological perspective addresses directly the problem of classroom control and group management procedures.

Classroom management researchers in this tradition study the way student cooperation and involvement is achieved so that important learning activities can be accomplished. The major function of the teacher from this point of view is to plan and orchestrate well-conceived group activities that flow smoothly. Misbehavior of students is conceived as actions that disrupt this activity flow. Examples of disruptions include students talking when quiet is desired, students not working on a seatwork assignment the teacher has given, or students getting out of their seats at inappropriate times. Teacher interventions in regard to student misbehavior, as will be described later, should be quick, often minor, and aimed at keeping the flow of learning activities and tasks on the right track.

> Researchers in the ecology and group process tradition are interested in how student cooperation and involvement are achieved in group settings.

**Kounin's Research.** The classic piece of research in the **classroom ecology** tradition was done in the late 1960s by Jacob Kounin and his colleagues. After several years of trying to understand classroom discipline, Kounin started to consider that maybe it was not the way teachers disciplined their students that was important but instead the way the classroom as a group was managed that made a difference. Kounin's work has greatly influenced the way we think about classroom management. His classic study is described in the Research Summary for this chapter. Many of Kounin's research findings are discussed in more detail later in the chapter.

**Doyle and Carter's Research.** Other researchers of particular interest who have used the ecological framework to guide their research are Walter Doyle and Kathy Carter (1984) at the University of Arizona. They were interested in how specific academic tasks are connected to student involvement and classroom management. To explore this topic,

# What Do Teachers Do to Create Well-Managed Classrooms?

*Kounin, J. S.* (1970). *Discipline and group management in classrooms.* New York: Holt, Rinehart & Winston.

The most challenging aspect of teachers' work is developing and maintaining a well-managed classroom. This challenge has led many researchers to examine how effective teachers manage their classrooms. The interesting result that stems from all this research is that good classroom managers actually prevent problems from occurring through the way they plan for and pace their lessons and the means they use to nip misbehavior in the bud. The classic study on this topic was done by Jacob Kounin in the 1960s.

**Problem and Approach:** After several years of trying to understand discipline in classrooms, Jacob Kounin started to consider that perhaps the key was not so much the way teachers disciplined individual students but, instead, the way they managed the whole classroom group. So, he decided to study group management. This is an interesting and important

study, because Kounin was one of the first researchers to go directly into classrooms and observe exactly what was going on. His study was also one of the first to use a video camera as an observation tool.

**Sample:** The sample of Kounin's study reported here consisted of forty-nine teachers and their students in upper elementary classrooms.

**Procedures:** Kounin developed elaborate procedures for observing classrooms, including videotaping teacher and student interaction and transcript analysis. Many variables were measured in the complete study. Here, only a few of the more important variables are described.

**Dependent Variables:** For Kounin, managerial success was demonstrated by classrooms in which work involvement was high and student deviancy was low.

1. Work involvement fell into three categories: (a) definitely doing the assigned work, (b) probably doing the assigned work, and (c) definitely not doing the assigned work.

2. Deviancy consisted of a three-category scheme: (a) student not misbehaving, (b) student mildly misbehaving, and (c) student engaging in serious misbehavior.

**Contextual Variables:** Kounin observed two types of learning activities: recitations and seatwork.

**Table 5.1** *Correlation of Selected Teacher Management Behaviors and Children's Behavior in Recitation and Seatwork Settings\**

| Dependent Variable | Recitation | | Seatwork | |
| --- | --- | --- | --- | --- |
| | Work Involvement | Freedom from Deviancy | Work Involvement | Freedom from Deviancy |
| Momentum | .656 | .641 | .198 | .490 |
| With-itness | .615 | .531 | .307 | .509 |
| Smoothness | .601 | .489 | .382 | .421 |
| Group alerting | .603 | .442 | .234 | .290 |
| Accountability | .494 | .385 | .002 | −.035 |
| Overlappingness | .460 | .362 | .259 | .379 |
| Challenge arousal | .372 | .325 | .308 | .371 |
| Overall variety and challenge | .217 | .099 | .449 | .194 |
| Class size (Range = 21–39) | −.279 | −.258 | −.152 | −.249 |

\*N = 49 classrooms (correlation of .276 is significant at .05 level).
Source: After Kounin (1970), p. 169.

**Independent Variables:** Kounin conceptualized eight different variables for describing the group management behavior of teachers.

1. *"With-itness."* The ability to accurately spot deviant behavior, almost before it starts.
2. *"Overlappingness."* The ability to spot and deal with deviant behavior while going right on with the lesson.
3. *Smoothness.* Absence of behaviors that interupt the flow of activities.
4. *Momentum.* Absence of behaviors that slow down lesson pacing.
5. *Group alerting.* Techniques used by teachers to keep noninvolved students attending and forewarned of forthcoming events.
6. *Accountability.* Techniques used by teachers to keep students accountable for their performance.
7. *Challenge arousal.* Techniques used by teachers to keep students involved and enthusiastic.
8. *Variety.* The degree to which various aspects of lessons differed.

**Pointers for Reading Research:** Up to this point in presenting statistics, researchers depended on mean scores and used *t* tests or analysis of variance (*f* tests) to see if mean scores between two groups were significant. To understand Kounin's study, a new statistic—the *correlation coefficient*, described in the Resource Handbook section on understanding research—needs to be reviewed. Remember, correlation refers to the extent of a relationship that exists between pairs of measures. The coefficient can range from +1.00 through .00

to −1.00. The sign does not have the traditional mathematical meaning. Instead, a plus sign represents a positive relationship, a minus sign a negative relationship. A .00 means no relationship exists, +1.00 means a perfect relationship exists, and −1.00 means a reverse relationship exists. Correlations can be tested for significance just as mean scores can.

**Results:** Table 5.1 shows the correlations Kounin found between various aspects of teacher management behavior and children's behavior during recitation and seatwork.

**Discussion and Implications:** Kounin's research provides a rich source of ideas for how teachers can approach the problem of classroom management. Table 5.1 shows that with-itness, momentum, overlappingness, smoothness, and group alerting all appear to increase student work involvement, particularly during recitation lessons. Similarly, with-itness and momentum decrease student deviancy. With-itness also decreases student deviancy in seatwork lessons, whereas variety appears to be the major behavior that helps promote work involvement in seatwork.

Note that all the relationships in the table, although not significant, are positive, except for the negative correlation coefficients for the relationships between accountability and freedom from deviancy during seatwork and those associated with class size. These negative correlations are small and what they mean essentially is that no relationships were found between those variables.

The implications for teacher behavior from Kounin's work are great and are described in some detail in the next section of this chapter.

they observed one junior high school English teacher and the students in three of her classes in a middle-class suburban school for a period of almost three months. The teacher, Mrs. Dee, was selected for study because she was an experienced teacher and she was considered to have considerable expertise in teaching writing to students.

This work is informative to the topic of classroom management because the researchers found that students had considerable influence over the task demands of the classroom. For instance, over a period of time Mrs. Dee assigned students a variety of major and minor writing tasks. Examples include writing an essay comparing Christmas in Truman Capote's story "A Christmas Memory" with Christmas today, writing a short story report, and writing descriptive paragraphs with illustrations. In some of the writing tasks, Mrs. Dee tried to encourage student creativity and self-direction, and to do that, she left the assignments somewhat open-ended. From detailed observations of Mrs. Dee's classroom, Doyle and Carter found, however, that students pressed to reduce the amount of self-direction and independent judgment in some of

Students have been shown to disrupt instruction by pretending to be confused.

the writing assignments. Students, even those considered very bright, used tactics such as asking questions or feigning confusion to force Mrs. Dee to become more and more concise and explicit. In other words, the students influenced the teacher to do more and more of their thinking.

Doyle and Carter also found that by asking questions about content and procedures, students, in addition to changing the assignment, also slowed down the pace of classroom activities. This was done to get an assignment postponed or just to use up class time. When Mrs. Dee refused to answer some of the students' delaying questions, things seemed only to get worse. Here is a direct quote from a report of what the researchers observed:

> Some students became quite adamant in their demands. . . . On such occasions, order began to break down and the normal smoothness and momentum of the classes were reinstated only when the teacher provided the prompts and resources the students were requesting. The teacher was pushed, in other words, to choose between conditions for students' self-direction and preserving order in the classroom. (p. 146)

Mrs. Dee was an experienced enough teacher to know that order had to come first or everything else was lost.

## Effective Teaching Research

Some classroom management researchers have been influenced by both behavioral theory and the ecological orientation. These researchers strived in the 1970s and 1980s to identify the behaviors of effective teachers, meaning teachers who could consistently produce high student engagement with academic activities. They pursued this approach because, as you read in Chapter 2, strong relationships had been found between student engagement and student achievement.

This research, which has spread over thirty years, has been led by Edmund Emmers, Carolyn Evertson, and several of their colleagues. Like Kounin before them, teacher-effectiveness researchers found strong relationships between student on-task behavior and a number of teacher behaviors. Specifically, when effective classroom managers were compared to ineffective classroom managers, the following teacher behaviors were observed.

1. The more effective classroom managers had *procedures* that governed student talk, participation, and movement; turning in work; and what to do during downtime.
2. Laboratory and group activities in the effective managers' classrooms ran smoothly and efficiently. *Instructions were clear*, and student *misbehavior was handled* quickly.
3. Effective managers had very *clear work requirements* for students and monitored student progress carefully.
4. Effective managers gave *clear presentations and explanations*, and their directions about note taking were explicit.

The child-centered perspective on classroom management views the chief source of the problem as irrelevant curricula and overemphasis on quietude and uniformity.

The implications of this research, along with recommendations for teachers, will be discussed in more detail in the next section.

## Child-Centered Traditions

Finally, there is a theoretical and research tradition that provides an alternative to behavioral and preventive perspectives. Relying on theories of John Dewey and humanistic psychologists, Abraham Maslow and Carl Rogers, current researchers such as Nel Noddings, Jeannie Oakes, and George Noblit argue that behavioral-minded researchers have it all wrong. Developing smooth-running classrooms or making lessons interesting, they argue, are simplistic solutions to much more complex problems. They agree with the observation made by John Dewey many years ago:

> The chief source of the "problem of discipline" in schools is that . . . a premium is put on physical quietude, on silence, on rigid uniformity of posture and movement; upon a machine-like simulation of the attitudes of intelligent interest. The teachers' business is to hold the pupils up to these requirement and to punish the inevitable deviations which occur. (Dewey in Kohn, 1996, p. 7)

This perspective argues for child-centered rather than subject-centered classrooms. Misbehavior, according to Oakes and Lipton (1999), "follows from instruction that attempts to coerce students, even if it is for their own and society's good" (p. 249), or, according to Kohn (1996), from situations "where we 'manage' behavior and try to make students do what we want . . . (rather than) . . . help them become morally sophisticated people who think for themselves and care about others" (p. 62). Curriculum should *not* be prescribed by teachers but instead should aim at promoting students' development and at meeting students' social and emotional as well as academic needs.

Child-centered educators do not have a set of specific guidelines for achieving effective classroom management, nor do they offer recipes for teachers to follow. Instead, as Nel Noddings (1992) has written, "schools should be committed to a great moral purpose: to care for children so that they too will be prepared to care" (p. 65). Caring and developing democratic classrooms become the alternative to preventive management and behavioral control.

Research in this tradition is often qualitative and ethnographic. A study done by George Noblit (1992) characterizes this approach. Noblit and his colleagues studied how two experienced inner-city teachers (one white, the other African American) developed caring relationships with their students. Noblit and his colleagues spent one full day every week for over a year in these teachers' classrooms and conducted interviews with teachers and children in the school. The vignettes displayed in Figure 5.1 illustrate how these teachers dealt with problem students and what it meant to develop "caring relationships."

# 🍎 *Preparing for Effective Classroom Management*

This section focuses directly on procedures beginning teachers can use to ensure effective classroom management. It is organized around four major topics: preventive classroom management, managing inappropriate and disruptive behavior, exhibiting confidence, and working toward caring communities and self-discipline.

## Preventive Classroom Management

Many of the problems associated with student misbehavior are dealt with by effective teachers through preventive approaches. Much of this section is based on the original research emanating from Kounin's work, and effective teaching research. The ideas and procedures are introduced here and revisited in later chapters in regard to management demands of particular approaches to teaching.

✔ **Check for Understanding**

- What are the three major theories that have guided classroom management research practices? What are the advantages and disadvantages of each?

- How did research conducted by Kounin, and Doyle and Carter demonstrate that optimal learning is most likely achieved in an orderly classroom?

- Which teaching variables defined in Kounin's classroom management approach appear to relate positively to student participation and optimal learning?

- What specific teacher behaviors lead to the most effective classroom management, according to teacher effectiveness researchers?

- What are the major features of classroom management from the perspective of child-centered theorists? Contrast child-centered views with those of behaviorists.

**Figure 5.1**  *Vignettes from Noblit's Study of Caring Teachers*

### Robert's Story

Robert was a challenge from his first day in Martha's classroom. He was a pudgy boy who had spent the previous school year at a special school for youths with severe behavioral problems. During the two years prior to that he had continually been removed from classrooms for exhibiting "inappropriate and aggressive" behavior.

Martha invested herself in helping him. She waited daily at the classroom door to greet Robert, and she always told him goodbye in the afternoon. She spent a few moments every day talking with him about anything and everything, from TV shows to his mother. And she firmly insisted that he participate in classroom activities—especially cooperative learning groups with the other children.

Because of the attention she paid to him, Robert slowly began to realize that Martha was committed to him. By November Robert had become a marginally accepted and fairly productive member of this class. He was still ornery and still had small outbursts in class, but he responded to Martha and to the other students in much more positive ways. Not once was Robert sent to the principal or suspended, a dramatic reversal for him. Martha was able to help Robert become a more academically and socially competent person despite the stigma of being labeled behaviorally disordered.

What was significant about Martha's influence on Robert was her dogged determination that he be given the opportunities to succeed in school and to attain social competence. There were no magic tricks, no technical fixes—just consistent, day-in and day-out, hour-to-hour, even minute-to-minute reminders to Robert to complete his work and respect others. She simply refused to give up on him. Martha explained, "I have a tendency not to give up on anybody. It is my responsibility."

Martha encouraged and enhanced Robert's social and academic growth despite the system. He usually participated in classroom discussions and activities, seemed to enjoy coming to school (in fact, never missed a day!), and appeared to have made a few friends in the class, all of whom showed up for his birthday party. Martha and Robert's caring relationship set a new context for Robert as a student. And within that context he was able to improve both his behavior and his academic achievement.

### John's Story

John had been mainstreamed into Pam's class. He had the unique ability of disappearing during any classroom event. He was painfully shy and would physically hide from interaction with Pam by lining up behind other students, dropping his head and shoulders below desk level, and so on. During group work, John would not talk or participate in any way beyond sitting with the other students. Pam decided it was her responsibility to help John become more a part of the class. She demanded that he take part by sitting up, attending to assigned tasks, and working with other students.

In addition to being stern with him, Pam moved his desk close to hers and kept him near her during small-group activities. She found that touching him was a key to his attending, and over time his response to her touching changed from alarm to acceptance and finally to a perception of support. Her hand on his shoulder would allow him to speak and to participate—and, by the end of the year, eye contact with Pam was sufficient assurance for him. Pam was tough but supportive in her caring for John, and he reciprocated.

Like Martha with Robert, Pam recognized John's need to become part of the class and disregarded the implicit belief that special children really do not belong in a regular classroom. Her concern for him, her fidelity to him rather than to a mandated curricular objective, guided her search for appropriate strategies to ensure his participation and inclusion in the class. Their relationship made the classroom a safe and nurturing environment for John and led him to take part in classroom activities and to complete academic work.

SOURCE: Adapted from Noblit (1992)

*Investing in kids*

**Establishing Rules and Procedures.** In classrooms, as in most other settings where groups of people interact, a large percentage of potential problems and disruptions can be prevented by planning rules and procedures beforehand. To understand the truth of this statement, think for a moment about the varied experiences you have had in non-school settings where fairly large numbers of people come together. Examples most people think about include driving a car during rush hour in a large city, attending a football game, going to Disneyland, or buying tickets for a movie or play. In all these instances, established rules and procedures indicated by traffic lights and queuing stalls help people who do not even know each other to interact in regular, predictable ways. Rules such as "the right of way" and "no cutting in line" help people negotiate rather complex processes safely and efficiently.

Think for a moment about what happens when procedures or rules suddenly break down or disappear. You can probably recall an instance when a power outage caused traffic lights to stop working or when a large crowd arrived to buy tickets for an important game before the ticket sellers set up their queuing stalls. Recently, a teacher was in Detroit for a conference, and her return flight was booked on an airline that had merged with another airline on that particular day. When the two airlines combined their information systems, something went wrong with the computers. This computer malfunction made it impossible for the ticket agents to know who was on a particular flight and prevented them from issuing seat assignments. The result was bedlam, full of disruptive behavior. People were shoving each other as individuals tried to ensure a seat for themselves; passengers were yelling at each other and at the cabin crew. At one point, members of a normally well-disciplined crew were even speaking sharply to each other. The incident turned out okay, because a seat was found for everyone. The boarding process, however, did not proceed in the usual orderly, calm manner because some well-known procedures were suddenly unavailable.

Classrooms in some ways are similar to busy airports or busy intersections. They, too, require rules and procedures to govern important activities. As used here, **rules** are statements that specify the things students are expected to do and not do. Normally, rules are written down, made clear to students, and kept to a minimum. **Procedures,** on the other hand, are the ways of getting work and other activity accomplished. These are seldom written down, but effective classroom managers spend considerable time teaching procedures to students in the same way they teach academic matter. Student movement, student talk, and what to do with downtime are among the most important activities that require rules to govern behavior and procedures to make work flow efficiently.

> **Classroom rules specify what students are expected to do and what they are *not* to do.**

***Student Movement.*** In many secondary classrooms, such as a science laboratory, the art room, or the physical education facility, and in all elementary classrooms, students must move around to accomplish important learning activities. They need to obtain or put away materials, sharpen pencils, form small groups, and so on.

Effective classroom managers devise ways to make needed movements by students flow smoothly. They organize queuing and distribution procedures that are efficient; they establish rules that minimize disruptions and ensure safety. Examples of rules include limiting the number of students moving at any one time and specifying when to be seated. How to line up, move in the halls, and go unattended to the library are procedures that assist with student movement.

> **Classroom procedures are established by teachers for dealing with routine tasks and coordinating student talk and movement.**

***Student Talk.*** Students talking at inappropriate times or asking questions to slow down the pace of a lesson pose a classroom management problem that is among the most troublesome to teachers. This problem can vary in severity from a loud, generalized classroom clamor that disturbs the teacher next door to a single student talking to a neighbor when the teacher is explaining an important idea.

Effective classroom managers have a clear set of rules governing student talking. Most teachers prescribe when no talking is allowed (when the teacher is lecturing or explaining), when low talk is allowed and encouraged (during small-group work or seatwork), and when anything goes (during recess and parties). Effective classroom managers also have procedures that make classroom discourse more satisfying and productive, such as talking one at a time during a discussion, listening to other people's ideas, raising hands, and taking turns.

**Downtime occurs when lessons are completed early or when students are waiting for upcoming events, such as moving to another class or going home.**

*Downtime.* A third area of classroom life for which rules and procedures are required is during **downtime.** Sometimes, lessons are completed before a period is over, and it is inappropriate to start something new. Similarly, when students are doing seatwork, some finish before others. Waiting for a film projector to arrive for a scheduled film is another example of downtime.

Effective classroom managers devise rules and procedures to govern student talk and movement during these times. Examples include: "If you finish your work, you can get a book and engage in silent reading until the others have finished." "While we wait for the film to start, you can talk quietly to your neighbors, but you cannot move around the room." "If your work is complete, please see if your neighbor needs your help." Table 5.2 shows a set of rules developed by one teacher and her students. Notice that the list is fairly brief and that it contains examples of what students should do and of behaviors that are inappropriate.

**Teaching Rules and Procedures.** Rules and procedures are of little value unless participants learn and accept them. This requires active teaching. Effective classroom managers generally establish only a few rules and procedures, then teach them carefully to students and make them routine through their consistent use. In most classrooms, only a few rules are needed, but it is important for the teacher to make sure students understand the purpose of each rule and its moral or practical underpinnings. Concepts and ideas associated with rules have to be taught just the same as any other set of concepts and ideas. For instance, very young children can see the necessity for

**Table 5.2** *Sample Rules for Classrooms*

| Rule | Examples of Dos and Don'ts |
| --- | --- |
| • Be respectful of rights of others. | Treat everyone with respect.<br>No name calling or teasing. |
| • Be polite and helpful. | Say please.<br>No fighting. |
| • Respect the properties of others. | Keep room clean.<br>Don't use others' supplies. |
| • Listen to others' ideas. | Pay attention when others are talking.<br>Don't call out or interrupt. |
| • Follow all school rules. | Use your hall pass.<br>Don't run in the cafeteria. |

keeping talk low during downtime, when it is explained that loud talk disturbs students in neighboring classrooms who are still working. Taking turns strikes a chord with older students who have heightened concerns with issues of fairness and justice. Potential injury to self and others can be given as the reason movement in a science laboratory has to be done a certain way. One point of caution about teaching rules should be noted, however. When teachers are explaining rules, they must walk a rather thin line between providing explanations that are helpful to students and sounding patronizing or overly moralistic.

> **As with any other subject, rules and procedures must be taught to students.**

Most movement and discourse procedures have not only a practical dimension but also a skill dimension that must be taught, like academic skills. In Chapter 12, several strategies will be described for teaching students how to listen to other people's ideas and how to participate in discussions that can be used by beginning teachers to help manage student talking. Student movement skills also need to be taught. Even with college-age students, it takes instruction and two or three practices to make getting into a circle, a fishbowl formation, or small groups move smoothly. Effective classroom managers devote time in the first week or so of the school year to teaching rules and procedures and then provide periodic review as needed.

**Maintain Consistency.** Effective classroom managers are consistent in their enforcement of rules and their application of procedures. If they are not, any set of rules and procedures soon dissolves. For example, a teacher may have a rule for student movement that says, "When you are doing seatwork and I'm at my desk, only one student at a time can come for help." If a student is allowed to wait at the desk while a first student is being helped, soon several others will be there too. If this is an important procedure for the teacher, then whenever more than one student appears, he or she must be firmly reminded of the rule and asked to sit down. If it is not important to the teacher, it should not be set forth as a rule. Another example is if a teacher has a rule that no talking is allowed when he or she is giving a presentation or explaining important ideas or procedures. If two students are then allowed to whisper in the back of the room, even if they are not disturbing others, soon many students will follow suit. Similarly, if the teacher wants students to raise their hands before talking during a discussion and then allows a few students to blurt out whenever they please, the hand-raising rule is soon rendered ineffective.

> **Maintaining consistency in applying rules and procedures is an aspect of classroom management that is often troublesome for beginning teachers.**

It is sometimes difficult for beginning teachers to establish consistency for at least two reasons. One, rule breaking normally occurs when more than one event is going on simultaneously. A novice teacher cannot always maintain total awareness of the complex classroom environment and thus does not always see what is occurring. Two, it takes considerable energy and even personal courage to enforce rules consistently. Many beginning teachers find it easier and less threatening to ignore certain student behavior rather than to confront and deal with it. Experienced teachers know that avoiding a difficult situation only leads to more problems later.

**Preventing Deviant Behavior with Smoothness and Momentum.** Another dimension of preventive classroom management involves pacing instructional events and maintaining appropriate **momentum.** The research by Doyle and Carter (1984) described how students can delay academic tasks, and Kounin's research (1970) pointed out the importance of keeping lessons going in a smooth fashion. Kounin also described how teachers themselves sometimes do things that interfere with the flow of activities. For example, a teacher might start an activity and then leave it in midair. Kounin labeled this

**A dangle is when a teacher starts an activity and then leaves it in midair.**

**A flip-flop occurs when a teacher starts an activity, then stops and starts another one, and then returns to the original activity.**

**Fragmentation occurs when a teacher breaks a learning activity into overly small units.**

**"Overdwelling" occurs when a teacher goes on and on after a subject or a set of instructions is clear to students.**

type of behavior a **dangle.** A dangle occurs, for example, when a teacher asks students to hand in their notes at the end of a lecture and then suddenly decides that he or she needs to explain one more point. Teachers also slow down lessons by doing what Kounin labeled **flip-flops.** A flip-flop is when an activity is started and then stopped while another is begun and then the original started again. A flip-flop occurs, for example, when a teacher tells students to get out their books and start reading silently, then interrupts the reading to explain a point, and then resumes the silent reading. Dangles and flip-flops interfere with the **smoothness** of classroom activities, cause confusion on the part of some students, and most important, present opportunities for noninvolved students to misbehave.

Kounin described two frequent types of lesson slow-down behaviors—**fragmentation** and **"overdwelling."** A teacher who goes on and on after instructions are clear to students is overdwelling. A teacher who breaks activities into overly small units, such as "sit up straight, get your papers out, pass them to the person in front, now pass them to the next person," and so on is fragmenting instructions. Slowing down momentum disrupts smoothness and gives uninvolved students opportunities to interrupt classroom activities. Table 5.3 summarizes and illustrates the common problems identified by Kounin that disrupt smoothness and momentum in lessons.

Minimizing disruptive and slow-down behaviors is difficult for beginning teachers to learn, as are many other effective management skills, because so many aspects of management are situational. Smoothness and momentum definitely vary with the nature of individual classes—what may be a dangle in one classroom may not be so in another, or what may be overdwelling with one group of students may be appropriate for another group.

**Orchestrating Classroom Activities During Unstable Periods.** Preventive classroom management also involves planning and orchestrating student behavior during unstable periods of the school day—periods of time when order is most difficult to achieve and maintain.

*Opening Class.* The beginning of class, whether it is the first few minutes of the morning in an elementary classroom or the beginning of a period in secondary schools, is an unstable time. Students are coming from other settings (their homes, the playground, another class) where a different set of behavioral norms apply. The new setting has different rules and procedures as well as friends who have not been seen since the previous day. The beginning of class is also a time in most schools in which several administrative tasks are required of teachers, such as taking roll and making announcements.

Effective classroom managers plan and execute procedures that help get things started quickly and surely. For example:

1. They greet their students at the door, extending welcomes to build positive feeling tones and to keep potential trouble outside the door.

**Table 5.3** *Common Problems in Maintaining Smoothness and Momentum*

| Problem | Definition |
| --- | --- |
| Dangle | Leaving a topic dangling to do something else. |
| Flip-flop | Starting and stopping an activity and then going back to it. |
| Fragmentation | Breaking instruction or activity into overly small segments. |
| Overdwelling | Going over and over something even after students understand it. |

2. They train student helpers to take the roll, read announcements, and perform other administrative tasks, so they can be free to start lessons.
3. They write instructions on the board or on newsprint charts so students can get started on lessons as soon as they come into the room.
4. They establish routine and ceremonial events that communicate to students that serious work is about to begin.

*Transitions.*  Citing research of Gump (1967, 1982) and Rosenshine (1980), Doyle (1986) said that "approximately 31 major **transitions** occur per day in elementary classrooms, and they account for approximately 15 percent of classroom time" (p. 406). There are fewer transitions in secondary classrooms, but they still are numerous and take considerable time. It is during transition periods (moving from whole group to small groups, changing from listening to seatwork, getting needed materials to do an assignment, getting ready to go to recess) when many disruptions occur. Learning to handle transitions is difficult for most beginning teachers. Prior planning and the use of cuing devices are two techniques that can help.

> **Transitions are the times during a lesson when the teacher is moving from one type of learning activity to another.**

Planning is crucial when it comes to managing transitions. Chapter 2 described how transitions must be planned just as carefully as any other instructional activity. At first, beginning teachers should conceive of each transition as a series of steps they want students to follow. These steps should be written down in note form and in some instances given to the students on the chalkboard or on newsprint charts. For example, making the transition from a whole-class lecture to seatwork might include the following steps:

*Step 1:* Put your lecture notes away and clear your desk.
*Step 2:* Make sure you have pencils and a copy of the worksheet being distributed by the row monitor.
*Step 3:* Begin your work.
*Step 4:* Raise your hand if you want me to help you.

As beginning teachers become more experienced with managing transitions, they will no longer need to list the steps for minor transitions and may instead rely on clear mental images of what is required.

**Cuing** and signaling systems are used by effective teachers to manage difficult transition periods. The best way to understand cuing is to think of it as an alerting device similar to the yellow light on a traffic signal or the "slow" sign on a curving road. Cues are used by teachers to alert students that they are about to change activities or tasks and to start getting ready. Here are some examples of cues.

- During a small-group activity, a teacher goes around to each group and announces, "You have five minutes before returning to the whole group."
- During a discussion activity, a teacher tells students, "We must end the discussion in a few minutes, but there will be time for three more comments."
- During a laboratory experiment, the teacher says, "We have been working for twenty minutes now, and you should be at least halfway done."
- In getting ready for a guest speaker, the teacher tells the class, "Our speaker will arrive in three minutes; let's straighten up the chairs and get ready to greet her."

Many teachers also develop a signal system for alerting students to a forthcoming transition or for helping them move through the steps of a transition smoothly. Signal systems are particularly effective with younger children and in classrooms where the activities are such that it is difficult to hear the teacher. The band instructor raising his or her baton is an example of a signal for students to get quiet and ready their instruments to play the first note. Figure 5.2 shows a set of hand signals developed by one

**Figure 5.2** *Examples of Signals for Communicating with Students*

**Rhythm or echo clapping** can be used to get attention of the students in the classroom. When the teacher claps four beats, the students respond with a two-clap echo, and this signals that all activity stops.

**Bell signaling** can be used to gain the attention of the students. Just a short ring will cue the students to stop all activities and listen (small hand bell).

**Light signaling** is often used by teachers and can be affective. The light switch is flicked once, quickly.

**Arm signals** can be used at times to gain the attention of students without having to use an audible signal. When children are in the hallway, lining up, or in the playground, the teacher raises an arm and this will cue the students to do the same and become quiet.

**Finger signals** can be used effectively in managing small groups, dismissing students, or conducting other tasks. When dismissing groups of students by areas, code the groups numerically and dismiss by signals.

**Looks** are often effective in gaining a student's attention. A quizzical or firm look may be all that is needed.

**Charts** can signal directions and important messages. Use a smiley face or sad face suspended from the ceiling. Flip to sad face when students' behavior is unacceptable; return to a smiley face when acceptable behavior occurs.

**Charts** that can tell students what to do when they finish work are very useful and assist students in becoming more independent and involved in purposeful activities. The ideas on these charts should be varied and changed frequently.

*(continued)*

**Figure 5.2** *Continued*

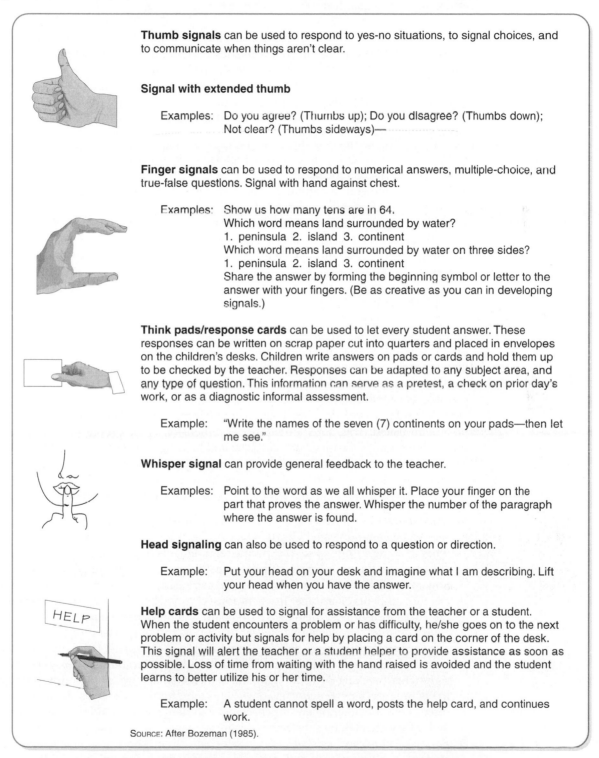

**Thumb signals** can be used to respond to yes-no situations, to signal choices, and to communicate when things aren't clear.

**Signal with extended thumb**

Examples:   Do you agree? (Thumbs up); Do you disagree? (Thumbs down); Not clear? (Thumbs sideways)—

**Finger signals** can be used to respond to numerical answers, multiple-choice, and true-false questions. Signal with hand against chest.

Examples:   Show us how many tens are in 64.
Which word means land surrounded by water?
1. peninsula  2. island  3. continent
Which word means land surrounded by water on three sides?
1. peninsula  2. island  3. continent
Share the answer by forming the beginning symbol or letter to the answer with your fingers. (Be as creative as you can in developing signals.)

**Think pads/response cards** can be used to let every student answer. These responses can be written on scrap paper cut into quarters and placed in envelopes on the children's desks. Children write answers on pads or cards and hold them up to be checked by the teacher. Responses can be adapted to any subject area, and any type of question. This information can serve as a pretest, a check on prior day's work, or as a diagnostic informal assessment.

Example:   "Write the names of the seven (7) continents on your pads—then let me see."

**Whisper signal** can provide general feedback to the teacher.

Examples:   Point to the word as we all whisper it. Place your finger on the part that proves the answer. Whisper the number of the paragraph where the answer is found.

**Head signaling** can also be used to respond to a question or direction.

Example:   Put your head on your desk and imagine what I am describing. Lift your head when you have the answer.

**Help cards** can be used to signal for assistance from the teacher or a student. When the student encounters a problem or has difficulty, he/she goes on to the next problem or activity but signals for help by placing a card on the corner of the desk. This signal will alert the teacher or a student helper to provide assistance as soon as possible. Loss of time from waiting with the hand raised is avoided and the student learns to better utilize his or her time.

Example:   A student cannot spell a word, posts the help card, and continues work.

Source: After Bozeman (1985).

experienced teacher to alert and assist his students with difficult transitions and to check their understanding of what is being taught.

*Closing Class.* The closing of class is also an unstable time in most classrooms. Sometimes the teacher is rushed to complete a lesson that has run over its allocated time; sometimes materials such as tests or papers must be collected; almost always students need to get their own personal belongings ready to move to another class, the lunchroom, or the bus. Effective teachers anticipate the potential management problems associated with closing class by incorporating the following procedures into their classroom organizational patterns:

- Leaving sufficient time to complete important closing activities, such as collecting books, papers, and the like.
- Making homework assignments early enough so that possible confusion can be cleared up before the last minute of class.
- Establishing routine procedures for collecting student work (such as placing a box by the door), so class time does not have to be used for this activity.
- Using alerting and cuing procedures to give students warning that the end of the class is approaching and that certain tasks need to be completed before they leave.
- Teaching older students that class will be dismissed by the teacher, not by the school bell or buzzer.

**Developing Student Accountability.** Every day teachers give their students assignments. Sometimes assignments are brief in duration and can be completed as seatwork. Others are more long term and require work at home. Most often, assignments provide students opportunities for practice, and this is an important aspect of the learning process, as later chapters will discuss. However, unless student work is handled consistently and unless students are held accountable for its completion, little learning will be accomplished. Therefore, an additional dimension of classroom management involves rules and procedures for managing and holding students accountable for their work. The following guidelines, which were adapted from the recommendations of Evertson and Emmer (1997) and Evertson, Emmer, Clements, and Worsham (1997), should be incorporated into the teachers' overall preventative management plan.

1. *Communicate assignments clearly and specify work requirements.* All assignments should be communicated clearly so all students have a full understanding about what they are supposed to do. Specific requirements must be clearly described, including such things as length, due date, neatness, spelling, grading procedures, and how missed work can be made up. Verbal explanations alone usually are not sufficient for students of any age. Teachers assist clarity when they describe assignments on worksheets or post them on a chalkboard or a newsprint chart.
2. *Have procedures for monitoring student work.* It is very important for teachers to be aware of student progress once assignments have been made. For seatwork, teachers can circulate around the room to check how things are going. For longer-term assignments, breaking down the assignment into smaller parts and requiring students to file progress reports every few days helps monitor their progress. Recitations and discussions are other means for checking if students understand their assignments and if they are making satisfactory progress.
3. *Be consistent in checking students' completed work.* In most classrooms the amount of student work is enormous. Teachers need procedures for collecting assignments, such as baskets or trays in front of the room, and others for returning corrected work in a timely fashion. Teachers also need a system for checking all work. Sometimes,

this can be accomplished by getting students to check each others' work. This is particularly appropriate for assignments for specific answers. Some assignments require careful reading by the teacher. All checking should be accomplished within a day or two after completion.

4. *Provide appropriate feedback on assignments.* Learning occurs when students receive feedback on their performance. All student work should be corrected and feedback should be given that is appropriate to the age of the students. This should occur as soon as possible after the assignment has been handed in. Often it is a good idea to spend class time going over assignments and discussing common errors or problems. Detailed guidelines for effective feedback are provided in Chapter 8.

## Managing Inappropriate and Disruptive Behavior

Preventive planning and skilled orchestration of classroom activities can prevent many of the management problems faced by beginning teachers, but not all. As in other social settings, every classroom will have a few students who will choose not to involve themselves in classroom activities and, instead, be disruptive forces. Disruptions can range from students talking when they are supposed to be listening to the teacher or refusing to go along with a small-group activity to yelling at the teacher and stomping out of the room. Managing disruptive behavior calls for a special set of understandings and a special repertoire of skills.

**The Causes of Misbehavior.**  Because beginning teachers have observed disruptive behavior in classrooms for many years as students, most can readily list the major causes of student misbehavior. These are the causes that appear on most lists: (1) students find schoolwork boring and irrelevant and try to escape it; (2) students' out of school lives (family or community) produce psychological and emotional problems that they play out in school; (3) students are imprisoned within schools that have authoritarian dispositions, which causes them to rebel; and (4) student rebelliousness and attention seeking are a part of the growing-up process.

Beginning teachers will want to think about the causes of inappropriate behavior, but they should beware of spending too much time on this type of analysis for two reasons. One, knowing the cause of student misbehavior, although helpful in analyzing the problem, does not necessarily lead to any change in that behavior. Two, dealing too much with psychological or sociological causes of misbehavior, particularly those that are not under the teacher's influence, can lead to acceptance and/or resignation. William Glasser (1986) made this point clearly:

> When a student is doing badly in school, we often point our fingers at a dismal home when the reason really is that the student does not find school satisfying enough for him to make an effort. There is no doubt that a student who cannot satisfy his needs at home may come to your class hungry for love and recognition and impatient that he can't quickly get what he wants. Rather than become discouraged, you should realize that if he can begin to satisfy his needs in your class, and if you are patient enough with his impatience, he has a good chance to learn enough to lead a productive life despite his home life. (p. 21)

**Dealing with Misbehavior.**  The general approach recommended to beginning teachers for dealing with disruptive behavior is not to search zealously for causes but, instead, to focus on the misbehavior itself and to find ways to change it, at least during the period of time the student is in the classroom. This approach emphasizes the importance of teachers accurately spotting misbehavior and making quick, precise interventions.

*Teachers who can spot disruptive student behavior quickly and accurately are called "with-it."*

***Being with It and Overlapping.*** You can all remember a teacher from your own school days who seemed to have "eyes in the back of her head." Kounin calls this skill "**with-itness.**" Teachers who are with it spot deviant behavior right away and are almost always accurate in identifying the student who is responsible. Teachers who lack this skill normally do not spot misbehavior early, and they often make mistakes when assigning blame.

"**Overlappingness**" is a second skill teachers use to spot and deal with deviant behavior. Overlapping means being able to spot a student acting inappropriately and inconspicuously deal with it so the lesson is not interrupted. Moving close to an offender is one overlapping tactic effective classroom managers use. Putting a hand on the shoulder of a student who is talking to his neighbor while continuing with instructions about how to do a project is another. Integrating a question intended to delay instruction or a "smart" remark right into an explanation about Edgar Allen Poe's syntax is a third example of overlappingness.

With-it and overlapping skills are difficult to learn, because they call for quick, accurate reading of classroom situations and the ability to perform several different teaching behaviors simultaneously. Once learned, however, they ensure more smoothly running lessons and classrooms.

***Responding Quickly to Desist Incidences.*** In classrooms, just as in any social setting, there are some participants who commit deviant acts. An example of deviant behavior on the freeway is driving ten or fifteen miles an hour above the speed limit; in church, it might be falling asleep during the sermon; in a library, it is talking loudly while others are trying to study. Those charged with the responsibility of enforcing rules and procedures may or may not choose to respond to each occurrence of deviancy. For example, most highway patrol officers will not stop a motorist for going seventy miles an hour on the freeway where the speed limit is sixty-five; most ministers don't confront a single parishioner who falls asleep; and those who talk very softly in libraries will probably not be reprimanded by the librarian. There are times, however, when those in charge will choose to respond to deviant behaviors. Kounin called this a **desist incident,** meaning an incident serious enough that, if not dealt with, will lead to further

*spotlight on Technology*

# Observing and Recording Student Behavior

One recommendation for teachers dealing with inappropriate classroom behavior is to become careful observers and recorders of student behavior. This aspect of behavior management is usually recommended by special education professionals and is very important in using positive and negative reinforcement. The premise is that recording student behavior can lead to seeing patterns of misbehavior and its relationship to certain events or times of day. This information can lead to a better understanding of a student's behavior and better use of reinforcement schedules.

One useful strategy for recording student behavior is an approach called ABC (antecedents-behaviors-consequences) analysis. Here is an example of ABC analysis provided by special educators Friend and Bursuck (1999):

Ms. Carlisle is observing Carlos. When the class is directed to form cooperative groups (**a**ntecedent), Carlos gets up from his seat and heads for the pencil sharpener (**b**ehavior). Ms. Carlisle tells Carlos to join the group (**c**onsequence). By keeping an ongoing ABC log of Carlos' behavior, Ms. Carlisle found out that whenever the class is transitioning from one activity to another, Carlos is likely to be off task. (p. 439)

Recording student behavior with so many other things going on is burdensome for the typical classroom teacher. However, several kinds of technology can be used to ease this burden somewhat. For instance, a file can be created on a laptop computer for keeping records and chronological ordering of ABC analysis. Event or wrist counters such as those used to keep score in golf can be used to keep track of particular student behaviors. For example, the teacher could click every time a student such as Carlos got out of his seat inappropriately. Similarly, a tape recorder can be used to record a student's inappropriate verbal behavior. This type of recording can then be used to discuss the behavior with the student and, when appropriate, with parents.

and widening management problems. The way desist incidents are identified and dealt with is the business of classroom management.

The way teachers respond to desist incidents can vary widely. Kounin (1970) identified several teacher **desist behaviors.** Three of these behaviors are illustrated in Table 5.4. Drawing on the work of Kounin, several different groups of procedures have been developed to deal with student misbehavior and to bring student attention back to a lesson once it has strayed. These include the Jones Model, the LEAST model, and Evertson

A desist incidence is a classroom occurrence serious enough that if not dealt with, it will lead to widening management problems.

**Table 5.4** *Examples of Teacher Desist Behaviors*

**Clarity**
The degree to which a teacher specifies what is wrong.

| | |
|---|---|
| Unclear desist: | "Stop that!" |
| Clear desist: | "Do not sharpen your pencil while I am talking." |

**Firmness**
The degree to which a teacher communicates "I mean it."

| | |
|---|---|
| Unfirm desist: | "Please don't do that." |
| Firm desist: | "I absolutely will not tolerate that from you!" |

**Roughness**
The degree to which a teacher expresses anger.

| | |
|---|---|
| Unrough desist: | "You shouldn't do that anymore." |
| Rough desist: | "When you do that, I get angry and I intend to punish you." |

**Table 5.5** *Three Models for Dealing with Student Misbehavior*

| Jones | Evertson and Emmer | LEAST |
|---|---|---|
| 1. Move close to where student is sitting. | 1. Ask student to stop the inappropriate behavior. Teacher maintains contact with child until appropriate behavior is correctly performed. | 1. **L**eave it alone. Is the behavior going to become troublesome? If not, ignore it. |
| 2. Make eye contact. | 2. Make eye contact with student until appropriate behavior returns. This is suitable when teacher is certain student knows what the correct response is. | 2. **E**nd the action indirectly. Distract student from the misbehavior by giving him or her something to do, preferably in a different area. |
| 3. Provide gentle pat on the shoulder, if needed. | 3. Restate or remind student of the correct rule or procedure. | 3. **A**ttend more fully. Get to know student better before you decide on a course of action. Is there something disturbing happening at home? Is there some kind of learning problem? |
| 4. Keep pace and momentum of lesson going. | 4. Ask student to identify the correct procedure. Give feedback if student does not understand it. | 4. **S**pell out directions. Remind student of what he or she should be doing. If necessary, also remind about consequences for failing to comply. |
| | 5. Impose the consequence or penalty of rule or procedure violation. Usually, the consequence for violating a procedure is simply to perform the procedure until it is correctly done. | 5. **T**rack the behavior. If this is a continuing problem, keep systematic records of the behavior and your actions to correct it. This can evolve into a contract with student. |
| | 6. Change the activity. Frequently, off-task behavior occurs when students are engaged too long in repetitive, boring tasks or in aimless recitations. Injecting variety is appropriate when off-task behavior spreads throughout a class. | |

and Emmer's model. The procedures for each model are summarized in Table 5.5. As you can see, the Jones model is primarily nonverbal and is useful for minor misbehavior. Procedures recommended by Evertson and Emmer concentrate on stopping inappropriate behaviors swiftly and making sure students understand what they are doing wrong. The LEAST model (an acronym for the steps teachers follow) includes procedures for minor misbehaviors as well as more serious problems that need to be handled

**Table 5.6** *Guidelines for Effective Praise*

| Effective Praise | Ineffective Praise |
|---|---|
| Is specific | Is global and general |
| Attends to students' accomplishments | Rewards mere participation |
| Helps students appreciate their accomplishments | Compares students with others |
| Attributes success to effort and ability | Attributes success to luck |
| Focuses attention on task-relevant behavior | Focuses attention on external authority |

over a period of time. Effective teachers create procedures that work for them, and these likely will include aspects of each of the models.

**Using Rewards.** A rather well-established principle in psychology is that when certain behaviors are *reinforced,* they tend to be repeated; conversely, behaviors that are not reinforced tend to decrease or disappear. This principle holds true for classrooms and provides teachers with one means for managing student behavior. The key to using **reinforcement principles** to influence student behavior obviously rests on the teacher's ability to (1) identify desirable behaviors, (2) identify appropriate reinforcers, and (3) skillfully use these reinforcers to strengthen and encourage desired behaviors.

**Praise.** The reinforcer most readily available to the classroom teacher is *praise.* However, there are important guidelines for the effective use of praise. For example, general praise, such as "great job," "oh, that's wonderful," or "excellent," is not very effective. Nor is insincere praise apt to have the desired effect. Jere Brophy reviewed a massive amount of research on the subject of praise and came up with the guidelines for teachers described in Table 5.6.

**Praise is the reward most readily available for teachers. However, praise must be used appropriately to be effective.**

**Rewards and Privileges.** Teachers can also encourage desirable behaviors through granting *rewards* and *privileges* to students. Rewards teachers have at their disposal include:

- Points for certain kinds of work or behavior that can enhance a student's grade.
- Symbols such as gold stars, happy faces, or certificates of accomplishment.
- Special honor rolls for academic work and social conduct.

Privileges that are at the command of most teachers to bestow include:

- Serving as a class leader or helper who takes notes to the office, collects or passes out papers, grades papers, runs the movie projector, and the like.
- Extra time for recess.
- Special time to work on a special individual project.
- Being excused from some required work.
- Free reading time.

**An overemphasis on external rewards can hinder student growth in self-management.**

A carefully designed system of rewards and privileges can help immensely in encouraging some types of behavior and reducing others. However, rewards and privileges will not solve all classroom management problems, and beginning teachers should be given two warnings. First, what is a reward or a privilege for some students will not be perceived as such by others. The age of students obviously is a factor; family, ethnic, and geographical background are others. Effective teachers generally involve their students in identifying rewards and privileges in order to ensure their effectiveness. Second, an overemphasis on extrinsic rewards can interfere with the teacher's efforts to promote academic work for its own sake and to help students practice and grow in self-discipline and management.

**Coercive Punishment and Penalties.** Rewards and privileges are used to reinforce and strengthen desirable behaviors. *Punishments* and *penalties* are used to discourage infractions of important rules and procedures. Socially acceptable punishments and penalties available to teachers are, in fact, rather limited and include:

- Taking points away for misbehavior that, in turn, affects students' grades.
- Making the student stay in from recess or after school for detention.
- Removing privileges.
- Expelling from class or sending a student to a counselor or administrator.

Beginning teachers should be careful about the types of punishments and penalties they establish. Researchers from the University of Texas offer the guidelines found in Figure 5.3.

✔ **Check for Understanding**

- What are the major steps teachers can take to prevent classroom management problems?

- What specific classroom times seem to lead to discipline problems? Why?

- What are some actions teachers commonly practice that can disrupt the momentum of lessons?

- What types of guidelines should a teacher clearly apply to ensure that students are accountable for their work? Do these approaches always work?

- What is the general approach for dealing with students who are disruptive? Do you agree? Why or why not?

- How would you justify the use of rewards in the classroom? What factors should a teacher consider to effectively use a reward system?

**Figure 5.3** *Guidelines for the Use of Penalties*

1. Use reductions in grade or score for assignment- or work-related behaviors such as missing or incomplete work.
2. Use a fine or demerit system to handle repeated violations of rules and procedures, particularly those involving willful refusal to comply with reasonable requests. Give them one warning, and if the behavior persists, assess a fine or demerit.
3. If you have a student who frequently receives penalties, try to set a more positive tone. Help the student formulate a plan to stop the inappropriate behavior.
4. Limit the use of penalties such as fines or checks to easily observable behaviors that represent major or chronic infractions of rules and procedures. The reason for this limitation is that penalty systems work only when they are used consistently. In order for this to take place, you must be able to detect the misbehavior when it occurs. If you cannot, you will find yourself constantly trying to catch students who misbehave.
5. Keep your classroom positive and supportive. Penalties should serve mainly as deterrents and should be used sparingly. Try to rely on rewards and personal encouragement to maintain good behavior.

Source: After Emmer et al. (1994), pp. 79–81.

## How Students Influence Classroom Behavior

Normally, we think about classroom management from the teacher's perspective and consider how teachers influence the learning environment and the management system. However, students also influence what goes on in the classroom, and effective teachers learn how to tailor their approach to classroom management to particular groups of students.

This idea was illustrated in a unique and interesting study conducted by Willis Copeland (1980). Copeland turned around the traditional research question, "What do teachers do to influence students?" and asked, "What do students do to influence the behaviors of their teachers?" Participants in Copeland's study were students in two middle-grade school classrooms—classrooms A and B—and two student teachers assigned to those classrooms, Beth and Al. Classroom A was in a racially and ethnically mixed school and had a large proportion of underachieving pupils. Classroom B was in a school in an affluent, upper-middle-class neighborhood and had highly motivated students. After two months of observing students and teachers in these classrooms, the student teachers switched assignments: Al in classroom A went to classroom B; Beth in classroom B went to classroom A. Again student and teacher behaviors were observed.

Copeland found that regardless of who the teacher was, Al or Beth, in classroom A, he or she adopted a more forceful questioning and management style toward the students. Similarly, in classroom B, regardless of whether Al or Beth was teaching, a more indirect questioning and responding management style was used. Copeland concluded from his study that behavior in classrooms is *bidirectional*, that is, behaviors of the participants are influenced not only by what the teacher does but also by what students do. In this situation, the academic abilities and development of the students themselves served to influence the student teachers' behaviors. Certain teacher behaviors (direct and forceful) seemed to work (at least were used) with the less-motivated students found in classroom A, while other behaviors (indirect) seemed to work and were used with the more-motivated students found in classroom B.

This is not to suggest that teachers should be mean or forceful with less-motivated students and more facilitating and indirect with those who are more motivated. Obviously, an important task for teachers with less-motivated students is find ways to increase their motivation. Nonetheless, this study is a reminder that teachers should have a rich repertoire of teaching and management strategies so they can tailor them to the needs of particular groups of students.

## 🍎 Classroom Management Programs

Over the past two decades, a spate of classroom management programs has been developed by psychologists, researchers, and educational practitioners. These programs stem from a specific theory or perspective and require schoolwide participation. Program creators develop materials to help teachers understand the program, and they provide training on how to use it. Though the effectiveness of particular programs has not always been studied, these programs nonetheless have been adopted and used widely. Four of these programs are described here to give beginning teachers a cursory understanding of what they may be confronted with in student teaching or their first teaching position.

### Traditional Programs Based on Reinforcement Theory

**Assertive Discipline.** Some classroom management and discipline programs have been built around the central concepts of the teacher acting in confident and assertive ways toward student misbehavior and administering predetermined penalties for infractions of classroom rules. During the past fifteen years, one of the more popular

**Assertive discipline is an approach to classroom management that emphasizes teachers insisting on appropriate student behavior and responding assertively to student infractions.**

programs based on these ideas has been developed by Lee Canter and Marlene Canter (1997). Called **assertive discipline,** the Canters' program maintains that teachers can gain control of their classrooms by insisting on appropriate student behavior and by responding assertively to student infractions.

Teachers (and sometimes whole schools) trained in assertive discipline start by developing a set of classroom and school rules deemed necessary for learning to occur. Consequences for disobedience are also clearly specified in advance. Students and their parents are then given clear explanations of these rules, and the consequences for infractions are explained. The Canters stress the importance of teachers following through with their rules, being consistent with administering consequences, and expecting support from parents.

*The Assertive Response Style.* At the center of the Canters' approach is their belief that teachers should respond to student misbehavior with an assertive style instead of responding passively or in hostile ways. Responding to student misbehavior with a rhetorical question such as, "Why are you doing that?" is an example of a passive style. A passive teacher, according to the Canters, is not using interpersonal influence effectively and appears wishy-washy to students. A hostile teacher, on the other hand, often responds angrily to student misbehavior and makes threats such as, "You'll be sorry you did that," or tries to produce guilt such as, "You should be ashamed of yourself." Passive and hostile styles are not effective, according to the Canters. Teachers who use a passive style are not communicating clearly to students what they expect, and the hostile style often produces meaningless threats that are difficult to enforce.

The assertive style calls for teachers to be very clear about their expectations and to respond to student misbehavior firmly and confidently. Teachers are counseled to specify the misbehaving student by name and to keep eye contact with the student. The Canters maintain that teachers should not accept excuses from misbehaving students. They argue that even though students may have inadequate parenting, special health problems, or great stress in their lives, these unfortunate circumstances should not excuse students from acting appropriately in the classroom or taking responsibility for their own behavior.

"The hardest part about goin' back to school is learning how to whisper again."

Reprinted with special permission of King Features Syndicate.

*Consequences.* Under the Canter approach, consequences are kept simple and are designed so their implementation will not cause severe disruption to ongoing instructional activities. Cangelosi (1988) reported one example of an assertive discipline program in a particular junior high school.

1. Each classroom teacher specifies for students the rules for classroom conduct.
2. The first time each day a student violates a rule during a particular class session, the teacher writes the student's name on a designated area of a chalkboard. The number of the rule that was violated is put next to the name. The teacher does not say anything.
3. The second time a student violates a rule (not necessarily the same rule), the number of that rule is added to the student's name on the board. Again, the teacher makes no other response to the off-task behavior.
4. Upon the third violation of the rules in the same class period, the student must leave the class and report to a detention room.
5. There are no penalties or requirements for students who have no more than one violation during any one class period.
6. Students with two violations are required to meet with the teacher after school to discuss the misbehavior and map out a plan for preventing recurrences.
7. The parent of students with three violations must appear at school to discuss the misbehavior and make plans for preventing recurrences (pp. 32 33).

Though the Canters' approach has been very popular, it also has its critics. Some teachers find it difficult to administer consequences without significantly disrupting their instructional programs. It takes time and energy, for instance, to write names on the chalkboard and to keep track of rule infractions. Also, some believe that the behavioristic approach behind assertive discipline puts too much emphasis on penalties and teacher-made rules and not enough emphasis on involving students in establishing their own classroom rules and learning how to be responsible for self-discipline. Finally, assertive discipline has not been evaluated thoroughly, and its effectiveness remains unclear.

**Dreikurs' Logical Consequences.** Chapter 3 provided a thorough description about how people's behavior can be attributed to goal-directed activity aimed at satisfying human motives and needs. In the 1960s, Dreikurs and his colleagues developed an approach to classroom discipline based on the idea that most student behavior, acceptable and unacceptable, stems from the fundamental need to belong and to feel worthwhile. According to Dreikurs, when the need to belong or feel worthwhile is frustrated through socially acceptable channels, students misbehave. Dreikurs categorized this misbehavior into four types: (1) attention getting, (2) power seeking, (3) revenge seeking, and (4) displays of inadequacy. Each instance requires a different response from the teacher. If a student is trying to get attention, the best thing to do, according to Dreikurs, is to ignore the behavior. If the student is trying to upstage or gain power over the teacher, the teacher should decline to get involved in the power struggle and try instead to find a way to give the student more influence and responsibility.

The Dreikurs approach is still used in some schools. Teachers trained in the approach learn how to identify the type of student misbehavior partly by getting in touch with their own emotional response. If the teacher feels "bugged," it is likely the student is seeking attention; if the teacher is getting angry, perhaps it is because the student is seeking power. Trained teachers also learn how to administer **logical consequences** according to the type of misguided goal behind the student's behavior. Logical consequences are punishments related directly to a misbehavior rather than the more general penalties of detention or reprimands used in many classrooms. Making a student who had written on the bathroom wall repaint the wall is a classic example of a logical consequence.

The Dreikurs approach emphasizes the importance of democratic classrooms in which students have a say in making the rules. Dreikurs views the logical consequence of misbehavior as more than just arbitrary punishment. He encourages teachers to administer logical consequences in a friendly and matter-of-fact manner, without elements of moral judgment. The long-range goal of this approach to discipline is to have students understand the reasons for their misbehavior and find ways to satisfy their self-worth and affiliation needs in socially acceptable ways.

The difficulties teachers have with the Dreikurs approach are twofold. Without extensive training, some find it difficult to develop the skill in identifying the specific motive that is causing the student to misbehave. Others find it difficult to identify logical consequences for many misbehaviors that occur in classrooms. For instance, what is the logical consequence for speaking out of turn? For sassing the teacher? For smoking in the halls or carrying a weapon to school? Nonetheless, some teachers who possess the necessary counseling skills have found the Dreikurs approach a powerful tool for dealing with disruptive students and helping them develop self-management skills.

## Programs That Aim Toward Self-Management and Community

There are also classroom management programs that have been built on premises stemming from humanistic psychology and child-centered, constructivist principles of teaching and learning.

**Glasser's Classroom Meeting.** Trained first as an engineer and later as a physician and clinical psychologist, William Glasser (1969, 1986, and 1992) has devoted much of his professional life to finding ways to make schools more satisfying and productive for students. Like Dreikurs, Glasser believes that most classroom problems stem from a failure to satisfy the basic need of students. In his early work, Glasser emphasized students' need for love and feelings of self-worth; in his later work, he expanded his list of basic needs to include survival and reproduction, belonging and love, power and influence, freedom and fun. Whereas Dreikurs proposes counseling and individual attention as a way to help students find ways to satisfy their needs, Glasser believes that school structures need to be modified. He proposed the **classroom meeting,** a regular 30-minute nonacademic period in which teachers and students discuss and find cooperative solutions to personal and behavior problems and in which students learn how to take responsibility for their own behavior and their personal and social development.

*Running Classroom Meetings.* A Glasser classroom meeting consists of six steps or phases (see Table 5.7). Note that for each phase there are specific things teachers need to do to make the meeting go successfully. In addition, there are several aspects of the total learning environment that need attention. When the classroom meeting is first being introduced and taught to students, the teacher keeps the learning environment tightly structured. More and more freedom can be given to students as they become successful in meetings. The teacher must maintain responsibility for ensuring partici-

**Table 5.7** *Syntax for the Glasser Classroom Meeting*

| Phase | Teacher Behavior |
|---|---|
| Phase 1: Establish the climate. | Using many of the strategies and procedures described in Chapter 3, the teacher establishes a climate in which all students feel free to participate and to share opinions and feedback. |
| Phase 2: Identify problems. | Teacher asks students to sit in a circle. Either the teacher or the students can bring up problems. Teacher should make sure that problems are described fully and in nonevaluative ways. Specific examples of the problems are encouraged. |
| Phase 3: Make value judgments. | After a specific problem has been identified, the teacher asks students to express their own values about the problem and the behaviors associated with it. |
| Phase 4: Identify courses of action. | Teacher asks students to suggest alternative behaviors or procedures that might help solve the problem and to agree on one to try out. |
| Phase 5: Make a public commitment. | Teachers asks students to make a public commitment to try out the new behaviors or procedures. |
| Phase 6: Provide follow-up and assessment | At a later meeting, the problem is again discussed to see how effectively it is being solved and whether commitments have been kept. |

pation, keeping student problem solving focused, and providing overall leadership. Usually, the teacher acts as discussion leader and asks students to sit in a circle during the classroom meetings. However, with younger students, participants sometimes sit on the floor, and with older students, the role of discussion leader is sometimes assumed by a student in the class.

*Suggestions for Starting and Running Classroom Meetings.* Effective execution of classroom meetings requires specific teacher actions before, during, and after the meeting. As much care and concern must go into planning and executing meetings as any other aspect of instruction.

*Planning.* In preparation for classroom meetings, teachers need to think through what they want the meeting to accomplish and have some problems ready for discussion in case none comes from students. Most important, overall planning must allow time for classroom meetings on a regular basis.

In elementary schools, many teachers who use classroom meetings start each day with this activity; others schedule it as a way to close each day; still others schedule classroom meetings on a weekly basis. In most middle and high schools, teachers schedule meetings less frequently, perhaps thirty minutes every other Friday, with special meetings if serious problems arise. The frequency of meetings is not as important as their regularity.

*Conducting the Meeting.* On the surface, the classroom meeting may look fairly simple and easy to conduct. In reality, it is very complex and calls for considerable skill on the part of the teacher. If a beginning teacher is in a school where classroom meetings

**Conducting a classroom meeting calls for considerable skill on the part of teachers. The rewards of this approach, however, are worth the effort.**

are common and students already understand their basic purposes and procedures, then the teacher can start meetings at the beginning of school. If not, then the recommendation is for beginning teachers to wait for a few weeks before introducing classroom meetings to students.

Most of the student and teacher skills needed for successful meetings are described elsewhere in *Learning to Teach*, particularly in Chapters 3 and 12. Some are repeated here, as they specifically relate to each phase of the classroom meeting.

1. *Establishing climate.* Before classroom meetings can be successful, the overall climate must be one that encourages participation in free and nonpunitive ways. Students also must be prepared in the appropriate mind-set to make meetings productive. Although classroom meetings can be used to build this kind of productive environment, some degree of trust must exist before meetings can be implemented. Many of the activities described in Chapter 3 are preludes to implementing classroom meetings.

2. *Identifying problems.* Students who have not been involved in classroom meetings need to be taught what constitutes a legitimate problem for the meeting. Problem-solving techniques can be taught, including giving students time to practice stating a problem, giving examples of a problem, and identifying the descriptive and value dimensions of a problem.

3. *Dealing with values.* The values surrounding most classroom behavior problems are very important, especially differences regarding the value of academic work. Put bluntly, some students do not value academic work as much as teachers do. At the same time, teachers may find an amazing similarity of values across racial, ethnic, and social-class lines regarding other aspects of classroom behavior. For example, most students, even at a very young age, see the moral and practical necessity of such rules as taking turns, listening, and showing respect to others. They also readily embrace most procedures that ensure safety and fairness. The classroom meeting can become an important forum for talking about value similarities and differences.

4. *Identifying alternative courses of action.* Except for very young children, most students can readily identify courses of action they, their teacher, or their classmates can take to resolve all kinds of classroom management problems. They know the reasons for rewarding desirable behavior and punishing disruptive behavior, and they also know the shortcomings of relying too heavily on these strategies. They even know what sort of alternative actions are available in classroom settings. During this phase of the classroom meeting, the teacher's primary role is to listen to alternative proposals, make sure everyone understands each one, and push for some type of consensus about which action students are willing to take. The teacher must also be clear and straightforward with students if a proposed action is definitely unacceptable, particularly if it goes against school policy. However, this does not exclude student efforts to get school policies changed.

5. *Making a public commitment.* A public commitment is nothing more than a promise by students, and in some instances the teacher, that certain attempts are going to be made to correct problem situations. Many teachers write these commitments on newsprint charts so that everyone in the class can remember them.

6. *Follow-up and assessment.* Once students have made a commitment to try out a new set of procedures and behaviors, it is very important that these commitments be followed and assessed. Specifically, teachers must remember the public commitments that were made and periodically come back to them in future classroom meetings. If commitments are not being kept or if the planned actions are not solving the problem, then additional time and energy must be given to the problem.

## The Caring Classroom

Finally, programs have been developed on constructivist, child-centered principles that aim at building threat-free learning communities and helping students make their own choices and develop self-management. These programs, advocated by reformers such as Kohn (1996), Noddings (1992), and Oakes and Lipton (1999), are more difficult to describe in a textbook than traditional classroom management programs. This is true because their developers emphasize no single alternative to more traditional approaches but instead argue that the alternatives are endless. Consistent with their perspective, constructivist, child-centered educators do not believe that their approach can be anchored in a set of simple recipes. However, they have enunciated principles for teachers to follow, such as those outlined by Kohn (1996):

- Act in ways that are socially just.
- Develop authentic relationships free of power and control.
- Allow students to construct moral meaning.
- Limit structures and procedures.
- Give students a say and have them solve problems together.

The meaning of teaching in socially just ways has been described by Oakes and Lipton (1999) as creating classrooms where teachers stand up for social justice and work to change the inequities that exist in the educational system. All talk and action in the classroom is aimed at understanding and working toward social justice. Here is what two teachers had to say about this perspective and its meaning for their approach to classroom management.

> I intend to break the cycle of an educational system that treats my current and future students as children who need to be controlled and "schooled." I intend to take advantage of my students' open-mindedness and susceptibility to instill in them a strong sense of social responsibility. My teaching means nothing if I am not leaving my students with unforgettable experiences and transformative dialogues through which they view themselves as conscious, competent participants in some larger reality—a community, which has the potential of being transformed only through their collaborative efforts. (Oakes & Lipton, p. 32)
>
> As a first-year teacher, I also cannot get discouraged if I am not able to create a socially just and democratic classroom in two weeks, or two months. The fact that the journey is a difficult one signifies its existence. I should keep this in mind and not get discouraged or overwhelmed. If you are passionately acting towards a just and transformative ideal, then you are a social justice advocate. (Oakes & Lipton, p. 33)

Developing authentic, caring relationships free of power and control is another principle that guides teachers in caring, child-centered classrooms. This means creating the type of learning community described in Chapter 3 in which teachers care for students and students care for each other in an atmosphere of participation and trust. These conditions can best be achieved if teachers limit the structure and procedures imposed on students. Kohn (1996), for example, says structures and restrictions should meet certain criteria. They are okay if they protect students, provide for flexibility, are developmentally appropriate, and lead to student involvement. They are inappropriate if they are simply to impose order or quiet voices, for adults only, or are developmentally inappropriate.

Finally, educators who argue for caring, child-centered classrooms have recommendations for dealing with disruptive and misbehaving students. Note the differences between Kohn's suggestions found in Table 5.8 and those described early in this chapter. Kohn's suggestions emphasize the importance of building a relationship, joining in mutual problem solving, and keeping punishments to a minimum.

### ✔ Check for Understanding

- What are the advantages and disadvantages of the assertive discipline approach in the classroom?

- How does Dreikurs explain misbehavior? In what ways do logical consequences teach a student to behave appropriately? Why do some teachers disagree with this approach?

- What teacher activities does Glasser's classroom meeting model require for successful classroom management? What factors contribute to a favorable meeting?

- What principles guide classroom management from a child-centered perspective? Do you think this approach will work? Why? Why not?

- Contrast Kohn's suggestion for dealing with disruptive behavior with the Canters' recommendations.

**Table 5.8** *Kohn's Ten Suggestions for Dealing with Disruptive or Misbehaving Students*

| | |
|---|---|
| Relationship | It is not possible to work with students who have done something wrong unless a trusting relationship has been developed. |
| Skills | Teachers need to help students develop the skills to solve problems and resolve conflicts. These would include listening skills and the ability to calm themselves and take another's point of view. |
| Diagnose | Teachers need to make sure they are accurately interpreting what is going on and are able to help students do their own analysis. |
| Question practices | Teachers need to look at their own practices and ask themselves if they are the cause of the misbehavior. |
| Maximize student involvement | Teachers need to be constantly on the lookout for ways to expand the role students play in making decisions. |
| Construct authentic solutions | Teachers and students need to develop real solutions to complex problems and not just a solution that can be done quickly. |
| Make restitution | Teachers should help students think about how they can make restitution and reparations for truly destructive actions. |
| Check back later | Teachers should encourage students to check back later to see if the solution and agreements are working. |
| Flexibility | Good problem solving for difficult situations requires flexibility about logistics and substance. |
| Minimize punitive impact | Sometimes there is no alternative to punishment. When that is the case, every effort should be made to minimize punishment through warm and regretful tones and confidence that problems eventually can be solved. |

Source: Kohn (1996), p. 47.

# 🍎 A Final Thought and Look to the Future

As with so many other aspects of teaching, approaches to classroom management are in a state of transition at the beginning of the twentieth-first century. What this means for a beginning teacher is that you will likely get your first job in a school where very traditional views of learning and classroom management prevail. Perhaps students will be treated as passive receptacles for teacher-constructed knowledge, and they will be expected to do what the adults in the school tell them to do. At the same time, many of you and others like you will have been influenced by a constructivist view of learning that holds that teachers should help students take active roles in constructing their own intellectual and moral meaning. This approach to teaching requires a different kind of classroom management system. It requires developing caring, learning communities in which students have a say in what they do and how they behave. It requires spending less time controlling students and more time helping them think for themselves and care for others. This will be the challenge of teaching and providing leadership for twenty-first-century classrooms.

## 🍎 Summary

### Perspective on Classroom Management

- Classroom management is not an end in itself but a part of a teacher's overall leadership role.
- Managerial and instructional aspects of teaching are highly interrelated and in real-life teaching cannot be clearly separated.
- Unless classroom management issues can be solved, the best teaching is wasted, thus making it possibly the most important challenge facing beginning teachers.

### Theoretical and Empirical Support

- A well-developed knowledge base on classroom management provides guidelines for successful group management as well as ways of dealing with disruptive students.
- A large portion of disruptive student behavior can be eliminated by using preventive classroom management measures, such as clear rules and procedures and carefully orchestrated learning activities.
- "With-itness," momentum, "overlappingness," smoothness, and group alerting all increase student work involvement and decrease off-task behavior and management problems.
- Effective managers have well-defined procedures that govern student talk and movement, make work requirements clear to students, and emphasize clear explanations.
- Researchers in the child-centered tradition study ways teachers develop threat free learning communities that allow students to make choices and develop self-management.

### Preparing for Effective Classroom Management

- Effective managers establish clear rules and procedures, teach these rules and procedures to students, and carefully

orchestrate classroom activities during such unstable periods as the beginning and end of class and transitions.
- Effective managers develop systems for holding students accountable for their academic work and classroom behavior.
- Regardless of planning and orchestration skills, teachers are still often faced with difficult or unmotivated students who choose to be disruptive forces rather than involve themselves in academic activity.
- Effective managers have intervention skills for dealing quickly with disruptive students in direct but fair ways.
- Teachers can encourage desirable behaviors by giving praise and granting rewards and punishments.
- Specific approaches to classroom management, such as assertive discipline, emphasize the importance of being clear about expectations and consistent in administering consequences.

### Classroom Management Programs

- In the long run, effective teachers find ways to reduce management and discipline problems by helping students learn self-management skills.
- As with other teaching functions, effective teachers develop an attitude of flexibility about classroom management, because they know that every class is different and plans, rules, and procedures must often be adjusted to particular circumstances.
- Although many aspects of thinking about classroom management can be learned from research, some of the complex skills of classroom orchestration will come only with extended practice and serious reflection.

##  Key Terms

| | | | |
|---|---|---|---|
| classroom management | downtime | overdwelling | desist behaviors |
| preventive management | momentum | transitions | reinforcement principles |
| reinforcement | dangle | cuing | assertive discipline |
| classroom ecology | flip-flop | with-itness | logical consequences |
| rules | smoothness | overlappingness | classroom meeting |
| procedures | fragmentation | desist incident | |

## 🍎 Books for the Professional

Emmer, E., Evertson, C., Clements, B., and Worsham, W. E. (1997). *Classroom Management for Secondary Teachers.* (4th ed.). Englewood Cliffs, N.J.: Prentice Hall.

Evertson, C., Emmer, E., Clements, B., and Worsham, M. (1997). *Classroom Management for Elementary Teachers.* (4th ed.). Englewood Cliffs, N.J.: Prentice Hall. These two volumes—one aimed at secondary teachers, the other at elementary teachers—describe in more detail many of the procedures and techniques described in this chapter. Growing out of a decade of research at the University of Texas, these books offer a comprehensive approach to classroom management from the perspective of teacher effectiveness. They stress the importance of teacher planning and organization as preventive management approaches.

Glasser, W. (1992). *The Quality School.* New York: Harper-Collins. Glasser's latest book extends earlier discussions about how to produce effective and satisfying classrooms to how to do the same thing schoolwide.

Glasser, W. (1986). *Control Theory in the Classroom.* New York: Harper & Row. Glasser's most recent work extends some of the basic ideas presented in *Schools Without Failure.* Most important are Glasser's recommendations for how schools can be restructured to provide more powerful settings for learning and how teachers can use the learning team and the cooperative learning strategies described in Chapter 11 of *Learning to Teach* to accomplish this restructuring.

Kohn, Alfie (1996). *Beyond Discipline: From Compliance to Community.* Alexandria, Va.: Association for Supervision and Curriculum Development. An excellent book describing how teachers can move from classroom management practices aimed at controlling and disciplining students to practices that build community and self-discipline.

Noddings, N. (1992). *The Challenge to Care in Schools: An Alternative Approach to Education.* New York: Teachers College Press. This book describes Nodding's ideas on how to develop classrooms and schools centered on the "ethic of caring," rather than on controlling.

Putnam, J., and Burke, J. B. (1992). *Organizing and Managing Classroom Learning.* New York: McGraw-Hill. This excellent book on classroom management for both elementary and secondary teachers shows how to set up and run a democratic classroom.

Weinstein, C. S., and Mignano, A. J., Jr. (1996). *Elementary Classroom Management: Lessons from Research and Practice.* (2nd ed.). New York: McGraw-Hill. This highly readable book on classroom management combines both the research and the wisdom of practice on this topic. It shows how various learning tasks make different demands on the management structure and how different management approaches are required.

## Reflection & Portfolio

# The Out-of-Control Classroom

A teacher in the school where you have just finished your student teaching has resigned at mid-year for personal reasons. The principal has asked if you would be willing to take her place until the end of the academic year. You are pleased to have been asked, but, you also know that the class has been completely out of control all fall. You have observed students in the class fighting with one another, and other teachers have told you that the teacher found them impossible to manage: they talk when they should be listening; they get up and move around the classroom regardless of what is going on; they are unruly and disrespectful. It is even rumored that this out-of-control situation is the reason behind the teacher's sudden departure. You know that if you take the position and are unsuccessful, your reputation and chances for future jobs will be ruined. Nonetheless, you decide that you can do it. But now you have to decide where to start and what to do.

Write a reflective essay about this situation that can be used in your portfolio to let others know about your overall views and approach to classroom management. You may wish to consider the following questions as you think through this problem: What would be your long-range goals for this group of students? What specific, short-term problems would you tackle first? Would you lean toward dealing with this situation using behavioral approaches? Or would you strive toward working toward self-management? When you have finished your portfolio entry, compare your views with those expressed by the two teachers below.

### Katherine Rims

"I have seen this type of out-of-control situation before, and it is difficult for any teacher to do anything about; it is particularly challenging for a beginner. I would take three immediate steps.

"First, I would set up an assertive management program. When kids are unruly and used to running the classroom, only a definite set of rules, an assertive response to misbehavior, and clearly defined consequences for misbehavior will bring this classroom back under the teacher's control. I would be firm without being mean. However, I would not allow a single transgression from expected behavior.

"A second action I would take is to talk to the principal and get her assurances that she would back me up if kids start challenging my authority, something that is likely to happen. Finally, I would write a letter to all the parents explaining my new classroom management system and encouraging them to support my efforts.

### David Morley

"I don't know all the reasons that this class has gotten out of control. However, I suspect three culprits—a curriculum not matched to the needs of the students, a lack of any kind of management system, and perhaps a teacher who didn't care for the students all that much.

"Here is what I would do: Before I accepted the job, I would have a long meeting with the principal, explain my classroom management philosophy, and ask for her support. I would describe changes that would have to made in the curriculum and in the overall structure of the classroom. If her support was not forthcoming, I would not accept the position. If she agreed to my approach, I would do three things.

"First, I would tell the students that I expected to win their respect and that I think they would be happier and learn more if we all got along with each other. I would spend at least one hour every morning for as long as it takes teaching students how to talk to one another and how to resolve conflicts. I would start formal "problem-solving groups" for the purpose of giving students a say in classroom rules and in what they are expected to learn. I would spend a lot of time getting students to talk about what they think is wrong and what they think we should do about it.

"Second, I would spend time talking to students trying to discover their interests and prior knowledge. The day-to-day curriculum would then be built around their interests and knowledge.

"Finally, I would ask all the parents to come to school to discuss the class. It is likely they know that things have been out of control. I would explain my approach, ask for their suggestions, and then close with some concrete steps they can take at home to help their sons or daughters be more effective students."

# Chapter 🍎 Six

# Assessment and Evaluation

## Reflecting on **Assessment and Evaluation**

The best way to approach this chapter is to reflect back on your own experiences as a student with assessment and evaluation. You have been tested hundreds of times during your years in school and college. The tests have ranged from simple pop quizzes to the high-stakes SATs. Also you have received grades many times. Sometimes you have received grades that you deserved; others have been unfair and reflected a bias against you. What have been your experiences with tests and grades?

🍎 *How did you react to testing situations and grades? Are you the kind of student who relishes a good, hard test and who feels a real sense of accomplishment when you do well? Or are you the kind of student who tenses up in testing situations and always comes away from the experience with negative feelings?*

🍎 *What do you think about standardized tests, such as IQ tests, state mastery tests, the SATs, or Praxis I and II for teachers? Do these tests ensure that students and teacher candidates learn what they are supposed to learn? Or do they simply get in the way of real learning and establish unfair barriers?*

🍎 *Have you thought about what kind of assessment system you are going to establish in your classroom? Do you look forward to being the type of teacher who is considered to have tough standards and grading policies? Are you going to use these to make students work hard? Or do you dread the whole idea of making judgments about students' work and plan to do everything you can to play down competition and make sure everyone passes your classes?*

**Assessing and evaluating students is one of the things teachers do that has important and lasting consequences for students.**

Leaders in almost all situations are responsible for assessing and evaluating the people who work for them. So too are teachers responsible for the assessment and evaluation of students in their classrooms, an aspect of their work that some find very difficult. Nonetheless, assessment, evaluation, and grading are of utmost importance to students and parents, and the way these processes are performed have long-term consequences. Assessment and evaluation processes also consume a fairly large portion of teachers' time. For instance, a review by Shaefer and Lissitz (1987) reported that teachers spend as much as 10 percent of their time on matters related to assessment and evaluation. Stiggins (1997) found that teachers could spend as much as one-third of their time on "assessment-related" activities. For these reasons, it is critical that beginning teachers build a repertoire of effective strategies for assessing and evaluating their students.

Although certain measurement techniques associated with assessment and evaluation are beyond the scope of this book, many basic concepts and procedures are well within the grasp of the beginning teacher. The first section of this chapter provides a perspective about why assessment and evaluation are important and defines several key concepts. This is followed by a section that samples the knowledge base on this topic. The final sections describe specific procedures beginning teachers can use for developing an overall assessment plan, making tests, and grading students as well as a discussion about schoolwide assessment and evaluation processes. A discussion also is included about some newer approaches to student assessment that are emerging in some schools.

## 🍎 *Perspective on Assessment and Evaluation*

If you think back to your own school days, you will recall the excitement (and the anxiety) of getting back the results of a test or of receiving your report card. When these events occurred, they were almost always accompanied by the student question, "Wadja get?" You also remember (in fact, you still hear) another favorite student question, "Is it going to be on the test?" These questions and the emotion behind them highlight the importance assessment and evaluation play in the lives of students.

### Importance of Assessment and Evaluation

Probably since the time the first test or the first grade was given, controversy has surrounded their use. For instance, some have argued that grades dehumanize education and establish distrust between teachers and students. Others have said that grading and comparing students leads to harmful anxiety and to low self-esteem for those who receive poor grades. Even those who acknowledge the importance of assessment and evaluation have often condemned current practices for the emphasis on testing basic skills out of context and the excessive competition that results. Still others have commented that grades are really a "rubber yardstick," measuring the whims of particular teachers rather than mastery of important educational goals. Today, teachers must test and evaluate, and they must respond to the use of standardized tests on their students and on themselves. This chapter strives to describe important contemporary features of assessment, testing, and evaluation. It also, as you will read, strives to encourage you to not accept the current situation uncritically and to consider alternative modes of assessment that may be more personalized, authentic, and fair. Regardless of the criticism and controversy surrounding this topic, the process of assessing and evaluating students has persisted and basic practices have remained essentially constant for most of the past century. Two important conditions of schools and teaching help explain this fact.

**Sorting Function of Schools.** Sociologists have observed that schools in large, complex societies are expected to help sort people for societal roles and occupational positions. Although some may wish for the day when better and fairer means are found for making these judgments, at present the larger society assigns the job of assessing and evaluating student growth and potential in large part to teachers. How well students perform on tests, the grades they receive, and the judgments their teachers make about their potential have important, long-run consequences for students. These judgments determine who goes to college, the type of college they attend, the careers open to them, and their first jobs, as well as the lifestyles they maintain. Enduring perceptions about self-worth and self-esteem can also result from the way students are evaluated in school. For these reasons, of all the leadership aspects of teaching, assessing and evaluating student growth and potential may be the most far-reaching. Teachers who do not take this aspect of their work seriously (regardless of reforms they may desire) are doing their students a great disservice. Still others argue that testing practices as they have evolved in the United States have been used to maintain the dominance of certain groups in society and prevent others from advancing. The unfairness and lack of social justice of this sorting function, criticism of current testing and grading practices, and suggested reforms will be discussed later in the chapter.

> **Although many wish it wasn't so, schools today help sort students for future opportunities.**

**Grade-for-Work Exchange.** Chapter 3 pointed out how classroom reward structures influence the overall learning community and how much of what students choose to do, or not do, is determined by what Walter Doyle labeled the "grade-for-work exchange." This idea described how students, like the rest of us, can be motivated to do certain things for extrinsic rewards. We may work hard and do what employers want so we will receive a merit raise; we may volunteer for community service hoping to receive public recognition for our work. This does not mean that our work has no intrinsic value or that altruistic reasons do not prompt us to help others. It simply means that for many people in our society, extrinsic rewards are valued and provide a strong incentive to act in particular ways.

Academic tasks such as completing assignments, studying for tests, writing papers, and carrying on classroom discourse is the work of students. Many teachers want their students to perform this academic work for the intrinsic value of learning itself. Although this is an admirable and, in many instances, attainable goal, grades remain important and should not be overlooked. It is important to remember that just as adults work for a salary, students work for grades. These exchanges are critically important and help explain some of classroom life.

> **Many students work for grades just as adults work for money.**

**Importance of Grades to Parents.** Parents are very concerned about their children's grades because they, more than their children, understand fully the important sorting function going on in schools. Most parents can recall critical judgments made about their work and the consequences these had for them. Similarly, they are keenly aware of the judgments being made when their child is placed in a lower-level reading group or a general math class instead of algebra.

*"Would you rather I be the smartest kid in the dumb group or the dumbest kid in the smart group?"*

SOURCE: (c) Lo Linkert, Phi Delta Kappan (May 1998)

Teachers have been known to complain about this type of parental concern, and sometimes these complaints are justified. For instance, some parents let unrealistic expectations for their children interfere with the teacher's professional judgment about the most appropriate level of work for their child. Conversely, other parents seem indifferent to their children's academic evaluation and offer little encouragement at home for doing good work or getting good grades.

Most parental concern, however, is natural and can be potentially beneficial. A growing literature (for example, Airasian, 1996) shows that parental concern about grades and performance can be tapped and used by teachers for the purpose of enhancing student learning. For example, involving parents in appropriate ways through homework is an excellent means of extending the teacher's instructional time. Several studies (Cooper, 1989, for example) have also shown that when teachers show regard for parental concerns by using more frequent reporting procedures and by getting parents to support the school's reward systems at home, these actions can result in more homework completed, better attendance, more academic engagement, and generally increased student output.

## Key Assessment and Evaluation Concepts

Assessment and evaluation are functions carried out by teachers to gather information needed to make wise decisions, and it should be clear by now that the decisions teachers make are important to students' lives. These decisions should be based on information that is relevant and as accurate as possible. Several key concepts can help you understand this topic more fully.

**Assessment is the process of collecting a full range of information about students and classrooms for the purpose of making instructional decisions.**

**Assessment.** The term **assessment** usually refers to the full range of information gathered and synthesized by teachers about their students and their classrooms. Information can be gathered on students in informal ways such as through observation and verbal exchange. It can also be gathered through formal means such as homework, tests, and written reports. Information about classrooms and the teacher's instruction can also be part of assessment. The range of information here can also vary from informal feedback provided by students about a particular lesson to more formal reports resulting from course evaluations and standardized tests.

**Evaluation.** Whereas assessment focuses on gathering and synthesizing information, the term **evaluation** usually refers to the process of making judgments, assigning value, or deciding on worth. A test, for example, is an assessment technique to collect information about how much students know on a particular topic. Assigning a grade, however, is an evaluative act, because the teacher is placing a value on the information gathered on the test.

Most evaluation specialists talk in terms of either formative or summative evaluations, depending on the use of the evaluation information. **Formative evaluations** are collected before or during instruction and are intended to inform teachers about their students' prior knowledge and skills in order to assist with planning. Information from formative evaluations is not used to make judgments about a student's work; it is used to make judgments about such matters as student grouping, unit and lesson plans, and instructional strategies. **Summative evaluations,** on the other hand, are efforts to use information about students or programs after a set of instructional activities has occurred. Its purpose is to summarize how well a particular student, group of students, or teacher performed on a set of learning goals or objectives. Summative evaluations are designed so that judgments can be made about accomplishments. Information obtained from summative evaluations is used by teachers to determine grades and to explain the reports sent to students and their parents. Table 6.1 compares key aspects of formative and summative evaluations.

**Information Quality.** If teachers make important decisions about students and about their teaching, it is only common sense that the information they use to make these decisions should be of high quality. Measurement and evaluation specialists use two technical terms to describe the quality of assessment information: **reliability** and **validity.**

A test is said to be reliable when it produces dependable, consistent scores for persons who take it more than once over a period of time. For instance, if a student took a test on Friday and then the same student took the test again the next Friday and received the same score, it is likely the test is reliable. If a group of students took the test one week and repeated the same test the following week and the rankings of the various students stayed about the same, it is even more likely that the test is reliable. A reliable test, thus, is one that measures a student's ability on some topic or trait consistently over time. A reliable test gives teachers accurate and dependable assessment information; however, it is important to remember that no single test can be expected to be perfect. Factors such as student guessing, mistakes made by teachers in scoring, as well as the students' feeling of well-being on the testing day all introduce error, inconsistency, and unreliability. Later, we will describe procedures that can cut down on the amount of error in tests.

**Evaluation is the process of making judgments, assigning value, or deciding on the worth of a particular program or approach or of a student's work.**

**Formative evaluation occurs before or during instruction and is used to assist with planning or making adaptations to instruction.**

**Summative evaluation is done after instruction to determine a program's effectiveness or the worth of student performance.**

**A test has reliability if it produces consistent results over several administrations.**

**A test is valid if it measures what it claims to measure.**

**Table 6.1** *Formative and Summative Evaluation*

| Type of Evaluation | When Collected | Type of Information Collected | How Information Is Used |
|---|---|---|---|
| Formative | Before or during instruction | Information about student prior knowledge and/or instructional processes | To assist teacher decision making |
| Summative | After instruction | Information about student and/or teacher performance | To assist making judgements about student or teacher accomplishments |

**Figure 6.1** *Quality of Assessment Information*

Reliability                    Validity

A test is said to be valid when it measures what it claims to measure. For example, a test that claims to measure students' attitudes toward mathematics is invalid if it really measures their attitude toward their mathematics teacher. Obviously, if a test is not measuring what it is intended to measure, the information it produces is of no value for teacher decision making. As you will see later, it is possible to increase the validity of tests and other assessment devices. Figure 6.1 illustrates the concepts of reliability and validity.

## 🍎 Theoretical and Empirical Support

The knowledge base for assessment and evaluation is immense. The underlying concepts used for measuring all kinds of traits and attributes, such as academic achievement, personality, and performance have long intellectual traditions. Similarly, technical topics associated with test construction, grading, and the use of evaluation information have been studied thoroughly for most of this century. Two lines of inquiry important to beginning teachers are sampled in this section: the effects of testing and grades on students and bias in teaching assessment.

### Effects of Grades and Testing on Students

For obvious reasons, one of the most important and frequently asked questions by beginning teachers is, Do tests, grades, and grading procedures influence student learning? Fortunately, this has also been a question of interest to educational researchers. Much is known about the effects of grades and other **extrinsic rewards** on students. However, a note of caution is in order about this research, because the issues involved are complex and intricate. As you will see, simple recipes do not exist.

One line of research stemmed from natural experiments that occurred in the late 1960s and the 1970s. During this period, several colleges and universities began the practice of giving students the choice of taking classes on a graded or a pass-fail basis. Several studies (for example, Gold et al., 1971) compared the students' performance, and the findings were pretty consistent: students performed better in graded situations than they did in pass-fail situations.

**Are Grades an Incentive?**  A persistent and troublesome problem for teachers is how to get students to do their homework. On the one hand, teachers would prefer that students complete assignments because of the work's intrinsic value. On the other hand, many experienced teachers would declare, "If I don't grade it, they won't do it." Francis Cullen and her colleagues (1975) conducted an interesting piece of research a few years ago that shed some light on this problem.

The researchers experimentally manipulated two types of incentives (positive and negative) to see what effects they would have on getting students to complete a simple library assignment. They studied 233 students in fourteen high school classes across three suburban schools. Students in the study were asked to complete a one-page library assignment. Although the assignment varied according to the subject of the class, it was the same for all classes in terms of length and difficulty. The fourteen classes were randomly assigned to three different categories: (1) positive-incentive group, where students were told if they handed in the assignment, they would receive X number of points on their final grade. If they did not complete the assignment, no points would be taken away; (2) negative-incentive group, where students were told that if they did not hand in the assignment, they would lose X number of points on their final grade; and (3) control group, where students were told that completing or not completing the assignment would not affect their grade.

Sixty-four percent of the students in the negative-incentive group completed the assignment compared to 42 percent in the positive-incentive group and only 14 percent in the control group. These data confirmed the researchers' hypothesis that grades used as negative incentives would be more powerful than grades used as positive incentives.

**Complexity of the Influence of Grades.**  The Cullen study seems to show grades can be a strong incentive for performing work. A beginning teacher, however, should be careful in interpreting this finding, because factors other than grades can affect performance. One key factor is how interesting or intrinsically motivating the assignment is in the first place. For example, in a rather well-known study, Lepper and her colleagues (1973) compared three groups of preschool children. Children were told they could draw pictures (an intrinsically interesting task for young children) during their free-play time. Children in one group were promised a reward if they drew a picture. Children in another group were told they would receive a surprise. Those in the third group were promised nothing. After this reward structure was introduced, the children were observed, and the amount of time they spent drawing pictures during free play was recorded. Those students who were promised a surprise or no reward at all spent almost twice as much time drawing as did students who had been promised a reward. These results, as you can see, are quite different from those of the Cullen study. Lepper and her colleagues explained their findings by pointing out that giving extrinsic rewards for something that is intrinsically interesting may actually have the opposite effect. This does not mean, however, as Lepper (1973) and others have explained, that extrinsic rewards should not be used. They are still needed for tasks that do not have high intrinsic motivation.

Another factor that influences the effects of grades on student learning is how students themselves perceive these grades in relation to the work they have performed. You remember reading in Chapter 3 that some students attribute their success or failure to their own hard work or lack thereof, whereas other students attribute it to luck. The grade and what it means will obviously be interpreted differently by each type of student.

> Rewards that are external to the activity itself, such as points, grades, or stars, are called extrinsic rewards.

> A set of complex factors affects the influence of grades and extrinsic rewards on the quality of student work.

**✔ Check for Understanding**

- In what ways have grades been shown to increase student performance? Why is overemphasis on the extrinsic grade reward system possibly a disadvantage?

- What subjective criteria have been shown to influence teachers when judging student work?

- What steps can teachers take to reduce the effects of bias when judging student work?

A student's past history with grades can also be a factor. Students who have a history of receiving high grades, for instance, have likely developed a positive view of themselves and will continue to aspire to and work for high grades. On the other hand, students who have histories of low grades come to see themselves as failures, and another low grade only confirms this perception. Obviously, the status parents and close friends attach to grades also influences students' attitudes.

*Effect of Testing.* As you will read in the next section, the use of standardized tests in schools is widespread today, and people in general think that if test scores are high, the school and its teachers are effective. Many instances have been reported where this is true (Education Trust, 1998; Schmoker & Marzano, 1999). However, for a variety of reasons, the effects of standardized tests may not always be as positive as some would believe.

One reason is that most standardized tests measure only a small range of abilities, mainly those that focus on quantitative and verbal tasks. And, as you read in Chapter 1, leading educators today believe that there are various forms of intelligence, including the eight types identified by Gardner (1994). Students who possess artistic, interpersonal, or intrapersonal abilities, for example, are at a disadvantage because these abilities are not measured on standardized tests.

Second, some educators are beginning to question whether frequent testing can actually impede meaningful education and student learning. This point of view is highlighted in the Research Summary for this chapter.

## Teacher Bias in Assessment and Grading

**In any assessment situation, the possibility of teacher bias is always a worry.**

From your own student experiences, you undoubtedly know how important it is for teachers to be perceived as fair and impartial in their treatment of young people. Being free from bias is particularly important when judging student work and assigning grades. Teacher bias is also a topic that has been extensively researched. Some of the most interesting studies were done by Starch and Elliot (1912, 1913), who showed the subjectivity of teachers in assessing and assigning grades to essay exams. In their first study, the researchers asked teachers in a number of different schools to grade student-produced essay exams in English. Later the researchers asked history and mathematics teachers to perform the same task. Starch and Elliot found that teachers used many different criteria when assessing essays, and consequently the scores or grades they gave to the same paper varied widely. On one English essay, for instance, the percentage of points awarded varied from 50 to 97. Similar studies conducted over the years continue to show that teachers hold different criteria for judging student work and that they are influenced by numerous subjective factors, such as the student's handwriting, whether or not the opinions expressed agree with those of the teacher, and the expectations teachers have for a particular student's work. (Remember the concept of self-fulfilling prophecy described in Chapter 4.) Fortunately, a number of strategies have been devised to reduce bias and subjectivity in assessment and grading. These procedures and techniques will be described more fully later in this chapter.

# Statewide and Schoolwide Assessment Programs

The following sections focus on strategies teachers can use to make assessment and evaluation both fair and productive. Statewide and schoolwide standardized assessment programs are described first, followed by specific procedures teachers can use to work with the results of standardized tests and communicate these to students, parents, and members of their communities.

Research Summary 6.1

# Personal Reflections of a Third Grade Teacher

*Angaran, Joseph.* Reflections in an age of assessment. *Educational Leadership* March 1999, 71–72.

Most of the research summaries in *Learning to Teach* are the result of the work of professional educational researchers, mainly individuals who work in university settings and conduct their research by watching and studying what goes on in schools. The knowledge we have about teaching, however, does not come only from this source. We also have what is called the "wisdom of practice." This Research Summary contains an example of this type of knowledge. It is the personal reflections of a third grade teacher in Eagan, Minnesota.

**Problem and Approach:** Joseph Angaran is concerned about what effect frequent testing and assessment may have on his students. In the twenty years he has been teaching, Angaran has observed some significant changes in the amount of time devoted to testing. He questions the usefulness and implications of the data being gathered, as well as the effect of the tests on his teaching and the learning of his students.

**Reflections and Conclusions:** "Every morning on my way to school, I pass by the marquee of a major entertainment complex. As I sit at the traffic light and patiently wait to begin my day, I glance at the marquee to watch announcements of upcoming events crawl across the screen in bright orange letters. I contemplate the enormity of the organization and the various set-up procedures each event must entail. . . .

"Soon, however, my thoughts become focused on the day ahead, and I wonder about the special events that dominate my date book and lesson planner. With increasing frequency, assessments are now the focus of my students' lives. When I glance at my calendar, I hardly ever see a week when I am not either preparing to test or formally assessing my students. This is a significant change since I began my teaching career nearly 20 years ago. I question the usefulness and the implications of the data we gather, as well as the effect these tests have on my teaching and on my students' learning.

"Teachers assess students by using an ever-increasing variety of tools. In my district, the average 3rd grader is evaluated with the following instruments: a national norm-referenced test for school achievement, a test to determine school ability, and two state-mandated tests in reading and math. In addition, classroom teachers are required to conduct a writing assessment and a test for oral retelling of a narrative or a descriptive text. . . .

"On some days, I merely facilitate movement among tests rather than encourage and enhance student learning. Being a teacher has been reduced to something akin to being a special events coordinator at the entertainment complex. Each test becomes another situation in which I must rearrange the classroom and its routines, coordinate test materials, and work to assuage the fears of the 8- and 9-year-olds whom I teach. The students sense underlying anxiety and apprehension despite assurances from me and their parents that we just want them to do their best. . . . Ironically, all this activity prepares them for hours of passivity. This extended amount of seat time flies in the face of what we know about how children learn. . . .

"Ostensibly, this test data will enable us to be better teachers, and it will give parents and the public a better idea of whether we are adequately preparing children for a place in society. In reality, however, the information overwhelms everyone. We now have more statistics on children than ever. Teachers are inundated with report after report, analysis after analysis, detail piled upon excruciating detail. Parents receive less information with even less interpretation of the results and, more important, no direct link to what they can do at home to help their child. The public often receives the most dramatic data taken out of context, misinterpreted, or sensationalized.

"Teachers are not provided enough time to analyze the test data and to translate the information into meaningful goals for their students. At times we seem to be putting the cart before the horse: Shouldn't we change the way we teach and then assess students? It doesn't make a lot of sense to continue to assess students when we are not given the time to modify our methodology. Without ample time to reflect and change, aren't we simply assessing either old practices or underfunded, undervalued, half-hearted attempts at educational change? . . . Without the time to examine our teaching practices and to work with our colleagues, we will continue to teach in the ways we were taught 20 or more years ago.

"In the rush to reform education, the classroom teacher's expertise and common sense have been pushed aside. . . . As professionals with extensive knowledge of child development and learning, we can determine what is best for our students. That does not mean that we will not listen to or accept information from others. It does mean, however, that we will know how to implement the most effective way to enhance student learning. After all, isn't that the goal of everyone?"

## Statewide and Schoolwide Use of Standardized Tests

Currently, it is common practice for states to use standardized tests to diagnose and evaluate students' academic progress. Called mastery or basic competency testing, these testing programs have evolved with the accountability movement discussed in Chapter 1. Today, tests are normally given to students in grades 4, 6, 8, and 10 in all fifty states. Although the tests vary from state to state, in the main they assess childrens' abilities in math, reading, and writing in the elementary grades. Grade 10 tests sometimes branch out into science, history, and geography.

The results of state tests are given to teachers, who can use them for diagnostic purposes. They are also given to students and their parents. In many states, test scores are summarized by school. Each school is compared to other schools in the state, and often these comparisons are published in the local newspaper. Figure 6.2 is an example from one state of the results teachers and parents receive.

The trend seems to be to make these tests more and more important in the lives of teachers and students and to use them to make high-stakes decisions. For example, schools in some communities have been taken over by the state government because their students have consistently done poorly on these tests. In some instances, students are required to pass statewide mastery tests before they are promoted to the next grade or awarded a high school diploma.

Many school districts also have standardized testing programs. In larger school systems, whole units of specially trained personnel exist to coordinate and manage this important educational activity. It is a rare school in which students are not tested at least yearly on such topics as study skills, reading, language acquisition, mathematical operations, verbal reasoning, and concept development. Sometimes schools use tests developed and distributed by national test publishers. Others use tests developed and distributed by state or district testing authorities. The results of tests are used to make judgments about the effectiveness of schools and teachers and, most important, to decide the future educational and job opportunities available to students.

Beginning teachers will not be required to select the tests to be used on a statewide or schoolwide basis, nor will they be held responsible for the administration, scoring, or initial interpretations of these tests. They will, however, be expected to understand the nontechnical aspects of the testing program, and they will be expected to use test results and to communicate these clearly to students and their parents. In many school districts, teachers are also being held accountable for their students' success on these tests.

*Standardized testing programs have important consequences in the lives of students and teachers.*

**Figure 6.2** *Sample State Mastery Test*

MASTERY TESTING PROGRAM
GRADE 8 REPORT

TEACHER:
SCHOOL:
DISTRICT:

| OBJECTIVE CLUSTERS TESTED | MASTERY CRITERIA | STUDENT SCORE |
|---|---|---|
| WRITTEN COMMUNICATION | | |
| 1. Prewriting/referencing | 11 of 15 | 13 |
| 2. Composing/revising | 11 of 15 | 12 |
| 3. Editing | 11 of 15 | 12 |
| TOTAL NUMBER OF OBJECTIVE CLUSTERS MASTERED (out of 3) | | 3 |
| READING COMPREHENSION | | |
| 1. Constructing Meaning | 7 of 10 | 9 |
| 2. Applying Strategies | 4 of 6 | 4 |
| 3. Analyzing, Elaborating, and Responding Critically | 10 of 14 | 11 |
| TOTAL NUMBER OF OBJECTIVE CLUSTERS MASTERED (out of 3) | | 3 |

| WRITING SAMPLE | STUDENT SCORE |
|---|---|
| Holistic Writing Score (Goal is 8 of 12) | 8 |

Your child has scored at or above the statewide goal in writing. Generally, students who score at this level produce fluent papers which contain somewhat well-developed responses. These papers are adequately elaborated with general and specific details. These papers show satisfactory to strong organizational strategy with a progression of ideas and transition.

| DEGREES OF READING POWER (DRP)™ | STUDENT SCORE |
|---|---|
| DRP Units (Goal is 64 DRP units) | 78 |

Your child has scored at or above the statewide goal for reading. Students who score at this level possess the knowledge and skills necessary to successfully perform the tasks and assignments appropriately expected of a student at this grade level with minimal teacher assistance. Generally, students who score at this level can comprehend textbooks and other materials used at grade eight or above.

| OBJECTIVES TESTED—MATHEMATICS | MASTERY CRITERIA | STUDENT SCORE |
|---|---|---|
| CONCEPTS | | |
| 1. Identify or extend patterns involving numbers and attributes | 4 of 6 | 4 |
| 2. Relate fractions, decimals and percents to their pictorial representation | 3 of 4 | 4 |
| 3. Rename fractions and mixed numbers as equivalent decimals and vice versa | 3 of 4 | 4 |
| 4. Rename fractions and decimals as equivalent percents and vice versa | 3 of 4 | 3 |
| 5. Identify points on number lines, scales and grids including fractions, decimals and integers | 3 of 4 | 3 |
| 6. Estimate the magnitude of mixed numbers and decimals | 3 of 4 | 4 |
| COMPUTATION AND ESTIMATION | | |
| 7. Add and subtract 2-, 3- and 4-digit whole numbers, money accounts and decimals | 3 of 4 | 4 |
| 8. Multiply and divide 2- and 3-digit whole numbers, money amounts and decimals by 1-digit whole numbers and decimals | 3 of 4 | 4 |
| 9. Multiply and divide whole numbers and decimals by 10, 100 and 1000 | 3 of 4 | 4 |
| 10. Add and subtract fractions and mixed numbers with reasonable and appropriate denominators | 3 of 4 | 4 |
| 11. Multiply whole numbers and fractions by fractions and mixed numbers | 3 of 4 | 3 |
| 12. Find percents of whole numbers | 3 of 4 | 4 |
| 13. Identify an appropriate procedure for making estimates involving whole number computation | 4 of 6 | 6 |
| 14. Identify an appropriate procedure for making estimates involving fraction and mixed number computation | 4 of 6 | 6 |
| 15. Identify an appropriate procedure for making estimates involving decimal computation | 4 of 6 | 6 |
| 16. Identify an appropriate procedure for making estimates involving percents | 5 of 7 | 6 |
| PROBLEM SOLVING/APPLICATIONS | | |
| 17. Solve problems involving order and magnitude of fractions | 3 of 4 | 3 |
| 18. Solve problems involving order and magnitude of whole numbers and decimals | 3 of 4 | 4 |
| 19. Solve problems involving rounding whole numbers and decimals | 3 of 4 | 4 |
| 20. Draw reasonable conclusions from graphs, tables and charts | 3 of 4 | 4 |
| 21. Create graphs from data | 3 of 4 | 4 |
| 22. Identify an appropriate number sentence to solve story problems | 3 of 4 | 4 |
| 23. Solve or estimate a reasonable answer to problems involving whole numbers, dollar amounts, including averaging | 3 of 4 | 3 |
| 24. Solve or estimate a reasonable answer to problems involving fractions, decimals and mixed numbers | 3 of 4 | 3 |
| 25. Solve or estimate a reasonable answer to problems involving ratios, proportions and percents | 3 of 4 | 3 |
| 26. Solve or estimate a reasonable answer to problems involving customary or metric units of measure | 3 of 4 | 2 |
| 27. Solve or estimate a reasonable answer to problems involving elementary notions of probability and fairness | 3 of 4 | 3 |
| 28. Solve or estimate a reasonable answer to problems involving means and medians of sets of data | 3 of 4 | 4 |
| 29. Identify needed information in problem situations | 3 of 4 | 3 |
| 30. Solve process problems involving the organization of data | 3 of 4 | 4 |
| MEASUREMENT/GEOMETRY | | |
| 31. Identify or draw geometric shapes and figures | 3 of 4 | 2 |
| 32. Identify or draw geometric transformations and symmetry | 3 of 4 | 4 |
| 33. Describe, model and classify shapes | 4 of 5 | 5 |
| 34. Measure and determine perimeters, areas and volumes | 3 of 4 | 4 |
| 35. Estimate lengths, areas, volumes and angle measures | 3 of 4 | 3 |
| 36. Identify appropriate metric or customary units of measure for a given situation | 3 of 4 | 4 |
| ALGEBRA | | |
| 37. Solve equations involving 1 step | 3 of 4 | 4 |
| 38. Use order of operations | 3 of 4 | 4 |
| 39. Use formulas to evaluate expressions | 3 of 4 | 3 |
| 40. Represent situations with algebraic expressions | 3 of 4 | 4 |

Your child has scored at or above the state goal for mathematics. Students at this level possess the knowledge and skills necessary to perform the tasks and assignments expected of 8th graders with minimal teacher assistance. Generally these students demonstrate well-developed computational skills, conceptual understandings and problem solving abilities.

TOTAL NUMBER OF OBJECTIVES MASTERED = 38
TOTAL STUDENT SCORE = 154
(Goal is 130 of 172)

## Nature of Standardized Tests

**Standardized tests,** as contrasted to tests made by teachers, are those that have been designed and validated by professional test makers for specific purposes such as measuring academic achievement or literacy levels. They can usually be administered in many different settings and still produce reliable information. In some instances, standardized tests also provide information about how some nationwide "norm group" performed on the test, thus providing a basis of comparison for students subsequently taking the test. Examples of standardized tests include the Stanford Achievement Test, the California Achievement Test, or the well-known Scholastic Aptitude Test (SAT) used by many colleges and universities in making entrance selections. Many of you took the SAT and soon will be taking Praxis, a standardized test on teaching developed and administered by the Education Testing Service (ETS).

## Norm-Referenced and Criterion-Referenced Tests

Today, two major types of standardized tests are used to measure student abilities and achievement. These are called norm-referenced and criterion-referenced tests. It is important to understand the differences between these two approaches to testing and to be able to communicate to others the assumptions, the advantages, and the disadvantages of each approach.

*Norm-referenced tests are standardized tests that evaluate a particular student's performance by comparing it to the performance of some other well-defined group of students.*

**Norm-referenced tests** attempt to evaluate a particular student's performance by comparing it to the performance of some other well-defined group of students on the same test. Most of the achievement tests you have taken as a student were norm-referenced. Your score told you how you performed on some specific topic or skill in comparison with students from a national population who served as the "norming" group for the test. Most norm-referenced tests produce two types of scores—a raw score and a percentile rank. The *raw score* is the number of items on the test a student answers correctly. The *percentile-rank score* is a statistical device that shows how a student compares with others, specifically the proportion of individuals who had the same or lower raw scores for a particular section of the test. Table 6.2 shows how raw scores are converted to percentile ranks on standardized, norm-referenced tests. Look at the student who answered thirty-eight out of the forty-eight test items correctly. You can see this score placed the student in the seventy-first percentile, meaning that 71 percent of the students in the norm group scored thirty-eight or lower on the test. If you look at the student who had a raw score of thirty on the test, you can see this converts to a percentile score of twenty-two, meaning that only 22 percent of the students in the norm group scored thirty or below.

*Criterion-referenced tests are those that evaluate a particular student's performance against a preestablished standard or criterion.*

Whereas norm-referenced tests measure student performance against that of other students, **criterion-referenced tests** measure it against some agreed-on level of performance or criterion. To show the major difference between a norm-referenced and criterion-referenced test, let us use as our example a runner's speed on the 100-yard dash. If a runner were compared to a larger group of runners using concepts from norm-referenced testing, the tester would report that a student who ran the 100-yard dash in thirteen seconds was in the sixty-fifth percentile for all other students in his or her age group. Using concepts from criterion-referenced testing, the tester would report that the established criterion for running a 100-yard dash was twelve seconds and that the student can now run it in thirteen seconds, one second short of criterion.

Generally, the content and skills measured on criterion-referenced tests are much more specific than on norm-referenced tests. Obviously, each provides different types of information for teachers to use. Figure 6.3 compares the differences in the kinds of information provided by the two kinds of tests. Note that on the norm-referenced test

**Table 6.2** *Conversion of Raw Scores to Percentile Ranks*

| Raw Score | Percentile Rank | Raw Score | Percentile Rank |
|:---:|:---:|:---:|:---:|
| 48 | | 34 | 44 |
| 47 | | 33 | 40 |
| 46 | | 32 | 36 |
| 45 | 99 | 31 | 30 |
| 44 | 96 | 30 | 22 |
| 43 | 93 | 29 | 18 |
| 42 | 90 | 28 | 15 |
| 40 | 81 | 27 | 11 |
| 39 | 76 | 26 | 7 |
| 38 | 71 | 25 | 4 |
| 37 | 65 | 24 | 3 |
| 36 | 56 | 23 | 1 |
| 35 | 49 | 22 | 1– |

**Figure 6.3** *Comparison of Information on a Norm-Referenced and Criterion-Referenced Test*

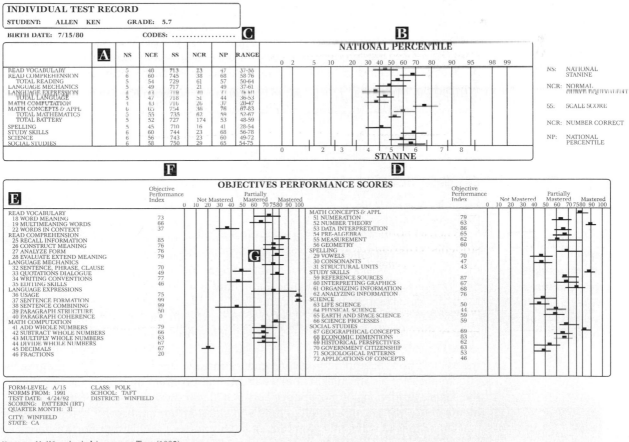

Source: California Achievement Test (1992).

(at the top of the figure), information is provided for more general categories, such as reading, language, and mathematics, and the student's performance is compared to national norms using percentile scores. The criterion-referenced test (at the bottom of the figure), on the other hand, indicates the level of mastery for very specific skills (such as editing skills) and reports the student's performance on an index ranging from zero (not mastered) to one hundred (completely mastered). Note also that results from the norm-referenced tests are reported in percentile ranks, whereas the results of the criterion-referenced test show the degree to which a particular student has mastered a specific skill. You will read later in this chapter how those who advocate assessment procedures that are more performance-based and authentic challenge the processes associated with both norm-referenced and criterion-referenced testing. But for now, let's consider the advantages and disadvantages of the two approaches.

## Advantages and Disadvantages of Different Approaches

*The SAT-9 does this*

If a teacher is interested in how his or her students compare to students elsewhere, results from norm-referenced tests are obviously called for. Norm-referenced tests allow comparisons within a particular school, district, or state. For example, achievement levels in all third grades in a particular district might be compared with those from other districts. Norm-referenced tests, however, will not tell very much about how well a specified set of school or teacher objectives are being accomplished; nor will they tell how students are currently doing in comparison to past performance on locally derived objectives.

Criterion-referenced tests, on the other hand, can provide information about a student's level of performance in relation to some specified body of knowledge or list of agreed-on objectives or standards. This is important information to have when making judgments about the effectiveness of particular instructional programs and activities. The results of criterion-referenced tests, however, do not allow for comparing the performance of students in a particular locale with national norms. More and more schools and teachers are using criterion-referenced tests because their information is better for diagnosing student difficulties and for assessing the degree to which schoolwide or systemwide purposes are being achieved.

## Communication of Standardized Test Results

**It is important that teachers communicate the results of standardized tests to parents and make sure they understand the limitations of these tests.**

It is important that teachers be able to explain the results of both norm-referenced and criterion-referenced tests in honest and straightforward ways. They may be asked to go over test scores with students, to explain test results to parents, and to interpret test scores that are published in the newspaper. Students and their parents need to know that a single score on a test does not pretend to measure all aspects of a person's abilities. At the same time, they need to know how standardized tests scores are used to make decisions that can affect students' lives.

Community members often need to be reminded of the strengths and limitations of particular testing programs and of the assumptions underlying all standardized tests. Educators have not done a very good job of explaining, in nontechnical terms, the assumptions behind norm-referenced testing and their limitations for judging the effectiveness of a particular school's educational program, nor have they explained the severe limitations of most paper-and-pencil standardized tests for making judgments about the multiple intelligences and skills of human beings. Knowledgeable teachers can find ways to communicate to parents and others that norm-referenced tests only compare students against a norm group and do not necessarily provide a good measure for how well a particular teacher, school, or system is achieving particular objectives. Teachers can also communicate to parents and the community that students' abilities and dispositions toward learning help determine how well they do on standardized tests and that a school with a predominance of less motivated students will never perform as well as schools with a predominance of highly motivated students. Finally, teachers can remind and caution parents and others about possible test bias as well as the narrow range of objectives that are actually measured on any standardized test.

## 🍎 A Teacher's Assessment Program

Whereas testing specialists have the major responsibility for statewide and systemwide testing, classroom teachers are responsible for the assessment, testing, and grading related to their specific courses. In general, a teacher's assessment activities are aimed at one of the following three goals: diagnosing prior knowledge and skills, providing corrective feedback, and making judgments and grading student achievement. These three purposes have some similarities but also some important differences.

### Diagnosing Prior Knowledge

To individualize instruction for specific students or to tailor instruction for a particular classroom group requires reliable information about students' capabilities and their prior knowledge. Both norm- and criterion-referenced standardized tests attempt to measure many areas of student achievement but are most highly developed and most readily available in reading, language development, and mathematics. Unfortunately, they are less available in other subject areas.

In many school systems, beginning teachers will be assisted by test and measurement personnel or by counseling and special education staff who have been specifically trained to help diagnose student capabilities and achievement. In other school systems, this type of assistance may not be available. If formal diagnostic information is not available, beginning teachers will have to rely on more informal techniques for assessing **prior knowledge.** For example, teachers can observe students closely as they approach a particular task and get some sense about how difficult or easy it is for them. Similarly, by listening carefully to students and by asking probing questions, teachers can get additional cues about students' prior knowledge on almost any topic. In fact, teacher and student questions are a major means of ascertaining student understanding. Verbal responses help teachers decide whether to move forward with the lesson or to back up and review. Nonverbal responses such as frowns, head nodding, puzzled looks, and the like also provide hints about how well students understand a topic. However, beginning teachers should be aware that sometimes these nonverbal behaviors can be misinterpreted.

Because many students will not admit their lack of knowledge or understanding in large groups, some teachers have found that interviewing students in small groups can be a good way to get the diagnostic information they need. This technique is particularly useful for getting information from students who do not participate regularly in classroom discussions or who give off few nonverbal signals. Student portfolios, described later, can also be used for diagnosing prior knowledge.

✔ **Check for Understanding**

- How have state testing programs impacted the curriculum and the way teachers teach?

- How do standardized tests differ from other types of testing methods?

- How do norm-referenced tests and criterion-referenced tests differ? What are the advantages and disadvantages of the two approaches?

- Why is it important that teachers have a thorough understanding of standardized testing methods and results?

*Prior knowledge* **refers to information and knowledge held by students before they receive instruction.**

## Providing Corrective Feedback

A second important purpose of assessment and evaluation is to provide students with feedback on how they are doing. As with diagnosing students' prior knowledge, this is easier to do for some topics and skills than others. Test makers have developed rather sophisticated and reliable procedures for measuring discrete skills such as word recognition or simple mathematical operations. It is also quite easy to collect information on how fast a student can run the 100-yard dash or how long it takes to climb a 30-foot rope. Biofeedback techniques are also available to help students monitor their own physical reactions to stress and certain types of exertion. However, as instruction moves from a focus on such basic skills and abilities to a focus on more complex thinking and problem-solving skills, the problem of providing **corrective feedback** becomes more difficult because there are fewer reliable tests and acceptable procedures for these more complex processes.

Chapter 8 provides some principles for giving feedback to students and explains the importance of feedback for student improvement. It also emphasizes that for corrective feedback to be useful, it must be immediate, frequent, and communicated in nonjudgmental ways.

### Check for Understanding

- What are the three major purposes of a teacher's own classroom assessment program?

- What methods and tools do teachers use to assess a student's prior knowledge?

- In what situations is corrective feedback most effective?

- Why is the reporting of grades such a critical responsibility of a teacher?

## Testing for Summative Evaluation and Reporting

For most beginning teachers, the bulk of their assessment time and energy goes toward assessing student progress, determining grades, and reporting progress. Although some teachers do not like this aspect of their work and find it time-consuming, it must be done and done well for reasons enumerated earlier and reiterated here. First, students expect their work to be evaluated, and they perform academic work for grades, as you have seen. Teachers who take this work-for-grade exchange lightly or who do it poorly are normally faced with serious classroom problems. Second, the larger society has assigned the job of making judgments about student achievement and ability to teachers. It is unjust if this aspect of the job is not done well.

The key concepts and procedures associated with the three major purposes of classroom assessment are summarized in Table 6.3. The next section provides more specific information about this aspect of the teacher's assessment program.

**Table 6.3** *Three Major Purposes of Classroom Assessment*

|  | **Diagnostic** | **Feedback** | **Reporting** |
| --- | --- | --- | --- |
| Function | Placement, planning, and determining the presence or absence of skills and prior knowledge | Feedback to student and teachers on progress | Grading of students at the end of a unit or semester |
| When used | At the outset of a unit, semester, or year, or during instruction when student is having problems | During instruction | At the end of quarter, semester, or year's work |
| Type of test | Standardized diagnostic tests; observations and checklists | Quizzes and special tests or homework | Final exams |
| Scoring | Norm- and criterion-referenced | Criterion-referenced | Norm- or criterion-referenced |

*Tailoring Teaching for Inclusive Classrooms*

# Using Assessment Information for Diagnosing Students with Disabilities

Today, beginning teachers can almost be assured that students with disabilities will be present in their regular classrooms. As you have read in previous chapters, inclusion of all students in the same classrooms has many advantages.

However, it also requires teachers to be able to deal with many different kinds of students and to have information about each. One set of assessment skills that is very important is in the area of diagnosis. In addition to information about academic abilities, several other kinds of assessment information are required if teachers are to work successfully with students who have special needs. These are summarized below.

In some schools, special educators and measurement experts will be present and will take the lead role in this aspect of teaching. In other schools, regular teachers will be required to participate directly in diagnosing student difficulties and using assessment information to tailor instruction for special-needs students.

| Category of Disability | Type of Assessment Information Required |
|---|---|
| Mentally retarded | Degree of intellectual ability, adaptive behavior, language functioning, and medical history |
| Hard of hearing/deaf | Audiological, intellectual, language, speech, and social and emotional development |
| Speech-impaired | Audiological, articulation, fluency, voice, language, and social and emotional development |
| Visually handicapped | Ophthalmological, intellectual, and social and emotional development |
| Seriously emotionally disturbed | Intellectual, medical, and social and emotional development |
| Orthopedically impaired and other health impairments | Medical, motor, adaptive behavior, and social and emotional development |
| Deaf-blind | Audiological, ophthalmological, language, medical, and adaptive behavior |
| Multiply handicapped | Medical, intellectual, motor, adaptive behavior, social and emotional development, language, speech, and audiological and ophthalmological, when appropriate |
| Gifted | Intellectual, creativity, and social and emotional development |

Source: Adapted from Friend and Bursuck (1999)

## 🍎 Specifics of Testing and Grading

The most important aspect of student assessment and evaluation in most classrooms involves the tests teachers make and give to students. Good test construction requires both skill and a commitment to this aspect of teaching. The general principles that follow offer beginning teachers some much-needed guidelines for constructing their own paper-and-pencil tests. Constructing more complex performance tests is discussed later.

## General Principles

Gronlund (1991, 1998) provided several principles that should guide teachers as they design an assessment system and create their own tests. Some of these principles are summarized as follows.

**Assess All Instructional Objectives.** An often-heard student complaint is that the test did not "cover what we covered in class." For whatever reasons, students who say this believe that they have been unfairly judged. Thus, Gronlund's first principle is that teachers should construct their test so it measures clearly the learning objectives they have communicated to students and the materials they have covered. In short, the test should be in harmony with the teacher's instructional objectives. For example, if the teacher completed a unit of work on the American colonial period and wants students to understand all aspects of this era, then the test should cover more than just the religious leaders of the period.

**Cover All Cognitive Domains.** Most lessons and units of instruction contain a variety of learning objectives ranging from the recall of factual information to the understanding, analysis, and creative application of specific principles. A good test does not focus entirely on one type of objective such as factual recall; rather, it measures a representative sample of the teacher's learning objectives. Measuring more complex skills such as higher-level reasoning is more difficult and time-consuming.

**Gronlund's general principles provide important guidance for teachers as they develop their assessment system.**

**Use Appropriate Test Items.** There are, as you know from your own experiences, many different kinds of test items and testing formats available to teachers. Some types of test items, such as matching or fill-in-the-blanks, are better for measuring recall of specific information; others, such as essay items, are better for tapping higher-level thinking processes and skills. A good test includes items that are most appropriate for a particular objective. More about this aspect of constructing tests is provided later.

**Make Tests Valid and Reliable.** A test is considered reliable when it produces dependable, consistent scores for persons who take it more than once over a period of time. A test is said to be valid when it measures what it claims to measure. Teacher-made tests that are clearly written and minimize guessing are generally more reliable than ambiguous ones that encourage guessing. Likewise, tests containing a fairly large number of items are generally more reliable than those with just a few items. A test that is well planned and covers the full range of objectives and topics is most likely to ensure validity. Teaching students the necessary skills to take the test also increases validity because, in some instances, students may know the information being tested but simply cannot read or interpret the questions. No single test, however, can give a completely accurate picture of what a student knows or can do. Thus, there is always the need to interpret results with caution and to rely on multiple sources of assessment information before making final judgments about a student's work.

**Although tests are used to grade students, they can also be used to improve student learning.**

**Use Tests to Improve Learning.** This final principle is meant to remind teachers that although tests may be used primarily to diagnose or assess student achievement, they can also be learning experiences for students. Going over test results, for instance, provides teachers with opportunities to reteach important information students may have missed. Debate and discussion over "right" answers can stimulate further study about a topic. Effective teachers integrate their testing processes into their total instructional programs for the purpose of guiding and enhancing student learning.

## Test Construction and Use

**Planning the Test.** In almost any class, teachers attempt to teach many different things. Some of what they teach is influenced by curriculum guides that have been developed in their district and by the textbooks available to them. Some things that are taught stem from a teacher's own interest and judgment about what is important; still others are influenced by what students are interested in and what they choose to study. Also, the instructional objectives of a particular course can cover a range of behaviors, including important facts about a topic, major concepts and principles, simple and complex skills, appreciations, and the ability to think critically and analytically. Obviously, every piece of information, skill, or higher-level process cannot be included on a particular test. Thus, decisions must be made about what to include and what to leave out. The **table of specifications** is a device invented by evaluation specialists to help teachers make these decisions and to determine how much space to allocate to certain topics and to the different levels of student cognitive processes (Bloom, Hastings, & Madaus, 1971; Gronlund, 1998). Table 6.4 shows a sample table of specification.

As you can see from this table, the teacher listed the major topics covered in the left-hand column. This particular table of specifications covers a unit of study on colonial America. It could have covered a day's work, a week's, or a whole course of study. Along the top of the table, the teacher listed the cognitive processes or student behaviors associated with the unit. Although other category systems could have been used, the teacher who constructed this table relied on Bloom's taxonomy, which was introduced in Chapter 2. Finally, within the table itself, the teacher placed numbers. These numbers represent the teacher's judgment about how many test items to include on the test for each of the topics and under each of the cognitive processes.

**Making the Test.** Once the teacher has decided which topics and cognitive processes to cover on a test, the next step is to decide on the test's format and the type of test

A table of specifications is a tool for constructing a test so it will have a balance of questions representing an array of instructional objectives and levels of student understandings.

**Table 6.4** *Table of Specifications*

Unit of work covered: _____

Anticipated time for taking the test: _____

| | Student Behaviors and Cognitive Processes | | | | | |
| | Knows/Recall of | | | Higher-Level | | |
| Topics/Content | Terms | Facts | Principles | Comprehension | Application | Evaluation |
|---|---|---|---|---|---|---|
| Colonial life | 1 | | | 1 | 1 | |
| New England town | | 1 | | 1 | 1 | |
| Southern plantation | | | 2 | 1 | 2 | |
| Clergy | | 1 | | | | |
| Transportation systems | | | 1 | 1 | 2 | |
| Children and education | | | 1 | 1 | | 1 |
| Indian warfare | | 2 | | | 1 | 1 |
| France and Spain | | 1 | 1 | | | 1 |
| Westward expansion | 2 | | | 1 | 1 | 2 |
| Total number of test items | 3 | 5 | 5 | 6 | 8 | 5 |

items to use. A major question is, Will the test be objective or essay? These are terms you are very familiar with from your prior experiences. However, it is important to point out that the term *objective,* as used here, means that answers to the items can be scored relatively free from bias. Like most other aspects of teaching, the choice of whether to use an objective or an essay test has important trade-offs, which are described here.

*Constructing and Scoring Objective Tests.* True-false, matching, multiple-choice, and fill-in-the-blanks are examples of test items that may be used on an **objective test.** The advantages of these types of test items are obvious. They allow greater coverage of the various topics a teacher has taught, and they can be easily and objectively scored. One disadvantage of objective tests is that it is difficult to write objective items that measure higher-level cognitive skills and processes. Another disadvantage is that good objective tests take a long time to construct. They simply cannot be put together in a few minutes the night before. Also, teachers always worry about the "guessing factor" associated with objective tests. This is particularly true when matching or true-false items are used. Finally, objective test items, regardless of how well constructed, can measure only a very limited range of understandings and skills. If a teacher decides to use the objective format, he or she must consider several factors as test items are prepared.

*True-False Items.* When the content of instruction or a learning objective calls for students to compare alternatives, true-false tests can be a useful means to measure their understanding. True-false tests are also useful as an alternative to a multiple-choice item if the teacher is having trouble coming up with several distracters. A good true-false item should be written so the choice is clear and the answer unambiguous. Look, for instance, at these examples of good and poor true-false items:

Good:  An island is a land mass that is smaller than a continent and is surrounded by water.
Poor:  Islands have been more important in the economic history of the world than have peninsulas.

The first example requires students to know the definition of the concept *island* as compared to other land forms. The answer is unambiguous. The second example, however, is very ambiguous. The word *important* would likely be interpreted in many different ways by students.

An obvious shortcoming with true-false test items is that students, whether they know the material or not, have a 50 percent chance of getting the correct answer.

*Matching.* When a teacher wants to measure student recall of a fairly large amount of factual information, matching items can be useful. Students are presented with two lists of items (concepts, dates, principles, names) and asked to select an item from one list that most closely matches an item from the other list. Most evaluation specialists caution against making either list too long—perhaps no more than six to eight items—or having more than one match for each set of items. As with true-false items, there is an element of guessing that the teacher needs to consider when choosing to use matching items. Below is an example of a matching question used by an English teacher who wanted to see if students knew the authors of the various literary works they studied.

*Directions:* Match the author listed in column B with the work he or she wrote, listed in column A.

| Column A | Column B |
|---|---|
| 1 _____ *Leaves of Grass* | A. Melville |
| 2 _____ *Walden* | B. Baldwin |
| 3 _____ *A Thousand Acres* | C. Smiley |
| 4 _____ *Moby Dick* | D. Bronte |
| 5 _____ *The Fire Next Time* | E. Whitman |
| 6 _____ *Jane Eyre* | F. Thoreau |

***Fill-in-the-Blanks.*** A third popular objective test format is fill-in-the-blank. This kind of test is rather easy to write, and it does a good job of measuring students' abilities to recall factual information. The element of guessing is virtually eliminated, because choices of possible correct answers are not provided. The tricks of writing good fill-in-the-blank items are to avoid ambiguity and to make sure questions have no more than one correct response. To show how two correct answers are possible, read the following example.

The Civil War battle of Antietam was fought in _____.

*Good test items are difficult and time consuming to prepare.*

Some students might write in "Maryland" (the place); others might write in "1862" (the date). Some subjects and instructional objectives lend themselves to clarity and this type of test item better than others.

*Multiple-Choice.* Multiple-choice items are considered by most evaluation specialists to be the best kind of objective test item. Multiple-choice items are rather robust in their use, and if carefully constructed, they minimize guessing. Also, if appropriately written, multiple-choice items can tap some types of higher-level thinking and analytical skills.

Multiple-choice items consist of providing students with three types of statement: a *stem*, which poses a problem or asks a question; the *right answer,* which solves the problem or answers the question correctly; and *distracters,* statements that are plausible but wrong. Although the number of distracters can vary, normally three or four are recommended.

Good multiple-choice items are difficult to write. The stem must provide enough contextual information so students thoroughly understand the problem or question being posed. At the same time, it must be written so that the correct answer is not easily revealed. Distracters must be such that they provide plausible solutions to students who have a vague or incomplete understanding of the problem, yet they must be clearly recognized as the wrong answer by students who have command of a topic. General guidelines for writing multiple-choice items include recommendations to:

> **Good multiple-choice questions are difficult to write.**

- Make the stem specific but with sufficient contextual information.
- Make all the distracters plausible and grammatically consistent with the stem.
- Make all aspects of the item clear so that students will not read more than was intended into the answer.

Stems should be straightforward and specific but provide sufficient context. Here is an example of a good stem:

Historians attached historical significance to the Battle of Antietam because

A. So many people were killed in the bloodiest battle of the Civil War.
B. It gave Lincoln the victory he needed to issue the Emancipation Proclamation.
C. Strategically, it was the strongest victory to that point by the Confederate Army.
D. It showed how vulnerable the North was to invasion by forces from the South.

And here is an example of a poor stem:

Antietam was

A. The bloodiest battle of the Civil War.
B. The battle that gave Lincoln the victory he needed to issue the Emancipation Proclamation.
C. The strongest victory to that point by the Confederate Army.
D. The battle that showed how vulnerable the North was to invasion by forces from the South.

Most Civil War historians point out that the Battle of Antietam was tactically a draw. Strategically, however, it was a Confederate defeat, and it did give Lincoln a victory he thought he needed before formally issuing the Emancipation Proclamation. The stem in the good example alerts students that it is the "historical significance" of the battle that they should consider. Those who had a good understanding of this specific era of the Civil War would know the link between Antietam and the Emancipation Proclamation. Without that context, however, distracter A might also be a very plausible answer, because the Battle of Antietam was the most costly in human life for a single day's engagement during the Civil War.

Just as the stem for a multiple-choice question needs to be carefully constructed, so too do the distracters. Two common errors made when writing distracters are lack of grammatical consistency and implausibility. Look at the example below.

Historians attached historical significance to the Battle of Antietam because

A. So many people were killed.
B. It gave Lincoln the victory he needed to issue the Emancipation Proclamation.
C. The Confederate Army.
D. Most Americans love bloody battles.

As you can see, several things are wrong with the distracters in this example. Distracters A, C, and D are much shorter than B. This may cue students to the right answer. Distracter C does not complete the sentence started in the stem, thus it is grammatically different from B, the right answer, and distracters A and D. Finally, for the serious student, distracter D could be eliminated almost immediately.

**Essay Tests.** Many teachers and test experts agree that **essay tests** do the best job of tapping students' higher-level thought processes and creativity. Obviously, this is a decided advantage of an essay test over an objective test. Another advantage is that it usually takes less time to construct. A note of caution, however. Good, clear essay questions don't just happen. And bear in mind the time it takes to construct sample answers and read and grade essay questions.

Essay tests have been criticized because they cover fewer topics than objective tests, they are difficult to grade objectively, and they may be heavily influenced by writing skills rather than knowledge of the subject. The first criticism can be resolved partially by using a combination of items—objective items to measure student understanding of basic knowledge and essay items to measure higher-level objectives.

As for grading bias, several guidelines have been developed by experienced teachers and evaluation specialists that help reduce the influence of writing prowess and grading bias.

1. *Write the essay question so it is clear and explains to students what should be covered in the answer.* For example, if the teacher wants students to apply information, the questions should say that; if the teacher wants students to compare two different ideas or principles, the question should state that clearly. For instance, "Discuss the Civil War" is too broad and does not tell students what to do. Consequently, answers will vary greatly and will be difficult for the teacher to score. On the other hand, "Describe and compare economic conditions in the North and the South during the 1840s and 1850s, and explain how these conditions influenced decisions by both sides to engage in civil war" describes more clearly the topics to be covered in the essay and the type of thinking about the topic the teacher wants.

2. *Write a sample answer to the question ahead of time and assign points to various parts of the answer.* Writing a sample answer can become a criterion on which to judge each of the essays. Assigning points to various aspects of the answer (for instance, five points for organization, five points for coverage, and perhaps five points overall) helps deal with the problem of uneven quality that may exist within a given answer. Students should be made aware of the point distribution if this technique is used.

3. *Use techniques to reduce expectancy effects.* Chapter 4 introduced the concept of expectancy effects—a phenomenon whereby teachers expect some students to do well and others to do poorly. Having students write their names on the back of their essays is one technique used to prevent this type of bias. However, this strategy has limited value because most teachers soon find they readily recognize a particular

**Essay tests, where students express their thoughts in writing, can tap complex ideas and concepts.**

**Writing sample answers and using holistic scoring are two techniques teachers can use to reduce bias in grading essay tests.**

student's handwriting. If the essay test has two or three questions, reading all the responses to a single question and then shuffling the papers before reading responses to the next question is another method teachers use to reduce expectancy effects. If teachers are working in teams, checking each other's grading is also helpful.

**The technique for grading essay questions or other written work that emphasizes looking at the work as a whole rather than at its individual parts is called holistic scoring.**

4. *Consider using holistic scoring.* Some evaluation specialists have argued that the best procedure for scoring essay questions and other types of student writing (reports, essays, etc.) is one they have labeled **holistic scoring.** The logic behind this procedure is that the total essay written by a student is more than the sum of its parts and should be judged accordingly. Teachers who use this approach normally skim through all the essays and select samples that could be judged as very poor, average, and outstanding. These samples then become the models for judging the other papers. Some teachers use this same process but add a second procedure of stacking the papers in appropriate piles as they read, for instance, an A pile, a B pile, and so on. They then reread selected papers from the various piles to check their initial judgments and to check for comparability of papers within a given pile.

Obviously, constructing essay items and making judgments about students' work this way can be difficult and time-consuming. The use of essay questions, however, remains one of the best means for measuring the more complex and higher-level abilities of students. Subjective grading will probably always be an unattractive feature of essay testing, but by employing the safeguards described here, this factor can be greatly reduced.

**Giving the Test.** The format of the test and the kind of coverage it provides are important ingredients. The conditions under which students take the test are equally important. As with many other aspects of teaching, having appropriate structures and routines can help make test taking a less stressful and more productive activity for students. Several guidelines stemming from the practices of effective teachers should be considered.

**Conditions of the testing situation are very important and can significantly influence how well students do.**

1. *Find ways to deal with test anxiety.* When confronted with a test, it is normal, and even beneficial, for students to be a little bit anxious. However, some students (often more than teachers suspect) experience a degree of test anxiety that prevents them from doing as well as they could. Effective teachers learn to recognize such students and help reduce anxiety in a number of ways. One way is to simply help students relax before a testing situation. Some teachers use humor and the release from tension it provides. Other teachers use simple relaxation methods, such as a few moments for reflection or deep breathing. Sometimes anxious students lack the requisite test-taking skills. Setting aside periods of instruction to help students learn how to pace themselves, how to allocate time during a test, how to make an outline for an essay question before writing, or how to skip over objective questions for which they do not know the answers, has been shown to reduce *test anxiety* and to improve test performance.

2. *Organize the learning environment for conducive test taking.* In Chapter 2, you read how critical the use of space is for instruction. In Chapter 3, other aspects of the overall learning community were discussed. The physical environment for test taking should allow students ample room to do their work; this in turn helps minimize cheating. Obviously, the test environment should be quiet and free from distractions.

3. *Make routines and instructions for the test clear.* Common errors made by beginning teachers include lack of carefully developed test-taking routines and unclear instructions. Most experienced teachers routinize the process of getting started on a test. They pass out the tests face down and ask students not to start until told to do so. This procedure is important for two reasons. One, it gives each student the same amount of time to complete the test. Two, it allows the teacher a chance to go over

the instructions with the whole group. In giving instructions for the test, experienced teachers know that it is important to go over each section of the test and to provide students with guidelines for how long to spend on each part. If a new format or type of question is being introduced, procedures and expectations need to be explained. Checking to make sure students understand the tasks they are to perform is another critical feature of getting students ready to take the test.

4. *Avoid undue competition and time pressures.* Unless teachers are using the cooperative learning strategies described in Chapter 10, there is always going to be some competition among students. Competition comes into focus most clearly during testing situations. Experienced teachers use a variety of means to reduce the effects of harmful competition such as grading to a criterion instead of on a curve (explained later); making the final grade for the course dependent on many samples of work, not just one or two tests; and having open discussions with students about competition and its effects on learning.

5. *Provide students with sufficient time.* Insufficient time is another factor that produces poor test performance. In fact, teachers often hear students complain, "I knew the stuff, but I didn't have enough time." Except in instances in which time is the criterion (for example, running the 100-yard dash), tests should be constructed so that students will have ample time to complete all aspects of the test. Beginning teachers often have trouble predicting the amount of time required for a particular test. Until these predictions become more accurate, a safe rule of thumb is to err on the side of having too much time. Making some of the tests "take-homes" is another way to avoid the pressures of time associated with test taking.

> Providing students with sufficient time to take a test is very important if teachers want students to perform well on their tests.

6. *Provide appropriate support for students with special needs.* Special-needs students, such as those who are blind or physically challenged in some other way, require special support when they are taking tests. Similarly, some otherwise capable students may have trouble reading quickly enough to complete a test in the time required. It is important for teachers to provide the special support (readers, more time, special tables) that special-needs students require.

## Grading

The logic behind norm-referenced and criterion-referenced testing also applies to the two major approaches to grading. **Grading on a curve** is a commonly used procedure in secondary schools and colleges, where students compete with each other for positions along a predetermined grading curve. A teacher following a strict interpretation of the grading-on-a-curve concept would give 10 percent of the students A's, 20 percent B's, 40 percent C's, 20 percent D's and 10 percent F's. Under this grading scheme, even students with a high degree of mastery of the testing material sometimes fall into one of the lower grading areas and vice versa.

> Grading on the curve is the practice of assigning grades so they will follow a normal curve.

An alternate approach to grading on a curve is **grading to criterion** or mastery. Teachers using this approach define rather precisely the content and skills objectives for their class and then measure student performance against that criterion. For example, in spelling, the teacher might decide that the correct spelling of 100 specified words constitutes mastery. Student grades are then determined and performance reported in terms of the percentage of the 100 words a student can spell correctly. A teacher using this approach might specify the following grading scale: A = 100 to 93 words spelled correctly; B = 92 to 85 words spelled correctly; C = 84 to 75 words spelled correctly; D = 74 to 65 words spelled correctly, and F = 64 or fewer words spelled correctly.

> Grading to criterion is the practice of assigning grades according to how well students do on a predefined set of objectives or standards.

Table 6.5 illustrates the differences between these two approaches for a particular group of students. As you can see, the two approaches produce different grades for

**Table 6.5** *Assigning Spelling Grades from Test Scores Using Two Approaches*

| | Grading on a Curve | | Grading to Criterion | |
|---|---|---|---|---|
| Eric | 98 | A | 98 | A |
| Maria | 97 | | 97 | |
| Ruth | 96 | B | 96 | |
| John | 96 | | 96 | |
| Tanisha | 96 | | 96 | |
| Sam | 95 | | 95 | |
| Denise | 92 | C | 92 | B |
| Mohammed | 90 | | 90 | |
| Louise | 90 | | 90 | |
| Elizabeth | 90 | | 90 | |
| Betty | 87 | | 87 | |
| Marcos | 87 | | 87 | |
| Martha | 86 | | 86 | |
| Tom | 83 | | 83 | C |
| Chang | 80 | D | 80 | |
| Dick | 78 | | 78 | |
| Beth | 73 | | 73 | D |
| Lane | 69 | | 69 | |
| Mark | 50 | F | 50 | F |
| Jordan | 50 | | 50 | |

individuals within the same class of students. Both grading on a curve and grading on mastery present some dilemmas for teachers. When grading on a curve, the teacher is confronted with questions about the relationship of grades to native ability. For example, should 10 percent of a class of very able students be given Fs? Should 10 percent of a class of learning-disabled students be given As?

Criterion testing and grading also present troublesome issues for teachers. If criterion levels are set in relation to what is realistic for a particular group of students, then able students should be expected to perform more work and at higher levels than their less-talented peers. However, when grades are assigned, the question arises: Should students who complete all work accurately, even though it is at a lower level, be given the same grade as students who complete all work accurately at a higher level?

Some schools and teachers have tried to resolve this dilemma by using a criterion-referenced report card that lists all the major objectives of the course. Rather than assigning a single grade for the entire course, the teacher assigns a number of grades or verbally describes a child's performance for each objective. This approach is also not trouble-free for teachers. Many parents are accustomed to the five-letter grading scale, because it is what they experienced when they were in school. Departures are confusing to them. Also, since a student's grade point average is traditionally used to determine admission to colleges and jobs, it is difficult to report a long list of performance measures that people in the outside world can understand.

# Test Generators and Electronic Grade Books

Most teachers today use a wide array of software programs that have been designed to help generate and score tests, record student grades and performance, and report results to students and their parents. Below are descriptions of how these work.

## Test Generators

Test generators allow teachers to create a bank of test questions that can then be organized for a particular test. This makes it easy to add and delete questions from year to year, as well as create more than one version of the same test to give to students who may be absent on the day the test is given. Some test generator software also provides printed answer keys for the test.

## Electronic Grade Books

Keeping records of student attendance and scores on tests is very time-consuming for teachers. It also requires great accuracy. Electronic grade books are similar to spreadsheet and database software programs. They allow scores, grades, and other statistical information to be recorded in the database, with calculations performed using the spreadsheet function of the grade book.

Grade book software also allows teachers to create reports with charts mapping student performance over time. This is an excellent way of generating reports for students and their parents and saves teachers many hours of work. Below is an example of a report generated by one grade book software program.

| William Course: SCID33 HIGH SCHOOL | | Crs:SCID33-Sec:1 | | | 1999/12/01 Section: 01 InteGrade Pro | |
|---|---|---|---|---|---|---|

| # | Task Type | Task Name | Score | Out of | Percent | Percent of Sprd |
|---|---|---|---|---|---|---|
| 1 | Homework | Topic Ques. pg 416 | 7 | 10 | 70 | 4 |
| 2 | lab/quiz | Extra Credit Presentations | | 0 | | 0 |
| 3 | lab/quiz | Constellation drawing | 10 | 10 | 100 | 2 |
| 4 | lab/quiz | Solar System Presentations | 95 | 100 | 95 | 21 |
| 5 | Homework | Topic Ques pg 420 | 10 | 10 | 100 | 4 |
| 6 | Homework | Topic Ques pg 427 | 10 | 10 | 100 | 4 |
| 7 | lab/quiz | Elipse Lab | 10 | 10 | 100 | 2 |
| 8 | Homework | topic Ques pg 407 | 5 | 10 | 50 | 4 |
| 9 | Test | TEST-Solar System | 95 | 100 | 95 | 60 |

**Student's Summary Grade:** **93**

**Missing Tasks:**

| # | Task Type | Task | Raw Score | Percent of Sprd |
|---|---|---|---|---|
| 2 | lab/quiz | Extra Credit Presentations | <empty> | 0 |
| | | Total Percentage Missing: | | 0 |

**Check for Understanding**

- What is the most important aspect of student evaluation?

- What are the major guidelines that teachers should follow when constructing tests?

- What are the purposes of a table of specifications?

- What are the characteristics and advantages of an objective test? Disadvantages?

- What guidelines should be followed by teachers attempting to eliminate subjective biases?

- What can be done by teacherms to create the most encouraging and stress-free test-taking environment?

- What are the two types of grading?

## Summary Guidelines for Testing and Grading

This section concludes with four summary guidelines that can assist teachers as they approach the task of working out their own testing and grading procedures.

**Test at All Levels.** A common mistake made by some teachers is to focus most test items on simple recall of information. It is easier to write and score this type of question because there is usually a single correct answer. However, if the teacher wants to extend student thinking and to promote higher-level thought processes, then test questions must require higher-level thinking. Bloom's taxonomy and a table of specifications, described previously, are devices that can assist teachers in constructing test items at various levels.

**Communicate Clearly to Students What They Will Be Tested On.** A favorite question from students is, "Will we be tested on this?" Effective teachers make it very clear to students which of the ideas presented in a lecture or found in the textbook will be included on the test. Some teachers will write key ideas from a lecture on the board or give them to students in a handout. Some provide the same kind of tool for information in the text. This communicates to students exactly what they are responsible for on the test. Other teachers spend time in review, outlining key ideas to be covered on the test. Still others provide study sheets with sample questions. The goal in each case is to alert students to what is expected of them.

Effective teachers also communicate to students the various levels of knowledge they will need to demonstrate and the amount of detail expected. If the students are expected to commit a list of facts to memory, they are told so; if they are expected to evaluate one idea and contrast it with another, they are told so. Starting with the fifth or sixth grades, students can be taught Bloom's classification system and use it as a guide for their own study, just as teachers use it as a guide for test construction.

**Use Multiple Measures.** Today, a vast array of learning outcomes exist for most subjects taught in school. These range from knowledge of basic facts and skills to more complex learning outcomes such as critical thinking and problem solving. Some kinds of measures work very well for assessing certain kinds of outcomes, such as multiple-choice questions for testing basic information; other kinds of outcomes, however, require measures such as essay questions and performance tests to adequately assess what students know and are able to do. Effective testing and grading policies require that teachers sample a wide range of possible student performances and use multiple assessment devices to measure important outcomes.

**Test Frequently.** Some teachers will wait until the end of an instructional unit to test students' knowledge acquisition. It is better to test students frequently for two reasons. First, frequent tests pressure students to keep up with what they are learning and provide them with feedback on how they are doing. Second, frequent testing provides the teacher with feedback on how well students are doing on key instructional objectives and allows reteaching of ideas students are not learning.

**Make Grading Procedures Explicit.** Regardless of the approach a teacher chooses to use in assigning grades, the exact procedures should be written down and communicated clearly to students and to their parents. Taking the mystery out of grading is one way to help students accomplish the work expected of them and is also a means of getting students to see the "fairness" of the grading system.

# 🍎 *A Look to the Future of Testing and Grading*

This chapter described the importance of assessment and evaluation mainly from the perspective of traditional practices. The effects of testing and grading on student learning have been explored, as has the importance these processes hold for parents and the long-run consequences they have for students.

This chapter has also pointed out that many aspects of testing and grading are controversial and have been for a long time. Perhaps your generation of teachers will find better and fairer ways to make judgments about the work of students. Perhaps methods will be invented that will keep the positive aspects of assessment and evaluation intact—providing feedback to students and their parents about work accomplished—but will eliminate the more destructive aspects of current practices. Some innovative processes and procedures exist. These may provide foundations on which to think about the future of assessment, evaluation, and grading.

Currently there appears to be a nationwide demand for more accountability by schools and teachers as well as a call for higher standards. There is a general belief that the emphasis over the past decade on minimal competencies measured with multiple-choice, standardized tests has raised the basic skill level of students slightly but has failed to promote and measure higher-level thinking and problem-solving skills. Many educators, parents, and test and measurement experts believe that this situation can be corrected by introducing new approaches to student assessment such as the use of authentic assessment, performance tasks, student portfolios, and grading for cooperative effort.

## Assessing Performance

Instead of having students respond to multiple-choice questions on paper-and-pencil tests, advocates of **performance assessments** want students to demonstrate that they can *perform* particular tasks, such as writing an essay, doing an experiment, interpreting the solution to a problem, playing a song, or painting a picture. Notice that the emphasis here is on testing procedural knowledge as contrasted to declarative knowledge.

Figure 6.4 compares a standardized test question and a multiday performance assessment on the concept *volume.* Note how thoroughly the task is described and how clearly the test developers present how to score the test.

*Performance assessments have students demonstrate their abilities to perform particular tasks in testing situations.*

**Figure 6.4** *Two Approaches to Testing Volume*

### Standardized Test Questions on Volume

1. What is the volume of a cone that has a base area of 78 square centimeters and a height of 12 centimeters?
   a. 30 $cm^3$
   b. 312 $cm^3$
   c. 936 $cm^3$
   d. 2808 $cm^3$

2. A round and a square cylinder share the same height. Which has the greater volume?

### A Multiday Performance Assessment on Volume

*Background:* Manufacturers naturally want to spend as little as possible not only on the product but on packing and shipping it to stores. They want to *minimize* the cost of production of their packaging, and they want to *maximize* the amount of what is packaged inside (to keep handling and postage costs down: the more individual packages you ship, the more it costs).

*Setting:* Imagine that your group of two or three people is one of many in the packing department responsible for m&m's candies. The manager of the shipping department has found that the cheapest material for shipping comes as a flat piece of rectangular paperboard (the piece of posterboard you will be given). She is asking each work group in the packing department to help solve this problem: *What completely closed container, built out of the given piece of posterboard, will hold the largest volume of m&m's for safe shipping?*

1. Prove, in a *convincing* written report to company executives, that both the *shape* and the *dimensions* of your group's container maximize the volume. In making your case, supply all important data and formulas. Your group will also be asked to make a 3-minute oral report at the next staff meeting. Both reports will be judged for *accuracy, thoroughness,* and *persuasiveness.*
2. Build a model (or multiple models) out of the posterboard of the container shape and size that you think solves the problem. The models are *not* proof; they will *illustrate* the claims you offer in your report.

Source: Wiggins (1993), p. 114.

*Authentic assessments have students demonstrate their abilities to perform particular tasks in real-life settings.*

This performance test has several features that are important and groundbreaking. It is an attempt to integrate several topics (science, writing, group work) into the assessment process rather than assessing specific skills. It requires students to perform a variety of tasks carried over several days rather than tasks that can be assessed in a few minutes. Additionally, it is an effort to measure complex intellectual skills and processes.

## Authentic Assessment

Performance assessments ask students to demonstrate certain behaviors or abilities in testing situations. **Authentic assessment** takes these demonstrations a step further and stresses the importance of the application of the skill or ability within the context of a real-life situation. Educational reformers such as Linda Darling Hammond (1997) and Jeannie Oakes (1999) argue that "meaningful performances in real-world" settings can more closely capture the richness of what students understand about how they can apply this knowledge than can testing for "bits and pieces" with conventional assessment procedures. Examples of authentic assessments include demonstrating work in exhibitions such as a science fair or art show, showing skill in a portfolio collection, performing in dance or music recitals, participating in debates, and presenting original papers to peers or parents.

## Designing and Scoring Performance and Authentic Assessments

You may ask why, if performance and authentic assessments have so many advantages over more traditional approaches, these approaches aren't used more often and why it took us so long to invent them. Most measurement experts agree (as do teachers who have tried to devise and use performance assessments) that performance tests take a great deal of time to construct and administer and that in most instances they are much more expensive. Think, for instance, how long it would take and the cost that would be involved to administer performance assessments to cover all the traditional topics currently found on the SAT. Further, the creation of good performance assessments requires considerable technical knowledge. For teachers who choose to begin constructing their own tests to measure student performance, Linn and Gronlund (1995) provided the following guidelines to improve the quality of these efforts.

1. Focus on learning outcomes that require complex cognitive skills and student performance.
2. Select or develop tasks that represent both the content and the skills that are central to important learning outcomes.
3. Minimize the dependence of task performance on skills that are irrelevant to the intended purpose of the assessment task.
4. Provide the necessary scaffolding for students to be able to understand the task and what is expected.
5. Construct task directions so that the students' task is clearly indicated.
6. Clearly communicate performance expectations in terms of the criteria by which the performance will be judged.

Many experts in authentic assessment (Wiggins, 1993, for example) argue that for authentic assessments to be effective, the criteria and standards for student work must be clear, known, and nonarbitrary. Students doing academic tasks need to know how their work will be judged in the same ways that divers and gymnasts competing in the Olympics know how their performances will be judged. Scoring rubrics is one technique assessment experts have derived to make criteria clear and nonarbitrary. A **scoring rubric** is a detailed description of some type of performance. It makes explicit the criteria that will be used to judge the performance. Rubrics can also be used to communicate criteria and standards to students before a performance. In the performing arts and sports (also in teaching), rubrics are often based on how an expert would perform. Students might be supplied with videotapes or other examples showing superior performance. A scoring rubric in an academic subject, such as history, is illustrated in Figure 6.5.

> **A scoring rubric is a detailed description of some type of performance and the criteria that will be used to judge it.**

## Student Portfolios and Narrative Descriptions

Closely related to performance and authentic assessment is the use of **student portfolios.** Many of you are already aware of the portfolio process in that it has been used in various fields of the visual arts for a long time. It is common practice for painters, graphic designers, and cartoonists, for example, to select illustrative pieces of their work and organize them into a portfolio that can be used to demonstrate their abilities to potential clients or employers. Often actors, musicians, and models use the same process.

Some schools, such as those in Winnetka, Illinois, and Manhattan, Kansas, have students develop portfolios to both assess and report student achievement. The portfolio in these schools consists of a sample of artifacts and reflections that represent what the student has done and can do across all subject areas. Here is a list of what the teachers in Manhattan have students include in their portfolios during the course of the school year: learning log entries, writing samples, spelling samples, handwriting samples, various text pages that students have mastered, audiotape recordings of readings, reports or demonstrations, videotape recordings of readings, reports or demonstrations, computer disks of various work, artwork, photographs, lists of books read, skills checklists, self-assessment sheets, outcome checklists, assessment narratives, and parents' reflections on the portfolio. In both Winnetka and Manhattan, students prepare their portfolios to be shared with parents and are guided by such questions as:

> **Portfolio assessment is a form of assessment that evaluates a sample of students' work and other accomplishments over time.**

How has my writing changed since last year?
What do I know about numbers now that I didn't know in September?
What is unique about my portfolio?

**Figure 6.5** *Scoring Rubric from an Advanced Placement History Exam*

*Questions:* "The economic policies of the federal government from 1921 to 1929 were responsible for the nation's depression of the 1930s." Assess the validity of this generalization.

### Scores

13–15   An accurate, well-written response that directly assesses the validity of the generalization. Demonstrates a clear understanding of governmental economic policies; for example, tariffs, probusiness legislation, and foreign debt. Uses at least three specific examples or covers many topics with an intelligent conclusion.

10–12   A good answer that attempts with some detail to assess the validity of the statement, if only implicitly. Should cover at least two areas of economic policy, but may contain a few minor errors of fact.

07–09   A reasonably coherent discussion, but with little analysis of economic issues. Answer is not fully developed; may discuss only one issue beyond the level of assertion; for example, laissez-faire policies. Or may give a coherent discussion of concepts without citing specific acts or policies.

04–06   Little if any assessment of the statement. An overgeneralized answer, without supporting evidence. . . . The stock market crash must be seen as not merely an event but a consequence of prior policies. . . .

Source: Wiggins (1993), pp. 52 and 53.

The idea here is to have students prepare their portfolios so that students reflect on their own learning. In addition, the teachers in Winnetka have combined portfolios, student reflections, and their own judgments into a visual reporting device, which is illustrated in Figure 6.6.

## Assessing Group Effort and Individually Contracted Work

In Chapter 10, you will read about cooperative learning procedures through which students are awarded points and grades for their work in teams and for their individual work. These procedures hold good potential for reducing the destructive process of comparing students with their peers as well as excessive competition.

Interest is also growing among educators today in using criterion-referenced evaluations. For instance, the creators and developers of mastery learning (Bloom, 1976; Guskey & Gates, 1986), the Keller (1966) plan, and individualized prescribed instruction (IPI) have shown how learning materials for some subjects can be broken down into smaller units of study and how students can be given the opportunity to work toward a specified objective (criterion) until they have mastered it. Grades under these systems are determined not by comparing students with their peers but by the number of objectives they have mastered. Systems in which teachers make contracts with

**Figure 6.6** *The Learning Experiences Form*

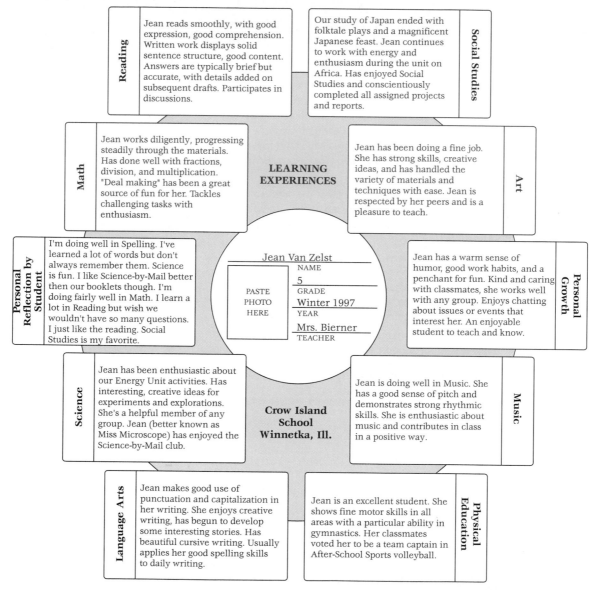

Source: After Hebert (1992), p.60.

individual students allow each student to compete with himself or herself on mutually agreed-on criteria rather than to compete with others. Grading for team effort and for individually contracted work, however, are difficult processes for teachers to implement by themselves. These experiments run strongly against current norms and traditions, and they require schoolwide policies and collegial support to be successful.

## Experimenting with New Approaches

Some beginning teachers will find themselves in schools in which a great deal of experimentation is going on with alternative assessments procedures. Others will find more traditional approaches being used. Alone, without the assistance of colleagues, it

is doubtful that beginning teachers can implement a complete alternative classroom assessment system. They can, however, experiment with pieces of alternative assessments. For instance, a science teacher could devise a few performance tests, described earlier, or a language arts or English teacher could make part of a student's grade depend on the performance of particular authentic writing tasks. Some use of portfolios can benefit almost every grade level in every subject area. These steps are movements in the right direction as your generation of teachers works to find better and fairer ways to assess and make judgments about the work of students.

## Assessment Bill of Rights

We conclude this chapter by returning to an admonition made at the beginning that assessment and evaluation are among the most important aspects of teachers' work and carry heavy responsibilities. Teachers must not only do this part of their job well but also must make sure that no harm comes to vulnerable students. Some assessment experts, such as Grant Wiggins, have proposed an "assessment bill of rights" (illustrated in Figure 6.7) to protect students from the potential harm that may come to them from educational testing.

**Figure 6.7**  *Assessment Bill of Rights*

All students are entitled to the following:

1. Worthwhile (engaging, educative, and "authentic") intellectual problems that are validated against worthy "real-world" intellectual problems, roles, and situations.
2. Clear, apt, published, and consistently applied teacher criteria in grading work and published models of excellent work that exemplifies standards.
3. Minimal secrecy in testing and grading.
4. Ample opportunities to produce work that they can be proud of (thus, ample opportunity in the curriculum and instruction to monitor, self-assess, and self-correct their work).
5. Assessment, not just tests: multiple and varied opportunities to display and document their achievement, and options in tests that allow them to play to their strengths.
6. The freedom, climate, and oversight policies necessary to question grades and test practices without fear of retribution.
7. Forms of testing that allow timely opportunities for students to explain or justify answers marked as wrong but that they believe to be apt or correct.
8. Genuine feedback: usable information on their strengths and weaknesses and an accurate assessment of their long-term progress toward a set of exit-level standards framed in terms of essential tasks.
9. Scoring/grading policies that provide incentives and opportunities for improving performance and seeing progress against exit-level and real-world standards.

Source: Wiggins (1993), p. 28.

### ✔ Check for Understanding

- What are some controversial aspects surrounding testing in our country, and what possible solutions can be considered to remedy these problems?

- How do performance assessments and authentic assessments differ from each other? How do they differ from standardized testing methods, and why are they harder to develop and administer?

- What is a student portfolio? How can it be used in a teacher's assessment program?

- What are the primary ideas behind the "Assessment Bill of Rights" developed by Wiggins?

# 🍎 *Summary*

### Perspective on Assessment and Evaluation

- Assessment and evaluation can be defined as functions performed by teachers to make wise decisions about their instruction and about their students. A fairly large portion of a teacher's time is consumed with assessment and evaluation processes.
- The consequences of testing and grading students are immense. They can determine the colleges students attend, the careers open to them, and the lifestyles they ultimately maintain.
- Evaluation specialists make key distinctions between formative and summative evaluation. Formative evaluation information is collected before or during instruction and is used to inform teachers about their students' prior knowledge and to make judgments about lesson effectiveness. Summative evaluation information is collected after instruction and is used to summarize how students have performed and to determine grades.
- Because the decisions made are so important, it is essential that the information used by teachers to make judgments be of high quality. Measurement specialists use two technical terms to describe the quality of assessment and evaluation information: reliability and validity.
- Reliability refers to the ability of a test or measurement device to produce consistent scores or information for persons who take the test more than once over a period of time.
- Validity refers to the ability of a test or other device to measure what it claims to measure.

### Theoretical and Empirical Support

- There is an extensive knowledge base about the technical aspects of assessment and evaluation.
- Studies show that external rewards, such as grades, can provide a strong incentive for students to perform work and can affect student learning.
- Studies also show that external rewards can sometimes have negative effects, particularly with tasks students find intrinsically interesting anyway.

### Statewide and Schoolwide Assessment Programs

- Most states today have testing programs that measure student achievement in grades 4, 6, 8, and 10. Information

from statewide tests is often used to compare how well schools are doing. In some instances, scores on statewide tests determine a student's promotion to the next grade or graduation from high school.
- Standards-based education and frequent testing are believed by many to have positive effects on student learning. Some leading educators and teachers, however, believe that frequent testing may also impede learning.
- Schoolwide assessment programs include the use of norm- and criterion-referenced tests usually chosen and administered by school district specialists.
- Norm-referenced tests evaluate a particular student's performance by comparing it to the performance of some other well-defined group of students.
- Criterion-referenced tests measure student performance against some agreed-on criterion.
- It is important that teachers understand the advantages and disadvantages of various types of schoolwide assessment procedures and be able to communicate these to students and their parents.

### A Teacher's Assessment Program

- The teacher's own classroom assessment program includes features for collecting information that can be used to diagnose students' prior knowledge and skills, to provide students with corrective feedback, and to make accurate judgments about student achievement.
- Formal tests to diagnose students' prior knowledge are more fully developed in fields such as mathematics and language arts. Asking questions, interviewing, and listening to students' responses as well as using portfolios are informal means of ascertaining what students know about a subject.
- Corrective feedback is most useful if it is immediate, frequent, and communicated in nonjudgmental ways.
- Testing students' progress and determining grades is an important aspect of teachers' work, and society expects it to be done well.

### Specifics of Testing and Grading

- A variety of guidelines exist for teachers to follow as they construct tests to measure student learning and make judgments and assign grades for student work.
- General principles for test construction consist of making test items in harmony with instructional objectives, cover-

ing all learning tasks, making tests valid and reliable, interpreting test results with care, and using the appropriate test items.

- A table of specifications is a device invented by evaluation specialists to help teachers determine how much space to allocate to various topics covered and to measure various levels of student cognitive processes.
- Teacher-made tests can consist of true-false, matching, fill-in-the-blanks, multiple-choice and essay items. Each type has its own advantages and disadvantages.
- Teacher bias in judging student work from essay questions is an important issue. To reduce bias, teachers should make their expectations for essay answers clear to students, write sample answers ahead of time, and use techniques to reduce expectancy effects.
- When giving tests, effective teachers find ways to reduce students' test anxiety, organize their learning environments to be conducive to test taking, make instructions clear, and avoid undue competition.
- Grading on a curve and grading to criterion or mastery are the two approaches used by classroom teachers. Each grading approach has its advantages and its shortcomings.
- Testing guidelines—making sure there is congruence between test items and what is being taught, testing fre-

quently, testing at all levels, being fair and impartial, and communicating clearly about testing and grading procedures—help teachers devise effective assessment and evaluation programs in their classrooms.

## A Look to the Future of Testing and Grading

- Currently, there appears to be a nationwide call for more accountability by schools and better and fairer ways to test and evaluate students.
- Performance and authentic assessments, as well as the use of portfolios, are likely to replace the more traditional paper-and-pencil tests in the near future.
- Performance and authentic assessments ask students to demonstrate that they can perform particular real-life tasks, such as writing an essay, doing an experiment, or playing a song.
- Developing performance and authentic assessment devices is a difficult and complex task, as is making sure these newer forms of tests are valid and reliable.
- New interest in accountability and testing has also led to the development of an "assessment bills of rights" to make sure that students are not harmed by educational testing procedures.

## Key Terms

| | | | |
|---|---|---|---|
| assessment | extrinsic rewards | table of specifications | performance assessment |
| evaluation | standardized tests | objective test | authentic assessment |
| formative evaluation | norm-referenced tests | essay test | scoring rubric |
| summative evaluation | criterion-referenced tests | holistic scoring | student portfolio |
| reliability | prior knowledge | grading on a curve | |
| validity | corrective feedback | grading to criterion | |

## 🍎 Books for the Professional

American Educational Research Association, American Psychological Association, and National Council on Measurement in Education (1985). *Standards for Educational and Psychological Testing*. Washington, D.C.: American Psychological Association. This important resource for teachers outlines the technical standards for test construction and for using test results.

Airasian, P. W. (1996). *Assessment in the Classroom*. New York: McGraw-Hill. This excellent text written specifically for teachers includes both formal as well as informal assessment procedures.

Gronlund, N. E., *Assessment of Student Achievement* (6th ed.). Boston: Allyn and Bacon, 1998. A very good standard text, recently updated, on how classroom teachers can assess learning outcomes.

Mitchell, R. (1992). *Testing for Learning: How New Approaches to Evaluation Can Improve American Schools.* New York: Free Press. This highly readable and up-to-date account of new approaches to student evaluation includes examples of best practice and presents the issues raised by different approaches to evaluation.

Rothman, R. *Measuring Up: Standards, Assessment and School Reform.* San Francisco: Jossey-Bass, 1995. An excellent book on alternative assessment strategies and how they can be used in schools.

Wiggins, G. P. (1993). *Assessing Student Performance.* San Francisco: Jossey-Bass. This book explores the purposes and aspects of testing and is filled with examples of newer approaches to assessment.

## Reflection & Portfolio

## Grading for Fairness and Learning

You have just met with the principal at the school where you have been hired for your first teaching position. You asked him about the school's grading and reporting policies. He said that teachers have considerable freedom. They are required to give A's, B's, C's, D's, and F's, and they must conform to the district's grading periods. Outside of these requirements, they can design their own system for how much weight to give to tests, quizzes, homework, participation, and the like. They can also decide whether to grade on a curve or on particular standards. He told you that most students in the school go to college and are very concerned about their grades. They and their parents are not afraid to complain if they believe a teacher has evaluated their work unfairly.

The principal encouraged you to talk to other teachers in the school, come up with your own approach for assessment and grading, and then discuss your plan with him. You have always believed that a teacher should have a grading system that is fair and acceptable to students. You also believe that a teacher's grading system should be one that will promote learning for all the students in a classroom.

Develop an assessment plan consistent with this teaching situation and your beliefs. You may wish to address the following questions in your plan before you compare it with the approaches used by the teachers below. What would be your overall approach? What weight would you give to tests, assignments, and projects? Would you give credit for participation? For effort? Would you hold all students to the same standards, or would you establish different standards for gifted students than for those who are learning disabled? How will you justify your system to your students? Their parents? Before you begin, consider how your assessment plan can become an important artifact in your professional portfolio and compare it to the ideas expressed by the experienced teachers below.

### Jane Fernandez

"I have spent many years developing what I think is a fair assessment system. I do not grade on a curve but instead on a set of flexible standards that I communicate to students at the beginning of the year. I test frequently, and tests count for 45 percent of the student's grade. Assignments and projects count for another 45 percent. Student participation, effort, and extra work count for 10 percent. My standards are flexible in that I expect more from students with high abilities than I do from students who have more difficulty learning or who have special needs. I differentiate my homework assignments and allow certain students more time to complete assignments. Whenever possible, I use performance and authentic assessment procedures and make some of these more difficult than others. Some of my colleagues think my system is unjust. However, I have found that most students understand the logic behind my practices and believe my approach is fair."

### William Fisher

"Some people tell me that my approach to assessment is old-fashioned. I believe strongly that students need to understand the "knowledge" that is supposed to be taught in my course. To get them to learn this content, I outline precisely what they are supposed to know and test weekly to find out how much they have learned. I also give mid-term and end-of-semester exams. Weekly quizzes count for 40 percent of the grade; the mid-term and the final exam together count for another 40 percent. Assignments count for 20 percent. I don't give extra credit, nor do I give credit for class participation. Everyone in the class is held to the same standards; they have the same assignments and take the same test.

"This approach has served me well over the years. The testing and grading system is easy to explain to students and their parents. Most students who are willing to put in the time can get an A or a B. I never ask trick questions, and I always make it very clear to students what's going to be on the tests. Students work very hard in my classes. Incentives work!"

# Part 2 🍎 *The Interactive Aspects of Teaching*

**P**art Two of *Learning to Teach* focuses directly on what most people think of as teaching—the actual face-to-face interaction between the teacher and the learner. Each of the six chapters describes one of six basic instructional approaches: (1) presentation; (2) direct instruction; (3) concept teaching; (4) cooperative learning; (5) problem-based instruction; and (6) discussion. You will find that the first three approaches are based primarily on teacher-centered principles of learning. These three models rely mainly on social learning theory and on behavioral and information processing theories of learning. The next three approaches are based on learner-centered principles. Learner-centered approaches rest on the philosophical perspective of John Dewey and other progressive educators and on cognitive and contructivist principles of learning. As you study these approaches, you will learn that each has been designed to achieve certain learning outcomes at the expense of others, and as such, each approach has advantages and disadvantages. No one approach is necessarily better than another. Appropriate use of each depends on the nature of the students in a classroom and the type of goals the teacher wants to achieve.

The various approaches described in Part Two are labeled *teaching models,* although other terms—such as *teaching strategies, teaching methods,* or *teaching principles*—share similar characteristics. The label *teaching model* was selected for two important reasons.

First, the concept *model* implies something larger than a particular strategy, method, or procedure. For example, as used here, the term *teaching model* encompasses a broad, overall approach to instruction rather than a specific strategy. Models of teaching have some attributes that specific strategies and methods do not have. The attributes of a model are a coherent theoretical basis; a point of view about what students should learn and how they learn; and recommended teaching behaviors and classroom structures for bringing about different types of desired learning.

Second, the concept of the teaching model serves as an important communication device for teachers. Joyce and Weil (1996) classified various approaches to teaching according to their instructional goals, their syntaxes, and the nature of their learning environments. Instructional goals specify the type of *student outcomes* a model has been designed to achieve. The use of a particular model helps a teacher achieve some goals but not others. A model's *syntax* is the overall flow of a lesson's activity. The *learning environment* is the context in which any teaching act must be carried out, including the ways students are motivated and managed.

Although there is nothing magical about these words or this classification system, they provide a language for communicating about various kinds of teaching activities, when they should occur, and why.

In describing the teaching models in the chapters that follow, we might seem to suggest that there is only one correct way to use a particular model. In some respects, this is true. If teachers deviate too far from a model's syntax or environmental demands, they are not using the model. On the other hand, once teachers have mastered a particular model, they often need to adapt it to their own particular teaching style and to the particular group of students with whom they are working. As with most other aspects of teaching, models are guides for thinking and talking about teaching. They should not be viewed as recipes to follow.

There is a substantial knowledge base for the instructional aspects of teaching, and there is the wisdom that has been accumulated by experienced teachers over the years. Part of the excitement and challenge in learning to teach is in figuring out the complexities of teaching, which the organizational pattern of a book cannot portray with complete accuracy.

# Chapter 🍎 Seven

# Presentation

## Reflecting on **Presentations**

Think of all the lectures you have heard in your lifetime. You can conjure up some that were stimulating, leaving you eager to learn more about the topic; others you remember may have been boring, leaving you fighting to stay awake; still others may have been humorous and entertaining, but you didn't learn very much. Before reading this chapter, take a few minutes to do the following:

🍎 *Make a list of the essential characteristics of the best lectures you have ever heard.*

🍎 *Make a similar list of the characteristics of the worst lectures you have ever heard.*

Now study your lists and consider what you think your teachers did to develop the best lectures and what they did or didn't do that produced poor lectures. How did the two types of lectures influence what you learned? Did you learn anything from the bad lecture?

Presentations or lectures by teachers comprise one-sixth to one-fourth of all classroom time. The amount of time devoted to presenting and explaining information increases at the higher grade levels of elementary school, in middle schools, and in high schools (Dunkin & Biddle, 1974; Rosenshine & Stevens, 1986). Some educators have argued that too much time is devoted to teachers talking, and over the years, considerable effort has gone into creating models aimed at decreasing the amount of teacher talk and making instruction more student-centered. Nonetheless, formal presentation of information remains the most popular model of teaching, and the amount of time devoted to it has remained relatively stable over time (Cuban, 1994).

> **Despite criticism, presentation or lecture maintains its popularity among teachers.**

The popularity of presenting and explaining is not surprising, since the most widely held objectives for education at the present time are those associated with the acquisition and retention of information. Curricula in schools are structured around bodies of information organized as science, mathematics, English, and the social sciences. Consequently, curriculum guides, textbooks, and tests routinely used by teachers are similarly organized. Further, many exams that students are required to take test primarily information. Experienced teachers know that exposition is an effective way of helping students acquire the array of information society believes it is important for them to know.

> **The appropriate use of the presentation model varies, depending on a teacher's objective and the particular students in the class.**

The purpose of this chapter is to introduce the **presentation teaching model** and tell how to use it effectively. We cannot judge the ideal amount of time a teacher should devote to this model. Instead, the model is described as a valuable teaching approach that can be used in all subject areas and at all grade levels. The appropriate use of the presentation model is situational; that is, its use depends on the objective the teacher is striving to achieve and the particular students with whom the teacher is working.

Fortunately, the knowledge base on teacher presentation and explanation is fairly well developed. Beginning teachers can learn this model quite easily. As you read this chapter and study the model, you will find much that is familiar. Some of the material you already know from speech classes taken in high school or college. Some of the difficulties of presenting you know from informal talks or speeches you have made. Although the goals of public speaking and classroom presentations are quite different, many of the basic communication skills are the same. We first provide a general overview of the presentation model using the analytical scheme described in the introduction to Part Two, namely, that a teaching model has three features: (1) the type of learner outcomes it produces; (2) its syntax or overall flow of instructional activities; and (3) its learning environment.

Following the overview, we take a brief look at the theoretical and empirical support for the presentation model, after which we provide a detailed discussion of how to conduct a presentation lesson. This same chapter structure will be followed in subsequent Part Two chapters.

## 🍎 *Overview of Presentation Teaching*

The specific presentation model highlighted here is an adaptation of what is sometimes called the advance organizer model. This model requires a teacher to provide students with advance organizers before presenting new information and to make special efforts during and following a presentation to strengthen and extend student thinking. This particular approach was chosen for two reasons. One, the approach is compatible with current knowledge from cognitive psychology about the way individuals acquire, process, and retain new information. Two, various components of the model have been

**Figure 7.1** *Presentation Teaching Aims at Accomplishing Three Learner Outcomes*

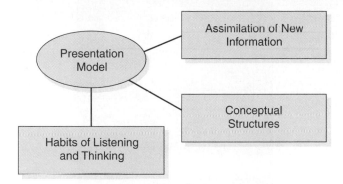

carefully studied over the past thirty years, thus giving the model a substantial, if not always consistent, knowledge base.

Briefly, the learning outcomes of the presentation model, shown in Figure 7.1, are rather clear and straightforward: namely, to help students acquire, assimilate, and retain new information, expand their conceptual structures, and develop particular habits of thinking about information.

Presentation is a teacher-centered model consisting of four major phases for teachers to follow. The flow proceeds from the teacher's initial attempt to clarify the aims of the lesson and to get students ready to learn, through presentation of an advance organizer and presentation of the new information, to the conclusion with interactions aimed at checking student understanding of the new information and extending and strengthening their thinking skills. When using the presentation model, the teacher strives to structure the learning environment tightly. Except in the final phase of the model, the teacher is an active presenter and expects students to be active listeners. Use of the model requires a physical learning environment that is conducive to presenting and listening, including appropriate facilities for use of multimedia technology.

> The presentation model requires a highly structured environment characterized by a teacher who is an active presenter and students who are active listeners.

**✓ Check for Understanding**

- What are the four phases of a presentation lesson?
- What learner outcomes characterize presentation lessons?
- What type of learning environment is required for an effective presentation?

## 🍎 *Theoretical and Empirical Support*

Three complementary sets of ideas have come together to provide the theoretical and empirical support for the presentation model of teaching. These include (1) the concept of **structure of knowledge,** (2) the psychology of **meaningful verbal learning,** and (3) ideas from **cognitive psychology** on how the human memory system works and how knowledge is represented and acquired. It is important to understand the ideas underlying these three topics because they provide the basis on which teachers choose, organize, and present information to students. They also support several features of the direct instruction and concept teaching models presented in Chapters 8 and 9, respectively.

### Structure and Organization of Knowledge

Knowledge of the world has been organized around various subject areas called *disciplines.* History is an example of a discipline that organizes knowledge using temporal concepts; biology organizes information and ideas about living things, and physics,

*Jerome Bruner was among the first to describe how important structure of knowledge is in education.*

about the physical world. The clustering of courses by academic departments in college catalogs is one illustration of the wide array of disciplines that exist. The classification of books in libraries according to subject matter under the Dewey decimal or Library of Congress system is another.

The disciplines, as they are defined at any point in time, constitute the resources on which most teachers and curriculum developers draw in making decisions about what knowledge should be taught to students. Over three decades ago, Ralph Taylor made this observation:

> From the standpoint of the curriculum, the disciplines should be viewed primarily as a resource that can be drawn upon for the education of students. Hence, we want to understand these resources at their best. . . . These disciplines at their best are not simply an encyclopedic collection of facts to be memorized but rather they are an active effort to make sense out of some portion of the world or of life. (Ford & Pugno, 1964, p. 4)

During the 1950s, several scholars and curriculum theorists started to study how disciplines were organized and what that organization meant to instruction. A book written by Jerome Bruner in 1960 called *The Process of Education* highlighted this research. This inquiry produced the idea that each discipline has a structure consisting of key concepts that define the discipline. Figure 7.2 shows a partial structure for information about American government.

Note that the illustration shows how the structure of government can be viewed as having several major ideas with a variety of subideas, such as citizen rights, amendment processes, and the various branches of government. It is not appropriate here to go into detail about the knowledge structures of various disciplines. However, it is important to emphasize that such structures exist and that they become a means for organizing information about topics, for dividing information into various categories, and for showing relationships among various categories of information.

The teaching implications of this structuring of knowledge are clear—the key ideas supporting each structure should be taught to students instead of lists of disparate facts or bits of information. For example, Bruner (1962) argued that knowing about a house "is not a matter of knowing about a collection of nails, shingles, wallboards, and windows" (p. 77). It is the total concept of house that is significant and important. The same can be said for examples from mathematics, economics, or botany.

**Figure 7.2** *A Partial Knowledge Structure for Representative Government*

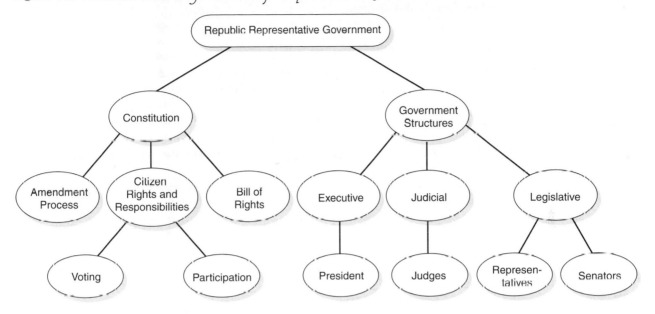

## Meaningful Verbal Learning

David Ausubel (1963), an educational psychologist, did some interesting ground-breaking work at about the same time. He was particularly interested in the way knowledge is organized hierarchically and how the human mind organizes ideas. He explained that at any point in time, a learner has an existing "organization . . . and clarity of knowledge in a particular subject-matter field" (p. 26). He called this organization a **cognitive structure** and believed that this structure determined a learner's ability to deal with new ideas and relationships. Meaning can emerge from new materials only if they tie into existing cognitive structures of prior learning.

Ausubel saw the primary function of formal education as the organizing of information for students and the presenting of ideas in clear and precise ways. The principal function of pedagogy, according to Ausubel (1963), is

> the art and science of presenting ideas and information meaningfully and effectively—so that clear, stable and unambiguous meanings emerge and . . . [are] retained over a long period of time as an organized body of knowledge. (p. 81)

For this learning to occur, according to Ausubel, the teacher should create two conditions: (1) present learning materials in a potentially meaningful form, with major and unifying ideas and principles, consistent with contemporary scholarship, highlighted rather than merely listed as facts; and (2) find ways to anchor the new learning materials to the learners' prior knowledge and ready the students' minds so that they can receive new information.

The major pedagogical strategy proposed by Ausubel (1963) is the use of **advance organizers.** It is the job of an advance organizer to

> delineate clearly, precisely, and explicitly the principal similarities and differences between the ideas in a new learning passage, on the one hand, and existing related concepts in cognitive structure on the other. (p. 83)

*An individual's cognitive structure determines his or her ability to deal with new information and ideas.*

*Advance organizers provide a device to help learners link new information to prior knowledge.*

More specific details about how to construct and present advance organizers are provided later in this chapter.

## Cognitive Psychology of Learning

A third stream of inquiry that helps explain how information should be presented to students grew out of the rapidly expanding field of cognitive psychology. Its frame of reference is important to teachers because it provides ways for thinking about how the mind works and how knowledge is acquired, organized, and represented in the memory system. As you read the key ideas here, you will observe how they are connected in many ways to Bruner's earlier concept of structure of knowledge and Ausubel's ideas about meaningful verbal learning.

Ellen Gagné (1985, 1993) and her colleagues have organized the ideas and research in the field of cognitive psychology that apply directly to teaching. The discussion that follows relies heavily on their work and their definitions of the different types of knowledge and how information is processed and represented in the memory system.

**Declarative knowledge is knowing about something, whereas procedural knowledge is knowing how to do something.**

**Conditional knowledge involves the process of deciding when to appropriately use declarative or procedural knowledge.**

Three Types of Knowledge. Learning theorists generally distinguish among three types of knowledge: *declarative knowledge, procedural knowledge,* and *conditional knowledge* (Marx & Winne, 1994; Ryle, 1949; R. Gagné, 1977; E. Gagné, 1985; and E. Gagné, et al., 1993). **Declarative knowledge** is knowledge *about something* or knowledge that something is the case. **Procedural knowledge** is knowledge about *how to do something.* **Conditional knowledge** is knowing when and why to use particular declarative or procedural knowledge. An example of declarative knowledge is knowledge about the three branches of government: that the legislative branch has two chambers (the House and the Senate) and that representatives to the House are elected to 2-year terms whereas senators are elected to 6-year terms. Procedural knowledge about this same topic is knowledge about how to go to the polling place and to vote on election day, how to write a letter to a senator, or if one is a senator, how to guide a bill through the Senate until it becomes a law. Conditional knowledge is knowing which of many political actions might be most effective in getting a desired piece of legislation passed. Table 7.1 summarizes the three types of knowledge and provides examples of each.

In addition, knowledge can be classified, as you read in Chapter 2, according to levels of complexity. At the lowest level is straightforward factual information, that is, simple declarative knowledge that one acquires but may or may not use. Memorizing the rules of poetry written in iambic pentameter is an example of factual knowledge. In contrast, the higher levels of knowledge generally involve using knowledge in some way, such as critiquing one of Robert Browning's poems or com-

**Table 7.1** *Three Kinds of Knowledge*

| Kinds of Knowledge | Definition | Example |
| --- | --- | --- |
| Declarative | Knowing about something or that something is the case | Rules of a game; definition of a triangle |
| Procedural | Knowing how to do something | Playing basketball; using a word processing program |
| Conditional | Knowing when to use particular declarative or procedural knowledge | When to dribble; when to subtract; when to highlight |

paring and contrasting it with the work of Keats. Often procedural knowledge requires the previous acquisition of declarative knowledge, in this case, basic concepts of poetry. Teachers want their students to have all three kinds of knowledge. They want them to acquire large bodies of basic declarative knowledge; they also want them to acquire important procedural and conditional knowledge, so they can take action and do things effectively.

The Resource Handbook explores in more detail the nature of knowledge and how it is acquired. We introduce the concept here because different types of knowledge are acquired in different ways. The presentation model described in this chapter is most useful in helping students acquire straightforward declarative knowledge. The direct instruction model described in Chapter 8, on the other hand, has been specifically designed to promote student learning of procedural and some types of conditional knowledge.

**Information Processing.** New knowledge (ideas and information) enter the mind through one of the senses—sight or hearing, for example—and are noted first by the learner's *working* or short-term memory. **Short-term memory** is the place where conscious mental work is done. For example, if you are solving the problem 26 × 32 mentally, you hold the intermediate products 52 and 78 in short-term memory and add them together there.

Information in short-term memory may soon be forgotten unless stored more deeply in **long-term memory.** Long-term memory can be likened to a computer. Information must first be coded before it can be stored and, although stored for perhaps a lifetime, cannot be retrieved unless first given appropriate cues. Information or ideas stored in long-term memory must also be retrieved to working memory before they can be used.

Figure 7.3 shows how short-term and long-term memory interact in instructional settings.

**Knowledge Representation.** Additional cognitive psychology ideas that help explain how the presentation model works involve the way knowledge is stored and represented in memory. Cognitive psychologists use the label **schema** to define the way people organize information about particular subjects and how this organization influences their processing of new information and ideas. Individuals' schema differ in important ways, and schemata (pl.) held about various topics prepare the learner to process new information and to see relationships. The more complete a person's **prior knowledge** and schema are for a particular topic, the easier it becomes to process new information and to see more abstract relationships. Although cognitive psychologists do not always agree about the exact way knowledge is represented in the memory system, they do agree that prior knowledge definitely filters new information and thereby determines how well new information presented by a teacher will be integrated and retained by a learner.

Teaching principles about presenting information growing out of ideas from cognitive psychology are important for teachers in four ways. One, it is important to know that knowledge is organized and structured around basic propositions and unifying ideas. However, individuals differ in the way their knowledge about particular topics is organized. Two, students' abilities to learn new ideas depend on their prior knowledge and existing cognitive structures. Three, the primary tasks for teachers in helping students acquire knowledge are:

1. organizing learning materials in a thoughtful and skillful way,
2. providing students with advance organizers that will help anchor and integrate new learning, and
3. providing them with cues for drawing information from their long-term to their working memories.

**Short-term memory is the place in the mind where conscious mental work is done.**

**Long-term memory is the place in the mind where information is stored, ready for retrieval when needed.**

**An individual's schema reflects the way information has been organized and stored in memory.**

*Prior knowledge refers to the information an individual has prior to instruction.*

**Figure 7.3**  *An Example of Short-Term and Long-Term Memory*

Suppose that a second-grade teacher wants Joe to learn the fact that the capital of Texas is Austin. The teacher asks Joe, "What is the capital of Texas?" and Joe says, "I don't know." At the same time Joe may set up an expectancy that he is about to learn the capital of Texas, which will cause him to pay attention. The teacher then says, "The capital of Texas is Austin." Joe's ears receive this message along with other sounds such as the other pupils' speech and traffic outside the school.

All of the sounds that Joe hears are translated into electrochemical impulses and sent to the sensory register. The pattern that the capital of Texas is Austin is selected for entry into working memory, but other sound patterns are not entered.

Joe may then code the fact that the capital of Texas is Austin by associating it with other facts that he already knows about Austin (e.g., that it is a big city and that he once visited it). This coding process causes the new fact to be entered into long-term memory. If Joe has already developed special memory strategies (which is somewhat unlikely for a second grader), his executive control process would direct the coding process to use these special strategies.

The next day Joe's teacher might ask him, "What is the capital of Texas?" This question would be received and selected for entry into short-term memory. There it would provide cues for retrieving the answer from long-term memory. A copy of the answer would be used by the response generator to organize the speech acts that produce the sounds, "Austin is the capital of Texas." At this point Joe's expectancy that he would learn the capital of Texas has been confirmed.

Source: After E. Gagné (1993), p. 78.

Finally, remember that cognitive structures change as a result of new information and thus become the basis for developing new cognitive structures.

## Empirical Support

The knowledge base on presenting and explaining information to learners has been developed by researchers working in several different fields, especially cognitive psychology and information processing, as described in the previous section. Other research comes from the study of teaching and has focused on such topics as set induction, use of prior knowledge, and advance organizers. Still other work has looked at teacher clarity and enthusiasm and how these attributes affect student learning. Since it is impossible to provide full coverage of this extensive research base, only selected works have been highlighted in this section.

**Establishing set is an important procedure teachers use at the beginning of a lesson for getting students ready to learn.**

**Prior Knowledge and Establishing Set.**  Research has been conducted during the past thirty years on the influence of prior knowledge for learning to read, learning to use new information, and learning to write. In general, this research points toward the importance of prior knowledge for learning new information and new skills.

One important teaching procedure for helping students use their prior knowledge is *induction* or **establishing set**, as it will be called here. Establishing set is a technique used by teachers at the beginning of a presentation to prepare students to learn and to establish a communicative link between the learners and the information about to be presented.

Several informative studies have been conducted on this topic. One of the most interesting was conducted in Australia by R. F. Schuck in the early 1980s. In a rather sophisticated experimental study, Schuck (1981) randomly assigned 120 ninth grade biology students to two groups. Teachers for the experimental group were given four hours of training on techniques for establishing set. When the experimental students' achievement was compared to that of the control students, Schuck found that the use of establishing set had a clear impact on student achievement. This impact existed not only immediately following instruction but also when students were tested twenty-four to twenty-six weeks later.

As you will see later, establishing set is not the same as an advance organizer, although both serve the similar purpose of using students' prior knowledge. By establishing set, teachers help students retrieve appropriate information and intellectual skills from long-term memory and get it ready for use as new information and skills are introduced. More information about and examples of establishing set are provided later.

**Using Advance Organizers.** As you read in the previous section, Ausubel saw the use of an advance organizer as a means to help make information meaningful to students. For Ausubel, an advance organizer consists of statements made by teachers just before actual presentation of the learning materials. These statements are at a higher level of abstraction than the subsequent information. Later in this chapter, advance organizers are defined more precisely; however, here it is important to say that advance organizers help students use prior knowledge just as establishing set does. They differ, however, in that they are tied more tightly to the subsequent information and provide an anchor for later learning.

> **Advance organizers are used to help make information more meaningful to students by relating prior knowledge to the new lesson.**

The Research Summary for this chapter (pages 242 to 243) presents Ausubel's seminal work on advance organizers, first published in 1960.

Since David Ausubel first published his results, other psychologists and educational researchers have been actively testing his hypothesis. Walberg (1986) reported that from 1969 to 1979, advance organizers were the subject of thirty-two studies. Walberg also described a synthesis of research done by Luiten, Ames, and Aerson (1980) that identified over 135 studies on the effects of advance organizers. Although not all the studies show the effectiveness of advance organizers, the findings seem to be consistent enough over time to recommend that teachers use advance organizers when presenting information to students.

**Teacher Clarity.** Using advance organizers, establishing set, and attending to prior learning all affect student learning. Another variable associated with the presentation of information that has been shown to influence student learning is **teacher clarity.** An important early study on teacher clarity was conducted by Hiller, Gisher, and Kaess (1969). They asked teachers to deliver two different 15-minute presentations to their students—one on Yugoslavia and the other on Thailand. Teachers were encouraged to make the presentations in their normal fashion. They studied five teacher presentation variables: verbal fluency, amount of information, knowledge structure cues, interest, and vagueness. The researchers found significant relationships on two factors: verbal fluency (clarity) and vagueness. The researchers suggested that lack of clarity in a presentation most often indicates that the speaker does not know the information well or cannot remember the key points. This, of course, suggests several steps for teachers who are about to present information to their students: (1) make sure the content is thoroughly understood, (2) practice and commit the key ideas to memory prior to presentation, or (3) follow written notes very carefully.

> **The clarity of a presentation is a very important factor in determining how much students will learn.**

*Research Summary 7.1*

# What Do We Know About Making Learning Meaningful?

*Ausubel, D. P. (1960).*

The use of advance organizers in the learning and retention of meaningful verbal material. *Journal of Educational Psychology,* 51, 267–272.

A common problem facing all teachers is how to make the information they want students to learn meaningful. Questions often asked are: Does the information have to be interesting to students? Does it need to connect to something they already know? Are there little things teachers can do that will make a difference?

**Problem and Approach:** Over forty years ago, David Ausubel asked the question, Does giving students an advance organizer to serve as an intellectual scaffold facilitate learning and retention of unfamiliar information? Ausubel's study is one of the oldest included in this book. It is here because it sparked a research interest in this problem and subsequently led to a substantial knowledge base on the effects of using advance organizers and of the importance of connecting new information to what students already know. It also demonstrated that sometimes a fairly small intervention by teachers can make a big difference in what students learn.

**Sample and Setting:** Ausubel studied 110 senior undergraduate students (78 women and 32 men) at the University of Illinois. The students were in teacher education and were enrolled in a course in educational psychology when they were asked to participate in the study.

**Procedures:** The researcher designed a 2,500-word learning passage on the topic of the "metallurgical properties of carbon steel." Emphasis of the content of the learning materials according to the researcher was on "basic principles of the relationship between metallic grain structures, on the one hand, and temperature, carbon content, and rate of cooling on the other." This topic was chosen because it had been determined that it was one that most liberal arts and teacher education majors would not be familiar with, an important condition if the central hypothesis was to be tested. Subjects were divided into two groups, experimental and control. The groups were matched on the basis of ability to learn unfamiliar material (test score on another passage of comparable difficulty). Each group then received the following treatments.

- Experimental group. The introduction to the steel learning materials for students in the experimental group contained a 500-word introductory passage with a substantive advance organizer—background material presented at a higher level of abstraction than information in the content of the materials to follow.
- Control group. The introduction to the steel learning materials for students in the control group provided historically relevant material and information in a 500-word passage but no advance organizer.

Both groups studied the learning materials for thirty-five minutes and then took a test on the materials three days later. The test consisted of thirty-six multiple-choice items covering the major principles and facts in the learning materials.

**Pointers for Reading Research:** There are no new concepts introduced in Table 7.2. Ausubel's study is rather straightforward. However, as with many studies during this era, Ausubel's subjects were college students. Results stemming from this type of population do not necessarily generalize to younger students and those with varying backgrounds typical of most elementary and secondary schools. It was not until the 1970s that large numbers of researchers left their own college classrooms and conducted investigations in the schools. This study is included here regardless of its weaknesses because of Ausubel's close association with the advance organizer model of teaching and because it has influenced so much later research.

**Table 7.2** *Retention Test Scores of Experimental and Control Groups on Learning Passage*

| Group | Type of Introduction | Mean | Standard Deviation |
|---|---|---|---|
| Experimental | Advanced organizer | 16.7* | 5.8 |
| Control | Historical overview | 14.1 | 5.4 |

*Significant at the .05 level.

**Results:** Table 7.2 shows the test scores of students in the experimental and control groups.

**Discussion and Implications:** As can be observed in Table 7.2, students who were given advance organizers before they read the 2,500-word passage on steel retained more information three days later as compared to students who were introduced to the learning materials with a historical passage. The weakness in Ausubel's study, as a test for the effectiveness of the advance organizer, is that the information was given to students in text, not verbally. Nonetheless, the principle is still the same. A word of caution: Ausubel's study should not be interpreted as proof that historical information is unimportant. Historical perspectives can be used, but they are not as effective as conceptual organizers in helping students integrate and retain meaningful verbal information.

*Teachers show enthusiasm for their subject by using uplifting language and dramatic body movement.*

In reviews of the research done over a long period of time, Rosenshine and Furst (1973) and Rosenshine and Stevens (1986) reported that "teacher clarity" has been a specific teaching trait that has shown up consistently as having an impact on student achievement.

**Teacher Enthusiasm.** An additional variable thought to influence teacher presentations is **teacher enthusiasm.** This is an interesting concept for two reasons. First, enthusiasm is often confused with theatrics and its associated distractions, and second,

✔ **Check for Understanding**

- Why is the concept "structure of knowledge" important to presentation teaching?

- What does Ausubel mean by "meaningful verbal learning"?

- What are the three types of knowledge?

- What is the difference between short-term and long-term memory? What roles does each play in the acquisition of new information?

- How can the research on prior knowledge, establishing set, and teacher clarity be used in planning a classroom presentation?

the research on the relationship between teacher enthusiasm and student learning is mixed.

*Effects of Enthusiasm.* In 1970, Rosenshine reviewed the research on teacher enthusiasm and reported that it showed pretty consistent relationships between teacher enthusiasm and student learning. Since that time, researchers have tried to study teacher enthusiasm and have developed training programs to help teachers become more enthusiastic in their presentations. For example, Collins (1978) developed and tested a training program that looked at a specific set of enthusiastic behaviors: rapid, uplifting, varied local delivery; dancing, wide-open eyes; frequent, demonstrative questions; varied, dramatic body movements; varied emotive facial expressions; selection of varied words, especially adjectives; ready, animated acceptance of ideas and feelings; and exuberant overall energy. Collins found that students in classes of enthusiasm-trained teachers did better than those in classes of untrained teachers.

However, in the mid-1980s, a study conducted by Bettencourt (see Borg and Gall, 1999) could find no difference between enthusiasm-trained and untrained teachers. Therefore, at this time, it appears that we should be careful about the importance of enthusiasm. Though enthusiasm seems to make a difference, the exact nature of enthusiasm and how much of it to use remain unknown.

## 🍎 *Planning and Conducting Presentation Lessons*

Understanding the theoretical and research bases underlying the teacher presentation model is not sufficient for its effective use. That requires expert execution of particular decisions and behaviors during the preinstructional, interactive, and postinstructional phases of teaching. This section describes guidelines for using the presentation model appropriately and effectively.

### Planning for Presentations

**Teaching is more than just talking. Successful lessons require extensive preparation involving multiple activities.**

Except for people who are really shy, it is quite easy for someone to get up in front of a class of students and talk for twenty to thirty minutes. *Talking, however, is not teaching.* Making decisions about what content to include in a presentation and how to organize content so it is logical and meaningful to students takes extensive preparation by the teacher. Four planning tasks are most important: (1) choosing objectives and content for the presentation, (2) determining students' prior knowledge, (3) selecting appropriate and powerful advance organizers, and (4) planning for use of time and space.

**Choosing Objectives and Content.** The objectives for presentation lessons consist mainly of those aimed at the acquisition of declarative knowledge. Figure 7.4 provides examples of typical objectives teachers might choose. However, the amount of declarative knowledge in any field is endless, and several principles can assist beginning teachers as they plan particular presentations or series of presentations.

**Power and Economy.** In Chapter 2, the concepts of power and economy were introduced as tools for curriculum selection. These concepts can also be used by teachers as they select content to include in a presentation. Remember the concept of power holds that only the most important and powerful concepts should be taught, rather than

**Figure 7.4** *Sample Instructional Objectives for a Presentation Lesson*

- Student will be able to describe the significance of the Fourteenth Amendment.
- Student will be able to identify the women authors of three nineteenth-century American novels.
- Student will be able to list the basic rules of ice hockey.
- Student will be able to define the meaning of photosynthesis.
- Student will be able to describe the contributions of three African Americans to United States history.

those of interest but not central to understanding the subject at hand. The economy concept recommends that teachers stay away from verbal clutter and limit their presentations to a minimum amount of information. Achieving economy and power in a presentation depends not so much on a teacher's delivery style as it does on planning. In fact, a carefully organized presentation read in a monotone might be more effective in producing student learning than a dynamic presentation void of powerful ideas, even though students may enjoy the latter more.

Conceptual Mapping. Another tool that is useful in deciding what to teach is that of **conceptual mapping.** Conceptual maps show relationships among ideas, and like road maps, they help users get their bearings. They also help clarify for the teacher the kinds of ideas to teach, and they provide students with a picture for understanding relationships among ideas. To make a conceptual map, you identify the key ideas associated with a topic and arrange these ideas in some logical pattern.

Determining Students' Prior Knowledge. Information given in a presentation is based on teachers' estimates of their students' existing cognitive structures and their prior knowledge of a subject. As with many other aspects of teaching, there are no clear-cut rules or easy formulas for teachers to follow. There are, however, some ideas that

*Lesson plans are based on a teacher's determination of students' prior knowledge.*

**Figure 7.5** *An Individual's Cognitive Structure with Respect to Representative Government*

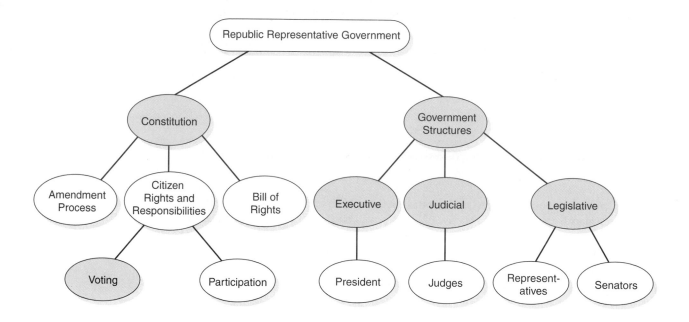

can serve as guides for practice as well as some informal procedures to be learned from experienced teachers.

*Cognitive Structures.* For new material to be meaningful to students, teachers must find ways to connect it to what students already know. Students' existing ideas on a particular topic determine which new concepts are potentially meaningful. Figure 7.5 illustrates how a student's cognitive structure might look in relation to certain concepts about government. Note that Figure 7.5 has the same information as Figure 7.2, but Figure 7.5 is being used to show that some concepts have been learned and others have not. Note also the illustrator's judgment (shaded areas) about which concepts will be relevant because of the student's prior knowledge.

*Intellectual Development.* Cognitive structures are influenced by students' prior knowledge. They are also influenced by maturation and development. Several theorists have put forth developmental theories, including Hunt (1974), Piaget (1954, 1963), and Perry (1969). Space does not allow a full discussion of the similarities and differences among developmental theories, but they agree that learners go through developmental stages ranging from very simple and concrete structures at early ages to more abstract and complicated structures later on. It is important that teachers tailor information they present to the level of development of the learners.

**Student's intellectual development and prior knowledge are important factors to consider when planning a presentation.**

Ideas about how students develop intellectually can assist teachers as they plan for a particular presentation; however, they cannot provide concrete solutions for several reasons. As experienced teachers know, development is uneven and does not occur precisely at any given ages. Within any classroom, a teacher is likely to find students at extremely varied stages of development. The teacher will also find some students who have developed to a high level of abstraction in some subjects, say history, and still be at a very concrete level in another subject, such as mathematics.

Another problem facing the teacher striving to apply developmental theories to planning for a particular presentation is the problem of measuring the developmental levels of students. Most teachers must rely on informal assessments. For example, teachers can watch students as they approach specific problem-solving tasks and make a rough assessment of the degree to which they use concrete or abstract operations. By listening carefully to students and asking probing questions, teachers can determine whether or not the information they are presenting is meaningful. Watching for nonverbal cues during a presentation, such as silence, frowns, or expressions of interest, can provide insights into what students are picking up from the presentation. Silence, for example, can mean that students are bored; most often it means they do not understand what the teacher is saying. It may be that part of the "art of teaching" and a major difference between expert and novice teachers is expert teachers' abilities to read subtle communication cues from students and then adapt their lessons so that new learning materials become meaningful.

> **Teachers can successfully ascertain student understanding of a lesson by asking questions and watching for nonverbal cues.**

Selecting Advance Organizers. The third planning task associated with the presentation model is choosing appropriate advance organizers. Remember, advance organizers become the hooks, the anchors, the "intellectual scaffolding" for subsequent learning materials. Ausubel suggested that advance organizers should be slightly more abstract than the content to be presented. More recent research (Mayer, 1984, for example) has suggested that concrete examples from the forthcoming lesson might work better than more abstract advance organizers. Regardless of the degree of abstraction, a good advance organizer contains materials familiar to students and is designed to relate to students' prior knowledge.

> **Advance organizers are scaffolds for new information. They are not merely a means of introducing a lesson.**

We should repeat one point here: The advance organizer *is not* the same as *other techniques* used by teachers *to introduce* a lesson, such as reviewing past work, establishing set, or giving an overview of the day's lesson. All of these are important for effective presentations, but they are not advance organizers. Following are three examples of advance organizers teachers have used in particular presentations to give you an idea of what they are.

*Example 1.* A history teacher is about to present information about the Vietnam War. After reviewing yesterday's lesson, telling students the goals of today's lesson, and asking students to recall in their minds what they already know about Vietnam (establishing set), the teacher presents the following advance organizer:

> I want to give you an idea that will help you understand why the United States became involved in the Vietnam War. *The idea is that most wars reflect conflict between peoples over one of the following: ideology, territory, or access to trade.* As I describe for you the United States' involvement in Southeast Asia between 1945 and 1965, I want you to look for examples of how conflict over ideology, territory, or access to trade may have influenced later decisions to fight in Vietnam.

*Example 2.* A science teacher is about to present information about foods the body needs to function well. After going over the objectives for the lesson, the teacher asks students to list all the food they ate yesterday (establishing set) and then presents the following advance organizer:

> In a minute, I am going to give you some information about the kinds of foods the body needs to function well. Before I do that, however, *I want to give you an idea that will help you understand the different kinds of food you eat by saying they can be classified into five major food*

*groups: fats, vitamins, minerals, proteins, and carbohydrates.* Each food group contains certain elements, such as carbon or nitrogen. Also, certain things we eat (potatoes, meat) are the sources for each of the elements in the various food groups. Now as I talk about the balanced diet the body needs, I want you to pay attention to the food group to which each thing we eat belongs.

*Example 3.* An art teacher is going to show and explain to students a number of paintings from different historical eras. After giving an overview of the lesson and asking students to think for a minute about changes they have observed between paintings done during different historical eras, the teacher presents the following advance organizer:

In a minute, I am going to show and talk about several paintings—some painted in France during the early nineteenth century, others during the late nineteenth and early twentieth century. Before I do that I am going to give you an idea to help you understand the differences you are going to see. *That idea is that a painting reflects not only the individual artist's talent but also the times in which it is created. The "times" or "periods" influence the type of techniques an artist uses as well as what he or she paints about and the type of colors used.* As I show you the various paintings, I want you to look for differences in color, subject of the painting, and specific brush techniques used by the artists and see how they reflect the artist's time.

**Effective presentations rely on the effective management of time and space.**

Planning for Use of Time and Space. Planning and managing time is very important for effective presentations. Two concerns should be foremost in teachers' minds: ensuring that allocated time matches the aptitudes and abilities of the students in the class, and motivating students so that they remain attentive and on-task throughout the lesson. Many teachers, particularly beginning teachers, underestimate the amount of time it takes to teach something well and are not always adept at checking how things are going as a lesson unfolds. Later in this chapter, assessment strategies that help teachers check for understanding are presented. Teachers use this assessment information to determine whether or not they have allocated sufficient time to a particular topic. Making sure that students understand the purposes of a presentation and tying lessons into their prior knowledge and interests are ways of increasing student attention and engagement. Guidelines for doing this also are provided in the next section.

Planning and managing space is equally important for a presentation lesson. In most situations, teachers prefer the *row and column formation* of desks illustrated in Figure 7.6. This is the most traditional way of arranging classroom space, and it was so prevalent during earlier times that desks in rows were attached to the floor so they couldn't be moved. This formation is best suited to situations in which students need to focus attention on the teacher or on information being displayed on the chalkboard, overhead projector, or computer projection devices.

**It is important to begin a lesson with an introduction that will capture students' attention and motivate them to participate.**

## Conducting Presentation Lessons

The syntax of a presentation lesson consists of four basic phases: (1) clarifying the aims of the lesson and getting students ready to learn; (2) presenting the advance organizer; (3) presenting the new information; and (4) checking students' understanding and extending and strengthening their thinking skills. Each phase and required teacher behaviors are illustrated in Table 7.3.

**Figure 7.6** *Row and Column Desk Formation*

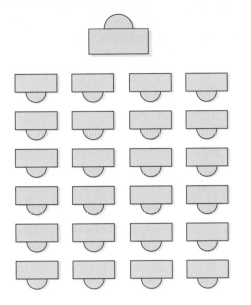

**Explaining Goals and Establishing Set.** Effective teaching using any instructional model requires an initial step by the teacher aimed at motivating students to participate in the lesson. Behaviors consistently found effective for this purpose are sharing the goals of the lesson with students and establishing a set for learning.

***Explaining Goals.*** In the discussion on motivation, you learned that students need a reason to participate in particular lessons and they need to know what is expected of them. Effective teachers telegraph their goals and expectations by providing abbreviated versions of their lesson plans on the chalkboard or on newsprint charts. Some teachers prefer newsprint charts because they can be made up the night before and posted on the wall, leaving the chalkboard free for other use; then they can be stored for future use. Effective teachers also outline the steps or phases of a particular lesson and the time required for each step. This allows the students to see the overall flow of a lesson and how the various parts fit together. Sharing the time parameters for the lesson also encourages students to help keep the lesson on schedule. Figure 7.7 shows how

**Table 7.3** *Syntax of the Presentation Model*

| Phase | Teacher Behavior |
|---|---|
| *Phase 1:* Clarify aims and establish set. | Teacher goes over the aims of the lesson and gets students ready to learn. |
| *Phase 2:* Present advance organizer. | Teacher presents advance organizer, making sure that it provides a framework for later learning materials and is connected to students' prior knowledge. |
| *Phase 3:* Present learning materials. | Teacher presents learning materials, paying special attention to their logical ordering and meaningfulness to students. |
| *Phase 4:* Check for understanding and strengthen student thinking. | Teacher asks questions and elicits student responses to the presentation to extend student thinking and encourage precise and critical thinking. |

**Figure 7.7** *Aims and Overview of Lesson on World War II*

**Today's Objective:** The objective of today's lesson is to help you understand how events and circumstances bring about change in the way people think about things.

**Agenda**

| | |
|---|---|
| 5 minutes | Introduction, review, and getting ready. |
| 5 minutes | Advance organizer for today's lesson. |
| 20 minutes | Presentation on the demise of the battleship and the concept of decisive engagement. |
| 15 minutes | Discussion for critical thinking. |
| 5 minutes | Wrap-up and preview of tomorrow's lesson. |

a social studies teacher shared her goals and the phases of her presentation with a group of eleventh grade students studying World War II.

Making students aware of what they are going to learn will help them make connections between a particular lesson and its relevance to their own lives. This motivates students to exert more effort. It also helps them to draw prior learning from long-term memory to short-term memory, where it can be used to integrate new information provided in a presentation.

*Establishing Set.* To get runners ready and off to an even start in a foot race, the command from the starter is "Get ready. . . . *Get set.* . . . Go!" The *get set* alerts runners to settle into their blocks, focus their attention on the track ahead, and anticipate a smooth and fast start.

Establishing set for a lesson in school is very much the same. Effective teachers have found that a brief review that gets students to recall yesterday's lesson or perhaps a question or anecdote that ties into students' prior knowledge is a good way to get started. Note the words used by the teacher in Figure 7.8 as she establishes set for her students.

Set activities also help students get their minds off other things they have been doing (changing classes in secondary schools; changing subjects in elementary schools; lunch and recess) and begin the process of focusing on the subject of the forthcoming lesson. These activities can also serve as motivators for lesson participation. Each teacher develops his or her own style for establishing set, but no effective teacher eliminates this important element from any lesson.

> Brief reviews that prompt students to reflect on a prior lesson or knowledge base have been found to be an effective way to start a new lesson.

**Presenting the Advance Organizer.** A previous section explained the planning tasks associated with choosing an appropriate advance organizer. Now consider how an advance organizer should be presented.

Effective teachers make sure the advance organizer is set off sufficiently from the introductory activities of the lesson and from the presentation of learning materials. As with the lesson goals, it is effective to present the advance organizer to students using some type of visual format such as a chalkboard, a newsprint chart, or an overhead projector. The key, of course, is that students must understand the advance organizer. It

**Figure 7.8** *Establishing Set Through Review*

Source: After E. Gagné (1993).

must be taught just as the subsequent information itself must be taught. This requires the teacher to be precise and clear.

**Presenting the Learning Materials.** The third phase of the model is the presentation of the learning materials. Remember how important it is for a teacher to organize learning materials in their simplest and clearest form using the principles of power and economy. The key now is to present previously organized materials in an effective manner, giving attention to such matters as clarity, examples and explaining links, the rule-example-rule technique, the use of transitions, and finally, enthusiasm.

*Clarity.* As described previously, a teaching behavior that has consistently been shown to affect student learning is the teacher's ability to be clear and specific. Common sense tells us that students will learn more when teachers are clear and specific rather than vague. Nonetheless, researchers and observers of both beginning and experienced teachers can find many instances of presentations that are vague and confusing. Vagueness

**Advance organizers should be set off from introductory activities and the subsequent presentation of learning materials.**

A teacher's ability to be clear and specific has continually been shown to have a positive impact on student learning.

occurs when teachers do not sufficiently understand the subjects they are teaching or when they lack sufficient examples to illuminate the subject.

Clarity of presentation is achieved through planning, organization, and lots of practice. Figure 7.9 provides suggestions to follow based on reviews of research by Rosenshine and Stevens (1986) and Cruickshank and Metcalf (1994).

*Explaining Links and Examples.* Effective presentations contain precise and accurate explaining links and examples. **Explaining links** are prepositions and conjunctions that indicate the cause, result, means, or purpose of an event or idea. Examples of such links include *because, since, in order to, if . . . then, therefore,* and *consequently.* Explaining links help students see the logic and relationships in a teacher's presentation and increase the likelihood of understanding.

Explaining links used in presentations helps learners understand cause and effect and other kinds of relationships.

Examples are another means used by successful presenters to make material meaningful to students. Good examples, however, are difficult for beginning teachers to think up and use. Following are guidelines that experienced teachers find useful in selecting examples:

* Identify the critical attribute(s) of the present learning.
* Select from students' own lives some previous knowledge or experience that exemplifies the same critical attribute.
* Check your example for distracters.
* Present the example.
* Label the critical attributes or elements in the example.
* Present exceptions.

**Figure 7.9** *Aspects of Clear Presentations*

1. Be clear about aims and main points.
   * State the goals of the presentation.
   * Focus on one main point at a time.
   * Avoid digressions.
   * Avoid ambiguous phrases.

2. Go through your presentation step by step.
   * Present materials in small steps.
   * Present students with an outline when material is complex.

3. Be specific and provide several examples.
   * Give detailed explanations for difficult points.
   * Provide students with concrete and varied examples.
   * Model or illustrate the idea whenever possible, and remember a picture is worth a thousand words.

4. Check for student understanding.
   * Make sure students understand one point before moving onto the next.
   * Ask questions to monitor student comprehension.
   * Ask students to summarize or paraphrase main points in their own words.
   * Reteach whenever students appear confused.

*Spotlight on Technology*

## Making Presentations Interactive

With computers and interactive multimedia, teachers can enhance their presentations and make them more interesting and thoughtful. Unlike the presentations that use overhead projectors or the chalkboard, computer-based presentations can be much more interactive, allowing the listener or viewer to be much more involved.

Three popular computer-based presentation tools on the market today are PowerPoint, ClarisWorks, and Persuasion. These software programs can be readily mastered by teachers and used regularly in classroom presentations. Today, many schools have the presentation software and computers to make this possible.

These technological tools are not only useful for teachers, students can also learn to use them to illustrate and enhance their own reports, stories, and projects.

Here is an example of an example. Say the teacher has been explaining the differences between mammals and reptiles to a group of young learners. She might proceed as follows:

- State an important generalization, such as "all mammals have warm blood."
- Then move to an example and say, "Examples of mammals you know about in your everyday lives include human beings, dogs, and cats. All these animals are mammals with warm blood."
- Finally conclude with, "Reptiles, on the other hand, are cold-blooded and are not mammals. One of the best known reptiles is the snake. Can you think of others?"

Another example of a teacher using an example follows:

There are important differences in the meanings of *climate* and *weather*. *Climate* means the overall pattern of weather a region experiences over many months and years. *Weather* is the day-to-day temperature and precipitation of a place.

Here is an example that will show you the difference between weather and climate. When Kevin and Krista visited Boston last summer, the weather was very hot, in the high 90s. We would not, however, say that Boston has a hot climate, because the weather in the winter can be very cold.

Presenting material clearly and using precise and accurate explaining links and examples require that teachers thoroughly understand both the materials being presented and the structure of the subject area being taught. For a beginning teacher having trouble, no solution exists except studying the content and the subject until mastery is achieved.

> Teachers must have a thorough understanding of the subject being taught in order to be able to present material concisely and completely.

*Rule-Example-Rule Technique.* A third technique used by effective presenters is the **rule-example-rule technique.** To apply this technique, perform the following steps.

*Step 1:* State the rule, such as "prices in a free market are influenced by supply and demand."

*Step 2:* Provide examples, such as: "When Americans in the early 1980s chose to use less oil (decrease in demand) and new oil fields were opened in coastal waters (increase in supply), the price of Middle Eastern oil went down." Or, "When there was a shortage of oil in the late 1990s (decrease in supply), the price of oil went up."

*Step 3:* Summarize and restate original rule, such as, "So, as you can see, the fluctuation of supply, along with people's desire for a product, influences what the price of a product will be."

Signposts and
transition statements
used in presentations
help learners move
from one topic to
another and alert
them to what is
important.

*Signposts and Transitions.* Particularly in longer presentations that contain several key ideas, effective presenters help learners capture main ideas and move from one part of the lesson to another by using **verbal signposts** and transitional statements. A signpost tells the learner what is important. Examples include statements such as "This is the main point I have been trying to make," "Please remember this point," and "The most important point to remember is. . . ."

Sometimes a transitional statement may be used to alert listeners to important points just made, such as "Now let me summarize the important points for you before I move on." In other instances, a transitional statement telegraphs what is to follow; for example, "We have just covered the important eras in Hemingway's life. Let's now turn to how his involvement in the Spanish Civil War influenced his writings." Or, "Now that we know the purposes of a conjunction, let's see how they work in some sample sentences." Transitional statements are important because they highlight the relationships among various ideas in a presentation, and they help display the internal organization of the information to learners.

*Enthusiasm.* As discussed in the research section, some evidence points to the importance of enthusiasm as an influence on student learning. However, results are somewhat contradictory.

Many teachers, particularly in secondary schools and colleges, argue that the key to effective presentation is for the presenter to use techniques and strategies borrowed from the performing arts. In fact, books have been written describing this approach, such as Timpson and Tobin's *Teaching as Performing* (1982). Emphasis is given to wit, energy, and charisma. Presentation is full of drama, anecdotes, and humor. However, this type of presentation can produce a positive evaluation from student audiences without regard for learning outcomes. This was seen in one well-known study in which a charismatic lecturer purposely gave an entertaining lecture without any real substance and got a very positive evaluation from a student audience (Naftulin et al., 1973). Such presentations do not necessarily lead to student acquisition of important information.

Although making presentations interesting and energizing for learners is desirable, a beginning teacher who has the skills to make such presentations should consider a note of caution. Too many theatrics may, in fact, detract from the key ideas a teacher is trying to convey and focus students' attention on the entertaining aspects of the presentation. This does *not* mean that teachers should not display enthusiasm for their subjects or a particular lesson. There is a fine line between the teacher who uses humor,

*Effective presenters walk a thin line between showing enthusiasm for their subject and performing solely for entertainment value.*

storytelling, and involvement to get major ideas across to students and the teacher who uses the same techniques for their entertainment value alone.

**Checking for Understanding and Extending Student Thinking.**  The final phase of a presentation lesson is to check to see if students understand the new materials and to extend their thinking about these new ideas.

*Checking for Understanding.*  It is obvious that if teachers do a lot of teaching but students are not learning, nothing has been accomplished. Periodically (weekly, unit-by-unit, each quarter), effective teachers use homework, tests, and other formal devices to find out what students understand and what they don't understand. Teachers should also use informal methods to check for understanding. Watching for verbal and non-verbal cues, described earlier, is one method teachers can use. When students ask questions that don't seem to connect to the topic, they are sending a verbal signal that they are confused. Puzzled looks, silence, and frowns are nonverbal signs that students are not "getting it." Eyes wide open in amazement, smiles, and positive head nodding all signal that understanding is occurring.

Experienced teachers become very effective in reading verbal and nonverbal cues; however, a surer means of **checking for understanding** is to ask students to make direct responses to statements or questions. Several easy-to-use techniques can become valuable pieces of the beginning teacher's repertoire. One is the technique of posing a question about the materials just presented and having students as a group signal their responses. Here are examples of how this works with younger students, as described by Madeline Hunter (1982):

> "Thumbs up if the statement I make is true, down if false, to the side if you're not sure."
>
> "Make a plus with your fingers if you agree with this statement, a minus if you don't, and a zero if you have no strong feelings."
>
> "Show me with your fingers if sentence 1 or sentence 2 has a dependent clause."
>
> "Raise your hand each time you hear (or see) an example of. . . ." (p. 60)

Note in the examples that students are encouraged to use the signal system to report confusion or things they are not quite sure of. These are areas, obviously, where teachers need to provide additional explanation. The signal system is even used at the college level, where students are appreciative of having their misconceptions cleared up immediately rather than having them revealed later on an important test. Choral responses (having students answer in unison) is another means to check for understanding, as is sampling several individuals in the class.

There are also several methods used by experienced teachers that are *not* very effective. For instance, sometimes a teacher will conclude a presentation and ask, "Now, you all understand, don't you?" Students normally perceive this as a rhetorical question and consequently do not respond. Asking more directly, "Now, does anyone have any questions?" is an equally ineffective way to check for student understanding. Most students are unwilling to admit publicly to confusion, particularly if they think they are the only ones who didn't understand what the teacher said or if they are afraid of being accused of not listening.

*Extending Student Thinking.*  Although an effective presentation should transmit new information to students, that is not the only goal for presenting and explaining information to students. More important, teachers want students to use and to strengthen their existing cognitive structures and to increase their ability to monitor their own

**Checking for understanding during presentations let teachers know if their students are grasping new information and ideas.**

*Tailoring
Teaching for
Inclusive
Classrooms*

## Adapting Presentations for Differing Student Abilities

Except in rare instances, no presentation will be equally suitable for all students in a class. Students will have different prior knowledge and different levels of intellectual development. They also will have differing learning styles and intelligences. Therefore, it is very important for teachers to tailor their lectures and presentations to meet the varying needs and backgrounds of the students in their class.

A number of ways exist in which teachers can adapt a presentation so it is relevant and meaningful to as many students as possible.

- *Make ready use of pictures and illustrations.* There is much truth to the saying that "a picture is worth a thousand words." Pictures and illustrations can illuminate ideas and concepts in a way that words cannot, particularly for younger children and students who do not deal well with abstractions. To test this recommendation, try to explain the color green to a 3-year-old using only words. Now do it again using pictures of the color green.

- *Use varying examples to make information meaningful to students with different degrees of prior knowledge on a subject.* This chapter has emphasized the importance of prior knowledge and the way it serves as a filter through which new information must pass. Information provided to students for which they have no prior knowledge will not be meaningful, and it will not be learned. The use of examples is one way that teachers help students to connect new information to what they already know. Since prior knowledge differs widely in most classrooms, using varying examples can help make information meaningful to all students.

- *Be more or less concrete to meet needs of differing levels of intellectual development.* Older and higher-achieving students can think more abstractly than can younger and most low-achieving students. When both are in the same classroom, it is important for teachers to explain ideas both concretely and abstractly.

---

**One of the best ways to get students to think about new information is to follow the presentation with questions and discussion.**

thinking. The best means for extending student thinking following a presentation of new information is through classroom discourse, primarily by asking questions and having students discuss the information. It is through this process that students integrate new knowledge with prior knowledge, build more complete knowledge structures, and come to understand more complex relationships. The techniques of asking appropriate questions and conducting effective discussions are among the most difficult for teachers to master and thus become the subject matter for Chapter 12.

## 🍎 Managing the Learning Environment

**Presentations break down if appropriate momentum is not maintained or if students behave in inappropriate ways, such as by talking or moving around the room.**

As described in Chapter 5, research has produced some general classroom management guidelines that apply to virtually all classrooms and all instructional models. These address the way teachers strive to gain student cooperation, the means they use to motivate students, the way they establish and teach clear rules and procedures, and the actions they take to keep lessons moving smoothly and at a brisk pace. Although these general aspects of classroom management are extremely important, it is equally important for teachers to recognize that management behavior varies depending on the instructional approach a teacher is using and the type of learning tasks that derive from that approach. What might be considered "out of control" in one instance might be "in order" in another. For instance, when the teacher is using the presentation model and talking to the whole class, it is not appropriate for students to be talking to each other.

*Effective presentation depends on an environment characterized by active student listening.*

**✓ Check for Understanding**

- What are the major issues to consider when planning a presentation?

- Why is a student's prior knowledge such a critical factor in what is learned from a presentation?

- What are the four phases of a presentation lesson, and what kinds of teaching behaviors are associated with each phase?

- What are the four key features of a clear presentation?

- What is the best seating arrangement for a presentation lesson?

- What role do "explaining links" and "examples" play in a presentation?

- Summarize why checking for student understanding is an important phase of a presentation lesson.

Talk, however, is appropriate, even required, during a lesson using small-group discussion. In this section, we describe the unique management requirements for the presentation model.

In a presentation lesson, a teacher generally structures the learning environment very tightly. In the early stages of the lesson, the teacher is an active presenter and expects students to be active listeners. Successful use of the model requires good conditions for presenting and listening; a quiet area with good visibility including appropriate facilities for using audio and visual aids. The success of the model also depends on students being sufficiently motivated to watch what the teacher is doing and to listen to what the teacher is saying. It is not a time for students to be sharpening pencils, talking to neighbors, or working on other tasks. Later, when students are asked to recite or to expand on what was presented, different management concerns will surface. In essence, the presentation model requires rules governing *student talk,* procedures to ensure good *pacing,* and methods for *dealing with misbehavior.*

Students talking at inappropriate times or asking questions that slow down the pace of a lesson are among the most troublesome management concerns during a teacher presentation. This problem can vary in severity from a loud, generalized classroom clamor that disturbs the teacher next door to a single student talking to a neighbor when the teacher is explaining or demonstrating an important idea. As described in Chapter 5, teachers are well advised to have a rule that prescribes no talking when they are explaining things, and this rule must be consistently reinforced. During the recitation phase of the lesson, students must be taught to listen to other student's ideas and to take turns when participating in a recitation or a discussion.

Presentation lessons break down when the instructional events become sluggish and appropriate momentum is not maintained. In Chapter 5, you read about how students in Mrs. Dee's classroom (Doyle & Carter, 1984) sometimes tried deliberately to break up the pace of instruction by asking questions and feigning confusion. This resulted in the teacher reducing the amount of content being taught and doing more and more of the students' thinking for them. Effective teachers spot this type of student behavior, nip it in the bud, and move on with a well-paced and smooth-flowing presentation. When misbehavior occurs, they deal with it firmly and quickly using desist behaviors described in Chapter 5.

## 🍎 *Assessment and Evaluation*

✔ **Check for Understanding**

- Describe the characteristics of the learning environment during a presentation lesson.

- What are the means teachers use to assess what students have learned from presentations?

The most important postinstructional tasks connected to the presentation model are testing and grading students on the information presented. Tests and grades are perhaps the most important feedback that teachers give to students, parents, and others associated with the schools, as you read in Chapter 6.

The presentation model is particularly adept at transmitting new information to students and at helping them retain that information. Therefore, the testing of students' knowledge acquisition and retention is the appropriate evaluation strategy for the model. This type of testing lends itself nicely to the paper-and-pencil tests with which you are familiar. In testing for student knowledge, however, several factors should be considered. Teachers should test at all levels of knowledge and not for simple recall of information. Furthermore, teachers should communicate clearly to students what they will be tested on. Finally, it is better to test frequently than to wait for midterm or final testing periods, particularly with younger students.

## 🍎 *Summary*

### Overview of Presentation Teaching

- Presentations, explanations, and lectures by teachers comprise a large portion of classroom time primarily because curricula in schools have been structured around bodies of information that students are expected to learn.

- The instructional goals of the presentation model are mainly to help students acquire, assimilate, and retain information.

- The general flow or syntax for a presentation lesson consists of four main phases: presenting objectives and establishing set, presenting an advance organizer, presenting the learning materials, and using processes to help extend and strengthen student thinking.

- Successful presentations require a fairly tightly structured learning environment that allows a teacher to effectively present and explain new information and the students to hear and to acquire the new information.

### Theoretical and Empirical Support

- The presentation teaching model draws its rationale from three streams of contemporary thought: concepts about the way knowledge is structured, ideas about how to help

students acquire meaningful verbal learning, and concepts from the cognitive sciences that help explain how information is acquired, processed, and retained.

- Bodies of knowledge have logical structures from which key concepts and ideas are drawn for teacher's presentations.

- Knowledge can be broken into three main categories: declarative knowledge, procedural knowledge, and conditional knowledge. Declarative knowledge is knowledge about something or knowledge that something is the case. Procedural knowledge is knowledge about how to do something. Conditional knowledge is knowing when to use particular declarative or procedural knowledge.

- People take in information and knowledge through their senses and transform it into short-term and long-term memory. Meaningful verbal learning occurs when teachers present major unifying ideas in ways that connect these ideas to students' prior knowledge.

- The empirical support for the presentation model is well developed. Studies have shown the positive effects of using advance organizers, connecting new information to students' prior knowledge, and presenting the information with clarity, enthusiasm, economy, and power.

## Planning and Conducting Presentation Lessons

- The planning tasks for the presentation model include carefully selecting content, creating advance organizers, and matching both to students' prior knowledge.
- Presenting information to students requires preparing students to learn from presentation as well as delivering learning materials.
- Clarity of a presentation depends on both the teacher's delivery and the teacher's general mastery of the subject matter being presented.
- Advance organizers serve as intellectual scaffolding on which new knowledge is built.
- Specific techniques used in presenting new material include explaining links, rule-example-rule, and verbal transitions.
- Teachers can help students extend and strengthen their thinking about new materials through discussion, questioning, and dialogue.

## Managing the Learning Environment

- In a presentation lesson, a teacher structures the learning environment fairly tightly and makes sure students are attending to the lesson.
- Most important, presentation lessons require clear rules that govern student talk, procedures to ensure a brisk, smooth pace, and effective methods for dealing with student off-task behavior or misbehavior.

## Assessment and Evaluation

- Postinstructional tasks of the presentation model consist mainly of finding ways to test for student knowledge acquisition. Because students will learn what is expected of them, it is important to test for major ideas. If testing is limited to the recall of specific ideas or information, that is what students will learn. If teachers require higher-level cognitive processing on their tests, students will also learn to do that.

## 🍎 Key Terms

| | | |
|---|---|---|
| presentation teaching model | procedural knowledge | teacher clarity |
| structure of knowledge | conditional knowledge | teacher enthusiasm |
| meaningful verbal learning | short-term memory | conceptual mapping |
| cognitive psychology | long-term memory | explaining links |
| cognitive structure | schema | rule-example-rule technique |
| advance organizer | prior knowledge | verbal signposts |
| declarative knowledge | establishing set | checking for understanding |

## 🍎 Books for the Professional

Bruner, J. (1960). *The Process of Education.* Cambridge: Harvard University Press. This classic influenced the curriculum reform movement of the 1960s, particularly in regard to the "structure of knowledge."

Cruickshank, D., and Metcalf, K. (1994). Explaining. In T. Husen and T. N. Postlewaite (eds.), *International Encyclopedia of Education.* (2nd ed.). Oxford: Pergamon Press. This book gives a straightforward presentation of the research and procedures to be used when explaining and presenting ideas to students in classrooms.

Gagne, E. D., Yekovick, C. W., and Yekovick, F. R. (1993). *The Cognitive Psychology of School Learning.* (2nd ed.). New York: HarperCollins. This is an excellent review of the research in cognitive psychology with particular attention to learning and how teachers can use this research in their day-to-day instruction.

Pearce, T. (1995). *Leading Out Loud: The Authentic Speaker, the Credible Leader.* San Francisco: Jossey-Bass. This book explores the relationship between speaking, communicating, and leadership. Although not written specifically for teachers, it is very relevant for teachers who want to consider the leadership functions of teaching.

Westra, M. (1996). *Active Communication.* Pacific Grove, Calif.: Brooks/Cole. Although not written specifically for a teacher audience, this book has some good information on public speaking and oral communication.

## Reflection & Portfolio

You work in a school where the principal believes that teachers spend too much time talking to kids. If she walks by your room and sees you lecturing, she frowns and lets you know her disapproval. Often at staff meetings, she voices the opinion that teachers should be "facilitators of learning" and not "fountains of information." You agree that teachers should do more than just talk to students; they should provide students with many active learning experiences. You also think that you need to use presentations on a regular basis if you are going to cover all the material in the curriculum guide and if your students are going to perform well on required standardized tests.

This situation seems to present you with a dilemma. On the one hand, you want the principal to think you are a good teacher; on the other, you feel strongly that presenting new information and ideas is central to the job of teaching.

Reflect on ways to deal with this situation. When you have finished, write up your ideas for an entry in your professional portfolio and compare them with the ideas expressed below by experienced teachers who have faced the same situation.

### Jason McDaniels

"I have worked for principals like the one described in this case. I have found that the best way to deal with this type of situation is to establish regular meetings with the principal and to explain to her my goals and objectives and how these are tied directly to student learning. It becomes a matter of demonstrating to the principal that some lecture is important and showing that my presentations produce results in student learning."

### Sun HoSo

"Unfortunately, some principals do not have a good understanding of the "teaching model" concept, nor do they understand that different approaches to teaching result in different outcomes. When I have been faced with this type of principal, I have found that I have to go over the models I use in my teaching and illustrate how these various approaches complement one another and how each lesson stems from important learning goals I hold for my students. In other words, I take it upon myself to educate the principal on the importance of repertoire and the mistake we make if we think there is one best way to teach."

# Chapter 🍎 Eight

# Direct Instruction

## Reflecting on Direct Instruction

Take a minute to list the things you remember your parents or teachers doing that helped you learn the following:

- 🍎 The first ten amendments to the Constitution
- 🍎 How to ride a bicycle
- 🍎 How to tie your shoelaces
- 🍎 The fifty state capitals
- 🍎 The multiplication tables

Were there particular steps or activities they used regardless of the subject? Were some things particularly helpful to your learning? What did these have in common? Were there things they did that hindered your learning?

Skills—cognitive and physical—are the foundations on which more advanced learning (including learning to learn) are built. Before students can discover powerful concepts, think critically, solve problems, or write creatively, they must first acquire basic skills and information. For example, before students can acquire and process large amounts of information, they must be able to decode and encode spoken and written messages, take notes, and summarize. Before students can think critically, they must have basic skills associated with logic, such as drawing inferences from data and recognizing bias in presentation. Before students can write an eloquent paragraph, they must master basic sentence construction, correct word usage, and the self-discipline required to complete a writing task. In essence, in any field of study, we must *learn the mechanics before the magic.*

**A major difference between novices and experts in any field is the degree to which they have mastered the basic skills of their trade.**

In fact, the difference between novices and experts in almost any field is that experts have mastered certain basic skills to the point where they can perform them unconsciously and with precision, even in new or stressful situations. For example, expert teachers seldom worry about classroom management, because after years of experience, they are confident of their group control skills. Similarly, top NFL quarterbacks read every move of a defense without thinking and automatically respond with skillful actions to a safety blitz or double coverage of prize receivers, something novice quarterbacks cannot do.

**The direct instruction model is an approach to teaching basic skills in which lessons are highly goal-directed and learning environments are tightly structured.**

This chapter focuses on a teaching model that is aimed at helping students learn basic skills and knowledge that can be taught in a step-by-step fashion. For our purposes here, the model is labeled the **direct instruction model.** This model does not always have the same name. Sometimes it is referred to as a *training model* (Joyce & Weil, 1996). Good, Grouws, and Ebmeier (1983) called theirs the active teaching model. Hunter (1982) labeled hers the mastery teaching model. And Rosenshine and Stephens (1986) called this approach explicit instruction.

This chapter begins with an overview of direct instruction, which is followed by a discussion of the theoretical and empirical support for the model. The chapter then gives concrete details about how to plan, conduct, and evaluate a direct instruction lesson. Case materials at the end of the chapter are provided to help you reflect on your own ideas about this approach to teaching.

## 🍎 Overview of Direct Instruction

Even though you may never have thought about direct instruction in any systematic way, you are undoubtedly familiar with certain aspects of it. The rationale and procedures underlying this model were probably used by adults to teach you to drive a car, brush your teeth, hit a solid backhand, write a research paper, or solve algebraic equations. Behavioral principles on which this model rests may have been used to correct your phobia about flying or wean you from cigarettes. The direct instruction model is rather straightforward and can be mastered in a relatively short time. It is a "must" in all teachers' repertoire.

**Direct instruction is an effective way to teach basic information and skills to students.**

As with other teaching models, direct instruction can be described in terms of three features: (1) the type of learner outcomes it produces; (2) its syntax or overall flow of instructional activities; and (3) its learning environment.

Briefly, direct instruction was designed to promote student learning of knowledge that is well structured and can be taught in a step-by-step fashion. The model is not intended to promote social learning or higher-level thinking. Direct instruction is a

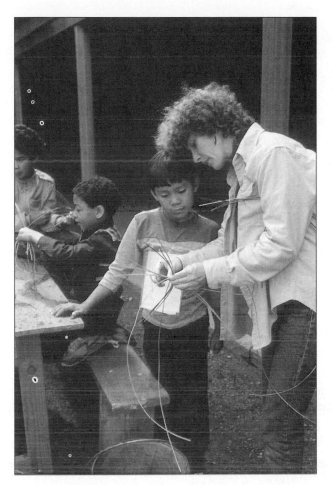

*The knowledge and skills taught in direct instruction lessons can be clearly explained or demonstrated.*

teacher-centered model that has five steps: establishing set, explanation and/or demonstration, guided practice, feedback, and extended practice. A direct instruction lesson requires careful orchestration by the teacher and a learning environment that is businesslike and task-oriented.

After taking a brief look at the theoretical and empirical support for direct instruction, we will provide a more detailed discussion on how to plan for, conduct, and evaluate direct instruction lessons.

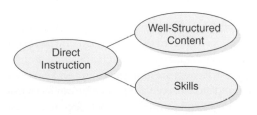

**Direct instruction aims at accomplishing two major learner outcomes: mastery of well-structured academic content and acquisition of all kinds of skills.**

✔ **Check for Understanding**

- What are the five phases of a direct instruction lesson?

- What are the learner outcomes of a direct instruction lesson?

- What type of learning environment is best for a direct instruction lesson?

## 🍎 Theoretical and Empirical Support

A number of historical and theoretical roots come together to provide the rationale and support for direct instruction. Some aspects of the model derive from training procedures developed in industrial and military settings. Barak Rosenshine and Robert Stevens (1986), for example, reported that they found a book published in 1945 entitled *How to Instruct* that included many of the ideas associated with direct instruction. For our purposes here, however, we will describe three theoretical traditions that provide the rationale for contemporary use of direct instruction: behaviorism, social learning theory, and teacher effectiveness research.

### Behavioral Theory

**Behavioral theories maintain that humans learn to act in certain ways in response to positive and negative consequences.**

Behavioral theories of learning have made significant contributions to direct instruction. Early behavioral theorists included the Russian physiologist Ivan Pavlov (1849–1936) and American psychologists John Watson (1878–1958), Edward Thorndike (1874–1949), and, more recently, B. F. Skinner (1904–1990). The theory is called **behaviorism** because theorists and researchers in this tradition are interested in studying observable human behavior rather than things that cannot be observed, such as human thought and cognition. Of particular importance to teachers is B. F. Skinner's work on operant conditioning and his ideas that humans learn and act in specific ways as a result of how particular behaviors are encouraged through reinforcement. You remember from Chapter 3 that the concept of reinforcement has a special meaning in behavioral theory. It means the use of consequences to strengthen particular behaviors either positively by providing some type of reward or negatively by removing some irritating stimulus.

As you will read later in this chapter, teachers who teach according to behavioral principles devise objectives that describe with precision the behaviors they want their students to learn; provide learning experiences, such as practice, in which student learning can be monitored and feedback provided; and pay particular attention to how behaviors in the classroom are rewarded.

### Social Learning Theory

**Social learning theory posits that much of what humans learn comes through the observation of others.**

More recently, theorists such as Albert Bandura have argued that classical behaviorism provides too limited view of learning, and they have used social learning theory to help study the unobservable aspects of human learning, such as thinking and cognition. **Social learning theory** makes distinctions between learning (the way knowledge is acquired) and performance (the behavior that can be observed). This theory also posits that much of what humans learn comes through the observation of others. According to Bandura, most human learning is done by selectively observing and placing into memory the behavior of others. Bandura (1977) wrote:

> Learning would be exceedingly laborious, not to mention hazardous, if people had to rely solely on the effects of their own actions to inform them of what to do. Fortunately, most human behavior is learned observationally through modeling: from observing others one forms an idea of how new behaviors are performed, and on later occasions this coded information serves as a guide for action. Because people can learn from example what to do, at least in approximate form, before performing any behavior, they are spared needless errors. (p. 22)

Unlike earlier behaviorists, social learning theorists believe that something is learned when an observer consciously attends to some behavior (e.g., striking a match) and then places that observation into long-term memory. The observer hasn't yet *performed* the observed behavior, so there have been no behavioral consequences (reinforcements), which behaviorists maintain are necessary for learning to occur. Nevertheless, as long as the memory is retained, the observer knows how to strike a match, whether or not he or she ever chooses to do so. The same claim can be said for thousands of simple behaviors such as braking a car, eating with a spoon, and opening a bottle.

According to Bandura (1986), observational learning is a three-step process: (1) the learner has to pay attention to critical aspects of what is to be learned; (2) the learner has to retain or remember the behavior; and (3) the learner must be able to reproduce or perform the behavior. Practice and mental rehearsals used in direct instruction are processes that help learners retain and produce observed behaviors. The principles of social learning translate into the following teaching behaviors:

- Use strategies to gain students' attention.
- Ensure that the observation is not too complex.
- Link new skills to students' prior knowledge.
- Use practice to ensure long-term retention.
- Ensure a positive attitude toward the new skill so students will be motivated to reproduce or use the new behavior.

More detail on how to apply the principles stemming from social learning theory will be provided in the section on how to conduct direct instruction lessons.

> Learning through observation involves three steps: attention, retention, and production.

## Teacher Effectiveness Research

The empirical support for the direct instruction model comes from many fields. However, the clearest empirical support for the model's classroom effectiveness comes from the **teacher effectiveness research** conducted mainly in the 1970s and 1980s, a type of research that studied the relationships between teacher behaviors and student achievement.

The study by Jane Stallings and her associates described in Chapter 2 illustrated the importance of time-on-task (Stallings & Kaskowitz, 1974). This study also contributed empirical support for the use of direct instruction. Remember that this study investigated elementary classrooms where teachers were using quite different approaches to instruction. Some teachers used highly structured and formal methods, while others used more informal teaching methods associated with the open classroom movement of the time. Stallings and her colleagues wanted to find out which of the various approaches were working best in raising student achievement. The behaviors of teachers in 166 classrooms were observed, and their students were tested for achievement gains in mathematics and reading. Although many findings emerged from this large and complex study, two of the most pronounced and long-lasting were the findings that time allocated and used for specific tasks was strongly related to academic achievement and that teachers who were businesslike and used teacher-directed (direct instruction) strategies were more successful in obtaining high engagement rates than those who used more informal and student-centered teaching methods.

Following this early work, literally hundreds of studies conducted between 1975 and 1990 produced essentially the same results, namely that teachers who had well-organized classrooms in which structured learning experiences prevailed produced higher student time-on-task ratios and higher student achievement than teachers who

> Teacher effectiveness research is an approach to studying teaching that looks at the relationship between teachers' observable behaviors and student achievement.

*Research Summary 8.1*

# How Do We Study Relationships Between Teacher Behavior and Student Achievement?

*Good, T. L., and Grouws, D. A. (1977).*
Teaching effect: A process-product study in fourth-grade mathematics classrooms. *Journal of Teacher Education,* 28, 49–54.

*Good, T. L., and Grouws, D. A. (1979).*
The Missouri mathematics effectiveness project: An experimental study in fourth-grade classrooms. *Journal of Educational Psychology,* 71, 355–362.

This chapter's research summary highlights, instead of a single study, a series of studies conducted by Good and his colleagues during the 1970s. His work is important for two reasons. One, it is a fine illustration of the process-product research, a unique approach to studying relationships between teacher behavior and student achievement. And two, it shows how knowledge is produced and refined over a number of years and through a number of studies.

**Problem:** Before the 1970s, many educational researchers focused mainly on teachers' personal characteristics and how they related to student learning. Researchers became disillusioned with this line of inquiry, and in the early 1970s, a new paradigm for research on teaching and learning emerged. Called **process-product research,** this approach to research had profound effects on our views of effective teaching. Process-product research was characterized both by the type of questions asked and by the methods of inquiry used by the researcher. The overriding question guiding process-product research was, What do individual teachers do that makes a difference in their students' academic achievement?

There are two key words in this question. One, the word *do,* suggests the importance of teachers' actions or behaviors, in contrast to earlier concerns about their personal attributes or characteristics. These teacher behaviors were labeled *process* by the researchers. The second key word is *achievement.* For the process-product researchers, achievement was

the *product* of instruction. In most instances, achievement was defined as the acquisition of those skills and that knowledge that could be measured on standardized tests. Teachers were judged effective if they acted in ways that produced average to above-average achievement for students in their class. Process-product research, thus, can be summarized as the search for those teacher behaviors (process) that led to above-average student achievement scores (product).

Process-product research was also characterized by particular methods of inquiry. Typically, process-product researchers went directly into classrooms and observed teachers in natural (regular) classroom settings. Teacher behaviors were recorded using a variety of low-inference observation devices, and student achievement was measured over several time periods, often at the beginning and end of a school year. Particular teacher behaviors were then correlated with student achievement scores, and successful and unsuccessful teacher behaviors were identified.

**Procedures:** Let's now look at what process-product research has contributed to our understanding of teacher effectiveness in general and to direct instruction specifically. Although hundreds of such studies were completed in the 1970s and 1980s, the work of Good and Grouws between 1972 and 1976 is illustrative of process-product research at its best, and it is illustrative of the type of evidence that supports the effectiveness of the direct instruction model.

**The Initial Study:** Between 1972 and 1973, Good, Grouws, and their colleagues studied over one-hundred third and fourth grade mathematics teachers in a school district that skirted the core of a large urban school district in the Midwest. The Iowa Test of Basic Skills was administered to students in their classrooms in the fall and spring for two consecutive years. From analyses of achievement gains made by students, the researchers were able to identify nine teachers who were relatively effective in obtaining student achievement in mathematics and nine teachers who had relatively low effectiveness. This led the researchers to plan and carry out an observational study to find out how the effective and ineffective teachers differed.

**The Observational Study:** To protect the identity of the "effective" and "ineffective" teachers, the researchers collected observational data from forty-one classrooms, including those in which the nine effective and nine ineffective teachers taught. Trained observers visited each classroom six or seven times during October, November, and

December of 1974. *Process* data were collected on many variables, including how instructional time was used, teacher-student interaction patterns, classroom management, types of materials used, and frequency of homework assignments. Student achievement was measured with the Iowa Test of Basic Skills in October 1974 and in April 1975. The classroom process data were analyzed to see if there were variables on which the nine high-effective and nine low-effective teachers differed.

**Results:** From the comparisons, Good and Grouws concluded that teacher effectiveness was strongly associated with the following clusters of behaviors.

- *Whole-class instruction.* In general, whole-class (as contrasted to small-group) instruction was supported by this study, particularly if the teacher possessed certain capabilities such as an ability to keep things moving along.
- *Clarity of instructions and presentations.* Effective teachers introduced lessons more purposively and explained materials more clearly than ineffective teachers did.
- *High performance expectations.* Effective teachers communicated higher performance expectations to students, assigned more work, and moved through the curriculum at a brisker pace than ineffective teachers did.
- *Task-focused but productive learning environment.* Effective teachers had fewer managerial problems than ineffective teachers. Their classrooms were task-focused and charac-

terized by smoothly paced instruction that was relatively free of disruptions.

- *Student-initiated behavior.* Students in effective teachers' classrooms initiated more interactions with teachers than students in the classrooms of ineffective teachers did. The researchers interpreted this as students' perceiving the effective teachers as being more approachable than the ineffective teachers.
- *Process feedback (knowledge of results).* Effective teachers let their students know how they were doing. They provided students with process or developmental feedback, especially during seatwork, and this feedback was immediate and nonevaluative.
- *Praise.* Effective teachers consistently provided less praise than ineffective teachers. This reflected the nonevaluative stance of the effective teachers. This finding flew in the face of the common wisdom at that time that praise was to be used by teachers very liberally. The result of process-product research showed that praise was effective only when used under certain conditions and in particular ways and that too much praise, or praise used inappropriately, did not promote student learning.

In sum, process-product researchers found that teachers who had well-organized classrooms in which structured learning experiences prevailed produced certain kinds of student achievement better than teachers who did not use these practices.

used more informal and less teacher-directed approaches. The Research Summary for this chapter describes briefly the nature of the research that produced these findings and provides an illustration of a group of studies conducted by Tom Good and his colleagues that also provide empirical support for the direct instruction model.

## 🍎 *Planning and Conducting Direct Instruction Lessons*

As with any approach to teaching, expert execution of a direct instruction lesson requires specific behaviors and decisions by teachers during planning, while conducting the lesson, and while evaluating its effects. Some of these teacher actions can be found in other instructional models, and other behaviors are unique to direct instruction. The unique features of conducting a direct instruction lesson are emphasized here.

✔ **Check for Understanding**

- What are the primary features of behaviorism?
- What is the critical feature of social learning theory?
- What characterizes the method of process-product research?
- How do most process-product researchers define achievement?

**Table 8.1** *Contrasting Objectives for Knowledge Acquisition and Skill Development*

| Knowledge Acquisition | Skill Development |
|---|---|
| 1. The student will be able to list the basic rules of ice hockey. | 1. The student will be able to pass while moving. |
| 2. The student will be able to identify the subjects in the following sentences:<br>  **a.** Whose brother are you?<br>  **b.** Ralph always walked to school.<br>  **c.** Josie loves to read mysteries. | 2. The student will supply an appropriate verb in the following sentences:<br>  **a.** Where _____ you?<br>  **b.** Ralph always _____ to school.<br>  **c.** _____ the apples to your sister. |
| 3. Given the equation $y = 2.6x + 0.8$, the student will correctly select the number corresponding to the $y$ intercept. | 3. The student will be able to solve for $x$ in the equation $9 = 2.6x + 0.8$. |

## Planning for Direct Instruction

**The direct instruction approach can be used to effectively teach both declarative and procedural knowledge.**

Chapter 7 introduced the concepts of declarative and procedural knowledge. Declarative knowledge, remember, is knowledge learners have about something, whereas procedural knowledge is knowledge about how to do something. The direct instruction model has been specifically designed to promote student learning of the procedural knowledge needed to perform simple and complex skills and of declarative knowledge that is well structured and can be taught in a step-by-step fashion. Table 8.1 contrasts the instructional objectives aimed at promoting knowledge acquisition with those aimed at skill development.

Differences can easily be observed in the two sets of objectives listed in Table 8.1. For instance, in the first set of objectives, the student is expected to know ice hockey rules. This is important declarative knowledge for students in a physical education class. However, being able to identify the rules does not necessarily mean that the student can perform any skills associated with ice hockey, such as passing while on the move, the content of the procedural knowledge objective found in column 2. Another example illustrating the differences in the two types of objectives is from the field of music. Many people can identify a French horn; some are even familiar with the history of the instrument. Few, however, have sufficient procedural knowledge to play a French horn well.

The direct instruction model is applicable to any subject, but it is most appropriate for performance-oriented subjects such as reading, writing, mathematics, music, and physical education. It is also appropriate for the skill components of the more information-oriented subjects such as history or science. For example, direct instruction would be used to help students learn how to make or read a map, use a timeline, or adjust a microscope to focus on a slide.

**Prepare Objectives.** When preparing objectives for a direct instruction lesson, the Mager format described in Chapter 2 is usually the preferred approach. Remember the STP guidelines specifying that a good objective should be *student*-based and specific, specify the *testing* situation, and identify the level of expected *performance*. The major difference between writing objectives for a skill-oriented lesson, unlike lessons with more complex content, is that skill-oriented objectives usually represent easily observed behaviors that can be stated precisely and measured accurately. For example, if the objective is to have students climb a 15-foot rope in seven seconds, that behavior can be observed and timed. If the objective is to have students go to the world globe and point out Kuwait, that behavior can also be observed.

Perform Task Analysis. **Task analysis** is a tool used by teachers to define with some precision the exact nature of a particular skill or well-structured bit of knowledge they want to teach. Some people believe that task analysis is something that is unreasonably difficult and complex, when in fact it is a rather straightforward and simple process, particularly for teachers who know their subjects well. The central idea behind task analysis is that complex understandings and skills cannot be learned at one time or in their entirety. Instead, for ease of understanding and mastery, complex skills and understandings must first be divided into significant component parts.

Task analysis helps a teacher define precisely what it is the learner needs to do to perform a desired skill. It can be accomplished through the following steps.

**Step 1:** Find out what a knowledgeable person does when the skill is performed.
**Step 2:** Divide the overall skill into subskills.
**Step 3:** Put subskills in some logical order, showing those that might be prerequisites to others.
**Step 4:** Design strategies to teach each of the subskills and how they are combined.

Sometimes a task analysis can take the form of a flow chart. This allows the skill and the relationships among subskills to be visualized. It also can show the various steps that a learner must go through in acquiring the skill. Figure 8.1 is a task analysis done this way. It shows the steps and subskills needed to perform a set of skills associated with playing ice hockey.

It would be a mistake to believe that teachers do task analysis for every skill they teach. Effective teachers, however, rely on the main concept associated with task analysis; that is, that most skills have several subskills and that learners cannot learn to perform the whole skill well unless they have mastered the parts.

Plan for Time and Space. Planning and managing time is very important for a direct instruction lesson. The teacher must ensure that time is sufficient, that it matches the aptitudes and abilities of the students in the class, and that students are motivated to stay engaged throughout the lesson. Making sure that students understand the purposes of direct instruction lessons and tying lessons into their prior knowledge and interests are ways of increasing student attention and engagement.

Planning and managing space is also very important for a direct instruction lesson. Many teachers prefer to use the more traditional row and column desk formation that was illustrated in Figure 7.6. This formation, you remember, is best suited to situations in which attention needs to be focused on the teacher or on information being displayed in the front of the room. A variant on the traditional row and column arrangement is the horizontal row desk arrangement illustrated in Figure 8.2 on page 273. Students sit quite close to each other in a fewer number of rows. This arrangement is often useful for direct instruction demonstrations in which it is important that students see what is going on or for them to be quite close to the teacher. Neither the row and column nor the horizontal arrangement is conducive to student-centered teaching approaches that depend on student-to-student interaction.

## Conducting Direct Instruction Lessons

Although experienced teachers learn to adjust their use of direct instruction to fit various situations, most direct instruction lessons have five essential phases or steps. The lesson begins with the teacher providing a rationale for the lesson, establishing set, and getting students ready to learn. This preparational and motivational phase is then followed by presentation of the subject matter being taught or demonstration of

**Task analysis involves dividing a complex skill into its component parts so it can be taught in a step-by-step fashion.**

**Figure 8.1** *Flow Chart of Skills for Ice Hockey*

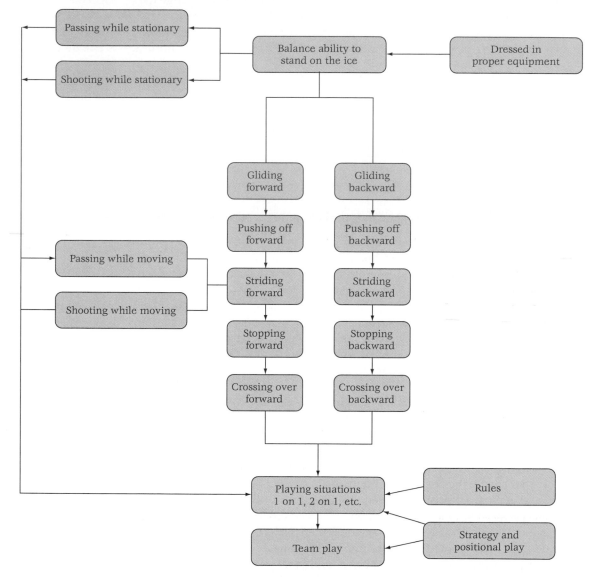

Source: Posner and Rudnitsky (1986), p. 77.

a particular skill. The lesson then provides opportunities for guided student practice and teacher feedback on student progress. In the practice-feedback phase of this model, teachers should always try to provide opportunities for students to transfer the knowledge or skill being taught to real-life situations. Direct instruction lessons conclude with extended practice and the transfer of skills. The five phases of the direct instruction model are summarized in Table 8.2.

**Provide Objectives and Establish Set.** Regardless of the instructional model being used, good teachers begin their lessons by explaining their objectives, establishing a learning set, and getting their students' attention. As previously described, an abbrevi-

**Figure 8.2** *Horizontal Desk Formation*

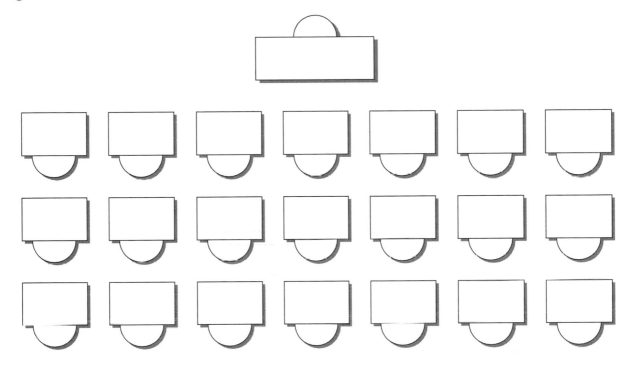

**Table 8.2** *Syntax of the Training Model*

| Phases | Teacher Behavior |
|--------|------------------|
| *Phase 1:* Clarify goals and establish set. | Teacher goes over goals for the lesson, gives background information, and explains why the lesson is important. Gets students ready to learn. |
| *Phase 2:* Demonstrate knowledge or skill. | Teacher demonstrates the skill correctly or presents step-by-step information. |
| *Phase 3:* Provide guided practice. | Teacher structures initial practice. |
| *Phase 4:* Check for understanding and provide feedback. | Teacher checks to see if students are performing correctly and provides feedback. |
| *Phase 5:* Provide extended practice and transfer. | Teacher sets conditions for extended practice with attention to transfer of the skill to more complex situations. |

ated version of the objectives should be written on the chalkboard or printed and distributed to students. In addition, students should be told how a particular day's objective ties into previous ones and, in most instances, how it is a part of longer-range objectives or themes. They should also be informed about the flow of a particular lesson and about how much time the lesson is expected to take. Figure 8.3 shows what a science teacher provided for her students before a lesson on microscopes.

**Figure 8.3** *Aims and Overview of Today's Lesson on Microscopes*

**Today's objective:** The objective of today's lesson is to learn how to bring into focus the lens on a compound light microscope so you can make an accurate observation of plant cells.

**Agenda**

| | |
|---|---|
| 5 minutes | Introduction, review, and objectives. |
| 5 minutes | Rationale. |
| 10 minutes | Demonstration of how to adjust lens on microscope—questions and answers. |
| 20 minutes | Practice with your microscope (I'll come around and help). |
| 10 minutes | Wrap-up and assignment for tomorrow. |

Giving the rationale and overviews for any lesson is important, but it is particularly so for skill-oriented lessons. Such lessons typically focus on discrete skills that students may not perceive as important but that require substantial motivation and commitment on their part to practice. Knowing the rationale for learning a particular skill helps to motivate and bring the desired commitment, unlike such general statements as "It's good for you," "You'll need it to find a job," or "It is required in the curriculum guide."

**Conduct Demonstrations.** The direct instruction model relies heavily on the proposition that much of what is learned and much of the learner's behavioral repertoire comes from observing others. Social learning theory specifically holds that it is from watching particular behaviors that students learn to perform them and to anticipate

"And then, of course, there's the possibility of being just the slightest bit too organized."

Reprinted by permission of Glen Dines/KAPPAN.

their consequences. The behaviors of others, both good and bad, thus become guides for the learner's own behavior. This form of learning by imitation saves students much needless trial and error. It can also cause them to learn inappropriate or incorrect behaviors. To effectively demonstrate a particular concept or skill requires teachers to *acquire mastery,* or a thorough understanding, of the concept or skills before the demonstration and to carefully *rehearse* all aspects of the demonstration before the actual classroom event.

*Acquiring Mastery and Understanding.* To ensure that students will observe correct rather than incorrect behaviors, teachers must attend to exactly what goes into their demonstrations. The old adage often recited to children by parents "Do as I say, not as I do" is not sufficient for teachers trying to teach precise basic information or skills. Examples abound in every aspect of human endeavor where people unknowingly perform a skill incorrectly because they observed and learned the skill from someone who was doing it wrong. The important point here is that if teachers want students to do something right, they must ensure that it is demonstrated correctly.

> **Effective demonstration requires a thorough mastery of what is being taught and careful rehearsal before the classroom event.**

*Attend to Rehearsal.* It is exceedingly difficult to demonstrate anything with complete accuracy. The more complex the information or skill, the more difficult it is to be precise in classroom demonstrations. Ensuring correct demonstration and modeling requires practice ahead of time. It also requires that the critical attributes of the skill or concept be thought through clearly and distinctly. For example, suppose you want to teach your students how to use a computerized system for locating information in the library and you are going to demonstrate how call numbers correspond to a book's location. It is important to prepare and rehearse so the numbering system demonstrated is consistent with what students will find in their particular library. If the demonstration consists of such steps as turning on the computer, punching in identifying information on the book, writing down the call number and then proceeding to the stacks, it is important that these steps be rehearsed to the point that none (such as writing down the call number) is forgotten during the actual demonstration.

## Providing Guided Practice.
Common sense says that practice makes perfect. In reality, this principle does not always hold up. Everyone knows people who drive their cars every day but who are still poor drivers or people who have many children but who are poor parents. All too often the assignments teachers give students do not really provide for the type of practice that is needed. Writing out answers to questions at the end of a chapter, doing twenty mathematics problems, or writing an essay does not always help students master important skills.

A critical step in the direct instruction model is the way the teacher approaches **guided practice.** Fortunately for teachers, a considerable amount of research evidence now exists that can guide efforts to provide practice. For example, we know that active practice can increase retention, make learning more automatic, and enable the learner to transfer learning to new or stressful situations. The following principles can guide the ways teachers provide for practice.

> **Guided practice increases retention, makes skills more automatic, and promotes transfer to new situations.**

*Assign Short, Meaningful Amounts of Practice.* In most instances, particularly with a new skill, it is important to ask students to perform the desired skill for short periods of time and, if the skill is complex, to simplify the task at the beginning. Brevity and simplification, however, should not distort the pattern of the whole skill.

*During guided practice, it is important for teachers to assist students, monitor how they are doing, and provide them with feedback.*

***Assign Practice to Increase Overlearning.*** For skills that are critical to later performance, practice must continue well beyond the stage of initial mastery. Many skills associated with the performing arts, athletics, reading, and typing have to be overlearned so they become automatic. It is only through **overlearning** and complete mastery that a skill can be used effectively in new situations or under stress. This ability to automatically perform a skill or combination of skills is what separates a novice from an expert in all fields. Teachers must be careful, however, because efforts to produce overlearning can become monotonous and actually decrease students' motivation to learn.

> Overlearning a skill produces the automaticity needed to use it in various combinations and in both novel and stressful situations.

***Be Aware of the Advantages and Disadvantages of Massed and Distributed Practice.*** Many schools in the United States have homework policies—the rule of thumb is about thirty minutes per night per subject for older students and at least a few minutes a night for younger students. Although homework can be valuable for extending student learning, a required amount of time each night can be harmful. The amount and timing of practice depend on many factors. Psychologists have typically defined this issue as **massed** (continuous) **practice** versus **distributed** (divided into segments) **practice.** Although the research literature does not give direct principles that can be followed in every instance, massed practice is usually recommended for learning new skills, with the caution that long periods of practice can lead to boredom and fatigue. Distributed practice is most effective for refining already familiar skills, again with the caution that the interval of time between practice segments should not be so long that students forget or regress and have to start over again.

> In general, massed practice is recommended when learning new skills and distributed practice when refining existing skills.

***Attend to the Initial Stages of Practice.*** The initial stages of practice are particularly critical, since it is during this period that the learner can unknowingly start using incorrect techniques that later must be unlearned. It is also during the initial stages of practice that the learner will want to measure success in terms of his or her performance as contrasted to technique. This issue is described more completely in the following section.

Check Understanding and Provide Feedback. This is the phase of a direct instruction lesson that most closely resembles what is sometimes called *recitation*. It is often characterized by the teacher asking students questions and students providing answers

## Software to Assist Skill Development

The direct instruction model is used mainly to teach basic skills. Today, software packages exist to assist teachers, particularly with drill and practice and through tutorials. *Drill and practice* software has been around for a good many years. Many of you have probably used it in school or at home. This software does not try to teach a new skill but instead provides users with practice opportunities and feedback. Programs are available mostly in mathematics, spelling, foreign languages, and other subjects where knowledge is well structured. Recently, some very effective software packages have been developed to teach students skills needed to operate a computer, such as keyboarding. The practice session in the typical drill and practice software provides students with a problem situation, asks them to choose a solution, and provides them with feedback on how they are doing. Correct solutions (answers) to problem situations allow students to move on to a more difficult situation. Incorrect answers prompt remedial problems for additional practice.

*Tutorials* differ from drill and practice in that they are designed to provide instruction on a given skill or topic. The tutorial is based on behavioral theories of learning. The topic is presented somewhat along the same lines as described in this chapter. The program leads students through the topic in small chunks and provides them opportunity for guided practice. The tutorial checks students' understanding and provides feedback. Like drill and practice programs, this type of program has been around for a long time. It was initially called programmed instruction.

To date, drill and practice and tutorial software programs have been used more widely in the home and industry than in classrooms. Parents, for example, have purchased software such as Mathblaster for their children to use, and many companies have used software in their employee education programs. Teachers, however, have been less quick to use these tools. A number of reasons might explain this lag, such as a lack of computers in classrooms or bad experiences with early programmed instruction software that focused on superficial problems and tasks. However, contemporary drill and practice and tutorial software can be powerful and flexible tools for teachers to use to help their students acquire basic information and skills. Students control the instruction, learn at their own pace, and can use the programs almost anywhere—at home, school, or work—there is a computer.

they deem to be correct. This is a very important aspect of a direct instruction lesson, because without knowledge of results, practice is of little value to students. In fact, the most important task of teachers using the direct instruction model is providing students with meaningful feedback and **knowledge of results.** Teachers can give feedback in many ways, such as verbally, by video- or audiotaping performance, by testing, or through written comments. Without specific feedback, however, students will not learn to write well by writing, read well by reading, or run well by running. The critical question for teachers is how to provide effective feedback for large classes of students. Guidelines considered important include the following.

*Guideline 1: Provide Feedback as Soon as Possible After the Practice.* It is not necessary that feedback be provided instantaneously, but it should be close enough to the actual practice that students can remember clearly their own performance. This means that teachers who provide written comments on essays should be prompt in returning corrected papers. It means they should immediately correct tests gauged to measure performance and go over them with students. It also means that arrangements for verbal, video, or audio feedback should be such that delay is kept to a minimum.

**Without knowledge of results (feedback), practice is of little value to students.**

For best results, feedback should be as specific as possible, be provided immediately following practice, and fit the developmental level of the learner.

*Guideline 2: Make Feedback Specific.*  In general, feedback should be as specific as possible to be most helpful to students. For example:

> "Your use of the word *domicile* is pretentious; *house* would do nicely."
> Instead of:
> "You are using too many big words."
> Or:
> "Your hand was placed exactly right for an effective backhand."
> Instead of:
> "Good backhand."
> Or:
> "Three words were spelled incorrectly on your paper: *Pleistocene, penal,* and *recommendation.*"
> Instead of:
> "Too many misspelled words."

*Guideline 3: Concentrate on Behaviors and Not Intent.*  Feedback is most helpful and raises less defensiveness with students if it is aimed directly at some behavior rather than at one's interpretation of the intent behind the behavior. For example:

> "I cannot read your handwriting. You do not provide enough blank space between words, and you make your O's and A's identical."
> Instead of:
> "You do not work on making your handwriting neat."
> Or:
> "When you faced the class in your last speech, you spoke so softly that most students could not hear what you were saying,"
> Instead of:
> "You should try to overcome your shyness."

*Guideline 4: Keep Feedback Appropriate to the Developmental Stage of the Learner.*  As important as knowledge of results is, feedback must be administered carefully to be helpful. Sometimes, students can be given too much feedback or feedback that is too sophisticated for them to handle. For example, a person trying to drive a car for the first time can appreciate hearing that he or she "let the clutch" out too quickly, causing the car to jerk. A beginning driver, however, is not ready for explanations about how to drop the brake and use the clutch to keep the car from rolling on a steep hill. A young student being taught the "i before e" rule in spelling probably will respond favorably to being told that he or she spelled *brief* correctly but may not be ready to consider why *receive* was incorrect.

Although incorrect performance must be corrected, teachers should try to provide positive feedback when students are learning new skills.

*Guideline 5: Emphasize Praise and Feedback on Correct Performance.* Everyone prefers to receive positive rather than negative feedback. In general, praise will be accepted whereas negative feedback may be denied. Teachers, therefore, should try to provide praise and positive feedback, particularly when students are learning new concepts and skills. However, when incorrect performance is observed, it must be corrected. Here is a sensible way to approach the problem of dealing with incorrect responses and performance:

1. Dignify the student's incorrect response or performance by giving a question for which the response would have been correct. For example, "George Washington would have been the right answer if I had asked you who was the first president of the United States."

2. Provide the student with an assist, hint, or prompt. For example, "Remember the president in 1828 had also been a hero in the War of 1812."
3. Hold the student accountable. For example, "You didn't know President Jackson today, but I bet you will tomorrow when I ask you again."

A combination of positive and negative feedback is best in most instances. For example, "You did a perfect job of matching subjects and verbs in this paragraph, except in the instance in which you used a collective subject." Or, "You were holding the racket correctly as you approached the ball, but you had too much of your weight on your left foot." Or, "I like the way you speak up in class, but during our last class discussion, you interrupted Ron three different times when he was trying to give us his point of view."

*Guideline 6: When Giving Negative Feedback, Show How to Perform Correctly.* Knowing that something has been done incorrectly does not help students do it correctly. Negative feedback should always be accompanied by teacher actions that demonstrate the correct performance. If a student is shooting a basketball with the palm of the hand, the teacher should point that out and demonstrate how to place the ball on the fingertips. If a writing sample is splattered with incorrectly used words, the teacher should pencil in words that are more appropriate. If students are holding their hands incorrectly on the computer keyboard, the correct placement should be modeled.

*Guideline 7: Help Students to Focus on Process, Not Outcomes.* Many times beginners want to focus their attention on measurable performance. "I just typed thirty-five words per minute without any errors." "I wrote my essay in an hour." "I drove the golf ball 175 yards." "I cleared the bar at four feet, six inches." It is the teacher's responsibility to get students to look at the *process,* or technique behind their performance, and to help students understand that incorrect techniques may achieve immediate objectives but will probably prohibit later growth. For example, a student may type thirty-five words per minute using only two fingers but will probably never reach one hundred words per minute using this technique. Starting the approach on the wrong foot may be fine for clearing the high jump bar at four feet, six inches, but will prevent ever reaching 5 five feet, six inches.

*Guideline 8: Teach Students How to Provide Feedback to Themselves and How to Judge Their Own Performance.* It is important for students to learn how to assess and judge their own performance. Teachers can help students judge their own performance in many ways. They can explain the criteria used by experts in judging performance; they can give students opportunities to judge peers and to assess their own progress in relation to others; and they can emphasize the importance of self-monitoring, goal setting, and not being satisfied with only "extrinsic" feedback from the teacher.

The process of assigning practice and giving students feedback is a very important job teachers have, and it requires learning a complex set of behaviors. A learning aid in the *Student Manual* is designed to help you observe how experienced teachers use practice and provide feedback.

## 🍎 *Managing the Learning Environment*

The tasks associated with managing the learning environment during a direct instruction lesson are almost identical to those used by teachers when employing the presentation model. In direct instruction, the teacher structures the learning environment very

---

**Negative feedback should be accompanied by demostrations of how to correctly perform the skill.**

✓ **Check for Understanding**

- What are the possible student outcomes of a direct instruction lesson?

- What are the major planning tasks associated with a direct instruction lesson?

- Why is task analysis an important planning tool for some types of direct instruction lessons?

- What are the five phases of a direct instruction lesson, and what kinds of teaching behaviors are associated with each phase?

- What are the major factors to consider when assigning guided practice? Independent practice?

- Summarize the guidelines for effective feedback.

## Tailoring Teaching for Inclusive Classrooms

# Varying Lessons to Meet Diverse Needs

In Chapter 4, we described several ways that children and youth can differ. These differences can include many things such as socioeconomic status, race or ethnicity, gender, ability, prior knowledge, cognitive style, and various disabilities. In Chapter 3, we described how students differ in terms of their motivational needs. Because of these differences, it is safe to conclude that no single lesson will ever be equally effective with all students. This is true with direct instruction lessons. Whereas we can provide information about how the model is supposed to work in general, in real teaching situations, it often does not work as planned. Effective teachers learn how to adapt their instruction to take into account student diversity. Below are some ways teachers can tailor direct instruction lessons.

### Vary the Structure of the Lesson

- Keep lessons for younger and low-achieving students very structured; keep objectives specific; use a moderately brisk pace.
- For older and higher-achieving students, promote extension of basic skill instruction and provide opportunities for exploration.

### Vary the Nature of Presentations and Demonstrations

- For younger and low-achieving students, highlight main ideas or procedures on the chalkboard or overhead pro-

jector. Confine presentations to only a few points or ideas. Make them short.
- For older and higher-achieving students, extend beyond basic ideas or skills.

### Vary the Nature of Interaction

- For all students, base instruction on students' prior knowledge; teaching what is already known will bore students; teaching ideas or skills for which insufficient knowledge exists is meaningless.
- Pay attention to cultural differences among racial and ethnic groups in terms of willingness to interact in front of others.

### Vary the Nature of Encouragement and Support

- Low-achieving and more dependent students will need continuous encouragement and support. The less students know, the more instructional support is required.
- Higher-achieving and more independent students value figuring things out on their own and may perceive too much teacher encouragement as interference. Many approaches can be successful when students know quite a bit about a subject.

### Vary the Use of Practice and Homework

- For lower-achieving students, make sure practice exercises are well understood and keep seatwork and homework assignments brief.
- For higher-achieving, more independent students, limit seatwork and keep homework challenging. Less review and independent practice are required.

---

**Homework is most often a continuation of practice and should involve activities that students can perform successfully.**

tightly and expects that students will be keen observers and listeners. Effective teachers use the methods described in Chapter 5 to govern student talk and to ensure that lesson pace is maintained. Misbehavior that occurs during a direct instruction lesson must be dealt with accurately and quickly.

Managing the independent practice aspect of direct instruction is something that teachers need to pay particular attention to. **Independent practice,** also called *seatwork* or *homework,* provides an opportunity for students to perform newly acquired skills on their own and, as such, should be viewed as a continuation of practice, not as a continuation of instruction. Also, homework and independent practice can be used as a way of extending student learning time. But teachers should not assign homework carelessly or frivolously. If a teacher doesn't value it, the students won't. Here are three general guidelines for independent practice given as homework.

1. *Give students homework they can perform successfully.* Homework should not involve the continuation of instruction but rather the continuation of practice or preparation for the next day's content.
2. *Inform parents about the level of involvement expected of them.* Are they expected to help their sons or daughters with answers to difficult questions or simply to provide a quiet atmosphere in which the students can complete their homework assignments? Are they supposed to check it over? Do they know the approximate frequency and duration of homework assignments?
3. *Provide feedback on the homework.* Many teachers simply check to determine whether homework was performed. What this says to the students is that it doesn't matter how it is done, as long as it is done. Students soon figure out that the task is to get something—anything—on paper, which sets a bad precedent. One method of providing feedback relatively easily is to involve students in correcting one another's homework.

## 🍎 Assessment and Evaluation

Chapter 6 emphasized the importance of matching testing and evaluation strategies to the goals and objectives for particular lessons and the inherent purposes of a particular model. Since the direct instruction model is used most appropriately for teaching skills and knowledge that can be taught in a step-by-step fashion, evaluation should focus on performance tests measuring skill development rather than on paper-and-pencil tests of declarative knowledge. For example, being able to identify the characters on the typewriter's keyboard obviously does not tell us much about a person's ability to type; however, a timed typing test does. Being able to identify verbs in a column of nouns does not mean that a student can write a sentence; it takes a test that requires the student to write a sentence to enable a teacher to evaluate that student's skill. Reciting the correct steps in any of the teaching models described in this book does not tell us whether a teacher can use the model in front of thirty students; only a classroom demonstration can exhibit the teacher's mastery of that skill.

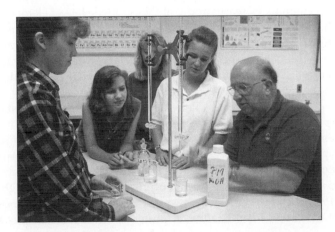

*Often the best test is one that allows individuals to demonstrate an authentic product.*

**Table 8.3** *Items for Knowledge Test and Skill Test*

**Knowledge Test**

1. How many players are there on an ice hockey team?
   a. 6
   b. 8
   c. 10
   d. none of the above

2. What is the subject of the following sentence?
   *"Mary's mother is an artist."*
   a. Mary
   b. mother
   c. an
   d. artist

3. At what point is the intercept located?
   a. 1    c. 3
   b. 2    d. 4

**Skill Test**

1. Demonstrate a pass while moving.

2. Correct the verbs, as needed, in the following sentences:
   a. Kim ran slowly to the store.
   b. Tommy said it was time to go.
   c. Levon sat joyfully to greet her day.
   d. "Please be noisier," said the teacher.

3. Solve for $x$ in the following equations:
   a. $2 = x + 4$
   b. $5x = 1 + (x/2)$
   c. $14 = 2x + 9x$
   d. $x/3 = 9$

Many times, performance tests are difficult for teachers to devise and to score with precision, and they can also be very time-consuming. However, if you want your students to master the skills you teach, nothing will substitute for performance-based evaluation procedures. Table 8.3 has examples of the type of test items that would be included on a skills test and contrasts those with items on the same topic that one would find on a knowledge test. Note that the test items correspond to the sample objectives in Table 8.1.

# 🍎 A Final Thought: Considering the Use of Direct Instruction

Teacher use of direct instruction comprises a large proportion of classroom time in American classrooms. The amount of time devoted to explaining information, demonstrating, and conducting recitations increases at the higher grade levels of elementary school, in middle schools, and in high schools. It is prevalent everywhere and remains the most popular teaching model. However, the model is not without its critics, and it will be important for you to be aware of the complaints that have been lodged against direct instruction and to explore your own views and values about the model and its use in your classroom.

The primary criticism of direct instruction is its emphasis on teacher talk. Most observers claim that teacher talk accounts for between one-half and three-fourths of every class period, and according to Cuban (1982, 1984), this phenomenon has remained constant during most of the past one-hundred years. Some educators argue that too much time is devoted to direct instruction. Others argue that the model is limited to teaching basic skills and low-level information and that it is not useful for accomplishing higher-level objectives. Still others criticize the model because of the behavioral theory underlying it. They argue that the model unavoidably supports the view that students are empty vessels to be filled with carefully segmented information rather than active learners with an innate need to acquire information and skills. Finally, there are those, including some of the model's early creators, who criticize direct instruction because of abuses in the way in which the model was implemented in many classrooms. For example, in one large public school system on the East Coast, every teacher was expected to give a direct instruction lesson every day. If a teacher used other approaches while being observed by a supervisor, the teacher received a negative evaluation. In another instance, teachers were required to write their objectives in behavioral format on the chalkboard every day, something never envisioned by the model's developers.

The continued popularity of explaining and demonstrating is not surprising, since the most widely held educational objectives are those associated with the acquisition of skills and the retention of basic information. Curricula in schools have been structured around bodies of information from the various academic disciplines—science, mathematics, English, and the social sciences. Consequently, curriculum guides, textbooks, and tests are similarly organized and are routinely used by teachers. Experienced teachers know that direct instruction is an effective way to help students acquire the array of basic information and skills believed by society to be important for students to know.

This book takes a balanced view toward direct instruction. As repeatedly stressed, direct instruction is just one of several approaches used by effective teachers. The real key to effective instruction is a teacher's ability to call on a varied repertoire of instructional approaches that permit a teacher to match instructional approaches to particular learning goals and to the needs of particular students.

> **Because direct instruction is the most popular teaching method, teachers should be aware of problems cited by critics.**

## 🍎 *Summary*

### Overview of Direct Instruction

- Acquiring basic information and skills are important goals of every subject taught in schools. In almost any field, students must learn the basics before they can go on to more advanced learning.
- The instructional effects of the direct instruction model are to promote mastery of simple and complex skills and declarative knowledge that can be carefully defined and taught in a step-by-step fashion.
- The general flow or syntax of a direct instruction lesson consists usually of five phases.
- The direct instruction model requires a highly structured learning environment and careful orchestration by the teacher. This tight structure does not mean it has to be authoritarian or uncaring.

### Theoretical and Empirical Support

- The direct instruction model draws its theoretical support from behavioral theory, social learning theory, and teacher effectiveness research.

- Direct instruction has been widely used and tested in school and nonschool settings. The model has strong empirical evidence to support its use for accomplishing certain types of student learning.

### Planning and Conducting Direct Instruction Lessons

- Preinstructional planning tasks associated with the model put emphasis on careful preparation of objectives and performing task analysis.
- The five phases of a direct instruction model are: providing objectives and establishing set; demonstration or explaining the materials to be learned; providing guided practice; checking for student understanding and providing feedback; and providing for extended practice and transfer.
- Conducting a direct instruction lesson requires teachers to explain things clearly; to demonstrate and model precise behaviors; and to provide for practice, monitoring of performance, and feedback.

- The use of practice should be guided by several principles: assigning short, meaningful amounts of practice; assigning practice to increase overlearning; and making appropriate use of massed and distributed practice.

## Managing the Learning Environment

- Direct instruction lessons require the unique classroom management skill of gaining students' attention in a whole-group setting and sustaining this attention for extended periods of time.
- Particular classroom management concerns include organizing the classroom setting for maximum effect; maintaining appropriate pace, flow, and momentum; sustaining engagement, involvement, and participation; and dealing with student misbehavior quickly and firmly.

## Assessment and Evaluation

- Assessment tasks associated with the model put emphasis on practice and on developing and using appropriate basic knowledge and performance tests that can accurately measure simple and complex skills and provide feedback to students.

## A Final Thought: Considering the Use of Direct Instruction

- Despite the variety of complaints that have been launched against direct instruction, it remains a very popular teaching model.

## 🍎 Key Terms

direct instruction model

behaviorism

social learning theory

teacher effectiveness research

process-product research

task analysis

guided practice

overlearning

massed practice

distributed practice

knowledge of results

independent practice

## 🍎 Books for the Professional

Cruickshank, D. R., Bainer, D., and Metcalf, K. (1999). *The Act of Teaching*. New York: McGraw-Hill. This book has a good chapter that describes the variations of the direct instruction model.

Gagné, R. M., and Briggs, L. J. (1979). *Principles of Instructional Design*. New York: Holt, Rinehart & Winston. This book contains very good chapters on designing instruction, particularly in terms of understanding task analysis and assessing student performance.

Good, T. L., Grouws, D., and Ebmeier, H. (1983). *Active Mathematics Teaching*. New York: Longman. This is one of the original descriptions of direct instruction.

Joyce, Bruce, and Weil, Marsha. (1996). *Models of Teaching*. (5th ed.) Boston: Allyn and Bacon. This book offers a good explanation of the direct instruction model.

In your first teaching position, you find yourself in a school where the teachers were trained over ten years ago in a particular approach to direct instruction. Although there has been considerable teacher turnover in the school, the direct instruction model seems to dominate all others and is used by all teachers in the school. Teachers are expected to develop lesson plans using behavioral objectives and follow the steps of the direct instruction model. The overall ethos of the school reflects an emphasis on teaching basic skills and viewing students as empty vessels to be filled with information.

You believe in teaching basic skills to students. However, you also believe that curriculum should be individualized for your students and that students should be allowed considerable autonomy in identifying their own goals, asking their own questions, and pursuing some of their own interests.

As you reflect on this situation and your approach to teaching, consider the following:

- Think about a unit you might teach at your grade level or teaching field. What do you want your students to get out of it? Write these goals down. Ask yourself which goals are dictated by your school's curriculum and which are dictated by the faculty's overall approach to teaching? By your own beliefs? By your students'? You might consider ranking these goals numerically.
- If you are in a field placement, share your goals with a fellow student or a teacher in the school. You might also discuss the goals with some students in the school. Get their opinion about which of the goals are the most important.

Now write down how you are going to approach your unit and which goals and approaches you will emphasize, remembering, of course, that your own personal views of teaching are at odds with those of the majority of teachers in your school. When you have finished, include your work as an entry in your professional portfolio and compare your thoughts with those of the teachers below who have faced the same situation.

## Sandy Marino

"I believe that children learn best when they are interested in a topic and when they can see its relevancy. It is important to relate subject matter to the students' daily lives and to arouse their curiosity about the topic. This can be done in a number of ways: using a thinking web to help them connect the topic to their daily lives, asking them a thought-provoking question, or engaging them in meaningful and relevant activities and materials.

"Therefore, in my eighth grade classes, I cover the school's curriculum and teach basic skills by involving my students in all aspects of planning and carrying out the instruction. I use more than one approach to instruction and try to accommodate as many learning styles and interests as possible. If the principal or some of my colleagues question my approach, I am ready to defend it. I have found that parents will also defend my approach when they hear their children say how much they enjoy my class and when my students perform well on mastery tests."

## Goodwin Roher

"I have been teaching third grade at my school for seven years. Our faculty has spent considerable time deciding together what we should cover and the approaches we should use with children. The teachers in grades 1 through 3 have spent considerable time aligning our reading, writing, and mathematics curriculum to the items on the state's mastery test given to all fourth graders. I think it is very important to cover all aspects of the school's curriculum, and the most effective way to do this is by direct teaching.

"I think catering to students' interest is also important, but only after they have mastered the basics. For example, I have interest centers in my classroom where students can pursue their interests once they have completed required work. I also use a teacher's aide to help students who fall behind in their work.

"I know this approach works. Students who have been in my classes consistently score above the state average on the fourth grade mastery test."

# Chapter Nine

# Concept Teaching

## *Reflecting on* **Concept Teaching**

Pick a concept from your teaching field for which you have a good understanding. Here are some examples:

🍎 *Mathematics—triangle*

🍎 *Economics—scarcity*

🍎 *Physical education—movement*

🍎 *Literature—love*

Write the concept on a piece of paper and make a web that shows other concepts that are related to the one you chose. Here is how a partial web for the concept of *scarcity* might look.

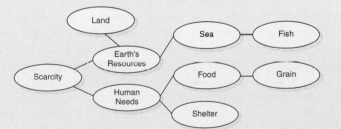

Next, consider how you might teach a young child about the concept of *scarcity*. Using a young child rather than an older one is good for this exercise because you will have to consider using means other than words to teach the concept. Think of the steps you might follow to teach the concept. In doing this, what did you learn about teaching a concept? Was it easier or more difficult than you thought it would be? What would you do differently next time?

The initial version of this chapter was written by Richard Jantz at the University of Maryland.

Most experienced teachers would agree that conveying information to students is very important but that teaching students how to think is even more important. Experienced teachers also know that concepts are the basic building blocks for thinking, particularly higher-level thinking, in any subject. Concepts allow individuals to classify objects and ideas and to derive rules and principles; they provide the foundations for the idea networks that guide our thinking. The process of learning concepts begins at an early age and continues throughout life as people develop more and more complex concepts, both in school and out. The learning of concepts is crucial in schools and in everyday life, because concepts allow mutual understanding among people and provide the basis for verbal interaction.

**Concepts are the basic building blocks for thinking and communication.**

The focus of this chapter is on **concept teaching** and how teachers can help students attain and develop the basic concepts needed for further learning and higher-level thinking.

The first section provides an overview of concept teaching, including the learning outcomes the model is designed to accomplish, the model's syntax, and the learning environment required to use the model effectively. This is followed by a discussion of the nature of concepts and the theoretical and empirical support for concept teaching. The final sections focus on the model itself and describe specific procedures used by teachers to plan, conduct, and evaluate concept teaching lessons.

# 🍎 Overview of Concept Teaching

"Ball." "Chair." "Box." "Table." "Crayon." Kim is naming things and placing objects into groups or classes. She is developing concepts. Combining something concrete, such as a ball, with an abstract quality, such as roundness, enables Kim to identify classes of objects, events, and ideas that differ from each other. By repeatedly sorting and classifying different balls, she can eventually form an abstract concept for these similar objects that allows her to think about them and, eventually, to communicate with others about them. But how can teachers help students learn concepts and develop conceptual understanding?

Concept teaching models have been developed primarily to teach key concepts that serve as foundations for student higher-level thinking and to provide a basis for mutual understanding and communication. (See Figure 9.1.) Such models are not designed to teach large amounts of information to students. However, by learning and applying key concepts within a given subject, students are able to transfer specific learnings to more general areas. In fact, without mutual understanding of certain key concepts, content learning in some subject areas is nearly impossible.

There are numerous approaches to concept teaching, but two basic ones have been selected for this chapter. These are labeled the *direct presentation* approach and the *concept attainment* approach. As will be described in detail later, the syntax for the two approaches vary slightly. Basically, however, a concept lesson consists of four major phases or steps: (1) present goals and establish set, (2) input examples and nonexamples, (3) test for concept attainment, and (4) analyze student thinking processes.

**The learning environment for concept teaching is moderately structured and teacher-centered.**

The learning environment for concept teaching might be described as moderately structured and teacher-centered. Transitions into and out of a concept lesson should be planned. The teacher makes judgments about which concepts to teach and where con-

**Figure 9.1** *Learner Outcomes of Concept Teaching*

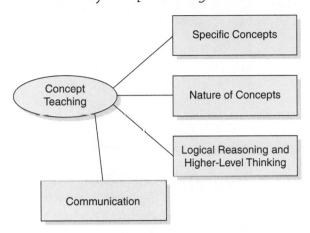

cept lessons should be sequenced within a larger unit of study. The teacher also selects the best examples and nonexamples of the concept based on the background and experiences of the students. During a concept lesson, there are numerous occasions when the teacher's main role becomes one of responding to student ideas, encouraging student participation, and supporting students as they develop their reasoning abilities. Checking for understanding and giving students opportunities to explore their own thinking processes also call for the teacher's support and encouragement. While a concept lesson is in progress, there is no time for casual talk with neighbors, studying other subject areas, or any other activity that might take attention away from the lesson.

✔ **Check for Understanding**

- What are the four phases of a concept lesson?
- What are the learner outcomes of a concept lesson?
- What type of learning environment works best for concept lessons?

## 🍎 *Theoretical and Empirical Support*

The theoretical and empirical support for concept teaching and learning is very extensive and covers a wide range of topics. This is because concept development and its relation to how the mind works have held the interest of theorists, philosophers, and researchers for centuries. Recently, this work has centered mainly in psychology and includes the contributions of Jean Piaget, Jerome Bruner, David Ausubel, and Howard Gardner, among others. Their studies showed how conceptual thinking develops in children and youth and how certain approaches to concept teaching affect these learning processes. In the sections that follow, we consider the relationship between concepts and higher-level thinking, the nature of concepts, and some of the knowledge we have about how best to teach concepts to students.

### Concepts and Higher-Level Thinking

Concept learning is more than simply classifying objects and forming categories. It is also more than learning new labels or vocabulary to apply to classes of objects and ideas. Instead, concept learning involves the process of constructing knowledge and organizing information into comprehensive and complex cognitive structures.

*Jean Piaget, a Swiss psychologist, had a lot of influence on our understanding of how conceptual thinking develops in children.*

As has been described in the chapters on presentation and direct instruction, students come into classrooms with a variety of prior experiences from which they have formed conceptions, or schemata, about the physical and social worlds. These schemata are a student's way of looking at the world. They help students explain and interpret what is happening in their lives. Sometimes the conceptions students hold are accurate; many times they are intuitive, naive, and, in fact, misrepresentations of reality. Misconceptions cannot be changed by simply presenting new information. Instead, change requires teaching processes that enable students to become aware of their existing schemata and help them to develop new concepts and reformulations of existing ways of thinking.

**Children's misconceptions about the world are pervasive. It is no simple matter to change their misconceptions.**

## The Nature of Concepts

**Concepts are devices used to organize knowledge and experiences into categories.**

In everyday usage, the term **concept** is used in several ways. Sometimes it refers to an idea someone has, such as, "My concept of how a president should act is straightforward." At other times it is used as a hypothesis; for example, "My concept is that we are always in debt because we spend too much on frills." When the term *concept* is used in connection with teaching and learning, it has a more precise meaning and refers to the way knowledge and experience are categorized.

Concept learning is essentially "putting things into a class" and then being able to recognize members of that class (R. Gagné, 1993). This requires that an individual be able to take a particular case, such as his or her pet dog Max, and place it into a general class of objects, in this case a class termed *dog*, that share certain attributes. This process requires making judgments about whether a particular case is an instance of a larger class.

**Concepts Themselves Can Be Placed into Categories.** Concepts, like other objects and ideas, can be categorized and labeled. Knowing the different types of concepts is important because, as is explained later, different types of concepts require different teaching strategies. One way of classifying concepts is according to the rule structures that define their use.

Some concepts have constant rule structures. The concept of *island*, for example, always involves land surrounded by water. A *triangle* is a plane, closed figure with three sides and three angles. The rule structures for these concepts are constant. Their critical attributes are combined in an additive manner and are always the same. This type of concept is referred to as a **conjunctive concept.**

Other concepts are broader and more flexible and permit alternative sets of attributes. Their rule structures are not constant. For example, the concept of a *strike* in baseball is based on a number of alternative conditions. A strike may be when a batter swings and misses, when an umpire determines that the pitch was in the strike zone even though the batter did not swing at the ball, or when the batter hits a foul ball. This type of concept is called a **disjunctive concept,** that is, one that contains alternative sets of attributes. The concept *noun* is another example of a disjunctive concept. It may be a person, a place, or a thing, but it cannot be all three at the same time.

A third type of concept is one whose rule structure depends on relationships. The concept *aunt* describes a particular relationship between siblings and their offspring. The concepts *time* and *distance* are also **relational concepts.** To understand either of these concepts, one must know the other, plus the relationship between them. For example, *week* is defined as a succession of days that has as its beginning point day one (usually Sunday) and as its ending point day seven (usually Saturday) and a duration of seven days.

**Concepts Are Learned Through Examples and Nonexamples.** Learning particular concepts involves identifying both *examples* and *nonexamples* of a concept. For instance, a cow is an example of a mammal but is a nonexample of a reptile. Australia is an example of a country in the Southern Hemisphere, but it is a nonexample of a developing country. Cotton and silk are examples of the concept *fabric,* but leather and steel are nonexamples. As we describe later, the way examples and nonexamples are identified and used by teachers is important in a concept lesson.

**Concepts Are Influenced by Social Context.** The critical attributes of a conjunctive concept, such as *equilateral triangle,* are fixed across social contexts. However, disjunctive or relational concepts, such as *poverty* or *literacy rate,* change from one social context to another. For example, poverty in the United States means something much different than poverty in a developing African country. Concepts with changing critical attributes are often found in the behavioral and social sciences and need an operational definition depending on the social context or cultural environment in which they are

> Concepts themselves can be categorized and labeled.

> Teachers should provide clear examples and nonexamples of what is being taught to ensure thorough understanding of the concept.

**Table 9.1** *Three Types of Concepts*

| Type | Characteristic | Example |
|---|---|---|
| Conjunctive | Constant rule structure | Island |
| Disjunctive | Alternative set of attributes | Strike in baseball |
| Relational | Rule structure depends on relationships | Aunt |

used. Consider the concept *aunt*. In some societies, *aunt* or *auntie* refers to any adult in the society who has some responsibility for caring for a particular child and has nothing to do with actual blood relationship. Consider also the geographical concepts *north* and *south* as they relate to climate. Children in the Northern Hemisphere are taught that as one goes south, the climate gets warmer. Obviously, this conceptual relationship would not hold true for children in Australia or Argentina. The labeling of concepts is also influenced by context. In England, a car's windshield is called a *windscreen,* and the trunk is called the *boot.* In both instances, the concepts are the same; the label is what is different.

**Social context and culture influence the definition and attributes of some concepts.**

**Concepts Have Definitions and Labels.** All concepts have names or labels and more or less precise definitions. For example, a relatively small body of land surrounded on all sides by water is labeled an *island.* Labels and definitions permit mutual understanding and communication with others using the concept. They are prerequisites for concept teaching and learning. Labels, however, are human inventions and essentially are arbitrary. Knowing the label does not mean a student understands the concept. This is what makes teaching concepts difficult.

**A concept's critical attributes are what distinguish it from all other concepts.**

**Concepts Have Critical Attributes.** Concepts also have attributes that describe and help define them. Some attributes are critical and are used to separate one concept from all others. For example, an *equilateral triangle* is a triangle with three equal sides. The **critical attributes** are that it must be a triangle and that each of the sides must be equal. Triangles without three equal sides are not equilateral triangles. In addition, if the concept is a subset of a broader concept, then it must also include the critical attributes of the broader concept. An *equilateral triangle* is a member of the class of concepts called *triangles* and thus must contain all the critical attributes of a triangle.

**Focusing exclusively on the critical aspects of concepts can result in confusion when learning new concepts.**

**Concepts Have Noncritical Attributes.** Some attributes may be found in some but not in all members of the class. These are called **noncritical attributes.** For example, size is a noncritical attribute of an equilateral triangle. All concepts have both critical and noncritical attributes, and it is sometimes difficult for students to differentiate between the two. For example, the concept *bird* is typically associated in most people's minds with the noncritical attribute flying. Robins, cardinals, eagles, and most other birds can fly. Flying, however, is not a critical attribute of birds, since ostriches and penguins cannot fly, yet they are still classified as birds. Focusing exclusively on critical attributes and typical members of a class can sometimes cause confusion when learning new concepts. Although flying is a noncritical attribute of birds, it is nonetheless typical of most birds and must be accounted for in teaching about them.

**Table 9.2** *Critical and Noncritical Attributes of Birds*

| Critical Attributes | Noncritical Attributes |
| --- | --- |
| Feathers | Feather color |
| Warm-blooded | Ability to fly |
| Feet | Webbed feet |

## Human Development and Concept Learning

Another important aspect underlying concept teaching comes from the field of human development. Research in this field, some of which dates back over half a century, has shown how age and intellectual development influence students' readiness and abilities to learn various types of concepts (Benjafield, 1992; Friedman, 1980; Piaget, 1954, 1963; Starkey, 1980; Welch & Long, 1940). This research has shown that children begin learning concepts at a very early age through object sorting and classifying activities and that concept learning continues throughout life. The way concepts are learned is affected by the learners' age, language development, and level of intellectual development. Theories of cognitive development of Jean Piaget and Jerome Bruner are important to teachers in regard to concept learning by students.

*The way concepts are learned is affected significantly by the learner's age and his or her levels of intellectual development.*

Swiss psychologist Jean Piaget developed a theory about how humans develop and make sense of their world. From Piaget's perspective, humans are always striving to make sense of their environment, and their biological maturation, their interaction with the environment, and their social experiences combine to influence how they think about things. The primary contribution of Piaget's ideas for teachers is his *stage theory of cognitive development*. According to Piaget, as children grow and mature, they pass through four stages of cognitive development: sensorimotor, preoperational, concrete operational, and formal operational. These stages and the kinds of thinking associated with each are illustrated in Table 9.3. As you can see, the type of learning that a person is capable of is linked to age. Younger children deal with their world in more concrete, hands-on ways, whereas older children and adults can engage in abstract problem solving.

An American psychologist, Jerome Bruner, also has provided a conceptualization about how children learn at different stages of maturation. Bruner (1966) identified three distinct modes of learning: (1) learning by doing, called the *enactive mode*, (2) learning by forming mental images, called the *iconic mode*, and (3) learning through a series of abstract symbols or representations, called the *symbolic mode*. As children grow older and progress through the grades, they depend less on the enactive mode and more on mental imagery and symbolic operations. In general, children under age 7 rely mainly on doing, or the enactive mode, for learning concepts. Children between the ages of 7 and 11 still rely on the enactive mode but begin learning concepts by forming mental images. Older children and early adolescents still use the iconic mode but increasingly rely on abstract symbols.

*Students use different modes of learning as they grow older.*

**Table 9.3** *Piaget's Stages of Cognitive Development*

| Stage | Age | Kinds of Thinking Abilities |
|---|---|---|
| Sensorimotor | Birth–2 years | Begins to recognize objects; can imitate. |
| Preoperational | 2–7 years | Develops use of language; begins ability to think symbolically; can see another person's point of view; lacks logical mental operations at this stage. |
| Concrete operational | 7–11 years | Can solve concrete problems in logical fashion; able to classify. |
| Formal operational | 11–15/adult | Can solve abstract problems in logical fashion; has concern for social issues. |

✔ **Check for Understanding**

- What kind of relationships exist between concepts and higher-level thinking?

- What are the critical features of different kinds of concepts?

- What are the differences between critical and noncritical attributes?

- What are Piaget's four stages of human development?

- What are the effects of early concept learning on later development?

**Time does not permit teaching every concept that exists in a field. Selecting appropriate concepts to teach is a major planning task for teachers.**

Research has shown that children can learn concepts at a fairly early age and that early concept learning facilitates what can be learned later on. A particularly interesting and important study (Novak & Musonda, 1991) on concept learning in science was selected for the Research Summary in this chapter (pages 295–296).

# 🍎 *Planning and Conducting Concept Lessons*

This section describes procedures and guidelines for planning and conducting lessons aimed at teaching concepts and the nature of concepts.

## Planning for Concept Teaching

During the planning phase of a concept lesson, teachers must make decisions about what concepts to teach and which approach to use. They must also do a thorough job of defining and analyzing concepts being taught and decide which examples and nonexamples to use and how best to present them to students during the lesson. These tasks are important and time-consuming. They make planning for a concept lesson very difficult, perhaps more so than planning for any other model of teaching.

*Selecting Concepts.* The curriculum is the primary source for selecting concepts to teach. Concepts may be embedded in textbooks, and the teacher's edition often provides guidance in selecting key concepts to teach. Take, for instance, the following passage on temperature and heat from a sixth grade science textbook.

> Objects that are moving can do work. You may think of work as doing chores such as washing the car or raking leaves. Scientists, however, define *work* as a force acting on an object and causing it to move. A falling hammer, for example, can do the work of driving a nail. Such work can be done because moving objects have energy. This energy of *motion* is called *kinetic energy.* The faster an object moves, the more kinetic energy it has. . . .
>
> Molecules, like all objects, have kinetic energy because of their motion. *Temperature* is a measure of the average kinetic energy of molecules. The higher the temperature, the faster the molecules in a given sample are moving, on the average. (Hurd et al., 1986, pp. 37–38)

In this passage, the concepts of *work, motion, kinetic energy,* and *temperature* are described. However, it is likely that most students will not understand these concepts thoroughly unless the concepts become the subjects of particular lessons taught by the teacher.

Local curriculum guides are another source for selecting concepts for instruction. In some cases, the key concepts will be listed as vocabulary to be developed in the unit. In other cases, concepts will be found within the main ideas or generalizations for a unit of study. For example, American history courses typically contain a unit on the westward movement. In this unit, students study why people migrated westward during the early eras of the nation's history. In the process, they study such key concepts as *migration, economic gain, religious freedom,* and *political freedom.* They also examine other concepts related to the unit's objectives, such as *expansion, self-sufficiency, heterogeneity, frontier, pioneer, pluralism,* and *terrain.* Obviously, all concepts cannot be taught in a single unit, and teachers must make decisions about which ones to single out for particular lessons.

Research
Summary
9.1

# Can Instruction at an Early Age Have Positive Effects on Learning Science Concepts?

*Novak, J. D., and Musonda, D. (1991).*
A twelve-year longitudinal study of science concept teaching.
*American Educational Research Journal, 28*, 117–115.

Do we sometimes underestimate young student's abilities to learn important concepts? That is the question that Novak and Musonda set out to examine over twenty years ago. Their study is interesting for two reasons. One, it shows that if taught properly, young children can learn basic science concepts and that this learning facilitates later concept development. Two, the study illustrates what can be learned if the same subjects are studied over a span of years rather than at just one point in time.

**Problem and Approach:** Using qualitative and quantitative methods, Novak and Musonda explored whether first and second grade students could be taught basic science concepts, and if so, whether their early science learning enhanced later understanding.

**Sample and Setting:** During 1971 through 1973, teachers in eleven first and second grade classrooms taught 191 students twenty-eight science lessons that had been developed by the researchers. Each lesson required between fifteen to twenty-five minutes to teach. A similar sample of forty-eight children, all from the same school, did not participate in the science lesson program and served as a comparison sample in the study. The study was conducted in the Ithaca, New York, public schools.

**Procedures:** Before the study, researchers developed twenty-eight science lessons, each built around a basic science concept. Examples of lesson topics included: classification of objects; how energy is stored; air molecules and movement; change and things that change them; energy and change. Lessons were presented with audiotapes and pictures, and students interacted with specially designed hands-on materials. Features of concept learning and the use of advance organizers were built into each science lesson. Students studied lessons one through sixteen in the first grade and lessons seventeen through twenty-eight in the second grade. The forty-eight comparison students received no science instruction during grades 1 and 2.

Students in the study were interviewed periodically, and their ideas were organized in concept maps or webs (see Figure 9.2). These maps were subsequently used by the researchers to assess changes in concept understanding from grade 1 through grade 12. As would be expected in a study of this duration, many students moved to other schools over the years, so the sample for the instructed group decreased from 191 to 38 and for the uninstructed group from 48 to 17 between grade 1 and grade 12.

**Results.** The results of the study reported here come primarily from data derived from the concept maps. Figure 9.2 illustrates what the concepts maps looked like; these were developed in grades 2 and 12 by Amy, one of the students in the study. As you can see, Amy's map becomes more lengthy as her understanding of science increases over the years. It also becomes more complex.

Using data available from the concepts maps for students (instructed and noninstructed) and matched according to grade point average, Novak and Musonda scored each student's science understanding at one of four different grade levels. In general, the researchers concluded that instructed students possessed more valid science concepts throughout their school years, and they held fewer misconceptions than noninstructed students did. Although wide variation existed for both groups, the instructed group consistently scored better.

**Discussion and Implications.** The remarkable findings of this study are twofold. One, young children have much concept learning potential that is often overlooked, and two, relatively few hours of science instruction in grades 1 and 2 pay off handsomely in learning about science later on in school. The study makes a strong statement about the importance of early science instruction and how this early instruction can have lasting impact.

**Figure 9.2** *Concept Maps for Amy in Grades 2 and 12*

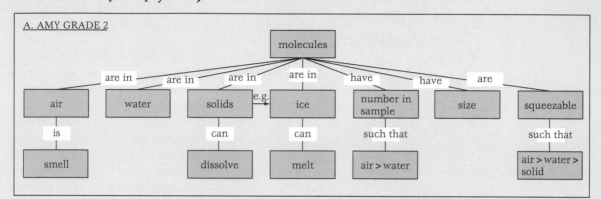

A. AMY GRADE 2

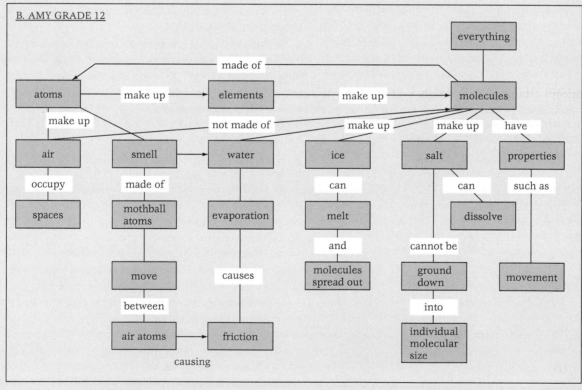

B. AMY GRADE 12

Source: Novak and Musonda (1991), pp. 137–138

Teachers also need to make decisions about which of the new vocabulary words need to be directly taught as concepts. Judgments are constantly being made as to which new terms are essential to understanding the important ideas of a lesson or a unit. If the students don't know the key concepts within a unit, then a lesson on the unknown concepts should be taught. Concept lessons should always be taught if the materials contain unfamiliar terms, a series of steps not known to students, or the use of some "rule" that is new to students.

In the process of selecting concepts to teach, it is important to remember a point made earlier: helping students understand a concept involves more than getting them to provide definitions of new vocabulary words.

**Deciding on an Approach.** A concept teaching lesson has several components. These include the name and definition of the concept, the concept's attributes (some that are critical and some that are not), and examples and nonexamples of the concept. There are several approaches for teachers to handle each of these components. As described earlier, this chapter focuses on two approaches, direct presentation and concept attainment.

The **direct presentation** approach employs a deductive *rule-to-example process* (Tennyson et al., 1983). This approach consists of the teacher first naming and defining the concept and then providing students with examples and nonexamples to reinforce their understanding of the concept. The focus is on labeling and defining the concept.

The **concept attainment** approach, on the other hand, turns this sequence around and uses an inductive *example-to-rule process* (Bruner, 1956). Examples and nonexamples of a particular concept are given first, and students discover or attain the concept themselves through the process of inductive reasoning. Labeling and defining the concept comes at the end rather than at the beginning of the lesson.

The approach a teacher uses depends on the *goals* being sought, the *students* being taught, and the *nature* of the concept. The direct presentation approach usually is best for the development of knowledge about a concept for which students have little or no previous understanding. The concept attainment approach is best when students have some understanding of the concept and the goals of the lesson are to explore the presence or absence of critical attributes of particular concepts and to learn the processes of inductive reasoning. Sometimes both approaches are used when students are learning complicated concepts.

**Defining Concepts.** Critical attributes, as you read earlier, are those attributes that are present in every example of a concept and distinguish it from all other concepts. For example, the concept *tree* might be defined as a "plant that lives for many years and has a single main stem that is woody." This definition includes the critical attributes *plant, lives for many years, single main stem,* and *woody.* These critical attributes define a concept, and consequently, students must understand them. However, noncritical attributes also enter into the picture. For example, size, shape, and color are noncritical attributes of trees. Blue lagoons, sandy beaches, and palm trees may be desirable on an island, but they are noncritical attributes. When learning concepts, students must not confuse the noncritical attributes, no matter how common, with the critical attributes of the concept.

The source of the definition for a concept and its critical attributes is also important. In some instances, concepts are defined in the glossaries of the students' textbooks, but

---

*Teachers must constantly make judgments as to which concepts must be mastered before moving to the next topic.*

*The direct presentation approach calls for teacher definition of a concept followed by appropriate provision of examples and nonexamples.*

*The concept attainment approach entails students deriving a concept themselves using inductive reasoning after being provided with examples and nonexamples.*

**Complex concepts from academic subjects need to be defined and taught appropriately for the age of the students.**

in other cases, they may be defined in the curriculum guides published by the local school districts. These definitions and critical attributes should be examined carefully. When defining concepts, it is important to recognize that some words used in the definition are irrelevant. For example, most dictionaries refer to the domesticated state of dogs. This is an interesting fact, but it is not what identifies a dog or separates dogs from cats. Essentially, there are three steps in defining a concept: (1) identify the concept's name; (2) list the critical and noncritical attributes; and (3) write a concise definition. For the *island* example, this would involve identifying the name as *island,* listing the critical attributes as land mass and water, and providing the following definition: "an island is a land mass that is smaller than a continent and is surrounded by water."

Analyzing Concepts. Once a concept has been selected and defined in terms of its critical attributes, the concept needs to be analyzed for examples and nonexamples. The selection of examples and nonexamples is probably the most difficult aspect of planning for a concept lesson. Examples serve as the connectors between the concept's abstraction and the learner's prior knowledge and experiences. Examples must be meaningful to the learner and must be as concrete as possible.

**Selecting good examples and nonexamples of a concept is one of the most challenging aspects of planning a concept lesson.**

Charts, diagrams, and webs as well as pictures should be used as visual examples of abstract concepts. They can also aid the teacher in analyzing the concept for instructional decisions. Table 9.4 contains an analysis of a set of concepts. Numbering the critical attributes and using the word *and* can be a reminder that all the critical attributes must be present to have an example of the concept.

Look at the example "Hawaii" in Table 9.4. It is a land mass not as large as a continent, there is a body of water nearby, and the water completely surrounds it. Each of the three critical conditions of an island is met; therefore, it is an example of the con-

**Table 9.4** *Analysis of Coordinated Concepts*

| Concept | Definition | Example | Nonexample | Critical Attributes |
|---------|------------|---------|------------|---------------------|
| Island | A land mass not as large as a continent, surrounded by water | Hawaii<br>Cuba<br>Greenland | Florida<br>Lake Erie<br>Australia | 1. Land mass (not continent), *and*<br>2. Water, *and*<br>3. Land surrounded by water. |
| Lake | A large inland body of water surrounded by land | Lake Huron<br>Great Salt Lake<br>Big Lake | Ohio River<br>Hawaii<br>pond | 1. Large inland body of water, *and*<br>2. Land, *and*<br>3. Water surrounded by land. |
| Peninsula | A land area almost entirely surrounded by water but having a land connection to a larger land mass | Florida<br>Italy<br>Delmarva | Cuba<br>Hudson Bay<br>Big lake | 1. Land connected to larger land mass, *and*<br>2. Water, *and*<br>3. Land surrounded almost entirely by water. |
| Bay | A body of water partly surrounded by land but having a wide outlet to the sea | Chesapeake Bay<br>Hudson Bay<br>Green Bay | Florida<br>lake<br>gulf | 1. Body of water connected to the sea by a wide outlet, *and*<br>2. Land, *and*<br>3. Water partly surrounded by land. |

cept. Teachers might also look at Florida as a nonexample of island. Land and water are present, but the land is not completely surrounded by water. All of the criteria are not met; therefore, Florida is a nonexample.

The isolation of the attributes is critical to the analysis and teaching of concepts. The teacher needs to decide if the attributes are critical and should be presented when matching examples and nonexamples, such as Hawaii and Florida, or if the attributes are noncritical and are best used in divergent examples after clear instances of the concept are presented.

## Choosing and Sequencing Examples and Nonexamples

The examples and nonexamples selected to illustrate a concept are very important. In general, it has been shown that initial examples should be familiar to the class. Students need to see typical examples clearly before they are ready to consider atypical ones. Similarly, students normally find it easier to identify a concept with its most immediate neighbors before relating it to more distant ones. If a robin is used as the best (most familiar) example of the concept *bird,* it is easier for the learner to distinguish close neighbors to robins, such as cardinals, sparrows, or bluebirds, than to distinguish more distant members, such as ducks, chickens, or penguins.

When selecting a set of examples, teachers will often make the noncritical attributes of the concept as *different* as possible. This helps students focus on the critical attributes common to each of the examples. For instance, if teachers are developing the concept of *island,* they might include Hawaii, a tropical island, and Greenland, which has a cold climate. The obvious differences in climates will help students focus their attention on the common attributes of these two examples. Likewise, when developing a set of examples for the concept *insects,* teachers might include water bugs and ants, which live in different environments but still have the same critical attributes.

When selecting a set of matched examples and nonexamples, teachers generally attempt to make the noncritical attributes of the pairs as similar as possible. This enables students to focus on the differences between the example and the nonexample. In the case of the concept of *island,* for example, the Florida peninsula and the Cuban island could serve as a matched pair because of the similarities in climate. Examples and nonexamples should be sequenced for presentation in a logical fashion, and normally sets should be ordered from the easiest to the more difficult. Teachers may also want to give cues to focus students' thinking before each set of three or four examples.

## Use of Visual Images

Using visual images affects the learning of concepts and supports the old adage that "a picture is worth a thousand words." For instance, Anderson and Smith (1987) studied how children come to understand science concepts such as *light* and *color.* They had 113 children in five classrooms study the following passage:

> Bouncing Light
>
> Have you ever thrown a rubber ball at something? If you have, you know that when the ball hits most things, it bounces off them. Like a rubber ball, light bounces off most things it hits.
>
> When light travels to something opaque, all the light does not stop. Some of this light bounces off. When light travels to something translucent or transparent, all the light does not pass through. Some of this light bounces off. When light bounces off things and travels to your eyes, you are able to see.

**Examples that are very different from each other will enable students to focus on common attributes of the concept.**

**Important planning tasks for teachers are choosing examples and nonexamples and deciding how to sequence them.**

**Visual aids and pictures have been shown to greatly facilitate student understanding of complex concepts.**

They found that only 20 percent of the students could understand that seeing is a process of detecting light that has been reflected off some object. However, in a second experiment, they used a visual aid such as the one illustrated in Figure 9.3. In contrast to the 20 percent who learned the concepts from reading about light, 78 percent of the students understood the concepts the teachers were trying to teach when visual aids were used to illustrate the concepts.

*Graphic organizers provide visual images and are a good way for students to link new information.*

**Graphic organizers** and conceptual webs are other forms of visual representation that can be useful. These devices can help highlight the critical attributes of a concept and make the concept more concrete for students. They can also provide students with an effective means for retrieving information from long-term memory so new concepts can be more easily understood.

There are normally four steps in constructing a web for a particular concept. These include:

**Step 1:** Create the core, which is the focus of the web. This would be the name of the concept.

**Step 2:** Construct strands branching out from the core. These strands are critical attributes of the concept.

**Step 3:** Draw strand supports, which connect the critical attributes to the concept.

**Step 4:** Identify the strand ties, which may show relationships among the various attributes.

**Figure 9.3** *Visual Depiction of the Role of Light in Seeing*

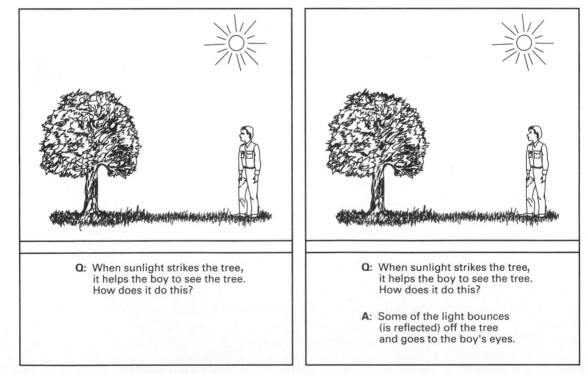

Source: After Richardson-Koehler (1987), p. 327.

**Figure 9.4** *Web of the Concept Equilateral Triangle*

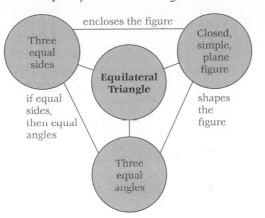

Figure 9.4 is a conceptual web of the concept *equilateral triangle*.

**Plan for Time and Space.** Just as with previous models, deciding on how to allocate sufficient time and how to use classroom space are important planning tasks for a concept lesson. Time requirements depend on the cognitive levels and abilities of the students as well as the complexity of the concept being taught. The most common error made by beginning teachers is underestimating the time it takes to teach even simple concepts thoroughly. Remember the earlier admonition that memorizing the definition of a concept is not the same as understanding it.

> A common mistake made by teachers is underestimating the time it will take to thoroughly teach even simple concepts.

The uses of space for concept teaching are similar to those described for the presentation and direct instruction models. Since concept teaching is teacher-directed, most teachers prefer to use the more traditional row and column formation illustrated in Chapter 7 or the horizontal desk formation described in Chapter 8. Both of these formations keep students' attention focused on the teacher and on information being displayed in the front of the room. Unfortunately, they are not ideal for the more interactive phases of a concept lesson.

## Conducting Concept Lessons

The four phases of a concept teaching lesson are outlined in Table 9.5. The sections that follow describe in some detail teacher and student behavior associated with each phase.

**Clarifying Aims and Establishing Set.** At the beginning of a concept lesson, just as with all types of lessons, the teacher needs to communicate clearly to students the aims of the lesson and how the lesson will proceed. The teacher might also go over the steps of the lesson and give students reasons why the concepts about to be taught are important to learn. Establishing set for a concept lesson requires procedures no different from those described in Chapters 7 and 8. Teachers get students ready to learn with a brief review, questions about yesterday's lesson, or an interesting anecdote that ties the forthcoming lesson into students' prior knowledge.

> Establishing set and preparing a class for the lesson to be taught is an important part of concept teaching.

*Tailoring Teaching for Inclusive Classrooms*

# Start Where the Students Are

Perhaps more than in any other situation, when teaching concepts, teachers must remain aware of the great diversity of their students and be ready to tailor their teaching to particular learners. One feature of diversity is the substantial variation in intellectual development and prior knowledge that will be found in most classrooms. As a result, some concepts will be meaningful and appropriate for some students, while they may be too difficult for and not within the experiences of others. One way teachers adapt instruction

"CITY CHILDREN HAVE TROUBLE WITH THE CONCEPT OF HARVEST."

(© Martha Campbell, from *Phi Delta Kappan*)

**Figure 9.5** *List of Easy and Difficult Examples and Nonexamples of Adverbs*

**Easy Examples**

1. You are so happy.
2. She has been absent lately.
3. Slowly, she walked home.
4. The train chugged loudly.

**Medium Examples**

5. Are you fighting mad?
6. Clouds gathered threateningly.
7. It was not difficult to explain.
8. The most dangerous weapon is a gun.

**Difficult Examples**

9. The small floral print looked pretty.
10. Cats are my number one favorite pet.
11. He wants the dark purple bicycle.
12. The book had three color pictures.

**Easy Nonexamples**

13. Sewing makes you happy.
14. She has been late.
15. She is slow
16. The loud train chugged.

**Medium Nonexamples**

17. Do you fight?
18. The threatening clouds gathered.
19. It is difficult to explain that *not* is a negative word.
20. Most guns are dangerous weapons.

**Difficult Nonexamples**

21. The small print looked pretty.
22. One special cat is my favorite pet.
23. He wants the dark trim to match.
24. The book had three pictures.

Source: After Merrill and Tennyson (1977), pp. 50–51.

to meet the needs of all learners is to consider the difficulty of the examples and nonexamples used in the concept lesson. Figure 9.5 illustrates easy, medium, and difficult examples and nonexamples for teaching the concept of *adverb*. Remember that an adverb is a word that modifies a verb, an adjective, or another adverb and functions to answer one of these questions: When? How? Where? or To what extent? The critical attributes are *modifies another word* and *function*.

Other features of diversity are the experiences students bring with them to the classroom and their cultural backgrounds. For example, conceptual understandings about the relationship between latitude and heat differ depending on which hemisphere we are in. Students in the Northern Hemisphere learn at a very early age to associate north with colder weather. This is exactly opposite for students who grow up in the Southern Hemisphere, where it gets colder as one goes south from the equator. Cultural differences can also influence one's understanding and perception of a particular concept. For example, Native Americans traditionally have a much different concept of time than do Americans who have European origins. It is difficult to illustrate something like the World Wide Web to an individual who has never seen a computer.

To be effective, teachers must remain aware of the vast differences among their students and never assume that any two students' understanding of a concept will be identical.

**Input of Examples and Nonexamples and Testing for Attainment.** The exact sequence for defining and labeling a concept or presenting examples and nonexamples varies according to the particular approach being used by the teacher. It is this internal arrangement and flow of activities that give each of the two approaches their unique character and allows each one to accomplish the particular learning outcomes for which it was designed.

**Table 9.5** *Syntax for Concept Teaching*

| Phase | Teacher Behavior |
| --- | --- |
| *Phase 1:* Clarify aims and establish set. | Teacher explains the aims and procedures for the lesson and gets students ready to learn. |
| *Phase 2:* Input examples and nonexamples. | In the direct presentation approach, teacher names the concepts, identifies the critical attributes, and illustrates with examples and nonexamples. |
| | In concept attainment, examples and nonexamples are given, and students inductively arrive at the concept and its attributes. |
| *Phase 3:* Test for attainment. | Teacher presents additional examples and nonexamples to test students' understanding of the concept. Students are asked to provide their own examples and nonexamples of the concept. |
| *Phase 4:* Analyze student thinking processes and integration of learning. | Teacher gets students to think about their own thinking processes. Students are asked to examine their decisions and the consequences of their choices. Teacher helps students integrate new learning by relating the concept to other concepts in a unit of study. |

*Some concepts are learned through student experimentation.*

**Lesson flow and sequence of concept teaching will vary depending on the topic and approach selected by the teacher.**

*Direct Presentation.* In the direct presentation approach, the internal flow of the lesson includes the following:

1. Naming the concept and providing students with a definition.
2. Identifying the critical attributes and giving examples and nonexamples of the concept.
3. Testing for concept understanding by getting students to provide examples and nonexamples.

Taking the concept *island* as analyzed in Table 9.4, a teacher using the direct presentation approach might proceed as follows:

- Tell students that they are going to learn the concept *island* and write the name of the concept on the board so that students can see the word.
- List the critical attributes: (1) land mass (not a continent), (2) water, (3) land surrounded by water.
- Show a simple drawing that contains only the critical attributes and point out each critical attribute. This could be followed by pictures of best examples, such as Hawaii, Greenland, or Cuba. As each picture is presented, point out the critical attributes again.
- Show students both examples and nonexamples of the concept and ask questions that force judgments about whether a new instance is an example or nonexample of the concept. Have students tell why or why not. Have students come up with their own example and nonexamples.

**Teachers using the concept attainment approach ask students to make decisions about examples once they demonstrate a basic understanding of a concept.**

*Concept Attainment.* In concept attainment, students already have some grasp of a concept or set of concepts and are asked to make decisions about whether or not particular examples are instances of a class. Teachers using the concept attainment approach would use the following steps.

1. Provide students with examples, some that represent the concept and some that do not. Best examples are clearly labeled *yes*, and carefully selected nonexamples are clearly labeled *no*.
2. Urge students to hypothesize about the attributes of the concept and to record reasons for their speculation. The teacher may ask additional questions to help focus students' thinking and to get them to compare attributes of the examples and nonexamples.

*Concepts are learned in and out of school.*

3. When students appear to know the concept, they name (label) the concept and describe the process they used for identifying it. Students may guess the concept early in the lesson, but the teacher needs to continue to present examples and nonexamples until the students attain the critical attributes of the concept as well as the name of the concept.

4. The teacher checks to see if the students have attained the concept by having them identify additional examples as *yes* or *no,* tell why or why not they are examples, and generate examples and nonexamples of their own.

> In the concept attainment approach, a concept is not labeled until students demonstrate understanding and have thought about critical attributes of the concept.

Concept attainment is an inductive process that assists learners in organizing data according to previously learned concepts. Unlike the direct instruction approach, the teacher provides a label and definition only after the students have engaged in the discovery of the critical attributes.

To illustrate the concept attainment approach, consider the following lesson, again using the concept *island.*

- The teacher shows a picture of an island and tells students this is an example of the concept. The teacher then shows a picture of a landform that is not an island and states that this is a nonexample of the concept.

- The teacher continues displaying pictures of islands and other landforms, telling students which are and which are not examples. Students are asked to guess what they think the concept is. All hypotheses and ideas are listed on the chalkboard. The teacher continues to present examples and nonexamples and asks students to reconsider their original hypotheses.

- Students are asked to state a definition of the concept and, if possible, label it. They also list the critical attributes of the concept.

- The teacher then shows additional pictures of islands and other landforms and asks students to identify each as a *yes* or *no.* The teacher also asks students to provide examples of islands they know about and instances of landforms that are not islands. Students explain why or why not.

**Check for Understanding**

- What are the major planning tasks associated with concept teaching?

- How do inductive concept lessons differ from those that use a deductive approach?

- What are the four phases of the concept teaching model, and what types of teacher behaviors are associated with each?

- What are things teachers should think about when adapting concept lessons for students of differing abilities?

- How does the use of examples and nonexamples differ in inductive and deductive concept lessons?

- Why is it important to help students analyze their own thinking processes?

**For the most part, the learning environment for concept teaching is fairly structured and teacher-centered.**

The major roles for the teacher during this aspect of a concept attainment lesson are to record student hypotheses and any critical attributes identified, to cue students, and to provide additional data if necessary.

**Analyzing Thinking and Integrating Learning.**  The final phase of both approaches to concept teaching emphasizes teacher-directed activities aimed at helping students to analyze their own thinking processes and to integrate newly acquired conceptual knowledge. To accomplish this, teachers ask students to think back and recount what was going through their minds as they were considering the concepts. What criteria did they use for grouping items? When did they first figure out the concept? How? What was confusing in the direct presentation lesson? How does the concept relate to other concepts they know about? Were they focusing on the concept as a whole or on a particular attribute? How did noncritical attributes affect attaining the concept? If they were going to teach the concept to a younger student, what would they do?

The intent of this type of questioning is to get students to think about their own thinking (termed *metacognition* and discussed in some detail in The Resource Handbook) and to discover and consider the patterns they use to learn and integrate new concepts into their cognitive frameworks. This phase of a concept lesson relies, obviously, on student discussion and participation. The guidelines for encouraging and facilitating student discussion and participation provided in Chapters 3 and 12 can also be used for this final phase of a concept teaching lesson.

## 🍎 Managing the Learning Environment

The tasks associated with managing the learning environment during a concept teaching lesson are very similar to those used by teachers when using the presentation or direct instruction models. This is particularly true when the teacher is using the direct presentation approach to concept teaching. For this approach, effective teachers structure the learning environment fairly tightly. While the lesson is in progress, they expect students to pay close attention to the lesson—to be keen observers and good listeners. Effective teachers use the methods described in Chapter 5 to govern student talk and to ensure that the pace of the lesson is maintained. Misbehavior that occurs during the lesson is dealt with accurately and quickly, also described in Chapter 5.

In concept attainment, on the other hand, students strive to discover or attain the concept themselves, and this inductive process requires discourse and discussion. There are times when the teacher's role is to encourage student interaction and to give them opportunities to explore their own thinking processes. Facilitating this student activity requires a less structured learning environment in which students can inquire and express their ideas freely. The management system required for more student-centered instructional activities will be described in greater detail in Chapters 10, 11, and 12.

## Illustrating Concepts with Technology

Good teachers have always known that a picture is worth a thousand words when teaching a difficult concept to students. Yet it is often difficult to find the right picture, one that will represent an abstract concept in a meaningful way. Technology can play a significant role in helping teachers find the right picture as well the right motion and the right sound.

Computer simulations, video clips, and CD-ROMs provide powerful means for bringing the outside world into the classroom and providing visual and auditory representations of abstract concepts. Often CD-ROM software programs are interactive and engage students by stimulating several senses through images, motion, and sound.

Let's consider an example. Trying to get students to visualize different eras in history and concepts that help explain life in other times is always difficult. "The Silk Road," a very interesting CD-ROM program developed in Canada, does an excellent job of bringing history into the classroom. Using still photographs, video clips, other types of moving images, and interesting text, "The Silk Road" shows life in thirteenth- and fourteenth-century Asia and the economic and social factors that gave rise to the rich trade route (called the Silk Road) between Asia and the Middle East and Europe. It does a masterful job of holding the user's interest while illustrating the effects of early trade on the development of the modern world. It was impossible to have this type of reality in classrooms a few years ago.

Similar CDs exist for just about every subject. You may wish review the National Gallery of Art CD or "Windows on Science," both of which use interesting collections of still photographs and video clips to illustrate hard-to-conceptualize concepts and ideas, respectively, in the fields of the visual arts and science.

## 🍎 *Assessment and Evaluation*

Many of the same ideas and strategies used in defining and analyzing concepts can be employed in evaluating students' understanding of concepts. However, when evaluating students' understanding of a concept, it is important that teachers ask the students to do more than merely define the concept with words.

To attain the higher levels of concept learning, students should be able to (1) define the concept and know its critical attributes, (2) recognize examples and nonexamples, and (3) evaluate examples and nonexamples in terms of their critical attributes. For example, with the concept of *island,* the learner, when given examples of islands, bays, lakes, and peninsulas, will (1) properly name and identify the islands, (2) name the critical attributes of islands and discriminate them from noncritical attributes, and (3) evaluate how the islands differ from bays, lakes, and peninsulas. In terms of the critical attributes of islands, for example, peninsulas are not completely surrounded by water.

There are a number of principles that teachers should consider when constructing tests of students' behaviors in the learning of concepts. For example, test items should include examples that measure students' abilities to generalize to newly encountered examples of a concept. The test items should also assess students' abilities to discriminate among examples and nonexamples. Tests might employ different formats, such as true-false, multiple-choice, matching, short answer, or short essay. Practice assessment activities, such as a variation of the "twenty questions" game, can be used to provide practice on students' knowledge of concepts. Figure 9.6 shows examples of multiple-choice items for assessing students' understanding of the concept of *inferring.*

**Check for Understanding**

• What are the key features of the learning environment for concept teaching?

• What factors should be considered when thinking about how to assess students' conceptual learning?

Concept lesson assessment should ensure that students are able to identify and discriminate among examples and nonexamples of the concept.

**Figure 9.6** *Example of Multiple-Choice Items to Assess Concept Understanding*

**Item to measure knowledge of the definition of the concept *inferring*:**

Which of the following is the best definition of *inferring*?

a. Using one or more of the senses to examine things carefully and to draw a conclusion.

b. Relating a scientific observation to something that is known, and drawing a conclusion.

c. Drawing a conclusion about what will happen without making a scientific observation.

d. Relating a scientific fact to something that is observed, and predicting the scientific outcome.

**Item to measure the ability to recognize examples and nonexamples of the concept:**

Some of the following stories describe inferring. Some stories do not. You must read each story carefully and then decide whether or not the person inferred. If the story describes inferring, blacken in the space for "Yes" on your answer sheet; if the story does not, blacken the space for "No".

a. Sandy observed many acorns underneath a tall tree. She knew that acorns fall from oaks.

b. Don looked carefully at a slice of bread and saw something green growing there.

c. Sam went to visit his uncle on the farm. He looked in the barn to see if his uncle was there.

d. Joe baked a cake. The cake did not rise. Joe knew that baking powder makes cakes rise.

**Item to measure the ability to discriminate the critical attributes of inferring:**

Which of the following tells about someone relating a scientific observation to something that is known?

a. Tom looked up information about African wildlife and gave a report on lions.

b. Mary drew pictures of three different types of clouds in the sky.

c. Bill saw some blue speckled eggs in a nest. He knew that robins lay blue speckled eggs.

d. Pam heard a noise in the dark room. She thought, "It must be a monster."

Source: After Klausmeir (1980).

# Summary

## Overview of Concept Teaching

- Concepts are the basic building blocks around which people organize their thinking and communication.
- Concept learning and logical thinking are critical goals for almost everything taught in schools. These become important scaffolding for building student understanding of school subjects. Concept learning is essentially a process of putting things into classes or categories.
- The instructional goals of concept teaching are mainly to help learners acquire conceptual understandings of the subjects they are studying and to provide a foundation for higher-level thinking.
- The general flow or syntax of a concept lesson consists of four major phases: present goals and establish set, provide examples and nonexamples, test for concept attainment, and analyze student thinking processes.
- Concept teaching requires a moderately structured learning environment.

## Theoretical and Empirical Support

- The theoretical and empirical support for concept teaching and learning is very extensive and covers a wide range of topics. Studies have shown how age and intellectual development influence readiness to learn concepts. Piaget's and Bruner's developmental theories are of particular importance to concept teaching and learning.
- A concept's critical attributes help define and distinguish it from other concepts. The various kinds of concepts include conjunctive concepts, disjunctive concepts, and relationship concepts. Students grasp general concepts mainly by being presented with specific examples and nonexamples of the concept.
- Studies have also shown how examples and nonexamples should be presented to maximize students' learning and how teachers can use such specific practices as visual images and graphic organizers to support concept learning.

## Planning and Conducting Concept Lessons

- Planning tasks for concept lessons include selecting concepts and choosing the most appropriate approach.
- There are several different approaches to teaching concepts. Two of the most prevalent are direct presentation

and concept attainment. In direct presentation, the teacher labels and defines the concept early in the lesson and then presents the best examples through exposition. In concept attainment, the teacher presents examples and nonexamples of a particular concept but does not define and label the concept until the end of the lesson.

- Concept analysis, selection of examples and nonexamples, and decisions regarding the sequence in which to present the examples are also important tasks teachers must perform during planning for a concept lesson.
- A concept lesson begins with the teacher telling students what the aims for the lesson are and getting them motivated and ready to learn.
- The exact sequencing for defining and labeling a concept and presenting examples and nonexamples varies according to the approach being used by the teacher. In direct presentation, the teacher presents the definition first, whereas in concept attainment, the teacher presents examples and nonexamples first and students discover and define the concept using an inductive process.
- Through questioning and discussion, teachers help students analyze their thinking processes and integrate new learning with old as the final phase of a concept lesson, regardless of approach.

## Managing the Learning Environment

- During the presentation and attainment phases of a concept lesson, the teacher maintains a structured learning environment. However, the final phases of a concept lesson encourage student interaction and require a more flexible, student-centered learning environment.

## Assessment and Evaluation

- As with other instructional models, the major postinstructional task is for teachers to match their testing programs to the model's particular goals.
- When evaluating students' understanding of a concept, it is important to ask students to do more than merely define the concept. Students should also be asked to demonstrate their knowledge of the concept's critical attributes and its relationship to other concepts.

# 🍎 Key Terms

| | | |
|---|---|---|
| concept teaching | relational concept | concept attainment |
| concept | critical attributes | graphic organizers |
| conjunctive concept | noncritical attributes | |
| disjunctive concept | direct presentation | |

# 🍎 Books for the Professional

Benjafield, J. G. (1992). *Cognitions*. Englewood Cliffs, N.J.: Prentice Hall. This is a good explication of how concepts are learned and their relationship to higher-level thinking.

Hyde, A. A., and Bizar, M. (1989). *Thinking in Context: Teaching Cognitive Processes Across the Elementary School Curriculum*. New York: Longman. This book provides a solid and contemporary theoretical framework about how to teach concepts and thinking skills to students. It shows how cognitive processes are linked to content in four important subject areas: reading and writing, mathematics, science, and social studies.

Joyce, B., and Calhoun, E. (1998). *Learning to Teach Inductively*. Boston: Allyn and Bacon. The authors of this little book provide a clear conceptual model and lots of examples of how to teach inductively and get elementary and high school students to think.

Tobin, K., Kahle, J. B., and Fraser, B. J. (1990). *Windows into Science Classrooms: Problems Associated with Higher-Level Cognitive Learning*. New York: Falmer Press. Although the focus of this book is on science classrooms, much of the research that is described and interpreted can be generalized to other types of classrooms where the teacher is interested in conceptual and higher-level learning.

Wiske, M. S. (ed.). (1998). *Teaching for Understanding*. San Francisco: Jossey-Bass. This is a book of readings in which contributors present innovative approaches that teachers can use to develop understanding on the part of students. It includes ways to choose curriculum topics, define goals, and design learning activities.

## Reflection & Portfolio

You are having a conversation with your cooperating teacher, and the topic of teaching concepts and higher-level thinking comes up. You say that you have not noted very many concept lessons in the classes you have observed over the past several weeks, and you wonder why. Your teacher responds by saying that with so much material to cover, she feels she and other teachers in the school can't justify the time it takes to plan and conduct good concept lessons. She goes on to say that many of the students in the school are of low ability and that she doesn't believe that they can benefit from lessons on concepts until they have mastered basic skills, mainly through the drill and practice of direct instruction. You don't argue with her, but her answer doesn't quite jibe with what you have been taught about concept teaching in your methods classes.

Reflect on this situation and write a reflective essay about how you will approach the teaching of concepts when you get your own classroom. In your reflective essay, you may want to consider the following questions: Why is concept teaching important or unimportant? What kind of student benefits from concept teaching and lessons aimed at higher-level thinking? If concept lessons take more time, how can a teacher justify their use? How central do you think concept teaching will be in your instructional repertoire? At the center? On the fringe? Depending on the students?

Compare your response to those provided by the two experienced teachers below and include your essay as an entry in your professional portfolio.

### Manos Alexandria

"I have always believed that the main thing I could do, regardless of the subject, is to help students get the big ideas. Further, I hold to the belief that when students discover or attain a concept on their own, real learning has taken place. It is important, regardless of the students' abilities, to involve them in problems vital to their lives and help them discover major concepts. It is important for students who lack basic skills to embed instruction of required skills within larger ideas and problems, not the other way around. It is critical to engage these students in dialogue rather than have them complete paper-and-pencil tasks."

### Susan Boadus-Garcia

"It has been my experience that many teachers spend too much time getting students to memorize lots of facts associated with a topic but not enough time on the major concepts and principles. I don't use the concept attainment approach all that often in my teaching. I do, however, spend a lot of time teaching the major concepts."

# Chapter ● Ten

# Cooperative Learning

## Reflecting on **Cooperative Learning**

Think about learning experiences you have had as a student where you were required to work with other students to complete a particular assignment. The experience may have been very brief, such as working on a few math problems with the student next to you, or it might have been extensive, requiring collaboration on a major term project.

Write down your thoughts on and reactions to these experiences by considering the following questions:

● *What did you like most about working on learning tasks with others? Least?*

● *Were the experiences you thought about valuable for you? Why? Why not?*

● *What do you think students learn when they work with others?*

● *Are there some aspects of learning together that are particularly effective? What are these?*

● *Are there some aspects of learning together that are particularly ineffective? What are these?*

Considering your answers, do you think you are a person who is prone to be positive toward cooperative learning? Or do you have some serious reservations?

The cooperative
learning model
requires student
cooperation and
interdependence in
its task, goal, and
reward structures.

The previous chapters described three models of teaching—presentation, direct instruction, and concept teaching. These models are used by teachers primarily to help students acquire new information, to learn important skills, and to think about and process information already acquired from prior learning. In essence, this is academic learning, and although this type of learning is extremely important, it doesn't represent the only goals for student learning. This chapter presents a model of instruction called *cooperative learning,* which goes beyond helping students learn academic content and skills to address important social and human relations goals and objectives.

The chapter begins with an overview of the instructional model, then presents its theoretical and empirical support. A section that describes the specific procedures used by teachers as they plan, conduct, and manage the learning environment during cooperative learning lessons follows. The final sections highlight the assessment and evaluation tasks associated with cooperative learning.

## 🍎 *Overview of Cooperative Learning*

All instructional models are characterized, in part, by their task structures, their goal structures, and their reward structures. **Task structures** involve the way lessons are organized and the kind of work students are asked to do. They encompass whether the teacher is working with the whole class or small groups, what students are expected to accomplish, and the cognitive and social demands placed on students as they work to accomplish assigned learning tasks. Task structures differ according to the activities involved in particular lessons. For example, some lessons require students to sit passively receiving information from a teacher's talk. Other lessons require that students complete worksheets, and still others require discussion and debate.

A lesson's **goal structure** refers to the amount of interdependence required of students as they perform their work. Three types of goal structures have been identified. Goal structures are *individualistic* if achievement of the instructional goal requires no interaction with others and is unrelated to how well others do. *Competitive* goal structures exist when students perceive they can obtain their goals if the other students fail to obtain theirs. *Cooperative* goal structures exist when students can obtain their goal only when other students with whom they are linked can obtain theirs. These three goal structures were illustrated previously in Chapter 3.

The **reward structure** for various instructional models can also vary. Just as goal structures can be individualist, competitive, or cooperative, so too can reward structures. Individalistic reward structures exist when a reward can be achieved independently from what anyone else does. The satisfaction of running a 4-minute mile is an example of an individualistic reward structure. Competitive reward structures are those for which rewards are obtained for individual effort in comparison to others. Grading on a curve is an example of a competitive reward structure, as is the way winners are defined in many track and field events. In contrast, situations in which individual effort helps others to be rewarded use cooperative reward structures. Most team sports, such as football, have a cooperative reward structure, even though teams may compete with each other.

Lessons organized around teacher-centered models are generally characterized by task structures by which teachers work mainly with a whole class of students or students work individually to master academic content. These goal and reward structures are based on individual competition and effort. In contrast, as its name implies, the co-

The terms *goal* and
*reward structures*
both refer to the
degree of
cooperation or
competition required
of students to
achieve their goals or
rewards.

**Figure 10.1** *Learner Outcomes for Cooperative Learning*

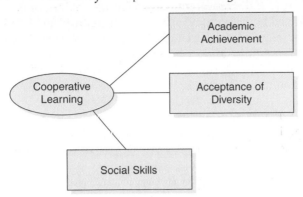

operative learning model is characterized by cooperative task, goal, and reward structures. Students in cooperative learning situations are encouraged and/or required to work together on a common task, and they must coordinate their efforts to complete the task. Similarly, in cooperative learning, two or more individuals are interdependent for a reward they will share, if they are successful as a group. Cooperative learning lessons can be characterized by the following features.

- Students work in teams to master academic goals.
- Teams are made up of high, average, and low achievers.
- Whenever possible, teams include a racial, cultural, and sexual mix of students.
- Reward systems are oriented to the group rather than the individual.

*} heterogen-
groupings*

All these features are explained more fully later in the chapter.

The cooperative learning model was developed to achieve at least three important instructional goals: academic achievement, acceptance of diversity, and social skill development (see Figure 10.1).

Although cooperative learning encompasses a variety of social objectives, it also aims at improving student performance on important *academic tasks*. Its supporters believe that the model's cooperative reward structure raises the value students place on academic learning and changes the norms associated with achievement. Slavin (1996) noted:

> Students often do not value their peers who do well academically, while they do value their peers who excel in sports. . . . This is so because sports success brings benefits to groups (the team, the school, the town), while academic success benefits only the individual. In fact, in a class using grading on the curve or any competitive grading or incentive system, any individual's success reduces the chances that any other individual will succeed. (p. 54)

Slavin, one of the founders of cooperative learning, believes that the group focus of cooperative learning can change the norms of youth culture and make it more acceptable to excel in academic learning tasks.

In addition to changing norms associated with achievement, cooperative learning can benefit both low- and high-achieving students who work together on academic tasks. Higher achievers tutor lower achievers, thus providing special help from peers who share youth-oriented interests and language. In the process, higher achievers gain academically, because serving as a tutor requires thinking more deeply about the relationships of ideas within a particular subject.

**The three instructional goals of cooperative learning are academic achievement, acceptance of diversity, and development of social skills.**

A second important effect of cooperative learning is wider acceptance of people who are different by virtue of their race, culture, social class, ability, or disability. Following the premises outlined by Allport (1954) over a half century ago, it is known that mere physical contact among different racial or ethnic groups or special-needs children is insufficient to reduce prejudice and stereotyping. Cooperative learning presents opportunities for students of varying backgrounds and conditions to work interdependently on common tasks and, through the use of cooperative reward structures, learn to appreciate each other.

A third and important goal for cooperative learning is to teach students skills of cooperation and collaboration. These are critical skills in a society in which much adult work is carried out in large, interdependent organizations and communities are becoming more culturally diverse and global in their orientations. Yet, many youth and adults alike lack effective social skills. This situation is evidenced by how often minor disagreements between individuals can lead to violent acts and by how often people express dissatisfaction when asked to work in cooperative situations.

Six major phases or steps are involved in a cooperative learning lesson. A lesson begins with the teacher going over the goals of the lesson and getting students motivated to learn. This phase is followed by the presentation of information, often in the form of text rather than lecture. Students are then organized into study teams. In the next step, students, assisted by the teacher, work together to accomplish interdependent tasks. Final phases of a cooperative learning lesson include presentation of the group's end product or testing on what students have learned and recognition of group and individual efforts. The six phases of a cooperative lesson are described in more detail later in the chapter.

The learning environment for cooperative learning is characterized by democratic processes and active roles for students in deciding what should be studied and how. The teacher provides a high degree of structure in forming groups and defining overall procedures, but students are left in control of the minute-to-minute interactions within their groups.

> The cooperative learning environment sets the stage for students to learn very valuable collaboration and social skills that they will use throughout their lives.

✔ **Check for Understanding**

- What are the key characteristics of cooperative learning, and how do these differ from other models of teaching?

- What are the six phases of a cooperative learning lesson?

- What are the major learner outcomes for cooperative learning?

- What type of learning environment works best for cooperative learning?

## 🍎 *Theoretical and Empirical Support*

The cooperative learning model did not evolve from one individual's theory or from a single approach to learning. Its roots go back to the early Greeks, but its contemporary developments can be traced to the work of educational psychologists and pedagogical theorists at the beginning of the twentieth century.

### Concept of the Democratic Classroom

In 1916, John Dewey wrote a book called *Democracy and Education*. Dewey's concept of education was that the classroom should mirror the larger society and be a laboratory for real-life learning. Dewey's pedagogy required teachers to create a learning environment characterized by democratic procedures and scientific processes. Their primary responsibility was to engage students in inquiry into important social and interpersonal problems. The specific classroom procedures described by Dewey (and his latter-day followers) emphasized small, problem-solving groups of students searching for their own answers and learning democratic principles through day-to-day interaction with one another.

*John Dewey*

Many years after Dewey's initial work, Herbert Thelen (1954, 1960) developed more precise procedures for helping students work in groups. Like Dewey, Thelen argued that the classroom should be a laboratory or miniature democracy for the purpose of study and inquiry into important social and interpersonal problems. Thelen, with his interest in group dynamics, put more structure on the pedagogy of group investigation and, as is described later, provided the conceptual basis for contemporary developments in cooperative learning.

The use of cooperative group work for Dewey and Thelen went beyond improving academic learning. Cooperative behavior and processes were considered basic to human endeavor, the foundation on which strong democratic communities could be built and maintained. The logical way to accomplish these important educational objectives, they believed, was to structure the classroom and students' learning activities so that they modeled the desired outcomes.

**Cooperative behavior was viewed by Dewey and Thelen as the foundation of democracy, and schools were seen as laboratories for developing democratic behavior.**

## Intergroup Relations

In 1954, the Supreme Court issued its historic *Brown* v. *Board of Education of Topeka* decision in which the Court ruled that public schools in the United States could no longer operate under a separate-but-equal policy but must become racially integrated. This led to subsequent decisions and actions by judicial and legislative bodies all across the country demanding that public school authorities submit plans for desegregation.

At the time, thoughtful theorists and observers warned that putting people of different ethnic or racial backgrounds in the same location would not, in and of itself, counteract the effects of prejudice or promote integration and better intergroup acceptance. They knew, for example, that the cafeteria in an integrated school might still be characterized by African American students sitting on one side of the room and white students on the other. They also knew that a community might be highly integrated but still have restaurants or churches patronized by only whites or only blacks.

A leading sociologist of the time, Gordon Allport, argued that laws alone would not reduce intergroup prejudice and promote better acceptance and understanding. Shlomo Sharan and his colleagues at Tel Aviv University in Israel (1984; 1992) have summarized three basic conditions required to counteract racial prejudice:

**Interethnic contacts occurring under conditions of equal status are needed to reduce racial and ethnic prejudice.**

(1) unmediated interethnic contact, (2) occurring under conditions of equal status between members of the various groups participating in a given setting, and (3) where the setting officially sanctions interethnic cooperation. (p. 2)

Much of the recent interest in the cooperative learning model has grown out of attempts to structure classrooms and teaching processes according to these three conditions. Robert Slavin's work, which is described later, was conducted in part in the inner cities along the eastern seaboard as part of integration efforts. The work of Sharan and his colleagues in Israel was prompted by that country's need to find ways to promote better ethnic understanding between Jewish immigrants of European background and those of Middle Eastern background. The work of David Johnson and Roger Johnson at the University of Minnesota explored how cooperative classroom environments might lead to better learning by and more positive regard toward students with special needs who were included (integrated) in regular classrooms.

## Experiential Learning

**Experiential learning in which individuals are personally involved in the learning provides theoretical support for cooperative learning.**

A third theoretical perspective that provides intellectual support for cooperative learning comes from theorists and researchers who are interested in how individuals learn from experience. Experience accounts for much of what people learn. For example, most people learned to ride a bicycle by riding one, and they learned about being a sister or brother by being one. Conversely, even though everyone can read books about marriage and child rearing, those who have married and raised children know that living these experiences is never the same as described in the books. Experience provides insights, understandings, and techniques that are difficult to describe to anyone who has not had similar experiences. Johnson and Johnson (1994), preeminent cooperative learning theorists, described experiential learning this way:

> Experiential learning is based upon three assumptions: that you learn best when you are personally involved in the learning experience, that knowledge has to be discovered by yourself if it is to mean anything to you or make a difference in your behavior, and that a commitment to learning is highest when you are free to set your own learning goals and actively pursue them within a given framework. (p. 7)

The concept of experiential learning is discussed further in subsequent chapters.

## Effects on Cooperative Behavior

Twenty-first century living is characterized by global, interdependent communities and by complex social institutions that require high degrees of cooperation among members. Consequently, most people prize cooperative behavior and believe it to be an important goal for education. Many of the schools' extracurricular activities, such as team sports and dramatic and musical productions, are justified on this basis. But what about activities within the classroom itself? Do certain types of activities, such as those associated with cooperative learning, have effects on students' cooperative attitudes and behaviors?

**The majority of studies done on the effects of cooperative learning show that it produces both academic and social benefits.**

Sharan (1984, 1992) and his colleagues have sought answers to this question for over a decade. They have worked on developing a particular approach to cooperative learning and testing it to see if its use would improve social relations among different Jewish subgroups in Israel. In one study, researchers randomly assigned thirty-three English and literature teachers to three training groups. Teachers in group 1 were taught how to fine-tune their whole-class teaching skills. Those in group 2 were taught how to use Slavin's Student Teams Achievement Divisions (STAD) (explained later), and those in group 3 were taught Sharan's Group Investigation (GI) approach to cooperative learning. The investigators collected massive amounts of information before, during, and after the experiment, including data from achievement tests, classroom observations, and cooperative behavior of students.

For the test of cooperative behavior, students were selected from classrooms using each of the three instructional approaches and were asked to engage in a task called "Lego Man." In six-member teams (each with three European and three Middle Eastern members), students were asked to plan how they would carry out a joint task of constructing a human figure from forty-eight Lego pieces.

Sharan's study showed clearly that the instructional methods influenced the students' cooperative and competitive behavior. Cooperative learning generated more cooperative behavior, both verbal and nonverbal, than whole-class teaching. Students from both cooperative-learning classrooms displayed less competitive behavior and more cross-ethnic cooperation than those who came from whole-class teaching classrooms.

## Effects on Interactions with Children Who Have Disabilities

Two decades after the Supreme Court ended separate-but-equal public schools, Congress in 1975 passed an equally historic piece of integration legislation. Titled the Education for All Handicapped Children Act and known as Public Law 94-142, this legislation required students with disabilities to be placed, whenever possible, into least restrictive environments. Instead of placement in special schools or classrooms (the approach used for most of the twentieth century), children with disabilities (approximately 12 percent of the student population) were to be included in regular classrooms. Obviously, this meant that regular classroom teachers now had children with physical, emotional, and mental disabilities in their classrooms.

*Cooperative learning helps students become engaged with one another*

Research Summary 10.1

# What Can Make Us Cheer for Our Peers with Special Needs?

*Johnson, R., Rynders, J., Johnson, D. W., Schmidt, B., and Haider S. (1979).*
Interaction between handicapped and nonhandicapped teenagers as a function of situational goal structuring: Implications for mainstreaming. *American Educational Research Journal, 16,* 161–167.

Just because people who are different from one another are placed in close proximity does not mean that they will interact in positive ways or shed their prejudice and negative stereotypes. An important question for educators and teachers is, What can we do to help students be more positive and more accepting toward peers who represent different racial backgrounds, come from different social classes, or who are disabled? Roger Johnson and David Johnson and their colleagues addressed this question in an important study that was creative in the way it sought answers to a complex problem in a very simple setting, a bowling alley.

**Problem and Approach:** The researchers wanted to find out the effects of various goal structures on the interactions between nondisabled junior high students and trainable mentally challenged students in a learning situation, in this instance, bowling classes.

**Sample:** Subjects in the study were thirty junior high students (ages 13 to 16, including fifteen boys and fifteen girls) from three midwestern junior high schools. Nine nondisabled students came from a public junior high school; nine other nondisabled students came from a private Catholic school. The twelve disabled students were from a special school for the mentally challenged. These students were able to communicate and understand instructions and that they did not have any physical disabilities that would prevent them from bowling.

**Procedures:** Students were divided randomly into learning teams of five. Each team contained three nondisabled students and two students with disabilities. Each of the learning teams was then assigned to one of three experimental conditions.

- *Cooperative condition.* Team members were instructed to "maximize" their team's bowling score at a criterion of fifty points improvement over the previous week. They were to help each other in any way possible.
- *Individualistic condition.* Students in these teams were instructed to "maximize" their individual scores by ten points over the previous week and to concentrate only on their own performance.
- *Laissez-faire condition.* Students were given no special instructions.

The three bowling instructors in the study were told what to say and were rotated across groups. All groups received the same amount of training over a 6-week period.

Trained observers, who were kept naive about the purpose of the study, watched the students bowl and recorded interactions among students in three categories: positive, neutral, and negative. Observations focused on the period of time from when a bowler stepped up to bowl until he or she stepped down from the bowling line.

**Pointers for Reading Research:** The researchers used the chi square ($\chi^2$) to test the significance of their results. This statistic is used by researchers when their data are of a particular type. It serves the same purpose as other tests of significance introduced earlier. The results as reported in this study are straightforward and easy to read and understand.

**Results:** Tables 10.1 and 10.2 show the results of the bowling study. Table 10.1 displays the frequency of homogeneous and heterogeneous interactions among the students in the three conditions. Table 10.2 displays data on "group cheers" for disabled students who threw strikes and spares over the course of the study.

**Discussion and Implications:** The data presented in Tables 10.1 and 10.2 are clear and straightforward. There were more interactions among students on the cooperative bowling team and, more important, more positive interactions that were both heterogeneous and homogeneous. Further study of their data revealed that "Each student with a disability on the average participated in 17 positive interactions with nondisabled peers per hour in the cooperative condition, 5 in the individualistic condition, and 7 in the laissez-faire condition" (p. 164).

The number of cheers given to disabled students in the cooperative condition gives additional support to the idea that

**Table 10.1** *Frequency of Homogeneous and Heterogeneous Interactions Within Conditions*

|  | Positive | | Neutral | | Negative | | Total |
|---|---|---|---|---|---|---|---|
|  | **Homo** | **Hetero** | **Homo** | **Hetero** | **Homo** | **Hetero** | **Total** |
| Cooperative | 495 | 336 | 67 | 47 | 4 | 10 | 959 |
| Individualistic | 243 | 92 | 61 | 17 | 15 | 11 | 439 |
| Laissez-faire | 265 | 136 | 75 | 49 | 9 | 6 | 540 |
| Total | 1003 | 564 | 203 | 113 | 28 | 27 | 1938 |

\*$X^2 = 86.87$, $p < 01$.

NOTE: Homogeneous interactions took place between nondisabled students and between disabled students; heterogeneous interactions took place between disabled and nondisabled students.
SOURCE: After R. Johnson et al. (1979), p. 165.

a cooperative goal structure is a means for getting positive response from nondisabled students toward their disabled peers.

This study, along with others that have produced similar results, has two important implications for teachers.

1. Individualistic and competitive goal structures associated with so many classroom learning tasks do not encourage positive interactions among people from differing backgrounds and conditions. Redefining the goal structure and making it more cooperative seems to help.
2. Severely disabled students, such as those who are mentally challenged, given the appropriate conditions, can be mainstreamed into learning settings with nondisabled students in ways that can benefit all.

**Table 10.2** *Frequency of Group Cheers Within Conditions*

| Condition | Frequency |
|---|---|
| Cooperative | 55 |
| Individualistic | 6 |
| Laissez-faire | 3 |

SOURCE: After R. Johnson et al. (1979), p. 165.

Just as theorists knew that racial integration would not end prejudice, there was considerable evidence in 1975 that placing disabled people (who have traditionally been perceived negatively) in close proximity to others would not end negative attitudes. In fact, some researchers argued that closer contact might even increase prejudice and stereotyping. A critical factor in producing more positive attitudes and behaviors seemed to be the way the interaction between disabled and nondisabled students was structured. David Johnson and Roger Johnson and several of their colleagues at the University of Minnesota studied how goal structures influence interaction in a unique and interesting way. Their study is summarized in the Research Summary for this chapter.

## Effects on Academic Achievement

One of the important aspects of cooperative learning is that while it is helping promote cooperative behavior and better group relations among students, it simultaneously helps students with their academic learning. Slavin (1986, 1995) reviewed studies investigating the effects of cooperative learning on achievement. These studies were done at all grade levels and included the following subject areas: language arts, spelling, geography, social studies, science, mathematics, English as a second language, reading, and writing. They were conducted in urban, rural, and suburban schools in the United States, Israel, Nigeria, and Germany. Of forty-five studies reviewed, thirty-seven of them showed that cooperative learning classes significantly outperformed control group classes in academic achievement. Eight studies found no differences. None of the studies showed negative effects for cooperative learning.

In a recent experiment, Slavin (1995) and his colleagues created an elementary school based on the concept of cooperation and cooperative learning. After the second year of implementation, students in the cooperative elementary school achieved significantly higher levels in reading vocabulary, reading comprehension, language expression, and math computation and application than their peers in a traditional elementary school did. They also displayed better social relations skills and were more accepting of disabled students.

Most developers of cooperative learning argue that learning in heterogeneous groups is beneficial for all students. It is assumed that students with lesser abilities learn more by working alongside those who have greater abilities and that the latter benefit from the process of serving as tutors to their less able peers. However, a small body of research (Robinson, 1990 and 1996) suggests that this is not always the case. Robinson reviewed the research on cooperative learning between 1967 and 1989. She concluded that intellectually gifted students do not necessarily benefit from working in heterogeneous groups. She further argues that using cooperative learning with talented students is a form of exploitation.

Although the research is not conclusive, beginning teachers who use cooperative learning should remain aware of possible unintended negative consequences.

To summarize, a strong theoretical and empirical framework for cooperative learning reflects the perspective that humans learn from their experiences and active participation in small groups helps students learn important social skills while simultaneously developing academic skill and democratic attitudes.

## ✔ Check for Understanding

- What philosophical and theoretical contribution did John Dewey and Gordon Allport make to the development of cooperative learning?

- Why are ideas from experiential learning important to cooperative learning?

- How strong is the empirical support for cooperative learning?

- On what effects of cooperative learning do researchers agree? Disagree?

# 🍎 *Planning and Conducting Cooperative Learning Lessons*

## Planning for Cooperative Learning

**Preparing cooperative learning lessons is somewhat different than planning other types of lessons.**

Many functions of teacher planning described in previous chapters can be applied to cooperative learning. However, cooperative learning requires some unique planning tasks as well. For example, time spent organizing or analyzing specific skills required of a direct instruction lesson may instead be spent gathering resource materials, text, or worksheets so that small groups of students can work on their own. Instead of planning for the smooth flow and sequencing of major ideas, the teacher may plan how to make smooth transitions from whole-class to small-group instruction. Following are some of the unique planning tasks and decisions required of teachers preparing to teach a cooperative learning lesson.

**Choose an Approach.** Although the basic principles of cooperative learning do not change, there are several variations of the model. Four approaches that should be part of the beginning teacher's repertoire are described here.

*Student Teams Achievement Divisions.* **Student Teams Achievement Divisions (STAD)** was developed by Robert Slavin and his colleagues at the Johns Hopkins University and is perhaps the simplest and most straightforward of the cooperative learning approaches (Slavin, 1995). Teachers using STAD present new academic information to students each week or on a regular basis, either through verbal presentation or text. Students within a given class are divided into four- or five-member learning teams, with representatives on each team of both sexes, various racial or ethnic groups, and high, average, and low achievers. Team members use worksheets or other study devices to master the academic materials and then help each other learn the materials through tutoring, quizzing one another, or carrying on team discussions. Individually, students take weekly or biweekly quizzes on the academic materials. These quizzes are scored and each individual is given an "improvement score." This improvement score (explained later) is based not on a student's absolute score but instead on the degree to which the score exceeds a student's past averages.

> In the STAD model of cooperative learning, students in heterogeneous teams help each other by using a variety of cooperative study methods and quizzing procedures.

*Jigsaw.* **Jigsaw** was developed and tested by Elliot Aronson and his colleagues at the University of Texas and then adapted by Slavin and his colleagues. Using Jigsaw, students are assigned to five- or six-member heterogeneous study teams. Academic materials are presented to the students in text form, and each student is responsible for learning a portion of the material. For example, if the textual material was on cooperative learning, one student on the team would be responsible for STAD, another for Jigsaw, another for Group Investigation, and perhaps the other two would become experts in the research base and history of cooperative learning. Members from different teams with the same topic (sometimes called the *expert group*) meet to study and help each other learn the topic. Then students return to their home teams and teach other members what they have learned. Figure 10.2 illustrates the relationship between home and expert teams.

Following home team meetings and discussions, students take quizzes individually on the learning materials.

> In the Jigsaw model, each team member is responsible for mastering part of the learning materials and then teaching that part to the other team members.

**Figure 10.2** *Illustrations of Jigsaw Teams*

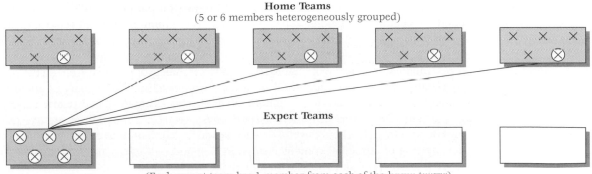

**Home Teams**
(5 or 6 members heterogeneously grouped)

**Expert Teams**

(Each expert team has 1 member from each of the home teams)

In Group
Investigation,
students not only
work together but
also help plan both
the topics for study
and the investigative
procedures used.

*Group Investigation.* Many of the key features of the **Group Investigation (GI)** approach were designed originally by Herbert Thelen. More recently, this approach has been extended and refined by Sharan and his colleagues at Tel Aviv University. Group Investigation is perhaps the most complex of the cooperative learning approaches and the most difficult to implement. In contrast to STAD and Jigsaw, students are involved in planning both the topics for study and the ways to proceed with their investigations. This requires more sophisticated classroom norms and structures than do approaches that are more teacher-centered.

Teachers who use the GI approach normally divide their classes into five- or six-member heterogeneous groups. In some instances, however, groups may form around friendships or around an interest in a particular topic. Students select topics for study, pursue in-depth investigations of chosen subtopics, and then prepare and present a report to the whole class. Sharan (1984) and his colleagues described the following six steps of the GI approach.

1. *Topic selection.* Students choose specific subtopics within a general problem area, usually delineated by the teacher. Students then organize into small two- to six-member task-oriented groups. Group composition is academically and ethnically heterogeneous.
2. *Cooperative planning.* Students and the teacher plan specific learning procedures, tasks, and goals consistent with the subtopics of the problem selected in step 1.
3. *Implementation.* Pupils carry out the plan formulated in step 2. Learning should involve a wide variety of activities and skills and should lead students to different kinds of sources both inside and outside the school. The teacher closely follows the progress of each group and offers assistance when needed.
4. *Analysis and synthesis.* Pupils analyze and evaluate information obtained during step 3 and plan how it can be summarized in some interesting fashion for possible display or presentation to classmates.
5. *Presentation of final product.* Some or all of the groups in the class give an interesting presentation of the topics studied in order to get classmates involved in each other's work and to achieve a broad perspective on the topic. Group presentations are coordinated by the teacher.
6. *Evaluation.* In cases where groups pursued different aspects of the same topic, pupils and the teacher evaluate each group's contribution to the work of the class as a whole. Evaluation can include either individual or group assessment, or both. (pp. 4–5)

In the structural
approach, teams may
have from two to six
members, and the
task structure may
emphasize either
social or academic
goals.

*The Structural Approach.* Another approach to cooperative learning has been developed over the past decade mainly by Spencer Kagan (1993, 1998). Although it has much in common with other approaches, the **structural approach** emphasizes the use of particular structures designed to influence student **interaction patterns.** The structures developed by Kagan are intended to be alternatives to the more traditional classroom structures, such as the recitation, in which the teacher poses questions to the whole class and students provide answers after raising their hands and being called on. Kagan's structures call for students to work interdependently in small groups and are characterized by cooperative rather than individual rewards. Some structures have goals for increasing student acquisition of academic content; other structures are designed to teach social or group skills. *Think-pair-share* and *numbered heads together,* described here, are two examples of structures teachers can use to teach academic content or to check on student understanding of particular content. *Active listening* and *time tokens* are examples of structures to teach social skills and are described later in the chapter.

**Figure 10.3** *Illustration of Think-Pair-Share*

Thinking

Pairing

Sharing

**Think-Pair-Share** The **think-pair-share** strategy has grown out of the cooperative learning and wait-time research. The particular approach described here, initially developed by Frank Lyman (1985) and his colleagues at the University of Maryland, is an effective way to change the discourse pattern in a classroom. It challenges the assumption that all recitations or discussions need to be held in whole-group settings, and it has built-in procedures for giving students more time to think and to respond and to help each other. Figure 10.3 illustrates how think-pair-share works. For instance, suppose a teacher has just completed a short presentation or students have read an assignment or a puzzling situation has been described. The teacher now wants students to consider more fully what has been explained or experienced. She chooses to use the think-pair-share strategy rather than whole-group question and answer. She employs the following steps.

**Step 1—Thinking:** The teacher poses a question or an issue associated with the lesson and asks students to spend a minute thinking alone about the answer or the issue. Students need to be taught that talking is not part of thinking time.

**Step 2—Pairing:** Next, the teacher asks students to pair off and discuss what they have been thinking about. Interaction during this period can be sharing answers if a question has been posed or sharing ideas if a specific issue was identified. Usually, teachers allow no more than four or five minutes for pairing.

**Step 3—Sharing:** In the final step, the teacher asks the pairs to share with the whole class what they have been talking about. It is effective to simply go around the room from pair to pair and continue until about a fourth or a half the pairs have had a chance to report.

**Numbered Heads Together** Numbered heads together is an approach developed by Spencer Kagan (1993) to involve more students in the review of materials covered in a lesson and to check their understanding of a lesson's content. Instead of directing questions to the whole class, teachers use the following four-step structure.

**Step 1—Numbering:** Teachers divide students into three- to five-member teams and have them number off so each student on the team has a different number between 1 and 5.

**Step 2—Questioning:** Teachers ask students a question. Questions can vary. They can be very specific and in question form, "How many states in the Union?" Or they can be directives, such as, "Make sure everyone knows the capitals of the five states that border on the Pacific Ocean."

**Step 3—Heads Together:** Students put their heads together to figure out and make sure everyone knows the answer.

**Step 4—Answering:** The teacher calls a number and students from each group with that number raise their hands and provide answers to the whole class.

Table 10.3 summarizes and compares the four approaches to cooperative learning.

**Choose Appropriate Content.** As with any lesson, one of the primary planning tasks for teachers is choosing content that is appropriate for the students given their interests and prior learning. This is particularly true for cooperative learning lessons, because the model requires a substantial amount of student self-direction and initiative. Without interesting and appropriately challenging content, a cooperative lesson can quickly break down.

Veteran teachers know from past experience which topics are best suited for cooperative learning, just as they know the approximate developmental levels and interests of students in their classes. Beginning teachers must depend more on curriculum guides and textbooks for appropriate subject matter. However, there are several questions that beginning teachers can use to determine the appropriateness of subject matter.

- Have the students had some previous contact with the subject matter, or will it require extended explanation by the teacher?
- Is the content likely to interest the group of students for which it is being planned?
- If the teacher plans to use text, does it provide sufficient information on the topic?
- For STAD or Jigsaw lessons, does the content lend itself to objective quizzes that can be administered and scored quickly?
- For a Jigsaw lesson, does the content allow itself to be divided into several natural subtopics?
- For a Group Investigation lesson, does the teacher have sufficient command of the topic to guide students into various subtopics and direct them to relevant resources? Are relevant resources available?

**Table 10.3** *Comparison of Four Approaches to Cooperative Learning*

| | STAD | Jigsaw | Group Investigation | Structural Approach |
|---|---|---|---|---|
| Cognitive goals | Simple academic information | Simple academic information | Complex academic information and inquiry skills | Simple academic information |
| Social goals | Group work and cooperation | Group work and cooperation | Cooperation in complex groups | Group and social skills |
| Team structure | 4–5 member heterogeneous learning teams | 5–6 member heterogeneous learning teams; use of home and expert teams | 5–6 member learning groups may be homogeneous | Varies—pairs, trios, 4–6 member groups |
| Lesson topic selection | Usually teacher | Usually teacher | Usually students | Usually teacher |
| Primary task | Students may use worksheets and help each other master learning materials | Students investigate materials in expert groups; help members of home group learn materials | Students complete complex inquiries. | Students do assigned tasks—social and cognitive |
| Assessment | Weekly tests | Varies—can be weekly tests | Completed projects and reports; can use essay tests | Varies |
| Recognition | Newsletters and other publicity | Newsletters and other publicity | Written and oral presentation | Varies |

**Form Student Teams.** A third important planning task for cooperative learning is deciding how student learning teams are to be formed. Obviously, this task will vary according to the goals teachers have for a particular lesson, and the racial and ethnic mix and the ability levels of students within their classes. Here are some examples of how teachers might decide to form student teams.

**How student teams are formed is an important planning task for teachers.**

- A fifth grade teacher in an integrated school might use cooperative learning for the purpose of helping students to better understand peers from different ethnic or racial backgrounds. He or she might take great care to have racially or ethnically mixed teams in addition to matching for ability levels.
- A seventh grade English teacher in a mostly middle-class white school might form student teams according to students' achievement levels in English.
- A tenth grade social studies teacher with a homogeneous group of students might decide to use Group Investigation and form teams according to student interest in a particular subtopic but also keep in mind mixing students of different ability levels.
- A fourth grade teacher with several withdrawn students in her class may decide to form cooperative teams based on ability but also to find ways to integrate the isolates with popular and outgoing class members.

- Early in the year, a teacher with several students new to the school might form learning teams on a random basis, thus ensuring opportunities for the new students to meet and work with students they don't yet know. Later, students' abilities could be used to form learning teams.

Obviously, the composition of teams has almost infinite possibilities. During the planning phase, teachers must delineate clearly their academic and social objectives. They also need to collect adequate information about their students' abilities so that if heterogeneous ability teams are desired, they will have the needed information. Finally, teachers should recognize that some features of group composition may have to be sacrificed in order to meet others.

**Develop Materials.** When teachers prepare for a whole-class presentation, a major task is to gather materials that can be translated into a meaningful lecture. Although teachers provide verbal information to students in a cooperative learning lesson, this information is normally accompanied by text, worksheets, and study guides.

**Providing interesting and developmentally appropriate study materials is important if student teams are to work independently.**

If students are to be given text, it is important that it be both interesting and at an appropriate reading level for the particular class of students. If study guides are to be developed by teachers, these should be designed to highlight the content deemed most important. Good study guides and materials take time to develop and cannot be done well the night before a particular lesson is to begin.

If teachers are using the Group Investigation method, an adequate supply of materials will have to be collected for use by student learning teams. In some schools, a beginning teacher can rely on the school librarian and media specialists for gathering materials. This normally requires the teacher to communicate clearly about the goals and objectives of a particular lesson and to be precise about how many students will be involved. For librarians and media specialists to be of maximum assistance requires enough lead time for them to do their work. Again, a beginning teacher should be cautioned about last-minute requests. The following guidelines are offered to get maximum assistance from school support staff when planning a cooperative learning lesson.

- Meet with the school librarian and media specialists at least two weeks before the lesson and go over your lesson objectives. Ask for their ideas and assistance.
- Follow up the meeting with a brief memo summarizing ideas, time lines, and agreements.
- Check back a few days before materials are needed to see if things are coming along as you expected and offer your assistance, if needed.
- If the materials are to be used in your room, ask the specialist to help you design a system for keeping track of materials. You may also ask the specialist to come into your room and explain the system to your students.

**If students have not had experience with cooperative learning, it is vital that the teacher orient them to its unique task, goal, and reward structures.**

**Plan for Orienting Students to Tasks and Roles.** It is important that students have a clear understanding about their roles and the teacher's expectations for them as they participate in a cooperative learning lesson. If other teachers in the school are using cooperative learning, this task will be easier because students will already be aware of the model and their role in it. In schools in which few teachers use the cooperative learning approach, beginning teachers will have to spend time describing the model to students and working with them on requisite skills. Chapters 3 and 12 describe procedures to increase communication within classroom groups, along with activities to build group cohesion. These are critical skills for students in classrooms in which teachers plan to use cooperative learning.

An important thing to remember for beginning teachers who have not used cooperative learning before and who are using it with students who are not familiar with the model is that at first it may appear not to be working. Students will be confused about the cooperative reward structure. Parents may also object. Also, students may not at first be very enthusiastic about the possibilities of small-group interactions on academic topics with their peers.

Using the cooperative learning model can be most difficult for a beginning teacher because it requires the simultaneous coordination of a variety of activities. On the other hand, this model can achieve some important educational goals that other models cannot, and the rewards of this type of teaching can be enormous for the teacher who plans carefully.

**Plan for the Use of Time and Space.** Another important planning task for cooperative learning is deciding how to use time and space. As described in Chapter 2, time is a scarcer commodity than most teachers realize, and cooperative learning, with its reliance on small-group interaction, makes greater demands on time resources than some other models of instruction do. Most teachers underestimate the amount of time for cooperative learning lessons. It simply takes longer for students to interact about important ideas than it does for the teacher to present the ideas directly through lecture. Making transitions from whole class to small groups can also take up valuable instructional time. Careful planning can help teachers become more realistic about time requirements, and it can minimize the amount of noninstructional time.

> **Cooperative learning lessons take more time than most other instructional models because they rely on small-group instruction.**

Cooperative learning requires special attention to the use of classroom space, along with moveable furniture. The **cluster seating** and **swing seating** arrangements are two ways experienced teachers use space during cooperative learning.

> **Cluster seating and swing seating arrangements lend themselves to ooopcrative learning because of their flexibility.**

*Cluster Seating Arrangement.* Seating clusters of four or six, such as those illustrated in Figure 10.4, are useful for cooperative learning and other small-group tasks. If the cluster arrangement is used, students may have to be asked to move their chairs for lectures and demonstrations so that all students will be facing the teacher.

**Figure 10.4** *Four- and Six-Cluster Seating Arrangements*

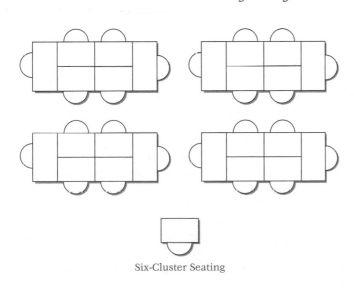

Six-Cluster Seating

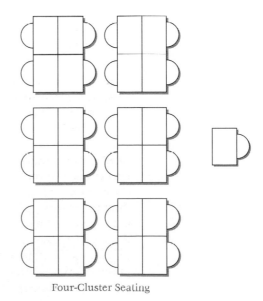

Four-Cluster Seating

**Figure 10.5** *The Swing Seating Arrangement*

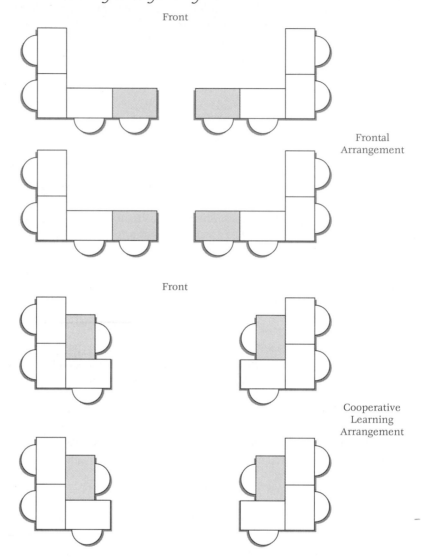

Swing Seating Arrangement. A particularly inventive approach with flexibility was developed by Lynn Newsome, a reading teacher in Howard County, Maryland. For cooperative learning, she uses a seating arrangement that allows her to "swing" from a direct instruction lesson to a cooperative learning lesson. Her desks are arranged in a wing formation, as shown in the top of Figure 10.5. On cue, students at the shaded wing desks move their desks to the arrangement shown in the bottom of Figure 10.5. Newsome reports that in both formations, she can "maintain eye contact with all students, and the room appears spacious" (MAACIE *Cooperative News*, p. 5).

## Conducting Cooperative Learning Lessons

The six phases of a cooperative learning lesson and associated teacher behaviors for each phase are described in Table 10.4. The first four phases are discussed in this sec-

## Forging New Relationships

Computers and associated technologies have become an integral part of our society. It is difficult to remember a time when we didn't have ATM machines, voice mail, cell phones, and an array of microprocessors to run our TVs, VCRs, and cars. It is equally difficult to remember when the words for books and term papers were written with pencils or on typewriters. Yet, schools have not embraced the use of technology as quickly as other institutions in our society. And many students know more about new technologies than some of their teachers. How can this be?

Some observers (Bagley & Hunter, 1992; Johanssen, 1996) believe that traditional classrooms will not accommodate the newer technologies and that these technologies will not be widely used in classrooms until we have major shifts in our views about classrooms and about learning. The more traditional views of learning (acquiring and storing new information) and classrooms (settings with competitive reward structures and for whole-class instruction) find little advantage in newer technologies. Instead, computers, CD-ROM software, and the World Wide Web, all of which are highly interactive and constructivist, work best in settings where students are working on small-group projects and where teachers are serving as facilitators as students discover and construct their own knowledge. In these classrooms, computers are organized in workstations, so students can easily work together in cooperative groups.

Perhaps as cooperative learning is used in more American classrooms, it will serve as a catalyst for wider use of computer and telecommunication technologies.

*Computers can assist with cooperative learning.*

tion. Testing and student recognition are described in the final section of the chapter, Assessment and Evaluation.

**Clarify Aims and Establish Set.** Some aspects of clarifying the aims for the lesson and establishing set are no different for cooperative learning than they were for other models. Effective teachers begin all lessons by reviewing, explaining their objectives in understandable language, and showing how the lesson ties into previous learning. Because many cooperative learning lessons extend beyond a particular day or week and

**Table 10.4** *Syntax of the Cooperative Learning Model*

| Phases | Teacher Behavior |
|---|---|
| *Phase 1:* Clarify goals and establish set. | Teacher goes over goals for the lesson and establishes learning set. |
| *Phase 2:* Present information | Teacher presents information to students either verbally or with text. |
| *Phase 3:* Organize students into learning teams. | Teacher explains to students how to form learning teams and helps groups make efficient transition. |
| *Phase 4:* Assist team work and study. | Teacher assists learning teams as they do their work. |
| *Phase 5:* Test on the materials. | Teacher tests knowledge of learning materials, or groups present results of their work. |
| *Phase 6:* Provide recognition | Teacher finds ways to recognize both individual and group effort and achievement. |

because the goals and objectives are multifaceted, the teacher normally puts special emphasis on this phase of instruction.

For example, when teachers are introducing a group investigation lesson for the first time, they will want to spend sufficient time with students to make sure specific steps and roles are clearly understood. This can also be the time when a teacher may want to talk about how students can take responsibility for their own learning and not rely solely on the teacher. It may also be a time to discuss how knowledge comes from many sources such as books, films, and one's own interactions with others.

**Clarifying aims for cooperative lessons is important because students must clearly understand the procedures and rules that will be involved in the lesson.**

If a teacher is about to introduce Jigsaw, he or she may want to discuss how people are required to work interdependently with others in many aspects of life and how Jigsaw gives students an opportunity to practice cooperative behaviors. Similarly, if the teacher's main objective is to improve relations between students from different ethnic backgrounds or races, he or she may want to explain this idea to students and discuss how working with people who are different from us provides opportunities to know one another better.

The important point with all these examples is that students are more likely to work toward important goals and objectives if the aims for the lesson have been explicitly discussed. It is difficult for students to perform a task well if they are unclear about why they are doing it or if the criteria for success are kept secret.

**Present Information Verbally or in Text.** Procedures and guidelines for presenting information to students will not be repeated here because that subject was covered extensively in Chapter 7. It is important, however, to provide some information about the use of text. Most of what is described here is not unique to the cooperative learning model and can be used by the beginning teacher in many situations involving text.

Teachers of young children know that relying on text to transmit content involves helping the children learn to read the assigned materials. Teachers in the upper grades and secondary schools (and college, for that matter) often assume their students can read and comprehend the assigned materials. Many times this is an incorrect assumption. If a cooperative learning lesson requires students to read text, then effective teachers, regardless of the age level of their students or the subject taught, will assume responsibility for helping students become better readers.

**Organize Students in Study Teams.** The process of getting students into learning teams and getting them started on their work is perhaps one of the most difficult steps for teachers using cooperative learning. This is the phase in a cooperative learning lesson where bedlam can result unless the transition is carefully planned and managed. There is nothing more frustrating to teachers than transitional situations in which thirty students are moving into small groups, not sure of what they are to do and each demanding the teacher's attention and help.

**Assist Team Work and Study.** Uncomplicated cooperative learning activities allow students to complete their work with minimum interruption or assistance by the teacher. For other activities, the teacher may need to work closely with each of the learning teams, reminding them of the tasks they are to perform and the time allocated for each step. When using the Group Investigation method, the teacher must remain constantly available to assist with resource identification. There is a fine line for the teacher to follow during this phase of a cooperative learning lesson. Too much interference and unrequested assistance can annoy students. It can also take away opportunities for student initiative and self-direction. At the same time, if the teacher finds that students are unclear about the directions or that they cannot complete planned tasks, then direct intervention and assistance are required.

🍎 *Managing the Learning Environment*

Unlike models described in the previous chapters, cooperative learning is a student-directed approach to teaching, and a cooperative learning environment requires attention to a unique set of rather difficult management tasks. For example, describing to students how to accomplish a complex group project is much more difficult than assigning them problems at the end of a textbook chapter. It is more difficult to organize students into study teams and to get them to cooperate than it is to get them to line up for recess or to sit and listen to the teacher. Consider, for example, the problems faced by Ken* when he tried to use cooperative learning as a student teacher.

> I couldn't wait to get my students into small groups. I didn't want to be like my cooperating teacher—she does all the talking and students are never allowed to work together. They seem so passive and so isolated from one another. Although she wasn't particularly enthusiastic about small-group work, she gave me her blessing. I was really excited. I was sure that the kids would respond well if they were given the chance to be active and to interact.
>
> I decided to use small groups in science, since my cooperating teacher has given me the most freedom in this area. (I think she doesn't like science and doesn't think it's all that important, so she lets me do whatever I want.) I told the kids that they could choose their own groups. I figured that being allowed to work with friends would be really motivating.
>
> Well, just getting into groups was chaotic. First, we had to move the desks from rows into clusters. Then there was lots of shouting and arguing about who was going to be in which group. The whole process took about 10 minutes and was really noisy. My cooperating

*Ken's story is a true one. It was told by Ken while he was doing his student teaching and was described by Weinstein and Migano (1993).

**The transition from whole-class instruction to small-group work must be carefully orchestrated.**

**Cooperative learning teachers need to be available to student teams, but students must also learn to depend on each other rather than on their teachers.**

✓ **Check for Understanding**

- What are the major planning tasks associated with cooperative learning lessons?

- How does planning for cooperative learning lessons differ from planning for direct instruction?

- What factors should be considered when choosing a particular cooperative learning approach? When choosing how to form learning groups?

- What are the six phases of a cooperative learning lesson, and what kinds of teacher behaviors are associated with each phase?

- How does the teacher role in cooperative learning differ from the role in direct instruction?

# Cooperation Supports Diversity

As when they use other approaches to teaching, cooperative learning teachers must find ways to adapt lessons to meet the needs of a diverse group of students. Many features of tailoring teaching for diversity that were described in earlier chapters hold true when using cooperative learning. However, this model presents some unique opportunities as well as particular problems for teachers.

The most important opportunity inherent in cooperative learning is the chance for students with special needs to work together in cooperative groups and on special projects with regular students. Cooperative learning is an important way for disabled students to participate fully in the life of the classroom.

However, teachers must adapt cooperative learning lessons, particularly if their classroom includes several learning-disabled students. Some examples of appropriate adaptations include:

- Provide more visual assists and explanation when making the transition from whole-group to small-group work.
- Be prepared to give assistance and supportive feedback to students who may be having difficulty but who are on the right track.
- Help nondisabled students understand how their disabled peers differ and what they can expect as they work together in learning groups.
- Help nondisabled students become familiar with aids for the disabled, such as hearing aids, sign language, and special computers.

teacher was *not* pleased, and I was really upset when I saw what happened. My class is real heterogeneous—I've got blacks, whites, Hispanics, Asian-Americans. Well, the groups turned out really segregated. They also tended to be just about all-boy or all-girl. Even worse—I have one mainstreamed girl in my class (she's learning disabled and really hyperactive), and nobody wanted to work with her at all. I ended up *making* a group take her, and they were pretty nasty about it. And there's another kid who's real shy and quiet; I had to get him into a group, too. It was really embarrassing for both of them.

Finally, I got everyone settled down and they started to work on the assignment. We've been talking about seeds and plants, and each group was supposed to plan an experiment that they would actually carry out to demonstrate what plants needed in order to grow. I emphasized that they were supposed to work together and make sure everyone contributed to the plan.

Well, it was a real mess. A couple of the groups worked out okay, but one group argued the whole time and never got anything written. In another group—all boys—they decided to just let the kid who was smartest in science plan the experiment. He kept coming up and complaining that no one else would do any work. And it was true. The rest just sat and fooled around the whole time. Another group had three girls and one boy. The boy immediately took charge. He dominated the whole thing; the girls just sat there and let him tell them what to do.

I had pictured everyone cooperating, helping one another, contributing ideas. But it didn't work out that way at all. And the noise—it just kept getting louder and louder. I kept turning off the lights and reminding them to use their "indoor voices." For a few minutes, they'd get quieter, but then it would get loud again. Finally, my cooperating teacher stepped in and yelled at everybody. I was really humiliated. I just couldn't control them. Right now, I'm pretty turned off to using cooperative groups. I think maybe she's right. Maybe these kids just can't handle working together. Maybe I should just go back to having everyone sit and listen to me explain the lesson. (pp. 176–177)

Many of the general management guidelines described in Chapter 5 as well as those related to presentation and direct instruction (Chapters 7 and 8) apply to cooperative learning lessons and could have assisted Ken with his management problems. When using any teaching model, it is important to have a few rules and routines that govern student talk and movement, keep lessons moving smoothly, maintain a general level of decorum in the classroom, and allow teachers to deal quickly and firmly with student misbehavior when it occurs. Management tasks unique to cooperative learning are helping students make the transitions from whole-class to cooperative learning groups, assisting students as they work in groups, and teaching students social skills and cooperative behavior.

## Help with Transitions

The process of getting students into learning groups and getting them started on their work is difficult. As Ken's story shows, this process can cause serious problems for the beginning teacher. Several simple but important strategies can be used by teachers to make transitions go smoothly.

1. *Write key steps on the blackboard or on charts.* Visual cues assist large groups of students as they move from one place in the room to another. Think of these as signs similar to those provided for people lining up to purchase theater tickets to a popular play or queuing procedures used at public events such as football games. Here is an example of such a display.

   **Step 1:** Move quickly to the location where your team's name has been posted on the wall.
   **Step 2:** Choose one team member to come up to my desk to gather needed learning materials.
   **Step 3:** Spend 10 minutes reading your particular assignment.
   **Step 4:** At my signal, begin your discussions.
   **Step 5:** At my signal return to your learning team and start presenting your information.

2. *State directions clearly and ask two or three students to paraphrase the directions.* Getting several students to repeat the directions helps everyone to pay attention and also gives the teacher feedback on whether or not the directions are understood.
3. *Identify a location for each learning team and have that clearly marked.* Left to their own devices, students at any age (even adults) will not evenly distribute themselves around a room. They will tend to cluster in areas of the room that are most easily accessible. For effective small-group work, teachers should clearly designate those parts of the room they want each team to occupy and insist that teams go to that particular location.

These procedures are highly prescriptive and structured. Once teachers and students become accustomed to working in cooperative learning groups, more flexibility can be allowed. However, for beginning teachers, and in the earlier stages of using cooperative learning, tightly structured directions and procedures can make lessons move much more smoothly and prevent the frustrations and discouragement experienced by Ken.

## Teach Cooperation

In many schools, students get few opportunities to work on common tasks, and subsequently, many students do not know how to work cooperatively. To help students

**Transition into small groups is helped by writing directions on the chalkboard, having students repeat them, and assigning each team a specific space.**

**First attempts at group learning will likely go smoothly if the teacher defines and calls for highly structured rules and procedures.**

*The sharing, participation, and communication skills needed in cooperative learning must be taught to students.*

cooperate requires attention to the kinds of tasks assigned to small groups. It also requires teachers to teach important social and group skills, such as the ones that follow.

**Structure lessons to require interdependence.**

**Task Interdependence.** As described earlier, cooperative learning requires that task structures be interdependent rather than independent. An example of an **independent task** is when teachers give each student a worksheet in math, divide them into groups, tell them they can help each other, but then require each student to complete his or her own worksheet, which will be graded individually. Although students may help one another, they are *not* interdependent to accomplish the task. This same lesson would become an **interdependent task** if the teacher divided the class into groups and required each group to complete one math worksheet with all member's names on it. Many teachers using cooperative learning for the first time fail to structure tasks so that they are interdependent, and they become frustrated when their students do not cooperate or choose to work alone.

Having group members share materials, as in the previous example, is one way to structure task interdependence; having pairs of students work on assignments together is another. A third way to structure interdependence around materials is to give some students the problems and others the answers and ask them to find a match between the two through discussion. The Jigsaw cooperative learning lesson, described earlier, is another way to create interdependence as group members are dependent on each other for information.

Role differentiation is another way to structure interdependence. During a group investigation project, for instance, one student might be responsible for typing the report on his or her word processor, another for creating transparencies to use in the presentation, and still another for delivering the actual presentation. Each group member is performing a specific task, but the success of the group as a whole depends on the cooperative and interdependent actions of all members.

**Social Skills.** Teachers should not assume that students have the requisite social or group skills to work cooperatively. Students may not know how to interact with one another, how to develop cooperative plans of action, how to coordinate the contributions of various group members, or how to assess group progress toward particular goals. To make cooperative learning work, teachers may need to teach a variety of group and social skills.

**Social skills** are those behaviors that promote successful social relationships and enable individuals to work effectively with others. Children can learn social skills from many different individuals: parents, child-care providers, neighbors, and teachers. Ideally, children progress from infants who possess few social skills to adults who have a rich repertoire of skills. However, many children and youth do not learn the requisite social skills to live and work together before they attend school. Skills found lacking in many children and youth include sharing skills, participation skills, and communication skills. It is important that teachers help students master these skills.

*Sharing Skills.* Many students have difficulty sharing time and materials. This complication can lead to serious management problems during a cooperative learning lesson. Being bossy toward other students, talking incessantly, or doing all the work for the group are examples of students' inabilities to share. Domineering students are often well intentioned and do not understand the effects of their behavior on others or on their group's work. These students need to learn the value of sharing and how to rein in their controlling behaviors. Two examples of lessons teachers can use to teach *sharing skills* are described here.

1. *Round robin.* Round robin is an activity that teaches students how to take turns when working in a group. The process is quite simple. The teacher introduces an idea or asks a question that has many possible answers. The teacher then asks students to make their contributions. One student starts, making his or her contribution, and then passes the turn to the next person who does the same. Turn-taking continues until every person in the group has had a chance to talk.
2. *Pair checks.* A way to help domineering students learn sharing skills is to have them work in pairs and employ the pair checks structure. The version of pair checks described here includes the eight steps recommend by Kagan (1993).

   **Step 1—Pair work:** Teams divide into pairs. One student in the pair works on a worksheet or problem while the other student helps and coaches.
   **Step 2—Coach checks:** The student who was the coach checks the partner's work. If coach and worker disagree on an answer or idea, they may ask the advice of other pairs.
   **Step 3—Coach praises:** If partners agree, coach provides praise.
   **Steps 4 through 6—Partners switch roles:** Repeat steps 1 through 3.
   **Step 7—Pairs check:** All team pairs come back together and compare answers.
   **Step 8—Teams celebrate:** If all agree on answers, team members do team handshake or cheer.

*Participation Skills.* Whereas some students dominate group activity, other students may be unwilling or unable to participate. Sometimes students who avoid group work are shy. Often shy students are very bright, and they may work well alone or with one other person. However, they find it difficult to participate in a group. The rejected student may also have difficulty participating in group activity. Additionally, there is the otherwise normal student who chooses, for whatever reason, to work alone and refuses to participate in cooperative group endeavors.

Making sure that shy or rejected students get into groups with students who have good social skills is one way teachers can involve these students. Structuring task interdependence, described previously, is another means to decrease the probability of students wanting to work alone. Using planning sheets where various group tasks are listed along with the students responsible for completing each task is a third way to

*Teachers should not assume that all of their students possess the social skills needed to effectively work in groups. Some may need help.*

*Before students can work effectively in cooperative learning groups, they must learn about each other and respect individual differences.*

*It is important for all students to participate fully in group activities. Teachers need to create situations that will help shy students participate fully and control the participation of domineering students.*

teach and ensure balanced participation among group members. *Time tokens* and *high talker tap out* are special activities that teach participation skills.

1. *Time Tokens.* If the teacher has cooperative learning groups in which a few people dominate the conversation and a few are shy and never say anything, time tokens can help distribute participation more equitably. Each student is given several tokens that are worth ten or fifteen seconds of talk time. A student monitors interaction and asks talkers to give up a token whenever they have used up the designated time. When a student uses up all of his or her tokens, then he or she can say nothing more. This, of course, necessitates that those still holding tokens join the discussion.

2. *High talker tap out.* It is not uncommon to find only a small percentage of the students participating in group work or discussions. One way to produce more balanced participation is to assign one student to keep track of each student's participation. If the monitor observes a particular student talking repeatedly, he or she can pass a note asking that student to refrain from further comments until everyone has had a turn. The monitor can also encourage shy students to take a turn in the same manner.

**Teachers should help students polish communication skills to ensure success in group learning environments.**

**Communication Skills.** It is quite common to find both younger and older students (adults also) lacking in important **communication skills.** We all have difficulty describing our own ideas and feelings so they are accurately perceived by listeners, and we have equal difficulty in accurately hearing and interpreting what others say to us. Cooperative learning groups cannot function very effectively if the work of the group is characterized by miscommunication. The four communication skills described in Chapter 12 (paraphrasing, describing behavior, describing feelings, and checking impressions) are important and should be taught to students to ease communication in group settings.

Often during classroom interaction, students are not listening to one another. Instead, they sit in the whole group with their hand in the air, waiting for their turn to speak, or in small groups where they may be talking or interrupting incessantly. One way to promote active listening is during some classroom discussions (those in which the main objective is learning to listen), insist that before a student can speak, he or she must first paraphrase what was said by the student who just finished speaking. More on teaching active listening and paraphrasing can be found in Chapter 12.

**Group Skills.** Most people have had experiences working in groups in which individual members were nice people and had good social skills, yet the group as a whole did not work well. Members may have been pulling in different directions, and consequently, work was not getting done. Just as individuals must learn social skills to interact successfully in group or community settings, groups as an entity must also learn **group skills** and processes if they are to be effective. Before students can work effectively in cooperative learning groups, they must also learn about one another and respect one another's differences.

**Students must show respect for each other for cooperative learning to work.**

*Team Building.* Helping build team identity and member caring is an important task for teachers using cooperative learning groups. Simple tasks include making sure everyone knows one another's names and having members decide on a team name. Having teams make a team banner or logo can also build esprit de corp among members. The following three activities can also be used to teach group skills and to build a positive team identity.

1. *Team interviews.* Have students in the cooperative learning teams interview one another. They can find out about other members' names, places they have traveled, special interests, or a favorite sport, holiday, color, book, movie, and so forth. Teachers can ask students to interview every student in the group and then share with the total group what they learned about group members and the group as a whole. A variation on this procedure is to have each student interview one other student in the team (or class) and then prepare an introduction for that person, which the student presents to the whole group or class.

2. *Team murals.* Teachers can ask students to use a variety of materials such as markers, crayons, chalk, paints, and pictures from magazines to make a mural illustrating how they would like their team to work together. Encourage all members to participate in making the mural. After it has been completed, have members discuss what they have done and explain their mural to members of other teams.

3. *Magic number 11.* Spencer Kagan (1993) described a team project in which students sit in a circle and hold out a clenched hand. They shake their hand up and down and say, "One, two, three." On the count of three, each student puts out so many fingers. The goal is to have all the fingers put out to add up to 11. No talking is allowed. After they succeed, the teams cheer.

**Teaching Social and Group Skills.** Teaching specific social and group skills is no different from teaching content-specific skills, such as map reading or how to use a microscope. Chapter 8 described the direct instruction model, which requires teachers to demonstrate and model the skill being taught and to provide time for students to practice the skill and receive feedback on how they are doing. In general, this is the model that teachers should use when teaching important social and group skills. The topic of teaching social and study skills to students is described in more detail in Chapters 11 and 12.

# 🍎 *Assessment and Evaluation*

For each of the models of teaching described previously, we emphasized the importance of using evaluation strategies that are consistent with the goals and objectives of a particular lesson and with the model's overall theoretical framework. For example, if the teacher is using presentation and explanation to help students master important ideas and to think critically about these ideas, then test questions asking students for both recall and higher-level responses are required. If the teacher is using the direct instruction model to teach a specific skill, a performance test is required to measure student mastery of the skill and to provide corrective feedback. All the examples and suggestions given in previous chapters, however, are based on the assumption that the teacher is operating under a competitive or individualistic reward system. The cooperative learning model changes the reward system and, consequently, requires a different approach to evaluation and recognition of achievement.

**Because of its cooperative task, goal, and reward structures, cooperative learning requires testing procedures different from those for a model built on competitive learning.**

## Test Academic Learning

For STAD and the Slavin version of Jigsaw, the teacher requires students to take quizzes on the learning materials. Test items on these quizzes must, in most instances, be of an objective type, so they can be scored in class or soon after. Figure 10.6 illustrates how individual scores are determined, and Figure 10.7 gives an example of a quiz scoring sheet.

**Figure 10.6** *Scoring Procedures for STAD and Jigsaw*

| | |
|---|---|
| **Step 1**<br>Established base line. | Each student is given a base score based on averages on past quizzes. |
| **Step 2**<br>Find current quiz score. | Students receive points for the quiz associated with the current lesson. |
| **Step 3**<br>Find improvement score. | Students earn improvement points to the degree to which their current quiz score matches or exceeds their base score, using the scale provided below. |

More than 10 points below base  _____ 0 points

10 points below to 1 point below base _____ 10 points

Base score to 10 points above base _____ 20 points

More than 10 points above base_____ 30 points

Perfect paper (regardless of base) _____ 30 points

SOURCE: After Slavin (1994), p. 19.

Slavin (1980, 1983, 1995), the developer of this scoring system, described it this way:

The amount that each student contributes to his or her team is determined by the amount the student's quiz score exceeds the student's own past quiz average. . . . Students with perfect papers always receive the . . . maximum, regardless of their base scores. This individual improvement system gives every student a good chance to contribute maximum points to the team if (and only if) the student does his or her best, and thereby shows substantial improvement or gets a perfect paper. This improvement point system has been shown to increase student academic performance even without teams, but it is especially important as a component of STAD since it avoids the possibility that low performing students will not be fully accepted as group members because they do not contribute many points. (p. 24)

A special scoring system does not exist for the Group Investigation approach. The group report or presentation serves as one basis for evaluation, and students should be rewarded for both individual contributions and the collective product.

### Assess Cooperation

Remember from earlier discussions that one of the primary goals of cooperative learning is social skill development, especially those skills that facilitate cooperation and collaboration. These skills are not as easy to assess as academic skills are, but students will not think they are important unless they are a part of the teacher's assessment system. Figure 10.8 identifies important collaborative skills that can be assessed and a rubric for doing so.

### Grade Cooperative Learning

In cooperative learning, teachers have to be careful about the their reward structure. It is important for teachers to reward the group product—both the end result and the cooperative behavior that produced it. Teachers also want to assess each member's contribution to the final product. These dual assessment tasks, however, can prove trou-

**Figure 10.7** *Quiz Score Sheet for STAD and Jigsaw*

| Student | Base Score | Quiz Score | Improvement Points | Base Score | Quiz Score | Improvement Points | Base Score | Quiz Score | Improvement Points |
|---|---|---|---|---|---|---|---|---|---|
| Date: May 23 | | | | Date: | | | Date: | | |
| Quiz: Addition with Regrouping | | | | Quiz: | | | Quiz: | | |
| Sara A. | 90 | 100 | 30 | | | | | | |
| Tom B. | 90 | 100 | 30 | | | | | | |
| Ursula C. | 90 | 82 | 10 | | | | | | |
| Danielle D. | 85 | 74 | 0 | | | | | | |
| Eddie E. | 85 | 98 | 30 | | | | | | |
| Natasha F. | 85 | 82 | 10 | | | | | | |
| Travis G. | 80 | 67 | 0 | | | | | | |
| Tommy H. | 80 | 91 | 30 | | | | | | |
| Edgar I. | 75 | 79 | 20 | | | | | | |
| Andy J. | 75 | 76 | 20 | | | | | | |
| Mary K. | 70 | 91 | 30 | | | | | | |
| Stan L. | 65 | 82 | 30 | | | | | | |
| Alvin M. | 65 | 70 | 20 | | | | | | |
| Carol N. | 60 | 62 | 20 | | | | | | |
| Harold S. | 55 | 46 | 10 | | | | | | |
| Jack E. | 55 | 40 | 0 | | | | | | |

SOURCE: After Slavin (1994), p. 20.

blesome for teachers when they try to assign individual grades for a group product. For instance, sometimes a few ambitious students may take on a larger portion of the responsibility for completing the group project and then be resentful toward classmates who made only minor contributions yet receive the same grade. Similarly, students who have neglected their responsibilities to the group effort may develop cynicism toward a system that rewards them for work they did not accomplish. Some experienced teachers have found a solution by providing two evaluations for students, one for the group's effort and one for each person's individual contribution.

*A special challenge for cooperative learning teachers is how to grade for both team and individual effort.*

## Recognize Cooperative Effort

Another important postinstructional task unique to cooperative learning is the emphasis given to recognizing student effort and achievement. Slavin and the Johns Hopkins developers created the concept of the weekly class newsletter for use with STAD and Jigsaw. The teacher (sometimes the class itself) reports on and publishes the results of team and individual learning in this newspaper.

The developers of the Group Investigation approach recognize team efforts by highlighting group presentations and by displaying the results of group investigations prominently in the room. This form of recognition can be emphasized even more by inviting guests (parents, students from another class, or the principal) to hear final reports. Newsletters summarizing the results of a class's group investigation can also be produced and sent to parents and others in the school and community. More is said about the topic of recognition in Chapter 11 on problem-based instruction.

**Figure 10.8** *Rubric for Cooperation and Collaboration*

**A. Works toward the achievement of group goals**

4 Actively helps identify group goals and works hard to meet them.
3 Communicates commitment to the group goals and effectively carries out assigned roles.
2 Communicates a commitment to the group goals but does not carry out assigned roles.
1 Does not work toward group goals or actively works against them.

**B. Demonstrates effective interpersonal skills.**

4 Actively promotes effective group interaction and the expression of ideas and opinions in a way that is sensitive to the feelings and knowledge base of others.
3 Participates in group interaction without prompting. Expresses ideas and opinions in a way that is sensitive to the feelings and knowledge base of others.
2 Participants in group interaction with prompting or expresses ideas and opinions without considering the feelings and knowledge base of others.
1 Does not participate in group interaction, even with prompting, or expresses ideas and opinions in a way that in insensitive to the feelings or knowledge base of others.

**C. Contributes to group maintenance.**

4 Actively helps the group identify changes or modifications necessary in the group process and works toward carrying out those changes.
3 Helps identify changes or modifications necessary in the group process and works toward carrying out those changes.
2 When prompted, helps identify changes or modifications necessary in the group process or is only minimally involved in carrying out those changes.
1 Does not attempt to identify changes or modifications necessary in the group process, even when prompted, or refuses to work toward carrying out those changes.

SOURCE: Adapted from Marzano, Pickering and McTighe (1993), pp. 87–88

✔ **Check for Understanding**

- What are the key features of the learning environment for cooperative learning?

- What factors should be considered when thinking about how to assess student achievement in cooperative learning?

- How does assessment and evaluation in cooperative learning differ from direct instruction?

- Why is grading for group effort controversial?

## 🍎 *Cooperative Learning: A Final Thought*

Cooperative learning should be a part of every beginning teacher's repertoire. Careful developmental work and empirical research have produced a model that helps to promote greater tolerance for differences, to teach important social and group skills, and to increase academic achievement. Inexperienced teachers, however, should be careful and should know about the difficulties involved in implementing cooperative learning in some settings.

In some communities, for instance, teachers may find strong resistance to the idea of cooperative reward structures. Many parents and community members value independent effort and believe these norms should be emphasized in schools preparing youth for an adult world characterized by competition. Many students, particularly those who excel in the more traditional, individualistic reward structures, will likewise object to approaches in which interdependent activities are valued and rewards are shared.

Some educators hold high expectations for cooperative learning as an effective means to increase positive student social behavior and to correct many of the social injustices that exist in our society. The model has demonstrated success in helping to accomplish these types of goals. However, educators should be careful not to overstate the benefits of the model and to educate citizens to recognize that no approach to teaching can solve long-standing social ills overnight.

# 🍎 *Summary*

### Overview of Cooperative Learning

- Cooperative learning is unique among the models of teaching because it uses different goal, task, and reward structures to promote student learning.
- The cooperative learning task structure requires students to work together on academic tasks in small groups. The goal and reward structures require interdependent learning and recognize groups as well as individual effort.
- The cooperative learning model aims at instructional goals beyond academic learning, specifically intergroup acceptance, social and group skills, and cooperative behavior.
- The syntax for cooperative learning models relies on small-group work rather than whole-class teaching and includes six major phases: present goals and establish set; present information; organize students into learning teams; assist team work and study; test on the materials; and provide recognition.
- The model's learning environment requires cooperative rather than competitive task and reward structures. The learning environment is characterized by democratic processes in which students assume active roles and take responsibility for their own learning.

### Theoretical and Empirical Support

- The intellectual roots for cooperative learning grow out of an educational tradition emphasizing democratic thought and practice, active learning, cooperative behavior, and respect for pluralism in multicultural societies.
- A strong empirical base supports the use of cooperative learning for the following educational objectives: cooperative behavior, academic learning, improved race relationships, and improved attitudes toward disabled children.

### Planning and Conducting Cooperative Learning Lessons

- Planning tasks associated with cooperative learning put less emphasis on organizing academic content and more

emphasis on organizing students for small-group work and collecting a variety of learning materials to be used during group work.
- One of the major planning tasks is deciding which cooperative learning approach to use. Four variations of the basic model can be used: Student Team Achievement Divisions, Jigsaw, Group Investigation, and structural approach.
- Regardless of the specific approach, a cooperative learning lesson has four essential features that must be planned: how to form heterogeneous teams, how students are to work in their groups, how rewards are to be distributed, and how much time is required.
- Conducting a cooperative learning lesson changes the teacher's role from one of center stage performer to one of choreographer of small-group activity.

### Managing the Learning Environment

- Small-group work presents special management challenges to teachers.
- During cooperative learning lessons, teachers must help students make transitions to their small groups, help them manage their group work, and teach important social and group skills.

### Assessment and Evaluation

- Assessment and evaluation tasks, particularly evaluation, replace the traditional competitive approaches described for earlier models with individual and group rewards, along with new forms of recognition.
- The use of newsletters and public forums are two devices teachers use to recognize the results of student work performed in cooperative learning lessons.

# 🍎 Key Terms

task structure

goal structure

individualistic goal structure

competitive goal structure

cooperative goal structure

reward structure

Student Teams Achievement Divisions (STAD)

Jigsaw

Group Investigation (GI)

structural approach

interaction patterns

think-pair-share

numbered-heads-together

cluster seating

swing seating

independent task

interdependent task

social skills

communication skills

group skills

# 🍎 Books for the Professional

Aronson, E., Blaney, S. C., Sikes, J., and Snapp, M. (1995). *The Jigsaw Classroom.* Beverly Hills, Calif.: Sage Publications. This book presents an in-depth discussion of the Jigsaw approach to cooperative learning, including results from research and detailed directions for teachers interested in the approach.

Johnson, D. W., and Johnson, R. T. (1998). *Learning Together and Alone. Cooperation, Competition, and Individualization* (4th ed.). Englewood Cliffs, N.J.: Prentice Hall. This book gives a detailed rationale for the goal and reward structures required for cooperative learning and provides many good ideas for teachers who want to implement cooperative learning in their classrooms.

Kagan, S. (1993). *Cooperative Learning.* San Juan Capistrano, Calif.: Resources for Teachers. A resource manual to assist teachers with using cooperative learning in their classrooms, this book is filled with lesson ideas and aids.

Slavin, R. (1995). *Cooperative Learning* (2nd ed.). New York: Longman. This book provides detailed rationale behind cooperative learning along with summaries of Slavin's research.

Slavin, R., Sharan, S., Kagan, S., Hertz-Lazarowitz, R., Webb, C., and Schmuck, R. (eds.). (1985). *Learning to Cooperate, Cooperating to Learn.* New York: Plenum Press. This is a book of readings by the major theorists and developers of cooperative learning. Rich in theory, it also provides practical approaches for teachers to follow.

## Reflection & Portfolio

In your first year of teaching, you find yourself in a middle school where teachers have not paid much attention to cooperative learning in the past. It is not that they are against cooperative learning; they simply have chosen to stick to more traditional, teacher-centered approaches. However, you had extensive exposure to this model in the school where you did your student teaching, and you believe strongly in the effectiveness of cooperative learning for goals you value as a teacher—teamwork and acceptance of diversity. You can't wait to get your students working in small groups.

During the second week of school, you introduce two cooperative learning projects in your seventh grade language arts class. You choose to use STAD to teach spelling, and you launch a long-term group investigation project in poetry. For spelling, you assign students to groups to ensure a good mix of abilities and ethnic-racial backgrounds; you allow the poetry groups to form according to students' interests, although you make it clear to students that you don't want any groups with all boys or all girls. You explain to your students that they will be tested in spelling weekly and that improvement and group effort will determine each person's grade. You make it clear that the group's effort in the poetry investigation is what will receive the highest reward.

During the first couple of weeks, you are *not* particularly happy about how things are going. Getting students to settle down and to work together has been somewhat difficult. They don't appear to be highly engaged, and you have received minor complaints about your grading system. However, you haven't taken these complaints too seriously, believing that things will get better soon.

On Monday of the fourth week of school, you get a note from the principal that she wants to meet with you after school. Of course, you are curious and a little worried about why she would want to meet with you. At the meeting, you are astounded. The principal tells you that a group of parents with very talented children visited the school last Friday to complain about your use of cooperative learning. They told her that their children were being penalized by having to work with less-talented students and that grading on group products was not fair. They expressed their belief that individuals should be rewarded for work they produce independent of others. The principal strongly recommended that you rethink your approach.

Reflect on this situation and consider what you would do. Is there a way to continue using cooperative learning without angering students, their parents, and the principal? Can you change your approach and still accomplish the teamwork and diversity goals you cherish? If you are in a field experience, share this situation with fellow students or your cooperating teachers before you compare your thoughts with the teachers below who have faced or known about similar situations. Be sure to write up your reflections on this situation as an exhibit in your professional portfolio.

### Rosemary Tambke

"Cooperative learning is good in theory, but it simply doesn't work in many real life settings. We live in a highly competitive world, and most parents want their children to learn how to compete successfully. Often, parents of talented students believe their children are slowed down if they have to spend too much time working in groups and helping other students. They believe grades should result from independent rather than group effort. When teachers are confronted with this situation, they must conform to the wishes of students and their parents and find ways other than to teach acceptance and cooperative learning teamwork. To do otherwise will court disaster for a beginning teacher."

### Amy Shin

"I have seen several situations such as this one, and normally, they involve beginning teachers who want to solve all the problems in education immediately. If I were the teacher in this situation, I would not give up on cooperative learning; instead, I would slow down. Teachers in this middle school have not used cooperative learning in the past, so group work and grading is new to students and to their parents. Instead of implementing a full-blown STAD approach and an extended group investigation, the teacher should get students comfortable working in pairs in low-stakes situations, perhaps using "think-pair-share" after reading a particular poem. The idea of cooperative grading should also be introduced gradually. This is a topic that should be explained, discussed, and perhaps debated with parents at the school's open house and in other settings; it is also one that should be discussed with other members of the faculty, including the principal. A teacher who wants to introduce cooperative learning in a school where it has not been used before should be prepared for the process to take as long as two or three years."

# Chapter ◉ Eleven

# Problem-Based Instruction

## Reflecting on Problem-Based Instruction

You have likely had teachers who spent a lot of time getting you to work on special projects and to take responsibility for your own learning. Instead of listening to lectures or participating in classroom discussions as a student In these teachers' classes, you were required to spend a lot of time in the library, on the Web, or out in the community. Instead of taking tests to determine your grade, you wrote reports or created other products that could be assessed. How did you react to these types of learning experiences?

◉ *Did you enjoy them? Or did you find them uninteresting and boring?*

◉ *What did you learn from these types of experiences? What didn't you learn that you should have?*

◉ *Were there aspects of these teachers' classes that you found particularly effective for you? Ineffective?*

Do the answers to these questions say anything about what you might do when you become a teacher? Will you use problem-based instructional strategies? Or are you more likely to stick with more teacher-centered approaches to instruction?

This chapter is about problem-based instruction (PBI) and its use in promoting higher-level thinking in problem-oriented situations, including learning how to learn. The model is referred to by other names, such as *project-based teaching, authentic learning,* and *anchored instruction.* Unlike the presentation or direct instruction models described in Chapters 7 and 8, in which the emphasis was on teachers presenting ideas or demonstrating skills, a teacher's role in problem-based instruction is to pose problems, to ask questions, and to facilitate investigation and dialogue. Most important, the teacher provides scaffolding—a supportive framework—that enhances inquiry and intellectual growth. Problem-based instruction cannot occur unless teachers create classroom environments in which an open and honest exchange of ideas can occur. In this respect, many parallels exist between problem-based instruction and classroom discussion, which is described in Chapter 12. You will note that problem-based instruction shares its intellectual roots with inquiry teaching and cooperative learning. In later sections, common features of all these methods are explored in more detail.

> **A teacher's role in PBI is to pose authentic problems, facilitate student investigation, and support student learning.**

As with previous chapters, we begin with an overview of problem-based instruction and a presentation of its theoretical and empirical underpinnings. A brief discussion of the model's historical traditions is also provided. This will be followed by sections that describe the specific procedures involved in planning, conducting, and evaluating problem-based learning. The chapter concludes with a discussion of how to manage the learning environment of problem-based instruction.

## 🍎 *Overview of Problem-Based Instruction*

The essence of problem-based instruction consists of presenting students with authentic and meaningful problem situations that can serve as springboards for investigations and inquiry. To illustrate this concept, consider the following scenario at an elementary school in a small town near Maryland's Chesapeake Bay.

> **The essence of problem-based instruction involves the presentation of authentic and meaningful situations that serve as foundations for student investigation and inquiry.**

[Ten]-year old Jamel rises to speak. "The chair recognizes the delegate from Ridge School," says the chair, a student from the local high school.

"I'd like to speak in favor of House Bill R130," Jamel begins. "This bill would tell farmers that they can't use fertilizer on land that is within 200 feet of the Chesapeake Bay because it pollutes the bay and kills fish. Farmers can still grow enough crops even if they don't plant close to water. We all will have a better life if we can stop pollution in the bay. I yield to questions."

A hand goes up. The chair recognizes a delegate from Carver School. "How does fertilizer harm the bay?" she asks. Jamel explains how the fertilizer supplies nutrients to algae, and when too much algae grows it deprives oysters, crabs, clams, and other marine life of oxygen.

A delegate from Green Holly School offers another viewpoint: "I'm a farmer," says 11-year old Maria. "I can hardly pay all my bills as it is, and I've got three kids to feed. I'll go broke if I can't fertilize my whole field." (Slavin, Madden, Dolan, & Wasik, 1994, pp. 3–4)

This debate continues for over an hour as students consider the problem of pollution and its relationship to the economy from the perspectives of farmers, commercial crabbers, business owners, and citizens who see pollution ruining the local tourist industry and the value of homes in the Chesapeake region.

These students are participating in "Roots and Wings," a PBI project developed at Johns Hopkins University. The purpose of "Roots and Wings" is to help students learn academic content and problem-solving skills by engaging them in real-life problem situations. This particular program, like other PBI projects, has certain characteristics that distinguish it from other teaching approaches.

## Special Features of Problem-Based Instruction

Various developers of problem-based instruction have described the instructional model as having the following features (Krajcik, 1999; Krajcik, Blumenfeld, Marx, & Soloway, 1994; Slavin, Madden, Dolan, & Wasik, 1992, 1994; Cognition & Technology Group at Vanderbilt, 1990)

- *Driving question or problem.* Rather than organizing lessons around particular academic principles or skills, problem-based instruction organizes instruction around questions and problems that are both socially important and personally meaningful to students. They address real-life situations that evade simple answers and for which competing solutions exist.
- *Interdisciplinary focus.* Although a problem-based lesson may be centered in a particular subject (science, math, social studies), the actual problem under investigation is chosen because its solution requires students to delve into many subjects. For example, the pollution problem raised in the Chesapeake Bay lesson cuts across several academic and applied subjects—biology, economics, sociology, tourism, and government.
- *Authentic investigation.* Problem-based instruction necessitates that students pursue *authentic* investigations that seek real solutions to real problems. They must analyze and define the problem, develop hypotheses and make predictions, collect and analyze information, conduct experiments (if appropriate), make inferences, and draw conclusions. The particular investigative methods used, of course, depend on the nature of the problem being studied.
- *Production of artifacts and exhibits.* Problem-based instruction requires students to construct products in the form of *artifacts* and *exhibits* that explain or represent their solutions. A product could be a mock debate like the one in the "Roots and Wings" lesson. It could be a report, a physical model, a video, or a computer program. Artifacts and exhibits, as will be described later, are planned by students to demonstrate to others what they have learned and to provide a refreshing alternative to the traditional report or term paper.
- *Collaboration.* Like the cooperative learning model described in Chapter 10, problem-based instruction is characterized by students working with one another, most often in pairs or small groups. Working together provides motivation for sustained involvement in complex tasks and enhances opportunities for shared inquiry and dialogue, and for the development of social skills.

**PBI lessons are organized around real-life situations that evade simple answers and invite competing solutions.**

**Student collaboration in PBI encourages shared inquiry and dialogue, and the development of thinking and social skills.**

Problem-based instruction was not designed to help teachers convey huge quantities of information to students. Direct instruction and lecture are better suited to this purpose. Rather, problem-based instruction, as illustrated in Figure 11.1, was designed primarily to help students develop their thinking, problem-solving, and intellectual skills; learn adult roles by experiencing them through real or simulated situations; and become independent, autonomous learners. A brief discussion of these three goals follows.

**Thinking and Problem-Solving Skills.** A bewildering array of ideas and words are used to describe the way people think. But what does thinking really involve? What are

**Figure 11.1** *Learner Outcomes for Problem-Based Instruction*

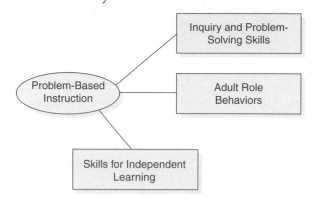

thinking skills, and particularly, what are **higher-order thinking** skills? Most of the definitions that have been provided describe abstract *intellectual processes* such as the following:

- Thinking is a process involving mental operations such as induction, deduction, classification, and reasoning.
- Thinking is a process of symbolically representing (through language) real objects and events and of using those symbolic representations to discover the essential principles of those objects and events. Such symbolic (abstract) representation is usually contrasted with mental operations that are based on the concrete level of facts and specific cases.
- Thinking is the ability to analyze, criticize, and reach conclusions based on sound inference or judgment.

Most contemporary statements about thinking recognize that higher-level thinking skills are not the same as skills associated with more routine patterns of behavior. They emphasize that even though precise definitions of higher-order thinking cannot always be found, we recognize such thinking when we see it in operation. Furthermore, higher-order thinking, unlike more concrete behaviors, is complex and not easily reduced to fixed routines. Consider the following statements of Lauren Resnick (1987) about what she defines as higher-order thinking:

- Higher-order thinking is *nonalgorithmic.* That is, the path of action is not fully specified in advance.
- Higher-order thinking tends to be *complex.* The total path is not "visible" (mentally speaking) from any single vantage point.
- Higher-order thinking often yields *multiple solutions,* each with costs and benefits, rather than unique solutions.
- Higher-order thinking involves *nuanced judgment* and interpretation.
- Higher-order thinking involves the application of *multiple criteria,* which sometime conflict with one another.
- Higher-order thinking often involves *uncertainty.* Not everything that bears on the task at hand is known.
- Higher-order thinking involves *self-regulation* of the thinking process. We do not recognize higher-order thinking in an individual when someone else "calls the plays" at every step.

*PBI projects resemble out-of-school learning situations more closely than they do the academic lessons that characterize most school learning.*

- Higher-order thinking involves *imposing meaning*, finding structure in apparent disorder.
- Higher-order thinking is *effortful*. There is considerable mental work involved in the kinds of elaborations and judgments required. (pp. 2–3)

Notice that Resnick used words and phrases such as *nuanced judgment, self-regulation, imposing meaning*, and *uncertainty*. Obviously, thinking processes and the skills people need to activate them are highly complex. Resnick also pointed out the importance of context when *thinking about thinking*. That is, although thinking processes have some similarities across situations, they also vary according to what one is thinking about. For instance, the processes we use to think about mathematics differ from those we use to think about poetry. The processes for thinking about abstract ideas differ from those used to think about real-life situations. Because of the complex and contextual nature of higher-order thinking skills, they cannot be taught using approaches suitable for teaching more concrete ideas and skills. Higher-order thinking skills and processes are, however, clearly teachable, and most programs and curricula developed for this purpose rely heavily on approaches similar to problem-based instruction.

**Higher-order thinking skills cannot be taught by using approaches designed for teaching concrete ideas and skills.**

**Adult Role Modeling.** Problem-based instruction also aims at helping students perform in real-life situations and learn important adult roles. In a speech entitled "Learning in School and Out," Resnick (1989) described how school learning, as traditionally conceived, differs in four important ways from mental activity and learning that occurs outside schools. Her four comparisons are paraphrased here.

1. School learning focuses on the individual's performance, whereas out-of-school mental work involves collaboration with others.
2. School learning focuses on unaided thought processes, whereas mental activity outside school usually involves cognitive tools such as computers, calculators, and other scientific instruments.
3. School learning cultivates symbolic thinking regarding hypothetical situations, whereas mental activity outside school engages individuals directly with concrete and real objects and situations.

✔ **Check for Understanding**

• What are the key characteristics of problem-based instruction, and how do these differ from other models of teaching?

• What are the five phases of problem-based lessons?

• What are the major learner outcomes of problem-based instruction?

• What type of learning environment works best for problem-based instruction?

4. School learning focuses on general skills (reading, writing, and computing) and general knowledge (world history, chemical elements), whereas situation-specific thinking such as whether to buy or lease a new car dominates out-of-school mental activity.

Resnick's perspective provides a strong rationale for problem-based instruction. She argues that this form of instruction is essential to bridge the gap between formal school learning and the more practical mental activity found outside school. Note how the features of problem-based instruction correspond to out-of-school mental activity.

• Problem-based instruction encourages collaboration and the joint accomplishment of tasks.
• Problem-based instruction has elements of an apprenticeship. It encourages observation and dialogue with others so that a student can gradually assume the observed role (scientist, teacher, doctor, artist, or historian, etc.).
• Problem-based learning engages students in self-selected investigations that enable them to interpret and explain real-world phenomena and to construct their own understanding about these phenomena.

Finally, problem-based learning strives to help students become independent and **self-regulated learners.** Guided by teachers who repeatedly encourage and reward them for asking questions and seeking solutions to real problems on their own, students learn to perform these tasks independently later in life.

Problem-based instruction usually consists of five major phases that begin with a teacher's orienting students to a problem situation and culminate with the presentation and analysis of student work and artifacts. When the problem is modest in scope, all five phases of the model may be covered in a few class periods. However, more complex problems may take as long as a full school year to accomplish. The five phases of the model are described in more detail later in the chapter.

**The classroom environment of PBI is student-centered and encourages open inquiry and freedom of thought.**

Unlike the tightly structured learning environment required for direct instruction or the careful use of small groups in cooperative learning, the learning environment and management system for problem-based instruction are characterized by open, democratic processes and by active student roles. In fact, the whole process of helping students become independent, self-regulated learners who are confident of their own intellectual skills necessitates active involvement in an intellectually safe, inquiry-oriented environment. Although the teacher and students proceed through the phases of a problem-based learning lesson in a somewhat structured and predictable fashion, the norms surrounding the lesson are those of open inquiry and freedom of thought. The learning environment emphasizes the central role of the learner, not of the teacher.

## 🍎 *Theoretical and Empirical Support*

Direct instruction, as you read in Chapter 8, draws its theoretical support from behavioral psychology and social learning theory. Teachers using direct instruction rely mainly on external stimuli, such as reinforcement, to maintain student cooperation and to keep them engaged in academic tasks. The teacher's role in a direct instruction lesson consists mainly of presenting information to students and modeling particular skills in a clear and efficient manner. Problem-based teaching, on the other hand, draws on **cognitive psychology** for its theoretical support. The focus is not so much on what students are doing (their behavior) but on what they are thinking (their cognitions) while they are doing it. Although the role of a teacher in problem-based lessons sometimes involves presenting and explaining things to students, it more usually involves serving as a guide and facilitator so that students learn to think and to solve problems on their own.

Getting students to think, to solve problems, and to become autonomous learners is not a new goal for education. Teaching strategies, such as *discovery learning, inquiry training,* and *inductive teaching* have long and prestigious histories. The *Socratic method,* dating back to the early Greeks, emphasized the importance of inductive reasoning and of dialogue in the teaching-learning process. John Dewey (1933) described in some detail the importance of what he labeled *reflective thinking* and the processes teachers should use to help students acquire productive thinking skills and processes. Jerome Bruner (1962) emphasized the importance of discovery learning and how teachers should help learners become "constructionists" of their own knowledge. Richard Suchman (1962) developed an approach called inquiry training in which teachers within a classroom setting present students with puzzling situations and encourage them to inquire and seek answers. For our purposes, problem-based instruction will be traced through three main streams of twentieth-century thought.

> **Problem-based instruction draws upon cognitive psychology for theoretical support.**

## Dewey and the Problem-Oriented Classroom

As with cooperative learning, problem-based instruction finds its intellectual roots in the work of John Dewey. In *Democracy and Education* (1916), Dewey described a view of education in which schools would mirror the larger society and classrooms would be laboratories for real-life inquiry and problem solving. Dewey's pedagogy encouraged teachers to engage students in problem-oriented projects and help them inquire into important social and intellectual problems. Dewey and his disciples, such as Kilpatrick (1918), argued that learning in school should be purposeful rather than abstract and that purposeful learning could best be accomplished by having children in small groups pursue projects of their own interest and choosing. This vision of purposeful or problem-centered learning fueled by students' innate desire to explore personally meaningful situations clearly links contemporary problem-based instruction with the educational philosophy and pedagogy of Dewey.

> **Dewey's view that schools should be laboratories for real-life problem solving provides the philosophical underpinning for PBI.**

## Piaget, Vygotsky, and Constructivism

Dewey provided the philosophical underpinnings for problem-based instruction, but twentieth-century psychology provided much of its theoretical support. The European psychologists Jean Piaget and Lev Vygotsky were instrumental in developing the concept of **constructivism** on which much of contemporary problem-based instruction rests.

Jean Piaget, a Swiss psychologist, spent over fifty years studying how children think and the processes associated with intellectual development. In explaining how the intellect develops in young children, Piaget confirmed that children are innately curious and are constantly striving to understand the world around them. This curiosity, according to Piaget, motivates them to actively *construct* representations in their minds about the environment they are experiencing. As they grow older and acquire more language and memory capacity, their mental representations of the world become more elaborate and abstract. At all stages of development, however, children's need to understand their environment motivates them to investigate and to construct theories that explain it.

**Constructivist theories of learning, which stress learners' need to investigate their environment and construct personally meaningful knowledge, provide the theoretical basis for PBI.**

The **cognitive-constructivist perspective** on which problem-based instruction rests borrows heavily from Piaget. It posits, as did he, that learners of any age are actively involved in the process of acquiring information and constructing their own knowledge. Knowledge does not remain static but instead is constantly evolving and changing as learners confront new experiences that force them to build on and modify prior knowledge. In the words of Piaget, good pedagogy

> must involve presenting the child with situations in which he himself experiments, in the broadest sense of that term—trying things out to see what happens, manipulating things, manipulating symbols, posing questions and seeking his own answers, reconciling what he finds one time with what he finds at another, comparing his finding with those of other children. (Duckworth, 1964, p. 2)

Lev Vygotsky was a Russian psychologist whose work was not known to most Europeans and Americans until recently. Like Piaget, Vygotsky believed that the intellect develops as individuals confront new and puzzling experiences and as they strive to resolve discrepancies posed by these experiences. In the quest for understanding, individuals link new knowledge to prior knowledge and construct new meaning. Vygotsky's beliefs differed from those of Piaget, however, in some important ways. Whereas Piaget focused on the stages of intellectual development that all individuals go through regardless of social or cultural context, Vygotsky placed more importance on the *social aspect of learning*. Vygotsky believed that *social interaction* with others spurred the construction of new ideas and enhanced the learner's intellectual development.

**The zone of proximal development is the label Vygotsky gave the zone between a learner's actual level of development and his or her level of potential development.**

A key idea stemming from Vygotsky's interest in the social aspect of learning was his concept of the **zone of proximal development.** According to Vygotsky, learners have two different levels of development: the level of actual development and the level of potential development. The *level of actual development* defines an individual's current intellectual functioning and the ability to learn particular things on one's own. Individuals also have a *level of potential development*, which Vygotsky defined as the level an individual can function at or achieve with the assistance of other people, such as a teacher, parent, or more advanced peer. The zone between the learner's actual level of development and the level of potential development was labeled by Vygotsky as the *zone of proximal development*.

The importance to education of Vygotsky's ideas is clear. Learning occurs through social interaction with teachers and peers. With appropriate challenges and assistance from teachers or more capable peers, students are moved forward into their zone of proximal development where new learning occurs.

## Bruner and Discovery Learning

**Discovering learning emphasizes active, student-centered learning experiences through which students discover their own ideas and derive their own meaning.**

The 1950s and 1960s saw significant curriculum reform in the United States that began in mathematics and the sciences but extended to history, the humanities, and the social sciences. Reformers strived to shift elementary and secondary curricula from a near-total focus on the transmission of established academic content to a focus on problem solving and inquiry. Pedagogy of the new curricula included activity-based instruction in which students were expected to use their own direct experiences and observations to gain information and to solve scientific problems. Textbooks were often abandoned in favor of lab manuals. Teachers were encouraged to be facilitators and question askers rather than presenters and demonstrators of information.

Jerome Bruner, a Harvard psychologist, was one of the leaders in the curriculum reform of this era. He and his colleagues provided important theoretical support for what became known as **discovery learning,** a model of teaching that emphasized the importance of helping students understand the structure or key ideas of a discipline, the need for active student involvement in the learning process, and a belief that true learning comes through personal discovery. The goal of education was not only to increase the size of a student's knowledge base but also to create possibilities for student invention and discovery.

When discovery learning was applied in the sciences and social sciences, it emphasized the *inductive reasoning* and *inquiry processes* characteristic of the scientific method. Richard Suchman (1962) developed an approach he called **inquiry training.** When using Suchman's approach, teachers present students with puzzling situations or **discrepant events** that are intended to spark curiosity and motivate inquiry. An example of one of Suchman's inquiry lessons with a discrepant event is described here.

> The teacher holds up a pulse glass. The pulse glass consists of two small globes connected by a glass tube. It is partially filled with a red liquid. When the teacher holds one hand over the right bulb, the red liquid begins to bubble and move to the other side. If the teacher holds one hand over the left bulb, the red liquid continues to bubble but moves to the other side.
>
> The teacher asks students, "Why does the red liquid move?"
>
> As students seek answers to this question, the teacher encourages them to ask for data about the pulse glass and the moving liquid, to generate hypotheses or theories that help explain the red liquid's movement, and to think of ways they can test their hypotheses or theories.

Contemporary problem-based instruction also relies on another concept from Bruner, his idea of **scaffolding.** Bruner described scaffolding as a process in which a learner is helped to master a particular problem beyond his or her developmental capacity through the assistance (scaffolding) of a teacher or more accomplished person. Note how similar Bruner's scaffolding concept is to Vygotsky's zone of proximal development concept.

The role of social dialogue in the learning process was also important to Bruner. He believed that social interactions within and outside the school accounted for much of a child's acquisition of language and problem-solving behaviors. The type of dialogue required, however, was not typically found in most classrooms. Many of the small-group strategies described in this text have grown out of the need to change the discourse structures in classrooms.

In sum, teachers using problem-based instruction emphasize active student involvement, an inductive rather than a deductive orientation, and student discovery or construction of their own knowledge. Instead of giving students ideas or theories about the world, which is what teachers do when using direct instruction, teachers using inquiry or problem-based learning approaches pose questions to students and allow students to arrive at their own ideas and theories. This approach has proven to be effective, as demonstrated in this chapter's Research Summary (pages 356 and 356).

## 🍎 *Planning and Conducting Problem-Based Lessons*

The concept of problem-based instruction is quite straightforward. It is not difficult to grasp the basic ideas associated with the model. Effective execution of the model, however, is more difficult. It requires considerable practice and necessitates making specific decisions during its planning and execution. Some of the teaching principles are similar to those already described for presentation, direct instruction, and cooperative learning, but others are unique to problem-based instruction. In the discussion that follows, emphasis is given to the unique features of problem-based instruction.

In the discussion that follows, emphasis is given to the unique features of problem-based instruction.

**A discrepant event is a puzzling situation that sparks curiosity and motivates inquiry into cause-and-effect relationships.**

**Scaffolding is the process in which a more knowledgeable person (teacher or student) helps a less knowledgeable person master a problem beyond his or her current level of functioning.**

✓ **Check for Understanding**

- What are the major intellectual roots for problem-based instruction?

- How does the theoretical perspective of constructivism inform problem-based instruction?

- What are the key ideas about problem-based instruction that stem from the work of Vygotsky? Piaget? Bruner?

- What does the concept of *scaffolding* mean, and how does it apply to problem-based instruction?

*Research Summary 11.1*

# What Do We Know About Problem-Based Instruction from Combining the Results of Many Studies?

*Albanese, M. A., and Mitchell, S. A. (1993).*
Problem-based learning: A review of literature on its outcomes and implementation issues. *Academic Medicine,* 68, 52–81.
*Bredderman, T. (1983).*
Effects of activity-based elementary science on student outcomes: A quantitative synthesis. *Review of Educational Research,* 53, 499–518.

The research boxes in previous chapters have each summarized the result of a single study. However, no single study on any topic or in any field provides definitive conclusions about the effects of a particular approach. The way to have confidence in conclusions is to combine the results of many studies. The process of combining results across several studies is called **meta-analysis.** Meta-analysis is a relatively new research methodology. Its development is generally attributed to Gene Glass (1976). Essentially, meta-analysis is a method of reviewing all experimental studies that have been performed over a period of time on a particular topic and then synthesizing the results of these studies. The mathematics of meta-analysis is beyond the scope of this discussion, but it involves computing what statisticians refer to as *effect size,* defined as a score that represents the strength of a treatment in an experiment or how much effect a particular approach has had. Researchers using meta-analysis examine the effect sizes from several experiments and, through this analysis, draw conclusions about particular teaching practices. Two important meta-analyses are described here to illustrate this type of research and to provide a partial picture about what kinds of instructional effects to expect from problem-based instruction.

## Bredderman's Meta-Analysis

Several process- and activity-based curricula were developed during the 1960s. Three such curricula involved science instruction for elementary students: Elementary Science Study (ESS), Science—A Process Approach (SAPA), and the Science Curriculum Improvement Study (SCIS). All three of these curricula were process-oriented, meaning that the emphasis was on how to discover and construct knowledge rather than on understanding predetermined content. All three were activity-based, meaning students used their own direct experience, observation, and experimentation to gain information and to solve scientific problems. In the early 1980s, Ted Bredderman studied the effects of the elementary science projects listed here by using meta-analysis techniques.

Bredderman (1983) began his study by identifying fifty-seven studies conducted between 1967 and 1978 that compared the effects of the new process and activity-oriented curricula with the effects of more traditional (content-based) science curricula. Over nine hundred classrooms and thirteen thousand students participated in these studies. Most of the studies were conducted after teachers were given special training on the new curricula. Studies analyzed by Bredderman typically compared the trained teachers with teachers in the same school or neighboring schools where the new curricula were not being used and who had received no special training. Bredderman was able to identify nine outcome variables across the fifty-seven studies:

- science content
- scientific method
- intelligence
- creativity
- perception
- logical development
- language development
- mathematics

Bredderman's meta-analysis provided some interesting results. The use of process- and activity-oriented science programs increased student achievement in all the outcome variables except logical development. The largest effects were found in three areas: understanding of scientific methods, intelligence, and creativity. Finally, when the process- and activity-based programs were compared to traditional programs in regard to student acquisition of science content, Bredderman noted that the activity-based curriculum produced only modest increases but did not produce negative effects. This led Bredderman to conclude that "the accumulating evidence on the science curriculum reform efforts . . .

consistently suggests that the more activity-process-based approaches to teaching science result in gains over traditional methods in a wide range of student outcomes" (p. 513).

### Meta-Analysis of Studies in Medical Education

Since the early part of the twentieth century, medical education consisted of students spending a good portion of their early years in lecture-based instruction to learn the biological foundations of medicine. During the past twenty-five years, however, medical education has undergone some major changes. The focus of reform has been on the methods used to teach the basic sciences and the manner in which clinical education is provided. Several medical schools in the United States and Canada have experimented with problem-based instruction as an alternative to the more conventional methods. The approach to problem-based instruction in medical education is similar to the model employed in K-12 education. It involves confronting medical students with an ill-defined problem and asking them to find workable solutions. Problem solving occurs through self-study and discussion in small groups often led by a faculty facilitator. Particular problems are presented to students before formal instruction on foundational science concepts. Thus, students are required to seek and construct their own knowledge through self-study and small-group interaction. Many medical educators believe that problem-based instruction makes students take greater responsibility for their own learning and results in greater mastery of important foundational content.

In 1993, two medical researchers, Mark Albanese and Susan Mitchell, completed a meta-analysis of studies that compared the outcomes of problem-based instruction to outcomes of conventional practices. They sought studies that had investigated such outcomes as student acquisition of basic science information, clinical abilities, thought processes (thinking ability), and student and faculty satisfaction. The researchers identified slightly over one hundred studies that compared problem-based instruction in medical education with conventional methods between 1972 and 1992.

The Albanese and Mitchell meta-analysis produced some interesting findings about the effects of problem-based instruction. Medical students trained with problem-based instruction methods performed better on clinical examinations than students trained with conventional methods. They were better at problem formation and tended to engage in more productive reasoning processes. On the other hand, students trained with problem-based instruction methods scored lower on basic science examinations and viewed themselves as less prepared in the basic sciences compared to students receiving the more conventional, lecture-based instruction. This latter finding led Albanese and Mitchell to conclude that although medical students prepared with problem-based methods may be better thinkers and more clinically adept than students prepared with conventional methods, they may have deficits in basic science knowledge. They also concluded that perhaps the best approach to use in medical education is to have a balance between lecture-based, teacher-directed approaches and student-centered, problem-based approaches. Note the similarity between the conclusion reached by Albanese and Mitchell and the one expounded in this text, that is, that different models of instruction are designed to accomplish different instructional goals. Good education proceeds when teachers have a rich repertoire of teaching models that can be used in a multifaceted instructional program.

## Planning for PBI Lessons

At its most fundamental level, problem-based instruction is characterized by students working in pairs or small groups to investigate ill-defined, real-life problems. Since this type of instruction is highly interactive, some believe that detailed planning is not necessary and perhaps not even possible. This simply is not true. Planning for problem-based instruction, as with other interactive, student-centered approaches to teaching, requires as much, if not more, planning effort. It is the teacher's planning that facilitates smooth movement through the various phases of problem-based lessons and the accomplishment of desired instructional goals.

**Because of its interactive nature, PBI requires as much, if not more, planning as more teacher-centered models.**

**Decide on Goals and Objectives.** Deciding on specific goals and objectives for a problem-based lesson is one of three important planning considerations. Previously, we described how problem-based instruction was designed to help achieve such goals as enhancing intellectual and investigative skills, understanding adult roles, and helping students to become autonomous learners. Some problem-based learning lessons may be aimed at achieving all these goals simultaneously. It is more likely, however, that teachers will emphasize one or two goals in particular lessons. For instance, a teacher may design a problem-based lesson on environmental issues. However, instead of having students simulate adult roles or seek solutions to environmental problems, as was the case in the "Roots and Wings" lesson, the teacher may instead ask students to conduct an online computer search of the topic in order to develop this type of investigative skill. Regardless of whether a lesson is focused on a single objective or has a broad array of goals, it is important to decide on goals and objectives ahead of time so they can be communicated clearly to students.

**Design Appropriate Problem Situations.** Problem-based instruction is based on the premise that puzzling and ill-defined problem situations will arouse students' curiosity and thus engage them in inquiry. Designing appropriate problem situations or planning ways to facilitate the planning process is a critical planning task for teachers. Some developers of problem-based instruction believe that students should have a big hand in defining the problem to be studied, because this process will foster ownership of the problem (Krajcik, 1994). Others, however, believe teachers should help students refine preselected problems that emanate from the school's curricula and for which the teacher has sufficient materials and equipment.

> **Some PBI teachers like to give students a strong hand in selecting the problem to be investigated because this increases their motivation.**

A good problem situation must meet at least five important criteria. First, it should be *authentic.* This means that the problem should be anchored in students' real-world experiences rather than in the principles of particular academic disciplines. How to deal with pollution in the Chesapeake Bay is an example of a real-life problem. Learning about the effects of sunlight on nutrients and algae in warm water is an example of an academic (scientific) problem in biology. Second, the problem should be somewhat ill defined and pose a sense of mystery or puzzlement. Ill-defined problems resist simple answers and require alternative solutions, each of which has strengths and weaknesses. This, of course, provides the fodder for dialogue and debate. Third, the problem should be meaningful to students and appropriate for their level of intellectual development. Fourth, problems should be sufficiently broad to allow teachers to accomplish their instructional goals yet sufficiently confined to make lessons feasible within available time, space, and resource limitations. Finally, a good problem should benefit from group effort, not be hindered by it.

Most puzzling situations either explore the cause-and-effect relationships within a particular topic or pose "why" or "what if" questions. The number of puzzling situations in any field is endless. As you approach choosing a particular situation for a lesson, consider these points:

- Think about a situation involving a particular problem or topic that has been puzzling to you. The situation must pose a question or problem that requires explanation through cause-and-effect analyses and/or provides opportunities for students to hypothesize and speculate.
- Decide if a particular situation is naturally interesting to the particular group of students with whom you are working, and decide if it is appropriate for their stage of intellectual development.

- Consider whether or not you can present the problem situation in a fashion that is understandable to your particular group of students and that highlights the "puzzling" aspect of the problem.
- Consider whether working on the problem is feasible. Can students conduct fruitful investigations given the time and resources available to them?

Obviously, many problem situations can be defined and posed to students. Indeed, the list is almost limitless. Following are several examples that have been reported by teachers. Some of these are tightly focused and can be completed in rather short periods of time. Others are more complex and require a whole course of study to complete.

*"Roots and Wings."* Sometimes simulated problem situations are used rather than real-life problems. In "Roots and Wings," developers created an integrated problem-based approach to learning elementary science, social studies, reading, writing, and mathematics. Here are two examples of the types of problems posed to students in this program.

- *World Lab.* Students assume the roles of various historical figures or contemporary occupational groups. They may be asked to solve the pollution problem in the Chesapeake Bay, to serve as advisors to the pharaohs of ancient Egypt, or to frame solutions to unfair taxes such as the American colonies did before the Declaration of Independence and the Revolutionary War.
- *Mathematics.* Mathematics for elementary students is moved from an abstract to a problem-solving focus. Students are asked to solve real-life math problems such as how to measure the depth of a pond or to estimate the time it would take for a ship to cross the Chesapeake Bay and are given many hands-on mathematics activities. The curriculum is also characterized by extensive use of calculators, computers, and math manipulatives.

*"Learning Expeditions."* Several school systems across the United States have been experimenting with a problem-based learning project called "Learning Expeditions" (see Rugen & Hart, 1994). Students involved in expeditionary learning are asked to inquire into stimulating problems and to find solutions through purposeful investigations and fieldwork. Some of the learning expeditions projects can be completed in three or four weeks; others last several months. Students are presented with ill-defined and open-ended themes or topics that cut across the traditional school subjects. Examples include such topics as urban renewal, pond life, or endangered species. From these more general topics, specific questions are posed. Examples of questions reported by teachers include the following:

- How can we tell when a community is thriving?
- What are the complex factors that influence pond life?
- How endangered are various species? How are endangered species affected by the complex interaction between humans and the environment?

As with other problem-based curricula, expeditionary learning strives to spark student interest by addressing authentic problem situations, helping students engage in field-oriented investigations, and helping them arrive at their own solutions.

*Rogue Ecosystem Project.* Teachers interested in environmental problems have been among the leaders in problem-based instruction. This is illustrated by the problem-based learning approach used by Hans Smith, a biology teacher at Crater High School in Central Point, Oregon.

**A good problem situation should be authentic, puzzling, open to collaboration, meaningful to the students, and consistent with the teacher's curriculum goals.**

**Sometimes simulated problem situations are more useful in the classroom than real-life problems.**

**Teachers involved in environmental issues have been leaders in the use of problem-based instruction.**

Smith designed an interdisciplinary course in which students meet for two hours each day and receive credit for biology, government, and health. The course is centered around two environmental themes—*watersheds* and the *life cycle of the Pacific salmon* (Smith, 1995). As part of their unit on watersheds, students work on a particular project that requires them to develop a plan for a campground using their scientific knowledge about the Rogue River and the watershed area it serves. Their plan must offer a complete environmental-impact study of campground construction and include interaction with the governmental agencies that approve campgrounds in the state of Oregon. Smith reported that these initial projects often prompt further inquiry and even more authentic studies such as:

• Studying other rivers in the region by taking stream surveys, testing water, mapping habitats, and determining pool and riffle ratios.
• Designing and building a student-operated fish hatchery in which two thousand coho salmon are raised and released each year.

Smith's use of problem-based instruction asks students to take on very large and complex problems and involves them over a rather long period of time. Smith is an example of a creative teacher willing to give students opportunities to perform numerous out-of-school adult roles such as testing water, constructing buildings, raising fish, writing reports, interacting with government agencies, and giving presentations.

**Organize Resources and Plan Logistics.** Problem-based instruction encourages students to work with a variety of materials and tools, some of which are in the classroom, others of which are in the school library or computer lab, and still others of which are located outside the school. Getting resources organized and planning the logistics of student investigations are major planning tasks for PBI teachers.

In almost every instance, PBI teachers will be responsible for an adequate supply of materials and other resources for use by investigative teams. In some instances, these materials may be included in particular curriculum projects such as with the "Roots and Wings" projects. Many science classrooms contain needed supplies and equipment to support student experiments and projects. Access in many schools to online and Internet data bases and CD-ROMs also facilitates problem-based instruction. When needed materials exist within the school, the primary planning task for teachers is to gather them and make them available to students. This normally requires working with school librarians and technology specialists. As described in Chapter 10, obtaining maximum assistance from librarians and technology specialists requires early notification by teachers about their plans. A series of meetings between the teacher and the specialists in which agreements are made about logistics, time lines, and rules for student conduct must be included in planning.

**Projects that require out-of-school investigations or collaboration present special challenges for PBI teachers.**

Sometimes students will need to do their investigative work outside the school. Students involved in the ecosystem project were encouraged to gather water samples, to present plans to local government units, and to release salmon. Some aspects of "Roots and Wings" involve interviewing local business and government leaders. Expecting students to work outside the confines of the school presents special problems for teachers and requires special planning. Teachers must plan in detail how students will be transported to desired locations and how students will be expected to behave while in nonschool settings. It also necessitates teaching students appropriate behavior for observing, interviewing, and perhaps taking photographs of people in the local community.

*Spotlight on Technology*

# The Web and Problem-Based Instruction

Until very recently, teachers who used problem-based approaches to teaching were pretty much limited to local libraries and communities as sources where their students could obtain information. All of this has changed dramatically over the past decade. Today, students can access information in libraries and communities all over the world through the Internet and the World Wide Web.

As you know, the Internet is a series of computer networks that connects computers around the globe and allows them to communicate with one another through a special electronic language. Once connected to the Internet, students can log into libraries around the world. Telnet, one of the typical and standard applications, allows students to access almost every large city or university library.

The World Wide Web (*WWW*) is the same as the Internet, except that it uses a communication language that can be accessed by a special piece of software called a web browser, which can display information in a variety of visual and auditory formats. The most popular browsers at the time this book is being written are Netscape Navigator and Microsoft's Internet Explorer. The Web is organized around literally millions of websites that are accessed through home pages; a home page is an introductory page that serves as a directory to categorized information that has been collected at the site. Through the use of hypertext links, information from one site can be linked to information in another, and users can move from one site to another merely by clicking the mouse button on words identified as links by color or underlining.

Because so much information is on the Web, it must be categorized and indexed similar to the way books are categorized and indexed by topics in a library. Users employ a device called a search engine to help locate information on specific topics. Browsers have search engines, and the Web has many independent search engines that can be accessed quickly. Users type in words or phrases that identify topics on which they want information. The search engine in turn provides a list of web addresses on the topic.

Students involved in an inquiry project can use the Web to access much of the information they need. Students in a history class can visit historical sites such as Gettysburg or museums such as the Smithsonian Institution. Art students can take virtual tours of the Louvre or the East Wing of the National Gallery. Science students can tour and secure data from NASA and scientific institutes around the world.

Teachers need to be cautious, however, when having students use the Web as a source of information. Everything found on the Web is not necessarily accurate. Information that appears in most scholarly journals and electronic databases, such as ERIC, is reviewed by peers, and its accuracy is checked before publication. Information that appears in mainline newspapers and magazines is reviewed by editors, and journalists are governed by a code of ethics that includes a commitment to report truthfully and accurately.

However, anyone can create a website, and there are no editors or panel of peers to hold web providers accountable. It is important that teachers point this out to their students and teach them how to evaluate the accuracy of the information they get from the Web.

*The World Wide Web is an excellent resource for PBI.*

## Conducting PBI Lessons

The five phases of problem-based instruction and required teacher behaviors for each phase are summarized in Table 11.1. Desired teacher and student behaviors associated with each of these phases are described in more detail below.

**Students need to understand that the purpose of PBI lessons is to learn how to investigate important problems and to become independent learners.**

**Orient Students to the Problem.** At the start of a problem-based lesson, just as with all types of lessons, teachers should communicate clearly the aims of the lesson, establish a positive attitude toward the lesson, and describe what students are expected to do. With students who are younger or who have not been involved in problem-based instruction before, the teacher must also explain the model's processes and procedures in some detail. Points that need elaborating include the following.

- The primary goals of the lesson are not to learn large amounts of new information but rather how to investigate important problems and how to become independent learners. For younger students, this concept might be explained as lessons where they will be asked to figure things out on their own.
- The problem or question under investigation has no absolute "right" answer, and most complex problems have multiple and sometimes contradictory solutions.
- During the investigative phase of the lesson, students will be encouraged to ask questions and to seek information. The teacher will provide assistance, but students should strive to work independently or with peers.
- During the analysis and explanation phase of the lesson, students will be encouraged to express their ideas openly and freely. No idea will be ridiculed by the teacher or by classmates. All students will be given an opportunity to contribute to the investigations and to express their ideas.

**Table 11.1** *Syntax for Problem-Based Instruction*

| Phase | Teacher Behavior |
|---|---|
| *Phase 1:* Orient students to the problem. | Teacher goes over the objectives of the lesson, describes important logistical requirements, and motivates students to engage in self-selected problem-solving activity. |
| *Phase 2:* Organize students for study. | Teacher helps students define and organize study tasks related to the problem. |
| *Phase 3:* Assist independent and group investigation. | Teacher encourages students to gather appropriate information, conduct experiments, and search for explanations and solutions. |
| *Phase 4:* Develop and present artifacts and exhibits. | Teacher assists students in planning and preparing appropriate artifacts such as reports, videos, and models, and helps them share their work with others. |
| *Phase 5:* Analyze and evaluate the problem-solving process. | Teacher helps students to reflect on their investigations and the processes they used. |

The teacher needs to present the problem situation with care or have clear procedures for involving students in problem identification. The guidelines provided in Chapter 8 on how to conduct a classroom demonstration can be helpful here. The problem situation should be conveyed to students as interestingly and accurately as possible. Usually being able to see, feel, and touch something generates interest and motivates inquiry. Often the use of discrepant events (a situation where the outcome is unexpected and surprising) can prick students' interest. For example, demonstrations in which water runs uphill or ice melts in very cold temperatures can create a sense of mystery and a desire to solve the problem. Short videotapes of interesting events or situations illustrating real-life problems such as pollution or urban blight are similarly motivational. The important point here is that the orientation to the problem situation sets the stage for the remaining investigation, so its presentation must capture student interest and produce curiosity and excitement.

**Organize Students for Study.**  Problem-based instruction requires developing collaboration skills among students and helping them to investigate problems together. It also requires helping them plan their investigative and reporting tasks.

*Study Teams.*  Many of the suggestions for organizing students into cooperative learning groups described in Chapter 10 pertain to organizing students into problem-based teams. Obviously, how student teams are formed will vary according to the goals teachers have for particular projects. Sometimes a teacher may decide that it is important for investigative teams to represent various ability levels and racial, ethnic, or gender diversity. If diversity is important, teachers will need to make team assignments. At other times, the teacher may decide to organize students according to mutual interests or to allow groups to form around existing friendship patterns. Investigative teams can thus form voluntarily. During this phase of the lesson, teachers should provide students with a strong rationale for why the teams have been organized as they have.

*Cooperative Planning.*  After students have been oriented to the problem situation and have formed study teams, teachers and students must spend considerable time defining specific subtopics, investigative tasks, and time lines. For some projects, a primary planning task will be dividing the more general problem situation into appropriate subtopics and then helping students decide which of the subtopics they would like to investigate. For example, a problem-based lesson on the overall topic of weather might be divided into subtopics involving acid rain, hurricanes, clouds, and so forth. The challenge for teachers at this stage of the lesson is seeing that all students are actively involved in some investigation and that the sum of all the subtopic investigations will produce workable solutions to the general problem situation.

For projects that are large and complex, an important task during this phase of instruction is to help students link the investigative tasks and activities to time lines. The Gantt chart shown in Figure 11.2 provides an example of how one teacher helped her class plan for a problem-based learning project in history. As described in Chapter 2, Gantt charts allow students to plan particular tasks in relation to when each starts and ends. They are constructed by placing time across the top of the chart and then listing the tasks down the side. X's denote the specific time assigned to accomplish particular tasks.

**Assist Independent and Group Investigation.**  Investigation, whether done independently, in pairs, or in small study teams, is the core of problem-based instruction.

**Figure 11.2** *Gantt Chart: Eighth Grade Local History Investigation*

This problem-based lesson has been designed to have students work in four teams for the purpose of investigating local history. The four investigative tasks are interviewing elderly people about the community; collecting appropriate information from old newspapers in the state's historical society; studying gravestones in the local cemetery; and collecting and reading early histories written about the area.

| Task | Time | | | |
|---|---|---|---|---|
| | March 10-15 | March18-23 | March 26-31 | April 3-7 |
| Orient students to problem situation. | xxx | | | |
| Organize study teams. | xxxxxxx | | | |
| Discuss with principal when students will be gone from school. | xx | | | |
| Gain permission from parents. | xxxxx | | | |
| Gain permission for visits from historical society. | xxx | | | |
| Have study teams plan their work. | | xxxxxxxx | | |
| Go over interviewing protocol. | | xx | | |
| Go over logistics for each type of visit. | | xx | | |
| Have teams do preliminary visit to make sure logistics are in place. | | xx | | |
| Have teams perform their investigative tasks. | | | xxxxxxxxxx | |
| Have teams prepare required artifacts/ exhibits. | | | | xxxx |
| Share artifacts/exhibits with parents and others. | | | | xxxx |

**Most problem-based situations involve data gathering, experimentation, hypothesis development, and solution analysis.**

Although every problem situation requires slightly different investigative techniques, most involve the processes of data gathering and experimentation, hypothesizing and explaining, and providing solutions.

*Data Gathering and Experimentation.* This aspect of the investigation is critical. It is in this step that the teacher encourages students to gather data and conduct mental or actual experiments until they fully understand the dimensions of the problem situation. The aim is for students to gather sufficient information to create and construct their own ideas. This phase of the lesson should be more than simply reading about the problem in books. Teachers should assist students in collecting information from a variety of sources, and they should pose questions to get students to think about the problem and about the kinds of information needed to arrive at defensible solutions. Students will need to be taught how to be active investigators and how to use methods appropriate for the problem they are studying: interviewing, observing, measuring, following leads, or taking notes. They will also need to be taught appropriate investigative etiquette.

*Hypothesizing, Explaining, and Providing Solutions.* After students have collected sufficient data and conducted experiments on the phenomena they are investigating,

*PBI projects culminate in the creation and display of artifacts such as reports, posters, physical models, and videotapes.*

they will want to start offering explanations in the form of hypotheses, explanations, and solutions. During this phase of the lesson, the teacher encourages all ideas and accepts them fully. As with the data-gathering and experimentation phases, teachers continue to pose questions that make students think about the adequacy of their hypotheses and solutions and about the quality of the information they have collected. Teachers should continue to support and model free interchange of ideas and to encourage deeper probing of the problem if that is required. Questions at this stage might include, "What would you need to know in order for you to feel certain that your solution is the best?" or, "What could you do to test the feasibility of your solution?" or, "What other solutions can you propose?"

Throughout the investigative phase, teachers should provide needed assistance without being intrusive. For some projects and with some students, teachers will need to be close at hand helping students locate materials and reminding them of tasks they are to complete. For other projects and other students, teachers may want to stay out of the way and allow students to follow their own directions and initiatives.

**Teacher support for the free exchange of ideas and the full acceptance of those ideas is imperative in the investigative phase of PBI.**

**Develop and Present Artifacts and Exhibits.** The investigative phase is followed by the creation of artifacts and exhibits. **Artifacts** are more than written reports. They include such things as videotapes that show the problem situation and proposed solutions, models that comprise a physical representation of the problem situation or its solution, and computer programs and multimedia presentations. Obviously, the sophistication of particular artifacts is tied to the students' ages and abilities. A 10-year-old's poster display of acid rain will differ significantly from a high school student's design for an instrument to measure acid rain. A second-grader's diorama of cloud formations will differ from a middle school student's computerized weather program.

After artifacts are developed, teachers often organize exhibits to display students' work publicly. These exhibits should take their audiences—students, teachers, parents, and others—into account. **Exhibits** can be traditional science fairs, where each student displays his or her work for the observation and judgment of others, or verbal and/or visual presentations, where ideas are exchanged and feedback is provided. The exhibition process is heightened in status if parents, students, and community members participate. It is also heightened if the exhibit demonstrates student mastery of particular topics or processes. Newsletters, such as those described in Chapter 10, offer another means to exhibit the results of students' work and to bring closure to problem-based projects.

*Analyze and Evaluate the Problem-Solving Process.* The final phase of problem-based instruction involves activities aimed at helping students analyze and evaluate their own thinking processes as well as the investigative and intellectual skills they used. During this phase, teachers ask students to reconstruct their thinking and activity during the various phases of the lesson. When did they first start getting a clear understanding of the problem situation? When did they start feeling confidence in particular solutions? Why did they accept some explanations more readily than others? Why did they reject some explanations? Why did they adopt their final solutions? Did they change their thinking about the situation as the investigation progressed? What caused this change? What would they do differently next time?

# 🍎 Managing the Learning Environment

Many of the general management guidelines described in Chapter 5 apply to the management of problem-based learning. For instance, it is always important for teachers to have a clear set of rules and routines, to keep lessons moving smoothly without disruption, and to deal with misbehavior quickly and firmly. Similarly, the guidelines for how to manage group work provided in Chapter 10 on cooperative learning also apply to problem-based learning instruction. There are, however, unique management concerns for teachers using problem-based instruction, and these are described here.

## Deal with Multitask Situations

**To make a multitask classroom work, students need to be taught to work both independently and together.**

In classrooms where teachers are using problem-based instruction, multiple learning tasks will be occurring simultaneously. Some student groups may be working on various subtopics in the classroom, while others may be in the library, and still others out in the community. Younger students may be using interest centers where students work in pairs and small groups on problems associated with science, math, language arts, and social studies before coming together to discuss their work with the whole class. To make a multitask classroom work, students must be taught to work both independently and together. Effective teachers develop cueing systems to alert students and to assist them with the transition from one type of learning task to another. Clear rules are necessary to tell students when they are expected to talk with one another and when they are expected to listen. Charts and time lines on the chalkboard should specify tasks and deadlines associated with various projects. Teachers should establish routines and instruct students how to begin and end project activities each day or period. They should also monitor the progress being made by each student or group of students during multitask situations, a skill that requires a high degree of with-itness, to use Kounin's term.

**Special management problems of PBI include adjusting to different finishing rates, monitoring student work, managing materials and equipment, and regulating movement outside the classroom.**

## Adjust to Differing Finishing Rates

One of the most complex management problems faced by teachers using problem-based learning is what to do with individuals or groups who finish early or lag behind.

Rules, procedures, and downtime activities are needed for students who finish early and have time on their hands. These include availability of high-interest activities such as special reading materials or educational games that students can complete on their own or (for older students) procedures for moving to special laboratories to work on other projects. Effective teachers also establish the expectation that those who finish early will assist others.

Late finishers present a different set of problems. In some instances, teachers may give lagging students more time. Of course, this action results in the early finishers having even more downtime. Teachers may alternately decide to get late finishers to put in extra time after school or on the weekend. However, this action is often problematic. If students are working in teams, it could be difficult for them to get together outside school. Furthermore, students who are falling behind often are those who do not work well alone and who need a teacher's assistance to complete important tasks and assignments.

## Monitor and Manage Student Work

Unlike some other types of instruction in which all students complete the same assignment on the same date, problem-based instruction generates multiple assignments, multiple artifacts, and often varying completion dates. Consequently, monitoring and managing student work is crucial when using this teaching model. Three important management tasks are critical if student accountability is to be maintained and if teachers are to keep a degree of momentum in the overall instructional process: (1) work requirements for all students must be clearly delineated, (2) student work must be monitored and feedback provided on work in progress, and (3) records must be maintained.

Many teachers manage all three of these tasks through the use of *student project forms.* Maintained on each individual, the student project form (Figure 11.3) is a written record of the work the individual or small group has agreed to complete, agreed-on time lines for completion, and an ongoing summary of progress.

## Manage Materials and Equipment

Almost all teaching situations require some use of materials and equipment, and managing these is often troublesome for teachers. A problem-based situation, however, places greater demands on this aspect of classroom management than other teaching models, because it requires the use of a rich array of materials and investigative tools. Effective teachers must develop procedures for organizing, storing, and distributing equipment and materials. Many teachers get students to help them with this process. Students can be expected to keep equipment and supplies organized in a science classroom and to distribute books and collect papers in other classrooms. Getting this aspect of management under firm control is very important, because without clear procedures and routines, teachers can be overwhelmed with problem-based lesson details.

## Regulate Movement and Behavior Outside the Classroom

When teachers encourage students to conduct investigations outside the classroom in such places as the library or the computer lab, they need to make sure that students understand schoolwide procedures for movement and use of these facilities. If hall passes are required, teachers must ensure that students use them appropriately. If movement

---

### ✔ Check for Understanding

- What are the key planning tasks associated with problem-based instruction?

- What are the five criteria for designing appropriate problem situations?

- What are the five phases of a PBI lesson, and what kinds of teacher behaviors are associated with each phase?

- Why is orienting students to problem-based lessons more complicated than with some other models of teaching?

- What major processes are involved as students pursue their inquiries in problem situations?

- How do artifacts and exhibits differ from more traditional term papers or reports?

**Teachers can modify lessons to adapt to the needs of disabled students.**

*Tailoring Teaching for Inclusive Classrooms*

# PBI, For All Students? Yes!

Sometimes problem-based instruction is viewed as a model more suited for students who are gifted and talented. This is not true. All students, regardless of their abilities, can benefit from PBI. In fact, less talented students often do not have the skills to work independently, making it all the more important for teachers to use approaches that develop these skills. However, when using PBI with students who are learning disabled or who lack skills for working independently, teachers should strive to adapt lessons in a variety of ways:

- Provide more direct instruction on particular investigation skills such as locating information, drawing inferences from data, and analyzing rival hypotheses.
- Take more time to explain PBI lessons and expectations for student work.
- Provide more time for students at each phase of their inquiries.
- Establish more precise time lines for checking progress and holding students accountable for work.

Observing students with special needs develop inquiry and problem-solving skills and become autonomous learners can be among a teacher's most rewarding experiences.

**Figure 11.3** *Student Project Form*

**Student's Name** _____
**Study Team's Name** _____
**Project Name and Scope:** _____
_____
_____
_____
_____

**Particular Assignments and Deadlines**

Project 1 _____
Feedback on 1 _____
Project 2 _____
Feedback on 2 _____
Project 3 _____
Feedback on 3 _____
Project 4 _____
Feedback on 4 _____
Final artifact or exhibit _____
_____

in halls is regulated, students must understand the rules associated with this movement. Similarly, teachers must establish rules and routines to govern student behavior when they are conducting their investigations in the community. For example, students should be taught the etiquette of interviewing and the need to obtain permission before looking at certain records or taking certain kinds of pictures.

# 🍎 *Assessment and Evaluation*

Most of the general assessment and evaluation guidelines provided in earlier chapters also pertain to problem-based instruction. Assessment procedures must always be tailored to the instructional goals the model is intended to achieve, and it is always important for teachers to gather reliable and valid assessment information. As with cooperative learning in which the instructional intents are *not* the acquisition of declarative knowledge, assessment tasks for problem-based lessons cannot consist solely of paper-and-pencil tests. The performance assessment and evaluation procedures described in Chapter 6 are the most appropriate ones to use with problem-based instruction. The work products created by students lend themselves nicely to performance assessment using scoring rubrics such as those described in Chapter 6 or checklists and rating scales described here. Further, performance assessment can be used to measure students' problem-solving potential as well as group work.

**The trend has been away from paper-and-pencil testing and toward performance assessments, which allow students to show what they can do when confronted with real problem situations.**

## Assess Understanding

Problem-based instruction goes beyond development of basic knowledge about a topic and aims instead at the development of rather sophisticated understandings of problems and the world that surround students. Figure 11.4 provides an example of testing for understanding rather than knowledge.

## Use Checklists and Rating Scales

Finding valid and reliable measurement techniques is one of the problems faced by teachers who want to use authentic assessment procedures. Some have turned to such fields as sports and the performing arts in which systems have been developed to measure complex performance tasks. Criterion-referenced checklists and rating scales are two devices that are often used in these fields. For example, individuals who judge diving or ice skating competitions use rating scales that compare individual performances to agreed-on standards. Rating scales are similarly used to evaluate musical or dance performances.

**Finding valid and reliable measurement techniques is a challenge faced by teachers who want to use problem-based instruction.**

Robert Rothman (1995) provided an example of a rating scale used by the teachers at Mark Twain Elementary School in Littleton, Colorado, to evaluate student work. Teachers there have developed a series of units that require students to address such real-world questions as, How are chimpanzees and people alike? How are wooden baseball bats made? How do parrots learn to talk? After completing their investigations, students write a report (artifact) about their topic using a computer; develop a visual representation (exhibit) of their topic; and deliver oral presentations to students, the principal, and a parent or community representative. The oral presentation is judged using the rating scale illustrated in Figure 11.5.

**Figure 11.4** *Example of Assessment Aimed at Understanding*

You are a prosecutor or a defense attorney in a trial brought by a parent group seeking to forbid purchase by your high school of a U.S. history textbook, excerpted below. (The book would be used as a *required supplement* to your current text, not in place of it.) You will present a 10-minute oral case, in pairs, to a jury, taking either side of the question, Is the book appropriate for school adoption and required reading? (supported by a written summary of your argument). You will be assessed on how well you support your claim about the accounts in the text, in response to the question, Are the accounts biased, inaccurate. or merely different from our usual viewpoint?

*On the American Revolution*

As a result of the ceaseless struggle of the colonial people for their political rights, the 13 colonies practiced bourgeois representative government by setting up their own local legislatures. As electoral rights were restricted in many ways in every colony, those elected to the colonial legislatures were mostly landlords, gentry, and agents of the bourgeoisie, without any representation whatsoever from the working people. These struggles reflected the contradictions between the colonies and their suzerain state. . . .

The British administration of the colonies was completely in the interests of the bourgeoisie in Britain. . . . The British colonial rule impeded development of the national economy in North America. It forced certain businesses into bankruptcy. As a consequence, contradictions became increasingly acute between the ruling clique in Britain and the rising bourgeoisie and broad masses of the people in the colonies. . . .

Heretofore [prior to the Boston Massacre], the struggle of the colonial people had been scattered and regional. In the course of the struggle, however, they summed up their experience and came to feel it necessary to stand together for united action. Thus in November 1772, a town meeting held in Boston adopted a proposal made by Samuel Adams to create a Committee of Correspondence to exchange information with other areas, act in unison, and propagate revolutionary ideas. . . . In less than 2 months, a Committee of Correspondence was formed by more than 80 cities and towns in Massachusetts, and later became the organs of revolutionary power. . . .

The Declaration of Independence was a declaration of the bourgeois revolution. The political principles enunciated in it were aimed at protecting the system of capitalist exploitation, legitimizing the interests of the bourgeoisie. In practice, the "people" referred to in the Declaration only meant the bourgeoisie, and the "right of the pursuit of happiness" was deduced from the "right of property" and intended to stamp the mark of legitimacy on the system of bourgeois exploitation. The Declaration was signed by 56 persons, of whom 28 were bourgeois lawyers, 13 were big merchants, 8 were plantation owners and 7 were members of the free professions, but there was not one representative of the working people.

During the time of the war, America began its westward expansion on a large scale. From the first, the colonies had been founded on the corpses of the Indians. . . . In 1779 George Washington sent John Sullivan with a force of soldiers to "annihilate" the Iroquois tribe settled in northern New York.

During the war patriotic women also played a big role. While men went to the front, they took over the tasks of production. They tilled fields and wove cloth, and sent food, garments, and other articles to the front. When Washington was in a precarious situation retreating into Pennsylvania with his army, the women of Philadelphia raised a huge fund to procure winter clothes for the revolutionary army.

After the outbreak of the war, America not only failed to organize the enslaved Negroes but guarded them even more closely, thus intensifying their oppression. This seriously impeded their participation in the war and was one reason why the war for Independence was slow in achieving victory. . . .

*Questions to Consider in Your Research and Presentation*

1. What can be said to be the most likely political influences on the authors' point of view? What evidence is there of those influences? How do they affect the authors' choice of language?
2. Why does it make sense, given the authors' perspective, that they pay particular attention to (a) the Committee of Correspondence, (b) the contribution of women, and (c) the plight of "Indians" and "Negroes""? Are the facts accurate? Do they warrant that much attention in your view?
3. You will be judged on the accuracy, aptness, and convincing qualities of your documentation, and the rhetorical effectiveness of *your* case. Be fair, but be an effective speaker and writer!

SOURCE: Wiggins (1993), pp. 212–213.

**Figure 11.5** *Sample Rating Scale for Oral Presentations*

| | | |
|---|---|---|
| 1. Student clearly describes the question and gives reasons for its importance. | Student states question but does not describe it or give reasons for its importance. | Student does not state question. |
| 2. Evidence of preparation and organization strong. | Some evidence of preparation and organization present. | No evidence of preparation or organization. |
| 3. Delivery engaging. | Delivery somewhat engaging. | Delivery flat. |
| 4. Sentence structure is correct. | Sentence structure is somewhat correct. | Sentence structure has many errors. |
| 5. Visual aid used to enhance presentation. | Visual aid referred to separately. | Visual aid is not mentioned. |
| 6. Questions from audience answered clearly and with specific information. | Questions from audience somewhat answered. | Questions from audience not answered. |

SOURCE: After Rothman (1995), pp. 12–13.

## Assess Adult Roles and Situations

Problem-based instruction, as you read at the beginning of this chapter, strives to engage students in learning situations that help them to learn about adult roles and to perform some of the tasks associated with these roles. Adult situations that might be learned and how they might be assessed are presented in Figure 11.6. Most of these situations can be assessed using the performance assessment tests, checklists, and rating scales described in the previous sections.

## Assess Learning Potential

Most tests, whether paper-and-pencil or performance-oriented, are designed to measure knowledge and skills at specific points in time. They do not necessarily assess learning potential or readiness to learn. Vygotsky's idea about the zone of proximal development, described earlier, has prompted measurement experts and teachers to consider how a student's learning potential might be measured, particularly potential

**Student presentations provide one source for assessment**

*Student presentations are fun, but also provide a rich source for assessment.*

**Figure 11.6** *Professional Roles and Situations That Can Be Assessed*

- *Attorney:* Show debate skills by playing characters in historical reenactments—Scopes trial; *Brown* v. *Board of Education.*
- *Ad agency worker:* Design advertising campaign; make book jackets.
- *Sociologist:* Design and conduct community survey; graph results.
- *Engineer:* Survey and map neighborhood.
- *Essayists:* Present conclusions in writing; write persuasive essay.
- *Historian:* Conduct oral history; critique textbooks for children.
- *Teacher:* Teach topic to a younger child.
- *Parent:* Get a young child to study.
- *Job applicant:* Prepare a portfolio, résumé.
- *Citizen:* Lead a group to closure; thoroughly rethink an issue; develop and effectively implement a plan; rate candidates; negotiate a dilemma; judge the adequacy of an emotional appeal; question the obvious.

SOURCE: After Wiggins (1993), pp. 222–224.

**✔ Check for Understanding**

- What are the key features of the learning environment for problem-based instruction?

- What are the unique management concerns for teachers using problem-based instruction?

- What factors should be considered when thinking about how to assess student learning in problem-based instruction?

- How does assessment and evaluation in problem-based instruction differ from the approach used in the more teacher-centered models?

that could be enhanced with the guidance of a teacher or more advanced peer. Readiness (learning potential) tests exist for reading and other language development areas. Assessment devices that present students with problem-solving tasks that diagnose their ability to benefit from particular kinds of instruction also exist. Assessment tasks that measure learning potential in most areas, however, are still in their infancy stage with much work yet to be done.

## Assess Group Effort

Chapter 10 on cooperative learning described assessment procedures used to assess and reward students for both individual and group work. These procedures can also be used for problem-based instruction. Assessing group effort reduces the harmful competition that often results from comparing students with their peers and makes school-based learning and assessment more like that found in real-life situations.

# 🍎 *Problem-Based Instruction: A Final Thought*

The current interest in problem-based instruction is quite extensive. The model is based on solid theoretical principles, and a modest research base supports its use. In addition, there appears to be considerable teacher and student enthusiasm for the model. It provides an attractive alternative for teachers who wish to move beyond more teacher-centered approaches to challenge students with the active-learning aspect of the model.

**There is considerable teacher and student enthusiasm for problem-based instructional approaches.**

However, problem-based instruction also has some obstacles to overcome if its use is to become widespread. The organizational structures currently found in most schools are not conducive to problem-based approaches. For instance, many schools lack sufficient library and technology resources to support the investigative aspect of the model.

The standard 40- or 50-minute class period found in most secondary schools does not allow time for students to become deeply involved in out-of-school activities. Additionally, since the model does not lend itself to coverage of a great deal of information or foundational knowledge, some administrators and teachers do not encourage its use. Drawbacks such as these cause some critics to predict that problem-based instruction will fare no better than Dewey's and Kilpatrick's *project method* or the *hands-on, process-oriented* curricula of the 1960s and 1970s.

# 🍎 *Summary*

## Overview of Problem-Based Instruction

- Unlike other models in which the emphasis is on presenting ideas and demonstrating skills, problem-based instruction has teachers present problem situations to students and get them to investigate and find solutions on their own.
- The instructional goals of problem-based instruction are threefold: to help students develop investigative and problem-solving skills, to provide students experiences with adult roles, and to allow students to gain confidence in their own ability to think and become self-regulated learners.
- The general flow or syntax of a problem-based lesson consists of five major phases: orient students to the problem; organize students for study; assist with independent and group investigations; develop and present artifacts and exhibits; and analyze and evaluate work.
- The learning environment of problem-based instruction is characterized by openness, active student involvement, and an atmosphere of intellectual freedom.

## Theoretical and Empirical Support

- Problem-based instruction has its intellectual roots in the Socratic method dating back to the early Greeks but has been expanded by ideas stemming from twentieth-century cognitive psychology.
- The knowledge base on problem-based instruction is rich and complex. Several meta-analyses done in the last few years provide a clear picture of the model's instructional effects.
- Over the past three decades, considerable attention has been devoted to teaching approaches known by various names—discovery learning, inquiry training, higher-level thinking—all of which focus on helping students become independent, autonomous learners capable of figuring things out for themselves.

## Planning and Conducting Problem-Based Lessons

- Major planning tasks associated with problem-based instruction consist of communicating goals clearly, designing interesting and appropriate problem situations, and logistical preparation.
- During the investigative phase of problem-based lessons, teachers serve as facilitators and guides of student investigations.

## Managing the Learning Environment

- Particular management tasks associated with problem-based instruction include dealing with a multitask learning environment; adjusting to different finishing rates; finding ways to monitor student work; and managing an array of materials, supplies, and out-of-class logistics.

## Assessment and Evaluation

- Assessment and evaluation tasks appropriate for problem-based learning necessitate finding alternative assessment procedures to measure such student work as performances and exhibits. These procedures go by the names of performance assessment, authentic assessment, and portfolios.

## 🍎 Key Terms

higher-order thinking

self-regulated learners

cognitive psychology

constructivism

cognitive-constructivist perspective

zone of proximal development

discovery learning

inquiry training

discrepant events

scaffolding

meta-analysis

artifacts

exhibits

## 🍎 Books for the Professional

Brooks, J. G., and Brooks, M. G. (1993). *In Search of Understanding: The Case for Constructivist Classrooms*. Alexandria, Va.: Association for Supervision and Curriculum Development. The authors describe how to set up a classroom based on constructivist principles and how to use strategies similar to those labeled "problem-based instruction" in this book. This is a very readable book.

Costa, A. L. (1985). *Developing Minds: A Resource Book for Teaching Thinking*. Alexandria, Va.: Association for Supervision and Curriculum Development. This is an excellent set of resources for teachers interested in making their classrooms more inquiry- and thinking-oriented.

Duckworth, E. (1987). *The Having of Wonderful Ideas and Other Essays on Teaching and Learning*. New York: Teachers College Press. This book is a collection of delightful and insightful essays on teaching and learning and using problem-based methods.

Kaplan, M. (1992). *Thinking in Education*. Cambridge, Mass.: Cambridge University Press. This book provides an excellent and contemporary analysis of what it means to teach children how to think and what needs to be done at all levels of education if we are to convert our classrooms into "communities for inquiry."

Krajcik, J., Czerniak, C. M. and Berger, C. F. (1998), *Teaching Children Science: A Project-Based Approach*. New York: McGraw Hill. This book is an excellent text on science teaching that details how to used problem-based instruction.

Resnick, L. B., and Klopfer, L. E. (eds.). (1989). *Toward the Thinking Curriculum: Current Cognitive Research*. Alexandria, Va.: Association for Supervision and Curriculum Development. The yearbook of ASCD provides an excellent review of the research in the cognitive sciences that has implications for both curriculum development in the various subject areas and teaching students how to think and inquire.

# Reflection & Portfolio

You have just finished grading the projects for your eleventh grade U.S. history class. You sigh. The work done by your students is very, very disappointing. Projects (research papers, video productions, portfolios, computer simulations) were supposed to be the results of a six-week unit on local history in which students researched a variety of local historical problems, linked these to current problems, and produced interesting and engaging artifacts and exhibits. Yet, the products you have just graded are not very good. Most students prepared reports of the more traditional term paper variety. These are not carefully done; they lack depth of analysis, and they are filled with grammatical and punctuation errors. Other products also appear to have been done in haste. Almost all of them lack creativity.

As a beginning teacher, this is your first attempt at using problem-based instruction. You are puzzled about why students didn't do better, and you start thinking about what has gone wrong. You ask yourself, "Did I provide sufficient directions to students about what they were supposed to do? Did I help them enough as they did their inquiries? Did I provide sufficient motivation?" Reflect on answers to these questions before you compare your thoughts to those of the teachers below. Also prepare your reflections as an exhibit in your professional portfolio.

## Jonas Kallen

"Poor work, regardless of the method a teacher is using, stems from a lack of motivation. When my students do poorly on assigned work, I normally assume that, for whatever reason, they were not vested in the topic or that the subject did not relate to their daily lives. Before launching a problem-based lesson on local history, a teacher should check to see what type of prior knowledge students have. Have they done similar projects in the past? Do they have relatives who have lived in the community for several generations? Posing interesting and provocative questions at the beginning of a project is a really good way to arouse curiosity and interest. Also, teachers should make sure as the project evolves that students are actively engaged and that activities are relevant."

## Ridaldo Sanchez

"In my experience, planning is the key to getting students to do good work on problem-based projects. Teachers can do many things to aid students in working and preparing projects. Some things I do include: (1) making sure I am clear in my own mind what I want the final projects to look like; (2) providing students with examples of various types of projects that I think are superior; (3) providing grading criteria in writing that specify the importance of projects being carefully written or produced with exacting standards for spelling, grammar, and so on.

"Also, when projects spread over several weeks like the ones in this situation, it is important to check student work and progress several times. Although this requires a little more work on the part of the teacher, providing feedback as work progresses results in superior student projects in the end."

# Chapter 🍎 Twelve

# Classroom Discussion

## Reflecting on Classroom Discussion

Surely you have had several teachers during your student career who made extensive use of discussion methods. Perhaps one was the type of teacher who came to class every day and presented you with provocative questions to talk about. Perhaps another started every class with a discussion about the previous night's homework.

Consider the many discussions you have participated in as a student:

🍎 *Did you participate widely in classroom discussions? Or were you a student who didn't participate much? If you didn't participate, do you know why?*

🍎 *Did you think your level of participation made any difference in how much you learned? Why? Why not?*

🍎 *Of the discussions you remember, which ones were most effective? Least effective?*

🍎 *What features did the effective discussions have in common?*

🍎 *What features did the ineffective discussions have in common?*

🍎 *What do you think students learn during discussions? What don't they learn?*

What do the answers you gave to these questions have to say about you and your views on classroom discussion? What do they say about how you might use discussion once you have your own classroom? Will you be a teacher who uses discussions often? Or will you tend to stay away from discussions and use other approaches instead?

In previous chapters specific teaching models were described, and you saw how at some point in most lessons, regardless of the model, dialogue or discussion was required. For instance, recitation, one type of teacher-student discourse, comes toward the end of presentation and direct instruction lessons as teachers strive to check for understanding and help students extend their thinking about particular information or concepts. Discussion occurs mainly in small groups during cooperative learning lessons, while the inquiry and problem-based lessons demand constant dialogue to accomplish the instructional goals of the model.

This chapter focuses on specifically *classroom discussion*. Discussion, you will find, is not exactly like the teaching models presented in previous chapters. Instead, it is a particular teaching procedure or strategy that can be used by itself or across a number of models. We will, however, use the same categories and labels to describe discussion as those used to describe previous teaching models.

> **Discussion is not really a full-blown teaching model; rather, it is a teaching procedure that is a crucial part of almost all teaching models.**

This chapter begins with an overview of classroom discussion, presents its theoretical and empirical support, and examines the specific procedures involved in planning, conducting, and evaluating classroom discussions. The final section highlights the importance of teaching students how to become effective participants in the classroom discourse system and describes how teachers can change some of the unproductive communication patterns that characterize many classrooms today.

## 🍎 *Overview of Classroom Discussion*

Classroom discussion and discourse are so central to all aspects of teaching, and effective use of classroom discussion requires an understanding of several important topics pertaining to classroom discourse and discussion. The dictionary definitions of *discourse* and *discussion* are almost identical: to engage in an orderly verbal interchange and to express thoughts on particular subjects. Teachers are more likely to use the term **discussion,** since it describes the *procedures* they use to encourage verbal interchange among students. Scholars and researchers are more likely to use the term **discourse,** since it reflects their interest in the *larger patterns* of exchange and communication found in classrooms. The term *discourse* is used to provide the overall perspective about classroom communication described in the section on theoretical support. The term *discussion* is used when specific teaching procedures are described.

> **Recitations are question-and-answer exchanges in which teachers check how well students recall factual information or understand a concept or idea.**

Sometimes discussions are confused with *recitations*. As is described in more detail later, discussions are situations in which teachers and students or students and other students talk with one another and share ideas and opinions. Questions employed to stimulate discussion are usually at a higher cognitive level. **Recitations,** on the other hand, are those exchanges, such as in a direct instruction lesson, in which teachers ask students a series of lower-level or factual questions aimed at checking how well they understand a particular idea or concept.

Discussions are used by teachers to achieve at least three important instructional objectives, as shown in Figure 12.1. First, discussion improves students' thinking and helps them construct their own understanding of academic content. As described in previous chapters, telling students about something does not necessarily ensure their comprehension. Discussing a topic helps students strengthen and extend their knowledge of the topic and increase their ability to think about it.

Second, discussion promotes student involvement and engagement. Research, as well as the wisdom of experienced teachers, demonstrates that for true learning to take place, students must take responsibility for their own learning and not depend solely

**Figure 12.1** *Learner Outcomes for Discussion*

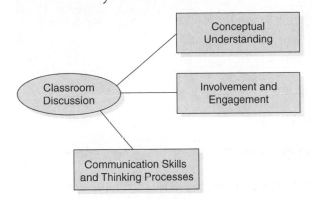

on a teacher. Using discussion is one means of doing this. It gives students public opportunities to talk about and play with their own ideas and provides motivation to engage in discourse beyond the classroom.

Third, discussion is used by teachers to help students learn important communication skills and thinking processes. Because discussions are public, they provide a means for a teacher to find out what students are thinking and how they are processing the ideas and information being taught. Discussions thus provide social settings in which teachers can help students analyze their thinking processes and learn important communication skills such as stating ideas clearly, listening to others, responding to others in appropriate ways, and asking good questions.

Most discussions follow a similar pattern, but variations do exist, depending on the teacher's goals for particular lessons and the nature of the students involved. Three variations will be described later in the chapter, but essentially, all three share the same five-phase syntax: explaining the aims of the lesson, focusing and holding the discussion, and bringing the discussion to a conclusion and debriefing it. These phases will be described in some detail later.

The learning environment and management system surrounding discussion are incredibly important. The environment for conducting discussions is characterized by open processes and active student roles. It also demands careful attention to the use of physical space. The teacher may provide varying degrees of structure and focus for a particular discussion, depending on the nature of the class and the learning objectives. However, in many ways, the students themselves control the specific minute-to-minute interactions. This approach to teaching requires a large degree of student self-management and control, a topic that is explored more fully later in this chapter.

## 🍎 *Theoretical and Empirical Support*

Much of the theoretical support for the use of discussion stems from the fields in which scholars study language, communicative processes, and patterns of exchange. These studies extend to virtually every setting in which human beings come together. To consider the role of language, think for a moment about the many everyday situations in which success depends largely on the use of language and communication. Friendships, for instance, are initiated and maintained mainly through language—friends talk and share experiences with one another. Families maintain their unique histories by

**Discussions are used to help students construct their own understanding and to improve communication and thinking skills.**

**Discussion-based teaching requires a great amount of student self-management.**

✓ **Check for Understanding**

- What are the five phases of a classroom discussion?

- What are the major learner outcomes for classroom discussions?

- What type of learning environment works best for classroom discussions?

*Discussion provides an opportunity for students to monitor their own thinking and for teachers to correct faulty reasoning.*

building patterns of discourse, sometimes even in the form of secret codes, that are natural to family members but are strange to outsiders, such as newly acquired in-laws. Youth culture develops special patterns of communication that provide member identity and group cohesion. The secret codes used by gangs are an example of communication used to maintain group identity. It is difficult to imagine a cocktail party, a dinner party, a church social, or any other social event existing for very long if people could not verbally express their ideas and listen to the ideas of others. The popularity of radio talk shows and computer networking adds additional evidence to how central interaction through the medium of language is to human beings.

Discourse through language is also central to what goes on in classrooms. Courtney Cazden (1986), one of America's foremost scholars on the topic of classroom discourse, wrote that "spoken language is the medium by which much teaching takes place and in which students demonstrate to teachers much of what they have learned" (p. 432). Spoken language provides the means for students to talk about what they already know and to form meaning from new knowledge as it is acquired. Spoken language affects the thought processes of students and provides them with their identity as learners and as members of the classroom group.

## Discourse and Cognition

A strong relationship exists between language and thinking, and both lead to the ability to analyze, to reason deductively and inductively, and to make sound inferences based on knowledge. Discourse is one way for students to practice their thinking processes and to enhance their thinking skills. Mary Budd Rowe (1986) summarized this important point nicely.

> To "grow," a complex thought system requires a great deal of shared experience and conversation. It is in talking about what we have done and observed, and in arguing about what we make of our experiences, that ideas multiply, become refined, and finally produce new questions and further explorations. (p. 43)

In some ways, discourse can be thought of as the *externalization of thinking*, that is, exposing one's invisible thoughts for others to see. Through discussions, then, teachers are given a partial window for viewing the thinking skills of their students and a setting for providing correction and feedback when they observe faulty, incomplete reasoning. Thinking out loud also provides students opportunities to "hear" their own thinking and to learn how to monitor their own thinking processes. Remember, learners don't acquire knowledge simply by recording new information on a blank slate; instead, they actively build knowledge structures over a period of time as they interpret new knowledge and integrate it into prior knowledge.

**Social Aspect of Discourse.** One aspect of classroom discourse, then, is its ability to promote cognitive growth. Another aspect is its ability to connect and unite the cognitive and the social aspects of learning. Indeed, the classroom discourse system is central to creating positive learning environments. It helps define participation patterns and, consequently, has a great deal of impact on classroom management. The talk of teachers and students provides much of the social glue that holds classroom life together.

> **In addition to promoting cognitive growth, discussion can also be used to further a positive social environment in the classroom.**

The cognitive-social connection is most clear in the way social participation affects thinking and cognitive growth. Lauren Resnick and Leopold Klopfer (1989) observed, for instance, that the

> social setting provides occasions for modeling effective thinking strategies. Skilled thinkers (often the instructor, but sometimes more advanced fellow students) can demonstrate desirable ways of attacking problems, analyzing texts, or constructing argument. . . . But most important of all, the social setting may let students know that all the elements of critical thought—interpretation, questioning, trying possibilities, demanding rational justification—are *socially valued*. (pp. 8–9)

## Teacher Talk

Working from a variety of perspectives and with diverse methods, researchers who study classroom discourse have found that most teachers talk a great deal and that a basic communication pattern exists in most classrooms. Also, they have found that this pattern is not necessarily the best one for promoting student thinking. This basic pattern of recitation, familiar to us all, is a teaching activity in which students in a whole-class setting are quizzed over their lessons by way of a question-answer format. Larry Cuban (1984) documented how the recitation pattern emerged early in the history of formal schooling and how it persisted throughout the twentieth century at almost all levels of schooling and across all academic subjects. Teacher dominance of classroom communication was also thoroughly documented by Ned Flanders in the late 1960s and early 1970s with numerous studies on teacher-student interaction. Flanders (1970) concluded that in most classrooms, two-thirds of the talk is by teachers. John Goodlad in his extensive study of schools made essentially the same observation in 1984.

> **Studies have repeatedly shown that teacher talk routinely constitutes about two-thirds to three-fourths of classroom discourse.**

The pattern is still very much with us today. In the 1990s, Richard and Patricia Schmuck visited and collected information on rural schools in the United States. They studied twenty-five school districts in twenty-one states. They interviewed 212 teenagers about their school experience and observed lessons in over thirty high school classrooms. In twenty-two out of the thirty classrooms, they reported seeing mainly recitation lessons. The Schmucks (1994) reported teachers talking three-fourths of the time and commented this was more than the two-thirds teacher talk Flanders observed three decades ago. Only twice did the Schmucks observe students talking in pairs, and only four times did they observe small-group interaction and exchange.

## Teacher Questioning

Recitation teaching relies on teachers talking and asking questions. The ways teachers ask questions and the types of questions they ask have been the focus of considerable inquiry and concern for quite some time. Mark Gall (1970), who has on several occasions reviewed the research on questioning, highlighted how frequently questions are asked in classrooms and, like Cuban (1994), illustrated how a persistent pattern has existed over time, mainly that teachers spend a large portion of school time talking and asking questions.

*Studies have resulted in conflicting conclusions regarding the benefits of higher-order questioning over fact-based question-and-answer sessions.*

Because questions are asked so often in classrooms, an obvious concern is what effects they have on student learning. In particular, what is the effect of factual and higher-order questions on student learning and thinking? For many years, the conventional wisdom held that higher-order questions lead to greater cognitive growth than that resulting from more concrete, factual questions. However, reviews of research in the early 1970s reported that no clear evidence existed one way or the other (Rosenshine, 1971; Dunkin & Biddle, 1974). By 1976, Barak Rosenshine was prepared to challenge the conventional wisdom when he concluded that "narrow" (factual) questions actually seemed to be the most useful, particularly when teachers provided immediate feedback about the correct and incorrect answers. It is important to point out that Rosenshine reviewed studies done in early-grade classrooms that had a large proportion of children from lower social and economic backgrounds. A few years later, in another review by Redfield and Rousseau (1981), the conclusion about the use of factual questions was challenged, and the researchers reported that asking higher-level and thought-provoking questions had positive effects on student achievement and thinking.

*Whether teachers should ask more higher-order or lower-order questions depends on their instructional objectives and on the students being taught.*

During the past decade, researchers have continued to study the controversy over the effects of question types on student achievement and thinking. A consensus appears to be emerging that the type of questions teachers ask should depend on the students with whom they are working and the type of educational objectives they are trying to achieve. Gall (1984; Gall & Gall, 1990), for example, interpreted this research in the following way.

- Emphasis on fact questions is more effective for promoting young children's achievement, which involves primarily mastery of basic skills.
- Emphasis on higher cognitive questions is more effective for students where more independent thinking is required.

In addition to the types of questions teachers ask, researchers have also been interested in the questions' level of difficulty and in teachers' overall pattern of questioning. **Level of difficulty** refers to students' ability to answer questions correctly regardless of cognitive level. Research on this topic has also produced mixed results. However, after a thorough review of the research, Jere Brophy and Tom Good (1986) concluded that three guidelines should be considered by teachers when deciding how difficult to make their questions:

- A large proportion (perhaps as high as three-fourths) of a teacher's questions should be at a level that will elicit correct answers from students in the class.
- The other one-fourth of the questions should be at a level of difficulty that will elicit some response from students, even if the response is incomplete.
- No question should be so difficult that students will not be able to respond at all.

The overall pattern of questioning is also important. All too often, the unspoken classroom discussion rules are that the teacher should ask all the questions, students should respond with right answers, and the teacher should repeat the questions if the answers

*Traditional teacher questioning patterns may lead to boredom and passivity.*

are wrong. Later, you will find that this kind of discussion pattern does not promote higher-level thinking or much real engagement.

## Wait-Time

A final important line of research in relation to classroom discussion and discourse focuses on the pace of interchange and a variable known as *wait-time*. **Wait-time** is the pause between a teacher's question and the student's response and between the response and the teacher's subsequent reaction or follow-up question. This variable was first observed in the 1960s, when considerable effort was under way to improve curricula in almost all academic subjects. These new curricula, particularly in the sciences and the social sciences, were developed to help students learn how to inquire and discover relationships among social and/or natural phenomena. The recommended method for virtually all curricula was inquiry or discovery-oriented discussions. However, researchers found that these types of discussions were not occurring. The research by Rowe on this important topic is highlighted in the Research Summary in this chapter (pages 384 and 385) for two reasons. Her investigations highlighted an important problem with classroom discourse and offered a cure. They also illustrated how research in education sometimes moves from observation of teacher behavior in regular classrooms to experimentation and the testing of new practices.

## 🍎 *Planning and Conducting Discussion Lessons*

As with the teaching models described in the preceding chapters, effective discussions require that teachers perform planning, interactive, management, and assessment tasks. Planning and interactive tasks are described in this section, followed by a discussion of management and assessment tasks.

## Planning for Discussion

Two common misconceptions held by many teachers are that planning for a discussion requires less effort than planning for other kinds of teaching and that discussions cannot really be planned at all because they rely on spontaneous and unpredictable

**Wait-time is the pause between the teacher's question and the student's response and between the student's response and the teacher's reaction.**

✔ **Check for Understanding**

- What relationships exist between language, discourse, and thinking abilities?

- Why is the cognitive-social connection important to the understanding of classroom discussion?

- How does the use of different kinds of questions produce different types of thinking on the part of students?

- Why is the concept of *wait-time* important when thinking about classroom discussion?

# When Can Slowing Down Increase Learning?

*Rowe, M. B. (1974).*
Wait-time and rewards as instructional variables, their influence on language, logic, and fate control. Part one: Wait-time. *Journal of Research in Science Teaching*, 11, 81–94.

Could it be that the absence of talk (pauses by the teacher) does more to influence discourse and complex thinking processes than its presence? That's what Mary Budd Rowe found in a series of interesting and important studies.

**Problem and Approach:** In Chapter 8, process-product research was introduced to show how researchers examine existing practices in a natural setting to discover relationships between teacher behavior and student learning. Other chapters, on the other hand, described how some knowledge has resulted from experiments and comparing the effects of innovative teaching practices. Sometimes a researcher may employ both observation in natural settings and experimentation with new practices. The classic study by Rowe and her colleagues on the discourse patterns of teachers is a good example of research that moved from observation of teachers in regular classrooms to experimentation with a new procedure.

**Sample and Setting:** This study actually progressed through two stages: (1) systematic observation of teachers in natural settings, and (2) planned experiments in which the researchers attempted to change the natural behavior of teachers.

**Natural Observations:** Discussion patterns were initially analyzed from 103 tapes made by thirty-six primary teachers in the New Jersey and New York region using the Science Curriculum Improvement Study (SCIS). The researchers also sought tapes of lessons from other parts of the country and at other grade levels. By the end of this stage of their inquiry, they had obtained over three hundred tapes from rural, suburban, and urban areas and from a variety of grade levels, including high school and college classes. Analysis of these lessons showed that the pace of instruction in most classrooms was very fast. In all but three classrooms, out of the hundreds studied, teachers displayed the following pattern.

- Teacher asked a question. Student must respond within at least one second.
- If student did not respond in one second, teacher repeated, rephrased, asked a different question, or called on another student (Wait-time 1).
- When a student did respond, the teacher reacted or asked another question within an average of 0.9 seconds (Wait-time 2).

The investigators concluded from this phase of their work that instruction in virtually all classrooms was very fast and without sufficient wait-time. They also concluded that in a few classrooms where they did find students engaged in inquiry, sustained conversation, speculation, and argument about ideas, the average wait-time hovered around three seconds. With this information, the researchers planned and conducted a series of controlled microstudies (1) to see if teachers could be taught to slow down the pace of their discussions by using wait-time, and (2) if the slower pace had an impact on discourse and cognitive processes.

**Procedures for the Microstudies:** Ninety-six teachers from two locations were recruited and trained to employ wait-times of at least three seconds. From a pool of lessons prepared by the researchers using various curricula and aimed at various grade levels, teachers were asked to teach six lessons to students who were assigned to four-member learning groups. Each lesson was recorded on audiotape. Tapes were transcribed and coded. The wait-time variables were measured using the following criteria.

- **Wait-time 1:** The time between when the teacher stops speaking and when either a student responds or the teacher speaks again
- **Wait-time 2:** The time between when a student stops speaking and when the teacher speaks

**Pointers for Reading Research:** The results of this study are descriptive and rather straight-forward. No new research concepts are introduced. However, Rowe's study is interesting in that it was conducted in stages. This illustrates how good research often moves from casual observations of phenomena in a natural setting to more systematic observation and only then to intervention and manipulation of important variables in controlled settings for the purpose of seeing if things can be changed for the better.

**Table 12.1** *Number of Questions and Typical Distribution of Question Types Before and After Wait-Time Training*

|  | Before Training | After Training |
|---|---|---|
| Mean number of questions per 15 minutes of transcript | 38 | 8 |
| Typical questions (%) |  |  |
| Rhetorical | 3 | 2 |
| Informational | 82 | 34 |
| Leading | 13 | 36 |
| Probing | 2 | 28 |

**Results:** Teacher behavior changed as a result of training to use longer wait-times. Table 12.1 shows the number of questions asked and the typical distribution of question types by teachers before and after wait-time training.

Notice the sharp drop in the number of questions asked by teachers after wait-time training. Also note that the number of informational questions declined while the number of probing and thought-provoking questions increased rather dramatically.

The researchers hypothesized that if teachers could slow down their pace, this behavior would impact on the way their students responded. Table 12.1 displays the results of Rowe's wait-time studies as they impact on what she called student outcome variables. Notice that this table compares the behaviors of only seventy-six of the ninety-five teachers who achieved criterion wait-times of three seconds or longer.

Table 12.2 shows these results when teachers started to use longer wait-times:

**Table 12.2** *Student Outcome Variables: Contrasts Between Tape 1 and Tape 6 of the Training Sequence for 76 of 95 Teachers Who Achieved Criterion Wait-Times of 3 Seconds or Longer*

| Student Variable | Tape 1 | Tape 2 |
|---|---|---|
| Length of response |  |  |
| Mean | 8 | 27 |
| Range | (3–12 words) | (14–39 words) |
| Number of unsolicited but appropriate responses |  |  |
| Mean | 5 | 17 |
| Range | (0–17) | (12–28) |
| Number of failures to respond |  |  |
| Mean | 7 | 1 |
| Range | (1–15) | (0–3) |
| Number of evidence-inference statements |  |  |
| Mean | 6 | 14 |
| Range | (0–11) | (6–21) |
| Number of solicitation, structuring, and reacting statements |  |  |
| Mean | 5 | 32 |
| Range | (1–6) | (11–46) |

- The length of student responses increased from eight words per response under the fast pace used by teachers to twenty-seven words. This signifies considerably longer statements by students after teachers are trained to use wait-time.
- The number of unsolicited but appropriate responses increased from a mean of five to a mean of seventeen.
- Failures to respond ("I don't know" or silence) decreased. In classrooms prior to training, the "no response" was as high as 30 percent of the time. This changed dramatically once teachers started to wait at least three seconds for students to think.
- When wait-time was lengthened, students provided more evidence type of statements to support the inferences they were making.

- With a slower pace, students asked more questions and the number of structuring and soliciting moves increased.

**Discussion and Implications:** What is striking about this study and other wait-time studies done since Rowe's initial work is (1) teachers, left to their natural inclinations, pace instruction too fast to allow much careful inquiry or serious dialogue, and (2) a rather simple intervention can bring rather striking changes in discourse patterns. Learning to wait results in fewer and different types of questions by teachers and, most important, different student responses. Given more time, students will less often fail to respond ("I don't know"), and they will increase the length of their responses. The quality of responses will also change. Students in classrooms in which teachers use wait-time engage in inquiry-oriented and speculative thinking.

**Proper planning for a discussion increases the opportunities for spontaneity and flexibility within the lesson.**

interactions among students. Both of these ideas are wrong. Planning for a discussion necessitates every bit as much effort, perhaps more, as planning for other types of lessons, and even though spontaneity and flexibility are important in discussions, it is a teacher's planning beforehand that makes these features possible.

**Consider Purpose.** Deciding that discussion is appropriate for a given lesson is the first planning step. Preparing the lesson and making decisions about what type of discussion to hold and specific strategies to employ are next. As described earlier, although discussions can stand alone as a teaching strategy, they are more frequently used in connection with other teaching models. Although the particular uses of discussion are practically infinite, teachers generally want their discussion to accomplish one of the three objectives described in the previous section: to check for student understanding of reading assignments or presentations through recitations, to teach thinking skills, or to share experiences.

**Teachers should plan discussions with their students in mind.**

**Consider Students.** Knowing about students' prior knowledge is just as important in planning a discussion as it is in planning other kinds of lessons. Experienced teachers know that they must also take into consideration their students' communication and discussion skills. They consider, for instance, how particular students in the class will respond differently to various kinds of questions or foci; they predict how some will want to talk all the time whereas others will be reluctant to say anything. When planning discussions, it is important to devise ways to encourage participation by as many students as possible, not just the bright ones, and to be prepared with questions and ideas that will spark the interest of a diverse student group. More is said about this aspect of discussion later.

**Choose an Approach.** As described previously, there are several different kinds of discussions, and the approach chosen should reflect a teacher's purposes and the nature of the students involved. Three approaches are discussed here.

*Recitations.* Although recitation is often overused, it nonetheless has its place. One important use is when teachers ask students to listen to or read about information on a particular topic. A reading assignment in history may vary in length from a paragraph to a whole book. A teacher's talk on ecosystems may be as long as a full-hour lecture or as short as five or ten minutes. Either can cover a variety of topics. Teachers generally ask students to read or listen with a definite purpose in mind. Sometimes it is to glean important information about a topic, whereas at other times it is to become familiar with a particular author, a specific type of literature, or a point of view or particular interpretation. Brief question-and-answer sessions (recitation discussions) about assigned reading materials or a lecture can provide teachers with a means of checking student understanding as well as motivating students to complete their reading assignments or to listen carefully when the teacher is talking.

**Brief question-and-answer or recitation sessions covering assigned materials are useful in checking student understanding and in motivating student work.**

*Inquiry or Problem-Based Discussion.* As described earlier, discussions are sometimes used to engage students in higher-order thinking and, thereby, to encourage their own intellectual investigation. Normally, such discussion is part of some type of problem-based teaching. Although a number of specific approaches have been developed, they all have a common syntax in which the teacher opens the lesson by presenting students with what Suchman (1962) labeled a *discrepant event* or what Palincsar and Brown (1989) called *mystery spots.* Both refer to puzzling situations that are not immediately explainable, such as water appearing to run uphill, metal changing shape when heated, and social data that confront conventional wisdom. Because these situations are puzzling to students and create cognitive dissonance, they provide a natural motivation to think. When using this approach, teachers encourage students to ask questions, to generate empirical data, and to formulate theories and hypotheses to explain the puzzling situation. In this type of discussion, teachers help students become conscious of their own reasoning processes and teach them to monitor and evaluate their own learning strategies.

**Problem-based lessons centered around a discrepant event encourage discussion and help students become aware of their own reasoning processes.**

*Sharing-Based Discussion.* Often teachers hold discussions for the purpose of helping students develop shared meaning from common experiences or to confront one another with differences of opinions. Younger children may be asked to talk about what they learned from their visit to the zoo or the apple farm. Older students may be asked to talk about what they learned from a science experiment they all performed or from a novel they read. Important current events such as a breakthrough in an arms treaty, new abortion legislation, or a natural disaster are often discussed in the classroom so that different points of view may be explored. Unlike recitation discussions, during which teachers ask students *to recall* specific information, or problem-based discussions, in which teachers get students *to reason,* sharing-based discussions help students *to form and to express thought and opinions independently.* Through dialogue about shared experiences and what these experiences mean, ideas are refined or expanded and questions are raised for future study.

**Sharing-based discussions help students form and express independent thoughts and opinions.**

**Make a Plan.** A lesson plan for a discussion consists of a set of objectives and a content outline. The plan should include not only the targeted content but also a well-conceived focus statement, the description of a puzzling event, and/or a list of questions. If the discussion is to follow a lecture, it is likely that the teacher already has the content firmly in mind and has explored the important conceptual relationships. When the discussion follows assigned readings, experienced teachers know that they must have extensive notes not only about specific facts but, more important, about the main ideas, points of view, and key relationships highlighted in the reading.

Sometimes teachers find using the *conceptual web* technique a useful planning device. As described in Chapter 9, a web provides a visual image of the characteristics and relationships around a central idea. Remember, to make a conceptual web, you identify the key ideas associated with a particular topic and arrange them in some logical pattern.

**Advance preparation and identification of questioning patterns can greatly improve the flow of a classroom discussion.**

Teachers will find that careful attention to preparation will help immensely as they strive to keep details straight for students and as they facilitate student understanding and higher-order thinking. For some types of discussions, asking students questions becomes a key feature. In preparing their questioning strategy, teachers need to consider both the cognitive level of questions and their level of difficulty.

During the past three decades, many systems have been developed for classifying the cognitive level of teacher questions. Most of the classification systems have similarities; all consider questions in terms of the cognitive processing they require students to perform. Bloom's *Taxonomy of Educational Objectives,* described in Chapter 2, can also be used by teachers to design questions for classroom discussions. Table 12.3 shows six categories of classroom questions and examples of each.

**A good discussion includes both lower- and higher-level questions.**

As described earlier, the research about the effects of using various types of questions is still unclear. However, beginning teachers should keep in mind one important truth, that is, that different questions require different types of thinking and that a good lesson should include both lower- and higher-level questions. One way to achieve this is to start by asking simple recall questions to see if students have grasped the basic ideas under consideration, follow with comprehension and analysis questions ("why" questions), and then conclude with more thought-provoking synthesis and evaluation questions.

In preparing the lesson plan and questioning strategies, remember to think through the issues associated with question difficulty. Experience helps teachers to know their

**Table 12.3** *Six Question Types According to Bloom's Taxonomy*

| Level | | Examples of Questions | Cognitive Processes |
|---|---|---|---|
| **Level 1** | Knowledge | Which region of the United States is Ohio in? What does $H_2O$ stand for? | Recalling factual information |
| **Level 2** | Comprehension | What is the difference between longitude and latitude? What is the book *The Old Man and the Sea* about? | Using information |
| **Level 3** | Application | If John has 12 feet of lumber, how many 2-foot-long boards can he make? | Applying principles |
| **Level 4** | Analysis | Why do you think the red liquid moves? Why do some trees lose their leaves in winter? | Explaining relationships or making inferences |
| **Level 5** | Synthesis | If the North had not won the Civil War, what would life be like in the United States today? What if John Brown had succeeded at Harpers Ferry? What might happen if the earth experienced a continuing warming trend? | Making predictions |
| **Level 6** | Evaluation | Which novel do you think is the best piece of literature? What do you think about the recycling program? | Making judgments or stating opinions |

**Figure 12.2** *U-Shaped Seating Arrangement*

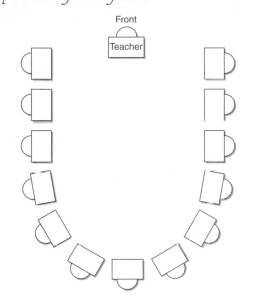

students and to devise questions of appropriate difficulty. Decisions about question type and difficulty can be better made during the quiet of advanced planning than during the discussion itself.

**Use Physical Space Appropriately.** Another planning task involves making arrangements for appropriate use of physical space. Earlier chapters explained how different seating patterns affect communication patterns within the classroom. The best seating arrangements for discussion are the U-shape and the circle formations illustrated in Figures 12.2 and 12.3. Both seating patterns allow students to see each other, an important condition for verbal interaction. Both can be accommodated in most classrooms. Each, however, has some advantages and disadvantages that should be considered.

The **U-shape seating pattern,** with the teacher situated in front at the open end of the U, gives a bit more authority to the teacher, an important feature when working with groups of students who lack discussion skills or where behavior management is a problem. The U-shape also allows freedom of movement for teachers. They have ready access to the chalkboard or flip charts, which may be important during the course of a discussion, and they can move into the U to make closer contact with particular students when that is needed. The disadvantage of the U is that it establishes some emotional distance between the teacher, as discussion leader, and students. It also puts considerable physical distance between students who are sitting at the head of the U and those sitting at the end.

The **circle seating pattern,** on the other hand, minimizes both emotional and physical distance among participants and maximizes opportunities for students to talk freely with one another. The disadvantage of the circle is that it inhibits the teacher from moving freely to the chalkboard or among students.

Many elementary and secondary schools today have furniture and other features that make movement from one seating arrangement to another possible. In some instances, however, teachers will be confronted with situations that severely limit this possibility. For example, some science laboratories and shop classes have fixed tables

*Teachers can improve class discussions by optimizing the use of physical space.*

*The best seating arrangement for a discussion is either a U-shape or a circle.*

**Figure 12.3** *Circle Seating Arrangement*

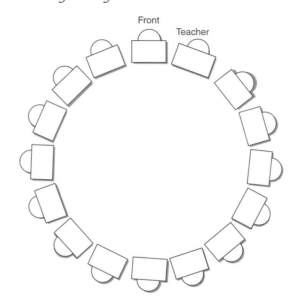

that make moving furniture impossible. Some drama and English classes may be held in the school's theater with fixed seating. These conditions require special problem solving on the part of teachers. Some experienced science teachers have students stand in a U-shape during discussion sessions; drama teachers and some elementary teachers have their students sit on the floor of the stage. The specifics of the classroom space and the teacher's own personal preferences certainly are strong considerations when making planning decisions about use of the space prior to a discussion.

## Conducting Discussions

> As discussion leader, a teacher should focus the discussion, keep it on track, encourage participation, and keep a visible record of it.

For whole-class discussions to be successful, some rather sophisticated communication and interaction skills are needed on the part of both teachers and students. It also requires norms that support open exchange and mutual respect. The syntax for most discussions consists of five phases: establishing set, focusing the discussion, holding the discussion, bringing it to a close, and debriefing. These five phases are summarized in Table 12.4. As discussion leader, a teacher also is responsible for keeping the discussion on track by refocusing student digressions, encouraging participation, and helping to keep a record of the discussions. All of these behaviors are described in some detail in the following sections.

**Establish Set and Focus the Discussion.**  Many classroom discussions are characterized by talk and more talk, much of which has little to do with either the main aims of the lesson or with encouraging student thinking. An effective discussion, just like an effective demonstration, is clearly focused and to the point. At the beginning, teachers must explain the purposes of the discussion and get students set to participate. They should also pose a specific question, raise an appropriate issue, or present a puzzling situation associated with the topic. These activities have to be in a form students can understand and respond to. Stating the focus question or issue clearly is one key to getting a good discussion started. Another way to establish set and spark student interest

**Table 12.4** *Syntax for Holding Discussion*

| Phase | Teacher Behavior |
|---|---|
| **Phase 1:** Clarify aims and establish set. | Teacher goes over the aims for the discussion and gets students ready to participate. |
| **Phase 2:** Focus the discussion. | Teacher provides a focus for discussion by describing ground rules, asking an initial question, presenting a puzzling situation, or describing a discussion issue. |
| **Phase 3:** Hold the discussion. | Teacher monitors students' interactions, asks questions, listens to ideas, responds to ideas, enforces the ground rules, keeps records of the discussion, and expresses own ideas. |
| **Phase 4:** End the discussion. | Teacher helps bring the discussion to a close by summarizing or expressing the meaning the discussion has had for him or her. |
| **Phase 5:** Debrief the discussion. | Teacher asks students to examine their discussion and thinking processes. |

is to relate the beginning discussion question or focus to students' prior knowledge or experiences.

**Hold the Discussion.** As a whole-class discussion proceeds, many circumstances can get it off track. In some cases, students will purposely try to get the teacher off the topic, as, for instance, when they want to talk about last Friday's ball game instead of the causes of World War I. Talking about Friday's game is fine if that is the objective of the lesson, but it is not appropriate if the aim is to encourage student reasoning.

A second example of wandering is when a student expresses an idea or raises a question that has little or nothing to do with the topic. This happens often, particularly with students who have trouble concentrating in school. It is also likely to happen with younger students who have not been taught good listening and discussion skills.

In both instances, effective teachers acknowledge what students are doing—"We are now talking about last Friday night's game" or, "You say your father had a good time in New York last weekend"—and then refocus the class's attention on the topic with a comment such as, "Talking about the game seems to be of great interest to all of you. I will let you do that during the last five minutes of the class period, but now I want us to get back to the question I asked you." or, "I know you are very interested in what your father did in New York, and I would love it if you would spend some time during lunch telling me more. Right now we want to talk about. . . ."

**Effective discussion leaders acknowledge students' offtrack remarks and then refocus their attention to the topic at hand.**

*Keeping Records.* Verbal exchange during a discussion proceeds more orderly if teachers keep some type of written record of the discussion as it unfolds. Writing students' main ideas or points of view on the chalkboard or flip charts provides this written record. Or it may consist of constructing conceptual webs that illustrate the various ideas and relationships being discussed.

A dilemma faced by beginning teachers in keeping a discussion record is how much detail to include and whether or not all ideas should be written down. These decisions, obviously, depend on the nature of the students involved and the purposes of the discussion. When a teacher is working with a group that lacks confidence in discourse skills, it is probably a good idea to write down as much as possible. Seeing many ideas

"Today I would like us to have a discussion on global warming. Let's begin by recalling what global warming is, as described in the article you read last night, and then move on to explore the various points of view on this topic and the one with which you most agree."

**Discussion proceeds in a more orderly fashion if some type of visible written record is kept as the discussion unfolds.** on the chalkboard or flip chart provides a public display of the many good thoughts that exist within the group and can encourage participation. With a more experienced and confident group, the teacher may want to list only key words, thus affording a more open exchange of ideas and opinions.

If the teacher has asked students specifically for their theories or ideas about a topic, it is important to list all ideas and treat these equally, regardless of their quality. On the other hand, if questions focus on direct recall of right answers, then only right answers should be recorded. How to respond to incorrect responses will be discussed in a moment.

*Spotlight on Technology*

# Discussing Online

The emergence of the Internet and the World Wide Web has made it possible for people to talk to one another in ways never before possible. Every day, literally millions of individuals enter web "chat rooms" and "discussion forums" for the purpose of expressing their views on a multitude of topics. Sometimes this exchange is between people who know each other; sometimes it is between strangers. Regardless, it highlights the importance of communication and the centrality of discourse in human communities.

Teachers have found they can use the popularity of online interaction among youth to accomplish some of the goals they have traditionally held for classroom discussions as well as to pursue goals not possible in pre-Internet times. Teachers report positive benefits of online communication and discussions. For instance, they can increase learning time. Some students may be motivated to continue talking about important topics online after the class is over. This has the effect of extending instructional time beyond the confines of the classroom walls. Online discussions can also increase participation. They allow certain students, perhaps those who are shy, to say things online they wouldn't say in class.

However, discussion conducted online may have a negative aspect. When students engage each other face-to-face, they can attend to the nuances of body language and observe the emotions that many topics generate, particularly those that are controversial and sensitive. Perhaps teachers and parents need to worry about students hiding behind their computer monitors and never acquiring skills to be effective in face-to-face situations.

If you are interested in online applications, you might want to check out the following websites: www.convene.com and www.linov.kuleuven.ac.be/BIC. ICQ and Instant Messenger are two currently popular discussion software programs.

*Listening to Students' Ideas.* A favorite discussion technique used by many teachers at the high school and college levels is "playing the devil's advocate." Teachers using this technique purposely take the opposite point of view from that being expressed by individual students or groups of students. Even though this approach can create lively exchange between a teacher and a few of the more verbal students, it does not work well with younger students or with many older students who lack good verbal and communication skills. Debate and argument arouse emotions, and despite their motivational potential may divert the students' attention from the topic. They also cause many less articulate or shy students to shrink from participation. If the teacher's goal is to help students understand a lesson and extend their thinking, then the teacher should listen carefully to each student's ideas. In this case, the teacher should remain nonjudgmental and inquiry-oriented, rather than challenging or argumentative.

> Free and open discussion is enhanced when teachers listen carefully and nonjudgmentally to students' ideas.

*Using Wait-Time.* Earlier we discussed how many teachers do not give students sufficient time to think and to respond. There are probably several reasons for this. One is the strong cultural norm in our society against silence. Silence makes many people uncomfortable and, consequently, they jump in to keep the conversation moving. Another is that waiting for student response can be perceived by teachers as threatening to the pace and momentum of a lesson. Additionally, silence or waiting can give uninvolved students opportunities to start talking or otherwise misbehaving. Although many contextual conditions influence wait-time, the general recommendations are for beginning teachers to practice waiting at least three seconds for a student's response, to ask the question again or in a slightly different way if there is no response, and never to move on to a second question without some closure on the first. The amount of wait-time should probably be less for direct recall questions and more for questions aimed at higher-level thinking and more complex content. After a student response, teachers should also wait a sufficient time before moving on.

> In most circumstances, teachers should practice waiting at least three seconds for a student's response.

*Responding to Student Answers.* When students respond correctly to teachers' questions, effective teachers acknowledge the correct answer with brief affirmations such as, "That's right," "Okay," or "Yes." They do not spend time providing overly gushy praise. Most teachers learn these behaviors quite quickly. However, responding to incorrect or incomplete responses is a more complicated situation. The guidelines described in Chapter 8 are repeated here.

1. *Dignify* a student's incorrect response or performance by giving a question for which the response would have been correct: For example, "George Washington would have been the right answer if I asked you who was the first president of the United States."
2. Provide the student with an *assist,* or prompt: For example, "Remember, the president in 1828 was also a hero in the War of 1812."
3. Hold the student *accountable:* For example, "You didn't know President Jackson today, but I bet you will tomorrow when I ask you again."

*Responding to Student Ideas and Opinions.* Although the art of questioning is important for effective discussions, other verbal behaviors by teachers are equally important, especially those for responding to students' ideas and opinions. These are responses aimed at getting students to extend their thinking and to be more conscious of their thinking processes. Statements and questions such as the following provide illustrations on how to do this.

*Being responsive to student ideas encourages participation.*

- Reflect on student ideas:
  "I heard you say. . . ."
  "What I think you're telling me is. . . ."
  "That's an interesting idea. I have never thought of it in quite that way. . . ."
- Get students to consider alternatives:
  "That's an interesting idea. I wonder, though, if you have ever considered this as an alternative. . . ."
  "You have provided one point of view about the issue. How does it compare with the point of view expressed by . . .?"
  "Evelyn has just expressed an interesting point of view. I wonder if someone else would like to say why they agree or disagree with her idea?"
  "Do you think the author would agree with your idea? Why? Why not?"
- Seek clarification:
  "I think you have a good idea. But I'm a bit confused. Can you expand your thought a bit to help me understand it more fully?"
- Label thinking processes and ask for supportive evidence:
  "It sounds to me like you have been performing a mental *experiment* with these data."
  "You have made a very strong *inference* from the information given you."
  "Can you think of an *experiment* that would put that hypothesis to a good test?"
  "What if I told you (give new information)? What would that do to your *hypothesis?*"
  "That's an interesting position. What *values* led you to it?"
  "If everyone held the *judgment* you just expressed, what would the result be?"

*Expressing Opinions.* Many beginning teachers are uncertain about whether or not they should express their own ideas and opinions during a discussion. Although teachers do not want to dominate discussions or make it appear that they are the only ones with good ideas, expressing ideas appropriately can be beneficial. It provides

**Student thinking can be extended by teacher actions that review student ideas, ask for alternative ideas, and/or seek clarification or supporting evidence.**

✔ **Check for Understanding**

- What are the major planning tasks associated with preparing for classroom discussion?

- How do the three approaches to discussion differ, and what should be considered when choosing a particular approach to use?

- What are the five phases of a discussion, and what kinds of teacher behaviors are associated with each?

# Watch for Cross-Cultural Differences

All communication in classrooms is difficult. It is particularly difficult during discussion because a particular set of rules exists for how to use language. As you read in Chapter 5 and this chapter, to be successful with classroom discussion, students must know when and how to communicate.

Students, however, differ in their understanding and use of classroom communication and participation structures. They also differ in their abilities to read subtle verbal and nonverbal clues about which rules are in effect at a particular time. Some

of these differences are cultural. For example, it has been reported that children from Micronesia and Polynesia as well as some African cultures often "chime in" during conversations, an act that may be perceived as interrupting by some teachers. Members of some cultures (some Native Americans, for example) often pause during a response, which is interpreted by some teachers as a sign they are done, when in fact they have more to say. Other communication differences stem from social class. Communication and participation structures in schools are similar to those of middle-class families. It is important for teachers when using discussion to be aware of their students' cultural and class backgrounds and to tailor lessons to meet particular needs. It is equally important to teach all students communication and participation patterns, such as not interrupting others, active listening, and taking turns, all of which are valued in the larger culture.

opportunities for teachers to model their own reasoning processes and to show students the way they tackle problems. It also communicates to students that the teacher sees himself or herself as part of a learning community interested in sharing ideas and discovering knowledge.

**End the Discussion.** As with other types of lessons, discussions need to be brought to proper closure. Effective teachers do this in a variety of ways. In some instances, they may choose to summarize in a few sentences what has been said and try to tie various ideas together or to relate them to the larger topic being studied. In other instances, teachers may want to close the discussion with a short presentation highlighting new or previously studied information. Some teachers ask students to summarize the discussion by posing a final question such as, "What is the main thing you got from our discussion today?" or, "What do you think was the most provocative point made during our discussion?"

## ✔ Check for Understanding

- What are the significant variables to consider when choosing a seating plan for discussion?
- What specific actions can teachers take to ensure effective discussions?
- What specific actions can teachers take to ensure broad participation in discussions?

**Debrief the Discussion.** From time to time discussions should be debriefed. Here, the focus is not on the content of the discussion but on the way the discussion proceeded. To conduct a successful **debriefing,** teachers must teach students the differences between the discussion itself and the debriefing and then pose questions such as: "How do you think our discussion went today? Did we give everyone a chance to participate? Did we listen to one another's ideas? Were there times when we seemed to get bogged down? Why? What can we all do next time to make our discussion more stimulating or provocative?"

## 🍎 *Managing the Learning Environment*

Many of the management tasks described in previous chapters also apply to discussion lessons. For example, pacing the lesson appropriately and dealing quickly and decisively with misbehavior are both essential teacher management behaviors when conducting a discussion. However, the most important management tasks are those aimed at improving discussion and discourse patterns in the classroom: teaching students specific discussion skills and establishing classroom norms that support productive discourse patterns. Several skills and norms are critical. In this section, skills and strategies to broaden participation, to promote interpersonal regard, and to heighten classroom thinking are described. Underlying the presentation is the premise that if discussion and discourse are to improve substantially, rather dramatic changes in the classroom discourse patterns must occur.

## Slow the Pace and Broaden Participation

An often heard statement of inexperienced teachers is, "I tried to hold a discussion, but no one said anything." It is not uncommon for discussions, even those led by experienced teachers, to follow a pattern in which the teacher's questions are all answered by less than a half dozen of the twenty-five to thirty students present. Remember the rapid discourse pattern described by Rowe earlier in this chapter? To broaden participation and get real discussions going requires substantial changes to this limited pattern of discourse. The pace must be slowed down and the norms about questioning and taking turns modified. Below are strategies that work and are used by experienced teachers.

**Think-Pair-Share.** The **think-pair-share** strategy was described in Chapter 10 as a cooperative learning structure that increased student participation. It is also an effective way to slow down the pace of a lesson and extend student thinking. This is true because it has built-in procedures for giving students more time to think and to respond and can affect the pattern of participation. For a description of the three-step think-pair-share strategy, return to Chapter 10.

**Buzz Groups.** The use of **buzz groups** is another effective means of increasing student participation. When using buzz groups, a teacher asks students to form into groups of three to six to discuss ideas they have about a particular topic or lesson. Each group assigns a member to list all the ideas generated by the group. After a few minutes, the teacher asks the recorders to summarize for the whole class the major ideas and opinions expressed in their group. Buzz groups, like think-pair-share, allow for more student participation with the learning materials and make it difficult for one or a few class members to dominate discussions. Using buzz groups can change the dynamics and basic patterns of classroom discourse and are easy for most teachers to use.

**Beach Ball.** A third technique, particularly effective with younger students, for broadening participation and promoting one person talking at a time is *beach ball*. The teacher gives the ball to one student to start the discussion with the understanding that only the person with the ball is permitted to talk. Other students raise their hands for the ball when they want a turn. Time tokens and high talker tap out, described in Chapter 10, are two other activities teachers can use to broaden classroom participation patterns.

## Increase Interpersonal Regard and Understanding

An open and honest communication process is perhaps the single most important variable for promoting positive classroom discourse and discussion. Fortunately, the way discourse occurs in classrooms can be greatly influenced by a teacher's leadership, particularly if he or she teaches skills that promote worthwhile **interpersonal communication** as well as a positive regard for it among students.

---

*Margin notes:*

Important management tasks faced by teachers involve the improvement of student discussion skills and controlling discourse patterns.

To broaden participation in discussions, the pace must be slowed down, and the norms for questioning and taking turns modified.

Since communication is essentially a process of sending and receiving messages, effective communication requires the sender of a message to express clearly what he or she intends to communicate and the receiver to interpret that message accurately. In reality, however, the message a person intends to send often is not the one the other person receives. The meaning intended in the sender's mind may not be accurately expressed or may be expressed in a manner that does not fit the receiver's prior experiences. Whenever either of these conditions occurs, a *communication gap* develops.

Following are four communication skills, described by Schmuck and Schmuck (1997), that people can use to make the process of sending and receiving messages more effective and thereby reduce the gap in communication. Two of these skills assist the sender; two assist the receiver.

**1. Paraphrase.** Paraphrasing is a skill for checking whether or not you understand the ideas being communicated to you. Any means of revealing your understanding of a message constitutes a paraphrase. Paraphrasing is more than word swapping or merely saying back what another person says. It answers the question "What exactly does the sender's statement mean to me?" and asks the sender to verify the correctness of the receiver's interpretation. The sender's statement may convey specific information, an example, or a more general idea, as shown in the following examples.

> *To improve communication, teachers can help students learn important communication skills.*

**Example 1**

Sender:   I'd sure like to own this book.

   You:   (*being more specific*) Does it have useful information in it?

Sender:   I don't know about that, but the binding is beautiful.

**Example 2**

Sender:   This book is too hard to use.

   You:   (*giving an example*) Do you mean, for example, that it fails to cite research?

Sender:   Yes, that's one example. It also lacks an adequate index.

**Example 3**

Sender:   Do you have a book on teaching?

   You:   (*being more general*) Do you just want information on that topic? I have several articles about it.

Sender:   No, I want to find out about cooperative learning.

**2. Describe Behavior.** In using a behavior description, one person reports specific observable behaviors of another person without evaluating them or making inferences about the other's motives. If you tell me that I am rude (a trait) or that I do not care about your opinion (my motivations) when I am not trying to be rude and do care about your opinion, I may not understand what you are trying to communicate. However, if you point out that I have interrupted you several times in the last ten minutes, I would receive a clearer picture of what actions of mine were affecting you. Sometimes it is helpful to preface a behavior description with "I noticed that . . ." or "I hear you say . . ." to remind yourself that you are trying to describe specific actions. Consider the following examples.

> "Jim, you've talked more than others on this topic."
> Instead of:
> "Jim, you always have to be the center of attention."
> Or:
> "Bob, I really felt good when you complimented me on my presentation before the class."

Instead of:
"Bob, you sure go out of your way to say nice things to people."

**3. Describe Feelings.** Although people often take pains to make sure that others understand their ideas, only rarely do they describe how they are feeling. Instead, they act on their feelings, sending messages that others draw inferences from. If you think that others are failing to take your feelings into account, it is helpful to put those feelings into words. Instead of blushing and saying nothing, try "I feel embarrassed" or "I feel pleased." Instead of "Shut up!", try "I hurt too much to hear any more" or "I'm angry with you."

**4. Check Impressions.** Checking impressions is a skill that complements describing your own feelings and involves checking your sense of what is going on inside the other person. You transform the other's expression of feelings (the blush, the silence, the tone of voice) into a tentative description of feelings and check it out for accuracy. An impression check describes what you think the other's feelings may be and does not express disapproval or approval. It merely conveys, "This is how I understand your feelings. Am I accurate?" Examples include the following.

> "I get the impression you are angry with me. Are you?"
> "Am I right that you feel disappointed that nobody commented on your suggestions?"

Often an impression check can be coupled easily with a behavior description, as in these examples.

> "Ellen, you've said nothing so far and seem upset with the class. Are you?"
> "Jim, you've made that proposal a couple of times. Are you feeling put down because we haven't accepted it?"

Teachers can learn and model these skills in their classrooms. They can also teach them directly to students, just as they teach many other skills. The direct instruction model described in Chapter 8 provides an appropriate strategy for teaching communication skills initially. A typical lesson is outlined in Figure 12.4.

*Developing the four communication skills suggested by Schmuck and Schmuck can assist the process of effectively sending and receiving messages.*

*Direct instruction can be used to teach specific communication skills.*

## Use Tools That Highlight Discourse and Thinking Skills

Frank Lyman and James McTighe have written extensively about the use of teaching tools, particularly visual ones, that help teachers and students learn discourse and thinking skills (Lyman, 1986; McTighe & Lyman, 1988; McTighe, 1998).

**Visual Cues for Think-Pair-Share.** The think-pair-share discussion strategy described previously (see Chapter 10) is not easy for students to use at first. Old habits, such as responding to teacher questions before thinking, or blurting out answers without waiting, are difficult to change. Lyman and teachers working with him have developed various ways of teaching students how to employ think-pair-share, particularly how and when to switch from one mode to another. A favorite strategy is to make and use **visual cueing** devices such as those illustrated in Figure 12.5.

**Thinking Matrix.** McTighe and Lyman (1988) also studied how to get students and their teachers to ask more questions that promote higher-level thinking and to analyze the nature of responses made to various types of questions. They created a device they call the **thinking matrix.** Lyman (1986) recommends that teachers create symbols that illustrate the various thinking processes described in Bloom's taxonomy and then

*Lyman and McTighe were particularly interested in the ways that visual tools and aids can be used by teachers.*

**Figure 12.4** *Typical Lesson Plan for Teaching Communication Skills*

**Step 1:** Introduce and explain the four communication skills, and define a topic for students to talk about.

**Step 2:** Have students get into groups of three for practice purposes. Each person in each trio is assigned a role—either sender, receiver, or observer. The sender begins a conversation and tries to describe his or her feelings or the receiver's behavior while discussing the topic. The receiver listens and either paraphrases or checks his or her impressions of the sender's feelings. The observer notes instances of communication skill use and instances where there are gaps in communication.

**Step 3:** Roles are exchanged so different people become senders, receivers, and observers.

**Step 4:** Finally, the teacher holds a class discussion about which skills are easy and which are difficult to learn and about how these skills can be applied in areas of classroom life as well as outside the classroom. During the discussion, the teacher should model use of the skills and encourage students to use them.

**Figure 12.5** *Cues for Using Think-Pair-Share*

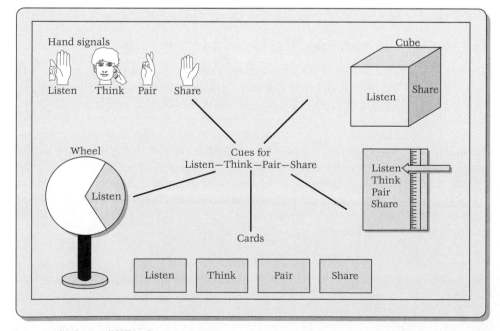

SOURCE: After Lyman (1985), p. 2.

**Figure 12.6**  *Teaching Thinking Skills with Question-Response Cues*

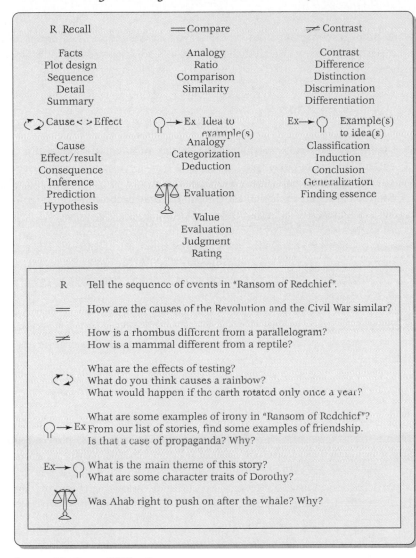

| R Recall | ═Compare | ⇄ Contrast |
|---|---|---|
| Facts | Analogy | Contrast |
| Plot design | Ratio | Difference |
| Sequence | Comparison | Distinction |
| Detail | Similarity | Discrimination |
| Summary | | Differentiation |

Cause ⟨ ⟩ Effect

| Cause | Idea to example(s) | Example(s) to idea(s) |
|---|---|---|
| Effect/result | Analogy | Classification |
| Consequence | Categorization | Induction |
| Inference | Deduction | Conclusion |
| Prediction | | Generalization |
| Hypothesis | Evaluation | Finding essence |

Value
Evaluation
Judgment
Rating

| R | Tell the sequence of events in "Ransom of Redchief". |
|---|---|
| ═ | How are the causes of the Revolution and the Civil War similar? |
| ⇄ | How is a rhombus different from a parallelogram? <br> How is a mammal different from a reptile? |
| ⟨⟩ | What are the effects of testing? <br> What do you think causes a rainbow? <br> What would happen if the earth rotated only once a year? |
| ○→Ex | What are some examples of irony in "Ransom of Redchief"? <br> From our list of stories, find some examples of friendship. <br> Is that a case of propaganda? Why? |
| Ex→○ | What is the main theme of this story? <br> What are some character traits of Dorothy? |
| ⚖ | Was Ahab right to push on after the whale? Why? |

SOURCE: After Lyman (1986), p. 3.

construct symbol cards that can be placed on the wall or held in the teacher's hand. During a discussion, teachers point to these symbols as they ask various types of questions. They also encourage students to categorize the questions they ask and the responses they give using the symbol cards. Figure 12.6 shows the symbol system developed by Lyman and teachers who work with him.

Teaching specific discourse skills is no different from teaching content-specific skills or social skills. As described in Chapter 8, the direct instruction model, which requires teachers to demonstrate and model the skill being taught and to provide time for students to practice the skill and receive feedback on how they are doing, is the best approach to use.

# 🍎 *Assessment and Evaluation*

As with the other teaching approaches, there are assessment and evaluation tasks for teachers to perform following a discussion. One is considering how a particular discussion should be followed up in subsequent lessons; the other is grading.

## Follow Up Discussions

Experienced teachers make both formal and mental notes for themselves following discussions. Sometimes these notes pertain to the content of the discussion and help determine subsequent lessons. For example, perhaps a discussion identifies some serious gaps in students' knowledge about a topic. Learning this might prompt a teacher to plan a presentation on a particular topic that came up in the discussion or to find suitable reading materials to assign students. A discussion can also identify aspects of a topic in which students are particularly interested. Teachers use the information they gain during discussions to plan lessons that will take advantage of this natural interest. The conduct of the discussion itself will give the teacher information about the strengths and weaknesses of students' thinking processes as well as the group's ability to engage in purposeful dialogue. Future lessons can then be planned to strengthen areas targeted for improvement.

Another aspect of following up a discussion is obtaining formal information from students about what they thought of the discussion and their role in it. The rating scale illustrated in Figure 12.7 can be an effective tool for gathering this type of assessment information.

## Grading Classroom Discussions

Grading classroom discussion can pose a perplexing problem for many teachers. On the one hand, if participation is not graded, students may view this part of their work as less important than work for which a grade is given. Remember the "work for grade exchange" concept described in Chapters 3 and 6? On the other hand, it is difficult to quantify participation in any satisfactory way. The questions teachers are confronted with when they try to grade discussions are: Do I reward quantity or quality? What

> Two ways to grade a discussion are to award bonus points for student participation and to have students do a reflective writing assignment based on the discussion.

**Figure 12.7** *Discussion Rating Scale*

**How Did You Feel About Today's Discussion?**

*Class's treatment of issues*
| superficial | 1 | 2 | 3 | 4 | 5 | thorough and deep |

*Helpfulness of discussion to your understanding*
| low | 1 | 2 | 3 | 4 | 5 | high |

*Your own level of engagement*
| low | 1 | 2 | 3 | 4 | 5 | high |

*The class's overall level of engagement*
| low | 1 | 2 | 3 | 4 | 5 | high |

*Quality of your own participation*
| poor | 1 | 2 | 3 | 4 | 5 | excellent |

SOURCE: After Wiggins (1993), p. 66.

constitutes a quality contribution? What about the student who talks all the time but says nothing? What about the student who is naturally shy but has good ideas?

There are two ways experienced teachers have confronted this grading dilemma. One is to give bonus points to students who consistently appear to be prepared for discussions and who make significant contributions. If this method is used, it needs to be discussed thoroughly with the class and opportunities provided that allow each student equal access to the bonus points available.

A second way to grade discussions is to use the discussion as a springboard for a reflective writing assignment. The grade in this instance is given not for participation but for the student's ability to reflect on the discussion and put in words what the discussion meant to him or her. When students know they are responsible for a postdiscussion reflective essay, this approach, when properly conceived and managed, can heighten student attention during the discussion and extend student thinking about the discussion after it is over. The obvious disadvantage of using this type of assignment is the time required to read and assign grades to the essays.

## 🍎 Classroom Discourse Patterns: A Final Thought

There is almost universal agreement among scholars and researchers that for real learning to occur, a different discourse pattern than the one currently found in most classrooms must be established. When asked about how they are going to teach, most beginning teachers will attest to the importance of providing opportunities for students to discuss important topics and to exchange ideas with each other and with the teacher.

Yet year after year, classroom observers say this is not happening. Teachers continue to dominate the talk that goes on in classrooms by presenting information and giving directions for students to follow. When they ask students questions, most of them are the kind that require direct recall rather than higher-level thinking, and if students don't answer immediately, another question is asked or another student called on. All this takes place at a very rapid pace. We know from research that teacher dominance of classroom discourse patterns and the rapid pace of this discourse are harmful. We also know that slowing down the pace of discourse and using different discourse patterns such as think-pair-share will produce more and better student thinking.

If this is true, why is it so difficult to change the discourse patterns in classrooms? Are there some underlying causes for this phenomenon? Do students really want to participate in discussions? Perhaps it is easier to sit and listen. Do teachers really want to have discussions? Perhaps it is easier just to talk. Will your generation of teachers accomplish the changes so many have talked about?

### ✓ Check for Understanding

- What are the key features of the learning environment for classroom discussions?

- What factors should be considered when thinking about how to assess student learning in classroom discussions?

**Although most teachers agree that classroom discussions are an important part of the learning process, actual discussion time is often quite limited.**

## 🍎 Summary

### Overview of Classroom Discussion

- Discourse and discussion are key ingredients for enhancing student thinking and uniting the cognitive and social aspects of learning.

- When experienced teachers refer to classroom discourse, they often use the label *discussion* to describe what they are doing. Classroom discussions are characterized by students and teachers talking about academic materials and by students willingly displaying their thinking processes publicly.

- Discourse can be thought of as externalization of thinking and has both cognitive and social importance.
- The primary instructional goals of a discussion lesson are to improve student thinking, to promote involvement and engagement in academic materials, and to learn important communication and thinking skills.
- The general flow or syntax for a discussion lesson consists of five major phases: provide objectives and set; focus the discussion; hold the discussion; end the discussion; and debrief the discussion.
- The structure of the learning environment for discussion lessons is characterized by open processes and active student roles.

### Theoretical and Empirical Support

- Studies for a good many years have described how discourse patterns in most classrooms do not afford effective dialogue among students or promote much discovery or higher-level thinking.
- A substantial knowledge base exists that informs teachers on how to create positive discourse systems and to hold productive discussions. Studies also provide guidelines about the types of questions to ask and how to provide appropriate pacing for students to think and to respond.
- Most classroom discourse proceeds at too rapid a pace. Teachers can obtain better classroom discourse by slowing down the pace and giving themselves and their students opportunities to think before they respond.

### Planning and Conducting Discussion Lessons

- An important planning task for a discussion lesson is deciding on which approach to use. There are several kinds of discussions. Major approaches include using discussion in conjunction with other teaching models; recitation discussions; discovery or inquiry discussions; and discussions to clarify values and share personal experiences.
- Other important planning tasks for teachers to consider include determining the purposes of the discussion; being aware of students' prior knowledge and discourse skills;

making plans for how to approach the discussion; and determining the type of questions to ask.

- Placing students in circles or using U-shape seating arrangements facilitates classroom discussions.
- Primary tasks for teachers as they conduct a discussion consist of focusing the discussion; keeping the discussion on track; keeping a record of the discussion; making sure students' ideas are listened to; and providing appropriate wait-time.
- Students' ideas should be responded to with dignity, and teachers should help students extend their ideas by seeking clarification, getting students to consider alternative ideas, and labeling thinking processes students are displaying.

### Managing the Learning Environment

- In general, discussion and classroom discourse patterns can be improved if teachers slow the pace and use methods to broaden participation and if they teach students to try to understand one another and have high interpersonal regard for each other's ideas and feelings.
- Teaching students four specific interpersonal communication skills (paraphrasing, behavior description, feeling description, and impression checking) can enhance the quality of classroom discourse and students' regard for each other.
- Specific visual tools such as the think-pair-share cueing device and the thinking matrix can help students learn discourse and thinking skills.
- For students to become effective in the discourse system and during specific discussions requires teaching student discourse skills just as directly as academic content and other academic skills are taught. The direct instruction model can be used to teach these important skills.

### Assessment and Evaluation

- Assessment and evaluation tasks appropriate for discussion consist of finding ways to follow up on discussions and to grade students for their contributions.
- Teachers use two ways to grade discussions: giving bonus points to students who consistently appear to be prepared and who make contributions, and grading reflective writing assignments based on the content of the discussion.

## 🍎 *Key Terms*

| | | |
|---|---|---|
| discussion | wait-time 1 | think-pair-share |
| discourse | wait-time 2 | buzz groups |
| recitations | U-shape seating pattern | interpersonal communication skills |
| level of difficulty | circle seating pattern | visual cues |
| wait-time | debriefing | thinking matrix |

## 🍎 Books for the Professional

Adger, C. T. (1995). *Engaging Students: Thinking, Talking, Cooperating.* Thousand Oaks, Calif.: Corwin Press. This book is filled with practical ideas for getting students to think and talk.

Hill, W. F. (1994). *Learning Through Discussion.* (3rd ed.). Thousand Oaks, Calif.: Sage. This book, recently revised, is one of the classics on how to use discussion in groups.

Resnick, L. B., and Kloper, L. E. (eds.). (1989). *Toward the Thinking Curriculum: Current Cognitive Research.* Alexandria, Va.: Association for Supervision and Curriculum Development. The yearbook of ASCD provides an excellent review of the research in the cognitive sciences that has implications for curriculum development in the various subject areas and for teaching students how to think.

Wilen, W. W. (ed.) (1990). *Teaching and Learning Through Discussion: The Theory and Practice of Discussion Method.* Springfield, Ill.: Charles C. Thomas. This is a very thorough book of readings covering all aspects of the discussion method.

## Reflection & Portfolio

For the third day in a row, you have begun your ninth grade science class by tossing out a provocative and challenging question. It has been your hope that you would be able to get a lively discussion going. Instead, you are met with deadly silence. Two or three students try to respond, but the others just sit there staring at you or looking down at their desks. You are embarrassed by the silence, but, more important, you are frustrated because your favorite classes as a student were those in which you could participate in lively debate. You believe strongly that effective teachers are those who have lively discussions in their classrooms.

You ponder this situation and ask yourself, "What's wrong? Perhaps my students are just a bunch of kids who don't care about science and care even less about talking about it. Perhaps everyone in my class is shy. Or perhaps I am doing something wrong."

Spend a few minutes reflecting on this situation and then compare your thoughts with the experiences of the teachers below. Also write up your reflections and include them as an exhibit in your professional portfolio.

### Rachael Aronson

"Every teacher has been faced with silence and blank faces in the process of trying to get students to participate in a discussion. The key to getting students to talk is to choose discussion topics that arouse their curiosity and relate to their daily lives. This doesn't mean choosing topics that are naturally interesting to youth culture, such as their favorite music or weekend sports events. Instead, it means taking the subject matter that is being studied and finding the aspect or theme that can be applied to everyday life. For example, if students are studying a unit on ecology in science, good topics for discussion are those that connect to what is going on today, such as 'How can we protect rivers and bays while still using them for commerce?' Or perhaps a question that focuses on evaluating some public policy, such as 'Should the flood control dams on the Columbia River be removed so salmon have an easier time getting to their spawning ground?' Sometimes I find the best discussions stem from questions for which there are no easy solutions and that call for speculation by students. For example, 'What do you suppose would happen if all the dams were removed from the Columbia River?'"

### Josh Zaird

"The trick for having a good discussion rests on two factors: creating a supporting classroom environment in which students feel comfortable with one another and teaching students to be good participants. I have found that helping students know other students in the class is an important first step toward full participation. I use the fishbowl technique to teach discussion skills. I have students get in two circles—an inner circle with five or six students and an outer circle with the remainder of the class. I sit in the inner circle, provide students in the inner circle with a discussion topic, and tell them they must discuss the topic for five minutes without my help. I tell the students in the outer circle that their job is to listen and to take notes on how the discussion is going. After the five minutes, I get students in both the inner and outer circles to report what they saw as the strengths and weaknesses of the discussion and to discuss what might be done to make the next discussion better. I continue this process every few days, rotating the students in the inner circle until all have had a chance to be discussants and all have been observers. This works with young children as well as adults. After four or five fishbowl sessions, everyone has sufficient discussion experience and skills to proceed with whole-class discussion on almost any topic."

# Part 3 ● *The Organizational Aspects of Teaching*

**P**art Three of *Learning to Teach* is devoted to the organizational aspects of teaching. Teachers, like other professionals, are expected not only to perform their primary responsibilities (in this case, providing instruction to students) but also to provide leadership to the organization as a whole. For teachers, this means working alongside others in the school—colleagues, administrators, parents, and students—to help set schoolwide expectations and gain clarity of purposes and actions.

The chapter that follows focuses on three specific aspects of schools: understanding schools as social organizations, providing leadership and working collaboratively with members of the school community, and helping schools improve. To perform these functions effectively, teachers must understand the nature of the school not only as a place where children come to learn but also as a place where adults work. Teachers also need specific organizational skills aimed at making work with others in the school productive.

As you read about and study these topics, you will discover two reasons they are so important. One, there appears to be a certain synergy at work in schools in which teachers and others have come together and made agreements about what is going to be taught, and this synergy makes a difference in how much students learn. Two, your ability to provide leadership and to relate to and work with others within the school and larger professional community will have a significant impact on your career. It is in this arena that you will become known to others and will build your professional reputation. Teachers who grow and progress in their careers are those who can enter into professional and schoolwide dialogue about educational issues.

# Chapter ☙ Thirteen

# School Leadership and Collaboration

## *Reflecting on* Schools as Places Where Adults Work

Before you read this chapter, consider the following situations, which are based on studies about what teachers do and how they spend their time.

**Neil** is a new third grade teacher at Holbrook Elementary School. He usually arrives at school about 7:30 A.M. This particular morning, Neil opens his room, then joins other third and fourth grade teachers who are planning a field trip to the local airport for their students to discuss how each of them is going to integrate this experience into their social studies curriculum. Back in his room in time to start class at 8:35 A.M., Neil spends the rest of the morning with his third graders. He is joined at several points by other adults. The principal drops in for a few minutes to observe and see if Neil needs any help. Two mothers join the class at 9:30 A.M. to assist Neil with his reading groups, and they stay through morning recess. The school's reading specialist comes by and tests a student who Neil thinks is having a severe word recognition problem. The special education resource teacher joins Neil's classroom to work for thirty minutes with two learning disabled students mainstreamed in Neil's room.

Over lunch, Neil talks with two second grade teachers about students of his who were in their classrooms last year. Neil stops at the library on his way back to his classroom to pick up a film he plans to show as part of his social studies unit and to remind the librarian that he will be bringing a small group of students to the library next Tuesday.

School lets out at 2:45 P.M.; Neil drops by the reading specialist's office to discuss the results of her testing before heading to the central office to participate on a science textbook selection committee. Neil was appointed to this committee by his principal because the principal knew that he had a very strong background in science and had worked at the Marine Biology Research Center for the past two summers.

**Helena** teaches tenth grade English at Cordoza High School. She, too, arrives at school about 7:30 A.M., and she meets with another new teacher to have a cup of coffee and discuss an exchange of teaching materials. Helen teaches three classes of sophomore English in the morning. Just before lunch, she is visited by her department chairperson, who is conducting one of his required formal observations of new teachers.

During her afternoon planning period, Helen and the department chair meet, and he gives her feedback on her lesson, pointing out that her lecture was brilliant but that her students took a long time getting to work in the small-group exercise she had planned.

After school, Helena meets for a few minutes with members of the school's debate team for whom she serves as advisor. On this day, Helena leaves her work with the debate team early because she wants to participate in the discussion on student advising planned for this week's faculty meeting. After the faculty meeting, Helena dashes home to have a quick dinner. The school's open house is this evening, and Helena has scheduled meetings with several parents to discuss their children's work.

Analyzing these typical days in the lives of two beginning teachers illustrates that they do many things in addition to interacting with students in classrooms. They meet with students about nonacademic tasks; they meet with fellow teachers and specialists within the school; they go to meetings; they work with parents; and they attend to their own learning. What do you think of these aspects of a teacher's work? How do you see yourself relating to the rapid pace and schedule of teaching? How do you see yourself relating to the noninstructional aspects of teaching? Working with fellow teachers? With parents? In the community?

*Schools are not only places where students learn; they are also places where teachers work.*

Previous chapters described what teachers do as they plan for and deliver instruction and manage complex classroom settings. Providing leadership and teaching students in classrooms, however, are not the only aspects of a teacher's job. Teachers are also members of an organization called *school* and as such are asked to perform important leadership functions at the school level, including working cooperatively with colleagues, serving on committees, and working with administrators and parents. The way these aspects of a teacher's job are performed makes a significant difference in the school's professional community and how students behave and what they learn. The way teachers carry out these functions also makes a significant difference in their own professional careers.

**Teachers are members of an organization called *school*, a place where many diverse organizational functions are performed.**

This chapter describes the work environment of schools and the corresponding culture of teaching. Emphasis is placed on the idea that schools are not only places where students come to learn; they are also places where adults work. After providing a conceptual framework for viewing schools as workplaces, we summarize the emerging knowledge base on the nature of teachers' work behavior and what makes some schools more effective than others. We conclude with a discussion of several important skills that beginning teachers need as they become fully involved in their first school and community.

## 🍎 *Perspective of Schools as Workplaces*

At this point in your career, it is likely that your view of schools stems mainly from many years of being a learner in classrooms. You are familiar with the classroom portion of the teacher's role, with the role of student, and with the way that students and teachers interact around academic tasks. However, you may not have had much chance to observe or reflect on schools as social organizations or on the nonclassroom aspects of a teacher's job. In fact, many people (including those in the media) rarely view schools from the perspective of the complex social organizations they are. This is unfortunate, because views of schools, stemming only from experiences as students, have caused misunderstanding on the part of many—teachers, parents, and policymakers—regarding school improvement efforts. Also, unrealistic views have led to many beginning teachers' disillusionment. The section that follows provides a view of schools that extends beyond the classroom doors.

## Schools Are Human Systems

In discussing schools, we take a perspective that schools are human systems that are influenced not only by the people who learn and work in them but also by the larger community and society. Schools are places where individuals do not act in totally free and disconnected ways but, instead, in more or less interdependent and predictable ways. Although individuals come together in schools to promote purposeful learning, each person does not chart his or her own course alone, nor do the actions of each have consequences only for that person. Also, as we describe later, the synergy developed by teachers acting in concert can have important consequences for student learning. To understand the human systems view of schools, think for a moment about the number of interdependent actions required to bring about a day's worth of instruction for students:

- Paper, pencils, and chalk have been ordered.
- Rooms have been cleaned.
- Curriculum guides have been prepared and textbooks ordered.
- Parents have chosen to send their children to school.
- Teachers have chosen to be professionally trained.
- Buses have been driven and breakfasts and lunches prepared.
- Schedules have been determined and children assigned to classes.
- Health services for students have been planned and managed.

This list could go on and on. The point, however, is that the contemporary school is a complex human system requiring its members to perform important functions in interdependent ways.

## Schools Have Histories and Cultures

**School culture consists of the ways members think about their actions and it reflects their beliefs, values, and history.**

Schools, like other organizations, have histories and cultures consisting of values, beliefs, and expectations that have developed and grown over time. The history of a school provides traditions and a multitude of routines—some good and some not so good—that are taken for granted by organizational members. The *culture of a school* provides the organizational arrangements that hold it together and give it power as a social entity. Lortie (1975) referred to culture as the "way members of a group think about social action; culture encompasses alternatives for resolving problems in collective life" (p. 216). Others have provided similar definitions, although they sometimes use different labels. Rutter and his colleagues (1979), for example, refer to the common values, beliefs, and ways of doing things as the school's **ethos;** Glass (1981) has called it *tone;* Joyce and his colleagues (1993) and Sergiovanni (1996) prefer the word *community.* Regardless of how it is labeled, **school culture** greatly influences what goes on in schools and determines expectations and roles for beginning teachers.

## Schools Have Features in Common with Other Organizations

In some ways, schools are similar to other organizations in society. For example, as in other organizations, members are directed toward the accomplishment of some goal. In a textile plant, the goal may be the production of men's shirts; IBM says information is its business. The overriding goals for schools are to provide *purposeful learning expe-*

*riences* and develop self-regulated learners. Members of schools—principals, teachers, and students—are rewarded, as are members in other organizations, when they strive for and accomplish common organizational goals. Similarly, they are punished when they fail. An example of a reward is experiments in some states in which teaching faculties are given merit increases if, as a group, they can lift achievement in their school above a set criterion. An example of punishment is instances in which teachers are dismissed if they cannot provide purposeful learning activities for their students.

Another organizational feature of schools similar to that found in other organizations is that coordination of effort is required. In addition to teachers, school staffs include curriculum coordinators, administrators, nurses, counselors, janitors, and other support personnel. Most of the people in schools, however, are students, and they too must be considered organizational members. Because school roles are specialized, routines and structures are created to help members carry out their special tasks in ways that will more or less facilitate what others are doing. The reason coordination of effort is not easy to accomplish in schools is described later.

> **The primary goal of schools is to provide a purposeful learning environment that leads to the development of self-regulated learners.**

## Schools Have Unique Features

Just as schools have features in common with other organizations, they also have features that are unique. It is the special features of schools that are most important for us to understand.

**Ambiguous and Conflicting Goals.** It has been stated several times in this book that the overriding goals of schools are to facilitate purposive learning for students and to develop self-regulated learners. Stated at this level of abstraction, most people would readily agree with these goals. However, when people in schools speak more precisely about what purposive learning means, many of their statements may seem ambiguous and may conflict with the aims of one group or another in the community.

Goal ambiguity can be illustrated with reference to citizenship education. Most people in Western societies believe that the schools should socialize students as good citizens who accept the values of democratic political systems and who embrace some degree of freedom in their own economic activities. However, how do school people, parents, and others know whether or not this goal is being accomplished? Parents, for example, are never sure their sons or daughters are embracing the values parents desire for them. Teachers seldom know how their former students behave as adult citizens. Do they vote, and are they participating community members?

> **Goal ambiguity and conflict are more prevalent in schools than in other organizations.**

As for goal conflict, do citizenship goals compete with academic learning goals? Which are most important, and how should time be allocated between the two? What constitutes good citizenship? Some argue that the most important aspect of citizenship education is the socialization of students into traditional values and beliefs. Some church-related and private schools are inclined toward this position. On the other hand, others argue that this approach to citizenship education is simply indoctrination and leads to narrowness and conformity. The good citizen, from this point of view, might be the critical thinker who questions existing values and structures and attempts to modify them.

**Compulsory Attendance.** A second special feature of schools is that their clients (the students) are compelled to be there. All states have compulsory attendance laws that require parents to send their children to school, normally until age 16. Although most people support these laws because they guarantee a minimum education for

**The fact that students are compelled to attend school makes for a unique type of client relationship not found in most other organizations.**

all children and help prevent forced child labor, they do create the problem of keeping unmotivated students involved in school life. Schools with large numbers of academically unmotivated students are often schools where teachers choose not to work. Recent innovations in some school systems, such as the creation of alternative and magnet schools, attempt to combat the compulsory nature of schooling by giving students and their parents more choices in the type of school the students attend. The fact still remains, however: students *must* go to school.

**Political Visibility.** Schools are highly visible and political in most communities. Many people take an active interest in their schools, and given local control, schools offer one of the few places where people in complex societies can have their voices heard. For example, it is quite easy in many communities to stay informed about school events since large portions of the daily newspapers are devoted to school news, including the school's budget. It is also easy to attend local school board or council meetings and voice opinions, just as it is easy to walk directly into most principals' offices without an appointment. The whole system is open and permeable. Some aspects of this situation are positive. Local control and the openness of the educational system have helped maintain strong support for education over the past century. At the same time, this situation leaves the school and those who work there vulnerable to political whims and sometimes unfair attacks.

**Schools Are Communities.** According to some observers, schools also differ from other organizations in that they are more like communities than modern bureaucracies (Bryk & Driscoll, 1988; Sergiovanni, 1996). Rather than being organizations governed by hierarchical control structures and formal systems of supervision, Sergiovanni argues, schools are communities built on shared purposes and mutual respect.

**In some ways, schools are more like communities than they are like modern organizations.**

> Communities are collections of individuals who are bonded together by natural will and who are together bound to a set of shared ideas and ideals. This bonding and binding is tight enough to transform them from a collection of "I's" into a collective we. As a "we," members are part of a tightly knit web of meaningful relationships. (p. 48)

Notice some of the words used by Sergiovanni: *bonded individuals, shared ideas,* and *collective we.*

Sergiovanni argues that over the past hundred years, modern organizations in business, the military, and the health fields have been constructed around formal and con-

*Schools offer one of the few places in our complex society where citizens can easily voice their opinions and views.*

tractual arrangements rather than conditions of shared values found in earlier times. Schools, he says, have mistakenly adopted these formal and contractual arrangements, and though these arrangements may make sense for businesses and hospitals, they do not work well for schools. Instead, they are the source of many of the problems found in today's school. Sergiovanni believes that schools are closer in character to the family, the neighborhood, and voluntary social groups—all organizations that have a special sense of shared values, belonging, and community.

The community metaphor for understanding schools is interesting and potentially powerful. And, as you will see later in this chapter, some research shows that schools where teachers share a common vision and shared values and have created a collaborative professional community characterized by a dialogue and sense of belonging produce higher student learning than schools in which relationships are more formal and contractual.

## Norms, Roles, and the Culture of Teaching

Another way to think about schools is to think about the norms, roles, and organizational arrangements that exist for the purpose of getting work accomplished. These will have strong influences on the experiences that beginning teachers have during both internships and their first year.

**Norms.** **Norms** are the expectations that people have for one another in particular social settings. They define the range of social behaviors that are allowed in given situations. Some norms are informal, such as the norm that prescribes a swimsuit rather than a cocktail dress on the beach. Some norms, however, are formal. For example, a person might not be arrested if he wore a tuxedo to the beach, but he would be if he broke a local ordinance that restricts bathing in the nude.

In schools, many formal and informal norms exist that affect teachers and students. For example, in some schools, new teachers will find norms supporting friendliness and openness that will make them feel welcome. In other schools, people may act toward one another in more reserved and formal ways. In some schools, norms to encourage experimentation may make beginning teachers feel comfortable in trying out new ideas, whereas in other schools, few risks will be encouraged. Two important norms associated with schools and the culture of teaching need highlighting, because they affect the lives of beginning teachers most directly.

> **Norms are the expectations that people have for one another in specific social settings.**

*Autonomy Norm.* In some ways, teachers have relatively little power and influence in the larger school system. However, they do have a great deal of influence in their own classrooms, supported by what has been labeled the **autonomy norm.** Teachers, including beginning teachers, do pretty much what they want to once they are in their classrooms and their doors are closed. In many schools, they alone are responsible for the day-to-day curricula and make almost all instructional decisions for themselves.

> **The expectation that educators are virtually free to teach as they please within the confines of their classrooms is known as the autonomy norm.**

*The Hands-Off Norm.* Closely paralleling the autonomy norm is a norm labeled by Lortie (1975), Sarason (1982), and Joyce, Hersh, and McKibbin (1993) as the **hands-off norm.** Not only are teachers given autonomy in their classrooms, but strong sanctions exist against interfering with other teachers in any but the most superficial ways. It is not appropriate, according to Lortie (1975), for teachers to ask for help, for example. Such a request suggests that the teacher is failing. Similarly, according to Feiman-Nemser and Floden (1986) and Little (1990), it is not permissible for teachers to tell a peer what to do or to suggest that he or she teach something differently.

> **The hands-off norm is the expectation in schools that teachers will not interfere in the work of other teachers.**

This is not to suggest to beginning teachers that colleagues within a particular school will be unfriendly or unsupportive. Teachers socialize a great deal with one another and on an emotional level are concerned and supportive of one another. Even so, teachers often avoid talking about instructional practices. It is important to point out that many contemporary school reform projects aim at breaking down the autonomy and hands-off norms by encouraging and helping teachers work together. We return to this idea later in the chapter.

**Roles.** Organizations and organizational culture also describe a teacher's role. The teacher's role, for example, includes norms about how teachers should behave toward students and students toward them, how teachers should interact with each other and with the principal, and how much teachers should participate in schoolwide problem solving and decision making. People in schools learn roles through interacting with each other.

**Contradictions in aspects of the teacher's role often cause anxiety for beginning teachers.**

Some aspects of the teacher's role are clear and straightforward. For example, it is clear that teachers should teach academic content to students and evaluate their students' progress. Some aspects of the teacher's role, however, are not so clear and sometimes provide contradictory expectations. Contradictions in role expectations cause anxiety and trouble for beginning teachers as they enter the school for the first time.

One of the most basic contradictions in the teacher's role stems from strong expectations that teachers should treat each child as an individual even though schools are organized so that teachers must deal with students in groups. This conflict is particularly acute with secondary teachers, who face as many as 150 to 180 students a day for rather brief periods of time. This role conflict, according to Lieberman and Miller (1992) and Little and McLaughlin (1993), is what makes teaching so personal, because to deal with the contradictory demands of individualization and group instruction requires the development of a teaching style that is "individual and personal."

A second basic contradiction in the teacher's role involves the degree of distance between teacher and students. On one hand, teachers are expected to maintain a certain social distance from students so authority and discipline can be maintained. In fact, as described in Chapters 3 and 5, control is often an overriding concern for beginning teachers, since they know they are being heavily judged on this score. On the other hand, most teachers know that they must form some type of bond with students in order to motivate them and help them to learn. Beginning teachers manifest the tensions of this role contradiction in a number of ways. They worry about whether or not they should allow students to call them by their first name or how friendly they should become with a particular student they really like and so on. Such tensions are quite normal, and only experience, it seems, provides the means for dealing with the many contradictions built into the teacher's role.

**School organizations are called cellular because teachers are independently responsible for organizing leadership and teaching functions within the "cells" of their own classrooms.**

**Cellular Organizational Structure.** Compared to most other organizations, schools are rather flat organizations. In elementary schools, there are mainly teachers and a principal, and in most secondary schools, one additional role, the department chair, is added. Some (Lortie, 1975; Joyce et al., 1993) have called this arrangement "cellular," that is, each classroom can be regarded as a cell within which the teacher is responsible for organizing the students, managing discipline, and teaching academic content. This arrangement, coupled with the hands-off norm, often creates an isolated work situation for teachers. They make independent decisions about when and how to teach each subject, and they do not ask other teachers for help. Joyce and his colleagues (1993) observed that this situation has made it customary for principals to relate to the teachers

Cellular Structure

one-to-one rather than as an organized faculty prepared to take collective responsibility. This professional isolation has led some observers to refer to teaching as a "lonely profession." With the addition of many new roles in schools over the past few years, such as special teachers and lead teachers of one kind or another, and new approaches for organizing curricula, it may be that the *cellular structure* of schools is changing. Currently, it remains the most common arrangement.

**Loosely Coupled Structure.** The school's cellular structure also causes an organizational arrangement that has been labeled **loosely coupled** (Weick, 1976; Bohman & Deal, 1991). This means that what goes on in classrooms is not very tightly connected to what goes on in other parts of the school. Teachers can and do carry out their own instructional activities independent of administrators and others. The central office may initiate new curricula or new teaching procedures, but if teachers choose to ignore these initiatives, they can. On the positive side, loose coupling allows considerable room for individual teacher decision making in situations where a substantial knowledge about "best" teaching practice is lacking. Conversely, loose coupling can stymie efforts to establish common goals and coordinated activities, something that is important for effective schooling, as you will see later.

Loosely Coupled

# 🍎 *Theoretical and Empirical Support*

Educators have for many years thought about the school as a formal organization. In fact, a very important book written by Waller in 1932 on the sociology of teaching provided many important insights into the nature of schools and of teaching. However, it is only in the last three decades that educators and educational researchers have started to highlight the importance of schools as workplaces and the importance of the organizational aspects of teaching. This section provides examples from fairly recent research about the nature of the work teachers do in schools and how one way this work is done can affect what students learn.

## Nature of Teachers' Work

Some people think that teachers' hours match those of the children they teach. Others think that teachers' work consists mainly of working with students. Experienced teachers do not agree with these perceptions. They know that teachers do many other things in addition to directly working with students. They also know that the time demands of teaching are quite great. Over the years, studies have supported this view.

Since 1961, the National Education Association (NEA) has surveyed teachers every five years and asked them to report the number of hours per week they spend on various teaching responsibilities. For more than thirty years, the findings of these reports have remained pretty consistent. Elementary teachers report that they work between

**✓ Check for Understanding**

- What is meant by saying that the school is a social system?

- How do culture, history, and ethos define many important functions and characteristics of a school?

- What features of schools make them different from other formal organizations?

- What norms tend to exist in schools that beginning teachers should anticipate?

- What aspects of a teacher's role are clear, and which tend to be more complex and contradictory?

- Why has teaching been called a "lonely profession"?

**Table 13.1** *Number of Hours per Week Spent on School-Related Responsibilities*

| | Total | Years of Teaching Experience | | Type of School | | | Size of Place | | |
| | | Less Than 10 | 10 or More | Elementary | Junior High | High School | Urban | Surburban | Rural |
| --- | --- | --- | --- | --- | --- | --- | --- | --- | --- |
| | | | | Percentage | | | | | |
| Fewer than 40 | 9 | 8 | 12 | 12 | 8 | 9 | 10 | 10 | 8 |
| 41 to 45 | 12 | 10 | 12 | 11 | 15 | 9 | 17 | 10 | 11 |
| 46 to 50 | 30 | 30 | 30 | 31 | 28 | 29 | 30 | 28 | 32 |
| 51 to 55 | 14 | 15 | 13 | 16 | 9 | 14 | 13 | 15 | 11 |
| More than 55 | 35 | 38 | 34 | 30 | 40 | 39 | 29 | 37 | 38 |
| Median | 50 | 54 | 50 | 51 | 51 | 55 | 50 | 55 | 51 |

Source: After Metropolitan Life (1995), p. 67.

*Teachers must be capable of juggling many different expected and unexpected activities within a typical workday.*

forty-five and forty-nine hours per week, whereas secondary teachers say that they work from forty-six to fifty hours per week (NEA, 1996; Metropolitan Life, 1995). A recent survey confirmed that the majority of teachers today spend at least forty-six hours in an average week on school-related responsibilities and over a third spend more than fifty-five hours per week (Metropolitan Life, 1995). Table 13.1 shows the number of hours per week teachers spend on school-related activities.

To validate these findings and to guard against inflated self-reporting, researchers have shadowed teachers to find out precisely what kind of work they do and for how long. In one particularly interesting study, Cypher and Willower (1984) shadowed five secondary teachers. They found that teachers averaged a 48.5-hour working week, spending approximately 38 hours in school and 10.5 hours in after-school work. The findings of Cypher and Willower's study combined with data from the Metropolitan Life (1995) survey are displayed in Table 13.2. Among other things, data in Table 13.2 show that most teachers spend less than 40 percent of their work week on instructional activity and that a sizable portion of their work consists of meetings and exchanges with other adults such as parents, the principal, and professional colleagues.

## Research on School Effectiveness

*School effectiveness research tries to uncover features that make some schools more effective than others.*

There is a growing belief that the overall culture and ethos of a school and what teachers do in concert contribute to what students learn as much as the performance of individual teachers does. During the past two decades, researchers have begun to supply empirical evidence in support of this perspective. Sometimes this research is called **school effectiveness research;** other times it is referred to as *organizational context research.*

Regardless of the specific label applied to it, this research has demonstrated pretty consistently that school culture and community, and the collective behavior of teachers, administrators, and parents can make an important difference in how much students learn. It points toward the importance of participants coming together and making schoolwide agreements about what should be taught, how it should be taught, and how people should relate to one another. It seems that there is a certain **synergy** work-

*Teachers work with students in extracurricular activities.*

**Table 13.2** *How Teachers Spend Their Time*

| Activity | Total Time in Minutes | Percentage of Time |
|---|---|---|
| Instruction | | |
|   Direct instruction | 95.4 | 20.6 |
|   Organizing | 15.9 | 3.4 |
|   Reviewing | 21.0 | 4.5 |
|   Testing | 22.9 | 5.0 |
|   Monitoring | 23.6 | 5.1 |
| Other work with students | | |
|   Study hall supervision | 17.4 | 3.8 |
|   Assemblies and clubs | 5.9 | 1.3 |
|   Control and supervision | 12.7 | 2.7 |
| Interaction with colleagues and others | | |
|   Planned meetings | 2.7 | 1.0 |
|   Unscheduled meetings | 46.5 | 10.0 |
|   Exchanges | 67.5 | 14.6 |
| Desk and routine work | 89.8 | 20.0 |
| Travel time | 24.6 | 5.3 |
| Private time | 16.2 | 3.5 |

Source: After Metropolitan Life (1995); Cypher and Willower (1984).

ing in schools that produces results that cannot be achieved when a teacher works alone on particularistic goals.

Additionally, this research emphasizes the people aspect of schooling. The quality of teaching and the professional community that exists within the school have been found to be more important than the amount of money spent on concrete, books, or paper. That does not mean that resources are not required for good schools; it just means that the amount of money spent on the school's library collection or the physical plant takes a backseat to the community that people within the school create.

Several groundbreaking studies in the late 1970s provided the first evidence on the importance of organizational features and processes. One study was done by an

**Synergy is at work in the school, which produces results that exceed what a teacher working alone could achieve.**

English child psychiatrist and his colleagues who studied twelve secondary schools in London (Rutter et al., 1979). Over a number of years, Rutter and his colleagues collected information about student behavior and achievement in and organization processes of a sample of high schools. The researchers found that student behavior and achievement varied markedly from school to school but that students were more likely to show good behavior and higher achievement in some schools than others. Better behavior and higher achievement were strongly related to aspects of the school's social organization, such as the degree to which a common ethos existed, the extent to which teachers held common attitudes, and the degree to which they behaved in consistent ways toward their students.

> **Behavior and achievement are strongly related to aspects of a school's social organization.**

Since Rutter's study, many other researchers have conducted similar studies with elementary and secondary schools in the United States (Brookover et al., 1979; Firestone and Rosenblum, 1988; Rosenholz, 1989). Almost all of these studies have produced similar results and conclusions, namely, that some schools develop cultures and communities that support student learning whereas other schools do not. The study by Valerie Lee and Julia Smith highlighted in the Research Summary for this chapter is an excellent example of a very recent study that illustrates the gains that can be achieved when teachers take collective responsibility for their students' learning.

## Features of Effective Schools

> **Effective school features are divided into two categories: those that deal with the social organization and those that deal with instructional and curriculum patterns.**

Several researchers have summarized the research on effective schools and the effects of school processes on student learning. One of the best summaries has been provided by Joyce, Hersh, and McKibbin (1993). Their review is summarized here and then used later as an organizer for considering the organizational skills required of teachers.

Joyce and his colleagues found that features of schools that were effective can be divided into two categories: those having to do with a school's *social organization* and those having to do with the school's *instructional* and *curriculum patterns*. These features are listed in Table 13.3 and described in more detail here.

Social Organization. Definitions of the social organizational attributes are listed here.

**Clear academic and social behavior goals.** Academic achievement is constantly emphasized, and teachers, parents, and students share common values and understandings about the school's achievement goals.

**Table 13.3** *Features of Effective Schools*

| Social Organization | Instruction and Curriculum |
|---|---|
| Clear academic and social behavior goals | High academic learning time |
| Order and discipline | Frequent and monitored homework |
| High expectations | Frequent monitoring of student progress |
| Teacher efficacy | Coherently organized curriculum |
| Pervasive caring | Variety of teaching strategies |
| Public rewards and incentives | Opportunities for student responsibility |
| Administrative leadership | |
| Community support | |

Source: After Joyce, Hersh, and McKibbin (1993).

*Research Summary 13.1*

# Working Together Makes a Difference

*Lee, V. E., and Smith, J. B. (1996).* Collective responsibility for learning and its effects on gains in achievement of early secondary school students. *American Journal of Education*, 104, 103–146.

The media often portray effective teachers through characters such as Jaime Escalante, of *Stand and Deliver* fame, who against great odds taught his East Los Angeles low-academic students advanced calculus. Or David Holland of *Mr. Holland's Opus*, who over a lifetime defended music education in his school and inspired his students through his singular devotion to their education and to their personal lives. It is true that individually inspiring teachers are effective, and we all remember them. At the same time, the collective, rather than individual, responsibility of teachers seems also to be crucial and provided the focus for a study by Valerie Lee and Julia Smith.

**Problem and Approach:** Lee and Smith began with the premise that the education of students revolves around the work done by teachers and that this work is pivotal in helping schools accomplish their main goal, student learning. But what does teachers' work consist of, and how is it organized? Specifically, what are the links between teachers' work lives and how much their students learn? These were questions that Lee and Smith set out to investigate using information from a large-scale study. The Lee and Smith study is important and was selected for inclusion here for two reasons. One, the results speak directly to the importance of the organizational aspects of teaching, and two, the study is a good illustration of how some research in education is conducted using already existing databases that are made available to the research community by governmental agencies.

**Sample and Setting:** The researchers used data from a nationally representative sample of 11,692 high school sophomores and 9,904 of their teachers. The sample was drawn from 820 schools and was part of the National Educational Longitudinal Study sponsored by the National Center for Education Statistics (NELS, 1988). This study surveyed over 22,000 students in 1988 when they were in the eighth grade and then again when they were sophomores in high school in 1990. Students in the sample were surveyed and tested, as were their teachers. Of the teachers who were studied, 31 percent taught mathematics, 32 percent English, 15 percent social studies, and 22 percent science. On average, the study contained data from about 12 teachers within each of the 820 schools.

**Procedures:** The researchers measured learning gains made by students between the eighth and tenth grades in four subjects: mathematics, reading, history, and science. In addition, they measured three features of teachers' work.

1. *Collective responsibility for student learning.* This feature measured how much teachers in schools believed individually and collectively that they were responsible for student learning and did not attribute learning difficulties to weak students or deficient home lives.
2. *Degree of staff cooperation.* This feature measured how well teachers and administrators got along, the supportiveness of the principal, and the degree to which teachers cooperated and had clarity about the schoolwide mission and goals.
3. *Amount of teacher control.* This feature measured teachers' perceptions about how much influence and control they had over conditions in their classrooms (e.g., curriculum and homework) and over policies affecting the whole school (e.g., discipline policy and ways students were grouped).

**Results:** There were many results of this large and complex study. For our purposes here, only a few findings will be highlighted. The first and most important finding of the study was that the achievement gains made by students were significantly higher in schools where teachers took collective responsibility for their students' academic successes and failures rather than blaming students. Table 13.4 shows the gains made by students between the eighth and tenth grades in the four subject fields and compares these gains in schools with high, medium, and low levels of teachers' collective responsibility for student learning. The data in Table 13.4 show that students gained most in all subject areas in the high-responsibility schools and least in the low-responsibility schools. The researchers reported that the differences among the three types of schools were statistically significant.

The researchers also found that the amount of staff cooperation made a difference in student achievement, but not nearly so much as collective responsibility did. Interestingly, this study did not find any relationship between the dimension of

**Table 13.4** *Mean Gains in Student Achievement for Sophomores Attending Schools with High, Medium, and Low Levels of Teachers' Responsibility for Student Learning*

| Subject | Level of Collective Responsibility for Learning | | |
| --- | --- | --- | --- |
| | **High** (*n* = 1,226) | **Medium** (*n* = 8,801) | **Low** (*n* = 1,665) |
| Math gain | 6.57 | 5.39 | 4.95 |
| Reading gain | 3.70 | 2.51 | 1.61 |
| History gain | 2.95 | 1.51 | 1.26 |
| Science gain | 3.43 | 1.54 | 1.33 |

Source: After Lee and Smith (1996), p. 119.

teacher control and student achievement. In other words, the amount of control and influence teachers had on classroom and schoolwide policies did *not* seem to effect the achievement of their students.

**Discussion and Implications:** This study has several important implications for teachers and for reform efforts aimed at school improvement. First, the findings emphasize the importance of teachers' work lives, particularly the beliefs they hold about their responsibility for student learning. This means that reform efforts involving new methods in classrooms or adopting new curriculum materials may not make much difference unless teachers' beliefs about their collective responsibilities for student learning also change.

Second, the results of this study provide support for the point of view that effective schools are more like caring communities than efficient bureaucracies and that caring, committed communities are more likely to occur in small settings rather than larger ones. So those school reformers who argue for making schools smaller may indeed be on the right track.

Finally, the study confirms what many people have believed for a long time—that the teacher is the most important ingredient in the mix of factors that influence a child's education. What is new, however, is the study's demonstration that it is teachers working together, not alone, which seems to be the crucial reason this is true.

**Order and discipline.** Basic rules of conduct have been agreed upon throughout the school, and teachers feel responsibility for enforcing behavioral norms both in their own particular classes and across the school.

**High expectations.** Teachers and other staff hold high standards for students. They convey to students an "I care" and can-do attitude and demand that each student aspire to excellence.

**Teacher efficacy.** Teachers also have high expectations for themselves and a strong belief that they can teach every child.

**Pervasive caring.** Teachers and other adults in the school develop a caring atmosphere. Their demands on students are not viewed as cruel and judgmental but as fair and caring. They communicate and celebrate student achievement.

**Public rewards and incentives.** Effective schools have devised ways to publicly reward student successes and achievements. Student work is displayed, honor rolls are published, and active communication exists between the school and parents.

**Administrative leadership.** Principals in effective schools care deeply about the school's academic programs. They support teacher and student efforts, and they help set the tone for high expectations and pervasive caring.

**Community support.** Staff in effective schools find ways to involve parents and community in the school's programs. This involvement goes beyond open houses to include such activities as school beautification, tutoring, and active fundraising for the school.

**Instruction and Curriculum.** The description of attributes associated with the instructional curriculum of effective schools includes the following.

**High academic learning time.** Teachers in effective schools have found ways to maximize the time devoted to academic learning. They waste little time getting classes started and move smoothly from one activity to another with minimum disruption. Schoolwide, they have found ways to keep administrative disruptions to a minimum.

**Frequent and monitored homework.** Homework is required and is checked by the teachers in effective schools. Checking and giving feedback to students is one way for teachers and other adults in the school to tell students they have high expectations and that they care.

**Frequent monitoring of student progress.** Through tests, quizzes, and informal devices, teachers keep track of student progress and give students and parents helpful feedback on this progress.

**Coherently organized curriculum.** The curriculum in effective schools is closely connected to the goals and objectives of the schools and is linked to the major evaluation and testing procedures. Teachers know what teachers at other levels or in other subjects are teaching and match their own instruction accordingly.

**Variety of teaching strategies.** Teachers in effective schools have broad repertoires of teaching strategies and employ these to help meet the school's instructional goals.

**Opportunities for student responsibility.** The adults in effective schools find ways to engage students in running their school through devices such as student government, and they encourage peer tutoring, hall monitoring, and other opportunities for students to engage in leadership behaviors.

# 🍎 *Organizational Skills for Teachers*

The perspectives and research on organizational context and effective schools are important for beginning teachers for several reasons. First, they can help round out your understanding of schools as social organizations, and second, they can serve as a reminder that your own classroom will be but part of a larger school effort. This research also draws attention to several contradictions that stem from the way schools have been organized. On one hand, it appears that effective schools are places where people have common goals, teachers have organized their curriculum coherently, and common rules and norms guide teachers' expectations for students, homework policies, and discipline. On the other hand, the cellular structure of schools and traditional

✓ **Check for Understanding**

- How does a teacher's typical workday differ from that perceived by the general public?

- What types of work do teachers do in addition to direct instruction with students? What percentage of time is spent outside of the classroom?

- What overall findings have been demonstrated by school effectiveness research?

- How do studies conducted by Rutter and others illustrate the importance of a cohesive school culture?

- What features characterize the social and instructional aspects of effective schools?

**The autonomous nature that governs interactions between teachers is contradictory to the conclusion that effective schools are coherently organized with common goals.**

*Spotlight on Technology*

## Making Grades and Homework a Click Away

One way that schools as a whole have made use of technology is through the development of websites where a variety of information can be made available to students and their parents. One of the most interesting applications is a school-based website that posts daily grades, attendance records, summaries of lesson plans, and particular teachers' homework assignments. This is made possible with software programs that link a teacher's electronic grade book to the website and allow students and parents access with a password.

These websites provide advantages for teachers, students, and parents. They allow teachers to keep everyone informed about what is going in their classrooms by posting comments on students' work for students and their parents to see. Students no longer have excuses for not knowing an assignment was due. Even if they have forgotten or have been absent, they can find the assignment and due date on their school and teacher's website. Similarly, they can keep track of their grades and where they stand in the class at all times.

Parents can monitor their children's work in a much more positive atmosphere. They can follow how their child is doing in school on a regular basis, thus preventing surprises associated with the quarterly report card.

To learn more about these websites, go to the website of ThinkWave.com, a software producer based in Sausalito, California.

---

norms that support teacher autonomy make it difficult for people in a school to create the conditions that will make their school effective.

The remainder of this chapter looks at specific organizational skills that will be of concern to beginning teachers. These are organized according to the other major *role holders* in schools with whom teachers are expected to work. As you read about these organizational skills, keep in mind the main idea from the effective schools research: namely, collective effort schoolwide can produce important conditions for student learning.

## Working with Colleagues

Establishing good working relationships with colleagues is an important challenge for a beginning teacher. Being successful in this endeavor requires an understanding of important norms governing collegiality and specific actions that can be taken.

**New teachers can attempt to overcome autonomy norms in schools by observing, discussing, and meeting with colleagues.**

**Norms.** When beginning teachers enter their first school, they should be aware of the norms that will govern many of the relationships between themselves and their colleagues. The hands-off norm, which allows colleagues within the school to be friendly and supportive but discourages specific suggestions about instructional practices, has already been described. The beginning teacher is likely to be included in lunchroom talk about school politics and the personalities of individual students but will not find much talk about curriculum or teaching methods. Beginning teachers will find they can ask colleagues to provide assistance in finding a place to live or locating a good doctor; they will not be able to ask for help (at least not very directly), however, if they are having a classroom management problem.

The cellular structure of most schools means that beginning teachers may be expected to work alone. They will not be observed by other teachers, nor will they be invited to observe their peers. Teaching success will be known only to students, spouses, or close friends; failures will be kept secret.

Possible Actions. All schools will not reflect the norms described in exactly the same way. Some schools, in fact, may have norms that support professional collegiality. Regardless of the situation, beginning teachers do have some latitude for working with colleagues in open and constructive ways. However, it may require well-planned initiatives on their part. The following activities are usually possible.

*Observing Other Teachers.* This book has stressed the importance of focused observation and reflection in the process of learning to teach. This process should continue for first-year teachers. In fact, many of the observation schedules provided can be used again and again—during early field experiences, during student teaching, and in the beginning years.

Beginning teachers who want to observe other teachers should inquire early about whether or not classroom visits and observations are acceptable practice in their schools. If they are, principals, department chairs, or lead teachers can facilitate observation opportunities. If norms prevent collegial observations, it is still likely that these can be done in other schools where the beginning teacher is not known. These visits will have to be arranged by principals or by system-level curriculum specialists because they will require substitute teachers.

*Discussing Educational Issues with Colleagues.* Even if school norms prevent widespread collegial interaction concerning the problems of teaching, most schools have at least a handful of teachers who like more discussion and collegiality. A beginning teacher can take the initiative in seeking out these teachers and promoting this type of exchange. Initial discussions may eventually lead to exchanges of materials and perhaps exchanges of classroom visits and observations.

Finally, beginning teachers can seek out other beginning teachers who have not yet been socialized into the hands-off norm and who are probably suffering from many of the same problems and concerns. It has happened that beginning teachers have established their own weekly study and support group where mutual concerns and teaching strategies are shared.

*Working in Small Groups and at Meetings.* It will be a rare school where a beginning teacher will not find at least a few meetings at which teachers come together for the purpose of mutual planning. Some beginning teachers may not feel comfortable speaking up at faculty assemblies, but they can seek out membership within numerous small groups in the school. In these small-group settings, they can promote collegial norms through modeling good group behavior, such as open communication and effective problem solving and decision making.

## Working with Administrators and Leadership Personnel

A second group of people beginning teachers need to relate to is the leadership personnel within the school. School norms govern these relationships also, and specific actions are required.

Norms. Most careful observers of teachers' relationships with principals and other school leaders have pointed out that norms governing these relationships are somewhat ambiguous (Carlson, 1996; Jensen, 1989; Walcott, 1973). On one hand, the school's professional ethos supports the concept of the principal serving as the school's instructional leader and as a role model for teachers. On the other hand, the hands-off

**New teachers can take several steps to build positive communication channels with the principal.**

norm applies to principals and other leadership personnel as well as to other teachers. Often this norm inhibits direct participation by principals in matters of curriculum or teaching strategies. Teachers, according to Feiman-Nemser and Floden (1986), want the principal to act as a

> buffer between themselves and outside pressures from district administrators, parents, and other community members. . . . In addition, they want the principal to be a strong force in maintaining student discipline—backing the teachers in their classroom discipline policies and maintaining consistent school-wide policies. In return for these services, the teachers are willing to cooperate with the principal's initiatives. (p. 509)

In many schools, norms do not support the direct involvement and participation of the principal in instructional activities, although this may be changing.

**Possible Actions.** Obviously, principals vary greatly in their educational beliefs and management styles. Some are very supportive, and some are not. Some have excellent organizational and interpersonal skills, and some don't. One principal's priorities and values will differ from another's. In some instances, these values and priorities will be consistent with the values and beliefs of a beginning teacher; in other cases, they will be diametrically opposed.

Several specific actions can be taken by beginning teachers to gain the support of the principal and to establish a positive working relationship, regardless of the type of person he or she turns out to be. These actions include the following.

- Initiate regular weekly meetings with the principal during the first few weeks to discuss expectations for teacher and student behavior, academic goals, and other features of the school. Find out the principal's thoughts on the attributes of effective schools and effective teaching.
- Keep the principal informed in writing about what you are doing in your classroom, particularly on such topics as special successes you have had, such as a good lesson; a complimentary note from a parent; any conflicts with students or parents; special events such as guest speakers, field trips, or parties you are planning.
- Invite the principal to your classroom, particularly for a lesson that is unique or special, and for parties in elementary schools or special celebrations in secondary schools.
- Write complimentary notes to the principal when he or she does something you like or something that is particularly helpful to you or one of your students.

All of these suggestions fall under the category of building positive communication channels between the beginning teacher and the principal. They are efforts by beginning teachers to get clear about the principal's expectations on the one hand and, on the other, to make sure the principal understands their instructional program and activities.

**Other School Leaders.** In many schools, beginning teachers work with other school leaders as well as the principal, including counselors, reading specialists, special education resource teachers, librarians, media specialists, and curriculum specialists. A beginning teacher should remember that roles within organizations are governed by norms that role holders shape as they interact with each other. This means that beginning teachers will have some latitude in their interactions with leadership personnel. These interactions could range from ignoring them completely to actively seeking out their support and assistance. The latter is recommended in most instances.

Beginning teachers should strive, in the very early weeks of school, to build positive working relationships with school leaders and specialists for several reasons. First, unlike teacher colleagues, leadership personnel often are expected to help beginning teachers and to provide help in confidential ways free of evaluation. Second, most counselors and resource teachers got to their current positions because they were effective classroom teachers who received advanced training. This means they probably possess important knowledge they can pass along to beginning teachers if appropriate relationships are established. Finally, resource personnel have more time to provide assistance and support than principals or other teachers in the school do. Beginning teachers should set up regular meetings with resource personnel to discuss roles and expectations, and they should try to keep these individuals informed of their classroom programs and activities.

## Working with Parents

Other important organizational members with whom beginning teachers will want to establish positive relationships are parents.

**Norms.** Teachers want the norms governing their relationships with parents to include both concern for the child and support for their instructional program. At the same time, many teachers do not want parents to interfere with their classrooms (see Feiman-Nemser & Floden, 1986; Davies, 1991). On the whole, teachers tend to keep a good distance between themselves and parents and, in fact, have little interaction with them. This is particularly true of teachers in middle and secondary schools.

Working with and for parents is an important organizational function of teaching, and a good relationship can create a strong support system for beginning teachers and their students. It can also be a very rewarding aspect of the teacher's work. Following are several ways beginning teachers can build positive, supportive relationships with parents or other significant adults in students' lives. Remember that, as with other aspects of teaching, guidelines for working with parents will vary from one context to another. You need to remain sensitive to the fact that in many communities, the two-parent home may no longer be the norm. You also need to recognize that even when two parents or adults live in the same home, it is likely that both are working.

**Possible Actions.** Teacher-parent interactions can take several forms, including reporting to parents, holding conferences with parents, and enlisting parents' help in school and at home.

*Reporting to Parents.* Remember the idea described in Chapter 6 that parents of children at any age want to know how their children are doing in school. The traditional report card is one means of giving parents this information. Experienced teachers, however, often use additional means to keep parents informed, because the formal report card is only issued quarterly and only summarizes progress in general terms.

Some teachers, particularly of younger children, try to make weekly or biweekly contact with parents through notes or telephone calls. Such contacts allow teachers to explain what is going on in their classrooms and how the parent's child is doing on specific lessons. Such frequent and regular contact provides the teacher with a natural means for communicating children's successes, not just their deficiencies, which often dominate more formal reports.

**Ideally, the norms governing parent-teacher relationships should combine concern for the student with support for the instructional program.**

**Teacher-parent interactions may include written reporting, conferencing, and requesting parent help when needed.**

Another means of parent communication—one that works well for middle and high school teachers who have many students—is the use of a weekly or monthly newsletter. The use of newsletters was described in Chapter 10. Following are suggestions to guide the production and circulation of classroom or schoolwide parent newsletters adapted from Bluestein (1982), Epstein (1988), and Henderson, Marburgaer, and Ooms (1986).

**Newsletters are a means of providing written updates to parents regarding activities in the classroom.**

- Your newsletters can be formal or informal. They should reflect a newspaper format with headings, and they should always be neatly and carefully done.
- The language of the newsletter should be suitable for the community and chosen with the parents' backgrounds in mind.
- Newsletters should be sent home consistently. Once a month is best in most situations. They can also be shared with other teachers and with the principal.
- Newsletters should be designed to provide information parents are interested in, such as what the class is studying; changes in formats or schedules; new goals and directions for the class; new rules; routines and expectations; and upcoming projects, programs, and events.
- A portion of the newsletter should be devoted to recognitions, such as for students or teams who have done good work, for parent helpers who have made significant contributions, and for others in the community who have visited or contributed to the class.
- Newsletters should contain samples of students' work, such as writings, poems, or projects. Make sure every student's work is included eventually.
- Newsletters can be used as a way to involve parents by inviting them to participate in class activities or to serve as classroom or school helpers.

*Holding Conferences with Parents.* Most beginning teachers will be involved with parent conferences. Teachers of younger children are sometimes required to make a home visit early in the school year and to hold quarterly in-school meetings with parents. Teachers of older students are normally given more latitude to initiate conferences as needed or when parents request them. In either event, holding parent conferences is an important organizational function of teaching and can provide valuable experiences for the teacher and the parents if done properly. This is also a function that some beginning teachers feel somewhat nervous about.

*Conferences provide a valuable opportunity for parents and teachers to develop a positive working relationship.*

Using information from the New Mexico Institute for Parent Involvement, Jane Bluestein (1982) and Fuller and Olsen (1998) suggested the following strategies for teachers to use for parent conferences:

*Preconference preparations include the following:*

1. Notify: Purpose, place, time, length of time allotted. Consider the parent's schedule and availability; offer choices of time whenever possible.
2. Prepare: Review child's folder, gather examples of work, and prepare materials. Be very familiar with the student's performance and progress before the parent arrives.
3. Plan agenda: List items for discussion and/or presentation.
4. Arrange environment: Comfortable seating, eliminate distractions. The parent is at an immediate disadvantage by being on your "turf." To help avoid power implications, arrange the environment so that you and the parent are on equal planes (same-sized chairs), sitting side-by-side at a table, as opposed to face-to-face across your desk.

*The actual conference includes the following:*

1. Welcome: Establish rapport.
2. State: Purpose, time limitation, note taking, options for follow-up. This is where you share information and present data. You may find note taking during the conference useful in recording your interactions—particularly the parent's feedback and responses. In addition, discuss various avenues you (each) may follow in future dealings with the student, including directions for your instruction and expectations.
3. Encourage: Information sharing, comments, questions.
4. Listen: Pause once in a while. Look for verbal and nonverbal cues. The above two recommendations support the concept of a conference being an *exchange* between the teacher and the parent.
5. Summarize.
6. End on a positive note.

*Postconference steps and recommendations include the following:*

1. Review conference with child, if appropriate.
2. Share information with other school personnel, if needed.
3. Mark calendar for planned follow-up. (pp. 385–386)

> Planning conference topics in advance can relieve the stress that beginning teachers may experience at meeting time.

### Enlisting Parents' Help in School and at Home.

A final way that beginning teachers can work with parents is by involving them as teachers and assistants, both in school and at home. This practice is more common in elementary and middle schools than in high schools. It is also easier in communities where *not all* the parents hold jobs. Regardless of the situation, beginning teachers will always find some parents or parent surrogates willing to help if proper encouragement is given. Some guidelines for involving parents include:

- **To assist with small groups.** Conducting small-group activities is difficult for teachers because there are so many simultaneous demands in the classroom. Effective teachers sometimes find parents who will come to the school and help on a regular basis. If beginning teachers choose to use parents in this way, they should consider the parents' schedules and plan some training so that parents know what is expected of them.

- **To assist with field trips and other special events.** Field trips and many other special events such as parties or celebrations take an extra set of hands. Again, with proper encouragement and training, parents can be most useful during these times.

> Teachers can develop positive relationships with parents by asking them for assistance at work or home.

- **As teacher aides.** Some teachers have found ways to use parents as aides in their classrooms, thus getting valuable assistance in correcting papers, writing and publishing class newsletters, organizing parties, and the like.
- **To help with homework.** Most parents feel a responsibility for helping their children with homework. Unfortunately, many do not know how to be helpful. Effective teachers teach parents how to teach their own children. This can also be done on a school-wide basis. This generally requires holding special evening sessions during which the teacher explains to parents what the homework is trying to accomplish, shows them how to help students practice, and provides them with guidelines for giving students feedback. Many of the skills described in this book can be taught to parents. Teaching parents teaching skills may be time-consuming, but it can extend the teacher's influence over student learning, perhaps more than any other single action.

## Working for School Improvement

Helping schools improve, as with other aspects of school leadership and collaboration, will not be the major concern of beginning teachers. It is, however, an area that beginners should know about. Making classrooms and schools better is a responsibility of teachers, and involvement, if only in a very small way, should start early in one's career.

**Why Improvement?** Schools as they exist today assumed their basic design in the late 1800s. Curiously, people are ambivalent about this design. Many citizens are comfortable with the familiar patterns of the schools they experienced as children, and they get upset with changes that challenge these basic patterns. For example, efforts to get rid of the "neighborhood school" concept, for whatever reasons, meet severe resistance in most communities. At the same time, citizens are quick to find fault with the schools when they fail to live up to contemporary expectations. Bruce Joyce and his colleagues (1993) caught the essence of this paradox when they wrote:

> Throughout history . . . [critics] . . . have found [the school] both too backward and too advanced. It falls behind the times and fails to keep us in simultaneous cadence. . . . Most citizens are cautious about educational innovation. People like the familiar old schoolhouse as much as they criticize it. They tend to believe that current problems in education are caused by changes (perceived as "lowering of standards") rather than because the old comfortable model of the school may be a little rusty and out-of-date. In fact, our society has changed a great deal since the days when the familiar and comfortable patterns of education were established, and many schools have become badly out of phase with the needs of children in today's world. (pp. 3–4)

Joyce and his colleagues are right. The world has changed considerably since the idea of formal schooling was first conceived. As you know, many aspects of peoples' lives and of their social institutions have transformed dramatically over the past quarter of a century. A shrinking world produced by new communication and transportation technologies has replaced older parochial views with more cosmopolitan outlooks and interests. Shifting population patterns have made diverse, multicultural communities the norm and have greatly increased social sensitivity. New information technologies that include telecommunication satellites, word processors, microcomputers, and the Internet have substantially changed the way information can be thought about and used. The printing technologies that only came into being during the last two hundred years, making possible the current system of schools and libraries, must now compete with electronic communications. It is possible right now, and affordable in the near future, for every classroom and home to have electronic access to the information and wisdom stored in the major libraries of the world. These changes provide the context in which education and schools must operate. They also influence the values and interests of the youth found in classrooms, as well as the values and beliefs you have about teaching and about schools.

Social changes are also accompanied by changes in childhood and adolescence. Youth mature sooner than in earlier times, and each generation is confronted with a different set of questions and priorities that must be addressed. Some years ago, American sociologist James Coleman (1972) illustrated this problem in an article entitled "The Children Have Outgrown the Schools." In this article, he argued that schools fail students because they are pursuing the wrong goals with inappropriate experiences. Schools were created at a time when the society, according to Coleman, was "information poor and action rich." This meant that people, including youth, had plenty of things to do but little information to assist them. Over time, however, society has become "information rich but action poor"—people now have access to all kinds of information but fewer opportunities for applying and acting on the information. Coleman suggested that modern curricula should require more opportunities for active learning and involvement rather than merely providing exposure to more and more information. He argued that it is no longer sufficient to view the transmitting of information as the only purpose of schooling. Programs are needed that provide youth with realistic links between education and daily living. Don Tapcott (1998) described a similar phenomenon in his book *Growing Up Digital,* namely, that schooling is out of touch with the realities of today's "net generation." How to adapt to these changes is a difficult, perplexing problem and a challenge for your generation of teachers.

**Possible Actions.** As a beginning teacher encountering your first classroom, you likely will be faced with many dilemmas and unanswered questions. You also will likely be troubled by some of the discrepancies between professional ideals and the realities you find. Some beginning teachers have been known to accept these realities with a sense of resignation or defeat. Others have faced the complexities of teaching with a desire for improvement. There are some concrete things teachers can do, even in their beginning years, that will establish healthy patterns and contribute to school improvement.

***Becoming a Student of One's Own Teaching.*** One means to improve classrooms is to become a student of one's own teaching. This type of activity is sometimes called **action research,** and it serves as a means for teachers to engage in critical inquiry into and reflection on the processes of teaching. The specifics of how to carry out action research projects are described in the Resource Handbook at the end of *Learning to Teach.*

***Working on the School Level.*** A beginning teacher's role in schoolwide improvement efforts at first involves being a thoughtful participant in proposals that come from others. Such proposals may involve policies for beginning teacher evaluation created by the state legislature, a new science curriculum adopted by the school district, or perhaps new approaches for classroom management offered by the principal. In all these instances, beginning teachers will be primarily on the receiving end. According to Fullan (1992), when teachers are faced with proposals for reform, they should consider individually and as a faculty several issues before deciding to commit themselves to the change effort. These issues include the following:

1. *Assess the nature of the proposed change.* Teachers need to give the proposed change careful study. They need to determine if it addresses an important need and if it has

been successful elsewhere. They also need to assess their own priorities. Teachers are faced with many changes all the time, and they can only put their energy into a few. In most instances, a faculty can only work on one or two improvement efforts at a time, and these are best accomplished when they are connected to the overall direction and vision of the school.

2. *Assess administrative support.* Some form of active support by administrators (superintendents and principals) is usually required for reform efforts to be successful. Although teachers may decide to go it alone, independent of their administrators, they should do so only after careful consideration of the risks involved with this type of action.

3. *Assess support by other teachers.* Most school improvement efforts require the support of most, if not all, the teachers in a school. If a single or a few teachers choose to initiate a project, it is wise to check out colleague support first and to stimulate support if it does not already exist before moving forward. School improvement is easier in schools in which teachers have a collaborative work culture.

✔ **Check for Understanding**

- What are some actions that can be taken to facilitate positive working relationships between beginning teachers and their colleagues?

- What are some actions that can be taken to facilitate positive working relationships between beginning teachers and their principals?

- What are some common parent-teacher interactions, and what can a teacher do to promote optimal relationships?

- Why do schools need to improve, and what are some actions beginning teachers can take to provide leadership for improvement?

*Exhibiting Leadership.* First impressions affect the way beginning teachers are received by professional colleagues both inside and outside school. One way that beginning teachers can become known among colleagues and win their regard is to exhibit leadership potential within the school or school system. Following are some examples, reported by principals and colleagues, of what several successful beginning teachers did to exhibit leadership during their first year.

- Elaine taught on a fifth and sixth grade teaching team that had a weak science curriculum. Elaine had majored in biology in college and had more science background than the other, more experienced teachers on the team. She volunteered to revise the science curriculum for the team and found suitable materials for teachers to use. This leadership was applauded by team members and made Elaine a highly valued and respected team member.

- Miguel was hired as a social studies teacher in a middle school. In discussions with students and colleagues, he found that for the previous three years, no one had paid any attention to the school's drama program. Miguel had been in numerous college plays and volunteered to head up the drama club and to sponsor a spring play. The play was a huge success, and Miguel won respect for his willingness to take on this schoolwide job.

- Valerie, a high school English teacher, was upset about the hall behavior of the students in the building wing where she had been assigned. After getting things off to a good start in her own class, she began discussing the hall problem with other teachers in the wing. Under her leadership, they established a set of rules for hall behavior and together agreed on ways to monitor student behavior between classes.

Obviously, beginning teachers should not overextend themselves by assuming too many leadership responsibilities. However, it is important to pick at least one project that has the potential for schoolwide attention and devote energy to getting successful results. Meeting the leadership challenges of teaching can be among the most rewarding accomplishments of a teacher's career.

# 🍎 *Summary*

## Perspective of Schools as Workplaces

- Schools are social organizations and, as such, are adult workplaces as well as places where students come to learn.
- People in schools act not in totally free and disconnected ways but in more or less interdependent and predictable ways.
- Schools have individual histories and cultures (tone, ethos) with norms and roles that influence school goals and processes and the way people work to achieve them.
- Although schools, like other organizations, are characterized by goals and control structures, they also have special features, such as goal ambiguity, compulsory attendance, political visibility, limited resources, and sense of community.
- Two important norms that regulate the culture of teaching and behavior in schools are the autonomy norm and the hands-off norm. The autonomy norm allows teachers to do pretty much what they want inside their classrooms. The hands-off norm sanctions teachers who try to interfere with other teachers' teaching methods or processes.
- Roles also define how teachers do their work. Some aspects of a teacher's role are contradictory; for example, the need to provide individual attention to students in group settings and the need to maintain a certain amount of social distance from students.

## Theoretical and Empirical Support

- Research on teachers' work lives has documented that teachers carry out many organizational functions in addition to working directly with students and that the time demands on teachers are quite extensive.
- A moderately strong knowledge base exists that helps explain why some schools are more effective than others. Some aspects of this research are still controversial.
- Research on schools has illustrated that while teaching performance in individual classrooms is very important, the way that principals, teachers, parents, and students all come together to define common goals, expectations, and procedures and the way teachers take collective responsi-

bility for student learning have substantial impact on what students learn.
- More effective schools have processes and procedures characterized by clear goals, high expectations, pervasive caring, strong leadership, community support, high academic learning time, frequent monitoring of student progress, coherent curricula, and variety in the methods used by teachers.

## Organizational Skills for Teachers

- Teachers contribute to effective schools by successfully working with colleagues; working with school leaders, such as the principal; working with parents; and providing leadership for school improvement.
- Establishing good working relationships with colleagues is very important and can be enhanced by observing other teachers in the school, volunteering to work on committees and task forces, and seeking out colleagues for discussion of educational issues.
- Teachers build good working relationships with principals and other leadership personnel by meeting with them regularly, keeping them informed about what they are doing in their classrooms, and participating in schoolwide activities.
- Parents will become partners in the teacher's classroom if they are kept informed about what is going on, made to feel welcome in the school and at conferences, and enlisted to help in their child's education at home and in school.
- Helping to improve classrooms and schools is an important aspect of the teacher's job.
- Improvement is needed because schools, in many instances, are out of phase with the needs of today's youth and do not live up to rising expectations people have for education.
- Teachers who choose to work toward school improvement can do so by becoming thoughtful and informed about change initiatives proposed by others and by helping to create and provide leadership for improvement projects.

## Key Terms

ethos

school culture

norms

autonomy norm

hands-off norm

loosely coupled

school effectiveness research

synergy

action research

## Books for the Professional

American Institute for Research (1999). *An Educators' Guide to Schoolwide Reform.* Arlington, Va.: Educational Research Services. This publication describes twenty-four school-wide programs aimed at improving and making schools more effective.

Fuller, M. L., and Olsen, G. (1998). *Home-School Relations: Working Successfully with Parents and Families.* Boston: Allyn and Bacon. A thoughtful guide with many specific details about how teachers can build productive relationships with parents, families, and communities.

Goodlad, J. I. (1984). *A Place Called School: Prospects for the Future.* New York: McGraw-Hill. This book reports a comprehensive study of the American school. It looks inside classrooms and schools with insightful detail and proposes ways effective schools can be achieved.

Jackson, P. W. (1968). *Life in Classrooms.* New York: Holt, Rinehart & Winston. *Life in Classrooms* is just what its name implies: a very careful description of what happens in elementary classrooms. This text is scholarly yet easy to read for beginning teachers.

Lieberman, A., and Miller, L. (1992). *Teachers—Their World and Their Work: Implications for School Improvement.* New York: City College Press. This is an excellent and very readable book on the social side of teaching, told from the perspective of the teachers.

Sarason, S. B. (1995). *Parental Involvement and the Political Principle.* San Francisco: Jossey-Bass. This book argues for radical new structures for governing schools and a much wider role for parents in the process.

Schmuck, R., and Runkel, P. (1995). *Handbook of Organization Development in Schools and Colleges.* Prospect Heights, Ill.: Waveland Press. This book presents a thorough analysis of schools as social organizations. It is filled with concrete suggestions for teachers to make their work with colleagues more effective and satisfying.

## Reflection & Portfolio

At the beginning of this chapter, you read about the busy work lives of two beginning teachers, both of whom were highly involved not only with their students but also with schoolwide activities. Now think about all aspects of a teacher's work and write a reflective essay on school leadership and collaboration in which you consider the following questions; What are your views on the noninstructional aspects of a teacher's work? Are these aspects important? Or do they take valuable time that could be spent with students? What about the effective school research? Do you believe that synergy can be created and student achievement enhanced when teachers work together? Or do you believe that the best way to improve student learning is to allow maximum autonomy for each teacher? When you begin your teaching career, which aspects of a teacher's work will you value the most? Which aspects will you find most troublesome? For example, do you look forward to working with colleagues and parents? Or do you think you will resent this type of work? You may wish to illustrate your reflections with photographs of schools, videos, papers, and other artifacts that will demonstrate to others your understanding of school as a place where teachers work and of the features that make some schools more effective than others. Finally, place this work in your professional portfolio and compare it with the views of the two teachers below.

*Elena Martinez*

"I really love working with my colleagues, and I seek out every opportunity to be involved with curriculum committees, school improvement task forces, and team teaching initiatives. I see this aspect of my work as a way to improve the whole school and in turn enhance what my students learn. These activities do not take away from the attention I pay to my students. Instead, they enrich my teaching. My work with colleagues is rewarding to me. I learn from other teachers, and they help me keep abreast of developments in my field. My work with parents provides me with insights about their children and about their community that I could obtain in no other way. I simply wouldn't work in a school where there wasn't a strong sense of collaboration and professional community."

*Peter Boros*

"I know some of my colleagues consider me old-fashioned and standoffish. I don't like to work with other adults all that much, and I find most committee work in this school to be a complete waste of time. The essence of teaching is the work I do every day with my students in my classroom. This is the reason I chose to enter teaching in the first place. I know and love history, and I am an excellent teacher. I don't want to have to compromise my approach to meet overall schoolwide goals. I don't want my colleagues telling me what to do."

# Resource Handbook

## 🍎 Contents

Chapter 1 of *Learning to Teach* described the importance of the knowledge base on teaching and learning and how educational research supports the practice of teaching and frees teachers from an overreliance on earlier common-sense and rule-of-thumb approaches. As with other complex human activities, research has its own rules and specialized language, which can be very confusing to the novice. Learning to learn from research requires some understanding of the methods and language used by researchers and an awareness of where to go for research information. A broad understanding of educational research is obviously beyond the scope of this book, but certain key concepts that are important for reading and understanding research are presented in this special resource section. The aim of this section is to help beginning teachers to use research, to read research reports with a critical eye, and to locate research results that may be needed to inform the practice of teaching.

## 🍎 *Key Research Concepts*

Researchers strive to find answers to *research problems* by posing particular *research questions*. The perspective taken by researchers and their definition of problems differ from the common usage of those terms. A problem, from the researcher's perspective, normally has three ingredients. It is clearly stated in question form, it focuses on relationships (particularly causal relationships) between two or more variables, and it implies the possibility of testing from a scientific perspective. Practical problems, on the other hand, although sometimes stated in question form, rarely focus on relationships that can be tested. Instead, they generally strive to state a discrepancy between the "way things are" and the way the problem solver would like them to be. To show the difference between a practical problem faced by teachers and a researchable problem posed by researchers, consider two types of questions that might be asked about student motivation. A teacher might ask a practical question, such as, "How can I get my unmotivated students to do their homework each night?" A researcher might ask a researchable question, such as, "What are the effects of two different reward systems (free time in school versus parental praise) on time devoted to homework by unmotivated students?" Both problems are clearly stated in question form, but only the latter focuses on relationships among variables and has a built-in procedure for investigation.

### Research Variables

When educational researchers study problems, they normally do so by thinking about variables within a particular situation that can help explain relationships and causation. A research **variable** is a characteristic of a person (teacher, student, parent) or some aspect of the environment (classroom, home, school) that can vary. Essentially, researchers try to sort out what goes with and influences what in the very complex environment of teaching and learning. They are also interested in arranging these variables into models that can explain teaching more fully. Much of the research during the last few decades has come from researchers who think about variables in a way similar to that shown in the model provided by Dunkin and Biddle (1974), displayed in Figure R1.1.

As you can see, this model organizes twelve sets of variables into four larger classes that were first named by Mitzel (1960).

**1.** *Presage variables.* These variables refer to the characteristics of teachers, namely their experiences, their training, and special properties they have such as skills and motivations.

**Figure R1.1** *Dunkin and Biddle Model for the Study of Classroom Teaching*

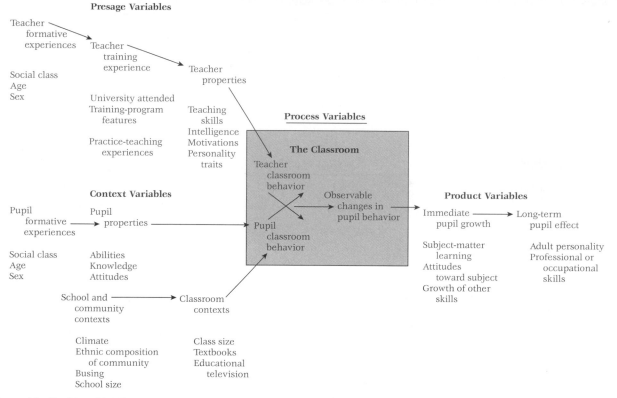

Source: After Dunkin and Biddle (1974), p. 38.

2. *Context variables.* These variables refer to the environment to which teachers must adjust, such as students' formative experiences, prior knowledge, students' abilities, and school, community, and classroom characteristics.

3. *Process variables.* These variables refer to the activities and procedures that occur in classrooms. They are variables associated with what teachers and students do. Process variables are those of most concern in this book.

4. *Product variables.* These variables refer to the outcomes of teaching and classroom interaction. They have been divided into two subsets by Dunkin and Biddle—immediate pupil growth and long-term effects. Two very important outcomes most teachers are concerned with are academic achievement and self-esteem.

Notice the arrows in the model. These are provided to show the presumed causative relationships among the variables. It is important to point out, however, as do Dunkin and Biddle (1974), that "each arrow is but a source of hypotheses and not a symbol of invariant truth." As they explained:

> For example, let us assume that teachers who come from middle-class backgrounds are known to approach pupils somewhat differently than those with lower-class backgrounds. Does this mean that social class "causes" differential classroom behavior? Indeed this interpretation might be correct. But it might also be true that teachers who come from middle- and lower-class backgrounds are more likely to attend different colleges and thus to

**Figure R1.2** *Conceptual Map of Research on Teaching*

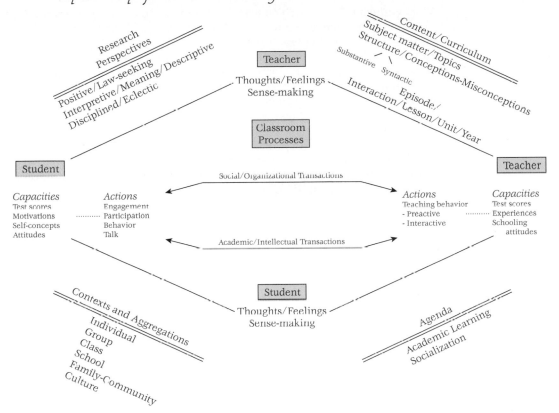

Source: After Shulman (1986), p. 9.

have had different experiences in teacher training; this latter factor, then, would be the actual cause of their different behaviors in the classroom. (p. 37)

Other researchers have developed models that differ from the one shown in Figure R1.1. For instance, Shulman (1986) constructed a model around the primary *participants* in the educational enterprise, namely students and teachers. Rather than assuming a causation that flows from the teacher to the learner, Shulman's model portrays teaching as an activity involving teachers and students working jointly. Teachers learn and students teach as the arrows in Figure R1.2 imply. In addition, the variables in Shulman's model extend beyond the observable behaviors of teachers and students and include their capacities (abilities and character), their thoughts and feelings, and their actions.

Researchers using Dunkin and Biddle's model strive to find relationships primarily between teacher behavior and subsequent student outcomes. Researchers using Shulman's model likely focus on a wider array of variables and explore multiple relationships, including the cognitions and feeling of students and their teachers as well as the multiple interactions found in classroom settings. Many other models strive to provide conceptual maps for the research on teaching. Although each has been constructed from its own point of view, all are attempts to show important relationships in the complex world of teaching and learning.

## Independent and Dependent Variables

When you read the research on teaching summarized in this book and elsewhere, you will often come across words such as *independent* and *dependent variable*. These are words used by researchers to describe a particular aspect of the variables they are studying. Strictly speaking, **independent variable** refers to a property that is the presumed *cause* of something, whereas **dependent variable** is the *consequence*. In the study of teaching, variables associated with teacher behavior (causes) are normally important independent variables, and student self-esteem or achievement (consequences) are important dependent variables.

Knowledge about teaching is really knowledge about the relationships between the many independent and dependent variables in the models displayed in Figures R1.1 and R1.2. Many of the relationships that appear to exist are only tentative and are always open to alternative interpretations. It is important to remember that an enterprise as complex as teaching does not always fall neatly into the models devised by researchers.

# Approaches to Educational Research

Educational researchers use several different approaches to study problems related to teaching and learning. The critical differences between the various approaches include the assumptions researchers make about the nature of scientific knowledge and the ways they design their studies, collect information, and interpret results.

## Assumptions About Scientific Knowledge

Today, researchers make different assumptions about the nature of the social world of education and about the nature of knowledge, and these assumptions influence the type of research they do. Some researchers, for instance, assume that the social world, in our case the world of schools and classrooms, has an *objective reality*. These researchers believe that schools, classrooms, teachers, and students exist independent of the researcher and that they are available for study in an objective, unbiased manner. Researchers who hold this perspective focus their research mainly on observable behaviors that can be measured. This perspective is often referred to as **positivism.** Much of the research that has been done in education over the past century rests on positivistic assumptions.

**Constructivism** is a different perspective about the social world and the nature of knowledge that has gained favor among the educational research community during the past thirty years. Researchers with this perspective believe that the social world does *not* exist independently but is instead constructed by the participant, mainly students, their teachers, and often the researcher himself or herself. This view of the social world is consistent with the constructivist principles of teaching and learning discussed elsewhere in *Learning to Teach*.

These perspectives about the social world and scientific knowledge are important because they influence the type of studies researchers conduct and the manner in which they analyze and report their results. Positivists, for instance, are more likely to conduct what has been labeled **quantitative research,** an approach to research that assumes an objective reality, that studies behavior in an objective fashion, and that uses statistical methods to analyze data. Constructivists, on the other hand, are more likely to conduct **qualitative research,** an approach that relies on holistic observations, reports data in verbal rather than quantitative form, and conducts the whole research process in a more personalized and interpretative fashion.

Currently, a great deal of debate goes on among researchers using these two approaches, and this debate is likely to continue. For our purposes here, it is probably safe to say that both perspectives and approaches can provide insights and discoveries that can improve classroom practice.

## Types of Research Studies

Let's now look more closely at some of the specific types of research used in education and reported in this book.

## Descriptive Research

Most of you can readily cite examples of **descriptive research,** not only in the field of education but in other fields as well. On any given day, you can pick up a newspaper and read the results of a survey someone has done. A survey is one type of descriptive research. Researchers adopting this approach commonly use questionnaires or interviews to gather information about the characteristics of some phenomenon or to measure people's opinions or attitudes on some subject.

Although it is difficult to do "good" survey research, the results of such research are easily understood. In most cases, the results are presented numerically and describe the number and percentage of people who have a specific characteristic or who believe in a particular way. The part of Lortie's study summarized in Chapter 1 is an example of one type of survey research. In that instance, information was collected by interview on why people chose to go into teaching. The well-known yearly survey conducted by Gallup to get citizens' opinions about the schools is another example of survey research.

Sometimes researchers using the descriptive approach are interested in a type of problem that can best be studied using qualitative methods through direct observation of a single case or a small number of cases. These approaches take the form of case studies or, in some instances, ethnographies. **Ethnography** is a word that comes from the field of anthropology and means an extensive study of an intact group of people, such as a culture, a society, or a particular role group. Normally, what a researcher does when conducting this type of research is to select from many possibilities what might be called a typical case and then to conduct in-depth observations of that single case. The aim of a case study, or an ethnography, is to collect extensive information so that a rich description and an in-depth understanding of the research problem will result. Examples of this type of research include the work of anthropologists such as Margaret Mead, who lived with and studied the people in Samoa to discover some of the important underlying patterns of that culture, and the work of Jean Piaget, who conducted in-depth case studies of children to discover how a young child's mind develops and grows.

As a rule, researchers using observational techniques must get quite close to the subjects they are studying. In fact, some become participants themselves and try to influence the problems they are studying.

As contrasted to collecting information using questionnaires or interviews, observation allows the researcher to study the point of view of a group or person and, in turn, construct a more complete picture of the situation. A weakness of this type of research, however, is that the researcher is only studying a single case or a small number of cases. Readers or users of this research must always ask how typical or representative the researcher's case was and whether the researcher's conclusions would hold up in other cases or other settings.

## Experimental Research

A second approach to research in education is the experiment. This is the traditional approach based on positivistic assumptions. Most readers are already familiar with the basic logic and procedures of this approach through their high school and college psychology, social science, and science classes. The results of this type of research are also frequently reported in the mass media.

The experimental study of teaching involves procedures in which the researcher, instead of describing or studying variables as they exist naturally in the world, sets up conditions so specified variables can be manipulated. Although there are over a dozen variations of educational experiments, the classical approach is for the researcher to perform three important acts: (1) to establish two groups believed to be the same; (2) to give one group (the experimental group) a special treatment and withhold the treatment from the other (the control group); and (3) to compare some measurable feature of the two groups to see if the treatment made any difference.

True experiments are difficult to do in education, because many of the problems teachers and researchers are interested in are not amenable to experiments for either logistical or ethical reasons. When they can be done, however, experiments produce powerful results, because they allow the researcher to draw conclusions about cause-and-effect relationships among variables. The educational problems most amenable to experimental manipulations are those associated with particular models and methods of teaching. The "bowling study" described in Chapter 10 is a good example of a cleverly constructed experiment.

## Correlational Research

Because so many aspects of teaching and learning cannot be studied experimentally, a third major research approach is often employed. Correlational research is used when the researcher explores the relationships between two or more variables that exist naturally and tries to sort out what goes with what. This approach is also familiar to most of you. Take, for example, the now well-known correlational studies showing strong relationships between cigarette smoking and certain diseases. Over many years, medical researchers have shown that people who smoke have a higher incidence of lung cancer and heart attacks than nonsmokers have. Nonetheless, the cause-and-effect relationship remains experimentally unproven because of the ethics of setting up a true experiment in which members of one group would be given a treatment that might lead to their deaths. Much of the research on effective teaching is also correlational research. For example, the many studies that show strong relationships between certain features of classroom management and student learning, such as those described in Chapter 5, are nearly all correlational.

In the study of teaching, the researcher is usually interested in finding relationships between some type of teacher behavior and student learning. Although very useful in education, it is important to keep in mind that correlational research does not establish cause and effect among variables, only relationships. More is said about this later.

## Causal-Comparative Research

Many times in education, variables of interest to the researcher cannot be manipulated, and data must be used from already defined groups. A method used to explore causal relationships in this situation is the causal-comparative method. In this type of research, unlike experimental research, the independent variable is not manipulated by the researcher because it already exists. Researchers compare two groups: subjects (normally in already existing groups) for whom a particular trait or pattern exists and similar subjects for whom it is absent. Two examples are given here. In both examples, the researcher studied variables that already exist and groups (classrooms) already defined.

- A researcher believes teachers are more critical toward Hispanic students than toward Anglo students. The researcher records teacher behaviors and then compares the teachers' interactions with the two groups. The independent variable in this case is ethnic origin—a trait in students that obviously already exists and is not manipulated.

- A researcher is interested in the attitudes of students toward school in two classrooms—one in which the teacher is using cooperative learning strategies, the other in which the teacher relies mainly on direct instruction. Attitudes are measured in the two classrooms and compared. Again, the independent variable (cooperative learning versus direct instruction) is a condition that already exists in the classroom and is not one the researcher manipulated.

In causal-comparative studies, differences between means are observed. The statistical tests employed are similar to those used in experimental research. This differs from correlational studies, in which the correlation coefficient is observed. Like correlational research, the results from causal-comparative studies are limited and must be interpreted with care, because it is not clear whether the variables observed are a cause or a result or whether some third factor is present that may be influencing both the independent and dependent variables.

# 🍎 *Statistical Concepts and Research Conventions*

The vast majority of educational research involves measuring individual or group traits that produce quantitative data. Over the years, researchers have developed statistical procedures to help organize, analyze, and interpret their data. To read and to use research requires an understanding of some of the basic procedures and agreed-on conventions used by researchers. There is nothing magical about statistics or about symbols used by researchers. They are merely a means to communicate clearly and objectively. They may, however, appear mysterious to the novice. Brief descriptions of several key ideas can help beginning teachers understand research and perhaps motivate further study.

## Sampling

Since it is obviously impossible to study all teachers or all students, educational researchers must, out of necessity, confine their studies to a small portion, or **sample**, of a total population. An example of this technique is the *sampling* done by market researchers to find out which TV shows people watch. From the millions of viewers at a given programming hour, researchers poll as few as fifteen hundred to two thousand persons selected from known segments of the viewing population. Users of market research ratings accept the results because they know that what the sample is watching represents (more or less) the habits of the total viewing audience.

The way a sample is selected is very important, because if it does not accurately represent the intended larger population, the results will obviously be biased. A famous mistake in sampling occurred in the 1948 presidential election when a sample of citizens drawn from telephone directories across the country the night before the election indicated that Thomas Dewey, the Republican candidate, would be elected. The next day, however, Harry Truman, the Democratic candidate, was elected. Upon analysis, the polling firm discovered that in 1948, many voters still did not have telephones, and those without phones, who could not be included in the sample, were more prone to vote Democratic. Drawing a sample from the telephone directory was not appropriate if the pollsters wanted to know what the total population of voters was going to do. When reading reports of educational research, it is important to study carefully the sampling techniques used by the researcher.

## Randomness

The concept of **randomness** is also very important in educational research. Usually random sampling or random assignment to groups means that individuals in any population have an equal chance of being selected for study. In survey research, this means that the researcher strives to define the total population of people he or she is going to study and then decides by chance which ones will be chosen for study. In experiments in which one group is to receive a special treatment and the other to serve as a control, the researcher is careful that subjects are assigned to one of the two groups on a random basis. The logic behind random sampling or random assignment to groups is that by using this procedure, the sample or the groups under investigation will have the same characteristics. This, however, is not always the case. For example, just as there is a chance, although very small, of flipping heads in a coin toss one hundred times in a row, there is also always a chance that a random sample will indeed not represent the total population or that two groups assigned at random will differ from one another in important ways.

## Numbers and Conventions

Researchers also use certain conventions to organize and report the results of their work to others.

**Mean Scores.** In many of the research studies summarized in this book as well as elsewhere, researchers report mean scores that allow comparison of one group with another. A **mean score** is nothing more than an average score and is calculated by adding all scores and dividing by the number of cases. The reporting convention of researchers is to use the symbol $\bar{X}$ or $M$ to designate the mean score and the symbol $N$ to communicate to readers the number of cases used to compute a particular mean. Mean scores are used to perform many of the statistical tests employed in educational research.

**Standard Deviation.** **Standard deviation (SD)** is another statistic that provides information about a set of scores. This statistic, found in many data tables, indicates the spread of a particular set of scores from the mean. Differences in means as well as differences in standard deviation are used to compute tests of statistical significance. The symbol SD is the most common convention for reporting standard deviation.

**Correlation and Correlation Coefficients.** **Correlation** expresses the degree to which a relationship exists between two or more variables. Familiar examples are the relationship between student IQ and student achievement, and the relationship between particular teaching behaviors (keeping students on task) and student achievement. Another is the relationship between a person's height and his or her performance on the basketball court.

To express these relationships in mathematical terms, researchers use a statistic called the **correlation coefficient.** A correlation coefficient can range from $+1.00$ through .00 to $-1.00$. The sign does not have the traditional mathematical meaning. Instead, a plus sign represents a positive relationship, a minus sign a negative relationship. Thus, .00 means no relationship exists, $+1.00$ means a perfect relationship exists, and $-1.00$ means a perfect reverse relationship exists. As observed in many of the studies summarized in this book, few instances are found in education (or any other aspect of human behavior) where perfect positive or negative relationships exist.

As described earlier, an important thing to remember about correlational studies and correlational coefficients is that even though they may show relationships among variables, they do not explain cause and effect. As an example, many studies show a positive relationship between students' time on task and academic achievement. Consequently, it is assumed that teachers who can keep students on task more will produce superior scores on achievement tests. Although this may be true, the time-on-task principle could be turned around. It could be logically argued that it is not time on task that produces achievement, but instead it is high-achieving students who produce high time-on-task ratios.

**Tests of Significance.** In any empirical research on human behavior, there is always the possibility that a specific outcome is the result of chance instead of some presumed relationship that is being studied. Researchers have developed a procedure called the *test of statistical significance* to help decide whether research results are indeed true or perhaps a matter of chance. Several different tests of significance are observed in the research reports found in this book. The main idea to remember is that when researchers use the word *significance,* they are using it differently than in common usage, where it normally means *important.* In the language of researchers, **significance** means the degree of truth rather than chance that they assign to their results. In general, researchers agree that differences between two sets of scores are statistically significant if they could occur by chance only 1 to 5 times out of 100. When you read the research reports in this text you will often see the notation $p < .01$ or $p < .05$. This means that the probability ($p$) of such results could occur by chance less than ($<$) 1 time out of 100 (.01) or 5 times out of 100 (.05).

# 🍎 *Reading and Keeping Abreast of Research*

## Reading Research with a Critical Eye

Most research in education today is subjected to a review process before it is published. Nonetheless, a teacher who is reading and using the results of research should learn to approach studies with a critical eye. Gall, Borg, and Gall (1996) listed a number of weaknesses that occur in research studies and reports. Part of their list is summarized briefly here.

- *Deliberate bias.* Although the goal of research is to discover truth, sometimes research is done to convince others of a point of view or of the effectiveness of a particular educational program.
  *Example:* Readers of research look to see if the researcher has anything to gain if the results turn out in a particular way. If so, the possibility of bias is greatly increased, and the study has to be examined very carefully. This does not mean, however, that all inventors of new programs or approaches who also conduct research on their inventions will deliberately bias the results. In most instances, they do not.
- *Nondeliberate bias.* Sometimes bias enters into research without the researchers' being aware of it. As with many other aspects of life, distortion can exist and influence us without our knowing it.
  *Example:* Look for emotional language and imbalanced presentation of research studies.
- *Sampling bias.* Sampling bias is something that plagues educational research, because it is so difficult to get random samples from total populations. However, as you learned in a previous section, if a sample contains bias, results can be spurious.
  *Example:* Studies in which volunteers have been used, where many subjects have been lost from the sample, or in which intact groups have been used for convenience purposes should raise red flags for readers and users of research.
- *Observer and measurement bias.* Human beings have a tendency to see what they want to see, hear what they want to hear, and remember what they want to remember. Even though researchers go to great lengths to guard against observer bias, they are always open to subtle error.
  *Example:* Looking at observation instruments or protocols to see if the researcher has included features to ensure objectivity or looking at interview questions for leading or threatening questions are means to check if observer bias has influenced the results of a study.

## Reading a Research Report: An Example

It is time now to see if you can apply these research concepts to an actual research report. Read the summary of the Johnsons' study (Research Summary 10.1 on pages 320 and 321) in Chapter 10. See if you can answer the following questions:

1. What assumptions about the nature of scientific knowledge are embedded in the study?
2. Is the study an example of descriptive, experimental, correlational, or causal-comparative research?
3. What variables were studied? Which variables are the independent variables? Which are the dependent variables?
4. Where would these variables fit in the Dunkin and Biddle research model? In the Shulman model?
5. How did the researchers use the mean statistic? From studying the scores and frequencies and tests of significance, what conclusions would you draw?
6. Based on your conclusion, what might you say about the impact of cooperative learning?
7. Which forms of bias do you find in the study? Deliberate bias? Nondeliberate bias? Observer bias? What about the sample? Is it biased?
8. What are the strengths of the study? What are the limitations?

## Keeping Abreast of Research

Once one starts teaching full time, it is sometimes difficult to keep up with research. There are just so many other things to do. Fortunately, there are special services available to teachers that can cut down the time needed to keep abreast of the research on teaching and learning. Beginning in the mid-1960s, the federal government became more interested in educational research and created several services to encourage the dissemination of educational research to classroom teachers. Two of these services can be useful to the beginning teacher.

**Regional Educational Laboratories.** Knowing that most research and research centers were not directly applicable to classroom teachers, regional educational laboratories were created in 1964 to translate research into classroom materials and strategies and to disseminate the results to teachers. Even though their budgets do not allow direct assistance in every classroom in their region, laboratory staffs hold many useful workshops and are eager to have classroom teachers visit their labs and learn about the work they are doing. These laboratories also provide opportunities for the more energetic teachers to participate in ongoing research and development projects. A complete list of centers and regional laboratories can be easily obtained in your library or on the Internet.

**Educational Research Information Centers.** Also in the mid-1960s, the federal government started to put together a network of educational research information centers called ERICs. Today, there are seventeen of these centers. ERICs are charged with three major tasks: (1) collecting the available knowledge on topics associated with various specialized areas of education, (2) organizing this information so it can be retrieved via computers from any place in the United States, and (3) summarizing these data in short bulletins and papers on topics of particular interest to teachers and other educators.

Today, all libraries in major universities and many large school districts or intermediate educational agencies have direct computer connections to the ERICs. To access these centers, you need only contact the person in charge of ERIC searches in your li-

**Figure R1.3** *E-mail Addresses for ERIC Subject Area Clearinghouses*

| ERIC Subject Area Clearinghouses | E-mail Address |
|---|---|
| Adult, Career, and Vocational Educational | ericave@postbox.acs. ohio-state.edu |
| Assessment and Evaluation | ericae@ericae.net |
| Community Colleges | ericcc@ucla.edu |
| Counseling and Student Services | ericcass@uncg.edu |
| Disabilities and Gifted Education | ericec@cec.sped.org |
| Education Management | ppiele@oregon.uoregon.edu |
| Elementary and Early Childhood Education | ericeece@uiuc.edu |
| National Parent Information Network | No e-mail available. |
| Higher Education | eriche@eric-he.edu |
| Information and Technology | eric@ericir.syr.edu, askeric@asskeric.org |
| AskERIC | askeric@askeric.org |
| Languages and Linguistics | eric@cal.org |
| Reading, English, and Communication | ericcs@indiana.edu |
| Rural Education and Small Schools | lanhamb@ael.org |
| Science, Mathematics, and Environmental Education | erics@osu.edu |
| Social Studies/Social Science Education | erocso@indiana.edu |
| Teaching and Teacher Education | query @aacts.nche.edu |
| Urban Education | ericcue@columbia.edu |

brary or school. That person will set up an appointment and discuss the type of topic about which you would like research information. The contact person can then perform online searches to give you an example of the types of articles and reports that are available. You can then order abstracts of the most relevant articles. Today, the ERIC collection is also available over the Internet. Individuals can visit the ERIC web site and perform online searches. AskERIC is also a service provided by the ERIC system. Users can ask questions related to education by sending an e-mail to askeric@ericir.sys.edu. Answers normally are provided within twenty-four hours. Users can also use the ERIC site to obtain sample lesson plans and other products on thousands of topics, as well as link to many other education websites and services. E-mail addresses for the various ERIC locations are provided in Figure R1.3.

## UNIT 2 *Action Research for Classroom Teachers*

Throughout *Learning to Teach*, the point of view has been that it is important for teachers to have a command of the knowledge base on teaching and that research is a valuable resource to guide teaching practices. In addition, Chapter 13 described the importance of teachers assuming responsibility and taking individual initiative for improving the classrooms and schools in which they work. A logical extension of these admonitions is the idea that teachers can become researchers for the purposes of improving their teaching and the learning environments in their classrooms. This resource unit provides the rationale for classroom research and describes how you can use action research for the purpose of improving your teaching.

## 🍎 *Perspective and Rationale*

When teachers engage in classroom research, it is commonly called **action research.** Sometimes it is referred to as **teacher research.** In many ways, action or teacher research is like any other research. It is the process of asking questions, seeking valid information, and interpreting and using the results. But it differs from some other kinds of research in that its goal is to produce valid information and knowledge that has immediate application—in this instance, for teachers or their students. And unlike some researchers, teacher researchers are more interested in knowledge about a specific situation (their own classroom) than about more general applications. In other words, action research is guided by the processes and standards of scientific inquiry, but it is not intended in most instances to inform the larger research or educational community. Instead, it is a process of acquiring information and seeking knowledge that will serve your own actions.

### A Short History

Action research as conceptualized and practiced today is the outgrowth of over a half century of thought that has been most influenced by the early traditions of John Dewey, Kurt Lewin, and Les Corey and his associates at Teachers College. More recently, the field has been influenced by Donald Schön, Chris Argyris, Sharon Oja, and Marilyn Cochran-Smith. Schön's ideas about reflective practice were introduced in Chapter 1. Argyris and colleagues (1985), who studied the traditions of action research, pointed out the importance of Dewey's contributions:

> Dewey (1929, 1933) was eloquent in his criticism of the traditional separation of knowledge and action, and he articulated a theory of inquiry that was a model both for scientific method and for social practice. He hoped that the extension of experimental inquiry to social practice would lead to an integration of science and practice. He based his hope on the observation that science . . . can become a mode of directed practical doing. This observation that experimentation in science is but a special case of human beings testing their conceptions in action, is at the core of the pragmatist epistemology. For the most part, however, the modern social sciences have appropriated the model of the natural sciences in ways that have maintained the separation of science and practice that Dewey deplored. Mainstream social science is related to social practice in much the same way that the natural sciences are related to engineering. This contrasts sharply with Dewey's vision of using scientific methods in social practice. (pp. 6–7)

### Why Action Research?

Today, the notion of teacher as researcher has gained widespread popularity in the United States, Great Britain, Canada, and Australia. In Great Britain, much of the interest has stemmed from the work of such people as Lawrence Stenhouse (1975, 1983, 1984), who has written widely about why action research is important, and David Hopkins (1985), who has provided concrete advice to teachers about how to conduct classroom research and use the results for school improvement. In the United States, many individuals, such as Oja and Smulyan (1989) and Cochran-Smith and Lytle (1993) have written about action research. In addition, the use of research and classroom teachers as action researchers has been high on the agenda of both major teacher associations, the American Federation of Teachers (AFT) and the National Education Association (NEA). (See Livingston & Castle, 1989, Ponessa, 1997) The individuals and organizations advancing action research worldwide base their argument on two common premises about the role of the teacher and the processes of improving classroom teaching.

**The Autonomous Professional.** Many thoughtful observers believe that the time has come for teachers to become autonomous professionals. By this, they mean that instead of teachers relying on principals, central office supervisors, or college professors to tell them what to do, they should instead have command of their own knowledge and information to support decisions they make about teaching practices. Stenhouse (1984) strongly supported this point of view.

> Good teachers are necessarily autonomous in professional judgement. They do not need to be told what to do. They are not professionally the dependents of researchers or superintendents, or innovators or supervisors. This does not mean that they do not welcome access to ideas created by other people at other places or in other times. Nor do they reject advice, consultancy or support. But they do know that ideas and people are not of much real use until they are digested to the point where they are subject of teachers' own judgement. . . . (p. 7)

For Stenhouse and others, the key to becoming an autonomous professional rests on teachers' disposition and ability to engage in self-study of their teaching and testing their classroom practices to see if they work. Obviously, this is a revolutionary view of teaching and one that departs dramatically from more traditional conceptions.

**Information Is Power.** In addition to the point of view that teachers should be autonomous professionals, action research is also based on several premises about the processes of school improvement and the power of valid information to bring about improvement. Change and improvement for individuals or organizations comes about only as people construct new realities to replace existing ones and thereby make proposed improvements meaningful to themselves. New realities are constructed from new information and knowledge that challenges current ways of thinking. Thus, one can think of action research as a way to help construct new realities about one's teaching. It is a way for teachers to:

- Collect *valid information* about their classrooms.
- Use this information to make *informed choices* about teaching strategies and learning activities.
- Share the information with students in order to gain their ideas and *internal commitment* to specified learning activities and procedures.*

## 🍎 *Doing Action Research*

To do action research requires choosing the type of inquiry in which to engage from among various forms and paying careful attention to several aspects of the action research process.

*The concepts of valid information, informed choice, and internal commitment come from Argyris (1970) and Schön (1987).

**Figure R2.1** *Framework and Types of Action Research*

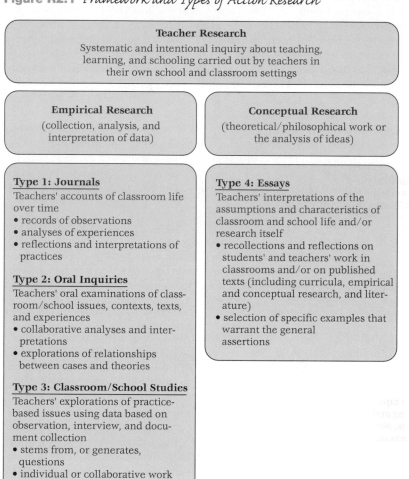

**Teacher Research**

Systematic and intentional inquiry about teaching, learning, and schooling carried out by teachers in their own school and classroom settings

**Empirical Research**
(collection, analysis, and interpretation of data)

**Conceptual Research**
(theoretical/philosophical work or the analysis of ideas)

**Type 1: Journals**
Teachers' accounts of classroom life over time
• records of observations
• analyses of experiences
• reflections and interpretations of practices

**Type 2: Oral Inquiries**
Teachers' oral examinations of classroom/school issues, contexts, texts, and experiences
• collaborative analyses and interpretations
• explorations of relationships between cases and theories

**Type 3: Classroom/School Studies**
Teachers' explorations of practice-based issues using data based on observation, interview, and document collection
• stems from, or generates, questions
• individual or collaborative work

**Type 4: Essays**
Teachers' interpretations of the assumptions and characteristics of classroom and school life and/or research itself
• recollections and reflections on students' and teachers' work in classrooms and/or on published texts (including curricula, empirical and conceptual research, and literature)
• selection of specific examples that warrant the general assertions

Source: After Cochran-Smith and Lytle (1993), p. 27.

## Types of Action Research

Marilyn Cochran-Smith and Susan Lytle (1993) provided a definition of teacher (action) research and categorized it into four types: journals, oral inquiries, classroom or school studies, and essays. These four types of research and what teachers do in each are described in Figure R2.1.

## Action Research Processes

In general, there is a flow or set of steps for initiating and completing an action research project. The three important parts of the process include deciding on problems to study and framing questions, collecting valid information, and interpreting and using this information for the purpose of improving one's teaching.

Action research starts with classroom situations that teachers find unsatisfactory and in need of improvement. The process consists of isolating a problem for inquiry, taking action, collecting data, observing what happens, and then reflecting on the

**Figure R2.2** *Kemmis and McTaggart's Conception of the Action Research Process*

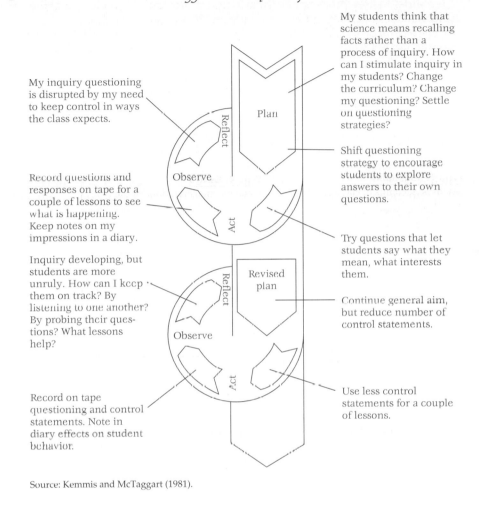

My students think that science means recalling facts rather than a process of inquiry. How can I stimulate inquiry in my students? Change the curriculum? Change my questioning? Settle on questioning strategies?

My inquiry questioning is disrupted by my need to keep control in ways the class expects.

Plan

Reflect

Observe

Shift questioning strategy to encourage students to explore answers to their own questions.

Record questions and responses on tape for a couple of lessons to see what is happening. Keep notes on my impressions in a diary.

Act

Try questions that let students say what they mean, what interests them.

Inquiry developing, but students are more unruly. How can I keep them on track? By listening to one another? By probing their questions? What lessons help?

Revised plan

Reflect

Observe

Continue general aim, but reduce number of control statements.

Record on tape questioning and control statements. Note in diary effects on student behavior.

Act

Use less control statements for a couple of lessons.

Source: Kemmis and McTaggart (1981).

whole process before recycling into further study. Australia's Kemmis and McTaggart (1981) illustrated their view of the action research process as shown in Figure R2.2.

## Problem and Question Formulation

**Overall Considerations.** A beginning teacher is confronted with literally hundreds of problems or questions that could be topics for action research. The most difficult part of an action research project, however, is identifying a specific problem for study and defining carefully the variables involved. David Hopkins (1985) identified five principles to use in deciding on a problem for study.

**1.** *The project should not interfere with the teacher's first job, which is teaching.* Obviously, there is no easy way to say whether an action research project will disrupt teaching. Hopkins reminds us that action research is used for the purpose of understanding and improving our teaching and not for the pleasure of doing research for its own sake.

2. *Methods of collecting data should not be too demanding of the teacher's time.* This, too, is a reminder to keep projects, particularly first efforts, rather simple so that the action research does not make undue demands on already busy schedules.

3. *The methods used should produce reliable and valid information.* Even though information generated from action research is to improve a particular teacher's practice rather than more generalizable results, the validity and reliability of the information are still important. If the methods are not rigorous and the information is not reliable and valid, the results will be of little value to anyone.

4. *The problem studied should be one to which the teacher is committed and that is capable of solution.* This is a reminder that if the problem is too complex or if it is influenced by factors over which the teacher has little control, then information collected, regardless of how valid or reliable, will make little difference.

5. *Ethical standards for research govern teachers' research, just as they do any other research.* Standards such as keeping people informed about purposes of the project, obtaining authorization before collecting sensitive information, maintaining confidentiality, and respecting the rights of subjects are just as important for teacher researchers to maintain as they are for other researchers.

**Getting to Specifics About Problems and Questions.** As with any research, a good problem for action research is one that can be stated in a question form, focuses on the relationships among variables, and has the possibility of testing. Remember from the previous resource unit the distinctions made between independent and dependent variables. An independent variable refers to some aspect or property of the problem that is the presumed cause (teacher behavior, for instance); a dependent variable is a consequence (student engagement or learning).

Sometimes problems or questions cannot be stated very clearly in the beginning. The problem is likely to consist of a general uneasiness a teacher has about a classroom situation. Things are just not working quite the way the teacher desires. Sometimes this general uneasiness about a problem or question can be transformed into something more specific by thinking about discrepancies or gaps that exist between the "way things are" and the "way you would like them to be." For instance, a teacher may have a situation in which only four or five students out of a class of twenty-five participate in discussions (the way things are). The desired state may be to have all students participate fully. The question for study thus becomes, "How can I increase participation in my classroom during discussion periods?"

Sometimes discrepancies exist between what we think we are doing and what we are actually doing. These too can become the focus for inquiry. As you will see in an example provided later, teachers may think they are interacting with all students in an equitable fashion but on careful study find that they indeed interact differentially with different types or groups of students. The first question that stems from this type of problem situation is, "Do I interact differentially with different types of students?" If so, a second question for study becomes evident: "How can I change my behavior?"

In general, the recommendation for beginning teachers is to tackle problems from their own immediate experiences and concerns and ask questions that can be tested with rather straightforward plans and data collection efforts. Some of these questions will be amenable to informal data collection and testing procedures; others will require more formal methods. Here are several categories of questions that have been posed by teacher researchers during student teaching or early in their careers.

1. *Questions associated with student opinions.* Sometimes teachers are not sure what their students think about their teaching or about life in their classrooms. Questions might include the following: "Do students have high opinions of my instruction?" "Do my students find the learning environment pleasant?" "Do my students find the learning environment challenging?" "Do my students have the perception that I am treating them fairly?"

**2.** *Questions associated with particular teaching strategies or procedures.* Another set of questions that are amenable to action research are those that provide descriptive information about what a teacher is doing; for example, "What type of questions do I use during a discussion?" "Who talks most in my classes?" "Do I question and respond to all students in an equitable fashion?" "Do I give all students fair access to public time?" "How long do I wait for students to respond after asking a question?" "What proportion of the day is devoted to my own talking? To student talking? To seatwork?" "When I give an assignment to be completed in class, what proportion of the students are on task?"

**3.** *Questions comparing different approaches or variations of the same approach over time or with different groups.* Good teachers have a variety of teaching strategies and procedures at their command. As emphasized many times in this book, they match appropriate strategies to particular learning situations or groups of students. Here are some obvious questions about this matching process: What is most appropriate? What produces the best results? Here are some examples of action research questions that aim at comparing different strategies or procedures: "If I use think-pair-share (described in Chapters 10 and 12) after lecturing or showing a film in my social studies class, will it result in more student participation and learning as compared to holding a whole-class discussion?" "If I make a contract (with a reward system built in) for my uninvolved students, will this increase their engagement in learning activities as compared to not having a contract system?" "If I use manipulatives and visual graphics when teaching a particular math concept, will students' test results be better as compared to just a straight verbal presentation?" "If I use direct instruction to teach a particular skill, will five independent practices be as effective as ten in helping students acquire proficiency?" "If I increase my wait-time to four seconds, will this change the nature of the discourse patterns in my classrooms as compared to a 2-second wait-time?"

## Gathering Information

Once a problem or question has been identified for inquiry, the next issue to be resolved by the teacher researcher is how to gather information. There are many techniques for doing this, some quite simple and others more complex. Five specific approaches to data collection are described below. The choice of which approach to use depends on the question being asked and the time teachers have to gather and analyze the information.

**Questionnaires.** When teachers want information about the attitudes or opinions of their students on some aspect of their teaching or classroom, the easiest and most economical way to gather this type of information is by giving students a questionnaire to fill out. Most of you are familiar with questionnaires about teaching, because you have been asked many times to fill out course evaluations in your college classes. Many examples of this type of questionnaire can be found in the accompanying manual. For example, Chapter 3 has a questionnaire to get information about how students feel about life in their classrooms. Chapter 4 has an example of a questionnaire to get perceptions students have about how fairly their teacher is treating them.

Questionnaire format normally poses a question or makes a statement with which respondents can agree or disagree. For example:

My teacher treats all students the same.

| Agree strongly | Agree | Neither agree nor disagree | Disagree | Disagree strongly |

or

Does the teacher help you when you are stuck?

| All the time | Most of the time | Sometimes/ sometimes not | Hardly ever | Never |
|---|---|---|---|---|

Many of the rules for constructing questionnaire items are the same as those described in Chapter 6 for constructing multiple-choice test questions. Remember to write questions that are simple and straightforward and make sure the response categories are consistent. When constructing a questionnaire for younger children, it is normal practice to use three rather than five response categories. For very young children, the happy, neutral, or sad face response categories illustrated in Figure R2.3 can be used.

Sometimes teachers prefer more open-ended responses. In this case, asking questions such as, "What did you like best about the lesson?" or "What did you like least?" provides valuable information. This type of item will provide more in-depth information and will not be biased by the response categories. However, it can be a bit more difficult to organize and interpret the responses from this type of question as compared to questions with definite response categories.

**Interviews.** Whereas questionnaires have the advantage of being easier to construct and score, they also have their disadvantages. One is never sure what students are actually thinking when they check one of the response categories. It is also difficult to write good questionnaire items that explore issues in any depth. An alternative way to collect information about student attitudes and opinions is to interview them.

Information can be obtained from students either individually or in small groups through an interview. As with questionnaires, it is important to write interview questions ahead of time and keep them straightforward and directed toward the question for which answers are sought. During the interview process itself, it is important to reassure students that they will not be punished for being candid, to employ good listening skills, and to emphasize how important their ideas are to you. The disadvantages of using interviews are that they are time-consuming (although the time factor can be reduced if students are interviewed in small groups), and it is frequently difficult to get students to express their true feelings and opinions candidly.

**Observations.** Many questions require some type of direct observation of teaching and student behavior. The procedures for observation and the recording devices can vary according to the type of question being asked. Normally, better information is acquired if a specific observation instrument is designed and used. Many specific observation instruments are provided in the accompanying manual. Their use (with adaptation) will help collect needed information for many of the questions posed by beginning teachers.

There are essentially three ways to collect information through observation. The choice again depends on the situation. One, the teacher may ask a colleague to observe classroom interactions and collect needed information. If this approach is used, the teacher researcher needs to make sure the colleague understands the observation instrument and can use it effectively.

**Figure R2.3** *Happy, Neutral, and Sad Face Responses*

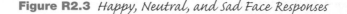

Many times it is better (and less threatening) to make audio or video recordings of a lesson and then observe and code specific behaviors from the videotapes or audiotapes. When verbal behavior of students or teachers is the subject of inquiry, audiotapes work fine. However, subtler nonverbal behaviors require video recordings. How one teacher used both audio and video recording to study his interactions with second grade students is described later.

Notes, Diaries, and Journals. Taking careful notes or keeping a diary or journal is a fourth way of collecting information about classroom events, your teaching, or your students' behavior. In general, observations must be committed to paper as soon as possible after an event, and they are more helpful if they are guided by a specific set of questions posed ahead of time as compared to more general observations that may come to mind. Notes and journals are particularly helpful for collecting information when the focus of inquiry is a particular student. They are also a good way to systematically study aspects of teaching that are not amenable to observation, such as your own thinking processes.

Standardized Tests. As described in Chapter 6, most states require all students to take standardized tests at various grade levels to demonstrate their mastery and achievement in reading, writing, mathematics, and often in social studies and science. To examine the effects of various approaches and practices being used in a school, teachers can use scores from these tests. For instance, teachers in a school may be disappointed by how their students are performing on the state's writing test. They decide to implement a writing-across-the-curriculum project. This approach requires teachers to have students do more writing in every subject area and to judge student work on common criteria. Obviously, student scores on the yearly standardized test would provide good insight into whether or not this new approach was making any difference.

## Interpreting and Using Information from Action Research

A final step in action research is to organize the results from a project and share it with others. Some teachers share the results with colleagues and use the data they have collected as a springboard for discussions about different approaches to teaching. Other teachers choose to share the results of an action research project with their students. The information collected in many projects can provide students with insights about their classroom and the teaching approaches being used by the teacher. This type of information can also help students gain commitment to learning activities found to be effective and provide a vehicle for them to think about and help plan classroom activities.

## 🍎 *Action Research: An Example*

This example is of an actual action research project done by a beginning teacher, David Weisz of Silver Spring, Maryland, while he was a student teacher in a second grade classroom (Weisz, no date).

## David's Questions

David was a very sensitive person and held strong beliefs about the importance of social justice in our society. He thought a lot about what teachers could do to promote justice and equality in their classrooms and was specifically concerned about his own treatment of students. His intentions were to treat all students equally and to communicate the same expectations to all students regardless of their abilities. He decided to study his use of questions and feedback in math groups from an equity perspective. He determined that the following questions would guide his action research project.

1. Do I favor students I perceive to be high achievers by directing more questions to them and by focusing high-level questions at them rather than at perceived low achievers and/or by giving them qualitatively or quantitatively better feedback?
2. Do I favor boys or girls in these same regards? (p. 2)

David explained that two things prompted his interest in this project. First, he had noticed during his student teaching the "relative ease with which a lesson can proceed if I focus exclusively or primarily on those students who appear to listen well, who have studied the materials, and who can be relied on to respond correctly or, at least, intelligently" (p. 2). He wondered if in his desire to have a smooth lesson he was favoring those whom he perceived as good students by asking them more questions and giving them more feedback and at the same time ignoring those students whom he perceived as not so good. He believed that teachers could be easily tempted into doing this as the pressures of teaching increase and wrote that he "wanted to avoid falling into this trap—or to get out of the trap if I've already fallen in it" (p. 2).
Second, David had studied gender differences in mathematics participation and written a paper on that topic for one of his college classes. He knew that some teachers show differential treatment to boys as compared to girls. He also had observed in a journal he kept that he was able to learn the names of the boys in his classes more readily than the names of the girls. So he wondered, "Will I be surprised to find that I differentiate between boys and girls in the questions I ask and the feedback I provide?" (p. 3).

## David's Data Collection Methods

To carry out his study, David made five audiotapes and one videotape of lessons he identified in advance as those in which he planned to have considerable teacher-student interaction. In addition, a week before taping, David identified the names of five students in the class whom he perceived to be high achievers and five whom he perceived to be low achievers. These perceptions were based on four weeks of experience with his students and knowing how well they did in mathematics. He reported, however, that he "quickly put this list away and tried not to think about it any more until the taping was finished" (p. 4). David knew if the names became too embedded in his mind, it could bias his interactions and diminish the value of the information he was about to collect.

Once he had his videotapes and audiotapes, David constructed and used a data sheet as shown in Table R2.1 to analyze his interaction with students.

## David's Results and Interpretations

After organizing his data and putting them in table format, David found that indeed he was showing slight differential treatment to high achievers as contrasted to low achievers and to boys as contrasted to girls. What is most interesting about David's action research project, however, is his careful and thoughtful interpretation of these data. His own words say it better than any summary: "There were certain areas where my treatment was not equitable (high- and low-order questions and the no-response, praise, and incorrect/dignified types of feedback)" (p. 7). David did not conclude from this information, however, that his differential treatment of students was necessarily bad teaching or unfair. Instead, he thought about what it meant and posed a question that even many professional researchers have ignored: "Is differential treatment always undesirable?"

**Table R2.1**  *David's Data Sheet for Coding Particular Types of Teacher-Student Interaction*

| Student's Name | Response Opportunities | Type of Questions | | Type of Feedback |
|---|---|---|---|---|
| | | High | Low | None + + − + − − + − |
| Coding schemes: | Response opportunity: | Student was called on by teacher. | | |
| | High questions: | Questions that required students to think | | |
| | Low questions: | Questions that required recall of information | | |
| | None: | Teacher moved on with no response. | | |
| | + + | Teacher praised a correct student response. | | |
| | − + | Teacher identified an incorrect response but dignified the error. | | |
| | − − | Teacher identified an incorrect response and was critical of the error. | | |
| | + | Teacher was positive but with no effect. | | |
| | − | Teacher was negative but with no effect. | | |

One important question which must be dealt with at the outset is whether an equal distribution of response opportunities, types of questions, and feedback is indeed desirable when comparing my treatment of perceived high achievers and perceived low achievers. Low achievers, high achievers and midrange achievers have different needs and may therefore require some kind of differential treatment: for example, low achievers may need more response opportunities, a more judicious blend of high order and low order questions, more praise—as long as it is measured and sincere—and more "dignifying" follow-up to incorrect responses. If I perceive certain students to be low achievers, would I be aiming at equal treatment of them vis-à-vis those I perceive to be high achievers, or *should I develop a more sophisticated approach to both the low achievers and the high achievers?*

A case then can be made for differential treatment of high and low achievers. The problem is, however, that when educational researchers find such differential treatment it often goes in the wrong direction—that is, it is often biased against low achievers. I refer, for example, to the work of Good and Brophy (1987). While equal treatment may not be ideal, it is nevertheless better than differential treatment that works against those who are perceived to be most in need of help. (p. 11)

So, David concluded that differential treatment may be desired as long as it is meeting individual needs and not always going against those of low ability. He turned next to his differential treatment of boys and girls and in this instance reaches a different conclusion.

Differential treatment on the basis of sex would seem to be much less defensible than differential treatment for perceived high and low achievers. What is significant in my results is that even though not great, it is the fact that in each case the imbalance in my treatment favored the boys: proportionately more of the total response opportunities went to boys, proportionately more high-order questions went to boys and substantially more low-order questions went to the girls. Again, while the differential is not large, the imbalance in all three instances works to the detriment of girls. Given the generally lower participation and achievement of girls in mathematics at higher levels, *I would have felt better had the imbalance gone the other way* (p. 13).

Finally, David concluded his thoughts about his action research project and set some goals for his teaching behavior in the future.

As I teach, I do not consciously think in terms of categories such as perceived high and low achievers and boys and girls. Nevertheless, the patterns found in the types of teacher-student interaction I studied in my action research indicated that, in some cases, I am interacting with students on the basis of these categorizations rather than on the basis of the individual student and thus may be communicating to them certain expectations for their performance based on these categorizations.

I am, now, as a result of this action research, more sensitive to the many ways that this can be done. I now must work to keep this sensitivity alive and ensure that I apply it in my teaching in the years ahead. (p. 13)

For those who choose to become students of their own teaching, David's action research project can be a model to follow. He chose to study a problem—differential treatment of students—that has been of concern to professional researchers for over two decades. It is also a problem in which teachers, regardless of their good intentions, find discrepancies between what they believe and what they actually do. David's use of audio and video recordings, along with the rather simple but effective coding scheme, produced objective information about his teaching behavior. The limited scope of the study and its overall design conform to the principles for action research described by Hopkins (1985). Most important, David's thoughtful interpretation of his results shows the significant progress he has made in his young career toward becoming a reflective, autonomous professional.

# UNIT 3 *Learning and Study Strategies*

Throughout *Learning to Teach,* the focus has been on what teachers do. This unit turns from a description of particular teaching strategies to a focus on student learning and study strategies. Thus, we shift our attention from looking primarily at what teachers do and think to what students do and think. The unit begins with an overview of learning and study strategies and their importance and then examines the theoretical support behind them. Next, arrays of learning and study strategies are examined, some dating back to ancient times and others the result of recent developments. The final section describes briefly how teachers teach learning strategies to students.

## 🍎 *Overview*

### Importance and Purposes of Strategy Instruction

You may ask, "Why include information on learning and study strategies in a book on teaching?" As emphasized throughout *Learning to Teach,* the ultimate purpose of teaching is to help students become independent and self-regulated learners. Therefore, one answer to the question is that good teaching includes teaching students how to think, how to remember, and how to monitor their own learning. Indeed, some educators believe, as do Weinstein and Meyer (1986), that it is strange that we expect students to learn yet seldom teach them about learning and that we require them to remember a considerable body of information yet seldom teach them the art of memory.

It is important for students to learn about the various learning and study strategies that are available as well as when to use them appropriately. In the past, such instruction was not always provided. Durkin (1978, 1979), for example, found that elementary teachers were good assignment givers but provided little instruction on how to study or learn. A study by Moely and colleagues (1986) reinforced this finding, as did Sirotnik's (1983) study of middle and high school teachers. More recently, this situation perhaps has improved as researchers and teachers have begun to develop specific learning strategies and to use them with students.

## Defining Learning Strategies

**Learning strategies** are the behaviors and thought processes used by students that influence what is learned, including memory and metacognitive processes. Students use these strategies to attack particular learning problems. For example, students are often assigned specific learning tasks, such as completing a worksheet in reading or locating source material for a history report. To complete these learning tasks requires engaging in particular thought processes and behaviors, such as skimming main headings, summarizing, and taking notes, as well as monitoring one's own thinking. So, to perform most assigned learning tasks, students must use several learning strategies.

## Self-Regulated Learners

The main purpose of strategy instruction is to teach learners to learn on their own. You remember from Chapter 1 that several terms are used to describe this type of learner, including *independent learner, strategic learner,* and *self-regulated learner.* This unit uses primarily the term *self-regulated learner,* which refers to the learner who can do four important things:

1. Accurately diagnose a particular learning situation;
2. Select a learning strategy to attack the learning problem posed;
3. Monitor the effectiveness of the strategy; and
4. Be motivated to engage in the learning situation until it is accomplished.

An example of a self-regulated learner is one who knows it is important to summarize or to ask questions while reading a passage in a book or listening to a teacher's presentation and one who is motivated to perform such an operation and monitor its success. This learner also knows when it is not important to employ a particular strategy, such as when the teacher is telling a joke or recalling an interesting experience.

## 🍎 *Theoretical Support for Learning Strategies*

Before we describe specific learning and study strategies, we will discuss the theory behind strategy instruction. This theory is important because it helps explain when particular learning and study strategies should be used by teachers and why they work the way they do. The support for learning strategies stems primarily from two theoretical sources, Vygotsky's work, described in Chapter 11, and contemporary cognitive psychology, introduced in Chapter 7. Remember that Vygotsky emphasized three main ideas: (1) the intellect develops as individuals confront new and puzzling ideas and link these ideas to what they already know; (2) interactions with others enhance intellectual development; and (3) a teacher's primary role is to serve as a helper and mediator of student learning. The contribution of cognitive psychology stems from those theories that explain how the mind works and how individuals acquire and process information. The perspectives offered by Vygotsky and more recent cognitive psychologists are important in understanding the use of learning strategies for three reasons. One, they highlight the important role that prior knowledge plays in the learning process. Two, they help us understand what knowledge is and the differences between various types of knowledge. And three, they help explain how knowledge is acquired by humans and processed in the mind's memory system.

**Figure R3.1** *Making Bridges Between the New and the Known*

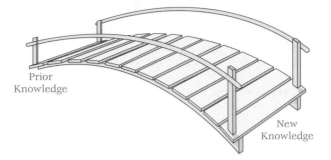

Prior
Knowledge

New
Knowledge

## Importance of Prior Knowledge

For many years—indeed, dating back to the early Greeks—philosophers and teachers have theorized that what individuals already know influences to a great extent what they can learn. One learns by associating new ideas with old ideas. Contemporary cognitive psychologists have refined these ancient truths and have shown more precisely how relating new information to information already stored in memory enhances learning.

Cognitive psychologists refer to the information and experiences stored in long-term memory as *prior knowledge.* Research has been conducted during the past three decades on the influence prior knowledge has on learning to read and write and learning to use new information of all kinds. A common finding that has emerged from this research is that a learner's prior knowledge controls new learning possibilities. That is, specific new knowledge—facts, concepts, and skills—cannot be learned until a foundation of related knowledge has been established. Figure R3.1 illustrates how important it is in teaching to help students build bridges between the new and the known.

## Kinds of Knowledge

You also read in Chapter 7 how knowledge can be divided into three categories: declarative knowledge, procedural knowledge, and conditional knowledge. Remember that **declarative knowledge** is knowledge a learner has about something or knowledge that something is the case. Knowing a poem, a group of facts, a list of dates, and the rules of a game are examples of declarative knowledge. In contrast, **procedural knowledge** is knowledge a learner has about how to do something. Being able to divide fractions, recite a poem, and play a game are examples of procedural knowledge. The third category of knowledge is referred to as **conditional knowledge,** which is knowing when to use particular declarative or procedural knowledge. Knowing when to apply a certain algorithm to solve a mathematics problem is an example of conditional knowledge, as is knowing when to use a particular learning strategy described in this unit.

## The Memory System

The role of prior knowledge and the way knowledge is represented in the mind are two important ingredients for understanding how individuals learn and how they employ particular learning strategies. How the memory system works is another. You were introduced to the *information processing* perspective of learning in Chapter 7. Remember that information-processing theorists rely heavily on the computer as the metaphor or analog for how the mind and its memory system work. From this perspective, infor-

**Figure R3.2** *Computers and Human Information Processing*

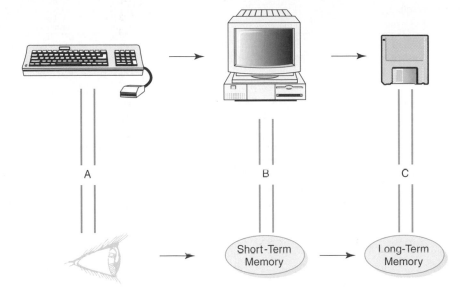

mation enters the mind through the senses (analogous to entering data using a computer keyboard) and is stored temporarily in a work space called **short-term memory** (the storage space on a desktop computer). From short-term memory, it is then transferred to **long-term memory** (a computer's hard disk) and stored (saved) until retrieved for later use. Figure R3.2 shows how a computer serves as a metaphor for the information-processing system.

**Short-Term and Long-Term Memory.** As Figure R3.2 suggests, new ideas and information begin as sensory input into our visual, auditory, tactile, and olfactory registers. Once the sensory input has been perceived and registered, it moves into short-term memory, the place in the mind where conscious mental work is done and input is either acted on in some way or forgotten. The storage space in short-term memory is very limited. However, it governs what learners attend to, how new information initially enters the memory system, and how it is subsequently transferred to long-term memory, the place where knowledge is stored permanently for later retrieval and use.

Getting students to activate prior knowledge and to focus their attention on particular learning materials is critical for bringing new information to short-term memory. However, information in short-term memory will soon be forgotten unless it is acted on by the learner. The more effort expended during this active processing phase in short-term memory, the better the chances are that the new information will be permanently transferred to long-term memory. This process of transferring new information from short-term memory to long-term memory is called **encoding.** Once in long-term memory, information is thought to be stored for a lifetime. However, storing information in long-term memory is meaningless unless ways can be found to activate and retrieve it. That, of course, is a major goal of teaching and of the several learning strategies presented in this unit.

**Knowledge Networks and Schemata.** The concepts of knowledge representation and schema theory were also introduced briefly in Chapter 7. Remember that cognitive psychologists believe that humans process knowledge in terms of basic units, called propositions and productions. **Propositions** are units of declarative knowledge, whereas

**Figure R3.3** *Reader Interacting with Text to Activate Schema and Learn New Information*

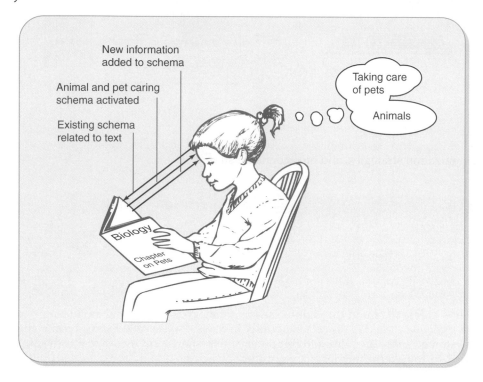

**productions** are the basic units of procedural knowledge. Together, they form **knowledge networks** that mentally link related concepts and bits of knowledge. The term *schemata* (the plural form of *schema*) refers to more complex knowledge structures, such as the vast array of concepts stored in long-term memory. A learner develops schemata through experience, and these, in turn, form the learner's prior knowledge. Some theorists have compared a person's schemata to a large filing system (Anderson & Pearson, 1984; Cooper, 1993). Various pieces of knowledge and information are stored in particular files (the schema). As new information or knowledge enters consciousness, the mind creates new files (new schema) or adds the information to existing files. Over a period of time, the whole filing system develops and expands. Mental systems, analogous to computer programs, are developed to make connections among the various files and to retrieve information from the filing system as needed. Figure R3.3 illustrates how a learner's filing system or schema influences understanding about a particular written passage.

In summary, knowledge enters short-term memory of the mind as sensory input. It is then encoded (transferred) and organized in long-term memory in the form of propositions, productions, and schemata. These knowledge networks are linked together in various relationships. Although psychologists do not always agree about the exact nature of the networks, there is a high degree of consensus that knowledge networks actively filter new information and thereby determine how well it will be received and retained by students.

# Types of Learning Strategies

Traditionally, students are asked to perform numerous learning tasks in school, such as practicing the multiplication tables, rehearsing a speech, writing in a journal, and collecting information on the World Wide Web. Although successfully completing these tasks is the most visible learning goal, a more important one is mastering the learning process itself: accurately diagnosing the learning situation, choosing an appropriate learning strategy, and monitoring the effectiveness of the strategy. This section describes how teachers can convert cognitive and information-processing theory into specific learning strategies for students. Detailed descriptions of four major types of learning strategies are given, including rehearsal strategies, elaboration strategies, organization strategies, and metacognitive strategies.

## Rehearsal Strategies

As you read in the previous section, for learning to occur, learners must act on the new information and connect it to prior knowledge. Strategies used for this encoding process are called **rehearsal strategies,** of which there are two kinds: *rote rehearsal* and *complex rehearsal.*

We are all familiar with the most basic of all rehearsal strategies, simply repeating out loud or subvocalizing information we want to remember. This is **rote rehearsal,** and it is used to remember phone numbers and directions to a particular location for a short period of time, say, when we don't have pencil and paper to write them down. We also use rote rehearsal to remember lists of items to buy at the store or chores that need to be done. Simply repeating information over and over helps keep simple information in short-term memory, but unless we elaborate on the information—link the phone numbers to something meaningful, for instance—there is little likelihood that it will transfer to long-term memory. Furthermore, simply repeating and vocalizing does not provide much assistance when more complex information is involved. A learner cannot remember all the words or ideas in a book simply by reading the book out loud.

Retaining more complex materials requires **complex rehearsal strategies** that go beyond merely repeating information. Underlining key ideas and making marginal notes are two complex rehearsal strategies that can be taught to students to help them remember more complex learning materials.

Underlining.  Underlining key ideas or text passages is a technique most students have learned by the time they reach college. Underlining helps students learn more from text for several reasons. First, it physically locates key ideas, thereby making review and memorization quicker and more efficient. Second, the process of selecting what to underline assists in connecting new information to existing knowledge. Unfortunately, students do not always use the underlining procedure very effectively. A common error is to underline almost everything. Obviously, this does not help highlight important information or allow for quick review before a test. Sometimes students also underline information that is irrelevant. This is particularly true of younger students who have difficulty determining what information is most and least important.

Marginal Notes.  Making marginal notes and other annotations helps supplement underlining and is another example of a complex rehearsal strategy. Figure R3.4 provides examples of marginal notes and other types of notations. Notice that the student circled words she didn't know, underlined important definitions, numbered and made a list of

**Figure R3.4** *Examples of Marginal Notes and Annotations*

| Type of Note or Annotation | | Example |
|---|---|---|
| Mark definitions | | The amount of time the teacher spends on <u>academic</u> tasks is called <u>allocated time.</u> |
| Circle unknown words. | | At least eleven of its (denizens) are on the federal list of endangered species. |
| Place asterisks next to important idea. | | *The system for making choices must be ethical. |
| Mark possible test item. | Test Item | How? Negotiate a favorable lease. |
| Number list (key ideas, causes, reasons). | | Weather patterns are influenced by 1) low pressure; 2) high pressure. |
| Note confusing passages | ?? do what?? | Rehearsal, particularly complex, strategies help students . . . |
| Mark summary statements. | | <u>New teachers are fortunate because they are starting their careers at an optimum time.</u> |
| Note similarities. | similar to Dewey? | Kilpatrick argued that learning should be purposeful. |

SOURCE: After McWhorter (1992), p. 319.

events, identified a confusing sentence, and wrote memory notes and comments. Rehearsal, particularly complex rehearsal strategies, helps students attend to specific new information and assists with encoding. It does not help students make new information more meaningful, however. This requires other, more complex learning strategies.

## Elaboration Strategies

**Elaboration strategies** make up the second category of learning strategies. As the name implies, elaboration is the process of adding detail so new information will become more meaningful, thereby making encoding easier and more definitive. Elaboration strategies help transfer new information from short-term to long-term memory by creating associations and connections between new information and what is already known. For example, relating a telephone number to a significant date such as one's birthday makes the number more meaningful and increases the likelihood that it will be retained in long-term memory. People use this strategy when creating PIN numbers for their bank cards or code numbers for voice mail accounts. These strategies use the mind's existing schemata to make sense out of new information. Note taking, the use of analogies, and the PQ4R method are three frequently used elaboration strategies.

Note Taking. A great deal of information is given to students through teacher presentations and demonstrations. Note taking assists students in learning this information

**Figure R3.5** *Example of Matrix Notes*

**Topic**    Loons and Cormorants

**Loons,** with their heavy, solid bones, enjoy a wet habitat. Loons range
between 30″–36″ and can be identified by their loud yodeling call.
They have a black-and-white checkerboard pattern.

**Cormorants** are heavy-bodied diving birds that paddle across the
water's surface. Cormorants are usually silent, and their size ranges
between 30″–36″. These birds are black with bare patches of
orange skin.

**Matrix Notes from Passage
on Loons and Cormorants**

| Similarities | Loon | Cormorant |
| --- | --- | --- |
| Structure | heavy, solid bones | heavy bodied |
| habitat | water | water |
| size | 30″–36″ | 30″–36″ |
| **Differences** | | |
| voice | loud, yodeling | silent |
| color | black/white | black/orange |

by compactly storing it for later review and rehearsal. Done correctly, note taking also helps organize information so that it can be processed and connected to existing knowledge more effectively. However, as with underlining, many students are ineffective note takers. Some students attempt to write down everything teachers say, whereas others have difficulty identifying relevant and important ideas. Effective note takers, on the other hand, capture the main ideas of a presentation in their own words in outline form so that they spend time making sense by synthesizing and summarizing important points and ideas. Kiewra (1989) suggested the use of **matrix note taking** as a way of elaborating and making comparisons within complex information. An example of this is shown in Figure R3.5.

**Analogies.**  Using analogies is another way of providing for elaboration. **Analogies** are comparisons made to show the similarities between like features of things or ideas that otherwise are different, such as a heart and a pump. Here are two more examples.

Our mind is like a computer that takes in and stores information. Our sensory registers are like the computer's keyboard where information enters. Information is stored in the mind's long-term memory just as it is stored on the computer's hard disk.

Schools are like factories. Students are the raw resources that are processed into a final product, an educated person.

When used as a learning strategy, note how analogies link new ideas—the way the mind or schools work—to already familiar ideas—the computer or factories.

**PQ4R.**  Another elaboration strategy that has long been very popular with teachers is the **PQ4R method** used to help students remember what they read. It is likely that you were taught this method during your elementary or middle school career. P stands for preview, Q for question, and the 4Rs consist of read, reflect, recite, and review (Robinson, 1961; Thomas & Robinson, 1972). A student using PQ4R would be instructed to approach a reading assignment using the following steps.

**Step 1:** *Preview* the reading assignment. Look at major headings and topics, read the overview and summary, and predict what the reading will be about.

**Step 2:** Consider the major topics and headings and ask *questions* for which the text might provide answers.

**Step 3:** *Read* the material. Pay attention to main ideas and seek answers to the questions posed.

**Step 4:** *Reflect* while reading. Create visual images from the text. Try to connect the new information in the text with what you already know.

**Step 5:** After reading, *recite* by answering the questions you asked out loud and without the book. Recall lists or other important facts included in the text either out loud or subvocally.

**Step 6:** *Review* by going back over the material, reread when necessary, and again answer the questions that were posed.

Previewing and asking questions before reading activates prior knowledge and starts the process of making connections between new information and what is already known. Looking at headings and major topics helps readers become aware of the organization of the new materials, thus facilitating its transfer from short-term to long-term memory. Recitation of basic information, particularly when accompanied by some form of elaboration, likewise enhances encoding.

## Organization Strategies

A third category of learning strategies involves what are referred to as organization strategies. As with elaboration strategies, these aim at helping learners increase the meaningfulness of new materials, mainly by imposing new organizational structures on the materials. **Organization strategies** may consist of regrouping or clustering ideas or terms or of dividing them into smaller subsets. They also consist of identifying key ideas or facts from a larger array of information. Outlining, mapping, and mnemonics are common organization strategies.

**Outlining.** In outlining, students learn to relate a variety of topics or ideas to some main idea. In traditional outlines, the only kind of relation is subordination of one topic to another. The first page of each chapter in this text shows an outline of the chapter and is there to give readers a preview of the key ideas and topics in the chapter and their relationship to each other. As with other learning strategies, students are rarely good outliners at first, but they can learn to write good outlines if they are given appropriate instruction and sufficient practice.

**Mapping.** Mapping, also called concept *webbing*, is an alternative to outlining. In some instances, mapping is more effective than outlining, particularly when the learning materials are complex. In Chapter 9, directions were provided on how to construct a concept map. Remember that the big job in developing a concept map is to show how main ideas and subparts of a topic or concept are related to one another. Figure R3.6 is an illustration of a concept map on stars.

**Mnemonics.** Mnemonics form a special category and technically can be classified as either elaboration or organization strategies. Essentially, **mnemonics** refers to techniques or strategies to assist memory by helping form associations that don't naturally exist. A mnemonic helps to organize information that reaches working memory in fa-

**Figure R3.6** *Example of a Concept Map*

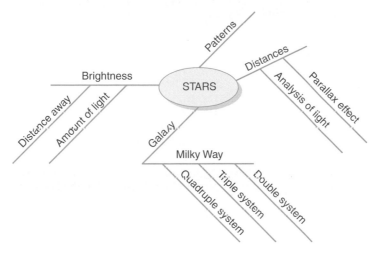

miliar patterns so that it more easily fits the schema pattern in long-term memory. Pattern recognition is an important part of connecting new information into long-term memory. Although you may never have labeled them as such, you have likely employed several different types of mnemonics in your life, both in and outside school. Several examples of this device are provided here.

*Chunking.* Because an individual's working memory has such limited capacity, it is difficult for most people to learn a long list of numbers such as those used to identify a credit card or an automobile registration. If, however, numbers can be placed in chunks, they are more easily remembered. For instance, most people can remember a ten-digit telephone number because it has been divided into three chunks: the area code (203), the neighborhood code (231), and the individual's four-digit number (2137). Thus, most people can remember 203-231-2137, whereas they have difficulty with 2032312137. Automobile license plate numbers are assigned using the same chunking principle, often three letters and three- or four-number combinations, such as LIA-6335. Vanity plates in which the letters and numbers are personally meaningful (e.g., one's initials and birth date) make the chunking product even more memorable.

*Acronyms.* Another mnemonic is the use of **acronyms** representing the first letter of each item in a list of items. Every Good Boy Does Fine (EGBDF) is a mnemonic used by beginning music students to remember the letters of the scale. HOMES is a familiar word to help us remember the names of the Great Lakes (Huron, Ontario, Michigan, Erie, Superior). Likewise, the first letters of the words Dad, Mom, Sister, Brother are used to help remember the steps in long division: divide, multiply, subtract, and bring down. Acronyms assist memory by making associations between new information and familiar information.

*Link-Word.* Perhaps the most well-known mnemonic used in school is the key-word or **link-word method.** Created initially by Richard Atkinson (1975) as a mnemonic to learn foreign language vocabulary, the link-word method teaches students how to create a mental image that links a familiar English word to an unfamiliar foreign language word. The example shown in Figure R3.7 consists of getting students to link the Spanish word *carta,* which means postal letter, to an image of a letter being transported in a shopping *cart.* Because the familiar image has the same sound as the foreign language

**Figure R3.7** *Example of the Link-Word Method*

*Carta* means letter

↓

(cart)

word being learned (*cart* and *carta*), both the meaning and the pronunciation of the new word are captured.

## Metacognitive Strategies

A fourth type of learning strategy has been labeled **metacognitive strategies.** *Metacognition* refers to learners' thinking about their own thinking and their abilities to use particular learning strategies appropriately. John Flavel (1985) provided a more complete definition when he wrote that metacognition is

> one's knowledge concerning one's own cognitive processes. . . . Metacognition refers, among other things, to the active monitoring and consequent regulation and orchestration of these processes in relation to the cognitive objective on which they bear, usually in the service of some concrete goal or objective. (p. 232)

Most authorities agree that metacognition has two components: knowledge about cognition and self-regulating mechanisms such as cognitive control and monitoring (Baker & Brown, 1984; Brown, 1982; Gagné, E., 1985, 1993). *Knowledge about cognition* consists of the information and understanding that a learner has about his or her own thinking processes as well as knowledge about various learning strategies to use in particular learning situations. An example is when a visually oriented student knows that making a conceptual map is a good way for him or her to understand and remember a large amount of new information. Knowledge about cognition is a form of declarative knowledge and, as such, can be taught to students like any other form of declarative knowledge.

The second component of metacognition, **cognitive monitoring,** is a learner's ability to select, use, and monitor learning strategies that are appropriate both for their own learning style and for the situation at hand. A visual learner's use of concept mapping is one example. Another example of this form of metacognition would be a learner's ability to select and to use an appropriate elaboration strategy (say, the link-word method) to accomplish a specific learning task (say, mastering a new foreign language word) and then to check the effectiveness of this method.

Table R3.1 lists the four types of cognitive strategies and provides examples of each. Students' success in school rests, to a large extent, on their proficiency to learn on their own and to monitor their own learning. This makes it important that the learning strategies described in the previous section be introduced to students starting in the early grades and continued throughout secondary and higher education.

**Table R3.1** *Four Categories of Cognitive Strategies*

| Strategy | Definition | Example |
|---|---|---|
| Rehearsal | Committing materials to memory by repeating them | Repeating a new phone number |
| Elaboration | Adding detail to new information and creating associations | Using mnemonic techniques and adding detail, such as relating a new phone number to one's Social Security number |
| Organization | Reorganizing or picking out main ideas from large bodies of information | Outlining, mnemonics, or mapping |
| Metacognition | Thinking about thinking and monitoring cognitive processing | Deciding that the best strategy for comprehending a body of new text is to create an outline of main ideas |

## Select Appropriate Strategies to Teach

At the minimum, students should be taught the study, learning, and memory strategies described in this unit. Younger students can be taught specific strategies such as outlining, mnemonic techniques, and PQ4R. Older students can then be taught how the memory system works and more advanced study and learning strategies, such as note taking, using marginal notes, and chunking. Students at every age should be introduced to such organization strategies as mapping and outlining. From the early grades, students should also be taught how to reflect on their metacognitive processes.

Using learning strategies effectively requires declarative, procedural, and conditional knowledge. Declarative knowledge about particular strategies should include how the strategy is defined, why it works the way it does, and how it is similar to or different from other strategies. For example, students need to know what matrix notes are and why this type of note taking is sometimes more effective in learning textual information than simple underlining is. They also need to know why underlining every word in a passage is not effective. Students require procedural knowledge as well, so they can use various learning strategies effectively. Knowing what a conceptual map is may be important declarative knowledge, but it is useless unless a student can actually make and use one. Finally, conditional knowledge is required so students know when and why to use particular strategies. For instance, students need to know when it is important to make matrix notes and when underlining will suffice.

## Choose an Instructional Approach

The process of teaching students learning strategies has been quite thoroughly studied (Collins & Brown, 1982; Duffy & Roehler, 1987; Palincsar & Brown, 1989; Pressley et al., 1991, 1998). For the most part, learning strategies consist of rather straightforward declarative and procedural knowledge. Teaching learning strategies, therefore, is not much different from teaching content-specific knowledge or skills such as map reading or how to use a microscope. Chapter 8 described a model of instruction for the acquisition of skills and well-structured declarative knowledge. Labeled the *direct instruction model*, it requires teachers to provide background information, to demonstrate the skill being taught, and then to provide time for students to practice the skill and receive feedback on how they are doing. In general, this is the model that teachers should use when introducing learning strategies to their students.

**Table R3.2** *Sequence of Lesson Topics and Activities for Elaboration Strategy Training Using Direct Instruction*

| Day | Topic | Activity |
|-----|-------|----------|
| Day 1 | What is an elaboration? | Explanation and guided practice |
| Day 2 | Why use elaborations? | Explanation and guided practice |
| Days 3–4 | Good elaborations generate much information. | Explanation and guided practice |
| Days 5–6 | Good elaborations organize information. | Explanation and guided practice |
| Day 8 | When to elaborate and how to recall | Guided and independent practice |
| Days 9–10 | Practice in deciding whether to elaborate and to recall | Independent practice |

Source: After E. Gagné (1985), pp. 298–299.

## 🍎 Teaching Learning Strategies

Sometimes it takes several days to teach a particular learning strategy. Ellen Gagné and her colleagues (1985) used the direct instruction approach to help seventh grade students understand and use elaboration strategies. They spent fifty minutes a day for ten days to accomplish their instructional objectives. Table R3.2 shows how they sequenced topics and activities over the ten days of instructional time.

## 🍎 A Final Thought

This Resource Handbook has explored various strategies aimed at helping students study and learn on their own. It has offered procedures for teaching learning strategies to students and for motivating them to become independent, self-regulated learners. It is important that all teachers help students learn how to learn. Meeting this challenge can be one of the most exciting and rewarding aspects of teaching.

# Glossary

**academic learning time** The amount of time a student is engaged in a particular subject or learning task at which he or she is successful.

**accountability** Holding teachers responsible for their teaching practices and for what their students learn.

**achievement motivation** The desire to take action and to excel for the purpose of experiencing success and feeling competent.

**acronym** A mnemonic that uses the first letter of familiar words to remember lists of names or other information.

**action research** Research conducted by teachers for the purpose of improving their own teaching or schools. Also called *teacher research.*

**action zone** The section of the classroom (normally the front rows and center columns) where students tend to be called on most often and most verbal interaction occurs.

**activity structures** Patterns of behavior that characterize what teachers do as they teach and what students do as they engage in learning tasks; can be viewed as the basic unit for planning.

**advance organizer** A statement made by teachers before a presentation or before having students read textual materials that provides a structure for new information to be linked to students' prior knowledge.

**affective domain** The domain that classifies objectives in the emotional response processes.

**affiliation motivation** The desire to take action for the purpose of experiencing friendship and close relationships with others.

**Americanization** The idea that one goal for education is to get minority groups to forsake their own cultures and assimilate into the dominant culture.

**analogies** An elaboration learning strategy that makes comparisons and shows the similarities between like features of things or ideas that otherwise are different.

**anticipatory set** Technique used by teachers at the beginning of a lesson to prepare students to learn and to establish a communicative link between the learner's prior knowledge and the new information to be presented. Same as *establishing set* and *set induction.*

**artifacts** The products produced by students in problem-based instruction, such as reports, videos, computer programs.

**art of teaching** A degree of accomplishment that allows basing complex decisions more on the teacher's experience than on research and scientific evidence.

**assertive discipline** An approach to classroom management that emphasizes teachers asserting their right to teach by insisting on appropriate student behavior and by responding assertively to student infractions.

**assessment** Process of collecting a full range of information about students and classrooms for the purpose of making instructional decisions.

**assigning competence** Drawing attention to special abilities and skills held by low-status students and bringing these to the attention of all students.

**assistive technologies** Special tools, mainly computer-related, to assist individuals who have special needs.

**attraction** The degree to which classroom participants respect and like one another.

**attribution theories** View of motivation that emphasizes the way individuals come to perceive and interpret the causes of their successes and failures.

**authentic assessment** Assessment procedures that have students demonstrate their abilities to perform particular tasks in real-life settings.

**authentic relationships** Relationships teachers build with their students in which both teachers and students treat each other as real and significant people.

**autonomous learner** A student who is motivated to take responsibility for his or her own learning and who has the skills and strategies to learn independently. See also *self-regulated learner.*

**autonomy norm** The expectation in many schools that teachers can do pretty much what they want within the confines of their classroom.

**available time** The part of the school day actually available for academic purposes.

**behavioral objective** A form for writing an instructional objective that emphasizes precision and careful delineation of expected student behaviors, the testing situation, and a performance criterion.

**behavior-content matrix** A planning tool that helps integrate instructional objectives, student behaviors, and course content.

**behaviorism** School of psychology emphasizing the importance of behavior and the external environment as a determinant of human behavior and learning.

**behavior modeling** Term used in social learning theory to describe how people learn as a result of observing others.

**best practice** Teaching methods, processes, and procedures that have been shown to be effective for helping students learn.

**causal-comparative research** Research that explores causal relationships when the independent variable cannot be manipulated.

**checking for understanding** Technique used by teachers to see if students have grasped newly presented information or skills.

**circle seating pattern** A seating arrangement used in discussion that places the teacher and students in a circle; maximizes free interchange among participants.

**classroom activities** Things students are expected to do in the classroom, such as listening, discussing, completing worksheets, and taking tests.

**classroom ecology** A way of looking at classrooms that is concerned mainly with how student cooperation and involvement are achieved.

**classroom management** The ways teachers organize and structure their classrooms for the purposes of maximizing student cooperation and engagement and minimizing disruptive behavior.

**classroom meetings** An approach to classroom management in which the teacher holds regular meetings for the purpose of helping students identify and resolve problem situations.

**classroom processes** Interpersonal and group processes that help classroom participants deal with issues of expectations, leadership, attraction, norms, communication, and cohesiveness.

**classroom properties** Distinctive features of classrooms, such as multidimensionality, simultaneity, immediacy, unpredictability, publicness, and history, that shape behavior of participants.

**classroom structures** The ways classrooms are organized around learning tasks and participation, and the ways goals and rewards are defined.

**classroom tasks** The work students are expected to do in classrooms and the cognitive and social demands placed on students as they perform particular lessons. See also *task structures.*

**cluster seating** Way to put desks in groups to facilitate cooperative learning and small-group lessons.

**cognitive-constructivist perspective** A view of learning that posits that learning occurs when learners are actively involved in the process of acquiring and constructing their own knowledge.

**cognitive domain** The domain in Bloom's taxonomy that classifies objectives in the thinking and reasoning processes.

**cognitive monitoring** Learners' abilities to select, to use, and to monitor appropriate learning strategies.

**cognitive processes** The thinking engaged in by teachers and students.

**cognitive psychology** Psychology of learning that focuses mainly on mental processes.

**cognitive strategies** Complex thinking strategies associated with receiving, storing, and retrieving information.

**cognitive structures** The way knowledge is organized and stored in the mind.

**competitive reward structure** Occurs when students perceive that they can obtain their goal if, and only if, the other students with whom they work fail to obtain their goals.

**complex rehearsal** A learning strategy, such as note taking and using analogies to encode complex information.

**concept attainment** An inductive approach to teaching concepts by which students derive the meaning and attributes of a concept from examples and nonexamples of the concept given by the teacher.

**concepts** Ways of organizing knowledge and experiences in categories within which items have common attributes.

**concept teaching** Approaches to teaching in which the emphasis is on helping students learn how to make and label categories of ideas, objects, and experiences.

**conceptual approach** An approach to multicultural education in which teachers incorporate a series of concepts associated with cultural pluralism into ongoing lessons.

**conceptual mapping** A technique of visually organizing and diagraming a set of ideas or concepts in a logical pattern so relationships can be readily observed. Also called *webbing*.

**conceptual web** See *conceptual mapping*.

**conditional knowledge** Knowledge about when it is appropriate to use particular declarative or procedural knowledge.

**conjunctive concept** A concept that has a constant rule structure.

**constructivism** A perspective of teaching and learning in which a learner constructs meaning from experience and interaction with others and the teacher's role is to provide meaningful experiences for students.

**constructivist perspective** A view that knowledge is often personal and that humans construct knowledge and meaning through experience.

**control group** Group of subjects that receives no special treatment during experimental research.

**cooperative goal or task structures** Occur when students perceive they can obtain their goal if, and only if, the other students with whom they work also obtain their goals.

**cooperative learning model** An approach to teaching in which students work in mixed-ability groups and are partially rewarded for group, rather than individual, effort and success.

**cooperative reward structures** Occur when students are interdependent for a reward they will share if they are successful as a group.

**corrective feedback** Information given to students about how well they are doing.

**correlation** A term used to express how two or more variables are related.

**correlational research** A type of research that investigates relationships between variables which exist naturally.

**correlation coefficient** Numbers ranging from +1.00 to −1.00 that describe the numerical relationship between variables.

**criterion-referenced grading** A practice in which criteria for success are defined in advance and all students have an opportunity to earn any possible grade.

**criterion-referenced test** A test that evaluates a particular student's performance against a preestablished standard or criterion.

**critical attribute** Feature of a concept that distinguishes it from all other concepts.

**cueing** A signal from teachers to alert or to set up situations for students in order to help them get ready to make an appropriate response.

**cultural deficit theory** The now-discredited theory that accounts for the low achievement of minorities by postulating some defect in their culture or race.

**cultural difference theory** The currently accepted theory that accounts for the low achievement of minorities by postulating that the discontinuity between home culture and school culture interferes with learning.

**cultural pluralism** An ideology encouraging minority cultures to maintain their distinctive identities within the larger culture and to value cultural diversity within societies.

**culture shock** The anxious emotional response to the ambiguity and disconfirmed expectations that come from dealing with unfamiliar cultures.

**dangle** When a teacher starts an activity and then leaves it in midair.

**debriefing** Way to assess the effectiveness of a classroom discussion by asking students what they thought of the discussion.

**declarative knowledge** Knowledge about something or that something is the case; knowledge of facts, concepts, or principles.

**demography** Study of population patterns; in education, this study is most concerned with size and distribution of school-aged children and youth.

**dependent variable** In research, the variable that may change as a result of the independent variable; the consequences of the independent variable.

**descriptive research** Research aimed at gathering detailed information about some phenomenon.

**desist** A teaching behavior aimed at stopping disruptive student behavior.

**desist incidence** A classroom incident serious enough that if not dealt with will lead to widening management problems.

**diagnostic test** Test used by teachers to determine students' prior knowledge and level of skill development. Information used to assist in planning.

**differential treatment** The difference in the educational experiences of the majority race, class, culture, or gender and those of minorities; that is, differences in quality of curriculum, instruction, classroom interaction, funding, enrollment, etc.

**dignifying errors** Technique used by teachers when responding to student answers that are wrong.

**direct instruction model** An approach to teaching basic skills and sequential material in which lessons are highly goal-directed and learning environments are tightly structured by the teacher.

**discourse** The larger patterns of verbal exchange and communication that occur in classrooms.

**discovery teaching or learning** An approach to teaching that emphasizes encouraging students to learn concepts and principles through their own explorations and to solve problems on their own.

**discrepant event** A puzzling situation that sparks curiosity and motivates inquiry into cause-and-effect relationships; used by teachers to engage students.

**discussion** A teaching method that relies on verbal exchange of ideas among students and the teacher.

**disjunctive concept** A concept that contains alternative sets of attributes.

**distracters** Plausible but wrong answers in a multiple-choice test question.

**distributed practice** Practice assigned to students to be done for brief periods spread over several sessions or periods of time.

**diversity** Refers to the variety among people that exists in schools and society.

**downtime** Time in classrooms when lessons are completed early or when students are waiting for upcoming events, such as moving to another class or going home.

**ecological system** A view of classrooms in which inhabitants (teachers, students, and others) interact within a highly interdependent environment.

**economy** Term used by Bruner to describe ways to limit the amount of materials to be taught at any one time.

**encoding** The process of transferring new information from short-term to long-term memory.

**endogenous** Qualities that are internal to a situation or have personal relevance.

**engaged time** The amount of time students actually spend on a particular subject or learning activity; also called *time on task.*

**equity** Refers to making conditions for everyone impartial, fair, just, and equal.

**ESL** Acronym for "English as a second language."

**essay test** An approach to testing in which students are required to express their thoughts in writing.

**establishing set** See *anticipatory set.*

**ethnography** Term from the field of anthropology to describe an extensive descriptive study of a single culture, society, or particular phenomenon.

**ethos** Common set of values, beliefs, and ways of doing things found in particular classrooms or schools. See also *school culture.*

**evaluation** Process of judging, assigning value, or deciding on the worth of a particular program or approach or of a student's work.

**example-to-rule** Technique of giving examples to students, helping them to come up with the rule or principle.

**exceptionality** Term used to define students who have special social, mental, emotional, or physical needs.

**exhibits** Displays of artifacts (products) students present that show their work from a problem-based lesson.

**exogenous** Word used to define qualities that are external to a situation or that have external causes.

**expectations** The amount and quality of work and behavior expected of students in classrooms and schools.

**expectations** Attitudes and beliefs teachers hold about the capabilities of their students.

**experiential learning** Theory of learning that explains how people learn from their experiences and subsequent reflections about their experiences.

**experiment** A type of research in which the researcher manipulates one or more variables so cause-and-effect relationships can be examined.

**experimental group** A group of subjects that receives a special treatment in experimental research.

**expert teachers** Experienced teachers who have mastered the art and science of teaching.

**explaining links** Prepositions or conjunctions used in a presentation that indicate the cause, result, means, or purpose of an event or idea.

**extending student thinking** Techniques used by teachers following a presentation to help students strengthen their understanding of the new material and to expand their cognitive structures.

**extrinsic motivation** Behavior caused by external factors such as rewards, punishments, or social pressures.

**extrinsic reward** A reward that is external to the activity itself, such as points, grades, or stars.

**feedback** Information given to students about their performance. Same as *knowledge of results.*

**feeling tone** The degree to which a learning environment or a particular learning task is perceived as pleasant or unpleasant.

**flip-flop** Occurs when a teacher starts an activity, then stops and starts another one, and finally returns to the original activity.

**flow experience** State when individuals feel total involvement and concentration and strong feelings of enjoyment as a result of a particular experience.

**formative evaluation** Evaluation that occurs before or during instruction and is used to assist with planning or making adaptations.

**fragmentation** Occurs when a teacher breaks a learning activity into overly small units.

**full bilingual program** A program in which instruction is carried out equally in two languages and the goals are full oral proficiency and literacy in both.

**Gantt chart** A planning technique to show pieces of work in relationship to one another and when each piece is expected to start and to finish.

**goal structures** The way that goals specify the degree of interdependence sought among students. There are three different types of goal structures: individualistic, competitive, and cooperative.

**grading on the curve** A practice of assigning grades so they will follow a normal curve.

**grading to criterion** Practice of assigning grades according to how well students do on a predefined set of objectives or standards.

**graphic organizer** A visual image presented to students to provide structure for new information about to be presented. Similar to an *advance organizer.*

**group development** Stages classroom groups go through in the process of developing into a cohesive and effective group.

**group investigation** An approach to cooperative learning in which students help define topics for study and then work together to complete their investigations.

**group processes** See *classroom processes.*

**group skills** Skills students have to participate effectively in groups.

**guided practice** Practice assigned to students to be completed under the guidance or watchful eye of the teacher.

**hands-off norm** Expectation in many schools that teachers will not interfere in other teachers' work.

**holistic scoring** Technique for grading essay questions or other written work that emphasizes looking at the work as a whole rather than at its individual parts.

**homework** Assignments that students are expected to complete outside of class.

**horizontal desk formation** Seating arrangement in which students sit close to one another in four or five rows; useful for direct instruction lessons.

**inclusion** Practice of including students, regardless of their disabilities, in regular classrooms.

**independent practice** Practice given to students to accomplish on their own without the teacher's guidance.

**independent variable** In research, the variable that is treated and presumed to cause some change in the dependent variable.

**individualistic reward structure** Occurs when achievement of the goal by one student is unrelated to the achievement of the goal by other students.

**individualized education plan (IEP)** A learning plan specifying long- and short-term educational goals for disabled students and agreed on by teachers, parents, and special educators.

**inductive reasoning** Process of coming up with general rules or principles based on information from specific examples or data.

**inductive teaching** See *inquiry teaching or training.*

**influence motivation** The desire to take action for the purposes of having control and a say in what's going on.

**information processing** The process used by the mind to take in, store, and retrieve information for use.

**inquiry teaching or training** An approach to teaching in which the emphasis is on helping students to inquire on their own and to develop such skills as asking questions and drawing conclusions from data.

**instructional effects** The learning goals a particular teaching model has been designed to achieve.

**instructional functions of teaching** Those aspects of teachers' work during which they are providing face-to-face instruction to students in classrooms.

**instructional objectives and goals** Statements that describe a teacher's instructional intents.

**interpersonal communication skills** Skills that promote honest communication and positive regard among students.

**intrinsic motivation** Occurs when people behave because the act brings personal satisfaction or enjoyment.

**jigsaw** An approach to cooperative learning in which students work in mixed-ability groups and each student is responsible for a portion of the material.

**journaling** A technique of writing on a regular basis one's thoughts and reflections about teaching experiences.

**knowledge acquisition** The process in which students acquire and assimilate new information and knowledge.

**knowledge base** Information, accumulated over time from research and the wisdom of experienced teachers, that informs teaching practices.

**knowledge networks** How information and related concepts are organized and linked together in the memory system.

**knowledge of results** Feedback given to students about their performance.

**knowledge representation** The way information is organized and stored in the memory system.

**leadership functions of teaching** Aspects of teachers' work, such as providing motivation and coordinating and controlling learning environments and activities.

**learning environment** The overall climate and structures of the classroom that influence how students respond to and remain engaged in learning tasks; the context in which teaching acts are carried out.

**least restrictive environment** The placement situation for disabled students that is the most normal and least confining based on the student's particular needs and problems.

**LEP** Acronym for "limited English proficiency."

**lesson plan** Organization for instruction for a particular lesson or period.

**lesson structures** The way learning activities and series of lessons are woven together.

**level of actual development** A concept attributed to Lev Vygotsky that identifies a learner's level of current intellectual functioning.

**level of concern** The amount of stress and anxiety students experience with a particular learning task.

**level of difficulty** Refers to how difficult a question asked of students is to answer.

**level of potential development** A concept attributed to Lev Vygotsky that identifies the level at which a learner could function intellectually with the assistance of a teacher or more advanced peer.

**link-word method** A mnemonic that creates a mental image linking a familiar word with an unfamiliar word; used mainly in foreign language instruction.

**logical consequences** Punishments administered for misbehavior that are directly related to the infraction.

**long-term memory** Place in the mind where information is stored, ready for retrieval when needed.

**loosely coupled systems** An organizational arrangement in which what goes on in one part of an organization is not very connected to what goes on in other parts of the organization.

**mainstreaming** Placing special-needs children in regular classes for full time or part time.

**massed practice** Practice assigned to students to be done during a single extended period of time.

**matrix note taking** An elaboration learning strategy and way of taking notes that places information in a matrix; facilitates encoding and making comparisons of complex information.

**mean score** The arithmetic average of a group of scores.

**melting pot** Ideology of education that believes the strengths of minority cultures should be blended into a new, single, superior culture.

**metacognition** Process of knowing and monitoring one's own thinking or *cognitive processes.*

**metacognitive strategies** Strategies used to recognize one's *cognitive processes* and ways to think about how information is being processed.

**mnemonics** A learning strategy to assist memory by forming associations between new materials and patterns that are familiar or already exist.

**momentum** Term used by Kounin to describe how teachers pace instruction.

**motivation** The process by which behavior is directed toward important human goals or toward satisfying needs and motives.

**multicultural education** An approach to teaching aimed at helping students recognize and value cultural diversity.

**needs disposition theory** Theory of motivation positing that people are motivated to take action to satisfy basic and higher-level needs.

**negative reinforcer** A stimulus such as punishment intended to eliminate or reduce undesirable behavior.

**noncritical attributes** Features found in some but not all members of a category.

**nonlinear planning** An approach to planning in which planners start with actions or activities deemed important and later attach goals to the action to help explain what happened.

**norm-referenced grading** A grading practice whereby students' scores are determined by comparison to others' in the class.

**norm-referenced test** A standardized test that evaluates a particular student's performance by comparing it to the performance of some other well-defined group of students.

**norms** The shared expectations students and teachers have for classroom behavior.

**novice teacher** A teacher who is just beginning and is still learning the art and science of teaching.

**objective tests** Tests with items that produce answers that can be scored with relatively little bias.

**objectivist perspective** A view that knowledge consists of "truths" and an objective reality that humans have access to and can learn through discovery and inquiry.

**observation** A research procedure in which the researcher watches and records behaviors; a procedure for learning to teach by watching, recording, and reflecting about teacher and student behavior in classrooms.

**opportunity to learn** The amount of time a teacher actually spends on academic tasks or activities.

**organizational functions of teaching** Those aspects of teachers' work involving interactions with other adults in the school setting for the purpose of schoolwide planning and coordination.

**organizational strategy** A class of learning strategies that helps increase the meaningfulness of new materials by imposing new and different organizational structures on the materials.

**overdwelling** Occurs when a teacher goes on and on after a subject or a set of instructions is clear to students.

**overlappingness** The ability of teachers to spot disruptive behavior and to deal with it without interrupting the flow of the lesson.

**overlearning** Working or practicing a task or skill until it is learned completely and can be performed automatically.

**participation structures** The established rules and processes that determine who can say what, when, and to whom during classroom discourse.

**pedagogy** The study of the art and science of teaching; also refers to the methods and approaches to instruction.

**performance assessment** Assessment procedures that have students demonstrate their abilities to perform particular tasks in testing situations.

**performance standard** A standard or goal students are expected to meet.

**planned academic time** The amount of time that teachers set aside for different subjects and activities.

**planning cycles** The spans of time considered for various aspects of planning: daily, weekly, unit, term, and yearly.

**portfolio** A collection of a student's work that demonstrates the student's ability to perform particular tasks.

**positive reinforcer** A stimulus such as a reward intended to get individuals to repeat desirable behavior.

**postinstructional planning** Teacher planning whereby decisions are made about how to provide feedback to students and how to assess and evaluate student learning.

**power** Term used by Bruner to describe the process of selecting only the most important (powerful) ideas and concepts to teach to students.

**PQ4R method** A strategy used to help learners remember what they have read; the letters stand for *preview, question, read, reflect, recite,* and *review.*

**practical arguments** Reasoning based on knowledge and beliefs that is used by teachers as they make pedagogical decisions.

**praise** Positive verbal and nonverbal statements offered by teachers as reinforcers to encourage and strengthen desirable student behaviors.

**preinstructional planning** Teacher planning conducted before instruction, during which goals, content, and approaches are decided.

**presentation teaching model** An approach to teaching wherein the primary emphasis is on explaining new information and ideas to students.

**preventive management** Perspective that effective classroom management can be achieved through good planning, interesting lessons, and effective teaching.

**principle** A cause-and-effect relationship between variables that has been established from results of several studies or experiments conducted over time.

**prior knowledge** Information and knowledge held by students before they receive instruction.

**privileges** Special activities and extra time bestowed by teachers to encourage desirable pupil behavior.

**problem-based instruction** Approach to teaching in which students investigate and study authentic and meaningful problem situations.

**problem solving** Finding ways to apply new solutions to complex problem situations rather than relying on fixed rules or recipes.

**procedural knowledge** Knowledge about how to do something. Can pertain to specific behavioral skills or to complex *cognitive strategies.*

**procedures** Systems established by teachers for dealing with routine tasks and coordinating student talk and movement.

**productions** The way basic units of procedural knowledge are organized and linked in the memory system.

**propositional network** Units or sets of interconnected knowledge. A proposition is the basic unit in a person's *cognitive structure.*

**psychomotor domain** The domain in Bloom's taxonomy that classifies objectives in the physical movement and coordination processes.

**punishments** Penalties imposed by teachers to discourage undesirable behaviors.

**randomness** Without a definite or biased pattern; the quality of being by chance.

**rational-linear planning** An approach to planning that focuses on setting goals and objectives first and then on selecting particular strategies or activities to accomplish these predetermined goals.

**reciprocal teaching** An approach to teaching reading in which peer teaching is used to help students master comprehension skills.

**recitation** An approach to teaching in which a teacher provides bits of information, asks questions, gets students to respond, and then provides feedback by praising or correcting.

**reflection** Careful and analytical thought by teachers about what they are doing and the effects of their behavior on their instruction and on student learning.

**rehearsal strategy** A learning strategy that assists the encoding process by connecting new information with prior knowledge.

**reinforcement** Consequences administered by teachers to encourage and strengthen certain desirable behaviors.

**relational concept** A concept whose rule structure depends on its relationship to other concepts.

**reliability** The degree to which a test produces consistent results over several administrations.

**repertoire** The number of teaching approaches and strategies that teachers are able to use to help students learn.

**reward structures** The ways in which rewards can be distributed within a classroom. There are three types: *individualistic, competitive,* and *cooperative.*

**role** Term used to describe a set of norms that details how various aspects of a particular job should be carried out.

**rote rehearsal** Strategies that help learners remember simple information by repeating aloud or to oneself information to be remembered.

**row-and-column desk formation** A classroom arrangement in which desks are organized in straight rows and columns; used effectively when a teacher is presenting or demonstrating and when student exchange is not required.

**rule-example-rule technique** A technique used when explaining something whereby the general principle or rule is given first, then elaborated on with specific examples, and finally summarized by a restatement of the rule.

**rules for behavior** Statements that specify expected classroom behaviors and define behaviors that are forbidden.

**sample** A group of subjects drawn from a larger population for the purpose of research.

**scaffolding** The process in which a learner is helped by a teacher or more accomplished person to master a particular problem beyond his or her current developmental level.

**schema, schemata** An individual's (teacher or student) knowledge structure or the way information has been organized and stored in memory.

**school culture** The ways members of a school think about social action; the embedded beliefs, values, and attitudes of members of a school. *Ethos, tone,* and *community* are often used to describe the same phenomenon.

**school effectiveness research** Research that tries to uncover features that make some schools more effective than others.

**school improvement** The process of helping schools change and adopt innovative practices.

**scientific basis of teaching** Teaching in which decisions are based on research and scientific evidence.

**scoring rubric** A detailed description of some type of performance and the criteria that will be used to judge it.

**seatwork** Independent work done by students, such as reading, answering questions, or completing worksheets.

**self-fulfilling prophecy** A situation in which teachers' expectations and predictions about student behavior or learning cause it to happen.

**self-management** An approach to classroom management in which teachers help students define problems, set their own goals, and monitor progress toward goal accomplishment.

**self-regulated learner** A learner who can diagnose a learning situation, select an appropriate learning strategy, monitor the effectiveness of the strategy, and remain engaged in the learning task until it is accomplished. See *autonomous learner.*

**set induction** See *anticipatory set.*

**short-term memory** The place in the mind where conscious mental work is done; also called *working memory.*

**single-group curriculum** An approach to multicultural education in which special units or courses are devoted to a particular group or culture.

**smoothness** The smooth flow and pacing of instructional events.

**social interaction** The interaction and exchange among individuals; Lev Vygotsky believed that interaction and exchange spurred learning and intellectual development.

**social learning theory** Perspective about learning that posits that much of what humans learn is through observation of others.

**social-system perspective** A way of viewing classrooms, schools, and other human organizations by considering how the various parts of the organization are interrelated and interdependent.

**socioeconomic status (SES)** Variations among peoples based on income, family background, and relative prestige within the society.

**Socratic method** An approach to teaching in which teachers help students think and inquire by asking questions that require inductive reasoning.

**stages of teacher concerns** A theory, attributed to Francis Fuller, explaining how teachers are concerned about different things as they learn to teach. The focus of concern is first on survival later on the teaching situation, and finally on pupil growth.

**stages of teacher development** A theory explaining how growth in teaching expertise occurs over time, progressing from one stage to the next stage in sequence.

**standard deviation** A measure that shows the spread of a set of scores from the mean.

**standardized tests** Tests that are normally designed by professional test makers for nationwide use and commercially distributed.

**statistical test and significance** Procedures used to determine whether results from research are indeed true or a result of chance.

**stem** A statement that poses a problem or asks a question in a multiple-choice test question.

**structural approach** Approach to cooperative learning attributed to Spencer Kagan.

**student accountability** Holding students responsible for their learning and their behavior.

**Student Teams Achievement Divisions (STAD)** An approach to cooperative learning in which students work in mixed-ability groups and rewards are administered and recognized for both individual and group effort.

**submersion approach** The now-illegal practice of simply placing limited English proficiency students in the classroom and expecting them to pick up English on their own without any formal teaching or other support from the school.

**success level** The level at which students succeed in academic tasks.

**summative evaluation** Evaluation done after instruction to determine program effectiveness or the worth of students' work.

**sustaining expectation effect** Occurs when teachers do not change their previous expectations about a student, even after the student's performance has improved or regressed.

**swing seating** Seating plan that allows easy movement of seats during cooperative learning lessons.

**synergy** Positive results achieved from working together or through combined action.

**syntax** The overall flow, sequence, or major steps of a particular lesson.

**systems analysis** Study and way of thinking about the relationships that exist between the interdependent parts of some whole.

**table of specifications** A tool for constructing tests that have a balance of questions, representing an array of instructional objectives and levels of student understandings.

**task analysis** A process for breaking down complex learning tasks into fundamental parts or subdividing complex skills into specific subskills so they can be mastered one at a time.

**task structures** The way lessons are arranged and the learning demands that lessons place on students.

**taxonomy** A classification system or device that helps arrange and show relationships among objects and ideas.

**taxonomy of educational objectives** A system developed by Benjamin Bloom for classifying objectives into three domains: *cognitive, affective,* and *psychomotor.*

**teacher clarity** Phrase used to describe the process of teachers giving presentations that are clear and free of ambiguity.

**teacher enthusiasm** A set of behaviors employed by teachers, such as using uplifting language and dramatic body movements, to make students interested in learning materials.

**teacher research** See *action research.*

**teaching model** A term used by Bruce Joyce to describe an overall approach or plan toward instruction. The attributes of teaching models are a coherent theoretical framework, an orientation toward what students should learn, and specific teaching procedures and structures.

**test anxiety** Phenomenon that occurs when students experience undue stress while taking a test and do poorly as a result.

**thinking matrix** A visual device to help students think about the types of questions and answers they provide during a discussion; used to teach thinking skills.

**think-pair-share** A technique used by teachers to slow down the pace of discourse and to increase student participation.

**time on task** See *engaged time.*

**timetabling techniques** Planning tools that chronologically map time relationships among various instructional activities.

**tone** See *ethos* and *school culture.*

**topical approach** An approach to multicultural education in which special lessons are devoted to studying heroes, holidays, art, literature, or the cuisine of a particular culture.

**transfer of learning** The process of applying knowledge or skills learned in one situation to new situations.

**transitional bilingual programs** Programs in which limited English proficiency students are initially provided instruction in their native language, with gradual increases in English until proficiency is achieved.

**transitions** The times during a lesson in which the teacher is moving from one type of learning activity to another.

**unit** An integrated plan for instruction covering several days and including several lessons aimed at a common set of goals and objectives.

**U-shape seating pattern** A seating arrangement used for discussions in which students' chairs form a U and the teacher is seated at the open end of the U.

**validity** The degree to which a test measures what it claims to measure.

**variable** A characteristic of a person or a physical or social situation that can change or vary from one instance to the next.

**verbal signposts** Statements made by teachers when explaining something that tells the student what is important or alerts them to important points coming up.

**visual cueing** Use of visual devices, such as hand signals, to inform students about what they should be doing.

**wait-time** The time a teacher waits for a student to respond to a question and the time a teacher waits before responding back.

**webbing** See *conceptual webbing*.

**with-itness** The ability of teachers to spot disruptive student behavior quickly and accurately.

**working memory** See *short-term memory*.

**zone of proximal development** A concept attributed to Lev Vygotsky that represents the area between a learner's level of actual development and his or her level of potential development.

# References

Abi-Nader, J. (1991). Creating a vision of the future: Strategies for motivating minority students. *Phi Delta Kappan, 72,* 546–549.

Adger, C. T. (1995). *Engaging Students: Thinking, Talking, Cooperating.* Thousand Oaks, Calif.: Corwin.

Airasian, P. (1994). *Classroom Assessment* (2nd ed.). New York: McGraw-Hill.

Airason, P. W. (1996). *Assessment in the Classroom.* New York: McGraw-Hill.

Albanese, M., and Mitchell, S. (1993). Problem-based learning: A review of literature on its outcomes and implementation issues. *Academic Medicine, 68,* 52–81.

Allen, V. (1991). Teaching bilingual and ESL children. In J. Flood, J. M. Jensen, D. Lapp, and J. R. Squire (eds.), *Handbook of Research on Teaching the English Language Arts.*

Allport, G. (1954). *The Nature of Prejudice.* Cambridge, Mass.: Addison-Wesley.

Alschuler, A. S., Tabor, D., and McIntyre, J. (1970). *Teaching Achievement Motivation: Theory and Practice in Psychological Education.* Middletown, Conn.: Education Ventures.

American Educational Research Association, American Psychological Association, and National Council on Measurement in Education. (1985). *Standards for Educational and Psychological Testing.* Washington, D.C.: American Psychological Association.

American Institute for Research. (1999). *An Educator's Guide to Schoolwide Reform.* Arlington, Va.: Educational Research Services.

Anderson, C. W., and Smith, E. L. (1983). Children's Conceptions of Light and Color: Developing the Concept of Unseen Rays. Paper presented at the annual meeting of the American Educational Research Association, Montreal, Canada.

Anderson, L. M. (1985). What are students doing when they do all that seatwork? In C. Fisher and D. Berliner (eds.), *Perspectives on Instructional Time.* New York: Longman.

Anderson, L. W., and Sosniak, L. A. (1994). *Bloom's Taxonomy: A Forty-Year Retrospective* (93rd yearbook of the National Society for the Study of Education, part II). Chicago: University of Chicago Press.

Angaran, Joseph. (1999). Reflections in an age of assessment. *Educational Leadership,* March, 71–72.

Anyon, J. (1980). Social class and the hidden curriculum of work. *Journal of Education,* 162, 67–69.

Arends, R. I. (1996). *Classroom Instruction and Management.* New York: McGraw-Hill.

Argyris, C. (1970). *Intervention Theory and Method.* Reading, Mass.: Addison-Wesley.

Argyris, C., Putnam, R., and Smith, D. M. (1985). *Action Science.* San Francisco: Jossey-Bass.

Aronson, E. (1997). *The Jigsaw Classroom: Building Cooperation in the Classroom.* (2nd ed.). New York: Longman.

Aronson, E., Blaney, S. C., Sikes, J., and Snapp, M. (1978). *The Jigsaw Classroom.* Beverly Hills, Calif.: Sage Publications.

Atkinson, J., and Feather, N. (1966). *A Theory of Achievement Motivation.* New York: Wiley.

Atkinson, J. W. (ed.). (1958). *Motives in Fantasy, Action and Society.* New York: Van Nostrand.

Atkinson, R. C. (1975). Mnemotechnics in second-language instruction. *American Psychologist,* 30, 821–828.

Ausubel, D. P. (1960). The use of advance organizers in the learning and retention of meaningful verbal material. *Journal of Educational Psychology,* 51, 267–272.

Ausubel, D. P. (1963). *The Psychology of Meaningful Verbal Learning.* New York: Grune & Stratton.

Baker, E. T. (1994). Meta-analytic evidence for non-inclusive educational practices: Does educational research support current practice for special needs students. Doctoral dissertation. Temple University, Philadelphia.

Baker, E. T., Wang, M. C., and Walberg, H. (1995). Synthesis of research: The effects of inclusion on learning. *Educational Leadership,* 52, 33–34.

Baker, L., and Brown, A. (1984). Metacognitive skills and reading. In P. D. Pearson, M. Kamil, R. Barr, and P. Mosenthal (eds.). *Handbook of Reading Research.* New York: Longman.

Bandura, A. (1977). *Social Learning Theory.* Englewood Cliffs, N.J.: Prentice Hall.

Bandura, A. (1986). *Social Foundations of Thought and Action.* Englewood Cliffs, N.J.: Prentice Hall.

Bank, J. A. (1994). *Multiethnic Education: Theory and Practice.* Boston: Allyn & Bacon.

Banks, J. (1995). *The Handbook of Research on Multicultural Education.* New York: Macmillan.

Banks, J. (1996). *Multicultural Education, Transformative Knowledge, and Action: Historical and Contemporary Perspectives.* New York: Teachers College Press.

Barker, R. G. (1968). *Ecological Psychology.* Stanford, Calif.: Stanford University Press.

Barzun, J. (1991). *Begin Here: The Forgotten Conditions of Teaching and Learning.* Chicago: University of Chicago Press.

Beane, J. A., Toepfer, C. F., and Alesi, S. J. (1986). *Curriculum Planning and Development.* Newton, Mass.: Allyn & Bacon.

Benjafield, J. G. (1992). *Cognitions.* Englewood Cliffs, N.J.: Prentice Hall.

Bennett, C. I. (1995). *Comprehensive Multicultural Education. Theory and Practice* (3rd ed.). Boston: Allyn & Bacon.

Berliner, D. C., and Biddle, B. J. (1995). *The Manufactured Crisis: Myths, Fraud, and the Attack on American Public Schools.* Reading, Mass.: Addison-Wesley.

Biklen, D. (1985). *Achieving the Complete School.* New York: Teachers College Press.

Blankenship, C., and Lilly, S. (1981). *Mainstreaming Students with Learning and Behavior Problems: Techniques for the Classroom Teacher.* New York: Holt, Rinehart, & Winston.

Bloom, B. S. (1976). *Human Characteristics and School Learning:* New York: McGraw-Hill.

Bloom, B. S. (ed.). (1956). *Taxonomy of Educational Objectives. Handbook 1: Cognitive Domain.* New York: David McKay.

Bloom, B. S., Hastings, T. J., and Madaus, G. F. (1971). *Handbook on Formative and Summative Evaluation of Student Learning.* New York: McGraw-Hill.

Bluestein, J. (1982). *The Beginning Teacher's Resource Handbook.* Albuquerque, N.M.: Instructional Support Services.

Bohman, L. G. and Deal, T. E. (1991). *Reframing Organizations.* San Francisco: Jossey-Bass.

Borg, W. R., and Gall, M. D. (1993). *Educational Research: An Introduction* (4th ed.). New York: Longman.

Boyer, E. L. (1983). *High School: A Report on Secondary Education in America.* New York: Harper & Row.

Bozeman, M. (1985). *Signaling in the Classroom.* (Mimeographed.) Salisbury, Md.: Salisbury State College.

Bramson, R. M. (1981). *Coping with Difficult People.* New York: Random House.

Bredderman, T. (1983). Effects of activity-based elementary science on student outcomes: A quantitative synthesis. *Review of Educational Research,* 53, 499–518.

Brenton, Myron (1970). *What's Happened to Teacher?* New York: Coward-McCann.

Brislin, R. W., Cushner, K., Cherrie, C., and Yong, M. (1986). *Intercultural Interaction: A Practical Guide.* Beverly Hills, Calif.: Sage Publications.

Brookover, W., Beady, C., Flood, P., Schweitzer, J., and Wisenbaker, J. (1979). *School Social Systems and Student Achievement: Schools Can Make a Difference.* New York: Praeger.

Brooks, J. G., and Brook, M. G. (1993). *In Search of Understanding: The Case for Constructivist Classrooms.* Alexandria, Va.: Association for Supervision and Curriculum Development.

Brophy, J. E. (1980). *Recent Research on Teaching.* East Lansing, Mich.: Institute for Research on Teaching, Michigan State University.

Brophy, J. E. (1981). Teacher praise: A functional analysis. *Review of Educational Research,* Spring, 5–32.

Brophy, J. E. (1983). Classroom organization and management. *Elementary School Journal,* 83, 265–286.

Brophy, J. E., and Good, T. L. (1974). *Teacher-Student Relationships: Causes and Consequences.* New York: Holt, Rinehart & Winston.

Brophy, J. E., and Good, T. L. (1986). Teacher behavior and student achievement. In M. C. Wittrock (ed.), *Handbook of Research on Teaching* (3rd ed.). New York: Macmillan.

Brophy, J. E., and Putnam, J. (1979). Classroom management in the early grades. In D. L. Duke (ed.), *Classroom Management.* Chicago: University of Chicago Press.

Brown, A., and Palincsar, A. (1985). *Reciprocal Teaching of Comprehension Strategies.* Technical Report no. 334. Champaign-Urbana, Ill.: University of Illinois.

Bruner, J. (1960). *The Process of Education.* Cambridge, Mass.: Harvard University Press.

Bruner, J. (1962). *On Knowing: Essays for the Left Hand.* Cambridge, Mass.: Harvard University Press.

Bruner, J. (1966). *Toward a Theory of Instruction.* Cambridge, Mass.: Harvard University Press.

Bruner, J. (1973). *Beyond the Information Given: Studies in the Psychology of Knowing.* New York: Norton.

Bruner, J. (1990). *Acts of Meaning.* Cambridge, Mass.: Harvard University Press.

Bruner, J. (1996). *The Culture of Education.* Cambridge, Mass.: Harvard University Press.

Bruner, J. (1998). *Acts of Meaning.* (2nd ed.) Cambridge, Mass.: Harvard University Press.

Bruner, J., Goodnow, J., and Austin, G. (1956). *A Study of Thinking.* New York: Wiley.

Bryk, A. S., and Driscoll, M. E. (1988). *The School as Community.* Madison: University of Wisconsin, National Center for Effective Secondary Schools.

Calberg, C., and Kavale, K. (1980). The efficacy of special versus regular class placement of exceptional children: A meta-analysis. *Journal of Special Education,* 14, 295–309.

Cangelosi, J. S. (1988). *Classroom Management Strategies: Gaining and Maintaining Students' Cooperation.* New York: Longman.

Canter, L., and Canter, D. M. (1976). *Assertive Discipline.* Los Angeles: Canter and Associates.

Canter, L., and Canter, D. M. (1995). *Lee Canter's Assertive Discipline.* Santa Monica, Calif.: Canter & Associates.

Canter, L., and Canter, D. M. (1997). *Assertive Discipline Positive Behavior.* Santa Monica, Calif.: Canter & Associates.

Carlson, R. (1996). *Reframing and Reform.* White Plains, N.Y.: Longman.

Carnegie Corporation. (1986). *A Nation Prepared: Teachers for the Twenty-First Century.* (1986). New York: Author.

Carroll, J. B. (1963). A model of school learning. *Teachers College Record,* 64, 723–733.

Cazden, C. B. (1972). *Child Language and Education.* New York: Holt, Rinehart & Winston.

Cazden, C. B. (1986). Classroom Discourse. In M. C. Wittrock (ed.), *Handbook of Research on Teaching* (3rd ed.). New York: Macmillan.

Cazden, C. B. (1988). *Classroom Discourse.* Portsmouth, N.H.: Heinemann.

Cazden, C. B., and Mehan, H. (1989). Principles from sociology and anthropology: Context, code, classroom, and culture. In M. C. Reynolds (ed.), *Knowledge Base for the Beginning Teacher.* New York: Pergamon Press.

Claiborn, W. L. (1969). Expectancy effects in the classroom: A failure to replicate. *Journal of Educational Psychology,* 60, 377–383.

Clark, C. M., and Lampert, M. (1986). The study of teacher thinking: Implications for teacher education. *Journal of Teacher Education,* 37, 27–31.

Clark, C. M., and Yinger, R. J. (1979). *Three Studies of Teacher Planning.* East Lansing, Mich.: Institute for Research on Teaching, Michigan State University.

Cochran-Smith, M., and Lytle, S. L. (1993). *Inside Outside: Teacher Research and Knowledge.* New York: Teacher College Press.

Cognition and Technology Group at Vanderbilt. (1990). Anchored instruction. Unpublished paper. Nashville, Tenn.: Vanderbilt University.

Cohen, E. (1994). *Designing Groupwork: Strategies for the Heterogeneous Classroom.* New York: Teacher College Press.

Coleman, J. (1961). *The Adolescent Society.* New York: Free Press.

Coleman, J. (1972). The children have outgrown the schools. *Psychology Today,* February, 72–82.

Coleman, J., Campbell, E., Hobson, C., McPartland, J., Mood, A., Weinfield, F., and York, R. (1966). *Equality of Educational Opportunity.* Washington, D.C.: U.S. Government Printing Office.

Collins, M. L. (1978). Effects of enthusiasm training on preservice elementary teachers. *Journal of Teacher Education,* 29, 53–57.

Combs, A. W. (1965). *The Professional Education of Teachers.* Boston: Allyn & Bacon.

Combs, A. W., Miser, A. B., and Whitaker, K. S. (1999). *On Becoming a School Leader.* Alexandria, Va.: Association for Supervision and Curriculum Development.

Comer, J. P. (1988). Educating poor minority children. *Scientific American,* 259 (5), 42–48.

Concept to guide multicultural education. Charles County, Md., Teacher Corp Project, no date.

Cooper, H. (1989). *Homework.* New York: Longman.

Cooper, H. M., and Good, T. (1983). *Pygmalion Grows Up: Studies in the Expectation Communication Process.* New York: Longman.

Cooper, J. D. (1993). *Literacy: Helping Children Construct Meaning* (2nd ed.). Boston: Houghton Mifflin.

Copeland, W. D. (1980). Teaching-learning behaviors and the demands of the classroom environment. *Elementary School Journal,* 80, 163–177.

Costa, A. L. (1985). *Developing Minds: A Resource Book for Teaching Thinking.* Alexandria, Va.: Association for Supervision and Curriculum Development.

Cruickshank, D., and Metcalf, K. (1994). Explaining. In T. Husen and T. N. Postlewaite (eds.), *International Encyclopedia of Education* (2nd ed.). Oxford: Pergamon.

Cruickshank, D. V., Bainer, D. L., and Metcalf, K. K. (1999). *The Act of Teaching* (2nd ed.). New York: McGraw-Hill.

Csikszentmihalyi, M. (1990). *Flow: The Psychology of Optimal Experience.* New York: Harper & Row.

Cuban, L. (1982). Persistent instruction: The high school classroom, 1900–1980. *Phi Delta Kappan,* 64, 113–118.

Cuban, L. (1984). *How Teachers Taught: Constancy and Change in American Classrooms, 1900–1980.* New York: Longman.

Cullen, F. T., Cullen, J. B., Hayhow, V. L., and Plouffe, J. T. (1975). The effects of the use of grades as an incentive. *Journal of Educational Research,* 68, 277–279.

Cummins, J. (1981). The role of primary language development in promoting educational success for language minority students. In California State Department of Education (ed.), *Schooling and Language Minority Students: A Theoretical Framework.* Los Angeles: National Evaluation, Disseminations, and Assessment Center, California State University.

Curtis, C. K., and Shaver, J. P. (1980). Slow learners and the study of contemporary problems. *Social Education,* 44, 302–309.

Cushner, K., McClelland, A., and Safford, P. (1996). *Human Diversity in Education: An Integrative Approach* (2nd ed.). New York: McGraw-Hill.

Cypher, T., and Willower, D. J. (1984). The work behavior of secondary school teachers. *Journal of Research and Development,* 18, 17–24.

Darling-Hammond, L. (ed.). (1996). *What Matters Most: Teaching for America's Future.* New York: Commission on Teaching and America's Future.

Darling-Hammond, L., Wise, A. E., and Klein, S. P. (1999). *A License to Teach.* San Francisco: Jossey-Bass.

Davies, D. (1991). Schools reaching out: Family, school, and community partnerships for student success. *Phi Delta Kappan,* 72, 376–382.

deCharms, R. (1976). *Enhancing Motivation.* New York: Irvington.

Deci, E. and Ryan, R. (1985). *Intrinsic Motivation and Self-Determination in Human Behavior.* New York: Plenum.

Denham, C., and Lieberman, A. (eds.). (1980). *Time to Learn.* Washington, D.C.: U.S. Department of Education.

Dewey, J. (1916). *Democracy and Education.* New York: Macmillan.

Dewey, J. (1929). *The Quest for Certainty.* New York: Minton, Balch.

Dewey, J. (1933). *How We Think* (rev. ed.). Lexington, Mass.: D.C. Heath.

Dewey, J. (1938). *Experience and Education.* New York: Macmillan.

Dilworth, M. E. (ed.). (1992). *Diversity in Teacher Education: New Expectations.* San Francisco: Jossey-Bass.

Doctorow, M., Wittrock, M. C., and Marks, C. (1978). Generative processes in reading comprehension. *Journal of Educational Psychology,* 70, 109–118.

Doyle, W. (1979). Classroom tasks and students' abilities. In P. L. Peterson and H. J. Walberg (eds.), *Research on Teaching: Concepts, Findings and Implications.* Berkeley, Calif.: McCutchan.

Doyle, W. (1980). *Classroom Management.* West Lafayette, Ind.: Kappa Delta Pi.

Doyle, W. (1986). Classroom organization and management. In M. C. Wittrock (ed.), *Handbook of Research on Teaching* (3rd ed.). New York: Macmillan.

Doyle, W. (1990). Themes in teacher education research. In W. R. Houston (ed.), *Handbook of Research on Teacher Education.* New York: Macmillan.

Doyle, W., and Carter, K. (1984). Academic tasks in classrooms. *Curriculum Inquiry,* 14, 129–149.

Dreikurs, R. (1968). *Psychology in the Classroom: A Manual for Teachers* (2nd ed.). New York: Harper & Row.

Dreikurs, R., and Grey, L. (1968). *A New Approach to Discipline: Logical Consequences.* New York: Hawthorne Books.

Duchastel, P. C., and Brown, B. R. (1974). Incidental and relevant learning with instructional objectives. *Journal of Educational Psychology,* 66, 481–485.

Duckworth, E. (1987). *The Having of Wonderful Ideas and Other Essays on Teaching and Learning.* New York: Teachers College Press.

Duckworth, E. (1991). Twenty-four, forty-two, and I love you: Keeping it complex. In K. Jervis and C. Montag (eds.), *Progressive Education for the 1990s: Transforming Practice.* New York: Teachers College Press.

Duffy, G., and Roehler, L. (1987). Improving reading instruction through the use of responsive elaboration. *Reading Teacher,* 40, 514–520.

Dunkin, M. J., and Biddle, B. J. (1974). *The Study of Teaching.* New York: Holt, Rinehart & Winston.

Eby, J. W. (1992). *Reflective Planning, Teaching, and Evaluation in the Elementary School.* New York: Macmillan.

Education Trust. (1998). *Education Watch, 1998.* Washington, D.C.: Author.

Elkind, D. (1997). Schooling and family in the postmodern world. *Phi Delta Kappan,* 18, 3–11.

Emmer, E. T., Evertson, C., and Anderson, L. M. (1980). Effective classroom management at the beginning of the school year. *Elementary School Journal,* 80, 219–231.

Emmer, E., Evertson, C., Clements, B., and Worsham, W. E. (1997). *Classroom Management for Secondary Teachers* (4th ed.). Englewood Cliffs, N.J.: Prentice Hall.

Emmer, E. T., Evertson, C., Sanford, J., and Clements, B. S. (1982). *Improving Classroom Management: An Experimental Study in Junior High School Classrooms.* Austin, Texas: Research and Development Center for Teacher Education, University of Texas.

Emmer, E. T., Evertson, C., Sanford, J., Clements, B. S., and Worsham, W. E. (1994). *Classroom Management for Secondary Teachers.* (3rd ed.). Englewood Cliffs, N.J.: Prentice Hall.

Epstein, J. L. (1988). How do we improve programs for parent involvement? *Educational Horizons,* 66, 58–59.

Evertson, C. M., and Emmer, E. T. (1982). Preventive classroom management. In D. Duke, (ed.), *Helping Teachers Manage Classrooms.* Alexandria, Va.: Association for Supervision and Curriculum Development.

Evertson, C. M., Emmer, E. T., Clements, B. S., and Worsham, W. E. (1997). *Classroom Management for Elementary Teachers* (4th ed.). Englewood Cliffs, N.J.: Prentice Hall.

Evertson, C. M., Emmer, E. T., Sanford, J. P., and Clements, B. S. (1983). Improving classroom management: An experiment in elementary classrooms. *Elementary School Journal, 84,* 173–188.

Evertson, E., Emmer, E., Clements, B., Sanford, J., and Worsham, M. (1994). *Classroom Management for Elementary Teachers* (3rd ed.). Englewood Cliffs, N.J.: Prentice Hall.

Feiman-Nemser, S. (1983). Learning to teach. In L. S. Shulman and G. Sykes (eds.), *Handbook of Teaching and Policy.* New York: Longman.

Feiman-Nemser, S., and Floden, R. E. (1986). In M. C. Wittrock (ed.), *Handbook of Research on Teaching* (3rd ed.). New York: Macmillan.

Fenstermacher, G. D. (1986). Philosophy of research on teaching: Three aspects. In M. C. Wittrock (ed.), *Handbook of Research on Teaching* (3rd ed.). New York: Macmillan.

Fenstermacher, G. D., and Soltis, J. F. (1986). *Approaches to Teaching.* New York: Teachers College Press.

Firestone, W. A., and Rosenblum, S. (1988). Building commitment in urban high schools. *Educational Evaluation and Policy Analysis, 93,* 285–299.

Fisher, C. W., and Berliner, D. (eds.). (1985). *Perspectives on Instructional Time.* New York: Longman.

Fisher, C. W., Berliner, D., Filby, N., Marliave, R., Cahen, L., and Dishaw, M. (1980). Teaching behavior, academic learning time, and student achievement: An overview. In C. Denham and A. Lieberman (eds.), *Time to Learn.* Washington, D.C.: National Institute of Education, Department of Education.

Flanders, N. A. (1970). *Analyzing Teaching Behavior.* Reading, Mass.: Addison-Wesley.

Flavel, J. (1985). *Cognitive Development* (2nd ed.). Englewood Cliffs, N.J.: Prentice Hall.

Fleener, A. (1989). *Sample Lesson Plan Format.* (Mimeographed). Minneapolis, Minn.: Augsburg College.

Ford, G. W., and Pugno, L. (eds.). (1964). *The Structure of Knowledge and the Curriculum.* Chicago: Rand McNally.

Fosnot, C. T. (1989). *Enquiring Teachers, Enquiring Learners.* New York: Teachers College Press.

Friedman, W. J. (1980). *The Development of Relational Understanding of Temporal and Spatial Terms.* (ERIC No. ED 178 176). Resources in Education.

Friend and Bursuck. (1999). *Including Students with Special Needs* (2nd ed). Boston: Allyn & Bacon.

Fullan, M. (1992). *The New Meaning of Educational Change* (2nd ed.). New York: Teachers College Press.

Fuller, F. (1969). Concerns of teachers: A developmental conceptualization. *American Educational Research Journal, 6,* 207–226.

Fuller, M. L., and Olsen, G. (1998). *Home-School Relations: Working Successfully with Parents and Families.* Boston: Allyn & Bacon.

Gage, N. L. (1978). *The Scientific Basis of the Art of Teaching.* New York: Teachers College Press.

Gage, N. L. (1984). *An Update of the Scientific Basis of the Art of Teaching.* (Mimeographed). Palo Alto, Calif.: Stanford University.

Gage, N. L. (ed.). (1963). *Handbook of Research on Teaching.* Chicago: Rand McNally.

Gagné, E. D. (1985). *The Cognitive Psychology of School Learning.* Boston: Little, Brown.

Gagné, E. D., Yekovick, C. W., and Yekovick, F. R. (1993). *The Cognitive Psychology of School Learning* (2nd ed.). New York: HarperCollins.

Gagné, R. M. (1977). *The Conditions of Learning and Theory of Instruction* (3rd ed.). New York: Holt, Rinehart & Winston.

Gagné, R. M. (1985). *The Conditions of Learning and Theory of Instruction* (4th ed.). New York: Holt, Rinehart & Winston.

Gagné, R. M., and Briggs, L. J. (1980). *Principles of Instructional Design* (2nd ed.). New York: Holt, Rinehart & Winston.

Gagné, R. M., and White, R. (1978). Memory structures and learning outcomes. *Review of Educational Research, 48* (2), 187–222.

Gall, J., and Gall, M. (1990). Outcomes of the discussion method. In W. W. Wilen (ed.), *Teaching and Learning Through Discussion: The Theory and Practice of the Discussion Method.* Springfield, Ill.: Charles C Thomas.

Gall, M. (1984). Synthesis of research on teachers' questioning. *Educational Leadership, 42,* 40–47.

Gall, M. D. (1970). The use of questions in teaching. *Review of Educational Research, 40,* 707–721.

Garcia, R. (1992). *Teaching in a Pluralistic Society. Concepts, Models, and Strategies.* New York: HarperCollins.

Gardner, H. (1983). *Frames of Mind.* New York: Basic Books.

Gardner, H. (1985). *The Mind's New Science.* New York: Basic Books.

Gardner, H. (1991). *The Unschooled Mind: How Children Think and How Schools Should Teach.* New York: Basic Books.

Gardner, H. (1993). *Multiple Intelligences: The Theory in Practice.* New York: Basic Books.

Gardner, H. (1994). Multiple intelligences: The theory in practice. *Teacher's College Record, 83,* 501–513.

Gardner, H. (1999). Who owns intelligence? *Atlantic Monthly,* February, 67–75.

Gardner, H., and Hatch, K. T. (1989). Multiple intelligences go to school. *Educational Researcher,* 18, 8–9.

Getzels, J. W., and Thelen, H. A. (1960). The classroom group as a unique social system. In N. Henry (ed.), *The Dynamics of Instructional Groups.* Chicago: National Society for the Study of Education, 59th Yearbook, Part 2.

Glass, G. (1981). Effectiveness of special education. Paper presented at Wingspread Conference, Racine, Wis.

Glass, G., Cahen, L., Smith, M. L., and Filby, N. (1982). *School Class Size: Research and Policy.* Beverly Hills, Calif.: Sage.

Glasser, W. (1969). *Schools Without Failure.* New York: Harper & Row.

Glasser, W. (1986). *Control Theory in the Classroom.* New York: Harper & Row.

Glasser, W. A. (1992). *The Quality School.* New York: HarperCollins.

Gold, R. M., Reilly, A., Silberman, R., and Lehr, R. (1971). Academic achievement declines under pass-fail grading. *Journal of Experimental Education,* 39, 17–21.

Good, T. L., and Brophy, J. E. (1987). *Looking in Classrooms* (4th ed.). New York: Harper & Row.

Good, T. L., and Grouws, D. A. (1977). Teaching effect: A process-product study in fourth grade mathematics classrooms. *Journal of Teacher Education,* 28, 49–54.

Good, T. L., and Grouws, D. A. (1979). The Missouri mathematics effectiveness project: An experimental study in fourth-grade classrooms. *Journal of Educational Psychology,* 71, 355–362.

Good, T. L., Grouws, D. A., and Ebmeier, H. (1983). *Active Mathematics Teaching.* New York: Longman.

Goodlad, J. (1975). *The Dynamics of Educational Change.* New York: McGraw-Hill.

Goodlad, J. (1984). *A Place Called School: Prospects for the Future.* New York: McGraw-Hill.

Goodlad, J. (1991). *Teachers for Our Nation's Schools.* San Francisco: Jossey-Bass.

Goodlad, J., and Klein, M. (1970). *Behind the Classroom Door.* Worthington, Ohio: Charles A. Jones.

Gould, S. J. (1996). *The Mismeasure of Man* (2nd ed.). New York: Norton.

Graham, S. and Weiner, B. (1996). Theories and principles of motivation. In D. Berliner and R. Calfee (eds.), *Handbook of Educational Psychology.* New York: Macmillan.

Griffith, D. P. (1992). Prenatal exposure to cocaine and other drugs:. Developmental and educational prognoses. *Phi Delta Kappan,* 74, 30–34.

Gronlund, N. E. (1991). *Constructing Achievement Tests* (3rd ed.). Englewood Cliffs, N.J.: Prentice Hall.

Gronlund, N. E. (1995). *How to Write and Use Instructional Objectives* (5th ed.). New York: Macmillan.

Gronlund, N. E. (1998). *Assessment of Student Achievement* (6th ed.). Boston: Allyn & Bacon.

Gronlund, N. E., and Linn, M. (1995). *Measurement and Assessment in Teaching* (7th ed.). New York: Macmillan.

Gump, P. V. (1967). *The Classroom Behavior Setting: Its Nature and Relation to Student Behavior.* Washington, D.C.: U.S. Office of Education.

Gump, P. V. (1982). School settings and their keeping. In D. L. Duke (ed.), *Helping Teachers Manage Classrooms.* Alexandria, Va.: Association for Supervision and Curriculum Development.

Guskey, T. R., and Gates, S. L. (1986). Synthesis of research on mastery learning. *Educational Leadership,* 43, 73–81.

Guthrie, G. P., and Guthrie, L. F. (1991). Streamlining interagency collaboration for youth at risk. *Educational Leadership,* 49 (1), 17–22.

Haberman, M. (1991). The pedagogy of poverty versus good teaching. *Phi Delta Kappan,* 72, 290–294.

Hallinan, M. T., and Sorensen, A. B. (1983). The formation and stability of instructional groups. *American Sociological Review,* 48, 838–851.

Heath, S. B. (1983). *Ways with Words: Language, Life and Work in Communities and Classrooms.* Cambridge, England: Cambridge University Press.

Hebert, E. A. (1992). Portfolios invite reflection—from student and staff. *Educational Leadership,* 49, 59–62.

Heider, E. R., Cazden, C. B., and Brown, R. (1968). *Social Class Differences in the Effectiveness and Style of Children's Coding Ability.* (Project Literacy Reports, No. 9). Ithaca, N.Y.: Cornell University.

Helmstetter (1996). *The Bell Curve: Intelligence and Class Structure in American Life.*

Henderson, A. T., Marburgaer, C. L., and Ooms, T. (1986). *Beyond the Bake Sale: An Educator's Guide to Working with Parents.* Columbia, Mo: National Committee for Citizens in Education.

Hill, W. F. (1994). *Learning Through Discussion* (3rd ed.). Thousand Oaks, Calif.: Sage Publications.

Hiller, J. H., Gisher, G. A., and Kaess, W. (1969). A computer investigation of verbal characteristics of effective classroom lecturing. *American Educational Research Journal,* 6, 661–675.

Hodgkinson, H. L. (1983). Guess who's coming to college? *Higher Education,* 17, 281–287.

Hodgkinson, H. L. (1992). *A Demographic Look at the Future.* Washington, D.C.: Institute for Educational Leadership.

Hopkins, D. (1985). *A Teacher's Guide to Classroom Research.* Philadelphia: Open University Press.

Housner, L. D., and Griffey, D. C. (1985). Teacher cognition: Differences in planning and interactive decision making between experienced and inexperienced teachers. *Research Quarterly for Exercise and Sport,* 56, 45–53.

Hunt, D. (1970). A conceptual level matching model for coordinating learner characteristics with educational approaches. *Interchange: A Journal of Educational Studies*, 1, 2–16.

Hunt, D. (1974). *Matching Models in Education*. Toronto: Ontario Institute for Studies in Education.

Hunter, M. C. (1982). *Mastery Teaching*. El Segundo, Calif.: TIP Publications.

Hunter, M. C. (1987). Beyond rereading Dewey: What's next? A response to Gibboney. *Educational Leadership*, 44, 51–53.

Hurd, D., et al. (1986). *General Science: A Voyage of Exploration*. Englewood Cliffs, N.J.: Prentice Hall.

Hvitfeldt, C. (1986). Traditional culture, perceptual style, and learning: The classroom behavior of Hmong adults. *Adult Education Quarterly*, 36, 65–77.

Hyde, A. A., and Bizar, M. (1989). *Thinking in Context: Teaching Cognitive Processes Across the Elementary School Curriculum*. New York: Longman.

Jackson, L. (1999). Doing school: Examining the effect of ethnic identity and school engagement in academic performance and goal attainment. Paper presented at the annual meeting of the American Educational Research Association, Montreal.

Jackson, P. W. (1968). *Life in Classrooms*. New York: Holt, Rinehart & Winston.

Jackson, P. W. (1986). *The Practice of Teaching*. New York: Teachers College Press.

Jacobs, H. H. (1997). *Mapping the Big Picture*. Alexandria, Va.: Association for Supervision and Curriculum Development.

Jencks, C., Smith, M., Ackland, H., Bane, M., Cohen, D., Gintis, H., Heyns, B., and Michelson, S. (1972). *Inequality: A Reassessment of the Effect of Family and Schooling in America*. New York: Basic Books.

Jensen, M. C. (1989). Leading the instructional staff. In S. C. Smith and P. K. Piele (eds.), *School Leadership: Handbook for Excellence*. Eugene, Ore.: ERIC Clearinghouse.

Jervis, K., and Montag, C. (eds.). (1991). *Progressive Education for the 1990s: Transforming Practice*. New York: Teachers College Press.

Johanssen, (1996) 10–33. (Dick Technology)

Johnson, D. W., and Johnson, F. P. (1975). *Joining Together: Group Theory and Group Skills*. Englewood Cliffs, N.J.: Prentice Hall.

Johnson, D. W., and Johnson, F. P. (1994). *Joining Together: Group Theory and Group Skills* (4th ed.). Englewood Cliffs, N.J.: Prentice Hall.

Johnson, D. W., and Johnson, R. T. (1998). *Learning Together and Alone* (4th ed.). Englewood Cliffs, N.J.: Prentice Hall.

Johnson, D. W., and Johnson, R. T. (1986). *Learning Together and Alone. Cooperation, Competition, and Individualization* (2nd ed.). Englewood Cliffs, N.J.: Prentice Hall.

Johnson, R., Rynders, J., Johnson, D. W., Schmidt, B., and Haider, S. (1979). Interaction between handicapped and nonhandicapped teenagers as a function of situational goal structuring: Implications for mainstreaming. *American Educational Research Journal*, 16, 161–167.

Jordan, J. (1988). Nobody mean more to me than you and the future life of Willie Jordan. *Harvard Educational Review*, 58, 363–374.

Joyce, B., and Calhoun, C. (1998). *Teaching for Understanding*. San Francisco: Jossey-Bass.

Joyce, B., Hersh, R., and McKibbin, M. (1993). *The Structure of School Improvement* (2nd ed.). New York: Longman.

Joyce, B., and Weil, M. (1972). *Models of Teaching*. Englewood Cliffs, N.J.: Prentice Hall.

Joyce, B., and Weil, M. (1996). *Models of Teaching* (5th ed.). Englewood Cliffs, N.J.: Prentice Hall.

Kagan, S. (1992). *Cooperative Learning*. San Juan Capistrano, Calif.: Resources for Teachers.

Kagan, S. (1998). *Cooperative Learning* (2nd ed.). San Juan Capistrano, Calif.: Resources for Teachers.

Kallen, H. M. (1924). *Culture and Democracy in the United States*. New York: Boni & Liveright.

Kaplan, L. (ed.). (1992). *Education and the Family*. Needham, Mass.: Allyn & Bacon.

Kaplan, M. (1992). *Thinking in Education*. Cambridge, England: Cambridge University Press.

Kay, H. (1991). Jason and Matt. In K. Jervis and C. Montag (eds.), *Progressive Education for the 1990s: Transforming Practice*. New York: Teachers College Press.

Keller, F. S. (1966). A personal course in psychology. In T. Urlich, R. Stachnik, and T. Mabry (eds.), *Control of Human Behavior*. Glenview, Ill.: Scott, Foresman.

Kemmis, S., and McTaggart, R. (1981). *The Action Research Planner*. Victoria, Australia: Deakin University Press.

Kilpatrick, W. (1918). The project method. *Teachers College Record*, 19, 319–333.

Klausmeier, H. (1980). *Learning and Teaching Concepts*. New York: Academic Press.

Koerner, B. I. (1999). Where the boys aren't. *U.S. News & World Report*, 8 February, 46–55.

Kohn, Alfie. (1995). *Punishment by Rewards: The Trouble with Gold Stars, Incentive Plans, A's, Praise and Other Bribes*. Boston: Houghton Mifflin.

Kohn, Alfie. (1996). *Beyond Discipline: From Compliance to Community*. Alexandria, Va.: Association for Supervision and Curriculum Development.

Kounin, J. S. (1970). *Discipline and Group Management in Classrooms*. New York: Holt, Rinehart & Winston.

Krajcik, J. (1994). Project-based instruction. Unpublished paper. Ann Arbor: University of Michigan.

Krajcik, J. S., Blumenfeld, P. C., Marx, R. W., and Soloway, E. (1994). A collaborative model for helping middle grade science teachers learn project-based instruction. *Elementary School Journal*, 94, 483–497.

Krajcik, J. S., Czemiak, C., and Berger, C. (1999). *Teaching Children Science: A Project-Based Approach.* Boston: McGraw-Hill.

Krug, M. (1976). *The Melting of the Ethnics.* Bloomington, Ill.: Phi Delta Kappa.

Ladson-Billings, G. (1994). *The Dreamkeepers: Successful Teachers of African American Children.* San Francisco: Jossey-Bass.

Languages spoken in U.S. homes. *Spokesman Review.* April 28, 1993, p. 2A.

Lee, V. E., and Smith, J. B. (1996). Collective responsibility for learning and its effects on gains in achievement of early secondary school students. *American Journal of Education*, 104, 1103–1146.

Leinhardt, G. (1989). Math lessons: A contrast of novice and expert competence. *Journal for Research in Mathematics Education*, 20, 52–75.

Lepper, M. R., Greene, D., and Nisbett, R. (1973). Undermining children's intrinsic interest with extrinsic reward: A test of the "overjustification" hypothesis. *Journal of Personality and Social Psychology*, 28, 129–137.

Lerup, L. (1977). *Building the Unfinished: Architecture and Human Action.* Beverly Hills, Calif.: Sage Publications.

Levin, H. M. (1987). Accelerated schools for disadvantaged students. *Educational Leadership*, 44, 19–21.

Lewin, K. (1951). *Field Theory in Social Psychology.* New York: Harpers.

Lewin, K., Lippitt, R., and White, R. (1939). Patterns of aggressive behavior in experimentally created social climates. *Journal of Social Psychology*, 10, 271–299.

Lieberman, A. (ed.). (1992). *The Changing Contexts of Teaching* (91st Yearbook of the National Society for the Study of Education). Chicago: University of Chicago Press.

Lieberman, A., and Miller, L. (1984). *Teachers, Their World, and Their Work.* Alexandria, Va.: Association of Supervision and Curriculum Development.

Lieberman, A., and Miller, L. (1992). *Teachers—Their World and Their Work: Implications for School Improvement.* New York: City College Press.

Linehan, M. F. (1992). Children who are homeless: Educational strategies for school personnel. *Phi Delta Kappan*, 74, 61–66.

Linn, M. C., and Hyde, J. S. (1989). Gender, mathematics, and science. *Educational Researcher*, 18 (8), 17–27.

Linn, R. L., and Gronlund, N. E. (1995). *Measurement and Assessment in Teaching* (7th ed.). Englewood Cliffs, N.J.: Prentice Hall.

Lippitt, R., and White, R. (1958). An experimental study of leadership and group life. In E. E. Macoby, T. M. Newcomb, and F. L. Hartley (eds.), *Readings in Social Psychology.* New York: Holt, Rinehart & Winston.

Little, J. W. (1990). The persistence of privacy: Autonomy and initiative in teachers' professional relations. *Teachers College Record*, 91, 509–536.

Little, J. W., and McLaughlin, B. (eds.). (1993). *Teachers' Work: Individuals, Colleagues and Contexts.* New York: Teachers College Press.

Livingston, C., and Castle, S. (eds.). (1989). *Teachers and Research in Action.* Washington, D.C.: National Education Association.

Lortie, D. C. (1975). *School-Teacher: A Sociological Study.* Chicago: University of Chicago Press.

Lotan, R. A., and Benton, J. (1990). Finding out about complex instruction: Teaching math and science in heterogeneous classrooms. In N. Davidson (ed.), *Cooperative Learning in Mathematics: A Handbook for Teachers.* Menlo Park, Calif.: Addison-Wesley.

Loucks-Horsley, S., and Hergert, L. F. (1985). *An Action Guide to School Improvement.* Alexandria, Va.: The Network and Association for Supervision and Curriculum Development.

Luiten, J., Ames, W., and Aerson, G. (1980). A meta-analysis of advance organizers on learning and retention. *American Educational Research Journal*, 17, 211–218.

Lyman, F. (1983). *Journaling Procedures.* (Mimeographed.) College Park, Md.: University of Maryland.

Lyman, F. (1985). *Think-Pair-Share.* (Mimeographed.) College Park, Md.: University of Maryland.

Lyman, F. (1986). *Procedures for Using the Question/Response Cues.* (Mimeographed.) College Park, Md.: University of Maryland and the Howard County Public Schools.

Lyman, F., Davie, A. R., and Eley, G. (1984). *Action Research by Student Teachers and Beginning Teachers: An Approach to Developing Problem Solving in the Classroom.* (Mimeographed.) College Park, Md.: University of Maryland.

Maccoby, E., Newcomb, T., and Hartley, E. (eds.). (1958). *Readings in Social Psychology* (3rd ed.). New York: Holt, Rinehart & Winston.

Macias, J. (1990). Scholastic antecedents of immigrant students: Schooling in a Mexican immigrant-sending community. *Anthropology and Education Quarterly*, 21, 291–318.

Madden, N. A., Slavin, R. E., Karweit, N. L., Dolan, L., and Wasik, B. A. (1992, April). Success for all: Longitudinal effects of a restructuring program for inner-city elementary schools. Paper presented at the annual meeting of the American Educational Research Association, San Francisco.

Mager, R. F. (1962). *Preparing Instructional Objectives*. Palo Alto, Calif.: Fearon Publishers.

Mager, R. F. (1984). *Preparing Instructional Objectives* (2nd rev. ed.). Palo Alto, Calif.: D. S. Lake.

Markle, S. (1975). They teach concepts, don't they? *Educational Researcher*, 4, 3–9.

Marshall, H. H. (1987). Motivational strategies of three fifth-grade teachers. *Elementary School Journal*, 88, 135–150.

Marzano, R., Pickering, D., and McTighe, J. (1993). *Assessing Student Outcomes*. Alexandria, Va.: Association for Supervision and Curriculum Development.

Marzano, R. J. (1992). *A Different Kind of Classroom: Teaching with Dimensions of Learning*. Alexandria, Va.: Association for Supervision and Curriculum Development.

Maslow, A. (1970). *Motivation and Personality* (2nd ed.). New York: Harper & Row.

Mayer, R. E. (1984). Aids to prose comprehension. *Educational Psychologist*, 19, 30–42.

McClelland, D. C. (1958). Methods of measuring human motivation. In J. W. Atkinson (ed.), *Motives in Fantasy, Action and Society*. New York: Van Nostrand.

McClelland, D. C. (1961). *The Achieving Society*. New York: Van Nostrand.

McCown, R. R., and Roop, P. (1992). *Educational Psychology and Classroom Practice: A Partnership*. Needham Heights, Mass.: Allyn & Bacon.

McLaughlin, D. (1995). Personal narratives for school change in Navajo settings. In D. McLaughlin and W. Tierney (eds.), *Naming Silenced Lives: Personal Narratives and Processes of School Change*. London: Routledge Press.

McTighe, J., and Lyman, F. T. (1988). Cueing thinking in the classroom: The promise of theory-embedded tools. *Educational Leadership*, 45, 18–24.

McWhorter, K. T. (1992). *Study and Thinking Skills in College*. New York: HarperCollins.

Mehrens, W. A., and Lehmann, I. J. (1984). *Measurement in Education and Psychology*. New York: Holt, Rinehart & Winston.

Merrill, M. D., and Tennyson, R. D. (1977). *Teaching Concepts: An Instructional Design Approach*. Englewood Cliffs, N.J.: Educational Technology.

*Metropolitan Life Survey of the American Teacher*. (1995). New York: Louis Harris & Associates.

Meyer, C. A. (1992). What is the difference between authentic and performance assessment? *Educational Leadership*, 49, 39–40.

Mitchell, R. (1992). *Testing for Learning: How New Approaches to Evaluation Can Improve American Schools*. New York: Free Press.

Mitzel, H. (1960). Teacher effectiveness. In C. W. Harris (ed.), *Encyclopedia of Educational Research* (3rd ed.). New York: Macmillan.

Moely, B. E., et al. (1986). How do teachers teach memory skills? *Educational Psychologist*, 21, 55–72.

Naftulin, D., Ware, J., and Donnelly, F. (1973). The doctor fox lecture: A paradigm of educational seduction. *Journal of Medical Education*, 48, 630–635.

National Center for Education and Statistics. (1996). *The Condition of Education*. Washington, D.C.: Author.

Needleman, H. L. (1992). Childhood exposure to lead: A common cause of school failure. *Phi Delta Kappan*, 74, 35–37.

Nettles, S. M. (1991). Community involvement and disadvantaged students: A review. *Review of Educational Research*, 61, 379–406.

Newcomb, T. M. (1961). *The Acquaintance Process*. New York: Holt, Rinehart & Winston.

Noblit, G. (1995). In meaning: the possibilities of caring. *Phi Delta Kappan*, 77, 682.

Noddings, N. (1992). *The Challenge to Care in Schools: An Alternative Approach to Education*. New York: Teachers College Press.

Noddings, N. (1995). Teaching themes of care. *Phi Delta Kappan*, 77, 676.

Novak, J. D., and Musonda, D. (1991). A twelve-year longitudinal study of science concept teaching. *American Educational Research Journal*, 28, 125–130.

Oakes, J. (1985). *Keeping Track: How Schools Structure Inequality*. New Haven, Conn.: Yale University Press.

Oakes, J. (1992). Can tracking research inform practice? Technical, normative, and political considerations. *Educational Researcher*, 21 (4), 12–21.

Oakes, J., and Lipton, M. (1999). *Teaching to Change the World*. Boston: McGraw-Hill.

Oja, S. N., and Smulyan, L. (1989). *Collaborative Action Research: A Developmental Approach*. New York: Falmer Press.

Palincsar, A., and Brown, A. (1989). Instruction for self-regulated reading. In L. Resnick and L. Kloper (eds.), *Toward the Thinking Curriculum: Current Cognitive Research*. Alexandria, Va.: Association for Supervision and Curriculum Development.

Palincsar, A. S., and Brown, A. L. (1984). Reciprocal teaching of comprehension-fostering and comprehension-monitoring activities. *Cognition and Instruction*, 1, 117–175.

Palincsar, A. S., and Klenk, L. J. (1991). Dialogues promoting reading comprehension. In B. Means, C. Chelemer, and M. S. Knapp (eds.), *Teaching Advanced Skills to At-Risk Students: Views from Research and Practice*. San Francisco: Jossey-Bass.

Pallas, A., Natriello, G., and McDill, E. (1989). The changing nature of the disadvantaged population: Current dimensions and future trends. *Educational Researcher*, 18, 16–22.

Pearce, T. (1995). *Leading Out Loud: The Authentic Speaker, the Credible Leader*. San Francisco: Jossey-Bass.

Peck (1992) 4–32.

Peddiwell, J. A. (1939). *The Saber-Tooth Curriculum*. New York: McGraw-Hill.

Perelman, L. (1992). *School's Out. Hyperlearning, the New Technology and the End of Education*. New York: William Morrow.

Perrone, V. (1991). *Expanding Student Assessment*. Alexandria, Va.: Association for Supervision and Curriculum Development.

Perry, W. (1969). *Forms of Intellectual and Ethical Development During the College Years*. New York: Holt, Rinehart & Winston.

Persell, C. H. (1977). *Education and Inequality*. New York: Free Press.

Peterson, P. L., Marx, R. W., and Clark, C. (1978). Teacher planning, teacher behavior and student achievement. *American Educational Research Journal*, 15, 417–432.

Phillips, S. (1972). Participant structures and communicative competence: Warm Springs children in community and classroom. In C. Cazden and D. Hymes (eds.), *Functions of Language in the Classroom*. New York: Teachers College Press.

Piaget, J. (1954). *The Construction of Reality in the Child*. New York: Basic Books.

Piaget, J. (1963). *Psychology of Intelligence*. Paterson, N.J.: Littlefield Adams.

Pogrow, S. (1990). Challenging at-risk students: Findings from the HOTS program. *Phi Delta Kappan*, 71, 389–397.

Popham, W. J. (1995). *Classroom Assessment: What Teachers Need to Know*. Needham Heights, Mass.: Allyn & Bacon.

Posner, G. J., and Rudnitsky, A. N. (1986). *Course Design: A Guide to Curriculum Development for Teachers* (3rd ed.). New York: Longman.

Pressley, M., et al. (1989). The challenges of classroom strategy instruction. *Elementary School Journal*, 58, 266–278.

Pressley, M., et al. (1991). *Cognitive Instruction that Really Improves Children's Academic Performance*. Cambridge, Mass.: Brookline.

Putnam, J., and Burke, J. (1992). *Organizing and Managing Classroom Learning*. New York: McGraw-Hill.

Putnam, J., and Burke, J. (1996). *Organizing and Managing Classroom Learning* (2nd ed.). New York: McGraw-Hill.

Pyle, A. (1997). Attacking the textbook crisis. *Los Angeles Times*. 29 September.

Redfield, D., and Rousseau, E. (1981). A meta-analysis of experimental research on teacher questioning behavior. *Review of Educational Research*, 51, 237–245.

Reed, S., and Sautter, R. C. (1990). Children of poverty: The status of 12 million young Americans. *Phi Delta Kappan*, 71, K1–K12.

Resnick, L. (1987). Learning in school and out. *Educational Researcher*, 16, 13–20.

Resnick, L. B. (1987). *Education and Learning to Think*. Washington, D.C.: National Academy Press.

Resnick, L. B., and Kloper, L. E. (eds.). (1989). *Toward the Thinking Curriculum: Current Cognitive Research*. Alexandria, Va.: Association for Supervision and Curriculum Development.

Reynolds, M. C. (ed.). (1989). *Knowledge Base for the Beginning Teacher*. New York: Pergamon.

Reynolds, M. C., Wang, M. C., and Walberg, H. J. (1987). The necessary restructuring of special and regular education. *Exceptional Children*, 53, 391–398.

Richardson, V. (ed.). *The Fourth Handbook of Research on Teaching*. New York: Macmillan.

Richardson, V. (ed.). *Handbook of Research on Teaching* (4th ed.). New York: Macmillan.

Richardson-Koehler, V. (ed.). (1987). *Educators' Handbook: A Research Perspective*. New York: Longman.

Rist, R. C. (1970). Student social class and teacher expectations: The self-fulfilling prophecy in ghetto education. *Harvard Education Review*, 40, 411–451.

Robinson, E. P. (1961). *Effective Study*. New York: Harper & Row.

Robinson (1990, 1996) 10–16.

Rosenbaum, J. E. (1976). *Making Equality: The Hidden Curriculum in High School Tracking*. New York: Wiley.

Rosenholz, S. (1989). *Teacher's Workplace: The Social Organization of Schools*. New York: Longman.

Rosenshine, B. (1970). Enthusiastic teaching: A research review. *School Review*, 78, 499–514.

Rosenshine, B. (1971a). Objectively measured behavioral predictors of effectiveness in explaining. In I. D. Westbury and A. A. Bellack (eds.), *Research into Classroom Processes*. New York: Teachers College Press.

Rosenshine, B. (1971b). *Teaching Behaviors and Student Achievement*. London: National Foundation for Educational Research.

Rosenshine, B. (1979). Content, time and direct instruction. In P. L. Peterson and H. J. Walberg (eds.), *Research on Teaching*. Berkeley, Calif.: McCutchan.

Rosenshine, B. (1980). How time is spent in elementary classrooms. In C. Denham and A. Lieberman (eds.), *Time to Learn*. Washington, D.C.: U.S. Department of Education.

Rosenshine, B., and Furst, N. (1973). The use of direct observation to study teaching. In R. M. W. Travers (ed.), *Second Handbook of Research on Teaching*. Chicago: Rand McNally.

Rosenshine, B., and Stevens, R. (1986). Teaching functions. In M. C. Wittrock (ed.), *Handbook of Research on Teaching* (3rd ed.). New York: Macmillan.

Rosenthal, R., and Jacobson, L. (1968). *Pygmalion in the Classroom*. New York: Holt, Rinehart & Winston.

Rothman, R. (1995). *Measuring Up: Standards, Assessment and School Reform*. San Francisco: Jossey-Bass.

Rowe, M. B. (1974a). Wait-time and rewards as instructional variables, their influence on language, logic, and fate control. Part one: Wait-time. *Journal of Research in Science Teaching,* 11, 81–94.

Rowe, M. B. (1974b). Relation of wait-time and rewards to the development of language, logic, and fate control. Part II: Rewards. *Journal of Research in Science Teaching,* 11, 291–308.

Rowe, M. B. (1986). Wait time: Slowing down may be a way of speeding up. *Journal of Teacher Education,* 37, 43–50.

Rugen, L., and Hart, S. (1994). The lessons of learning expeditions. *Educational Leadership,* 52, 20–23.

Russell, T., and Munby, H. (eds.). (1992). *Teachers and Teaching: From Classroom to Reflection.* New York: Falmer Press.

Rutter, M., Maughan, B., Mortimore, P., Ouston, J., and Smith, A. (1979). *Fifteen Thousand Hours: Secondary Schools and Their Effects on Children.* Cambridge, Mass.: Harvard University Press.

Ryan, K., Newman, K., Mager, G., Applegate, J., Lasley, T., Flora, R., and Johnston, J. (1980). *Biting the Apple: Accounts of First Year Teachers.* New York: Longman.

Ryle, G. (1949). *The Concept of Mind.* London: Hutchinson's University Library.

Sadker, M. (1985). *Women in Educational Administration.* Washington, D.C.: Mid-Atlantic Center for Sex Equity.

Sadker, M., and Sadker, D. (1990). *Sex Equity Handbook for Schools* (2nd ed.). New York: Longman.

Santrock, J. W. (1976). Affect and facilitative self-control. Influence of ecological setting, cognition, and social agent. *Journal of Educational Psychology,* 68 (5), 529–535.

Sarason, S. (1971). *The Culture of School and the Problem of Change.* Boston: Allyn & Bacon.

Sarason, S. (1982). *The Culture of School and the Problem of Change* (2nd ed.). Boston: Allyn & Bacon.

Sarason, S. D. (1995). *Parental Involvement and the Political Principle.* San Francisco: Jossey-Bass.

Schlosser, L. K. (1992). Teacher distance and student disengagement: School lives on the margin. *Journal of Teacher Education,* 43, 128–140.

Schmoker, M., and Marzano, R. (1999). Realizing the promise of standards-based education. *Educational Leadership,* 57, 177–121.

Schmuck, R., and Runkel, P. (1995). *Handbook of Organization Development in Schools and Colleges.* Prosper Heights, Ill.: Waveland Press.

Schmuck, R. A., Runkel, P., Arends, J., and Arends, R. (1977). *The Second Handbook of Organization Development in Schools.* Palo Alto, Calif.: Mayfield.

Schmuck, R. A., and Schmuck, P. A. (1992). *Small Districts, Big Problems.* Newbury Park, Calif.: Corwin Press.

Schmuck, R. A., and Schmuck, P. A. (1997). *Group Processes in the Classroom* (7th ed.). Dubuque, Iowa: Brown & Benchmark.

Schön, D. A. (1983). *The Reflective Practitioner.* San Francisco: Jossey-Bass.

School choice. (1999). *Education Week,* 16 October, 1.

Schuck, R. (1981). The impact of set induction on student achievement and retention. *Journal of Educational Research,* 74, 227–232.

Schulman, L. S. (1986). Paradigms and research programs in the story of teaching: A contemporary perspective. In M. C. Wittrock (ed.), *Handbook of Research on Teaching* (3rd ed.). New York: Macmillan.

Schulman, L. S. (1987). Knowledge and teaching: Foundations of the new reform. *Harvard Education Review,* 57, 1–22.

Schwab, J. J. (coordinator). (1965). *Biological Sciences Curriculum Study: Biology Teachers' Handbook.* New York: Wiley.

Sergiovanni, T. (1996). *Leadership for the Schoolhouse.* San Francisco: Jossey-Bass.

Shaefer, W., and Lissitz, R. (1987). Measurement training for school personnel: Recommendations and reality. *Journal of Teacher Education,* 38, 57–63.

Shanker, A. (1995). Full inclusion is neither free nor appropriate. *Educational Leadership,* 52, 18–23.

Shapiro, N. S., and Levine, J. L. (1999). *Creating Learning Communities.* San Francisco: Jossey-Bass.

Sharan, S., Kussell, P., Hertz-Lazarowitz, R., Bejarano, Y., Raviv, S., and Sharan, Y. (1984). *Cooperative Learning in the Classroom: Research in Desegregated Schools.* Hillsdale, N.J.: Erlbaum.

Sharan, S., and Sharan, Y. (1976). *Small Group Teaching.* Englewood Cliffs, N.J.: Education Technology.

Shavelson, R., and Baxter, G. (1992). What we've learned about assessing hands-on science. *Educational Leadership,* 49, 20–25.

Sirotnik, K. A. (1983). What you see is what you get. *Harvard Educational Review,* 54, 16–32.

Sizer, T. (1984). *Horace's Compromise: The Dilemma of the American High School.* Boston: Houghton-Mifflin.

Skinner, B. F. (1956). *Science and Human Behavior.* New York: Macmillan.

Slavin, R. (1980). Effects of individual learning expectations on student achievement. *Journal of Educational Psychology,* 72, 520–524.

Slavin, R. (1983). *Cooperative Learning.* New York: Longman.

Slavin, R. (1984). Students motivating students to excel: Incentives, cooperative tasks and student achievement. *Elementary School Journal,* 85, 53–62.

Slavin, R. (1986). *Student Team Learning* (3rd ed.). Baltimore: Center for Research on Elementary and Middle Schools, Johns Hopkins University.

Slavin, R. (1994). *Using Student Team Learning* (4th ed.). Baltimore: Johns Hopkins University.

Slavin, R. (1995). *Cooperative Learning* (2nd ed.). Boston: Allyn & Bacon.

Slavin, R. (1996). *Every Child, Every School: Success for All.* Thousand Oaks, Calif.: Corwin Press.

Slavin, R., Madden, N., Dolan, L., and Wasik, B. (1992). *Success for All.* Arlington, Va.: Educational Research Services.

Slavin, R., Madden, N., Dolan, L., and Wasik, B. (1994). Roots and wings: Inspiring academic excellence. *Educational Leadership, 52,* 10–14.

Slavin, R., Sharan, S., Kagan, S., Hertz-Lazarowitz, R., Webb, C., and Schmuck, R. (eds.). (1985). *Learning to Cooperate, Cooperating to Learn.* New York: Plenum Press.

Sleeter, C. E., and Grant, C. A. (1988). *Making Choices for Multicultural Education: Five Approaches to Race, Class, and Gender.* Columbus, Ohio: Charles M. Merrill.

Smith, H. (1995). Rogue eco-system project. *Educational Connection, 1,* 3–4.

Sorensen, A. B., and Hallinan, M. T. (1986). Effects of ability grouping on growth in academic achievement. *American Educational Research Journal, 23,* 519–542.

Spaulding, C. L. (1992). *Motivation in the Classroom.* New York: McGraw-Hill.

Stallings, J., and Kaskowitz, D. (1974). *Follow-Through Classroom Observation Evaluation 1972–1974.* (SRI project URU-7370). Stanford, Calif.: Stanford Research Institute.

Starch, D., and Elliot, E. C. (1912). Reliability of grading high school work in English. *Scholastic Review, 20,* 442–456.

Starch, D., and Elliot, E. C. (1913). Reliability of grading high school work in history. *Scholastic Review, 22,* 676–681.

Starkey, D. (1980). *The Origins of Concept Formation: Object Sorting and Object Preference in Early Infancy.* (ERIC No. ED 175555: Resources in Education).

Staub, D., and Peck, C. A. (1995). What are the outcomes for nondisabled students? *Education Leadership, 52,* 36–41.

Steele, C. M. (1992, April). Race and the schooling of Black Americans. *Atlantic Monthly,* 68–78.

Stenhouse, L. (1975). *An Introduction to Curriculum Research and Development.* London: Heinemann.

Stenhouse, L. (1983). *Authority, Education and Emancipation.* London: Heinemann.

Stenhouse, L. (1984). Artistry and teaching: The teacher as focus of research and development. In D. Hopkins and M. Wideen (eds.), *Alternative Perspectives on School Improvement.* New York: Falmer Press.

Stiggins, R. J. (1987). Profiling classroom assessment environments. Paper presented at the annual meeting of the National Council on Measurement in Education, San Francisco.

Stiggins (1997) 6–3.

Stipek, D. J. (1988). *Motivation to Learn: From Theory to Practice.* Englewood Cliffs, N.J.: Prentice Hall.

Stipek, D. J. (1996). Motivation and instruction. In D. Berliner and R. Calfee (eds.), *Handbook of Educational Psychology.* New York: Macmillan.

Stover, L. T., Neubert, G. A., and Lawlor, J. C. (1993). *Creating Interactive Environments in the Secondary School.* Washington, D.C.: National Education Association.

Suchman, R. (1962). *The Elementary School Training Program in Scientific Inquiry.* Report to the U.S. Office of Education. Urbana: University of Illinois.

Swing from wings. (1990, February). Mid-Atlantic Association for Cooperation in Education Cooperative News.

Taba, H. (1996). *Teaching Strategies and Cognitive Functioning in Elementary School Children.* San Francisco: San Francisco State University.

Tapscott, D. (1998). *Growing Up Digital: The Rise of the Net Generation.* New York: McGraw-Hill.

Tennyson, R. (1978). Pictorial support and specific instructions as design variables for children's concept and rule learning. *Educational Communication and Technology: A Journal of Research and Development, 26,* 291–299.

Tennyson, R., and Cocchiarella, M. (1986). An empirically based instructional design theory for teaching concepts. *Review of Educational Research, 56,* 40–71.

Tennyson, R., Youngers, J., and Suebsonthi, P. (1983). Concept learning by children using instructional presentation forms for prototype formation and classification-skill development. *Journal of Educational Psychology, 75,* 280–290.

Thelen, H. A. (1954). *Dynamics of Groups at Work.* Chicago: University of Chicago Press.

Thelen, H. A. (1960). *Education and the Human Quest.* New York: Harper & Row.

Thomas, E. L., and Robinson, H. A. (1972). *Improving Reading in Every Class: A Sourcebook for Teachers.* Boston: Allyn & Bacon.

Timpson, W. M., and Tobin, D. N. (1982). *Teaching as Performing.* Englewood Cliffs, N.J.: Prentice Hall.

Tobin, K. (1990). Teacher mind frames and science learning: Beliefs about teaching and learning. In K. Tobin, J. B. Kahle, and B. J. Fraser, (eds.), *Windows into Science Classrooms: Problems Associated with Higher-Level Cognitive Learning.* New York: Falmer Press.

Tobin, K., Kahle, J. B., and Fraser, B. J. (eds.). (1990). *Windows into Science Classrooms: Problems Associated with Higher-Level Cognitive Learning.* New York: Falmer Press.

Travers, R. M. (ed.). (1973). *Second Handbook of Research on Teaching.* Chicago: Rand McNally.

Tyler, R. W. (1950). *Basic Principles of Curriculum and Instruction.* Chicago: University of Chicago Press.

U.S. Department of Commerce, Bureau of the Census. (1990). *Statistical Abstract of the United States*. Washington, D.C.: U.S. Government Printing Office.

U.S. Department of Education. (1996). *Youth Indicators, 1996*. Washington, D.C.: U.S. Government Printing Office.

U.S. Department of Education. (1998). *Conditions of Education, 1998*. Washington, D.C.: U.S. Government Printing Office.

U.S. Department of Education, Office of Bilingual Education and Minority Language Affairs. (1998). *Facts About Limited English Proficient Students*. Washington, D.C.: U.S. Government Printing Office.

Veenman, S. (1984). Perceived problems of beginning teachers. *Review of Educational Research, 54*, 143–178.

Villegas, A., and Watts, S. M. (1991). Life in the classroom: The influence of class placement and student race/ethnicity. Paper presented at the annual meeting of the American Educational Research Association, Chicago.

Villegas, A. M. (1991). *Culturally Responsive Teaching*. Princeton, N.J.: Educational Testing Service.

Wadsworth, B. J. (1989). *Piaget's Theory of Cognitive Development* (4th ed.) New York: Longman.

Walberg, H. J. (1986). Syntheses of research on teaching. In M. C. Wittrock (ed.), *Handbook of Research on Teaching* (3rd ed.). New York: Macmillan.

Walcott, H. (1973). *The Man in the Principal's Office: An Ethnography*. New York: Holt, Rinehart & Winston.

Waller, W. (1932). *The Sociology of Teaching*. New York: Russell & Russell.

Wang, M. C., Reynolds, M., and Walberg, H. (1995). Serving students at the margin. *Educational Leadership, 52*, 12–17.

Wang, M. C., Walberg, H. J., and Reynolds, M. C. (1992). A scenario for better—not separate—special education. *Educational Leadership, 50*, 35–38.

War Manpower Commission (1945). *The Training Within Industry Report*. Washington, D.C.: Bureau of Training.

Warren, D. (ed.). (1989). *American Teachers: Histories of a Profession at Work*. New York: Macmillan.

Weick, K. E. (1976). Educational organizations as loosely coupled systems. *Administrative Science Quarterly, 21*, 1–19.

Weick, K. E. (1979). *The Social Psychology of Organizing* (2nd ed.). Reading, Mass.: Addison-Wesley.

Weiner, B. (ed.). (1974). *Achievement Motivation and Attribution Theory*. Morristown, N.J.: General Learning Corporation.

Weinstein, C. F., and Mayer, R. F. (1986). The teaching of learning strategies. In M. C. Wittrock (ed.), *Handbook of Research on Teaching*. New York: Macmillan.

Weinstein, C., and Mignano, A. J. (1997). *Elementary Classroom Management* (2nd ed.). New York: McGraw-Hill.

Weinstein, C. S., and Mignano, A. J., Jr. (1996). *Elementary Classroom Management: Lessons from Research and Practice* (2nd ed.). New York: McGraw-Hill.

Weisz, D. n.d. *Action Research Project: Equitable Distribution of Questioning and Feedback in the Classroom*. (Mimeographed.) College Park: University of Maryland.

Welch, L., and Long, L. (1940). The higher structural phases of concept formation. *Journal of Psychology, 9*, 59–95.

Westra, M. (1996). *Active Communication*. Pacific Grove, Calif.: Brooks/Cole.

Wiggins, G., and McTighe, J. (1998). *Understanding by Design*. Alexandria, Va.: Association for Supervision and Curriculum Development.

Wiggins, G. P. (1993). *Assessing Student Performance*. San Francisco: Jossey-Bass.

Willen, W. W. (ed.) (1990). *Teaching and Learning Through Discussion: The Theory and Practice of Discussion Method*. Springfield, Ill.: Charles C Thomas.

Wise, A. (1995). NCATE's emphasis on performance. *NCATE Quality Teaching, 5*, 1–12.

Wiske, M. S. (ed.). (1998). *Teaching for Understanding*. San Francisco: Jossey-Bass.

Wittrock, M. C. (ed.). (1986). *Handbook of Research on Teaching* (3rd ed.). New York: Macmillan.

Worthen, B., White, K., Fan, J., and Sukweeks, R. (1999). *Measurement and Assessment in Schools* (2nd ed.). New York: Longman.

Yinger, R. (1980). A study of teacher planning. *Elementary School Journal, 80*, 107–127.

Zahorik, J. (1970). The effects of planning on teaching. *The Elementary School Journal, 71*, 143–151.

# Photo Credits

CHAPTER 1:
Opener: Michael Newman/PhotoEdit
p. 5 Bettmann/Corbis; p. 10 Bob Daemmrich; p. 15, 25
    Elizabeth Crews

CHAPTER 2:
Opener: Joel Gordon
p. 41 Michael Dwyer/Stock Boston, p. 47 Elizabeth
    Crews; p. 68 Bob Daemmrich

CHAPTER 3:
Opener:Joel Gordon
p. 77, 83, 96, 101 Bob Daemmrich; p. 105 Elizabeth Crews

CHAPTER 4:
Opener Joel Gordon
p. 113 Bob Daemmrich, p. 124, 142 Elizabeth Crews;
    p. 147 Bob Daemmrich

CHAPTER 5:
Opener: Myrleen Ferguson/PhotoEdit
p. 157, 174 Bob Daemmrich

CHAPTER 6:
Opener: Bob Daemmrich
p. 200 Bob Daemmrich; p. 211, 219 Elizabeth Crews;
    p. Bob Daemmrich

CHAPTER 7:
Opener: Bob Daemmrich
p. 236 AP/Wide World Photos; p. 243 Elizabeth Crews;
    p. 245 Bob Daemmrich; p. 254 Elizabeth Crews; p. 257
    Bob Crist/CORBIS

CHAPTER 8:
Opener: Mary Kate Denny/PhotoEdit
p. 265 Elizabeth Crews; p. 276 Bob Daemmrich; p. 281
    CORBIS

CHAPTER 9:
Opener: Richard Hutchings/PhotoEdit
p. 290 Bettmann/Corbis; p. 304, 305 Bob Daemmrich

CHAPTER 10:
Opener: Vic Bider/PhotoEdit
p. 317 Corbis/Bettmann; p. 319, 331, 336 Bob Daemmrich

CHAPTER 11:
Opener: Bob Daemmrich
p. 351 Bob Daemmrich/Stock Boston; p. 361, 365, 371
    Elizabeth Crews

CHAPTER 12:
Opener: Richard Hutchings/PhotoEdit
p. 380, 383, 395 Elizabeth Crews

CHAPTER 13:
Opener: Michael Newman/PhotoEdit
p. 411 Mark Burnett/Stock Boston, p.;nt414 Najlah
    Feanny/Stock Boston; p. 419 Fredrik Bodin/Stock
    Boston; p. 428 Bob Daemmrich/The Image Works

# Name Index

# Subject Index

Note: Pages in *italics* indicate illustrations; those followed by t indicate tables.